ExamSim

Experience realistic, simulated exams on your own computer with Osborne's interactive ExamSim software. This computer-based test engine offers knowledge and scenario-based questions like those found on the actual exams. ExamSim also features a review mode that helps build your testing confidence by allowing you to analyze the questions you missed.

Knowledge-based questions present challenging material in a multiple-choice format. Answer treatments not only explain why the correct options are right, they also tell you why the incorrect answers are wrong.

EXAM QUESTIONS

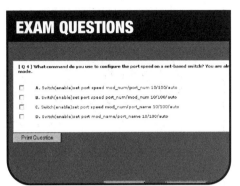

Realistic **scenario-based questions** challenge your ability to analyze and synthesize complex information in realistic scenarios similar to those on the actual exams.

Additional CD-ROM Features

- Complete hyperlinked **e-book** for easy information access and self-paced study

System Requirements:

A PC running Internet Explorer version 5 or higher

The **score report** provides an overall assessment of your exam performance as well as performance history.

SCORE REPORT

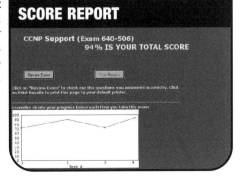

CCNP™ Support
Study Guide

(Exam 640-506)

CISCO® CERTIFIED NETWORK PROFESSIONAL

CCNP™ Support
Study Guide

(Exam 640-506)

Syngress Media, Inc.

Osborne/McGraw-Hill

Berkeley New York St. Louis San Francisco Auckland Bogotá Hamburg London Madrid Mexico City
Milan Montreal New Delhi Panama City Paris São Paulo Singapore Sydney Tokyo Toronto

Osborne/**McGraw-Hill**
2600 Tenth Street
Berkeley, California 94710
U.S.A.

For information on translations or book distributors outside the U.S.A., or to arrange bulk purchase discounts for sales promotions, premiums, or fund-raisers, please contact Osborne/**McGraw-Hill** at the above address.

CCNP™ Support Study Guide (Exam 640-506)

1234567890 DOC DOC 0198765432109

Book p/n: 0-07-212544-6 and CD p/n: 0-07-212545-4
parts of ISBN: 0-07-212546-2

Publisher Brandon A. Nordin	**Editorial Management** Syngress Media, Inc.	**Technical Reviewer** Frank Jimenez
Vice President and Associate Publisher Scott Rogers	**Project Editor** Maribeth A. Corona	**Copy Editor** Darlene Bordwell
Editorial Director Gareth Hancock	**Acquisitions Coordinator** Jessica Wilson	**Production and Editorial** Black Hole Publishing Services
Associate Acquisitions Editor Timothy Green	**Series Editor** Mark Buchmann	**Series Design** Roberta Steele
	Technical Editor Neil Lovering	**Cover Design** Greg Scott

This book was published with Corel VENTURA™ Publisher.

About Syngress Media

Syngress Media creates books and software for Information Technology professionals seeking skill enhancement and career advancement. Its products are designed to comply with vendor and industry standard course curricula, and are optimized for certification exam preparation. You can contact Syngress via the Web at www.syngress.com.

Contributors

John Barnes (CCNA, CCNP, CCSI) currently works as an instructor and consultant for www.CertaNet.com. John has over 10 years experience implementing and troubleshooting local and wide area networks, combined with 4 years experience as an instructor. He is currently pursuing the CCIE certification. John currently lives in Dallas, Texas, and enjoys spending time with his wife Tina and daughter Sydney.

Ricardo Daza (CISSP, CCNP (LAN-ATM, Voice Access), CCDA, SCNA (Solaris 7), IBM CSE (AIX 4.3 Sys Admin, AIX Firewall), MCSE+I, MCT, CNA) is a Channel Systems Engineer for Cisco Systems (http://www.cisco.com/), working out of Cisco's Seattle, Washington, office. He has over 10 years of computer consulting experience and has passed 9 Cisco Certified Exams including the CCIE Written Qualification Exam (lab scheduled for later this year). During his career, Ricardo has worked on many extensive and diverse projects, including network infrastructure and security analysis, network design and implementation, network management and documentation, project management and end-user training. He is proficient in a number of different vendor products ranging from Cisco, Microsoft, Sun, Novell, IBM, Bay, and 3Com to name a few.

Don Dettmore (CCNP, MCSE, CNE) does network design for a leading worldwide IT Solutions provider to the financial industry. He is currently working on two network implementations with Fortune 500 companies. Don has been working with computers for over 10 years, and doing network design and administration for the last 5. In addition to the CCNP, he also holds the CNE and MCSE certifications.

Brad Ellis (CCIE#5796, MCSE, MCNE, CCDP) works as a Senior Network Engineer for SequoiaNET.com, an Auburn Hills, Michigan, based consulting company. He has over 7 years of experience in IT including large-scale routing, remote access, voice over IP, VPN, and firewall design/implementation. Brad holds a B.S. in Electrical Engineering and a B.S. in Computer Engineering. He is also a partner and technical advisor for www.ccbootcamp.com and www.optsys.net. Brad may be contacted at bellis@optsys.net.

Michelle Famiglietti (CCNP, CCDA) is Network Manager at Financial Technologies, Inc. (http://www.financialtech.com/), located in Chantilly, Virginia,. She is responsible for the operation and design of the network infrastructure. Michelle has over 10 years of experience in the network field and for the last several years has focused on Cisco technologies. With previous experience at two Fortune 500 companies, Michelle has had the opportunity to troubleshoot a wide variety of hardware and software. Michelle lives with her husband Matthew in Falls Church, Virginia. She can be reached at ciscobabe@usa.net or at her Web site http://mfamiglietti.home.mindspring.com/.

Nick Guy (CCNP, MCSE) is Manager of Network Operations for Northwest Link (http://www.nwlink.com) in Bellevue, Washington. Nick has worked extensively with the provision and upkeep of the Frame Relay, DSL, and dialup services that Northwest Link offers. Nick lives with his wife Marsha and 9-year-old son in Seattle, Washington. Nick can be reached via nick@nwlink.com or nick@as-it-happens.com between OS upgrades.

Edward Moss (CCNP, CCDP, CNE) recently joined SBC DataComm Global Accounts as a Systems Engineer. He has over 15 years of experience in the network industry and has specialized in Cisco and Novell networks. Formerly with Experian as a Network Engineer, he has worked on many large-scale and mission critical projects providing LAN and WAN infrastructure design, configuration, implementation, and support services. Ed also founded, and presently heads the Omaha Cisco User Group (http://omaha.ciscousers.org) and is currently working towards his CCIE certification. He can be reached at ed@teklnk.com.

James Placer (CCDP, CCNP Voice Access, NNCDS, NNCSS, MCSE) is a Network Design Engineer employed by Interactive Business Systems, Inc. (http://www.ibs.com/) Enterprise Networking Group (http://www.ibsentg.com), located in Livonia and Kalamazoo, Michigan. He designs, troubleshoots, and implements large-scale LAN and WAN networks based primarily on Cisco Systems and Nortel Networks platforms. He has over 14 years of experience in the computer systems and networking fields. James lives with his wife Kathy just outside the town of Allegan, Michigan and can be reached at jplacer@ibsentg.com.

Vijay Ramcharan (CCNP, CCDP, MCSE) is an Information Systems Manager in New York City. He has over 4 years of experience in small- as well as large-scale environments and started his networking career by providing technical support in a Windows environment. Over the years Vijay has worked on diverse projects, including database implementation, EDI, and Y2K migration. He is currently pursuing the CCIE R/S certification. Vijay lives with his wife Sharon in Queens, New York, and is now enjoying the first addition to their family, baby Jessica. He can be reached at vijayr@donnaricco.com.

Technical Editor

Neil Lovering (CCIE #1772) is a co-founder of CertaNet, Inc. He has been involved in the networking arena for more than 10 years. He has been a Cisco Certified Systems Instructor for more than 5 years and has taught thousands of students network design, configuration, and troubleshooting techniques. He has been a consultant on many large network design projects and specializes in OSPF and BGP implementation. Neil has been a technical writer, editor, and course designer for many years.

Technical Reviewer

Frank Jimenez (CCIE #5738, CCDP, CCNP, MCNE, MCSE, MCP+I) is employed as a Systems Architect at CompuCom Systems, Inc. (http://www.compucom.com), headquartered in Dallas, Texas. He has over 8 years of experience designing networks to support corporate internetworking, messaging, and management solutions. Frank lives with his wife Diana and three children in Dallas, and can be contacted via email at ccie5738@hotmail.com.

Series Editor

Mark Buchmann (CCIE, CCSI) is a Cisco Certified Internetworking Expert (CCIE) and has been a Certified Cisco Systems Instructor (CCSI) since 1995. He is the owner of MAB Enterprises, Inc., a company providing consulting, network support, training, and various other services. Mark is also a co-owner of www.CertaNet.com, a company providing online certification assistance for a variety of network career paths including all the various Cisco certifications.

In his free time he enjoys spending time with his family and boating. He currently lives in Raleigh, North Carolina. Mark is Series Editor for Syngress Cisco books.

ACKNOWLEDGMENTS

W e would like to thank the following people:

- All the incredibly hard-working folks at Osborne/McGraw-Hill: Brandon Nordin, Scott Rogers, Timothy Green, Gareth Hancock, and Jessica Wilson.
- The Black Hole Publishing Services staff for their help in fine tuning the project.

CONTENTS AT A GLANCE

CONTENTS

PREFACE

his book's primary objective is to help you prepare for and pass the CCNP Support Exam 640-506. We believe that the only way to do this is to help you increase your knowledge and build your skills. After completing this book, you should feel confident that you have thoroughly reviewed all of the objectives that Cisco has established for the exam.

In This Book

This book is organized around the topics covered within the CCNP Support Exam administered at Sylvan Testing Centers.

In Every Chapter

We've created a set of chapter components that call your attention to important items, reinforce important points, and provide helpful exam-taking hints. Take a look at what you'll find in the chapters:

■ Each chapter begins with the **Certification Objectives**—what you need to know in order to pass the section on the exam dealing with the chapter topic. The Certification Objective headings identify the objectives within the chapter, so you'll always know an objective when you see it!

EXERCISE 1-1
■ **Certification Exercises** are interspersed throughout the chapters. These are step-by-step exercises. They help you master skills that are likely to be an area of focus on the exam. Don't just read through the exercises; they are hands-on practice that you should be comfortable completing. Learning by doing is an effective way to increase your competency with the language.

■ **From the Classroom** sidebars describe the issues that come up most often in the training classroom setting. These sidebars give you a valuable perspective into certification- and product-related topics. They point out common mistakes and address questions that have arisen from classroom discussions.

■ S & S sections lay out specific scenario questions and solutions in a quick-to-read format.

SCENARIO & SOLUTION

You have just taken over as the network administrator and have no information on the password for one of your 3600 series routers. What is a possible solution?	Perform the password recovery process on the 3600 series router.
You have been informed that a new remote location needs connectivity. It will require ISDN access and a four-port hub. What model of router would provide a solution here?	The 803 and 804 both provide for ISDN with a four-port hub.
An OC-1 connection is being installed at your central location that now employs a 2600 series router. What changes will need to be made at the central site to accommodate this connection?	A 3600 series with the HSSI port will be needed here.

■ The **Certification Summary** is a succinct review of the chapter and a re-statement of salient points regarding the exam.

 ■ The **Two-Minute Drill** at the end of every chapter is a checklist of the main points of the chapter. It can be used for last-minute review.

 ■ The **Self Test** offers questions similar to those found on the certification exam. The answers to these questions, as well as explanations of the answers, can be found in Appendix A. By taking the Self Test after completing each chapter, you'll reinforce what you've learned from that chapter, while becoming familiar with the structure of the exam questions.

Some Pointers

Once you've finished reading this book, set aside some time to do a thorough review. You might want to return to the book several times and make use of all the methods it offers for reviewing the material:

1. *Re-read all the Two-Minute Drills,* or have someone quiz you. You also can use the drills as a way to do a quick cram before the exam.

2. *Review all the S & S scenarios* for quick problem solving.

3. *Re-take the Self Tests.* Taking the tests right after you've read the chapter is a good idea, because it helps reinforce what you've just learned. However, it's an even better idea to go back later and do all the questions in the book in one sitting. Pretend you're taking the exam. (For this reason, you should mark your answers on a separate piece of paper when you go through the questions the first time.)

4. *Complete the exercises.* Did you do the exercises when you read through each chapter? If not, do them! These exercises are designed to cover exam topics, and there's no better way to get to know this material than by practicing.

INTRODUCTION

How to Take a Cisco Certification Examination

This introduction covers the importance of your CCNP certification and prepares you for taking the actual examination. It gives you a few pointers on methods of preparing for the exam, including how to study and register, what to expect, and what to do on exam day.

Catch the Wave!

Congratulations on your pursuit of Cisco certification! In this fast-paced world of networking, few certification programs are as valuable as the one offered by Cisco.

The networking industry has virtually exploded in recent years, accelerated by nonstop innovation and the Internet's popularity. Cisco has stayed at the forefront of this tidal wave, maintaining a dominant role in the industry.

The networking industry is highly competitive, and evolving technology only increases in its complexity, so the rapid growth of the networking industry has created a vacuum of qualified people. There simply aren't enough skilled networking people to meet the demand. Even the most experienced professionals must keep current with the latest technology in order to provide the skills that the industry demands. That's where Cisco certification programs can help networking professionals succeed as they pursue their careers.

Cisco started its certification program many years ago, offering only the designation Cisco Certified Internetwork Expert (CCIE). Through the CCIE program, Cisco provided a means to meet the growing demand for experts in the field of networking. However, the CCIE tests are brutal, with a failure rate of over 80 percent. (Fewer than 5 percent of candidates pass on their first attempt.) As you might imagine, very few people ever attain CCIE status.

In early 1998, Cisco recognized the need for intermediate certifications, and several new programs were created. Four intermediate certifications were added: CCNA (Cisco Certified Network Associate), CCNP (Cisco Certified Network Professional), CCDA (Cisco Certified Design Associate), and CCDP (Cisco

Certified Design Professional). In addition, several specialties were added to the CCIE certifications; currently CCIE candidates can receive their CCIE in five areas: Routing and Switching, WAN Switching, ISP-Dial, SNA/IP Integration, and Design.

I would encourage you to take beta tests when they are available. Not only are the beta exams less expensive than the final exams (some are even free!), but also, if you pass the beta, you will receive credit for passing the exam. If you don't pass the beta, you will have seen every question in the pool of available questions, and can use this information when you prepare to take the exam for the second time. Remember to jot down important information immediately after the exam, if you didn't pass. You will have to do this after leaving the exam area, since materials written during the exam are retained by the testing center. This information can be helpful when you need to determine which areas of the exam were most challenging for you as you study for the subsequent test.

Why Vendor Certification?

Over the years, vendors have created their own certification programs because of industry demand. This demand arises when the marketplace needs skilled professionals and an easy way to identify them. Vendors benefit because it promotes people skilled in their product. Professionals benefit because it boosts their careers. Employers benefit because it helps them identify qualified people.

In the networking industry, technology changes too often and too quickly to rely on traditional means of certification, such as universities and trade associations. Because of the investment and effort required to keep network certification programs current, vendors are the only organizations suited to keep pace with the changes. In general, such vendor certification programs are excellent, with most of them requiring a solid foundation in the essentials, as well as their particular product line.

Corporate America has come to appreciate these vendor certification programs and the value they provide. Employers recognize that certifications, like university degrees, do not guarantee a level of knowledge, experience, or performance; rather, they establish a baseline for comparison. By seeking to hire vendor-certified employees, a company can assure itself that not only has it found a person skilled in networking, but also it has hired a person skilled in the specific products the company uses.

Technical professionals have also begun to recognize the value of certification and the impact it can have on their careers. By completing a certification program, professionals gain an endorsement of their skills from a major industry source. This endorsement can boost their current position, and it makes finding the next job even easier. Often a certification determines whether a first interview is even granted.

Today a certification may place you ahead of the pack. Tomorrow it will be a necessity to keep from being left in the dust.

CCNP @dvice

Signing up for an exam has become easier with the new Web-based test registration system. To sign up for the CCNP exams, access http://www.2test.com, and register for the Cisco Career Certification path. You will need to get an Internet account and password, if you do not already have one for 2test.com. Just select the option for first-time registration, and the Web site will walk you through that process. The registration wizard even provides maps to the testing centers, something that is not available when you call Sylvan Prometric on the telephone.

Cisco's Certification Program

Cisco now has a number of certifications for the Routing and Switching career track, as well as for the WAN Switching career track. While Cisco recommends a series of courses for each of these certifications, they are not required. Ultimately, certification is dependent upon a candidate's passing a series of exams. With the right experience and study materials, you can pass each of these exams without taking the associated class.

Table i-1 shows the Cisco CCNP 2.0 exam track.

The Foundation Routing and Switching exam (640-509) can be taken in place of the Routing, Switching, and Remote Access exams.

As you can see, the CCNA is the foundation of the Routing and Switching track, after which candidates can pursue the Network Support path to CCNP and CCIE, or the Network Design path to CCDA, CCDP, and to CCIE Design.

Please note that if you have taken CCNP exams from the 1.0 track (Exam #'s 640-403, 640-404, 640-405, 640-440) you may take the remainder of your exams from the 2.0 track, but you will be certified as a CCNP 1.0.

TABLE i-1	Exam Name	Exam #
CCNP 2.0 Track	CCNA 2.0	640-507
	Routing	640-503
	Switching	640-504
	Remote Access	640-505
	Support	640-506

CCNP Online

In addition to the technical objectives that are being tested for each exam, you will find much more useful information on Cisco's Web site at http://www.cisco.com/warp/public/10/wwtraining/certprog. You will find information on becoming certified, exam-specific information, sample test questions, and the latest news on Cisco certification. This is the most important site you will find on your journey to becoming Cisco certified.

CCNP Advice

When I find myself stumped answering multiple-choice questions, I use my scratch paper to write down the two or three answers I consider the strongest, and then underline the answer I feel is most likely correct. Here is an example of what my scratch paper looks like when I've gone through the test once:
21. B or <u>C</u>
33. <u>A</u> *or C*
It is extremely helpful to you mark the question and then continue. You can return to the question and immediately pick up your thought process where you left off. Use this technique to avoid having to reread and rethink questions.

You will also need to use your scratch paper during complex, text-based scenario questions to create visual images to help you understand the question. For example, during the CCNP exam you will need to draw multiple networks and the connections between them or calculate a subnet mask for a given network. By drawing the layout or working the calculation while you are interpreting the question, you may find a hint that you would not have found without your own visual aid. This technique is especially helpful if you are a visual learner.

Computer-Based Testing

In a perfect world, you would be assessed for your true knowledge of a subject, not simply how you respond to a series of test questions. But life isn't perfect, and it just isn't practical to evaluate everyone's knowledge on a one-to-one basis. (Cisco actually does have a one-to-one evaluation, but it's reserved for the CCIE Laboratory exam, and the waiting list is quite long.)

For the majority of its certifications, Cisco evaluates candidates using a computer-based testing service operated by Sylvan Prometric. This service is quite popular in the industry, and it is used for a number of vendor certification programs, including Novell's CNE and Microsoft's MCSE. Thanks to Sylvan Prometric's large number of facilities, exams can be administered worldwide, generally in the same town as a prospective candidate.

For the most part, Sylvan Prometric exams work similarly from vendor to vendor. However, there is an important fact to know about Cisco's exams: they use the traditional Sylvan Prometric test format, not the newer adaptive format. This gives the candidate an advantage, since the traditional format allows answers to be reviewed and revised during the test. (The adaptive format does not.)

CCNP
advice

Many experienced test takers do not go back and change answers unless they have a good reason to do so. You should change an answer only when you feel you may have misread or misinterpreted the question the first time. Nervousness may make you second-guess every answer and talk yourself out of a correct one.

To discourage simple memorization, Cisco exams present a different set of questions every time the exam is administered. In the development of the exam, hundreds of questions are compiled and refined, using beta testers. From this large collection, a random sampling is drawn for each test.

Each Cisco exam has a specific number of questions and test duration. Testing time is typically generous, and the time remaining is always displayed in the corner of the testing screen, along with the number of remaining questions. If time expires during an exam, the test terminates, and incomplete answers are counted as incorrect.

CCNP Advice

I have found it extremely helpful to put a check next to each objective as I find it is satisfied by the proposed solution. If the proposed solution does not satisfy an objective, you do not need to continue with the rest of the objectives. Once you have determined which objectives are fulfilled you can count your check marks and answer the question appropriately. This is a very effective testing technique!

At the end of the exam, your test is immediately graded, and the results are displayed on the screen. Scores for each subject area are also provided, but the system will not indicate which specific questions were missed. A report is automatically printed at the proctor's desk for your files. The test score is electronically transmitted back to Cisco.

In the end, this computer-based system of evaluation is reasonably fair. You might feel that one or two questions were poorly worded; this can certainly happen, but you shouldn't worry too much. Ultimately, it's all factored into the required passing score.

Question Types

Cisco exams pose questions in a variety of formats, most of which are discussed here. As candidates progress toward the more advanced certifications, the difficulty of the exams is intensified, through both the subject matter and the question formats.

CCNP Online

In order to pass these challenging exams, you may want to talk with other test takers to determine what is being tested, and what to expect in terms of difficulty. The most helpful way to communicate with other CCNP hopefuls is the Cisco mailing list. With this mailing list, you will receive e-mail every day from other members, discussing everything imaginable concerning Cisco networking equipment and certification. Access http://www.cisco.com/warp/public/84/1.html to learn how to subscribe to this source of a wealth of information.

True/False

The classic true/false question format is not used in the Cisco exams, for the obvious reason that a simple guess has a 50 percent chance of being correct. Instead, true/false questions are posed in multiple-choice format, requiring the candidate to identify the true or false statement from a group of selections.

Multiple Choice

Multiple choice is the primary format for questions in Cisco exams. These questions may be posed in a variety of ways.

Select the Correct Answer   This is the classic multiple-choice question, in which the candidate selects a single answer from a minimum of four choices. In addition to the question's wording, the choices are presented in a Windows radio button format, in which only one answer can be selected at a time. The question will instruct you to "Select the best answer" when they are looking for just one answer.

Select the Three Correct Answers   The multiple-answer version is similar to the single-choice version, but multiple answers must be provided. This is an all-or-nothing format; all the correct answers must be selected, or the entire question is incorrect. In this format, the question specifies exactly how many answers must be selected. Choices are presented in a check box format, allowing more than one answer to be selected. In addition, the testing software prevents too many answers from being selected.

Select All That Apply   The open-ended version is the most difficult multiple-choice format, since the candidate does not know how many answers should be selected. As with the multiple-answer version, all the correct answers must be selected to gain credit for the question. If too many answers or not enough answers are selected, no credit is given. This format presents choices in check box format, but the testing software does not advise the candidates whether they've selected the correct number of answers.

Make it easy on yourself and find some "braindumps." These are notes about the exam from test takers, which indicate the most difficult concepts tested, what to look out for, and sometimes even what not to bother studying. Several of these can be found at http://www.dejanews.com. Simply do a search for CCNP and browse the recent postings. Another good resource is at http://www.groupstudy.com. Beware however of the person that posts a question reported to have been on the test and its answer. First, the question and its answer may be incorrect. Second, this is a violation of Cisco's confidentiality agreement, which you as a candidate must agree to prior to taking the exam. Giving out specific information regarding a test violates this agreement and could result in the revocation of your certification status.

Freeform Response

Freeform responses are prevalent in Cisco's advanced exams, particularly where the subject focuses on router configuration and commands. In the freeform format, no choices are provided. Instead, the test prompts for user input, and the candidate must type the correct answer. This format is similar to an essay question, except the response must be specific, allowing the computer to evaluate the answer.

For example, the question

Type the command for viewing routes learned via the EIGRP protocol.

requires the answer

show ip route eigrp

For safety's sake, you should completely spell out router commands, rather than using abbreviations. In this example, the abbreviated command **SH IP ROU EI** works on a real router, but is counted as wrong by the testing software. The freeform response questions almost always are answered by commands used in the Cisco IOS. As you progress in your track for your CCNP you will find these freeform response question increasingly prevalent.

Fill in the Blank

Fill-in-the-blank questions are less common in Cisco exams. They may be presented in multiple-choice or freeform response format.

Exhibits

Exhibits, usually showing a network diagram or a router configuration, accompany many exam questions. These exhibits are displayed in a separate window, which is opened by clicking the Exhibit button at the bottom of the screen. In some cases, the testing center may provide exhibits in printed format at the start of the exam.

Scenarios

While the normal line of questioning tests a candidate's "book knowledge," scenarios add a level of complexity. Rather than asking only technical questions, they apply the candidate's knowledge to real-world situations.

Scenarios generally consist of one or two paragraphs and an exhibit that describes a company's needs or network configuration. This description is followed by a series of questions and problems that challenge the candidate's ability to address the situation. Scenario-based questions are commonly found in exams relating to network design, but they appear to some degree in each of the Cisco exams.

CCNP
Advice

You will know when you are coming to a series of scenario questions, because they are preceded by a blue screen, indicating that the following questions will have the same scenario, but different solutions. You must remember that the scenario will be the same *during the series of questions, which means that you do not have to spend time reading the scenario again.*

Studying Techniques

First and foremost, give yourself plenty of time to study. Networking is a complex field, and you can't expect to cram what you need to know into a single study session. It is a field best learned over time, by studying a subject and then applying your knowledge. Build yourself a study schedule and stick to it, but be reasonable about the pressure you put on yourself, especially if you're studying in addition to your regular duties at work.

CCNP ☜
ⓐdvice

One easy technique to use in studying for certification exams is the 30-minutes-per-day effort. Simply study for a minimum of 30 minutes every day. It is a small but significant commitment. On a day when you just can't focus, then give up at 30 minutes. On a day when it flows completely for you, study longer. As long as you have more of the flow days, your chances of succeeding are extremely high.

Second, practice and experiment. In networking, you need more than knowledge; you need understanding, too. You can't just memorize facts to be effective; you need to understand why events happen, how things work, and (most important) how and why they break.

The best way to gain deep understanding is to take your book knowledge to the lab. Try it out. Make it work. Change it a little. Break it. Fix it. Snoop around "under the hood." If you have access to a network analyzer, like Network Associate Sniffer, put it to use. You can gain amazing insight to the inner workings of a network by watching devices communicate with each other.

Unless you have a very understanding boss, don't experiment with router commands on a production router. A seemingly innocuous command can have a nasty side effect. If you don't have a lab, your local Cisco office or Cisco users' group may be able to help. Many training centers also allow students access to their lab equipment during off-hours.

Another excellent way to study is through case studies. Case studies are articles or interactive discussions that offer real-world examples of how technology is applied to meet a need. These examples can serve to cement your understanding of a technique or technology by seeing it put to use. Interactive discussions offer added value because you can also pose questions of your own. User groups are an excellent source of examples, since the purpose of these groups is to share information and learn from each other's experiences.

The Cisco Networkers conference is not to be missed. Although renowned for its wild party and crazy antics, this conference offers a wealth of information. Held every year in cities around the world, it includes three days of technical seminars and presentations on a variety of subjects. As you might imagine, it's very popular. You have to register early to get the classes you want.

Then, of course, there is the Cisco Web site. This little gem is loaded with collections of technical documents and white papers. As you progress to more advanced subjects, you will find great value in the large number of examples and reference materials available. But be warned: you need to do a lot of digging to find the really good stuff. Often your only option is to browse every document returned by the search engine to find exactly the one you need. This effort pays off. Most CCIEs I know have compiled six to ten binders of reference material from Cisco's site alone.

Scheduling Your Exam

The Cisco exams are scheduled by calling Sylvan Prometric directly at (800) 829-6387. For locations outside the United States, your local number can be found on Sylvan's Web site at http://www.prometric.com. Sylvan representatives can schedule your exam, but they don't have information about the certification programs. Questions about certifications should be directed to Cisco's training department.

This Sylvan telephone number is specific to Cisco exams, and it goes directly to the Cisco representatives inside Sylvan. These representatives are familiar enough with the exams to find them by name, but it's best if you have the specific exam number handy when you call. After all, you wouldn't want to be scheduled and charged for the wrong exam (for example, the instructor's version, which is significantly harder).

Exams can be scheduled up to a year in advance, although it's really not necessary. Generally, scheduling a week or two ahead is sufficient to reserve the day and time you prefer. When you call to schedule, operators will search for testing centers in your area. For convenience, they can also tell which testing centers you've used before.

Sylvan accepts a variety of payment methods, with credit cards being the most convenient. When you pay by credit card, you can even take tests the same day you call—provided, of course, that the testing center has room. (Quick scheduling can be handy, especially if you want to retake an exam immediately.) Sylvan will mail you a receipt and confirmation of your testing date, although this generally arrives after the test has been taken. If you need to cancel or reschedule an exam, remember to call at least one day before your exam, or you'll lose your test fee.

When you register for the exam, you will be asked for your ID number. This number is used to track your exam results back to Cisco. It's important that you use the same ID number each time you register, so that Cisco can follow your progress. Address information provided when you first register is also used by Cisco to ship certificates and other related material. In the United States, your Social Security number is commonly used as your ID number. However, Sylvan can assign you a unique ID number if you prefer not to use your Social Security number.

Table i-2 shows the available CCNP 2.0 exams and the number of questions and duration of each. This information is subject to change as Cisco revises the exams, so it's a good idea to verify the details when you register for an exam.

In addition to the regular Sylvan Prometric testing sites, Cisco also offers facilities for taking exams free of charge at each Networkers Conference in the United States. As you might imagine, this option is quite popular, so reserve your exam time as soon as you arrive at the conference.

Arriving at the Exam

As with any test, you'll be tempted to cram the night before. Resist that temptation. You should know the material by this point, and if you're too groggy in the morning, you won't remember what you studied anyway. Instead, get a good night's sleep.

Arrive early for your exam; it gives you time to relax and review key facts. Take the opportunity to review your notes. If you get burned out on studying, you can usually start your exam a few minutes early. On the other hand, I don't recommend arriving late. Your test could be canceled, or you might be left without enough time to complete the exam.

When you arrive at the testing center, you'll need to sign in with the exam administrator. In order to sign in, you need to provide two forms of identification. Acceptable forms include government-issued IDs (for example, passport or driver's license), credit cards, and company ID badge. One form of ID must include a photograph.

TABLE i-2   Cisco Exam Lengths and Question Counts

Exam Title	Exam Number	Number of Questions	Duration (minutes)	Exam Fee (US$)
Routing 2.0	640-503	80	90	$100
Switching 2.0	640-504	80	90	$100
Remote Access 2.0	640-505	80	90	$100
Support 2.0	640-506	80	90	$100

Aside from a brain full of facts, you don't need to bring anything else to the exam. In fact, your brain is about all you're allowed to take into the exam. All the tests are closed book, meaning that you don't get to bring any reference materials with you. You're also not allowed to take any notes out of the exam room. The test administrator will provide you with paper and a pencil. Some testing centers may provide a small marker board instead.

Calculators are not allowed, so be prepared to do any necessary math (such as hex-binary-decimal conversions or subnet masks) in your head or on paper. Additional paper is available if you need it.

Leave your pager and telephone in the car, or turn them off. They only add stress to the situation, since they are not allowed in the exam room, and can sometimes still be heard if they ring outside the room. Purses, books, and other materials must be left with the administrator before you enter. While you're in the exam room, it's important that you don't disturb other candidates; talking is not allowed during the exam.

In the exam room, the exam administrator logs onto your exam, and you have to verify that your ID number and the exam number are correct. If this is the first time you've taken a Cisco test, you can select a brief tutorial for the exam software. Before the test begins, you will be provided with facts about the exam, including the duration, the number of questions, and the score required for passing. Then the clock starts ticking, and the fun begins.

The testing software is Windows-based, but you won't have access to the main desktop or to any of the accessories. The exam is presented in full screen, with a single question per screen. Navigation buttons allow you to move forward and backward between questions. In the upper right corner of the screen, counters show the number of questions and time remaining. Most important, there is a Mark check box in the upper left corner of the screen—this will prove to be a critical tool in your testing technique.

Test-Taking Techniques

One of the most frequent excuses I hear for failing a Cisco exam is "poor time management." Without a plan of attack, candidates are overwhelmed by the exam or become sidetracked and run out of time. For the most part, if you are comfortable with the material, the allotted time is more than enough to complete the exam. The trick is to keep the time from slipping away when you work on any one particular problem.

Your obvious goal in taking an exam is to answer the questions effectively, although other aspects of the exam can distract from this goal. After taking a fair number of computer-based exams, I've developed a technique for tackling the problem, which I share with you here. Of course, you still need to learn the material. These steps just help you take the exam more efficiently.

Size Up the Challenge

First take a quick pass through all the questions in the exam. "Cherry-pick" the easy questions, answering them on the spot. Briefly read each question, noticing the type of question and the subject. As a guideline, try to spend less than 25 percent of your testing time in this pass.

This step lets you assess the scope and complexity of the exam, and it helps you determine how to pace your time. It also gives you an idea of where to find potential answers to some of the questions. Often the answer to one question is shown in the exhibit of another. Sometimes the wording of one question might lend clues or jog your thoughts for another question.

Imagine that the following questions are posed in this order:

Question 1: Review the router configurations and network diagram in exhibit XYZ (not shown here). Which devices should be able to ping each other?

Question 2: If RIP routing were added to exhibit XYZ, which devices would be able to ping each other?

The first question seems straightforward. Exhibit XYZ probably includes a diagram and a couple of router configurations. Everything looks normal, so you decide that all devices can ping each other.

Now consider the hint left by Question 2. When you answered Question 1, did you notice that the configurations were missing the routing protocol? Oops! Being alert to such clues can help you catch your own mistakes.

If you're not entirely confident with your answer to a question, answer it anyway, but check the Mark check box to flag it for later review. If you run out of time, at least you've provided a first-guess answer, rather than leaving it blank.

Take on the Scenario Questions

Second, go back through the entire test, using the insight you gained from the first go-through. For example, if the entire test looks difficult, you'll know better than to spend more than a minute or so on each question. Break down the pacing into small milestones; for example, "I need to answer 10 questions every 15 minutes."

At this stage, it's probably a good idea to skip past the time-consuming questions, marking them for the next pass. Try to finish this phase before you're 50 to 60 percent through the testing time.

By now, you probably have a good idea where the scenario questions are found. A single scenario tends to have several questions associated with it, but they aren't necessarily grouped together in the exam. Rather than rereading the scenario every time you encounter a related question, save some time by answering the questions as a group.

Tackle the Complex Problems

Third, go back through all the questions you marked for review, using the Review Marked button in the question review screen. This step includes taking a second look at all the questions you were unsure of in previous passes, as well as tackling the time-consuming ones you postponed until now. Chisel away at this group of questions until you've answered them all.

If you're more comfortable with a previously marked question, unmark it now. Otherwise, leave it marked. Work your way now through the time-consuming questions, especially those requiring manual calculations. Unmark them when you're satisfied with the answer.

By the end of this step, you've answered every question in the test, despite your reservations about some of your answers. If you run out of time in the next step, at least you won't lose points for lack of an answer. You're in great shape if you still have 10 to 20 percent of your time remaining.

Review Your Answers

Now you're cruising! You've answered all the questions, and you're ready to do a quality check. Take yet another pass (yes, one more) through the entire test, briefly rereading each question and your answer. Be cautious about revising answers at this point unless you're sure a change is warranted. If there's a doubt about changing the answer, I always trust my first instinct and leave the original answer intact.

Trick questions are rarely asked, so don't read too much into the questions. Again, if the wording of the question confuses you, leave the answer intact. Your first impression was probably right.

Be alert for last-minute clues. You're pretty familiar with nearly every question at this point, and you may find a few clues that you missed before.

The Grand Finale

When you're confident with all your answers, finish the exam by submitting it for grading. After what will seem like the longest ten seconds of your life, the testing software will respond with your score. This is usually displayed as a bar graph, showing the minimum passing score, your score, and a PASS/FAIL indicator.

If you're curious, you can review the statistics of your score at this time. Answers to specific questions are not presented; rather, questions are lumped into categories, and results are tallied for each category. This detail is also given on a report that has been automatically printed at the exam administrator's desk.

As you leave the exam, you'll need to leave your scratch paper behind or return it to the administrator. (Some testing centers track the number of sheets you've been given, so be sure to return them all.) In exchange, you'll receive a copy of the test report.

This report will be embossed with the testing center's seal, and you should keep it in a safe place. Normally, the results are automatically transmitted to Cisco, but occasionally you might need the paper report to prove that you passed the exam. Your personnel file is probably a good place to keep this report; the file tends to follow you everywhere, and it doesn't hurt to have favorable exam results turn up during a performance review.

Retesting

If you don't pass the exam, don't be discouraged—networking is complex stuff. Try to have a good attitude about the experience, and get ready to try again. Consider yourself a little more educated. You know the format of the test a little better, and the report shows which areas you need to strengthen.

If you bounce back quickly, you'll probably remember several of the questions you might have missed. This will help you focus your study efforts in the right area. Serious go-getters will reschedule the exam for a couple of days after the previous attempt, while the study material is still fresh in their minds.

Ultimately, remember that Cisco certifications are valuable because they're hard to get. After all, if anyone could get one, what value would it have? In the end, it takes a good attitude and a lot of studying, but you can do it!

CISCO® CERTIFIED NETWORK PROFESSIONAL

1

Support Resources for Troubleshooting

CERTIFICATION OBJECTIVES

Companies in today's business world seem to more often merge, be acquired, or acquire other companies. Overnight, the size of a network can double. Even without corporate mergers, small companies to large enterprises want to stay on the edge of technology with faster servers, networks, voice and video integration, redundant systems, and more reliable infrastructure. Even in a "stable" environment, without significant change, there is often a steady increase of users, systems, and resources. As a result, it might be easy for a network manager to lose sight of the direction the network is taking.

It is obvious that our networks are growing, and even small changes can severely stress them—at the very least, degrading their performance and at times rendering the networks and systems attached to them useless. Nearly every network has become mission critical at some point, and we must strive to reduce the amount of system downtime.

What does it mean when your network is down? How much does it cost if your entire company misses one hour of work, or an entire day? What would it cost you in regard to customer confidence if your customers learned your network was down for an extended period of time?

This chapter presents an overview of some of the tools that are available to help you troubleshoot and maintain greater control over your network and, as a result, reduce the amount of unscheduled downtime. These tools include applications and resources from Cisco as well as third-party companies. This chapter covers a range of items from Internet resources to hardware diagnostics and protocol analyzers to modeling and monitoring tools.

CERTIFICATION OBJECTIVE 1.01

Types and Purposes of Troubleshooting Tools

"Like all other arts, the Science of Deduction and Analysis is one which can only be acquired by long and patient study, nor is life long enough to allow any mortal to attain the highest possible perfection in it." —*Sherlock Holmes*

Troubleshooting in itself is an art. It is how we apply our knowledge of networking that provides us with our skills in deduction. The tools we have provide us with the means, or the science, to prove our deductions. The tools presented here will more quickly help narrow the list of possible solutions to your network problems.

Media Test Equipment

In most cases, troubleshooting starts with the Physical Layer, and cable testers can offer a wide range of functionality along with a wide range of prices. One of the most basic and inexpensive tools available is a *volt-ohm meter (VOM)*, or a *digital multimeter (DMM)*. This simple piece of equipment can quickly provide information about the Physical Layer of the network. These meters are able to test basic continuity and measure AC and DC voltage, current, and resistance. In some cases, they can also measure inductance and capacitance.

Basic *cable scanners* often operate as a pair of devices, one at each end of a wire, with light-emitting diodes (LEDs) that check continuity. Certain combinations of LED colors indicate proper operation or show if the cable is wired incorrectly.

Higher-level cable scanners also often include automated tests to provide greater detail and depth of information. This includes testing a variety of media such as unshielded twisted-pair (UTP), shielded twisted-pair (STP), and coaxial cables. Cable scanners can often provide a wire map that tells us if the wiring is correct, if it us using EIA-TIA 568 A/B or USOC wiring schemes, and if there are shorts, opens, or crossed pairs on a cable. Higher-end cable scanners also include *time-domain reflectometers (TDRs)*, which can tell how long a cable is and if there is a short or open along the cable. Other functions also include information on near-end crosstalk (NEXT) and attenuation at various frequencies or speeds such as 10MHz or 100MHz. The term *crosstalk* refers to the tendency of signals to "jump" pairs near the ends of wires, where the pairs have been separated and untwisted. *Attenuation* is the tendency for signals to get weaker over distance.

At the high end of the cable scanner range are some devices that provide greater detail—not at only at the Physical Layer, but also at the Transport and Network Layers. These devices are often capable of displaying Media Access Control (MAC) addresses, Internet Protocol (IP) addresses, ranges, and subnet information, along with network utilization. Information provided can include utilization by device and diagnostic information, with possible solutions to common problems. Test equipment in this category might even be able to interact with a Domain Name Server (DNS) and possibly basic Transmission Control Protocol/Internet Protocol (TCP/IP) tests such as PING. Most of this test equipment is primarily for cables (copper twisted pair and coax), but there are also similar devices for testing single-mode and multimode optical fiber or attachments specifically for fiber.

Some of the more popular companies that produce these types of cable scanners include the following:

- Fluke (www.fluke.com)
- Microtest (www.microtest.com)
- AVO International (www.avointl.com)
- Datacom Technologies (www.datacom.textron.com)

exam
Ⓦatch

Be familiar with basic Physical Layer cable specifications such as maximum length for various technologies such as 10Base-T, 100Base-T, and multimode and single-mode fiber for both full- and half-duplex operation.

Network Monitors

Network monitors are to networks what fire detection systems are to buildings. In a building, the fire detection system is always operating, and by monitoring the system, you can determine if there is fire or smoke on a particular floor or specific area. Some systems even report information from temperature sensors and determine if water is flowing to the sprinkler system in a specific area.

The network monitor nearly parallels the fire detection system. Network monitors continuously track information on each individual segment of the network, including monitoring protocols, packet size, flow, errors, and other statistics.

A network monitor also helps define a baseline for the network. A *baseline* is merely a snapshot or statistical average of the normal status or performance of the network. The network monitor can compare ongoing network events to the baseline and alert a network manager to events that might be abnormal, such as excessive errors, retransmissions, or bandwidth utilization.

Network monitors can also provide us with historical and trending information. Based on the information provided, we can more reliably determine when a particular segment should be split or migrated to a higher bandwidth.

Network monitors are typically deployed on critical—and in some cases, all—segments of a network, including wide area links and remote locations. Each monitor sends its information to a central collection or management system and can be queried for more detailed information, if needed.

on the **Job**

Some protocol analyzers such as Network Associates' Distributed Sniffer also can function as a network monitor. Such a network monitor, working in conjunction with a collector or management console such as NetScout (www.netscout.com), can help you collect an extensive historical record of your network.

Protocol Analyzers

Another important tool for the network manager is the *protocol* or *packet analyzer*. These devices are also commonly called "sniffers," although Sniffer is also the name of a product from Network Associates (previously Network General). The generic term *sniffer* is frequently used to mean a packet analyzer, much as "Kleenex" is used for tissue.

A protocol analyzer is to a network what an EKG is to the heart. The primary purpose of a protocol analyzer is to capture packets on a specific segment of a network. By reviewing this traffic, you can view the contents of each packet. Very basic functions of protocol analyzers include monitoring real-time statistics such as packets or frames per second, bandwidth utilization, and distribution of packets of various sizes.

Most protocol analyzers can display packets in various modes. This includes summary views, which normally display source and destination addresses and port numbers. The heart of protocol analysis is the actual decoding of a packet. This decoding can be displayed in a raw hexadecimal format, usually with its translation or interpretation of the data so we can better understand the packet contents.

Some protocol analyzers, such as Network Associates' Sniffer Pro product, include an expert analysis function. Using this feature, you can come up with possible solutions or recommendations regarding the operation of the network after several minutes of capturing data.

Protocol analyzers are tremendously helpful, but only if you know how to use them. Do not expect to use a packet analyzer for the first time and have everything be crystal clear to you. As with any tool, you will need to spend some time getting familiar with its operation. The best time to do this is when the network is operating normally. For protocol analyzers, this usually means you should be able to narrow down the output to include only what you need to see and then be able to understand that output. The two tasks are somewhat similar. The scope of the number and type of packets must be narrowed, so as not to be overwhelmed by the sheer number of packets. In order to specify what packets you want to see, you need to know something about the protocol you are trying to monitor—which is the first step to understanding the packets themselves. This means knowing which MAC addresses to look for, which Layer 3 protocol addresses to look for, and which socket or port numbers to look for. For example, you might need to monitor how Dynamic Host Configuration Protocol (DHCP) transactions occur between the client and server because workstations are no longer obtaining addresses automatically.

The best way to learn how to use your packet analyzer is to put it to work monitoring a protocol that is running properly. As with most tools, it is best not to try and learn how to use the packet analyzer while you are working on a problem. If you have been following the Cisco certification track, this likely is not a problem, since many examples of protocol analyzer output have been presented throughout your training. Don't forget that several questions on the tests will be based on packet analyzer output.

exam
ⓦatch

Cisco IOS-based DEBUG commands can effectively produce the same raw output as a protocol analyzer. Be prepared to see several decode screen shots and be able to identify information in the network and data link headers (for example, frame types).

EXERCISE 1-1

Using Troubleshooting Tools

Scenario: A workstation on your network has been experiencing very poor network performance when communicating with other systems. The workstation is functioning properly, and performance is good after the station is moved to another network connection. What is the most likely cause of the original performance issues, and how can it be tested?

Solution: Besides configuration issues, the most common problems are related to cabling. Using a cable scanner, test the wiring between the workstation and the hub. This includes any patch cables that are attached to the workstation and the hub. It is important to note that a simple "wire map" or continuity check might not be a sufficient test, and other factors could induce problems. A TDR might be required to ensure that the cable length does not exceed the maximum specifications, and "noise" could be induced on the line by being in close proximity to electrical wiring and equipment such as fluorescent lighting.

SCENARIO & SOLUTION

Why does troubleshooting typically start at the Physical Layer?	Other than configuration errors, the most common faults are found at the Physical Layer. These faults can include faulty cables, failed transceivers and network adapters, and the like. Operation of the Physical Layer of the Open Systems Interconnection (OSI) model must be confirmed before we can ensure that the other layers are operating properly.
What is a "baseline" and how do I use it?	A baseline shows what is "normal" for your network. A baseline can be taken on many different variables, such as bandwidth, error rate, or CPU utilization. By comparing a snapshot of the current value of a variable against the baseline, you can determine when the network is not operating properly. When used over time, these snapshots could show a trend and can be used for future planning.
Is a cable scanner or TDR really necessary for troubleshooting?	In a small network that experiences few changes, most likely not. However, in larger networks, use of a cable scanner can save considerable time. You can quickly check cables between end stations and hubs, and you can easily determine if there is a cable fault. For new installations using TDR, the total length of a cable can be determined to see if it falls within the acceptable length.

CERTIFICATION OBJECTIVE 1.02

Network Management Systems

We all know that businesses rely more on networks, which are more complex than ever before. They're also more visible than ever before. As a result, administrators need to be able to quickly identify when a problem occurs and where it is and be able to effect their repair rapidly. Consequently, network management has become more than just an option or an afterthought for a network. Network management is nearly a necessity and must be designed along with the network, from the ground up.

Network management is much more than a series of icons displayed on a screen. Network management is a proactive tool. It consists of several individual areas:

■ Inventory management

■ Configuration management

■ Security management

■ Performance management

■ Fault management

These subdivisions reduce the total cost of ownership and provides a way to do things more easily. Using these tools, administrators can monitor, configure, and administer a wide array of devices.

Before we cover the finer points of network management, it is helpful to understand some of the basic building blocks of network management. These building blocks include Management Information Base (MIB), Standard Network Management Protocol (SNMP), and remote monitoring (RMON).

Management Information Bases

A *Management Information Base (MIB)* is a database of objects for a specific device. MIB 1 includes 114 standard objects that are considered essential for either fault or configuration management. MIB II extends MIB I and has 185 objects defined. Other standard MIBs include RMON, host, router, and switch. Most companies use proprietary MIBs, which are extensions of standard MIBs that work in conjunction with the company's hardware,

Simple MIB variables include:

■ **Router**   Free buffers, congestions, errors, dropped packets

■ **Switch**   Dropped packets, error rates

■ **Hub**   Collisions

■ **Server**   Disk utilization, CPU utilization

FROM THE CLASSROOM

Documenting the Network

Often, documenting the network is an afterthought. That's a mistake. Even during the most basic stages of network design and implementation, documentation is critical.

Even more critical than creating the documentation is its maintenance. As a general rule, do not create documentation that will not be maintained. This might sound harsh, but no documentation might be better than inaccurate documentation. For example: a network management system reports that a specific segment of the network is experiencing a high error rate. Based on this information and your documentation, a technician sets out to a specific wiring closet to monitor the network with a protocol analyzer—only to

find that there is no problem, only normal utilization and no errors. After reporting this situation, the technician learns that he was directed to the wrong segment. The end result: network users and applications continue to suffer because the documentation had not been updated.

While troubleshooting various issues, we often go from one possible solution to another, without documenting our changes. Again, this results in lost time, since we might lose track of exactly what we did and have to reproduce our efforts later. After changes have been made in the network, all applicable documentation needs to be updated to reflect the current configuration of the network and equipment.

—*Edward Moss, CCNP, CCDP, CNE*

Simple Network Management Protocol

Simple Network Management Protocol (SNMP) is an Application Layer protocol designed for message exchange. SNMP can provide significant information about a device through polling. *Polling* is the mechanism that allows for retrieval of MIB information by using a GET function. SNMP is used to retrieve MIB information as well as update operating parameters on remote systems from one common location.

SNMP functions are typically broken into two default categories, or *communities*, which are normally defined as *public* and *private*. Using public queries, you can normally obtain basic operational information from a network device. The private community is normally reserved for changing the operational parameters of a network device, such as system passwords. Often, the words *public* and *private* are the default community strings or passwords for these functions and should be changed.

Although a wealth of information can be obtained using SNMP, it does not lend itself well to proactive monitoring. This is because regular polling from a central management console can consume significant bandwidth, which might become critical if monitored from a remote location across a slow wide area network (WAN) link.

Remote Monitoring

Remote monitoring (RMON) was designed to support proactive monitoring of network traffic but not the network devices themselves. RMON provides the ability to set thresholds. When a threshold has been exceeded, the RMON agent alerts the *Network Management System (NMS)* and reports the alarm. RMON enables:

- Network fault diagnosis
- Planning
- Performance tuning

RMON1 Groups

Currently RFC 1757 defines nine RMON groups and monitors only the first two layers of the OSI model, or the Physical and the Data-Link Layers. These nine groups are:

- **Statistics**   Real-time current statistics
- **History**   Statistics over time
- **Alarm**   Predetermined threshold watch
- **Host**   Tracks individual host statistics
- **HostTopN**   *N* statistically most active hosts
- **Matrix**   A<>B - Conversion statistics
- **Filter**   Packet structure and content matching
- **Capture**   Collection for subsequent analysis
- **Event**   Reaction to predetermined conditions

Currently RFC1513 defines an additional group to the RMON 1 specification:

- **TokenRing**   Token Ring RMON extensions

RMON2 Groups

RMON2 is an addition to the RMON specification, not a replacement for it. An additional nine groups (for a total of 19) were added to the specification. RMON2 also provided for the monitoring of Layers 3 through 7, allowing RMON to monitor the entire OSI model. The RMON2 specification is covered in RFC 2021 and includes the following groups:

- **protocolDir**   Probes master list of protocols.
- **protocolDist**   Segment protocol statistics.
- **addressMap**   Host-to-MAC address-matching list.
- **nlHost—Host in/out**   Network Layer statistics.
- **nlMatrix—A<>B**   Network Layer statistics.
- **alHost—Host in/out**   Application Layer statistics.
- **alMatrix—A<>B**   Application Layer statistics.
- **usrHistory**   Data logging—user-specified carryables.
- **probeConfig**   Probes configuration standards.

4 RMON Groups Enabled by Default in Catalyst Switches

All Cisco IOS software images, at a minimum, include some RMON support. This support includes RMON alarms and event groups. These groups can be coupled with existing Cisco MIB variables.

Be warned that unlike SNMP, the RMON process can be very processor intensive and could severely impact the performance of the device.

on the
ĵob

For cost-conscious customers, an application called the Multi-Router Traffic Grapher (MRTG) is available under the GNU General Public License and can be found at http://ee-staff.ethz.ch/~oetiker/webtools/mrtg/mrtg.html. Using this utility, users can produce effective graphs of traffic and error rates, CPU, memory, and modem pool utilization—or virtually any other variable available— through SNMP. Users can generate graphs, which can be viewed with a Web browser, showing traffic seen during the last seven days, the last four weeks, and the last 12 months by consolidating the data collected. Keep in mind that regular polling of network devices increases the amount of traffic on the network.

CiscoWorks

Everyone wants up-to-date and accurate information on all devices in the network. This is often a rare achievement; in most organizations it is difficult to obtain a simple inventory of devices. With this in mind, imagine how enormous the task would be to manually compile the inventory, list of interfaces, amount of memory, IOS version, and so on—and then keep it updated. CiscoWorks is able to assist us in completing this monumental task.

CiscoWorks is Cisco's SNMP management product. More accurately, it is Cisco's *collection* of SNMP management products. This section of the chapter provides a short introduction to CiscoWorks 2000, the latest version of CiscoWorks. This product is fairly complex, and it would take a book or two to cover it comprehensively. In fact, network management is a specialization track for both CCNP and CCIE. Here, the suite of CiscoWorks products is presented with descriptions of their general capabilities, providing you with some of the information on which you might be tested.

Resource Manager Essentials

Previous versions of CiscoWorks required a third-party resource manager. For SNMP software, a *resource manager* is the portion of the software that is responsible for discovering SNMP devices and for doing the basic polling function. One example of such software is Hewlett-Packard's OpenView. On top of the resource manager is usually some sort of graphical map of the network, employing various shapes and colors to indicate equipment types, link types, and the state of the network. Some SNMP management software also includes *element managers,* which are usually device-specific software used for specialized management functions. For example, an element manager might manage the modem settings of a modem pool device. Typically, element managers can be launched by making a selection from a graphical map.

Resource Manager Essentials (RME) contain many elements. Among these are Inventory Manager, Change Audit Service, Device Configuration Manager, Availability Manager, Syslog Analyzer, Cisco Management Connection, and CCO Service tools:

■ **Inventory Manager**   Maintains an up-to-date hardware and software inventory.

- **Change Audit Service**   Displays comprehensive reports of software, hardware, and configuration changes, when they were made and by whom, and if they were made from the command-line interface (CLI) or a CiscoWorks 2000 application.

- **Device Configuration Manager**   Maintains an active archive of router and switch configurations, allowing you to search for specific configuration specifications and compare configuration files.

- **Software Image Manager**   Simplifies and speeds software image analysis and deployment.

- **Availability Manager**   Highlights critical devices' ability to respond.

- **Syslog Analyzer**   Isolates network error conditions and suggests probable causes.

- **Cisco Management Connection**   Builds Cisco Management Connections to your favorite management applications.

Resource Manager also provides tools that directly link to Cisco Connection Online (CCO), which can greatly reduce the amount of time you spend searching for diagnostic information. RME also can also be used to track SMARTnet contracts and directly submit Cisco Technical Assistance Center (TAC) problem reports and track open bugs on IOS and Catalyst releases.

CiscoWorks for Switched Internetworks

CiscoWorks for Switched Internetworks, or *CWSI* (pronounced "swizzy") is a suite of network management applications that allow you to configure, monitor, and manage a switched internetwork. CiscoWorks 2000 includes its own resource manager, so no additional software purchase is necessary. If you desire, CiscoWorks 2000 can also run on top of a number of other resource managers such as OpenView and Tivoli as well as exchange management information with these management platforms. The main view into CiscoWorks is CWSI.

CiscoView

CiscoView, Cisco's most widely deployed device management platform, is entirely Web based and browser accessible. CiscoView allows you to graphically view virtually any Cisco device, including routers, switches, access servers, hubs, and concentrators. At a glance, you can view the status of individual interfaces and ports to quickly grasp critical and essential information.

The CiscoView application allows greater capabilities than simply viewing device status. With Read Only and Read/Write security options, users also have the ability to modify configurations such as trap, IP route, virtual local area network (VLAN), and bridge configurations.

VLAN Director

The VLAN Director application enables you to display, configure, modify, and manage VLANs in your network by providing a graphical mapping utility for Cisco Catalyst switches. For example, VLAN Director can be used to discover and document your present VLAN configuration. To simply change the configuration—for example, if you wanted to add a port to a VLAN—all you need to do is drag a port icon from CiscoView to the appropriate VLAN name in VLAN Director.

Traffic Director

Traffic Director allows you to monitor and record critical information about network usage, events, and trends. You can then analyze this information to identify and isolate potential network problems.

Traffic Director is a centralized database that collects SNMP and RMON data from agents that are located at various points on a network. These agents include switches, routers, and specialized probes.

You can perform simple functions such as monitoring network traffic and measuring data flow, as well as setting thresholds and generating alarms when the thresholds are exceeded.

Traffic Director can also act as a distributed protocol analyzer by selectively gathering network traffic as frames from any operational segment protocol, node, or conversation. Each agent will then store this information in an internal file and send the file to the Traffic Director console when requested. The Protocol Decode application then reads the file and presents each packet in a raw data (byte) form or the full seven-layer decode.

ATM Director

ATM Director discovers asynchronous transfer mode (ATM) switches, physical links, and permanent and switched virtual connections and provides performance monitoring of ATM switches and links within the ATM network. ATM Director also displays ATM VLANs and Private Network-to-Network Interface (PNNI) components and their status in the network.

on the job *CiscoWorks for Windows is a product suite suited to small and medium-sized businesses, whereas Cisco Works 2000 is oriented toward large enterprise networks. CiscoWorks for Windows includes Whats-Up Gold from Ipswitch Inc., Cisco View, Threshold Manager (to configure RMON enabled devices), and utilities to execute a variety of SHOW commands.*

NetSys

Fixing network problems can be both time consuming and very costly. Often, changes are made on a remote router that could result in loss of communication to that router. If no one with the necessary technical expertise is at the site, and without a redundant link or out-of-band management, there might no way to repair the damage other than to dispatch an engineer to the site or ship replacement equipment.

According to Cisco, most reported network problems are configuration related. More than 40 percent of Cisco's technical support calls involve device misconfigurations. Errors that affect connectivity can be fairly obvious and easy to locate, but as networks grow in complexity, the chance of making latent errors increases significantly. Latent errors are typically not found right away and can be very difficult to isolate. Latent errors often come to the surface when additional, seemingly minor changes are made or the network comes under heavy load.

Cisco's NetSys Baseliner helps alleviate the problems that can arise from configuration changes by allowing configurations and changes to be made offline, before committing them to the live network. NetSys Baseliner creates a model of your network by using system configuration files. The network can then be viewed graphically as configured, not planned or discovered. NetSys Baseliner then checks for more than 100 common yet difficult-to-isolate configuration problems, providing a more complete understanding of how the network functions.

NetSys Baseliner also proactively monitors configuration changes by maintaining a historical record of each device's configuration. You can generate many reports that provide an overview of the network's health. These reports can immediately isolate the sources of errors and assist in problem resolution by detailing the exact Cisco IOS commands that have changed in each configuration file.

When used properly, NetSys is a tool that aids in network design, analysis, redesign, and stress testing, providing information on the performance of a network.

CiscoWorks 2000 is a suite of applications, not a single product. Cisco maintains several product numbers for various versions of the suite. For example, CiscoWorks suites are available for LAN or WAN solutions. The LAN suite includes applications for advanced management of Catalyst switching platforms. The WAN suite includes applications more suited to traffic management and access control as well as applications to administer the routed infrastructure.

Be prepared to answer several questions relating to Cisco management tools. Questions will most likely be general in nature and ask such things as when it would be appropriate to use a specific application. For example, VLAN Director is used to manage VLAN configurations.

SCENARIO & SOLUTION

Which tools will help me build a visual map of my network?	Most any SNMP management package with an autodiscovery feature can provide this type of map. CiscoWorks for Windows and CiscoWorks 2000 are just some of the applications available.
How can I view the values of MIBs on my equipment?	Many applications are available. CiscoWorks for Windows includes Whats-Up Gold by Ipswitch software. This application can send the necessary SNMP commands to view the MIB variables. Other applications such as the MRTG can query many variables on a regular basis and graphically display the results over time.
I want to use CiscoWorks 2000 to manage my network. Which product do I need?	This used to be very confusing because there was no single product called CiscoWorks 2000. CiscoWorks is a suite of applications. Cisco now provides this product in two primary versions, *Routed WAN Management* and *LAN Management*. Additional information can be found at *www.cisco.com/warp/public/44/jump/ciscoworks.shtml.*

EXERCISE 1-2

Network Management

Scenario: You want to monitor the amount of traffic on several segments of your network to create a baseline. Which application would be the most appropriate to perform this function?

Solution: The most appropriate application would be Traffic Director. Traffic Director allows you monitor and record critical information about network usage, events, and trends. These data are collected from agents, such as switches, routers, and specialized probes, via SNMP and RMON. Other applications can also provide similar functionality, but many of these utilize SNMP only and query each device often. This increased amount of traffic, especially for a large number of devices, can have significant impact on the performance of the network.

CERTIFICATION OBJECTIVE 1.03

Cisco Connection Online

Cisco recognizes that each customer is unique and presents a distinct set of requirements, from size and operational necessity of each customer's network to the design of the infrastructure and the level of support needed to maintain that infrastructure.

Cisco Connection Online (CCO) is the foundation of a suite of interactive network applications that provide access to a wealth of resources via the Internet. Cisco is committed to providing customer satisfaction, and CCO is designed to meet that goal.

CCO offers Internet commerce and technical support applications that provide immediate online access to the same knowledge base that are available to Cisco technical assistance service representatives. By delivering all the functionality required to design, implement, and support Cisco products and systems, these applications help users speed the resolution of network issues and work more proactively to improve network performance and uptime.

CCO provides users with two levels of access:

- **Guest Access** The general public can review company and product information as well as most product documentation.

- **Registered Access** Registered customers have either purchased a support contract or are authorized Cisco Partners. Registered users have access to all the guest information as well as advanced online services, software, and utilities. Varying levels of registered access are tailored to the levels of Cisco resellers and Cisco employees.

exam
ⓌatchＷatch

Remember that CCO is accessible both online and via CD. Information on the CD is updated monthly, and the online version is updated continuously.

Infrastructure

CCO can be accessed with virtually any Web browser and is available in a variety of languages, including English, Chinese, French, Russian, Italian, Spanish, German, Korean, and many others.

Cisco maintains primary support centers in San Jose, California; Research Triangle Park, North Carolina; Brussels, Belgium; and Sydney, Australia. Cisco also maintains several points of presence for content in countries throughout the world, providing users quicker access to system documentation.

Documentation

CCO provides access to Cisco's entire library of end-user documentation, selected product news, and bug databases that are updated constantly. Among the documents are:

- Router, switch, and hub installation guides
- IOS release notes, configuration guides, command references, and summaries
- Debugging references and error messages
- Cisco MIB

Cisco's documentation is also available on CD and is packaged with most core products; it is also available by subscription. Subscriptions are updated and shipped monthly.

Marketplace

Cisco's Marketplace is one method via which users can order networking products, training materials, subscriptions, and promotional merchandise.

Using the Marketplace configuration tools, users can select a product to be configured, such as a router or a switch. The configuration tools then display a list of product bundles. Users complete the configuration with the other necessary components such as IOS versions and feature licenses, power supplies, cables, the Network Processing Engine, and port adapter options. The configuration is then verified to ensure the capabilities of the chassis have not been exceeded nor anything left out that is necessary for operation.

Like most of the online offerings, Marketplace is available 24 hours a day, seven days a week.

Software Center

The primary purpose of Cisco's software center is to deliver software upgrades and solutions for a variety of products. Users can quickly access a wide range of software products—from Cisco IOS software for use on routers, switches, and gateway platforms to network management and security applications for workstation servers. Other software found here includes internetworking protocol suites for host systems and software utilities such as the Router Software Loader (RSL) and Cisco ConfigMaker.

The software center also provides information required to upgrade various platforms. For example, certain images might require a specific ROM image, amount of Flash memory, or RAM. Some documentation is included in this area, such as the *IOS Reference Guide*, which contains information about Cisco IOS software, including the Cisco IOS release process, release-naming conventions, software maintenance numbering conventions, and the relationship between various Cisco IOS releases.

Bug Toolkit

The Bug Toolkit is an integrated set of applications allowing users to quickly identify, evaluate, categorize, and track defects that could impact a user's network.

Bug Navigator II

The Bug Navigator II utility searches for known bugs based on software version, feature set, and keywords. The resulting matrix shows when each bug was integrated or fixed, if applicable.

Bug Watcher

With Bug Watcher, users can create "bins" that can "watch" or monitor the status of any number of defects. Bins can be generated from Bug Navigator as a result of a search or can be directly edited within the tool to add specific bug IDs. Bins can also be updated by search agents that monitor the Bug database on an ongoing basis for new bugs that match profiles defined in Bug Alerts. When configured correctly, the Bug Watcher can notify users via e-mail of any potential bugs or issues that match a specific platform or IOS.

Troubleshooting Engine

The troubleshooting engine helps users solve common problems quickly and easily. Users are able to provide information on the symptoms of their problem in conjunction with IOS revision, hardware platform, and general technology.

The troubleshooting engine returns links to resources that best match your search criteria. From the results screen, you can select a resource or enter additional information to refine your search results even more.

The Cisco Technical Assistance Center also provides a list of top issues with answers to the most common questions asked of the TAC for specific technologies.

Stack Decoder

Users turn to the Stack Decoder in rare circumstances, such as when a Cisco router encounters a set of conditions it has not been programmed to handle. In these situations, the router generates a stack trace.

Stack traces can be displayed by executing the privileged command SHOW STACK from the exec prompt of the router. The stack trace is an important feature of the Cisco IOS that allows the subsequent diagnosis and repair of the underlying cause.

Cisco considers a software defect to be any situation that results in a stack trace and restart not due to a hardware failure.

Once the trace has been analyzed, Stack Decoder presents a list of potential resolutions. This list normally includes a list of Bug IDs. From examining this list and comparing details such as IOS revision, platform, and conditions described in the bug summary, the root cause of the crash should become evident.

Open Forum

The Open Forum is an interactive tool that taps the technical knowledge and expertise of many network professionals. CCIEs participate in the Open Forum by answering questions submitted by customers. It is important to remember that these CCIEs might or might not work for Cisco, and the Open Forum is provided to Cisco customers as a service. The answers provided in the forum do not necessarily represent the views of Cisco.

Case Management Toolkit

The Case Management Toolkit allows customers to open, query, and update cases with the TAC. Before opening a case online (even before calling TAC), users should query both the Open Forum and the Troubleshooting Engine. Remember, Cisco has stated that more than 40 percent of all problems opened with the TAC are related to misconfigurations, and the majority of these issues can be resolved with the online tools provided on CCO.

When a case is opened, be prepared to provide the maintenance contract number, the product serial number, and the priority of the issue, based on the following guidelines:

- **Priority 1**   An existing network is down or there is critical impact to business operations. Cisco and the customer will commit any necessary resources to resolving this issue.

- **Priority 2**   The network is operational; however, it is severely degraded by inadequate performance. The customer's business is also severely impacted. Resources will work on resolving this issue during normal business hours.

- **Priority 3**   The network performance is impaired, but most business operations remain functional. Resources will work on resolving this issue during normal business hours.

■ **Priority 4**   The customer requires information or assistance on Cisco product capabilities, installation, or configuration. There is no or little impact to the customer's business. Resources will be assigned to these issues during normal business hours.

A word of advice: do not rely on e-mail or the case manager to open Priority 1 or Priority 2 issues.

Customers can also query or update cases that have been opened. Customers can query the history and status of any case (including closed cases) assigned to a contract number. Customers can view the information that TAC representatives have entered into the ticket, which includes the time of events as they occur, escalations, and the like.

Cisco Technical Assistance Center

The Cisco Technical Assistance Center (TAC) is at the heart of Cisco's online offerings. When a problem arises that an engineer cannot resolve with the tools available online, customers with support contracts have the option to contact TAC directly. This most often occurs with Priority 1 or 2 incidents.

To effectively work on an incident, the Cisco Support Engineer (CSE) requires information relating to the incident. If you have effectively researched the problem, you should have most of this information already. In this information, you should have compiled a list of symptoms, such as performance issues, loss of connectivity, and so on.

Specific information required by Cisco CSE includes the following:

■ Version information, including platform and IOS revisions (obtained from the SHOW VERSION command) and firmware revisions (obtained using the SHOW CONTROLLERS command).

■ Current configuration of each router involved (obtained by issuing the SHOW RUNNING-CONFIG command).

■ An accurate network topology map, showing device connectivity and related Network Layer protocols. This map should also include any key servers or hosts.

- If the issue is related to spontaneous device reloads or system halts, the device stack information (from the SHOW STACKS command) might be requested.

- In rare instances, often as a last resort, a core dump could be requested. The WRITE CORE command can be used if the router is malfunctioning but has not completely crashed. The EXCEPTION DUMP *IP-ADDRESS* global command sets the router to capture a core dump to a Trivial File Transfer Protocol (TFTP) server. Keep in mind that if the router is severely malfunctioning or there is no network connectivity, it will not be possible to capture the core dump.

exam
ⓦatch

Be able to identify common commands that you might need to use when requested by Cisco TAC.

SCENARIO & SOLUTION

How do I get a subscription to TAC?	Each Cisco product falls into a service category. For example, an 801 router falls into Category 1; most 2500 series routers are in Category 4, and a 3640 is Category 10. You can purchase from Cisco or a reseller a one- or three-year support contract based on the service category of the product. Using the support contract number, you are granted access to TAC and additional areas of CCO not generally available to the public, such as the software subscription service.
I have a minor problem and need some more information before I continue. It's not a service issue, so I can't open a case with TAC. How can I get more information?	You can research your topic on the Cisco Open Forum. If you cannot find a suitable answer, you can present your own question. Questions are answered in the forum by CCIEs, who are more than willing to help.

EXERCISE 1-3

CCO

Scenario: You are encountering a problem with the configuration of a router. The configuration appears to be correct, but the network is not functioning as expected. What resources are available to resolve this problem, and what would be the most appropriate resource to start with?

Solution: Again, verify your configuration with documentation. CCO's Troubleshooting Engine can also provide some insight to common issues that you might have overlooked. If you are convinced that the configuration is correct, CCO's Bug Toolkit might be able to provide further information if the issue is related to a bug that has been reported and identified. Researching the CCO's Open Forum or presenting your question there could also provide an answer. As a last resort, you can open an incident with Cisco TAC.

CERTIFICATION SUMMARY

This chapter has provided a view into some of the options and resources available for troubleshooting and maintaining a network—from the physical infrastructure to network management, supporting documentation, and network modeling.

Network modeling and simulation tools such as NetSys Baseliner can assist you in both building a network and planning changes. Cable testers can be used to certify the physical infrastructure as cables are newly installed or as the integrity of cables must be established.

Network management tools such as CiscoWorks allow the network to be proactively monitored by polling statistics on a regular basis via SNMP. As critical events occur throughout the network, RMON agents can notify the network management system in real time.

As problems arise on the network, it might be necessary to use protocol analysis tools to gain a greater insight to what is actually occurring on the network. By capturing, viewing, and analyzing frames from a network segment, experienced users can gain the benefit of detailed information on the network.

By taking the knowledge learned from these initial troubleshooting steps, users can query the online tools on CCO. Issues can be researched and questions presented to the Open Forum. Effectively using the Troubleshooting Assistant, Bug Toolkit, and Stack Decoder can yield a number of potential solutions to virtually any issue. Possible solutions include an IOS upgrade available from the Software Library.

Again, many problems can be researched, diagnosed, and resolved using the tools described in this chapter; however, at times, customers are unable to resolve issues themselves. In these instances, an incident can be opened with Cisco TAC, either online or over the telephone. The information collected during the troubleshooting process will serve as the base information for TAC. Based on the priority of the issue, Cisco Technical Assistance Representatives will work around the clock to get it resolved.

Using the CCO Case Management Toolkit, customers can directly interact with the TAC staff until the issue is resolved.

TWO-MINUTE DRILL

Here are some of the key points from each certification objective in Chapter 1.

Types and Purposes of Troubleshooting Tools

❑ Troubleshooting typically begins at the Physical Layer.

❑ Network monitors provide a baseline and historical and trending information.

❑ A baseline is a statistical average of the normal status or performance of the network.

❑ A time-domain reflectometer (TDR) can be used to measure the length of a cable and identify any opens and shorts in it.

❑ Protocol analyzers are used to capture packets on a network segment so they can be examined in greater detail.

Network Management System

❑ Network management consists of: Inventory management; Configuration management; Security management; Performance management; and Fault management.

❑ A Management Information Base (MIB) is a database of objects for a specific device.

❑ SNMP is the mechanism that allows for the retrieval if MIB information.

❑ Remote monitoring (RMON) agents are implemented in software for a specific hardware platform to provide proactive monitoring of a network.

❑ RMON1 defines nine groups and monitors the first two layers of the OSI model (Physical and Data-Link Layers).

❑ An additional group was added to the RMON1 specification (for a total of 10 groups) that defines the Token Ring extensions.

❑ RMON2 added an additional nine groups to the original RMON1 specification and provides for monitoring of all seven layers of the OSI model.

❑ Catalyst switches include the RMON *alarms* and *event* groups, by default.

❑ The RMON process can be very processor intensive.

Cisco Connection Online

❑ CCO is the foundation of a suite of interactive network applications available via the Internet or CD.

❑ CCO provides access to Cisco's entire library of end-user documentation.

❑ Cisco's Marketplace is one method via which users can order networking products, training materials, subscriptions, and promotional merchandise.

❑ The primary purpose of the software center is to deliver software upgrades and solutions for a variety of Cisco products.

❑ The Bug Toolkit is an integrated set of applications allowing users to quickly identify, evaluate, categorize, and track defects that could impact their networks.

❑ The Case Management Toolkit allows customers to open, query, and update cases with Cisco's TAC.

SELF TEST

The following questions will help you measure your understanding of the material presented in this chapter. Read all the choices carefully because there might be more than one correct answer. Choose all correct answers for each question.

Types and Purposes of Troubleshooting Tools

1. At what layer of the OSI model does most troubleshooting begin?

   A. Layer 3, Network

   B. Layer 7, Application

   C. Layer 1, Physical

   D. Layer 2, Data Link

2. A cable is suspected of being defective. What type of test equipment can be used to verify its operation? Choose all that apply.

   A. Oscilloscope

   B. Volt-ohm meter or digital multimeter

   C. Time-domain reflectometer

   D. Protocol analyzer

3. In what situation would it be most appropriate to create a baseline of a network?

   A. When the network is under peak load.

   B. When the network is operating correctly.

   C. When the network is not functioning correctly.

   D. When the network is idle or at lowest utilization.

4. Which application would be most useful in creating a baseline of a network?

   A. Network monitor

   B. Protocol analyzer

   C. Cable tester

   D. Traffic generator

5. What function does a protocol analyzer provide?

   A. Creates a baseline

   B. Produces a detailed inspection of packets

   C. Monitors MIB variables

   D. Traces the route a packet takes through a network

6. What is the best way to learn how to use a protocol analyzer?

   A. Read the documentation.

   B. Monitor a working network.

   C. Monitor a failing network.

   D. Monitor for "top talkers."

7. One of the most important tasks performed when using a protocol analyzer is which of the following?

   A. Keeping copies of the packets

   B. Narrowing down what is being monitored

   C. Sending SNMP requests

   D. Printing packets

Network Management Systems

8. SNMP can be used for which of the following? Choose all that apply.

   A. Configuring network equipment

   B. Resetting router passwords

   C. Collecting statistical information

   D. All of the above

9. A network needs to be monitored and alerts need to be sent to a management console when set thresholds are exceeded. Which application is best suited for this task?

   A. SNMP

   B. RMON

   C. MIBs

   D. Protocol analyzer

10. RMON1 monitors which of the following layers of the OSI model? Choose all that apply
   A. Layer 1
   B. Layer 2
   C. Layer 3
   D. Layer 4

11. True or false: the RMON2 specification replaces RMON1 functionality.
   A. True
   B. False

12. What default RMON groups are enabled on Catalyst switches?
   A. Events
   B. Statistics
   C. Alarm
   D. History

13. Your network is experiencing slow and sluggish performance. Which application can act as a distributed protocol analyzer?
   A. VLAN Director
   B. Cisco View
   C. Resource Manager Essentials
   D. Traffic Director

Cisco Connection Online

14. How is "registered" access to CCO determined for Cisco customers?
   A. By purchasing a support contract
   B. By registering a Cisco product
   C. By obtaining CCNP certification
   D. By purchasing an IOS upgrade

15. In preparing a proposal for your management, you need to research additional information for a Cisco product you believe would help network performance. Where can you find the latest documentation and product information?

A. Cisco Product Catalog

B. Cisco Documentation CD

C. CCO

D. Cisco Technical Forum

16. Where can you go to locate Cisco software upgrades?

A. CCO Software Center

B. Cisco Technical Assistance Center

C. CCO documentation

D. Cisco Bug Toolkit

17. What Cisco utility notifies you when there might be a service-affecting issue with a specific product?

A. Open Forum

B. Bug Toolkit

C. Troubleshooting Assistant

D. Compatibility Advisor

18. When is it most appropriate to use the Troubleshooting Engine?

A. When TAC is not available.

B. When you don't have a support contract.

C. When you are solving complex problems.

D. When you are solving simple problems.

19. When may a Cisco TAC engineer request an exception dump?

A. When a router's system software completely fails

B. When a router's system software partially fails

C. When a TFTP server is not available

D. When the software is operating correctly and all interfaces fail

LAB QUESTION

What information should be collected prior to contacting Cisco TAC to open an incident?

SELF TEST ANSWERS

Types and Purposes of Troubleshooting Tools

1. ☑ **C.** Layer 1, Physical. Most network troubleshooting efforts begin at the Physical Layer.
   ☒ **A, B,** and **D** are incorrect because operation of the lower layers must be validated before you can be sure upper layers are operating correctly.

2. ☑ **B** and **C.** Volt-ohm meter or digital multimeter and time-domain reflectometer. A VOM/DMM provides basic continuity testing, among other functions. A TDR is used to find opens and shorts in a cable as well as cable length.
   ☒ **A** and **D** are incorrect. An oscilloscope displays waveforms, or, more specifically, levels of intensity over time. A protocol analyzer is used to view the details of a specific protocol.

3. ☑ **B.** When the network is operating correctly. A baseline is merely a snapshot or statistical average of the normal status or performance of the network.
   ☒ **A, C,** and **D** are incorrect because these events do not provide an accurate reference for what is normal for a network. Given a long enough period to create a baseline, peak and idle times will be included.

4. ☑ **A.** Network monitors are designed to provide historical and trending information. When a network monitor is used as a reference, it becomes easy to detect when the network exceeds normal operation given a specific day or time.
   ☒ **B** is incorrect because a protocol analyzer is used primarily to view specific packets. **C** is incorrect because a cable tester's primary purpose is to test the Physical Layer of the network. **D** is incorrect because a traffic generator is used to introduce traffic to a network segment, often for "stress testing."

5. ☑ **B.** Produces a detailed inspection of packets. The primary purpose of a protocol analyzer is to capture packets on a specific segment of a network so they can be inspected in greater detail.
   ☒ Although a protocol analyzer can be used to some extent to create a baseline, **A** is incorrect because baselines are often created over several days. A protocol analyzer is more a focused tool that provides an immediate snapshot of the network that can be compared against a baseline. **C** is incorrect because MIBs are monitored using SNMP, typically by a network management system. **D** is incorrect because a protocol analyzer can monitor only the segment of the network to which it is connected and is limited to viewing and evaluating the contents of packets on that segment.

6. ☑ **B.** Monitor a working network. By monitoring a working network, you can realize the proper "order" of things. By knowing the proper operation, you will find it easier to determine when the network is not operating correctly.

   ☒ **A** and **D** are incorrect because, although reading the documentation and monitoring for "top talkers" might be helpful, they provide no basis for your specific network. **C** is incorrect because, in most critical situations, time is of the essence, and it might be difficult to determine what is or is not correct operation for the network.

7. ☑ **B.** Narrowing down what is being monitored. The scope of the number and type of packets must be narrowed so as not to be overwhelmed by the sheer number of packets.

   ☒ **A, C,** and **D** are incorrect because protocol analyzers typically do not send SNMP requests and, although printing or keeping copies of packets could be helpful, they are not as important.

Network Management Systems

8. ☑ **D.** All of the above. SNMP is an Application Layer protocol that allows access to a network device's MIBs. These MIB objects can be polled to gather statistical data or can be set to configure a device, including system passwords.

   ☒ There are no incorrect answer choices for this question.

9. ☑ **B.** RMON. Remote monitoring is enabled by a software agent running on a network device. This agent monitors the device's status. If thresholds carry from acceptable limits, the agent notifies the management console.

   ☒ **A, C,** and **D** are incorrect because SNMP is used by a remote application to poll MIBs on a network device, and protocol analyzers are used to examine the contents of individual packets.

10. ☑ **A** and **B.** Layer 1 and Layer 2 are correct because RMON1 monitors only the first two layers of the OSI model, as defined in RFC 1757.

    ☒ **C** and **D** are incorrect because Layers 3 and 4 of the OSI model are addressed in the RMON2 specification.

11. ☑ **B.** False. RFC 2101 defined RMON2 as an extension to RMON1, allowing all seven layers of the OSI model to be monitored.

    ☒ **A,** true, is incorrect because the RMON2 specification does not replace RMON1 functionality.

12. ☑ **A** and **C** are correct because Catalyst switches include RMON1 groups Alarms and Events.

    ☒ **B** and **D** are incorrect because the Statistics and History RMON groups are available only with the purchase of additional options for Catalyst switches.

13. ☑ **D.** Traffic Director has the capability to act as a distributed protocol analyzer.
☒ **A** is incorrect because VLAN Director allows for the configuration and viewing of VLANs throughout the network. **B** is incorrect because Cisco View can view and configure network devices. **C** is incorrect because Resource Manager Essentials is the portion of the software that is responsible for discovering SNMP devices and for doing the basic polling function.

Cisco Connection Online

14. ☑ **A.** By purchasing a support contract. Customers receive registered access to CCO by purchasing a support contract.
☒ **B, C,** and **D** are incorrect because purchasing a Cisco product does not entitle the customer to registered access, nor does purchasing an IOS upgrade. (However, registered users with access to the Software Center can access IOS upgrades.) The only certification that allows registered access to CCO is CCIE.

15. ☑ **C.** CCO provides access to Cisco's entire library of end-user documentation, selected product news, and bug databases that are updated constantly.
☒ **A, B,** and **D** are incorrect because the Cisco Product Catalog describes the networking products currently offered. The Cisco Documentation CD contains most of the data required, but it is updated only monthly and might not contain the latest information. The Cisco Technical Forum is a subset or portion of CCO and is used primarily for troubleshooting, not product information.

16. ☑ **A.** The CCO Software Center provides information required to upgrade the software for various platforms.
☒ **B** and **D** are incorrect as these resources assist in locating a bug or problem that could require a software upgrade. **C** is incorrect because CCO documentation might only provide information regarding software releases.

17. ☑ **B.** The Bug Toolkit allows users to quickly identify, evaluate, categorize, and track defects that could impact a user's network. Bug Alert agents in the toolkit can notify you of any issues that relate to a specific platform and issue.
☒ **A** is incorrect because the Open Forum allows users to present questions that are answered by qualified CCIEs. **C** is incorrect because the Troubleshooting Assistant is used to solve relatively simple networking issues. **D** is incorrect because the Compatibility Advisor is used to test whether a configuration is valid with a target version of a Catalyst Supervisor Engine or operating system.

18. ☑ **D.** When you are solving simple problems. The Troubleshooting Engine simulates steps a Cisco TAC engineer would take when diagnosing a problem. The Troubleshooting Engine is used to resolve the most common configuration and performance issues.
    ☒ **A** is incorrect because TAC is available 24 hours a day, seven days a week. **B** is incorrect because registered access to CCO is required to access the Troubleshooting Engine, and a support contract is required for registered access to CCO. **C** is incorrect because the Troubleshooting Engine resolves relatively simple issues.

19. ☑ **B.** When a router's system software partially fails.
    ☒ **A, C,** and **D** are incorrect because if there is a complete failure or the router is unable to communicate with the designated TFTP server, the router will be unable to write the core dump.

LAB ANSWER

1. Your support contract number should be located to provide to TAC to ensure that the incident can be opened in a timely manner.

2. Identify the extent of the issue. Is this to be a Priority 1, 2, 3, or 4 incident?

3. Obtain basic documentation of your network, primarily a current diagram showing the network connectivity.

4. Obtain information from all applicable routers that could be experiencing problems. This includes the output from the following commands:

   ■ SHOW VERSION
   ■ SHOW RUNNING-CONFIG
   ■ SHOW CONTROLLERS
   ■ SHOW STACKS

5. If possible, have a method for Cisco TAC to connect to your network or router. Most common methods include Internet access and direct modem access to the AUX port of the router.

2

Using Troubleshooting Methods

O nly a few years ago, it was fairly uncommon for a company to have a dedicated connection to the Internet. It was also uncommon for a company to have a dedicated connection to another company. In many companies, networks did not even exist. Usually one or two people in the company had a knack with computers and ended up working on the network, even though their "real" jobs were unrelated. Most of the problems were fairly simple, and when they were not, these companies called on consultants.

Today, most companies have networks in place, and many have a variety of types of networks, often interconnected. Every connection to the network is a problem waiting to happen. Every network connected to another network is also a problem waiting to happen. In a properly managed network, the number and types of problems will be relatively limited. In an improperly managed network or in an internetwork consisting of components not entirely under your control, the numbers and types of problems will be more expansive. Early networks were often unstable. For that reason, today's users are quick to assume that a problem they encounter has its root in the network and they frequently do not check anything before calling for help. This is the glorious truth of networking.

As the number of connections to a network grows, so too grows the need for a consistent troubleshooting methodology. As the complexity of the network increases, the value increases dramatically. One of the most rewarding reasons for following a consistent troubleshooting methodology is that it will help you isolate the problem more quickly, which will keep end users from calling every five minutes to find out when the problem will be fixed.

This chapter reviews the problem-solving model and goes over each step in detail, with real-life examples. By the time we are finished, you should be able to identify the major components of the problem-solving model and provide examples of each.

CERTIFICATION OBJECTIVE 2.01

The Problem-Solving Model

Without realizing it, you probably already have a problem-solving model that you follow every time you encounter a problem. For simple problems, some answers are so obvious that you might think you are skipping some steps. Actually, you do not really skip the steps; it just appears that you do.

Let us look first at a simple problem with which most of us have dealt and fit it into the model with which we will work. Consider the example in the following Lost Keys Scenario. We already know what the problem is, so we do not bother to ask ourselves the obvious question "What is the problem?" Our minds have already processed the question and come up with the answer, so what comes to mind is the thought "I cannot find my keys." Refer to the following Scenario & Solution.

SCENARIO & SOLUTION

Define the problem.	I cannot find my keys.
Gather facts.	The last time I had them I was walking in the door to the house.
Consider possibilities based on facts.	I could have left them in the door. I could have laid them on the table in the entry. I could have left them in a coat pocket.
Create an action plan.	Check the front door. Check the table in the entry. Check the coat pocket.
Implement the action plan.	Check each place listed in the action plan.
Observe the results.	They were not in the front door. They were not on the table in the entry. They were not in the coat pocket.
Iterate the process (if necessary).	In this case, it is still necessary because I have not found the keys.
Consider possibilities based on facts.	I had groceries in my hand, so I could have left the keys in the kitchen. The phone was ringing as I walked in the door, so the keys could be by the telephone.
Create an action plan.	Check in the kitchen. Check by the telephone.
Implement the action plan.	Check each place listed in the action plan.
Observe the results.	They were not in the kitchen. They were by the telephone.
Iterate the process (if necessary).	In this case, it is no longer necessary because I found the keys.
Document the facts when resolved.	The keys were found by the telephone.

Each step in the Lost Keys Scenario probably seemed very familiar to you. In a simple case of lost keys, it might be obvious to say that you cannot fix a problem if you do not know what caused the problem. It is very easy to jump to conclusions about the cause of a problem without gathering all the relevant information, though. In the best case, jumping to conclusions causes additional work for you but no harm to the network. In the worst case, it exacerbates the problem or creates a new problem overlaid on the original problem. Without following each step in order, you can end up chasing your tail. A number of examples are examined throughout this chapter as we investigate each step in detail.

EXERCISE 2-1

Generic Troubleshooting Lab: Yippee.net

The following exercise is intended to give you the opportunity to begin thinking about a problem in terms of the generic methodology just presented. As the chapter progresses, hands-on lab exercises will enhance your understanding of the problem-solving methodology.

You are the new network engineer at Yippee, Inc. The company grew rapidly and now has about 20 remote offices, most of which connect to the corporate office in San Francisco using Frame Relay over Cisco routers. Transmission Control Protocol/Internet Protocol (TCP/IP) is the only protocol that crosses the wide area network (WAN). A dedicated 128k Frame Relay connection to the Internet is protected by a Cisco PIX firewall.

Each office has a single NT file server that is used for file and print sharing. In addition, an e-mail server is located in each office. The name of the file/print server at the remote office is the same as the name of the remote office. For example, the server in Atlanta is named ATLANTA.

All shared servers (intranet, database, and Web servers) are located in the San Francisco office. The following are the server names and functions: YIPPEE-MAIL is the corporate e-mail server. All Internet e-mail and intercorporate mail goes through this mail server. YIPPEE-IN is the intranet server. YIPPEE-DB is the corporate database server, and YIPPEE is the public Web server.

Figure 2-1 shows the setup for the network described in this lab.

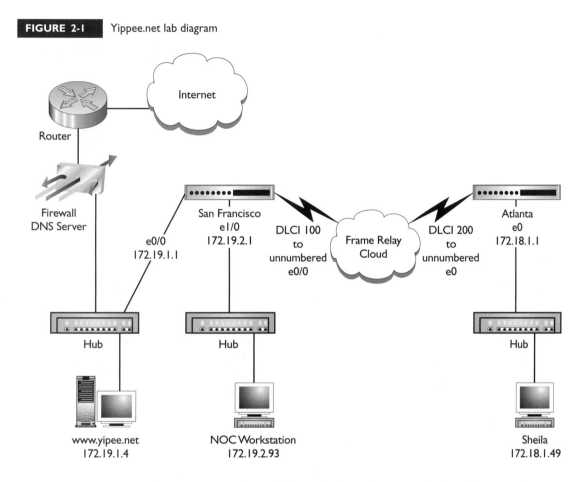

FIGURE 2-1   Yippee.net lab diagram

You have just received a call from Sheila in the regional sales office in Atlanta. Sheila states that she is unable to get to the www.yippee.net site using her Web browser. Working with another individual, simulate a troubleshooting scenario and fill in Table 2-1.
Solution:
The results of this exercise will vary widely. The following answer is just one of many possibilities. During the simulation, the following information is gathered in order to define the problem:

1. Sheila is the only one in the office today, so we do not know whether or not others in the same office are affected by the problem that she is experiencing.

TABLE 2-1   A Troubleshooting Scenario List

Step	Example
Define the problem.	
Gather facts.	
Consider possibilities based on facts.	
Create an action plan.	
Implement the action plan.	
Observe the results.	
Iterate the process (if necessary).	
Consider possibilities based on facts.	
Create an action plan.	
Implement the action plan.	
Observe the results.	
Iterate the process (if necessary).	
Document the facts when resolved.	

2. Sheila is at a small sales office in Atlanta. The Yippee.net Web server is located at the corporate office in San Francisco.

The problem is defined as follows: "At least one user in Atlanta is unable to access the Yippee.net Web server in San Francisco."

The following information is gathered during the fact-gathering phase:

1. There have been no power outages or storms in the area.

2. Sheila was on the Yippee.net Web site earlier this morning.

3. Sheila is able to access her local e-mail server and her local file server but reports that she has not received any e-mails since about 10:00 a.m. EST.

4. Sheila states that to her knowledge, nothing has changed.

5. We have Sheila open her Web browser and try to access the Yippee.net Web site. She gets an error message that states, "The page you are looking for is

currently unavailable." We have Sheila try to open the Web site www.hooya.com. She gets the same error message.

6. Sheila has an IP address of 172.18.1.49 and a gateway of 172.18.1.1. She is able to ping her gateway. This tells us that her connection to the LAN is good.

7. Sheila is unable to ping www.yippee.net and states that she receives an error message indicating "Unknown host www.yippee.net." This tells us that her Domain Name Server (DNS) resolution is not working, either.

8. The address of the host www.yippee.net is 172.19.1.4. We ask Sheila to ping this address and the ping request times out. Next we ask Sheila to run a traceroute, which times out after reaching her gateway.

9. We are able to ping the Web server locally from our workstation, 172.19.2.93. This tells us that the Web server is responding to TCP/IP traffic. We are also able to open the Web page, which tells us that the Web server is responding to HTTP traffic.

10. The connection from Atlanta to San Francisco is a 56k Frame Relay circuit.

11. A check of the router in San Francisco shows the PVC is active, which tells us that the Frame Relay circuit is functioning properly on the San Francisco end. Checking the statistics on the PVC, we can see that inbound traffic counters are incrementing, but the outbound traffic counters are not incrementing.

12. We are unable to Telnet to the router in Atlanta, so we dial in to the router. A check of the router in Atlanta shows the PVC is active, which tells us the Frame Relay circuit is functioning properly on the Atlanta end. Checking the statistics on the PVC, we can see that the outbound traffic counters are incrementing, but the inbound traffic counters are not incrementing.

13. We are unable to ping Sheila's workstation from our workstation. A traceroute fails at the local router.

14. The problem definition is revised to state that "TCP/IP traffic between Atlanta and San Francisco is not functioning properly."

15. Checking the show CDP neighbors in both routers, we can see that each router sees the other and that the IP addresses visible are the correct IP addresses.

16. Checking the show IP route tables in both routers, we can see that all the appropriate routes are visible in each router.

17. Checking the running configuration in each router, we can see that no configuration changes were made in the Atlanta router in the last three weeks, but a configuration change was made in the San Francisco router at 6:55 a.m. PST, just 5 minutes before the problem was noticed in Atlanta.

18. The problem is characterized as a constant acute problem because of its sudden onset and the fact that it can be observed at any time.

19. Comparing the previous configuration to the current configuration in the San Francisco router, we can see that the change made was an access list applied to the serial interface connecting to Atlanta.

Next, we consider possibilities based on facts.

1. We have established that Frame Relay is working (show CDP neighbors), so the circuit and the associated Layer 2 Frame Relay functionality are not likely to be the issue.

2. We have established that there was a configuration change made in the San Francisco router shortly before the problem was noticed in Atlanta. The access-list change is most likely the cause of the problem.

Next, we create an action plan:

1. The hypothesis is that there is an error in the access list. If we correct the error, IP traffic from Atlanta to San Francisco will be restored.

2. In order to modify the access list, we will need to:

   a. Remove the access list from all interfaces on the router where it is applied.

   b. Remove the access list from the router.

   c. Rebuild the access list from scratch, with the proposed modifications.

   d. Reapply the access list to each interface on the router on which it was originally applied.

   e. Verify that everything is still working at all other locations.

   f. Verify that TCP/IP traffic from Atlanta to San Francisco is now restored.

3. We have two recovery plans:

   a. Keep a copy of the current access list, which appears to affect only San Francisco, and reapply this access list.

b. Apply a copy of the previous access list, taken from the last backup.

4. Our change control process requires that we notify the director of operations before any changes are made, even in the event of an emergency, so our action plan includes this step. The risks are defined as low, since only internal company connections are affected by the modifications and the activity should be nonintrusive.

As we implement the action plan, we follow each step defined in order, carefully observing the effects of each change on the performance of the network. We see no signs of new problems introduced. Having implemented the action plan, we can observe that TCP/IP traffic is now going both directions between San Francisco and Atlanta. We call Sheila back to see if she is now able to access www.yippee.net. Sheila reports that she is able to access the Web site and that she also seems to be receiving new e-mail now.

We verify that we can now run a traceroute to Sheila's workstation from ours. Since the problem is resolved, we do not need to iterate the process.

Finally, we document the problem that was observed and how it was resolved, communicating with the other members of the department so that they are aware of the problem for future reference.

Why Use a Methodology?

A problem-solving model in some ways is nothing more than common sense. As the lost keys example demonstrates, there is nothing mysterious about the model. At first, some of the steps might seem so basic that they are a waste of time. With more complex problems, however, each of these steps is crucial to arriving at the right solution. Formalizing these common sense steps allows you to focus on the problem instead of the process. Here are some reasons to follow a methodology:

- Allows you to focus on the problem, not the process
- Ensures that you are working on the problem, not a symptom of the problem
- Allows you to arrive at a more accurate diagnosis more quickly
- Facilitates the implementation of corrective measures

Flowchart the Troubleshooting Process

Figure 2-2 presents a flowchart demonstrating the problem-solving methodology.

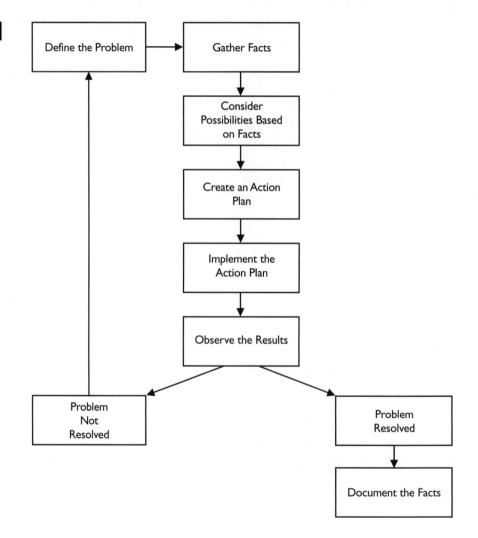

FIGURE 2-2

A generic
flowchart of the
problem-solving
model

CERTIFICATION OBJECTIVE 2.02

Defining the Problem

A typical support call might come from an end user who says something like this: "The network is down." Your job is to figure out exactly what that means. If you like to read mystery novels to try to solve the crime before the books' detectives do, you are well on your way to defining the problem because you know the key questions any good detective will ask. Here are some key questions to help you with the definition process.

Who Is Affected by the Problem?

Most networks are hierarchical. A *hierarchy* is a top-to-bottom structure with specific data paths for different parts of the structure. In a typical organization, the corporate headquarters is at the top of the hierarchy. Within the corporate headquarters there may be multiple organizations, sometimes divided along departmental lines. Feeding out of the corporate headquarters are links to regional offices, which often have links to multiple offices behind them. In most cases, not everyone is affected by a problem, so one of the best ways to begin to define the problem is to determine which group(s) are affected.

Having said that, before assuming that any group is affected, you can ask simple questions of the end user to determine whether or not the problem is affecting only a single user. Even though in most cases the network is not at fault if only a single user is affected, you will often be expected to prove it. Regardless, you should still be able to explain why the network is not the culprit.

The rule of thumb is to start with the end user and work your way out, first to the department, then to multiple departments at the same location, then to the entire location, then to the region, and so on. Let us assume that Sally has called and stated that the network is down. You might start with a series of questions like those referenced in the following Scenario & Solution questions.

SCENARIO & SOLUTION

Are you the only one having a problem?	No.
Who else is having a problem?	I know Jane mentioned she is also having this problem.
Anybody else?	I don't know.
Could you ask a few people?	Sure. Hold on … Yes, it seems that everyone on this floor is having the same problem.
What about on the other floors?	I don't know.
Would you mind checking?	Sure. Hold on … No, it seems that it is just the people on this floor.

As seen from the Sample User Definition Questions, the end user does not know that the problem is affecting a larger group until you ask her to find out. Knowing the number of users affected and their location(s) will help you when time comes to determine what is causing the problem. Now it is known that everyone on the floor Sally works on is having the same problem. We still do not really know what the problem is, but we know it affects a specific population of end users.

Most companies do not have network or systems engineers in every office location. Often, all support is provided remotely. In every office there is usually one person who ends up dealing with computer questions. It might be the secretary, or it might be a manager. Depending on who you are speaking with and their experience with computers, you might have to provide more or less detailed explanations. You will also need to keep in mind that the listener must interpret every sentence, and interpretations of even simple questions and answers can vary widely. I might ask you if anyone else is having a problem, and you might interpret it as though I asked whether or not *anyone* is having exactly the same problem. Although the questions are similar, they are not entirely the same. You will find that some users challenge your skills in communication. Over time, you can develop the end users' knowledge and understanding by building good relationships with them. After awhile, you might have them so well trained that they call you with the IP address and tell you which groups are affected without you having to ask. Of course, depending on the problem, the IP address might not be helpful information! Still, it pays to help users understand what information you need to help them resolve problems and to build good relationships with them so that they want to help you help them.

Undoubtedly you have followed good network operations procedures by fully documenting every component of your network. Hard as it might be to believe, in many organizations network documentation is the first thing that slides when time is short, and some organizations never had any network documentation to begin with. Those who do not have documentation on which to rely will have to discover the relevant components of the network dynamically. This chapter quickly walks through the process of how you might go about this and points out a couple of ways to keep the end user from knowing that you do not have a clue as to how the network elements are connected.

As a good network engineer, you already know the most basic of troubleshooting tools: *traceroute*. This is a wonderful way to figure out where the user is in relation to you. First, though, you have to figure out the IP address of the workstation in question. Depending on how IP addresses are assigned in your organization, getting the IP address of the workstation might be a simple matter—or it might not.

A fair number of companies use static IP addresses. A *static IP address* is one that is permanently reserved for use by one workstation. Some companies are meticulous at maintaining an accurate list of which workstation has which IP address and who is assigned to use that workstation. The list might be maintained as a flat text file in a database, or the addresses might be added to the DNS server, depending on the company. If you are lucky enough to work at an organization that knows exactly who has which workstation and the IP address of all workstations, think twice before changing jobs. The rest of the world seems to be scrambling just to keep up with which IP addresses have been given out; companies often do not know which workstation is using a particular address, much less the name of the user.

Other companies use *Dynamic Host Configuration Protocol (DHCP)*, a protocol that allows IP addresses to be assigned dynamically. This means that each time the workstation is powered on, it could be assigned a different IP address. If the workstation names and their users are meticulously assigned by the network administrator, you could go to the DHCP server (assuming you have access to it) and find out which IP address was assigned to the workstation in question. Alas, many companies never change the workstation name when it is assigned to a new user, and others use workstation names with no relevance to the name of the end user.

Another protocol, *Dynamic Domain Name Server (DDNS)*, combines DHCP functionality with the *Domain Name Server (DNS)*. DNS provides name resolution, and one of its long-standing drawbacks until the advent of DDNS was that any device receiving an address assigned by a DHCP server could not be added to the DNS server. This meant that a large number of workstations could not be addressed by name. DDNS resolves this issue by dynamically updating the DNS server with the workstation name and its IP address as the address is assigned. A few large companies have implemented DDNS. If workstation names are logically assigned, you might be able to figure out the IP address by the workstation name.

If you have not yet been able to determine the workstation's IP address to run the traceroute, you might have to ask the user. Some users may be reticent to answer what they consider to be basic questions, but most will be more than happy to walk through any settings on their workstation if they think you will be able to help them. If you do have to ask the user for his or her IP address, it never hurts to verify the gateway and subnet mask at the same time if a DHCP server does not assign those.

Once you have obtained the IP address, you can then run a traceroute. In some organizations, the router names are added to DNS, and if you are lucky, the router names will be fairly meaningful. If the network is truly down, you will not get what you are looking for (the node name of the router connected to the user's segment). But if the network is up, you will hopefully get the node name of the router and have already started part of the test process at the same time.

If the traceroute fails, you can ask Sally for the IP address of the gateway and do an *name server lookup (NSLOOKUP)*, a command available on Windows NT as well as Unix systems to query the DNS server for the name associated with an IP address. If you are running Windows 95, 98, or 2000 or an Apple machine, a number of shareware programs are available that will allow you to do an NSLOOKUP from your workstation. If your DNS administrator has not added your routers to the name server, you will have to find another way of figuring out where Sally is located. If you have a telecommunications background, you might have already thought of asking for Sally's phone number, and that could still work. Unfortunately, with the advent of IP phones, the phone number might not be meaningful in this context anymore. You could ask Sally for the name of her file server, which in many organizations will have a great name such as "Texas." Of course, you could ask Sally to tell you where she is calling from.

Knowing that Sally is located in Texas is only half the battle, though. You still have to "connect the dots" from Texas to your office in New York. A traceroute will either fill in all the missing blanks or tell you where the path is failing. At this point, if you are unable to run a successful traceroute, you might want to research the route without keeping Sally on the line.

Figure 2-3 illustrates the results of the TRACERT command when issued from a Windows 98 workstation.

From the traceroute to www.cisco.com, we can tell that the IP address of the Web site is 198.133.219.25. We can also tell that there are 16 hops from the workstation to the Web site. Although one of the routers is not defined in the domain name server (207.69.220.65), most are, and we can tell that we move through the Mindspring network to the BBN Planet network and finally to the Cisco network. Note on Line 14 that the output shows "Request Timed Out." This message often indicates that the next hop is not reachable, but it is also displayed

FIGURE 2-3   A sample traceroute

when the engineer responsible for the router (or firewall) has specifically prohibited responding to the traceroute with the identity of the network device.

The traceroute shown in Figure 2-3 clearly demonstrates that the physical and logical connectivity from the client to the server is intact and operational. In other words, if the user has reported an inability to open the Web site from his or her browser, the problem is something other than the routed path.

What Are the Symptoms?

Of all the questions you will have to answer, this one will be the most challenging. If you have worked in the environment for a long time, you might have the advantage of knowing something about your users and their applications. If you have just joined the company or if you work in a company providing services to users outside the company, however, you might need to draw the relevant information out of the end user.

on the
Job

You will always want the end user to walk through the entire problem with you from start to finish. If the user is experiencing a problem from within an application that is trying to access the network, find out what application, what resource the user is trying to access on the network, and the exact symptom he or she is able to observe when it fails. If you can, try following along with the user on your own workstation. That might not be possible if the user is running a custom application or trying to access a resource you do not have security privileges to access. But if you can follow along, it will help you understand what the end user is seeing.

Some companies install remote-control software on the end users' workstations, allowing network and systems engineers to remotely monitor the keystrokes and screen of the workstation. This can be helpful if the user is describing a problem that you are not able to replicate but the user is able to replicate.

Ultimately, you need to understand what the end user is experiencing, when it is happening, and if the user has a theory regarding why it is occurring; the latter is always helpful to hear, although it can be unreliable, depending on the end user's knowledge level.

Defining the Normal Operational Baseline

Hopefully, defining the normal operational baseline has already been done as part of general network management procedures within the organization. The ultimate goal is to develop an understanding of how the present situation (defined by the end user as a problem) compares to normally observable operations. Defining the normal operational baseline has two components:

- Know what the end user (subjectively) considers normal.
- Know what historical measurements have (objectively) been demonstrated to be normal.

First, it is important to understand what the end user or the organizational unit perceives as normal. We cannot simply say that because the users in Dallas are not complaining when bandwidth utilization exceeds 70 percent of capacity, the users in Los Angeles should not consider such utilization levels a problem. It might be that the users in Dallas have decided to sacrifice performance for the sake of cost. It is possible that the users in Dallas are not using any real-time applications, but the users in Los Angeles are using time-sensitive applications. The end user will often volunteer information along these lines. If not, make sure you understand why the end user considers the current conditions abnormal.

Second, verify the end user's observations through objective measurements. You might discover that network utilization has recently started spiking above 70 percent on Friday afternoons. You now know that there is definitely a measurable change in the network, and you have also gained valuable information regarding patterns and time frames. On the other hand, you might discover that the network utilization has been significantly above 70 percent for the last six months. How you define the problem and respond to it could change dramatically, depending on what you find when you look at the baseline.

Defining What Could Possibly Go Wrong in the Network

Given the description of the problem, what you know about the network, and about the application(s) involved, you need to list what the problem might be. For example, if an end user from Dallas calls and says that every time he tries to open a document located on a file server in New York he gets an error message, you would develop a list of potential problems: the problem could be that the file server is down. The network connection(s) could be down. The user's password could have expired. The user might not have an account on the file server. The user's application could be at fault. Do not limit the list to problems that could be caused by a network failure.

Defining Exactly What Is Wrong

A good definition does not assume the cause of the problem. An example of a good definition is something like, "None of the users in Texas can access the e-mail server in New York." It would be inappropriate to say, "The line from Texas to New York is down." That sounds like a good definition, but it is really a statement of cause. If you jump ahead in the process that way, you might not be working on the right problem. It is entirely possible that the line from Texas to New York *is* down, but we do not know that is not the cause of the e-mail problem the users in Texas are experiencing.

In order to arrive at a good definition, you need to know who is affected, what is affected, and how the current situation is different from what is considered normal.

EXERCISE 2-2

Problem Definition

This hands-on lab exercise is the first in a series of exercises that will walk through the complete problem resolution process, from problem definition to documentation. For this exercise, you need two routers with Ethernet interfaces, a hub, and, of course, an Ethernet workstation. Your lab will be set up like the network in Figure 2-4.

In the examples that follow, the first router is a 2500 series router and the second is a 2600 series router. The syntax for the Ethernet port is slightly different, but you

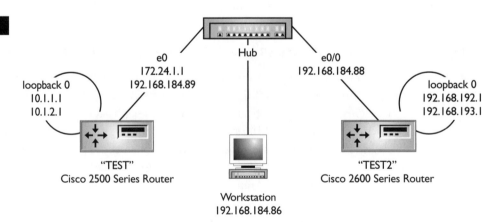

FIGURE 2-4

Test Lab
Network

e0
172.24.1.1
192.168.184.89

loopback 0
10.1.1.1
10.1.2.1

Hub

e0/0
192.168.184.88

loopback 0
192.168.192.1
192.168.193.1

"TEST"
Cisco 2500 Series Router

Workstation
192.168.184.86

"TEST2"
Cisco 2600 Series Router

should be able to complete these exercises with either model router without any difficulty.

The first router should be have the following configuration:

```
service timestamps log datetime
hostname Test
enable password cisco
ip subnet-zero
interface Loopback0
 ip address 10.1.2.1 255.255.255.0 secondary
 ip address 10.1.1.1 255.255.255.252
 no ip directed-broadcast
no shutdown
interface Ethernet0
 ip address 192.168.184.89 255.255.255.240 secondary
 ip address 172.24.1.1 255.255.255.0
 no ip directed-broadcast
 no shutdown
router eigrp 200
 network 10.0.0.0
 network 172.24.0.0
 network 192.168.220.0
router rip
 redistribute eigrp 200
 network 192.168.184.0
ip classless
line vty 0 4
 password cisco
 login
```

The second router should have the following configuration:

```
service timestamps debug uptime
service timestamps log datetime
hostname Test2
enable password cisco
interface Loopback0
 ip address 192.168.193.1 255.255.255.0 secondary
 ip address 192.168.192.1 255.255.255.0
no shutdown
interface Ethernet0/0
 ip address 192.168.184.88 255.255.255.240
no shutdown
router rip
```

```
 redistribute connected
 network 192.168.184.0
ip classless
line vty 0 4
 password cisco
 login
```

1. Connect the Ethernet port of each router to the hub. Connect the Ethernet port of the workstation to the hub. Set the workstation's TCP/IP address as 192.168.184.86 with a subnet mask of 255.255.255.240 and the gateway address of 192.168.184.89.

2. Connect the console cable to the first router, TEST.

3. From a terminal emulator on your workstation, log in to the TEST router. Ping the following addresses from the TEST router: 192.168.184.88, 192.168.192.1, and 192.168.193.1.

4. Move the console cable to the second router, TEST2.

5. From a terminal emulator on your workstation, log in to the TEST2 router. Ping the following addresses from the TEST2 router: 192.168.184.89, 172.24.1.1, 10.1.1.1, and 10.1.2.1.

6. Define the problem. (We will resolve the problem as we move through the remainder of the chapter.)

Solution:

First we need to define who is affected. In our case, TEST2 cannot ping any valid addresses on TEST1, so TEST2 is the "who" that is affected.

Second, we need to know what is not working. We know that we cannot ping. If you took it a step further, you would have discovered that no form of IP traffic can go from TEST2 to TEST. So the "what" that is affected is IP traffic. It should be fairly obvious that IP traffic should be able to go from TEST2 to TEST.

Third, we need to know when the problem started. Since we just put in these two routers, we know that the problem started when they were put in. In other words, the setup never worked.

With this information, we can now define the problem as "Since the two routers were installed, no IP traffic has been able to go from the TEST2 router to the TEST1 router."

CERTIFICATION OBJECTIVE 2.03

Gathering Facts

Once you have defined the problem, it is time to begin gathering the facts associated with the problem. There is a fine line between the two steps. The easiest way to understand the difference is by deciding which question you are trying to answer:

- What is not working?
- Why is it not working?

If you are answering the first question, you are defining the problem. If you are answering the second question, you are gathering the facts. As you gather the facts, you might find that you need to refine or revise your original problem definition.

Never Assume Anything

Sometimes the most obvious questions go unasked. Failing to ask whether the power cord is plugged into the wall or whether the telephone cord is plugged into the modem can result in many hours of unnecessary work. We do not like to ask, because it can feel like we are insulting the end user by asking such simple questions. Most users do think to check basic physical connectivity before calling for assistance. Still, every network administrator encounters those users who do not check. You might have just installed the equipment yesterday afternoon or been on the premises this morning. Still, you should check. Even if you know the user, you should always ask. Remember, as you ask, be tactful and courteous. This is especially important if the user has already spoken to other engineers or administrators asking for help. It helps to apologize before asking the questions. Some users will inevitably be irritated, no matter how you phrase your questions, but most will realize that you are simply following good troubleshooting procedures.

Always remember that if you are relying on an end user to verify physical connectivity, you need to be very explicit regarding what you want checked. Even if you describe a V.35 cable in great detail, including color, weight, what each end looks like, and where it should be connected, the user might report back regarding the RS232 cable instead. If you can possibly verify physical connectivity yourself, in person, do so. If not, walk through the steps with the user to check connectivity.

Have the user describe what he or she can see. Then, repeat back to the user what he or she described and ask any questions to clarify, until you are comfortable that you understand what the user has described. Finally, take everything you hear with a grain of salt. This is not to say that the person on the other end of the phone line is stupid. In almost every case, you will be talking to a bright, educated individual. However, that individual has not been trained to work on a network, just as we were not trained to be accountants.

When Did the Problem Start?

In the case of troubleshooting, timing really is everything. First and foremost, try to find out exactly when the problem started. Users do not always know when "the network went down," but you can build a realistic timeline by asking just two questions:

- When was the last time it worked?
- When did you first notice it was not working?

Follow those questions by checking the SYSLOG server or, in the absence of a SYSLOG server, the router and switch logs. Depending on the timeline, you might not be able to rely on the log files in a router or switch, though. Sometimes you can track down the timeline by checking other information that has a time stamp. Table 2-2 is a list of other resources worth checking to narrow down to a more specific time.

If you know that the frame relay PVC changed status 21 minutes ago and the end user reported the problem 15 minutes ago, the two factors are probably related. If you know that every time you do a SHOW IP BGP NEIGHBOR command you see that the neighbor status is only 2 minutes old, you likely have a problem between the two neighbors. Knowing the time frame helps reduce the scope of possible problems you must consider.

Has Anything Changed?

The sequence of events can be more important than the events themselves. We need to know who did what when. Do not limit the questions to things that happened in the last hour. This is especially important if a problem is reported in the beginning of a week. For example, you might receive a call on Tuesday saying that "No one can get to the mainframe." After having done your research, you learn that there is a

TABLE 2-2 Time Discovery Grid

What to Check	What It Tells You	Why It Is Helpful
SHOW LOG	When circuit outages occurred and the sequence of those outages.	You can pinpoint a specific time when a reportable event occurred.
SHOW VERSION	How long the router or switch has been active.	The device might have lost power recently and the counter information will be more informative. The device might have reloaded for less acceptable reasons, such as a bus error, as well.
SHOW FRAME PVCS	How long since the PVC last changed status.	You can match a network outage to the trouble report to see if there is a correlation, or you can eliminate a network outage as the source of the problem.
SHOW PROCESSES CPU	CPU utilization for 5 seconds, 1 minute, and 5 minutes.	If there is a serious problem, you can see whether CPU utilization has spiked in the last 5 minutes.
SHOW DLSW PEERS	How long each DLSW peer has been active.	Short DLSW peer times are an indication of a recent outage of some sort.
SHOW IP ROUTE	How long each IP route has been active.	IP route age for link-state routing protocols can provide a clue regarding when a problem most recently occurred.
SHOW IP [EIGRP | OSPF | APPLETALK | BGP] NEIGHBOR	How long each IP EIGRP, OSPF, AppleTalk, or BGP Neighbor has been active.	Short neighbor status can provide a clue regarding when a problem most recently occurred.

DLSW connection for TN3270 traffic to the mainframe from Hawaii to California. No one else is having a problem getting to the mainframe, only the users in Hawaii are. You have checked the router logs and nothing has gone down. Your DLSW connections show active peers on each end, and you can ping all the way through to the mainframe. What could possibly be wrong?

You need to be able to narrow down the possibilities, and the most likely culprit is something that was changed fairly recently. Between the "last time that it worked" and "the first time they noticed it was not working" lies the source of most

FROM THE CLASSROOM

Setting the Time with Cisco Routers and Switches

Cisco routers and switches don't keep time when they are powered off. Instead, they are programmed to activate with a date programmed into the IOS. The date that appears can vary depending on the device. For example, a 4700 router might boot up thinking it is 12:00 a.m. on Thursday, November 21, 1996, while a 2500 router might boot up thinking it is 12:00 a.m. on March 1, 1995. There is no way to change the default date in a router or switch. If you want the correct date to appear, you have two choices. First, you can Telnet to the device after every reboot and manually set the correct date and time. Alternatively, you can use Network Time Protocol (NTP) to configure the router or switch to query an NTP server for the current time.

Having the correct time in the router will not affect the operation of the router, but it is helpful when you are troubleshooting problems. It is more important to have a time stamp on the log entries so that you can see exactly when each entry occurred. This is not the default on Cisco routers, so you should add the following statement to your configuration: "service timestamps log datetime." This statement tells the router to insert a time stamp at the beginning of a log entry.

So what do you do if you have set the time and added the "service timestamps log datetime" statement in your configuration, but nothing shows up in the log? Check to make sure that you have "logging buffered" set in your configuration. If not, the only logging will appear on the console. If you have turned on debugging and you want the output to appear on your Telnet session, you can use the command TERMINAL MONITOR. Be careful, though, because you could lose your Telnet session with all the output and not be able to enter any new commands. Finally, if you are working on the console and all those log messages are driving you crazy, you can turn off the logging to the console by typing **no log console** into your configuration.

—*Michelle Famiglietti, CCNP, CCDA*

problems. All you have to do now is ask the right questions of the right people to find out all the intricate, minuscule changes that were made during that time period and you are halfway to solving the problem. If you had to bet on which change was the most likely culprit, put money on the one preceded by the phrase "All I did was change …."

In particular, when dealing with a WAN problem, end users rarely think to mention that a severe storm passed through the area, with multiple lightning strikes. Occasionally they might comment that the power was out overnight. This is one case in which a casual conversation about the weather could really pay off.

Consider the following real-life problem (the names have been changed to protect the guilty). Ron called the help desk at 9:00 a.m. on Monday morning and stated that he could no longer reach the server JOB, which, according to the documentation, is accessed by going through an extranet connection. The user reported that the problem "just started this morning" at 8:00 a.m. Following initial questioning, you determined that none of the users in Ron's department (accounting) could access this server, but they are able to access other network services such as e-mail, the Internet, and their network file shares.

Additional questioning revealed that the last time Ron actually tried to reach the server was the previous Wednesday. We now have a problem definition as follows: "None of the users in the accounting department is able to reach the extranet server JOB. The last successful access of the server was last Wednesday, and the first time the users noticed they were unable to access the server was at 8:00 a.m. today."

Now the fun begins. First, we assume nothing. Toward this end, we pull out our documentation regarding the connection, who accesses this particular connection, and how they access the connection. We ask Ron to walk through what he is doing on his workstation and describe each step to us. In this case, Ron is using a special application provided by the vendor called JOB-APP. Ron double-clicks on the icon for JOB-APP. Ron reports that JOB-APP appears to try to run but after a long period of time finally reports the following error message: "Unable to Reach Server. Please try again later." From our documentation we can see that the application runs over TCP/IP and that there is a firewall between the user and the circuit connecting to the extranet vendor's location.

Since we have already checked to see if Ron can access the Internet, we know that his TCP/IP stack is functioning. However, we are not going to assume that everything is properly configured, so we ask Ron to open a DOS prompt and run a traceroute to the inside address of the firewall, 172.20.5.254. The traceroute fails at the gateway just before the firewall, 172.20.5.1. According to the documentation, Ron should be able to successfully complete a traceroute to the firewall. So we now have our first clue.

In this particular case, instead of completing the "gather the facts" phase of the problem-solving model, we decide that there must be a problem with the firewall and go on to spend several hours working on the "problem." Finally, finding no problem with the firewall, we decide that additional information is required and continue the "gather the facts" phase. While still looking at the firewall, we check the firewall log and are able to determine that the last transmission of data through the firewall occurred on Friday afternoon at around 4:30 p.m.

We call Ron back to find out if he knew of anything that might have changed over the weekend. At this point, Ron replies that the local network administrators had worked on all the workstations in the department over the weekend and mumbles something about "Ethernet." We know that a number of workstations at Ron's office were being converted from Token Ring to Ethernet, and we also know that this would mean the workstations would show up on a different IP network segment. The documentation reveals that the firewall was configured to speak only with a specific IP network segment, and the real problem begins to emerge. There is nothing wrong with the firewall; it is performing exactly as configured. The problem is that the Ethernet conversion project failed to recognize that a change would be required to this firewall to allow traffic to pass from the new network to the extranet server.

Characterizing the Problem

Every problem can be characterized in two ways, both of which involve time. The two ways are as follows: how frequently the problem can be observed and how frequently the problem has occurred. In grasping this concept, there are four key terms to understand: constant problems, intermittent problems, chronic problems, and acute problems.

Is the Problem Constant or Intermittent?   The easiest problems to define and to resolve are those that are constant. A *constant problem* started at a specific point in time and continues to exist, so it is easier to examine. An *intermittent problem* comes and goes, often at irregular intervals, and is therefore harder to isolate and resolve.

Is the Problem Chronic or Acute?   A *chronic problem* is one that comes with its own life history. Any unsolicited reference to a previous point in time often indicates that the problem could be chronic in nature and should be probed for additional information. Telltale phrases accompany reports of chronic problems: "Every time this happens …," "Usually when I call …," "What they said last time …," "This always seems to happen when …," and so on. The word *chronic* does not refer to a problem that first occurred only recently and has continued for several days.

By contrast, an *acute problem* is one that just recently started and has not previously appeared specifically as described in this situation. The user often expresses surprise at an acute problem and is most often frustrated by a chronic problem.

If we combine these terms, we end up with the following possible combinations:

- **Chronic constant** An example of a chronic constant problem is, "Since last month the network has been running really slow all the time."

- **Chronic intermittent** An example of a chronic intermittent problem is, "Every so often I cannot get on the Internet."

- **Acute constant** An example of an acute constant problem is, "Since 2:00 p.m. today I have not been able to get on the Internet."

- **Acute intermittent** An example of an acute intermittent problem is, "Since this morning I have been having trouble getting on the Internet; I can get to some Web sites but not others."

The most challenging problem to resolve is a chronic intermittent problem. It is hard to catch an intermittent problem when it is occurring, and if it is chronic, that means it has been going on for a while and there is usually no clear time frame during which to research what might have caused the problem.

Defining What Still Works Despite the Reported Problem

The vast majority of reported network problems are partial failures. That is, almost everything is working except certain pieces, which could be a group of servers, a group of users, a group of sites, or the like. In defining the problem, we have clearly specified what is *not* functioning. We still need to identify what *is* working. In other words, if the problem is defined as "No user on the fifth floor in the Texas office can get to the e-mail server," we imply that the users can get to other devices. The ultimate objective in creating this list is to be able to use it to eliminate or target possible sources of the problem.

For example, if you work in an organization with multiple protocols, it would be a good idea to find out if there is a problem with all protocols or just one. If you work in an organization with distributed servers, are all the servers unreachable, or is it just an isolated segment? If you are troubleshooting an Internet connectivity problem, you might want to check to see if the problem is just HyperText Transfer Protocol (HTTP) or whether other protocols within the TCP/IP protocol suite are affected as well.

For organizations with dedicated Internet connections, end users will frequently report that "the Internet is down" whenever they cannot reach a Web site. Keep in mind that end users do not know how the underlying protocols communicate or even how the network is physically connected from their site to the Internet. Another common occurrence is for an end user to report that a file server is down. For this reason, the simple process of opening a browser yourself and trying to reach the site the user is trying to reach can be an invaluable time-saver. When Bill calls and says that he cannot reach www.funstuff.org, open a browser and see for yourself what happens. It stands to reason that if you can get to the site, the Internet must not be down. (Well, that might not be entirely true, since there could be problems in portions of the Internet, but at least you have verified that you have a good connection while Bill does not—in other words, there is a problem on Bill's end but not at the Internet connection.) What if you cannot get to www.funstuff.org, either? Here's the key piece to remember: just because you cannot get to a specific site does not mean that the Internet is down. As you gather the facts, check to see if you can get to other Web sites, such as www.youshouldbeworking.com.

Another real-life example illustrates a more complex problem and highlights why it is important to verify even the basics. John called the e-mail administrator, Ray, to report that he had received a call from a vendor stating that e-mails to John from the vendor were being returned as undeliverable. Ray investigated the problem and discovered that about half the outbound e-mails were failing and that only a small number of inbound e-mails were being received.

Ray reported the problem to the network engineer, Sally. At almost the same time, sporadic reports were being received from all over the company that some Internet sites were unreachable, but others were not. As the day went on, the number of reports escalated dramatically. The circuit was stable, and communications to the Internet carrier were reliable. Traffic volume was down significantly, however. The Internet carrier investigated and reported that all the BGP routes were being properly advertised and that it could find no problem.

By Day Two of this situation, the number of inbound e-mails was down to a trickle. Surely it was a problem with the e-mail server. Ray checked; no, nothing had changed in a week. Ray insisted it must be a problem with the firewall. Sally checked; no, nothing had changed in over 10 days; no inbound packets were coming in. Sally called the Internet carrier back. Still no diagnosis, and still no clear definition of the problem had been arrived at. There did not seem to be a pattern, other than what worked in the morning might not work in the afternoon, and once something stopped working it never started working again.

By Day Three, nothing other than some Web browsing was working. Finally, one engineer began to check each required component in order. The circuit had already been verified. The BGP routes had been verified. What about the domain name? What about the IP address registry? A quick check on the Internet revealed that the controlling authority had disabled the domain name. Further research revealed that the name had been disabled through a spoofed e-mail to the authority. The Internet was not down, but a component required for Internet access was no longer available.

Comparing Findings to the Network Baseline

A *baseline* is a series of measurements taken over a known period of time. Ideally, the performance of the network during this period of time is considered optimal at best and acceptable at worst. The objective of a baseline is to provide a point of reference for the future, when problems occur or when you are planning for additional traffic requirements on the network.

exam
ⓦatch

Baselining your network provides critical network analysis information for problem isolation and resolution. Baselining also provides essential data for monitoring the health of your network.

From a troubleshooting standpoint, the most common reason for comparing your current situation to a baseline is for user complaints that involve phrases such as "The network is slow" or "It takes longer than usual." These are basically performance complaints from end users. You could also use a network baseline to troubleshoot performance degradation that has been highlighted by a programmer building new code, by a network management station such as OpenView or NetView, by other network engineers, or by yourself when working on another problem or installation.

The end-user complaint regarding slow performance is fairly simple to address. Here are the basic scenarios with which you will end up:

■ This is the normal behavior of the network.

■ The network utilization has steadily increased and is now reaching the limits of its capacity as measured by end-user acceptance.

■ There is a spike in network utilization due to unusual circumstances.

■ A problem with a nonnetwork device is impacting the performance of the network.

■ There is a problem in or between components of the network.

So how does a network baseline help you figure out which scenario you are dealing with? Common sense dictates that if you know what is "normal" within the network and you compare what is normal to what is currently observed, you can tell whether or not there has been a change and whether or not that change is significant.

We can see from the monthly baseline graph in Figure 2-5 that historically, the traffic to this location has not exceeded 5.6k. Comparing this data to the current weekly graph in Figure 2-6, we see that it is evident that traffic has more than doubled, peaking as high as 16k. If you know your network, figuring out which scenario these graphs represent will be simple. If you are new to your network, you need to consider each scenario and try to identify the most likely scenario using any historical data available to you. Let's consider each of the possible options individually.

Is it possible that this is the normal behavior of the network? In most cases, a spike in one week that is not seen in historical monthly reports is probably not the normal behavior of the network. Under some circumstances, though, it could be normal behavior. For example, some seasonal businesses have quarterly or annual spikes in traffic, corresponding with the peaks in business activity. Some businesses run a promotion for a week. In these cases, perhaps this spike is not a problem at all.

FIGURE 2-5	`Monthly' Graph (2 Hour Average)

A monthly
baseline graph

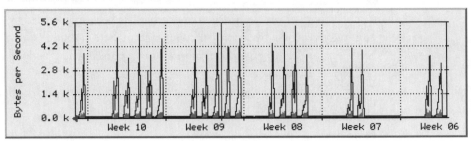

Max In: 554.0 B/s (0.3%)   Average In:121.0 B/s (0.1%)   Current In:57.0 B/s (0.0%)
Max Out:5322.0 B/s (2.8%) Average Out:505.0 B/s (0.3%) Current Out:59.0 B/s (0.0%)

FIGURE 2-6	`Weekly' Graph (30 Minute Average)

A weekly graph

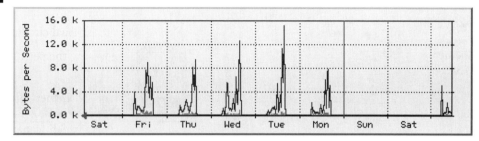

Max In:1036.0 B/s (0.5%)   Average In:148.0 B/s (0.1%)   Current In:59.0 B/s (0.0%)
Max Out: 15.1 kB/s (7.8%) Average Out:751.0 B/s (0.4%) Current Out:60.0 B/s (0.0%)

If the circuit was just upgraded because the link was saturated, the increase in traffic could be a good sign.

Has the network utilization steadily increased, and is it now reaching the limits of its capacity as measured by end-user acceptance? In the two graphs, there does not appear to be anything steady about the increase. It appears that the traffic jumped overnight. Of course, the dates are not included on the graphs, so we could be considering a monthly graph from two months ago and a weekly graph from this past week. If we assume that the two graphs represent adjacent time periods, the answer is that the spike is probably not part of a steady increase. If they are separated by a period of time, we need to see the graphs for the intervening time period to answer this question.

Is there a spike in network utilization due to unusual circumstances? Again, if we assume that the graphs in Figures 2-5 and 2-6 represent adjacent time periods, it is possible that there is an unusual circumstance. For example, a patch could have been released for an application provided by the company and made available via File Transfer Protocol (FTP) to outside customers. The marketing department might be running daily e-mail campaigns. However, if the pattern continues beyond a defined period of time, it is less likely to be due to unusual circumstances. Figure 2-7 is more representative of an unusual period of bandwidth utilization.

In Figure 2-7, we can see that the inbound and outbound traffic spiked at 100 percent and stayed at that level for a measurable period of time. If the traffic in only one direction had spiked at 100 percent, we might hypothesize that a large FTP was in progress during these times. Since both directions spiked, we might assume that FTP could not be the culprit. In this particular case, however, the traffic

FIGURE 2-7

Evidence of
unusual
bandwidth
utilization

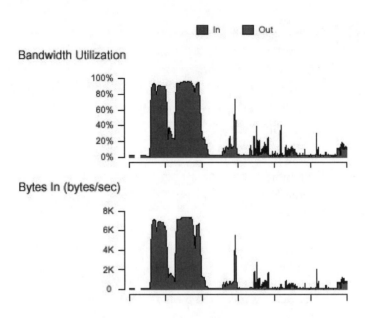

measurements were for a router in England, which was the intermediate router for traffic from the United States to France.

The culprit turned out to be a 4GB FTP transfer from the United States to France across a T1 line in England, and the period of time in the graph represented seven days. If you have the opportunity to investigate while such a traffic spike is occurring, the router can provide the source and destination addresses as well as the number of packets transmitted when IP accounting (IPX accounting works as well) is turned on at the appropriate interface. Just remember to make sure that the CPU utilization of the router is not high when doing so or you might lose access to the router to turn the accounting feature back off. If you are running Cisco Express Forwarding (CEF, an advanced switching feature), you can see this information for IP without turning on accounting.

Is there is a problem with a nonnetwork device that is impacting the performance of the network? This situation is most likely to be seen in a LAN, although the problem is not exclusive to LANs. Increased traffic can be observed because of invalid routes injected into the network by unauthorized devices on the LAN. For example, in one case, after significant investigation it was determined that a dual-attached NT server on the LAN had the IP routing feature enabled. Although the router was not configured to "listen" to RIP broadcasts from the LAN, the workstations on the LAN automatically picked up the extra routes and began to send all the traffic destined for the remote offices to the NT server. A traceroute from the router revealed nothing unusual, but a traceroute from the client workstation revealed the offending device.

In another case, a Novell server, NOVELL1, was configured to use 802.3 instead of 802.2. A second Novell server on the network, NOVELL2, was configured with both 802.2 and 802.3 protocols. NOVELL1 was being routed through NOVELL2 to a remote Novell server in Canada, NOVELL3, which was also running 802.3, to join the Novell tree. In this case, IPX accounting determined that the source and destination addresses of the high-traffic devices and coordination with the network administrators responsible for the servers allowed identification of the source of the problem.

Is there a problem in or between components of the network? Changes in traffic patterns can be the result of an incorrect configuration of a single network device. Improperly redistributing static routes can result in traffic from the core of the network being routed through a remote facility. The statement IP CLASSLESS in a single router on the edge of the network can result in an increase in network traffic being improperly routed through the remote router instead of through the core of the network, if all the other routers have the NO IP CLASSLESS statement. Knowing which network devices were recently installed, reconfigured, or removed can be helpful in tracking down the source of such a problem.

EXERCISE 2-3

Gathering the Facts

When we left our last exercise, we had just defined the problem: "Since the two routers were installed, no IP traffic has been able to go from the TEST2 router to the TEST1 router." Continuing with the previous lab setup, gather the relevant facts.
Solution:

We need to answer several questions. When did the problem start? It first started when the routers were put in. Has anything changed? Yes, we installed two new routers. The problem can be characterized as constant acute, so it should be relatively easy to troubleshoot. Defining what still works is where things start to become interesting.

1. From your workstation's DOS prompt, ping the following addresses (on the TEST router): 192.168.184.89, 172.24.1.1, 10.1.1.1, and 10.1.2.1. Everything works.

2. From your workstation's DOS prompt, ping the following addresses (on the TEST2 router): 192.168.184.88, 192.168.192.1, and 192.168.193.1. Everything works.

3. In the previous exercise you logged in to the TEST2 router and were able to successfully ping the addresses from the TEST2 router: 192.168.184.89, 172.24.1.1, 10.1.1.1, and 10.1.2.1.

4. If you use the SHOW CDP NEIGHBOR DETAIL command on each router, you will begin to see why there might be a problem. Here is the output from each router:

```
Test>show cdp neighbor detail
-------------------------
Device ID: Test2
Entry address(es):
 IP address: 192.168.184.88
Platform: Cisco 2612, Capabilities: Router
Interface: Ethernet0, Port ID (outgoing port): Ethernet0/0
Holdtime : 161 sec

Version :
Cisco Internetwork Operating System Software
IOS (tm) C2600 Software (C2600-I-M), Version 11.3(4)T1, RELEASE SOFTWARE (fc1)

Copyright (c) 1986-1998 by Cisco Systems, Inc.
Compiled Wed 01-Jul-98 11:48 by phanguye
advertisement version: 1

Test2>show cdp neighbor detail
-------------------------
Device ID: Test
Entry address(es):
 IP address: 172.24.1.1
Platform: Cisco 2500, Capabilities: Router
Interface: Ethernet0/0, Port ID (outgoing port): Ethernet0
Holdtime : 139 sec

Version :
Cisco Internetwork Operating System Software
```

```
IOS (tm) 2500 Software (C2500-I-L), Version 12.0(3)T, RELEASE SOFTWARE (fc1)
Copyright (c) 1986-1999 by Cisco Systems, Inc.
Compiled Mon 22-Feb-99 17:42 by ccai
```

Notice that the two routers are able to communicate using CDP (Layer 2) but not TCP/IP. If you look carefully at the IP address reported, you will see that one router is using 192.168.184.88 as its primary Ethernet address while the other is using 172.24.1.1 as its primary Ethernet address.

Neither router has a default gateway, as can be seen from the results of the SHOW IP ROUTE command:

```
Test>show ip route
Codes: C - connected, S - static, I - IGRP, R - RIP, M - mobile, B - BGP
    D - EIGRP, EX - EIGRP external, O - OSPF, IA - OSPF inter area
    N1 - OSPF NSSA external type 1, N2 - OSPF NSSA external type 2
    E1 - OSPF external type 1, E2 - OSPF external type 2, E - EGP
    i - IS-IS, L1 - IS-IS level-1, L2 - IS-IS level-2, * - candidate default
    U - per-user static route, o - ODR, P - periodic downloaded static route
    T - traffic engineered route

Gateway of last resort is not set

R   192.168.192.0/24 [120/1] via 192.168.184.88, Ethernet0
R   192.168.193.0/24 [120/1] via 192.168.184.88, Ethernet0
    172.24.0.0/16 is variably subnetted, 2 subnets, 2 masks
D      172.24.0.0/16 is a summary, Null0
C      172.24.1.0/24 is directly connected, Ethernet0
    10.0.0.0/8 is variably subnetted, 3 subnets, 3 masks
C      10.1.2.0/24 is directly connected, Loopback0
D      10.0.0.0/8 is a summary, Null0
C      10.1.1.0/30 is directly connected, Loopback0
    192.168.184.0/28 is subnetted, 1 subnets
C      192.168.184.80 is directly connected, Ethernet0

Test2>show ip route
Codes: C - connected, S - static, I - IGRP, R - RIP, M - mobile, B - BGP
    D - EIGRP, EX - EIGRP external, O - OSPF, IA - OSPF inter area
    N1 - OSPF NSSA external type 1, N2 - OSPF NSSA external type 2
    E1 - OSPF external type 1, E2 - OSPF external type 2, E - EGP
    i - IS-IS, L1 - IS-IS level-1, L2 - IS-IS level-2, * - candidate default
    U - per-user static route, o - ODR

Gateway of last resort is not set
```

```
C  192.168.192.0/24 is directly connected, Loopback0
C  192.168.193.0/24 is directly connected, Loopback0
   192.168.184.0/28 is subnetted, 1 subnets
C     192.168.184.80 is directly connected, Ethernet0/0
```

We can also see that TEST has more routes than TEST2.

If we turn on DEBUG IP RIP in TEST2, we know that at a minimum of every 30 seconds we should see some events on the console. Clearly, we can see that TEST2 is sending RIP packets but not receiving any:

```
Test2#debug ip rip
RIP protocol debugging is on
Test2#
23:25:20: RIP: sending v1 update to 255.255.255.255 via Ethernet0/0 (192.168.184.88)
23:25:20:   network 192.168.192.0, metric 1
23:25:20:   network 192.168.193.0, metric 1
23:25:47: RIP: sending v1 update to 255.255.255.255 via Ethernet0/0 (192.168.184.88)
23:25:47:   network 192.168.192.0, metric 1
23:25:47:   network 192.168.193.0, metric 1
23:26:16: RIP: sending v1 update to 255.255.255.255 via Ethernet0/0 (192.168.184.88)
23:26:16:   network 192.168.192.0, metric 1
23:26:16:   network 192.168.193.0, metric 1
23:26:44: RIP: sending v1 update to 255.255.255.255 via Ethernet0/0 (192.168.184.88)
```

Here's the output from the TEST router:

```
Test#debug ip rip
RIP protocol debugging is on
Test#
23:37:29: RIP: sending v1 update to 255.255.255.255 via Ethernet0 (192.168.184.89)
23:37:29: RIP: build update entries - suppressing null update
23:37:38: RIP: received v1 update from 192.168.184.88 on Ethernet0
23:37:38:   192.168.192.0 in 1 hops
23:37:38:   192.168.193.0 in 1 hops
23:37:38: RIP: Update contains 2 routes
23:37:55: RIP: sending v1 update to 255.255.255.255 via Ethernet0 (192.168.184.89)
23:37:55: RIP: build update entries - suppressing null update
```

Clearly, both routers are sending RIP routes, but if we look closely, we see that the RIP update from TEST includes no routes. Instead, it includes "suppressing null update."

CERTIFICATION OBJECTIVE 2.04

Considering Possibilities Based on Facts

This is the time to let your imagination run wild. The more bizarre or complex the problem, the more opportunity you will have to speculate. General brainstorming principles should apply at this point; nothing should be discounted until examined. As with brainstorming, this process has some guiding principles to follow.

Comparing What Still Works to What Could Go Wrong

Since you have gone through the previous steps in the troubleshooting process, you have already developed your list of what is working and your list of what is not working. Here we want to identify any relationships within each list and identify what is different between the two lists (besides the fact that everything in one list works and everything in the other list does not work).

Eliminating Possible Points of Failure

It is often easier to determine what is working than to quickly identify what is not working. Eliminating from your list those parts of the network that are functioning properly allows you to more clearly focus your investigation on the possible source of the trouble.

Considering Each Component of the Network

Thinking through how the devices in the network are physically and logically connected can be helpful. Every network is composed of similar components. From the end-user workstation (or the dumb terminal, in some networks) to the server or mainframe, you can list and consider each individual component. Consider the diagram in Figure 2-8.

The problem could be with the workstation, the cable, the hub or switch, the router, the public or private network, and so on. Using your network map, start with the end user and follow the path from the end user to the unreachable destination. Once you have identified a suspect component within the network, continue checking the remaining components. Network failures sometimes involve multiple components. For example, there could be a circuit failure and a failure

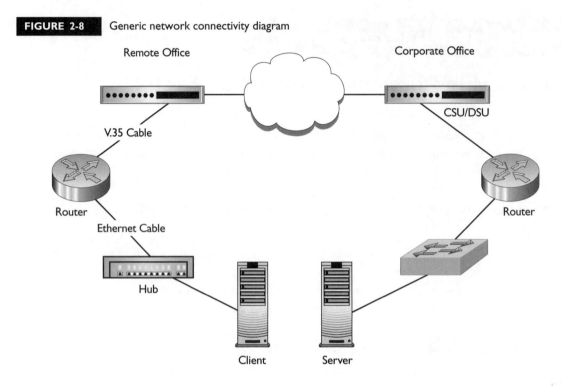

FIGURE 2-8   Generic network connectivity diagram

within the channel service unit/data service unit (CSU/DSU) at the same time. This is especially likely if the cause of the trouble is a lightning strike.

Creating a List of Possible Trouble Areas

From observation of the network, comparing it to the baseline, and gathering relevant facts, you should now be in a position to begin to hypothesize regarding the possible source of the problem. In order to eliminate possible points of failure, you had to consider each device along the network path and determine that it was functioning properly or set it aside for further consideration. At this point, you need to consider more carefully those possible trouble areas that were not eliminated.

Identifying the OSI Layer

There is a good reason that a discussion of the Open Systems Interconnection (OSI) layer appears at the beginning of just about every network book. When you are faced with a problem, one of the best ways to eliminate possible causes is to eliminate each OSI layer in a step-by-step fashion. This holds true for the process of defining the problem as well. The end user will not be able to answer this question on his or her own without prompting, but the skillful troubleshooter will guide the end user through the process and in doing so will arrive at the proper layer.

As you think about the problem, consider whether this is likely to be a Physical Layer problem, a data layer problem, a network problem, and so forth. Your thought process might go something like this: "If she can ping the server, Layer 3 is probably not the problem." Or "If I can see the SAPs in the router in New York, it is probably not a problem with the server itself (Layers 1 and 2)." Or, "If the interface is down, there is probably a problem in Layer 1."

Within each device could be multiple components, any one of which could be functioning improperly. For example, the workstation includes a network interface card (NIC) or a modem, if dealing with a dial problem; the networking or communications software; the operating system; the application(s); and so on.

Methodically looking at each item on the list, think about how likely it is to be the cause of the problem. Each will be considered relatively more or less likely to be accurate.

EXERCISE 2-4

Considering the Possibilities

Continuing with the previous lab setup, consider the possible causes of the problem.
Solution:

We know that the connection from one router to the other is valid (SHOW CDP NEIGHBOR validates Layer 2 connectivity), so the problem is not likely to be the interface, the cable, or the hub.

We know that TCP/IP is working in one direction but not the reverse. This appears to be a Layer 3 (routing) problem. From the facts previously gathered, we can quickly come up with at least three possible causes of the problem:

- It is possible that the lack of a default gateway is the cause of the problem.

- It is possible that the primary address on the Ethernet interface of each router needs to be in the same network.

- It is possible that a configuration error is preventing the routes from being advertised from the TEST router.

Creating an Action Plan

In the middle of a crisis, it is tempting to throw planning aside and rush in to try to fix the problem. Temptation is just another word for trouble, though. An action plan is a series of steps to test a hypothesis or to resolve a problem. A good plan accomplishes two very important goals. First, you are forced to think through the process, and as you do so, you discover one of three things:

- You realize that what you thought was causing the problem is only a symptom of the problem.

- You realize that what you thought would verify the problem will not have the desired end result.

- You create a well-designed test plan.

Creating a Plan on How to Test Each Possible Problem

As you plan your testing, you will find that you go through the same process each time. Let's look at the components of a good test plan. Briefly, they are:

1. Define the hypothesis.

2. Define each individual step.

3. Define expected results.

4. Define a recovery plan.

5. Define and communicate the risks.

Define the Hypothesis

A *hypothesis* is nothing more than an educated guess. You will not know until you have tested it whether or not it was valid. Before you can test a hypothesis, you must have a clear understanding of what you expect to find. When a scientist creates a hypothesis, he or she specifies both the cause and the effect of an activity or process. An example of a poorly defined hypothesis is, "There is a spanning-tree problem on the switch." A hypothesis is often presented in the form of "if…then" statements. A better hypothesis would state that "If we change the priority of Port 1 on the switch, then spanning-tree will stabilize."

In networking, a well-defined hypothesis might be, "The workstation is unable to reach the e-mail server because there is no host file on the workstation or because the e-mail server is not defined in the DNS server." It is possible to test a hypothesis without resolving the problem. Your hypothesis might be, "If we check the firewall logs, we will find that we have an unusually high number of packets coming from the Hooya mail server."

Define Each Individual Step

Once you have a clearly defined hypothesis, you need to map out each step required to verify the hypothesis. You might have only one step, but in most cases you will have multiple steps. In our preceding e-mail example, we could go two ways, depending on our company policy. We could define the e-mail server in the DNS, or we could add a statement in the host file on the workstation. Either way, we would detail the specific changes to be made. In our firewall example, we would specify that we will open the firewall logs for the last three days (or whatever was deemed appropriate) and compare the number of packets from the Hooya mail server to our network baseline information.

Define Expected Results

Once the change(s) have been implemented, you need to be able to verify whether or not the expected results were achieved. In order to do this, you need to know before you begin what you should see when you are finished. You also need to know when you can expect to see the results. In our e-mail example, the expected results might be, "The workstation will immediately be able to ping the mail-server by name, and the mail client will be able to connect to the server." For our firewall example, we might say, "We will see at least 25 percent more packets from the Hooya mail server over the last three days compared with the previous three-day period."

You might not see results immediately, especially in the case of an intermittent problem. For example, if you are dealing with a problem with the network being "slow" every Monday, you might have to wait until the following Monday to observe the effects of your changes. If you are dealing with an intermittent problem in the Frame Relay network that happens at random intervals, your expected results could be that "The problem will not reoccur" and the interval might be over a period of 10 days.

Define a Recovery Plan

If we have made any changes in the process of verifying (or disproving) our hypothesis, we need to be prepared to undo them. In the case of a host file or DNS change, the back-out process will be fairly simple. At some point, however, it is likely that you will implement an IOS upgrade as part of this process. How will you roll back to the previous IOS, if necessary? How will you know whether or not it is necessary to back out? You should have the answers to these questions before proceeding.

Define and Communicate the Risks

There is almost always a risk that service will be adversely affected when you make a change in a network device. The risk could be extremely low, or it could be very high. If you change the bandwidth statement on an interface in a router running Open Shortest Path First (OSPF), there is the potential that the traffic patterns will be changed as a result. The risk varies significantly depending on the network layout, and it is your responsibility to assess the risk for your organization. Likewise, if you find that you need to modify the spanning-tree parameters in your corporate switches, you need to assess the likelihood that the tree will need to reconverge, resulting in a relatively brief but unavoidable denial of service to network users.

on the **job**

Depending on the organization and its tolerance for risk, you might need to communicate the anticipated changes and the associated potential risks to others within the organization. Some companies have formal change-control meetings and require that no changes be implemented without first being approved through the change-control process. The more bureaucratic the organization (read: the government), the more likely you need to follow a defined change-control process. Other companies have no change-control meetings but expect management to be notified of any changes that have the potential to result in denial of service. Still others don't care what changes are made as long as the network is operational during normal business hours. You might or might not have the authority to implement any change above a certain level of risk. You need to know what is expected within your company and follow the appropriate company procedures.

Sequencing the Possible Problems, With the Most Likely First

If you think the problem is probably a bad cable, but it could be a bad port on the switch, it makes sense to replace the cable or at least test the cable in some way before replacing the switch or changing ports on the switch. After working on the same types of problems repeatedly, you will become more accomplished at pinpointing the problem with your first hypothesis. Partly, this happens because you learn along the way, and partly it is because you see the same problem over and over again. After a while you will know that it is rarely a "bad port" on a switch that is to blame for a workstation being unable to communicate on the network. Because it is always a possibility that the problem is with the port on the switch, however, we should keep it on the list of things to check, but only after ruling out the more likely problems, such as a bad cable, incorrect network settings on the workstation, the wrong virtual LAN (VLAN) on the switch, and so on.

Consider the following situation. The Frame Relay circuit in your South Carolina office has failed. The router was supposed to automatically initiate dial backup to the host office in Georgia, but this did not occur. You have now resolved the problem with the Frame Relay circuit and need to address the problem defined as, "The dial backup from South Carolina to Georgia is not occurring when the Frame Relay circuit goes down." You have listed the following possibilities (not all possibilities are listed here):

- The basic rate interface (BRI) line on the router in South Carolina could be down.
- The primary rate interface (PRI) line on the router in Georgia could be down.
- The configuration in the router in South Carolina could be incorrect.
- The configuration in the router in Georgia could be incorrect.

If both routers have been in place for a period of time and dial backup has previously been activated successfully, the hypotheses listed above are sequenced in order of the most likely. If dial backup has never been activated successfully, a configuration error could be more likely.

If you are using the BACKUP INTERFACE command on a serial interface, the BRI interface will be placed in standby mode, and it is not possible to verify whether or not the line is functional. Here is what it would look like in the router:

```
Test2600#sh in bri0/0
BRI0/0 is standby mode, line protocol is down
```

A simple test plan for the first hypothesis might look like this:

1. Dial in to the router. (We do not want to risk losing our connection to the router while we are testing.)

2. Remove the configuration statement BACKUP INTERFACE BRI0/0 from Serial 0/0.

3. SHOW INTERFACE BRI0/0 to see if the line appears to be up. If the line is up, we will see:

   ■ BRI0 is up, line protocol is up (spoofing)

4. If the line is down, we will see:

   ■ BRI0 is down, line protocol is down

5. Replace the statement BACKUP INTERFACE BRI0/0 on Serial 0/0.

You might notice that the action plan did not involve shutting down the serial interface to see if the BRI line came up. Although shutting down the serial interface would have the same effect, it would also have the effect of denying network services to end users at the location during testing. You could implement such an action plan only while manually dialed in to the router (since you would lose your Telnet connection) and while no users were at the facility and while no unattended data transfers were occurring. This is an unlikely combination in most networks.

Astute readers will have noticed that a number of pieces were missing from the preceding action plan. Some of the pieces that need to be added before the plan should be executed include a time frame for the process, a list of potential risks associated with the plan, a recovery plan, and communicating with the facility.

exam
ⓦatch

Whenever possible, an action plan should be minimally intrusive while still being effective.

If the BRI line in South Carolina is down, the follow-up action plan will include reporting trouble on the line to the carrier as well as verifying that there is not a physical connection problem. If the BRI line is not plugged into the router, you will have the same symptoms. In some cases, you can use the SHOW CONTROLLERS command to verify whether or not a cable is physically connected to the router, as demonstrated in this output from our TEST router:

```
TEST2500#show controllers serial 2
CD2430 unit 0, Channel 0, Revision A5
Channel mode is synchronous serial
idb 0xC2328, buffer size 1524, RS-232 DCE cable, clockrate 9600
```

In the case of BRI, the SHOW CONTROLLERS command will not provide information about an attached cable.

You can use DEBUG ISDN q931, DEBUG ISDN q921, and DEBUG ISDN EVENTS as additional troubleshooting tools. Always remember that DEBUG is a dangerous command to use in a production environment, and be extremely conservative when deciding whether or not it is safe to use.

EXERCISE 2-5

Creating an Action Plan

Continuing with the previous lab setup, create an action plan to address the two most likely causes of the problem:

- It is possible that the primary address on the Ethernet interface of each router needs to be in the same network.

- It is possible that a configuration error is preventing the routes from being advertised from the TEST router.

Solution:
Action Plan #1

Hypothesis: Making the 192.168.184.89 address on the Ethernet interface of the TEST router the primary address will resolve the routing problems previously identified.

If the primary address on the Ethernet interface of each router needs to be in the same network, we need to change the TEST router's Ethernet configuration so that it looks like this:

```
interface Ethernet0
 ip address 192.168.184.89 255.255.255.240
 ip address 172.24.1.1 255.255.255.0 secondary
```

The steps necessary to make these changes are as follows:

1. Remove the secondary address from the Ethernet interface:
   interface Ethernet0
   no ip address 192.168.184.89 255.255.255.240 secondary

2. Overwrite the primary address on the Ethernet interface:
   interface Ethernet0
   ip address 192.168.184.89 255.255.255.240

3. Enter the 172.24.1.1 address as a secondary address:
   interface Ethernet0
   ip address 172.24.1.1 255.255.255.0 secondary

4. Check to make sure the 192.168.184.0 and the 172.24.0.0 networks are still included in the routing statements in the router by using the SHOW RUN command. You should see:
   ```
   router eigrp 200
    network 10.0.0.0
    network 172.24.0.0
    network 192.168.220.0
   router rip
    redistribute eigrp 200
    network 192.168.184.0
   ```
   If you do not see this output, add the appropriate statements to the router.

5. Once these changes are made, you should be able to successfully ping all addresses from each router.

6. The changes required are intrusive in nature, so all users on the Ethernet segment should be advised that they will lose connectivity to other locations during the modifications. The risks are low if changes are made through a direct console cable, higher if made through a dial connection. These changes should not be made through a telnet connection since TCP/IP connectivity to the Ethernet interface will be affected.

Our recovery plan will be implemented if the change has a negative impact on existing traffic. The recovery plan is to change the configuration back to the way it was when we started. To prepare for the recovery plan, we will make a backup of the current configuration.

Action Plan #2

Hypothesis: A configuration error on the TEST router is preventing the TEST router from advertising the IP routes to the TEST2 router. The TEST router should have the statement "redistribute connected" under the "router rip" section of the configuration.

The steps required to implement this change are very simple:

1. In configuration mode, enter the following commands:
   router rip
   redistribute connected

2. Check to make sure that everything that was working is still working.

3. Check the routing tables in each router to make sure that the routes still look correct.

4. Once this change is made, you should be able to successfully ping all addresses from each router.

5. The change is not intrusive in nature, but any time you redistribute, you run a risk of introducing new routing problems. All users on the Ethernet segment should be advised that they could lose connectivity to other locations during the modifications.

Our recovery plan will be implemented if the change has a negative impact on existing traffic. The recovery plan is to change the configuration back to the way it was when we started. To prepare for the recovery plan, we will make a backup of the current configuration.

We next need to sequence our action plans. The most likely resolution is Action Plan #2, so in the real world we would implement Action Plan #2 first. However, for the purposes of our lab, we set the sequence as Action Plan #1, followed by Action Plan #2.

CERTIFICATION OBJECTIVE 2.06

Implementing the Action Plan

When a problem is relatively simple, it is easy to know when to implement the action plan. Once we have the action plan, there is no question that it is time to proceed.

In the case of a complex problem, when you are not sure whether or not you are on the right track, it can be harder to know whether or not you should proceed. What if you have widespread reports of problems and you are unable to find a pattern to them? What if you are dealing with a chronic intermittent problem and you have not been able to actually observe the problem while it is occurring? In these cases, the process does not change. Once you have a theory about a possible cause and you have an action plan to test the theory, it is time to implement your plan.

exam
ⓦatch

It is not necessary to be certain that you have identified the cause of the problem before implementing your plan. It is only necessary to have a clearly defined hypothesis and an action plan to test the hypothesis.

Implementing the action plan is a complete process within itself, as demonstrated in Figure 2-9.

Like the problem-solving model itself, the execution of an action plan is iterative; you must work through each step in succession until all the steps have been completed.

Executing Each Action Plan

Your action plan should have a clearly defined start time and an expected duration. While you execute the action plan, it is important that you ensure that no other changes are taking place at the same time. In a large organization, this means that you need to inform other engineers before you begin. If your organization has a change-control process, you need to communicate the anticipated start and end times. When dealing with a problem, you sometimes have little opportunity to follow the formal change-control process, but it is critical that you know what else is happening in the network that could skew the outcome.

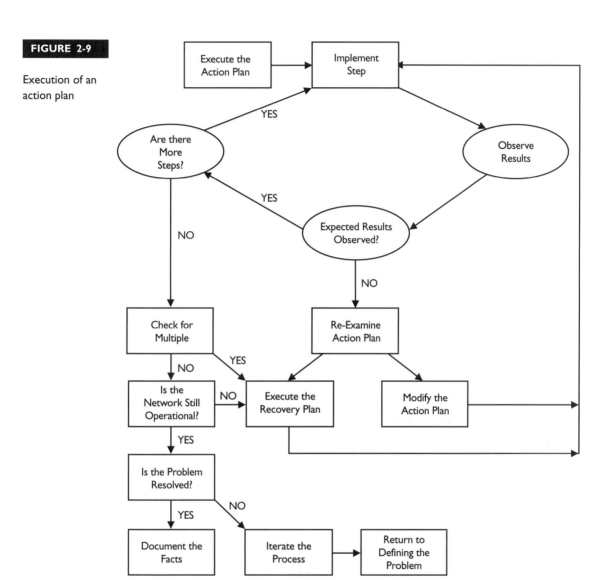

FIGURE 2-9

Execution of an action plan

Within an Action Plan, Change Only One Variable at a Time

As you work through your action plan, it might seem logical to work through every step of the plan and then check the results. If you do so, however, you might miss important clues along the way. Implement a step, verify that the outcome of that step occurred as expected, then move to the next step. If you need to upgrade the

IOS on a router and you have reached the point at which you have finished loading the new IOS in the router, you should verify that the CHECKSUM reported by the router matches what you expected. If it does, move to the next step in the process. If it does not, check your back-out plan.

Testing Each Plan to Check for Multiple Failures

As you defined your action plan, you prepared a list of the risks associated with implementing the plan. As you now implement the plan, be on the lookout for any indication that the risk is becoming a reality. In addition, be on the lookout for other problems—problems that you did not anticipate.

For example, if you plan to apply an AppleTalk RTMP filter to reduce WAN traffic, you should have a clear list of all the zones that should be visible in each part of the network. When you deny a cable range, you also deny the zones within that cable range, so you should make sure that you have not denied any partial zones that are needed. In such a case, include checking to make sure the filter is providing the expected results by doing a SHOW APPLE ROUTE. You will also want to do a SHOW APPLE ZONE and compare the results of both commands to your prepared set of expected results.

CERTIFICATION OBJECTIVE 2.07

Observing the Results

Plan in advance to pay attention to the details, not just the big picture. Build into your action plan time between each step to look at all the relevant information. If you are troubleshooting an AppleTalk connectivity problem between two routers, be certain to use the SHOW APPLETALK NEIGHBORS command and review the output on each router. You should also observe the output of the SHOW APPLETALK ZONE and SHOW APPLETALK ROUTE commands, and possibly the SHOW APPLETALK ARP command.

After Each Variable Change, Ensure That the Network Is Still Operational

At this point, there is one basic question, which can be stated in two ways. One, is everything that was working before still working? Two, did I break anything new?

Here we want to go back to the list of things that were working and make sure that each is still working. This process generally involves using the appropriate SHOW commands on the routers and/or switches. For example, if you add a new static IP route to the router, you probably want to use the SHOW IP ROUTE command in two or more routers in the network to ensure that the network is still operational. If you do not intend to redistribute the route, the new static route should not appear in the other routers, but it should appear in the router where the command was entered. If you are redistributing the route, the new route should appear in the other routers, but other routes should not be affected. It might require communication with the end user between each step, depending on the nature of the problem you are troubleshooting. However, in most cases, you should not rely on the end user to verify that the network is operational.

Correcting the Individual Problem, Ensure That the Network Is Still Operational

It is said that the best way to learn what *not* to do is to do it once and suffer the consequences. Anyone who has ever had the experience of fixing a problem, going home thinking he or she was a hero, and then being paged at 3:00 a.m. because instead he or she caused a new problem will remember this lesson. It is easy to fix one problem and cause a new one without realizing it. Knowing what was working when you started gives you a ready-made list of things to check after you "correct" the problem.

After Each Action Plan, Ensure That the Network Is Still Operational

Regardless of whether or not a specific action plan resolved the individual problem, check to make sure that everything else is still working before proceeding to the next action plan.

In some cases, it might be appropriate to leave in changes that were implemented, even if the problem was not resolved. Consider a problem with packets being dropped somewhere in the network. Assume that you have hypothesized that implementing custom queuing will resolve the problem. You have implemented custom queuing, but the problem is still not resolved. You might decide that custom queuing has improved performance, even though it did not resolve the specific problem. Before proceeding to the next action plan, you should check to make sure that traffic being handled by the default queue is not adversely affected or, if it is, that any agreed-on service levels are not adversely affected.

EXERCISE 2-6

Executing the Action Plan

Continuing with the previous lab setup, implement Action Plan #1.
Solution:

First, connect the console cable to the console port of the TEST router and log in to the router in enable mode.

Next, enter the following commands:

```
configure terminal
interface ethernet0
no ip address 192.168.184.89 255.255.255.240 secondary
ip address 192.168.184.89 255.255.255.240
ip address 172.24.1.1 255.255.255.0 secondary
```

Next, use the SHOW RUN command to verify that the routing statements are still in place:

```
router eigrp 200
 network 10.0.0.0
 network 172.24.0.0
 network 192.168.220.0
 !
router rip
 redistribute eigrp 200
 network 192.168.184.0
```

Next, observe the results. From a terminal emulator on your workstation, log in to the TEST2 router. Ping the following addresses from the TEST2 router: 192.168.184.89, 172.24.1.1, 10.1.1.1, and 10.1.2.1. The results are shown in Figure 2-10.

We can now ping 192.168.184.89, but we still cannot ping the other addresses. In other words, Action Plan #1 did not resolve the problem, although there is some improvement.

Having verified that everything else appears to be functioning, there is no need to implement our recovery plan.

FIGURE 2-10 Observe the results: Action Plan #1

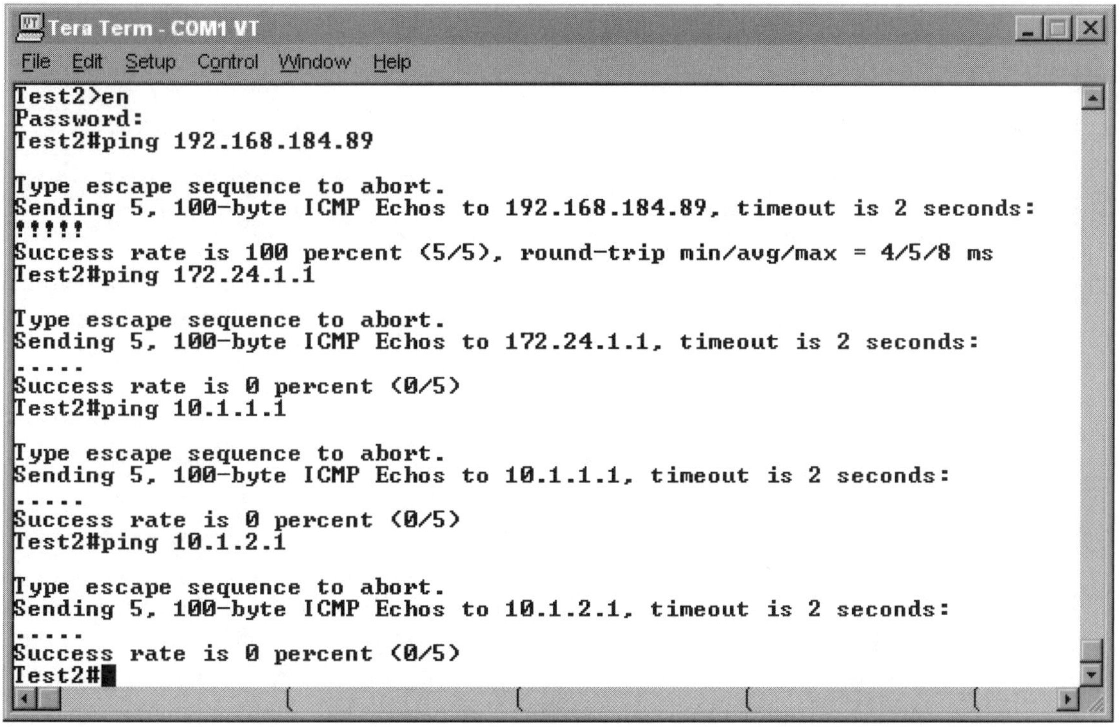
Tera Term - COM1 VT
File Edit Setup Control Window Help
Test2>en
Password:
Test2#ping 192.168.184.89
Type escape sequence to abort.
Sending 5, 100-byte ICMP Echos to 192.168.184.89, timeout is 2 seconds:
!!!!!
Success rate is 100 percent (5/5), round-trip min/avg/max = 4/5/8 ms
Test2#ping 172.24.1.1
Type escape sequence to abort.
Sending 5, 100-byte ICMP Echos to 172.24.1.1, timeout is 2 seconds:
.....
Success rate is 0 percent (0/5)
Test2#ping 10.1.1.1
Type escape sequence to abort.
Sending 5, 100-byte ICMP Echos to 10.1.1.1, timeout is 2 seconds:
.....
Success rate is 0 percent (0/5)
Test2#ping 10.1.2.1
Type escape sequence to abort.
Sending 5, 100-byte ICMP Echos to 10.1.2.1, timeout is 2 seconds:
.....
Success rate is 0 percent (0/5)
Test2#

CERTIFICATION OBJECTIVE 2.08

Iterating the Process

If you have defined multiple action plans and the first action plan does not resolve the problem, you need to repeat the process, returning to the original definition of the problem. Although you could decide that the definition of the problem has not changed, you might find that after implementing the recently completed action plan, you have a new understanding of the problem and will want to make some adjustments.

exam
⚠️atch

After completing the action plan, if the problem is not resolved, you will return to the problem definition phase of the problem-solving model, even if you have multiple action plans defined.

If There Are Multiple Action Plans, Execute Each Independently

Some problems require many hours, days, or even weeks to resolve. However, the vast majority of problems can be resolved in a relatively short span of time. At first glance, it might appear that executing multiple action plans simultaneously will speed the process, but doing so can actually slow it down significantly. Consider this scenario: if John is reconfiguring the line card on the switch on the second floor while Sarah is replacing the Supervisor Module in the switch on the first floor, and if the problem is still not resolved, how do you observe the effects of each action independently? The answer is that you cannot. If you do not know which action had which effect, you cannot effectively troubleshoot a problem by implementing multiple actions simultaneously. Regardless of how many engineers are working on the problem, each action plan should be executed at a distinctly separate time, and everyone working on the problem should be advised before any action plan is executed so that they can ensure they do not interfere with the implementation of the plan.

Even though it is certainly important to make sure that every measure is taken to ensure the fastest possible resolution of a problem, it is even more important to be able to identify the specific action that *did* resolve the problem. The phrase "The problem is fixed; who cares what caused it?" is inappropriate and irresponsible. Problems repeat themselves for a variety of reasons. Having seen a problem once and knowing what resolved it the first time will speed the resolution process in the future. Just remember to be careful not to assume the current problem is the same as the last problem!

on the

()ob

The more individuals involved in working on a problem, the greater the risk of multiple action plans being executed simultaneously. Likewise, in a team environment, it is important to know who is responsible for decisions. When time is of the essence, it is critical to stop and decide who will make the decisions. It is easy to feel that you are "in over your head" when a problem is severe and to allow others to dictate what steps should be taken. Rely on your instincts, and don't be afraid to speak up.

Several years ago, I as a manager was faced with a crisis. The vice president and the director of my division were both involved. Neither had formal training in networking, and they were making contradictory decisions. One brought in a consultant who did not know anything about the network. The other wanted to proceed in a way that didn't make sense to me. My coworker spoke up, but in the confusion of the situation I kept my mouth shut. For three days the company was unable to function, even though the number of affected users could have been dramatically reduced by swapping two Catalyst 5500s until we were able to diagnose the problem. In our case, too many cooks did spoil the broth!

EXERCISE 2-7

Iterating the Process

Continuing with the previous lab setup, iterate the process, ending with the implementation of Action Plan #2.

Solution:

First, review the current problem definition to determine whether or not it should be refined based on the outcome of Action Plan #1. The current problem definition is, "Since the two routers were installed, no IP traffic has been able to go from the TEST2 router to the TEST1 router." This problem definition is still appropriate.

Second, we want to make sure that we did not overlook any relevant facts. Based on the currently available information, it does not appear that any new facts will provide better information. Reviewing what we did when we considered the possibilities, implementing Action Plan #2 still appears to be a wise move. We have already created Action Plan #2, so the next step is to implement it.

Connect the console cable to the console port of the TEST router. Log in to the router in enable mode. Enter the following commands:

```
configure t
router rip
redistribute connected
```

Next, observe the results. From a terminal emulator on your workstation, log in to the TEST2 router. Ping the following addresses from the TEST2 router: 192.168.184.89, 172.24.1.1, 10.1.1.1, and 10.1.2.1. The results are shown in Figure 2-11.

It appears that the problem is now resolved. Finally, we want to make sure that everything else is still working. From your workstation's DOS prompt, ping the

FIGURE 2-11 Observe the results: Action Plan #2

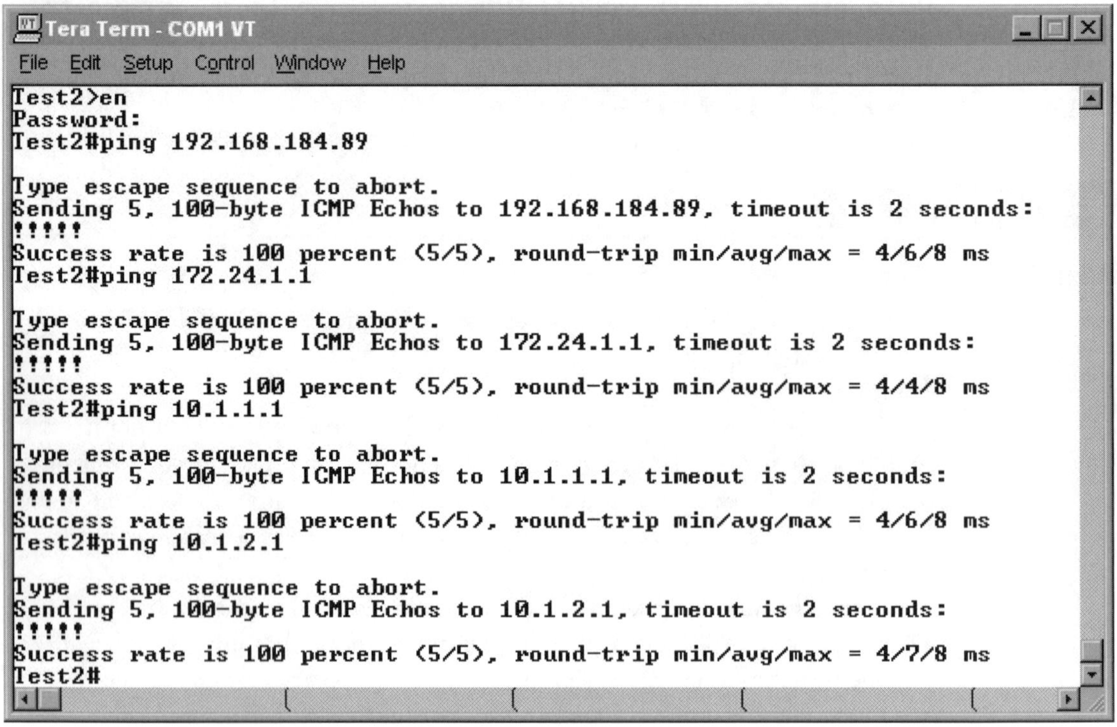

```
Tera Term - COM1 VT                                                    _ □ ×
File  Edit  Setup  Control  Window  Help
Test2>en
Password:
Test2#ping 192.168.184.89

Type escape sequence to abort.
Sending 5, 100-byte ICMP Echos to 192.168.184.89, timeout is 2 seconds:
!!!!!
Success rate is 100 percent (5/5), round-trip min/avg/max = 4/6/8 ms
Test2#ping 172.24.1.1

Type escape sequence to abort.
Sending 5, 100-byte ICMP Echos to 172.24.1.1, timeout is 2 seconds:
!!!!!
Success rate is 100 percent (5/5), round-trip min/avg/max = 4/4/8 ms
Test2#ping 10.1.1.1

Type escape sequence to abort.
Sending 5, 100-byte ICMP Echos to 10.1.1.1, timeout is 2 seconds:
!!!!!
Success rate is 100 percent (5/5), round-trip min/avg/max = 4/6/8 ms
Test2#ping 10.1.2.1

Type escape sequence to abort.
Sending 5, 100-byte ICMP Echos to 10.1.2.1, timeout is 2 seconds:
!!!!!
Success rate is 100 percent (5/5), round-trip min/avg/max = 4/7/8 ms
Test2#
```

following addresses (on the TEST2 router): 192.168.184.88, 192.168.192.1, and 192.168.193.1. Everything works.

Log in to the TEST2 router and ping the addresses from the TEST2 router: 192.168.184.89, 172.24.1.1, 10.1.1.1, and 10.1.2.1. Our problem is resolved!

CERTIFICATION OBJECTIVE 2.09

Documenting the Facts

When everything is finally back to "normal," it might seem like overkill to document what happened. There is always more pressing work, and documentation never feels very important. It is certainly not what most people enjoy. This is especially true if you worked through the night to fix the problem. Maybe you are the only network engineer at the company, so you do not think it is important to document what happened because you will remember what happened later on.

There are some excellent reasons that it is important to document the problem, the action plans, the observed results, and the final resolution. When I was just starting out in this field, I had a boss whose pet phrase was, "Document as though you are going to get hit by a bus on the way home." He was not morbid; he simply understood the realities of life. You never know what will happen next. You might not be at work tomorrow, for a variety of reasons—you could go on vacation, you could be home sick, you could decide to change jobs, you could transfer to another division. Even if you are still in the same job in three years, you might not remember the details of this situation later on. The bottom line is that your brain is not the appropriate place to document corporate history.

There is a difference between simply knowing that a problem occurs frequently and being able to identify the specific dates and times when it happened. If the circuit from Los Angeles to Seattle is frequently down, for example, and you finally decide to complain to the long distance carrier, you need the details associated with each problem. These details include not only dates, times, and descriptions of the problems, but the names of the carrier's employees you spoke with, the names of supervisors, and other details that are easy to forget.

The process of documenting the problem forces you to focus on the event and gives you an opportunity to consider whether remedial steps can be taken to prevent the problem from occurring in the future. This is also your opportunity to review your problem-solving methodology and refine it for future use.

Documenting Each Change Made to the Network

It is a good practice to keep notes throughout the entire problem-solving process. In your notes, include all the information you have gathered as well as every single change made, in the order it was made, along with the reason for the change and the effect of the change. When the problem is finally resolved, you can use these notes to put together formal documentation for future reference.

In addition to documenting the problem and actions taken to resolve the problem, you need to update your documentation for each component of the network to reflect the current configuration. If you physically replaced a component in the network, update the documentation with the current serial number and acquisition date. Update maintenance records appropriately as well. Document the disposition of any equipment removed from the network and the reason for its removal. If you remove a line card from a switch because there are three bad ports on it, for instance, you will want to be reminded of this action before you install the card somewhere else. Otherwise, you will be troubleshooting the same problem all over again.

Finally, make sure that a new backup configuration is stored in a safe location. Documentation is more than just the text explanations, network diagrams, and other information. Your backup is part of your documentation. It is good practice to maintain rotating copies of backups.

EXERCISE 2-8

Documenting the Facts

Document the facts regarding the lab we have worked on throughout this chapter.
Solution:

A problem was reported on the morning of June 8. It was determined to be a configuration error on the TEST router that prevented routes from being properly advertised to the TEST2 router.

To resolve this problem, the following changes were made to the TEST router on June 8 at 3:00 p.m. EST.

Original Configuration

```
interface Ethernet0
 ip address 192.168.184.89 255.255.255.240 secondary
 ip address 172.24.1.1 255.255.255.0
router rip
 redistribute eigrp 200
 network 192.168.184.0
```

Revised Configuration

```
interface Ethernet0
 ip address 192.168.184.89 255.255.255.240
 ip address 172.24.1.1 255.255.255.0 secondary
router rip
 redistribute eigrp 200
 network 192.168.184.0
 redistribute connected
```

CERTIFICATION SUMMARY

The generic problem-solving model is a tool that is flexible enough to be used for both simple and complex network problems. This tool can help speed the problem-solving process by allowing you to focus on the problem instead of the process itself. The model is a road map for you to follow. It has a number of key components.

In the discovery phase, you define the problem. Make sure you understand who is affected and what the problem is. Next, gather facts regarding the problem and the circumstances surrounding the problem. As you gather facts, you can begin to consider the various possibilities. As you create your action plan, you need a clearly defined hypothesis and expected results.

In the implementation phase, as you execute the action plan, you will observe the results of each step, observe the results of the completed action plan, and make decisions along the way about whether to implement a recovery plan or iterate the process, or that the problem is now resolved.

In the completion phase, you will verify that the problem is resolved and document the facts regarding the problem and all associated changes for future reference.

✓ TWO-MINUTE DRILL

Here are some of the key points from each certification objective in Chapter 2.

The Problem-Solving Model

❑ The problem-solving model is a template based on commonsense principles.

❑ The problem-solving model allows you to focus on the problem instead of the process.

❑ The problem-solving model can help you arrive at a more accurate diagnosis more quickly.

Defining the Problem

❑ A good problem definition is a statement of observable information, not the possible cause of the problem.

❑ A good problem definition includes the observable symptoms (what is wrong) and who is affected.

❑ Compare the reported problem to the normal operational baseline.

Gathering Facts

❑ Find out when the problem occurred and what changes, if any, occurred around the same time.

❑ Characterize the problem as constant or intermittent.

❑ Characterize the problem as chronic or acute.

❑ Find out what is still working, and compare that to what is not working.

❑ Whenever possible, independently verify observable facts reported by end users.

Considering Possibilities Based on Facts

❑ Compare what still works to what could go wrong.

❑ Eliminate possible points of failure.

Creating an Action Plan

- ❏ An action plan is a detailed list of steps to be taken.
- ❏ For each step in an action plan, the expected results should be defined.

Implementing the Action Plan

- ❏ Implement each step individually.
- ❏ Observe the results of each individual step and compare them to the expected results.

Observing the Results

- ❏ After the complete action plan has been implemented, compare the results to the expected results.
- ❏ After each change, ensure that the network is still operational.
- ❏ Once the problem is corrected, ensure that the network is still operational.

Iterating the Process

- ❏ If there are multiple action plans, execute each one independently.
- ❏ Re-evaluate the definition of the problem and the potential causes based on the observed results.

Documenting the Facts

- ❏ Document the problem as it was observed, the action plan(s) that were taken to resolve the problem, and the actual cause of the problem.
- ❏ Document each change made in the network.

SELF TEST

The following questions will help you measure your understanding of the material presented in this chapter. Read all the choices carefully because there might be more than one correct answer. Choose all correct answers for each question.

The Problem-Solving Model

1. What are good reasons to follow a problem-solving methodology? Choose all that apply.

   A. It ensures that you are working on the problem, not a symptom of the problem.

   B. It allows you to focus on the process.

   C. It facilitates the implementation of corrective measures.

   D. It allows you to arrive at a more accurate diagnosis more quickly.

2. Arrange the following components of the problem-solving model in the proper order.

   A. Observe the results

   B. Iterate the process

   C. Consider possibilities based on facts

   D. Create an action plan

   E. Document the facts when resolved

   F. Implement the action plan

   G. Define the problem

   H. Gather facts

3. What is the difference between defining a problem and gathering the facts?

   A. When you gather the facts, you try to figure out what caused the problem instead of when the problem started.

   B. When you gather the facts, you try to figure out who is affected rather than what is not working.

   C. When you define a problem, you try to figure out what is not working rather than who is affected.

   D. When you define a problem, you try to identify what is not working rather than why something is not working.

Defining the Problem

4. John called on Tuesday morning and indicated that he cannot access the e-mail server in Colorado. No one else in his office, located in Utah, can access the e-mail server. Monday was a holiday, and most people in the office took Friday off. No one is certain when he or she was last able to receive mail. Everyone is able to access other network services. Based on this scenario, pick the best problem definition.

   A. No one in Utah has been able to check his or her e-mail since Thursday.

   B. The network connection to Utah went down between Thursday and Tuesday.

   C. The e-mail server in Colorado is down.

   D. No one in Utah is able to access the e-mail server in Colorado. The problem began sometime between Thursday and Tuesday.

5. Which one of the following statements is a good problem definition?

   A. The network is slower than usual.

   B. Since last night, users on the first floor in the New York office cannot get to the intranet server in Dallas.

   C. Nothing is working.

   D. The Internet is down.

6. What is *not* a key question to ask in order to define a problem?

   A. Who is affected?

   B. When did the problem start?

   C. What are the symptoms?

   D. How does this situation differ from what is normal?

Gathering Facts

7. What is a network baseline?

   A. A series of measurements taken over a known period of time

   B. A series of measurements showing the highest traffic volume each day

   C. Daily measurements taken over a known period of time

   D. Daily measurements showing the lowest traffic volume each day

8. When an end user reported a problem, she stated, "The last time this happened, someone reset the router and everything was fine." Choose the best follow-up question.

   A. Do you know if they reloaded the router or just reset the IP routes?

   B. What do you mean, "They reset the router"?

   C. What was wrong with the router?

   D. Does this happen often?

9. What is the most difficult kind of problem to troubleshoot?

   A. Chronic intermittent

   B. Chronic constant

   C. Intermittent constant

   D. Chronic acute

Considering Possibilities Based on Facts

10. What should you do once you have identified a suspect component within the network?

   A. Identify the OSI layer

   B. Create a list of possible trouble areas

   C. Continue checking the remaining components

   D. Create an action plan

11. As you look at the network diagram in Figure 2-12, in what order would you consider whether or not each of the following devices was directly related to a problem involving failed communications between the client and the server?

   A. End-user workstation, Ethernet cable to hub, hub, Ethernet cable to remote router, remote router, V.35 cable to remote DSU, cable to remote demarc, circuit, corporate cable to demarc, corporate DSU, corporate V.35 cable to router, corporate router, corporate Ethernet cable to router, corporate switch, Ethernet cable to server, server.

   B. Circuit, end-user workstation, server, Ethernet cable from workstation to hub, Ethernet cable to server, Ethernet cable to remote router, corporate Ethernet cable to router, V.35 cable to remote DSU, cable to remote demarc, hub, remote router, corporate cable to demarc, corporate DSU, corporate V.35 cable to router, corporate router, corporate switch.

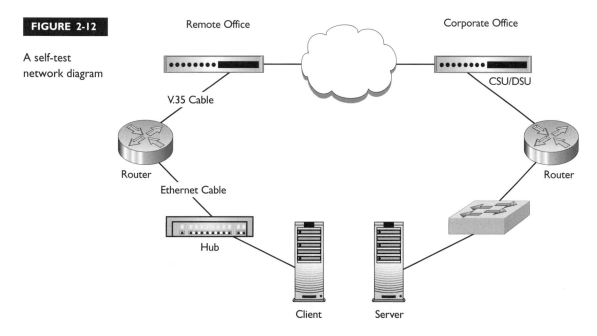

FIGURE 2-12

A self-test
network diagram

Remote Office

Corporate Office

CSU/DSU

V.35 Cable

Router

Router

Ethernet Cable

Hub

Client

Server

C. Circuit, end-user workstation, server, Ethernet cable to hub, hub, Ethernet cable to remote
router, remote router, V.35 cable to remote DSU, cable to remote demarc, corporate cable
to demarc, corporate DSU, corporate V.35 cable to router, corporate router, corporate
Ethernet cable, corporate switch, Ethernet cable to server.

D. End-user workstation, Ethernet cable to hub, hub, Ethernet cable to remote router, remote
router, V.35 cable to remote DSU, cable to remote demarc, circuit, corporate cable to
demarc, corporate DSU, corporate V.35 cable to router, corporate router, corporate
Ethernet cable, corporate switch, Ethernet cable to server, server.

Creating an Action Plan

12. Which one of these is *not* a step in defining an action plan?

    A. Define expected results

    B. Define what could possibly go wrong in the network

    C. Sequence the possible problems, with the most likely first

    D. Communicate the risks

13. Which of the following would be a better action plan to verify that a backup BRI line is operational?

   A. Add the configuration statement SHUTDOWN to Serial 0/0 and SHOW INTERFACE BRI 0/0 to verify that the interface is up. Ping the remote end of the BRI connection. Remove the statement SHUTDOWN from interface Serial 0/0.

   B. Dial in to the router. Add the configuration statement SHUTDOWN to Serial 0/0 and SHOW INTERFACE BRI 0/0 to verify that the interface is up. Ping the remote end of the BRI connection. Remove the statement SHUTDOWN from interface Serial 0/0.

   C. Remove the configuration statement BACKUP INTERFACE SERIAL 0/0 from BRI0/0 and SHOW INTERFACE BRI 0/0 to verify that the interface is up. Replace the statement BACKUP INTERFACE SERIAL 0/0.

   D. Dial in to the router. Remove the configuration statement BACKUP INTERFACE BRI 0/0 from Serial 0/0 and SHOW INTERFACE BRI 0/0 to verify that the interface is up. Replace the statement BACKUP INTERFACE BRI 0/0.

14. What step is missing from the action plan in the Question 13?

   A. Define the baseline

   B. Document the facts

   C. Communicate the potential risks to the facility

   D. Iterate the process

15. What is an action plan?

   A. A series of steps to test a hypothesis or to implement a solution

   B. A series of steps to resolve a problem

   C. A series of steps to define a problem

   D. A series of steps to identify the cause of a problem

Implementing the Action Plan

16. Which statement defines an appropriate way to implement an action plan?

   A. Implement all the steps, then check the results.

   B. Implement a step, verify the outcome of that step, and then move to the next step.

   C. Implement a series of steps, verify the outcome of those steps, and then move to the next series of steps.

   D. Implement all the action plans, then check the results.

17. If you apply an AppleTalk RTMP filter to reduce WAN traffic, how might you test your plan for multiple failures?

   A. Ask the end users if they are noticing any problems.

   B. Use the SHOW APPLE ROUTE and SHOW APPLE ZONE commands, then compare the output to the previously defined expected results.

   C. Use the SHOW APPLE INTERFACE command to see if there are any problems.

   D. Use the CLEAR APPLE RTMP command, then check to see if any errors are reported by the router.

Observing the Results

18. You have added the following statement to a router in your network: IP ROUTE 192.168.254.0 255.255.255.0 192.168.12.10. What might be the next step in your action plan?

   A. Save the configuration to memory by doing a WRITE MEMORY to ensure that the modified configuration is not lost if power is lost.

   B. Enter CLEAR IP ROUTE * at the command line to ensure that the new route is activated.

   C. Use the SHOW IP ROUTE command in two or more routers in the network to ensure that the network is still operational.

   D. Ping 192.168.254.1 to see if the command worked.

19. You have added the following statement to a router in your network: IP ROUTE 192.168.254.0 255.255.255.0 192.168.12.10. You are not using the REDISTRIBUTE command. How might you check to see whether or not there were any unexpected results?

   A. Use the SHOW IP ROUTE command in two or more routers in the network to make sure the route is not there.

   B. Enter CLEAR IP ROUTE * at the command line and observe the output.

   C. Save the configuration to memory by doing a WRITE MEMORY and observe the output.

   D. Ping 192.168.254.1 to see if the command worked.

Iterating the Process

20. After completing the first action plan, if the problem is not resolved, which phase of the problem-solving model will you return to if you defined multiple action plans?

   A. Problem-definition

   B. Iteration

    C. Consider the possibilities

    D. Implement the action plan

21. You have defined three action plans: verify that the BRI is operational, manually initiate a dial test, and debug the CHAP sequence. Which of the following statements is correct?

    A. Three different people should execute each plan simultaneously so that all the variables can be considered.

    B. The same person should execute each plan simultaneously so that no variable is missed.

    C. Three different people should execute each plan without telling the others when they will execute the plan, so no one person knows the results of the others' tests.

    D. It does not matter how many people execute the plans as long as they are executed independently so that the results of each plan can be observed without interference from the other plans.

Documenting the Facts

22. Once the problem is resolved, what should you do? Choose all that apply.

    A. Update the maintenance records

    B. Move on to the next problem

    C. Update the network diagrams

    D. Create a new backup

23. When should you document changes to the network?

    A. At the end of each month

    B. Every hour

    C. After every change

    D. When there are no more problems waiting to be addressed

LAB QUESTION

Using the same physical lab setup that has been used throughout the chapter, turn on IP accounting in the TEST router. Initiate a Trivial File Transfer Protocol (TFTP) transfer of the router's current configuration to the workstation. Initiate a TFTP transfer of the router's IOS from the TEST router to the workstation. When the TFTP has completed, display the IP accounting statistics. What device(s) have generated the most traffic, according to the IP accounting statistics? What did you expect to see?

SELF TEST ANSWERS

The Problem-Solving Model

1. ☑ **A, C, and D.** All are benefits of using the problem-solving model. If you are working on a symptom of the problem, you might never reach a point at which you can resolve the problem. If you are focusing on the problem instead of the process and have a clearly defined problem and hypothesis, you will be able to build a better action plan to resolve the problem more quickly.

   ☒ **B** is incorrect because the problem-solving model allows you to focus on the problem *instead of* the process. If you are spending your time trying to decide what your next step should be when you have not gathered any facts yet, you will not be very effective in solving the problem.

2. ☑ **G, H, C, D, F, A, B, E.** This is the correct order. You must define the problem before you can gather any facts. Once you have gathered the facts, you can consider possibilities based on facts. Until you have considered possibilities based on facts, you cannot create an action plan. Once the action plan is created, you can implement the plan, observing the results. You iterate the process if necessary, depending on the results observed. Once the problem is resolved, you should document the facts for future reference.

   ☒ If you try to implement the steps in any other order, you will create more work for yourself and it will take longer for you to resolve the problem at hand.

3. ☑ **D.** When you define a problem, you try to identify what is not working rather than why something is not working. This answer is correct because a good problem definition does not assume the cause of the problem. Instead, a good problem definition clearly identifies what is not working as well as who is affected and when the problem started.

   ☒ **A** appears to be correct on the surface because the statement itself is correct. However, the distinction between defining the problem and gathering the facts does not involve the question of when the problem started. **B** is incorrect because when you are gathering the facts, you are not trying to figure out who is affected; that is part of the problem-definition process. Figuring out what is not working is also part of the problem-definition process, not of the process of gathering the facts. **C** is incorrect because when you define a problem, you try to figure out *both* what is not working *and* who is affected.

Defining the Problem

4. ☑ **D.** No one in Utah is able to access the e-mail server in Colorado. The problem began sometime between Thursday and Tuesday. This answer is correct because a good problem definition includes who is affected ("no one in Utah"), what is not working ("unable to access the e-mail server in Colorado"), and when the problem began ("sometime between Thursday and Tuesday"). If any of the three components are missing, the problem definition is incomplete.

   ☒ **A** appears to be a complete problem definition, but without clearly stating which e-mail server the users access, we have not defined exactly what is failing. If the users in Utah access different e-mail servers—for example, one in Colorado and the other in Texas—and neither is working, this is a different problem entirely. **B** is incorrect because the phrase "the network is down" is a statement of cause rather than a statement of the problem itself. **C** is incorrect because it is a statement of cause rather than a statement of the problem itself.

5. ☑ **B.** Since last night, users on the first floor in the New York office cannot get to the intranet server in Dallas. This answer is correct because it includes all the required components for a good problem definition: who is affected? The users on the first floor in New York. What is not working? They cannot get to the intranet server in Dallas. When did the problem start? Last night.

   ☒ **A** is incorrect because it is a subjective observation and it is not clear which network or what part of the network, does not include a statement regarding who is affected, and does not specify when the problem started. **C** is incorrect because it is vague. If everything is down, it should be clearly specified, as in this example: "No one can reach any network device at any location. This problem started about 5 minutes ago." **D** is incorrect because it is too vague and does not include a statement of who is affected or when the problem started. It is also an assumption of the cause of the problem rather than a clear definition of the problem. The Internet is a large collection of networks; for this statement to be true, every single network throughout the Internet would have to simultaneously lose its connectivity to the Internet. A better statement is, "No one in the company can access the Internet. The problem was reported about 15 minutes ago."

6. ☑ **B.** When did the problem start? This is the correct answer because it is the only question you would *not* ask during the "define the problem" phase. This is a question you would ask during the "gather the facts" step.

   ☒ **A, C,** and **D** are not the correct answers because these are all questions that you would ask when defining the problem.

Gathering Facts

7. ☑ **A.** A series of measurements taken over a known period of time. A network baseline can be taken over any period of time, but the period of time must be known. The number of measurements is nonspecific since different periods of time should be measured in different ways. If you take 30 measurements over the course of a day, you could use that for a single-day network baseline. If you take 30 measurements over the course of a month, you could use that as a monthly network baseline.

☒ **B** is not correct because a network baseline includes all the measurements taken, regardless of whether they show high or low traffic volume. **C** is not correct because the frequency of measurements is nonspecific. **D** is not correct because the frequency of measurements is nonspecific. It is also incorrect because a network baseline includes all the measurements taken, regardless of whether they show high or low traffic volume.

8. ☑ **D.** Does this happen often? The key phrase is "The last time this happened," which indicates that this might be a chronic problem. In a large organization in which many engineers work on different problems, you might not know the history of various problems reported from the field. Even if you have checked the documentation and there is no indication of recent problems, this is the most appropriate question to ask.

☒ **A** and **C** are not good questions to ask because the end user should not be expected to know exactly what an engineer did to resolve a given problem. **B** might be okay, but it would be better to ask, "Who reset the router?" and then follow up with the engineer who did so.

9. ☑ **A.** Chronic intermittent. A chronic problem is more difficult to troubleshoot than an acute problem because there is no clearly defined starting point from which to begin the investigation. An intermittent problem is more difficult to troubleshoot than a constant problem because it is difficult to examine the problem while it is occurring. The combination of chronic and intermittent is therefore the most difficult to troubleshoot.

☒ **B** is incorrect because a constant problem is easier to examine while it is occurring than an intermittent problem. **C** and **D** are incorrect because the combinations are not valid. A problem cannot be both intermittent and constant, nor can it be both acute and chronic.

Considering Possibilities Based on Facts

10. ☑ **C.** Continue checking the remaining components. This is the correct answer because network failures sometimes include multiple components. If you continue to check the remaining components, you might discover additional suspect components that need to be considered.

    ☒   **A** is incorrect because the OSI layer is considered while creating a list of possible trouble areas. **B** is incorrect because you create the list of possible trouble areas after considering all the possibilities based on facts. **D** is incorrect because the action plan is created later in the process.

11. ☑   **A.** End-user workstation, Ethernet cable to hub, hub, Ethernet cable to remote router, remote router, V.35 cable to remote DSU, cable to remote demarc, circuit, corporate cable to demarc, corporate DSU, corporate V.35 cable to router, corporate router, corporate Ethernet cable to router, corporate switch, Ethernet cable to server, server. This is the correct answer because the list of components starts from the end user's workstation, works through each component of the network in the order encountered, and finally reaches the server.

    ☒   **B, C,** and **D** are incorrect because each of them either works through the process in the wrong order or eliminates some of the components. Every component of the network must be considered.

Creating an Action Plan

12. ☑   **B.** Define what could possibly go wrong in the network. This is the correct answer because it is the only one that is not a step in defining an action plan. You define what could possibly go wrong in the network as part of the "define the problem" phase.

    ☒   **A, C,** and **D** are all part of creating an action plan, so none of these is the correct answer.

13. ☑   **D.** Dial in to the router. Remove the configuration statement BACKUP INTERFACE BRI 0/0 from Serial 0/0 and SHOW INTERFACE BRI 0/0 to verify that the interface is up. Replace the statement BACKUP INTERFACE BRI 0/0. An action plan should always take into account the potential risks, so in this case you would definitely want to dial in to the router first, removing the statement from the serial interface, checking the status of the BRI line, then replacing the statement on the serial interface.

    ☒   **A** is incorrect because an action plan should be as unobtrusive as possible. Shutting down the serial interface would have a negative impact on existing traffic. In addition, without dialing into the router first, you are at risk of losing your connection to the router to bring it back up later. **B** is incorrect because an action plan should be as unobtrusive as possible. Shutting down the serial interface would have a negative impact on existing traffic. **C** is incorrect because there is a risk of losing connectivity to the router while you make the changes. In addition, the backup interface statement would not appear on the BRI0/0 interface, so this answer is technically incorrect as well.

14. ☑   **C.** Communicate the potential risks to the facility. Every action plan should include communicating the potential risks to the facility. In this case, if the backup interface statement is removed from the router and there really is a circuit outage, dial backup will not take place.

☒ **A** is incorrect because the baseline is defined as part of the "define the problem" phase. By the time you have reached the action plan, you should have already completed this process. **B** is incorrect because you document the facts after the problem has been resolved, not as part of the action plan. **D** is incorrect because the process is iterated only after the action plan is implemented.

15. ☑ **A.** A series of steps to test a hypothesis or to implement a solution. This is the correct answer because an action plan is designed to test a hypothesis or to implement a solution.
☒ **B** is incorrect because although the hope is that implementing a solution will resolve a problem, it is not known that it will do so until the plan is implemented. If the problem is not resolved, it was still an action plan. **C** is incorrect because the problem should already be defined by this point in time. **D** is incorrect because although the plan can test a hypothesis that might prove the cause of the problem, it will not define the cause of the problem.

Implementing the Action Plan

16. ☑ **B.** Implement a step, verify the outcome of that step, and then move to the next step. When implementing each step, you need to stop and observe the results before moving to the next step. If you move too quickly through an action plan, you might miss important clues or create a new problem without realizing it.
☒ **A** and **C** are incorrect because an action plan should be implemented one step at a time, not as a series of steps. **D** is incorrect because each action plan should be executed independently so that you can observe the results after each plan is implemented.

17. ☑ **B.** Use the SHOW APPLE ROUTE and SHOW APPLE ZONE commands, then compare the output to the previously defined expected results. This is the correct answer because it is the only one that includes SHOW commands that would display the new routing table and the current zone information.
☒ **A** is incorrect because you should ask the end users for feedback only if you cannot obtain the relevant information directly from the network equipment. **C** is incorrect because using the SHOW APPLE INTERFACE command will not provide information regarding the routing table and zones available, so the relevant information will not be verified. **D** is incorrect because when you are clearing the routes in a router, no error messages are reported unless the command is incorrectly entered. The only way to see if there are problems with the routing table is to look directly at the routing table.

Observing the Results

18. ☑ **C.** Use the SHOW IP ROUTE command in two or more routers in the network to ensure that the network is still operational. This is the correct answer because, even more important than verifying whether or not an action had the desired effect, you should always check to make sure the network is operational and that you have not created a new problem. If you have added a static route in the router and are not redistributing routes, make sure that the new static route is not being propagated through the rest of the network. Likewise, if you are redistributing routes, make sure that the new route is being propagated through the rest of the network.

    ☒ **A** is incorrect because you never want to save a configuration change until you have verified that you have not introduced a new problem into the network and that the desired effect has been achieved. **B** is incorrect because there is no need to clear the routes in order to activate a new static route. **D** is incorrect because even if you cannot ping the destination address, the command might still have been effective. Likewise, being able to ping the destination address does not prove that a new problem has not been introduced into the network.

19. ☑ **A.** Use the SHOW IP ROUTE command in two or more routers in the network to make sure the route is not there. If you are not redistributing the route, it should not appear in other routers in the network. If the route does appear elsewhere, you have an unexpected result.

    ☒ **B** is incorrect because there is no output when clearing the IP routes in a router, so you will not be able to observe anything. **C** is incorrect because when you save a configuration to memory, the router does not check to see if there are problems with the configuration, so you would not be able to observe anything. **D** is incorrect because verifying that a command had the desired effect does not verify that undesirable side effects were not introduced into the network at the same time.

Iterating the Process

20. ☑ **A.** Problem definition is correct because after implementing each action plan you should return to the "define the problem" phase, every time, at least to confirm that your initial definition and understanding are still accurate and to determine whether any additional facts should be gathered before implementing the next action plan.

    ☒ **B** is incorrect because there is no iteration phase. **C** is not correct because there is no need to consider the possibilities at this point in the process. **D** is incorrect because after completing an action plan, even if there are multiple action plans, the next step in the process is to define the problem.

21. ☑ **D.** It does not matter how many people execute the plans as long as they are executed independently so that the results of each plan can be observed without interference from the other plans. It does not matter how many people execute the action plans, but it does matter that each plan be executed independently so that the results can be observed without any interference from the other plans.

    ☒ **A** is incorrect because action plans should never be executed simultaneously. **B** is incorrect because there is no requirement that the same person execute each action plan and because each action plan should be executed independently instead of simultaneously. **C** is incorrect because communicating with other engineers working on the problem is critical to ensuring that the plans are not executed simultaneously. **C** is also incorrect because all engineers working on a problem should be made aware of the results of all action plans.

Documenting the Facts

22. ☑ **A, C, and D.** Update the maintenance records, update the network diagrams, and create a new backup. Once a problem is resolved, the maintenance records should be updated with any changes in serial numbers, hardware configuration, or operating system software. The network diagrams should be updated with any changes. A new backup should be created.

    ☒ **B** is incorrect because if the documentation is not completed when the problem is fresh in your mind, it will not get done, be incomplete, or be inaccurate.

23. ☑ **C.** After every change. Every time you make a change to the network, you should document the change, along with the reason for the change.

    ☒ **A** is incorrect because if you wait until the end of each month, many of the details will be lost forever, and many changes will be overlooked entirely. **B** is incorrect because even if a network changes frequently, hourly updates might not be necessary. **D** is incorrect because if you wait until there are no more problems to be addressed, you will never document anything.

LAB ANSWER

1. Start a TFTP program on the workstation

2. Log in to the TEST router in enable mode

3. Ensure that you can ping the workstation from the TEST router

4. Add the following statements to the configuration of the router:

```
interface ethernet 0
ip accounting
```

5. While in enable mode, enter the following command:

```
Test#copy run tftp
Address or name of remote host []? 192.168.184.86
Destination filename [running-config]? Test-config
!!
965 bytes copied in 6.320 secs (160 bytes/sec)
Test#copy flash tftp
Source filename []? c2500-i-l_120-3_T.bin
Address or name of remote host []? 192.168.184.86
Destination filename [c2500-i-l_120-3_T.bin]?
!!!!!!!!!!!!!!!!!!!!!!!!!!!!!!!!!!!!!!!!!!!!!!!!!!!!!!!!!!!!!!!!!!!!!!!!!!!!!!!
(output deleted)
!!!!!!!!!!!
6186488 bytes copied in 78.236 secs (79313 bytes/sec)
Test#sho ip accou
  Source        Destination      Packets        Bytes

Accounting data age is 2
```

You might have been surprised to see no traffic in the statistics. This is because traffic initiated by the router is treated differently from traffic moving from one interface to another. In order to see IP accounting information, the traffic must cross through the interface.

3

LAN
Troubleshooting
Problem Areas

CERTIFICATION OBJECTIVES

The growing complexity of LANs in corporations means that network administrators face challenging aspects of their jobs that were not as common in earlier years. LANs today encompass a wide range of technologies, from intranets to firewalls and VLANs. Problems that were easily pinpointed in the past are no longer so easy to spot and correct. This increased complexity in the LAN requires efficient and quick action in order to correctly diagnose and solve problems.

The importance of the Physical Layer in troubleshooting cannot be overlooked. Any good troubleshooter knows that the first place to start looking for possible solutions to a connectivity problem is the Physical Layer. Well over half of most connectivity failures can be attributed to Physical Layer faults. If you can eliminate the Physical Layer as the location of failure when you are troubleshooting, you can be sure that you have half the problem already solved.

A good understanding of the OSI model is also essential to pinpointing the cause of problems. After all, if you cannot be sure where in the model the problem lies, what method will you use to eliminate the possible causes of the problem? How can you know what successive steps to take to eliminate a particularly bothersome connectivity issue that just does not go away? Efficient and successful troubleshooting begins with a good grasp and appreciation of the OSI model. This chapter examines the first two layers of the OSI model in detail, along with some technologies that are used in those layers. Problems and their solutions associated with these technologies are also discussed.

on the *job*

One of the most troublesome problems I've seen occurred when a desktop lost connectivity with the rest of the network and all possible solutions— cable, duplex settings, drivers, IP address and subnet mask settings—were tried, all to no avail. Even the status LEDs seemed operational. Finally, after changing the network card itself, all the problems disappeared. As an aside, the network card happened to be a generic, no-brand-name part.

CERTIFICATION OBJECTIVE 3.01

Physical Layer Responsibilities

The Physical Layer resides at Layer 1 of the seven-layer OSI model (see Figure 3-1). As its name suggests, the Physical Layer is primarily concerned with the physical characteristics of the transmission medium. Pin-outs, cable characteristics, various types of connectors, and voltage are all parts of Physical layer specifications. Clocking or clock rate is also a characteristic of the Physical layer. For example, in an Ethernet network using twisted-pair cabling, binary computer data consisting of ones and zeros must be converted into a sequence of voltages that are transmitted along a length of wire, received by an end station, and converted from voltage sequences into ones and zeros again. Specifications for clocking are included in the framing format and control mechanisms defined in the interface standards themselves. At the Physical layer, devices such as hubs or repeaters are used for connectivity.

Figure 3-1 is a simple layout of the OSI model. A brief description of each layer is provided beside each layer. The examples given in each layer should be sufficient to make the functions of the layers clear.

FIGURE 3-1		
The layers of the OSI model	Application	Applications that require communications capabilities. Examples: WWW, FTP, SMTP, Telnet
	Presentation	Data formats and also encryption. Examples: Character sets, file formats like .doc, .xml
	Session	Defines control of conversations between stations. Examples: RPC, named pipes, IPC
	Transport	Error control and recovery, connection/nonconnection oriented protocols. Examples: TCP, UDP
	Network	Delivery and addressing of packets from one node to the next. Examples: IP, IPX, AppleTalk
	Data Link	Concerned with protocols that specify how data is to be transferred across specific media. Examples: HDLC, SDLC
	Physical	Deals with the physical characteristics of the transmission medium. Examples: V.35, Ethernet, FDDI

Note: The Physical Layer is not responsible for encapsulation of any kind. What this means is that the Physical Layer adds no headers or trailers to frames. Encapsulation or the addition of headers and/or trailer information is done only at higher layers of the OSI model. The goal, of course, was to make the model as efficient as possible. Because the Physical Layer is not involved in any additional work of encapsulation, it is free to transmit data as quickly as possible.

exam
ⓦatch

Watch out for cabling issues when you are troubleshooting. One of the most common problems that you can encounter is the use of patch cables from a pile somewhere in a storage room. Straight-through and crossover cables have totally different functions. Learn to recognize straight-through cables and crossover cables on sight. You can learn how to do this by visiting www.cisco.com/univercd/cc/td/doc/product/lan/cat3ks/c3ksug/cat3ksa.htm and looking at the pin-outs for the cables. Straight-through cables can be determined by looking at the connectors at the ends of the cable with the flat, pin side toward you. Look at the colors of the cables: if both connectors match left to right (or right to left), the cable is straight through. The most common colors from left to right are:

Orange/white: Thick orange, thin white
Orange: Solid
Green/White: Thick green, thin white
Blue: Solid
Blue/white: Thick blue, thin white
Green: Solid
Brown/white: Thick brown, thin white
Brown

This is the easiest way to determine whether or not a cable is straight through or crossover.

Datagrams, Packets, and Frames

More than likely, everyone has heard the terms *datagrams, packets,* and *frames*. But are you aware of how these components fit into the OSI model?

First, we need to begin by examining the *protocol data unit (PDU)*. A PDU is used to describe a number of bytes that include the header and trailer of a layer, all other encapsulated headers, and user data. From the perspective of the successive lower layer, the headers and data from the higher layers are just large chunks of data:

■ PDUs from the Transport Layer are referred to as *segments*.

- PDUs from the Network Layer are called *packets*.
- PDUs from the data-link and Physical Layers are called *frames*.

It is also important to note that at each successively lower layer, data is broken down into smaller, more uniform sizes to facilitate transmission onto the respective media. Each individual section of the data that is broken up receives its own headers and trailer. For frames that do not meet the minimum size limitations when broken up or segmented, padding is added to meet those requirements.

Exercise 3-1 demonstrates the importance of knowing what type of cable to use, whether straight-through or crossover.

EXERCISE 3-1

Testing Connectivity with Cable Pin-outs

Get a crossover cable and a straight-through cable. Make a crossover cable if you do not have one by following these steps:

1. Wire one end as straight through, as shown in the preceding Exam Watch. Wire the other end using the guide below:
    Pin 1: Green/white
    Pin 2: Green
    Pin 3: Orange/white
    Pin 4: Blue
    Pin 5: Blue/white
    Pin 6: Orange
    Pin 7: Brown/white
    Pin 8: Brown

2. Patch in a PC that was previously connected to the switch via straight-through cable with the crossover cable. Did all the status and link LEDs go out?

Straight-through and crossover cables are not interchangeable. Be well aware of the differences between the two. Straight-through cables are used to connect unlike devices—a NIC to a hub, for example. Crossover cables are used to connect like devices, such asa hub to a hub. Learn the function of each of the wires. They prove a valuable asset when you are troubleshooting.

Data-Link Layer Responsibilities

The data-link layer of the OSI model resides at Layer 2. As shown in Figure 3-2, the data-link layer has been subdivided by the IEEE into two additional layers: the Media Access Control (MAC) Layer and the Logical Link Control (LLC) Layer. Shown in the OSI model earlier, the data-link layer deals with specifications that detail how data is to be transferred across specific types of connections and media. The asynchronous transfer mode (ATM) specification, for example, specifies a 53-byte packet size consisting of a 48-byte payload and a 5-byte header. Standards or protocols such as IEEE 802.2 and IEEE 802.3 are also defined at this layer. Devices such as bridges and Layer 2 switches operate at the Data-Link Layer.

Note: You are probably thinking that the word *protocol* is used only in reference to TCP/IP, NetBEUI, RIP, OSPF, and the like. The word *protocol* can be used to refer to any standard or specification. For example, ATM is not often thought of as a protocol, but that is exactly what it is.

Depending on the protocol or specification being used, the Data-Link Layer can also provide error and flow control and bit synchronization between end stations to ensure successful delivery of packets. The Data-Link Layer is the link between the physical nature of Layer 1 and the data-oriented higher layers of the OSI model. The Data-Link Layer is therefore also responsible for converting the data from the upper layers into the signals required by the Physical Layer. In addition, the Data-Link Layer creates packet headers and checksum trailers, encapsulates datagrams into frames, and performs error

FIGURE 3-2		
The two sublayers of the Data-Link Layer		Network
		LLC
	Data Link	MAC
		Physical

detection. Hardware addresses are also mapped with IP addresses (commonly known as *Address Resolution Protocol,* or *ARP*) at this layer. For half-duplex Ethernet networks, the Data-Link Layer monitors the transmission medium using the Carrier Sense, Multiple Access with Collision Detection (CSMA/CD) protocol and determines when the medium is free so that data can be transmitted.

The following scenario illustrates some of the functions of the Data-Link Layer: Suppose that Host A wants to send a message to Host B. A message created by Host A passes down from the Application Layer of the OSI model to the lower layers. Each successive layer from the Transport Layer down to the Data-Link Layer receives the data from the previous layer and encapsulates it by appending its own header to the data. The Data-Link Layer receives the data from the Network Layer. The Data-Link Layer appends the data frame with source and destination MAC addresses (MAC address information is a function of the Data Link protocol—ARP), along with data field information, and a CRC trailer is created. At this point, the Data-Link Layer puts the frame on the network for transmission. As the message is being received on Host B, the Data-Link Layer of Host B reads the incoming frame. If the MAC address in the destination field is its own, the Data-Link Layer processes the incoming information. A CRC is then performed on the frame, comparing the results to information in the frame trailer. If the information matches, the header and trailer are removed in order to forward the data information to the next layer (the Network Layer). On the other hand, if the information is different, a request is sent to the sending station for a retransmission of the message.

MAC Layer

The MAC sublayer is the first layer between the Physical Layer and the upper layers. MAC Layer functions are outlined in the following sections.

Sending Station

- Receives data from the LLC sublayer and adds a preamble and start of frame (SOF) delimiter

- Inserts source and destination MAC addresses

- CRC information is placed into the Frame Check Sequence (FCS) field of the Ethernet frame

- Monitors transmission medium for collisions and opportunities to transmit data

Receiving Station

- Determines whether frames received are error free by looking at the FCS.

- Monitors broadcasts.

- Determines whether a frame received is intended for the station by looking at the Destination MAC address field. If the frame is not intended for the station, it is dropped. If the frame is intended for the station, the source and destination MAC addresses are removed along with the preamble, SOF delimiter, and FCS, and the remaining data is passed up to the LLC Layer.

MAC Address Types

Hardware MAC addresses that are encoded by the card manufacturer onto the unit can be referred to as *NIC addresses, burned-in addresses, hardware addresses, unicast addresses, Ethernet addresses,* or *Token Ring addresses.* In the past, MAC addresses were usually encoded onto a network interface card (NIC) by means of a nonreprogrammable computer chip—hence the name *burned-in address (BIA).* Today, however, on some of the newer NICs, the administrator can change MAC addresses. It is hardly ever necessary to change this address; it is generally safer to stick with the address given by the manufacturer.

exam
Ⓦatch

You should be able to at least tell the difference between a broadcast MAC address and a unicast MAC address in a protocol analyzer decode of packets. Remember that a broadcast MAC address has a value of FFFFFFFFFFFF in hexadecimal format.

Along with the unicast hardware address, there can be all or a combination of the following types of MAC addresses on your network:

- **Broadcast address**   Means "all" devices on a LAN.

- **Multicast address**   Means that a particular group of devices across LANs receives the transmission.

- **Functional address**   Used in Token Ring networks to represent devices, which are serving a particular function. For example, the Active Monitor on a Token Ring LAN has a functional address.

on the
Job

I remember a situation early in my networking days; I had to oversee the move of a number of workstations from one location to another. The two locations happened to be connected by bridges. When the workstations were in their new location, I couldn't get them to recognize the network. In my utter confusion, I forgot that bridges contain a table of the MAC addresses of the workstations and that the bridges still "thought" that the workstations were on their old side of the network. After mulling over the problem overnight, I realized that the bridges were the cause of the trouble. I reset them, and the problem was solved.

Now that you know all about MAC addresses, Exercise 3-2 demonstrates the use of a protocol analyzer in capturing and displaying a frame that is broadcast to all stations on a LAN.

EXERCISE 3-2

Decoding Broadcast Packets Using a Protocol Analyzer

1. Obtain and install a protocol analyzer on a desktop. Microsoft provides one for free with its Windows NT Server OS that captures data entering and leaving the desktop on which it is installed. This one is used for this exercise. Many others are available on the Web for trial periods.

2. Begin a capture. Refer to Figure 3-3 for a screenshot from Network Monitor.

3. Stop and view the capture by clicking on the eyeglass button. This takes you to a list of all captured frames. See Figure 3-4.

4. Double-click on a frame that has a destination MAC address of *BROADCAST. This brings up the window shown in Figure 3-5, which has details about that particular frame.

5. As you can see, the broadcast frame has a destination address of FFFFFFFFFFFF. This means that all stations on the LAN receive this packet.

For the exam, you should be able to tell the difference between broadcast and unicast frames. The screenshots highlight the important part of identifying a broadcast address. Learn to recognize broadcast MAC addresses and unicast MAC addresses.

FIGURE 3-3

Capture window
of Microsoft
Network
Monitor

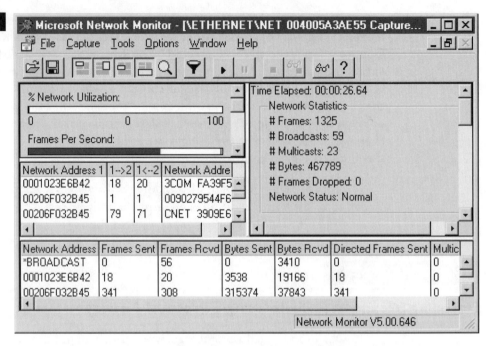

FIGURE 3-4

Network
Monitor capture
summary

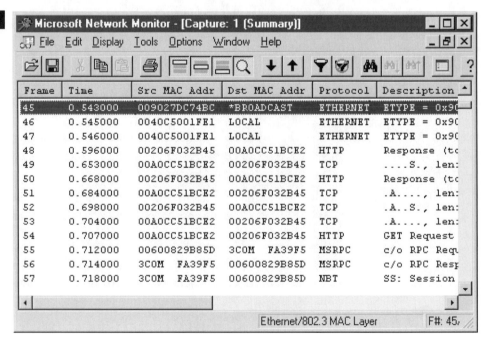

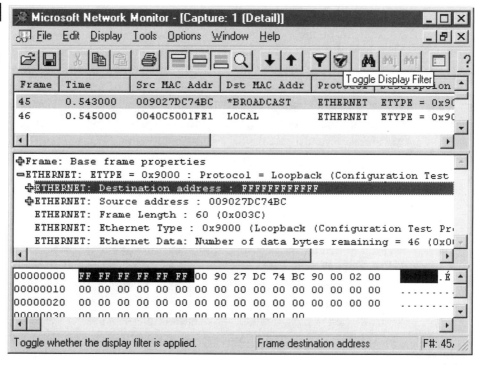

FIGURE 3-5

Network
Monitor captured
frame detail

Logical Link Layer

The Logical Link Layer is defined in the IEEE 802.2 standard. Most people know of the LLC Layer but find it difficult to explain its function. LLC specifies the mechanisms for addressing stations across the media and for controlling the exchange of data between those stations. LLC includes connection-oriented as well as connectionless methods of data transfer.

Connectionless data transfer methods use LLC Type 1; connection-oriented methods use LLC Type 2. In essence, the LLC sublayer generates and interprets commands to control the flow of data, including recovery operations for error detection. Detecting errors in data does not necessarily equate to the recovery of those errors. Most protocols, including Token Ring 802.5 and Ethernet 802.3, do not make provisions for error recovery. However, both Token Ring 802.5 and Ethernet 802.3 have an option in LLC Type 2 for error recovery. Network Basic Input/Output System (NetBIOS) and Systems Network Architecture (SNA) are two typical higher-layer protocols that use LLC2.

To simplify your understanding of the application of LLC, consider the following exercise. Suppose that Server A sends some SAP packets (using Novell's IPX/SPX) to Server B. Server A and Server B each have one NIC, bound to several network protocols, such as IPX/SPX, TCP/IP, and NetBEUI. Now, when those packets get over to Server B, how will the Data-Link Layer of Server B know which network protocol should receive the data from those packets so that it will be correctly understood? Should it just hand over the data and by some unknown method the correct protocol gets the data? No, of course not. This is where the LLC Layer comes in. The LLC Layer in Ethernet and Token Ring provides two fields in its header that identify the type of data that is in the data field. These two fields are the Destination Service Access Point (DSAP) and the Source Service Access Point (SSAP). The DSAP field identifies which higher-layer protocol should receive the data; the SSAP identifies the source protocol.

LAN administrators supporting NetBIOS and SNA traffic across LAN segments should be familiar with LLC. Most often, you will see LLC2 used when SNA traffic is traversing your network. There is also a possibility that you can see it directly encapsulated into Frame Relay. For example, a router simply forwards LLC2 frames and often implements LLC link stations. NetBIOS uses LLC to locate resources, and then LLC2 connection-oriented sessions are established.

LLC Type I Operation

Ethernet can carry multiple Network Layer protocols. A station that has multiple Network Layer protocols must be able to distinguish which of those protocols should get data that is received from another station on the network. This decision is based on the frame EtherType and/or DSAP field of the frame. The EtherType field contains values (not in bits or bytes) greater than 1500 (0x05DC hexadecimal). Values lower than 1500 are used to indicate the length of a frame.

Note: The EtherType field is not used in Token Ring. Token Ring exclusively uses the LLC DSAP and SSAP fields.

Figure 3-6 shows an IP packet with the illustrated LLC Layer.

FIGURE 3-6

LLC1 operation in an IP packet

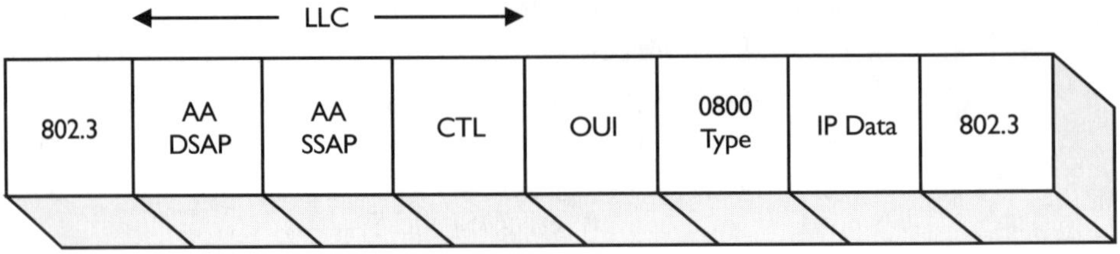

| 802.3 | AA DSAP | AA SSAP | CTL | OUI | 0800 Type | IP Data | 802.3 |

The IEEE defined a special way for using EtherType values in conjunction with LLC. The Subnetwork Access Protocol (SNAP) header was added as an enhancement to the LLC Layer. The LLC Layer actually consists of the DSAP, SSAP, and CTL fields. The SNAP application was presented to simplify network protocols' adjustment to the new frame formats introduced by the IEEE 802.2 committee at the time. SNAP allows for Ethernet vendors to quickly switch their drivers and network protocols over the IEEE 802.*x* packet format without rewriting the program code.

A value of 0xAA of the DSAP and SSAP fields in Figure 3-6 indicates that another set of headers is present above the usual 3 bytes of LLC headers. This value of 0xAA indicates the presence of the SNAP header, consisting of an organizationally unique identifier (OUI) and a Type field. The Type field is 0x0800 hexadecimal, which is 2048 in decimal—more than the 1500 value mentioned previously. This Type identifier specifies that the protocol is IP. The CTL field has a value of 0x03 in the case of IP, which helps distinguish the various protocols that are running. RFC 1700 provides a list of EtherType values. Figure 3-7 is a representation of the LLC Layer in an IPX packet. Notice the absence of the SNAP header.

The reason for this absence is the fact that IPX/SPX takes direct advantage of the DSAP and SSAP fields. Therefore, no layering is needed as in the case of IP. 0xE0 in the DSAP and SSAP fields in Figure 3-7 represent Novell's IPX protocol, which makes you think: why would IP need to use a SNAP header as opposed to taking advantage of the DSAP and SSAP fields the way IPX does? Actually, this was tried. The IETF used a SAP value of 0x60 to represent IP. This made it possible to layer IP directly over the LLC header. This is documented in RFC-948. However, RFC-948 made no provisions for the use of other protocols in the TCP/IP stack. For example, ARP still had to use 802.2 specifications to obtain MAC address information; that information could then be included in 802.3 encapsulation of the IP packets. This not very elegant solution led to the development of the SNAP header and the use of the EtherType field and is defined in RFC-1948.

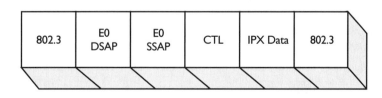

| 802.3 | E0 DSAP | E0 SSAP | CTL | IPX Data | 802.3 |

LLC Type 2 Operation

LLC2 provides the functionality needed for reliable data transfer (quite similar to Layer 4 function). LLC2 also allows for error recovery and flow and congestion controls. The protocol supports specific acknowledgments connection establishment as well as providing for flow control, making sure that the data arrives in the order in which it was sent. The LLC2 service, therefore, incurs more overhead than LLC1.

The connection-oriented services are used in LAN services today. The protocols that do not invoke a Transport or Network Layer (NetBIOS and NetBEUI) are the most common protocols that require the use of LLC2. Windows NT, Solaris, IBM Warp Server, and others use this type of connection. Most Network Layer protocols such as TCP/IP and IPX/SPX do not use this mode of LLC and have Network, Transport, and Session Layers built into the protocol, which provide error detection and correction. Therefore, these protocols have no use for the connection-oriented mode of LLC2.

Now that you have an idea of the services provided by Layer 2, refer to the following Scenario & Solution.

CERTIFICATION OBJECTIVE 3.03

Ethernet/IEEE 802.3

Ethernet—and specifically, the IEEE 802.3 standard—refers to a set of rules that have been established for data transmission at the Physical Layer and the MAC

SCENARIO & SOLUTION

What mode of LLC do Network Layer protocols such as TCP/IP and AppleTalk use?	LLC1. TCP/IP and AppleTalk use their own error recovery mechanisms.
What layer does a station use when determining if a packet belongs to it?	Stations use the Data-Link Layer to determine if the MAC address is their own.
What protocol does a station use for finding out the MAC address of another station?	ARP is used to find the MAC address for a station from TCP/IP addresses.

portion of the Data-Link Layer of the OSI model. Nodes on an Ethernet network implement a simple rule: listen before speaking. As you already know, Ethernet uses shared media. This means that all stations on a particular segment have equal opportunity to use the media for transmission. Only one station can transmit at any one time, however. Stations use the CSMA/CD protocol to determine whether another station is using the transmission medium. If a station that wants to use the media finds that the media is free by using CSMA/CD, it begins sending data. If two stations send data at the same time, a collision occurs and the stations wait a period of time before they retransmit.

Many network administrators believe that CSMA/CD is better utilized in an environment in which the cable length is short. When there is increased traffic volume on an Ethernet LAN, the chance for collision increases because that collision domain is being utilized more frequently. Of course, decreasing the number of collisions means that the size of the collision domain must also be reduced. Using switches or bridges reduces collision domains.

Exercise 3-3 demonstrates how the number of collisions increases when the transmission medium is heavily utilized in a shared environment.

EXERCISE 3-3

Collision Increase Due to a Large File Transfer on a Shared Medium

1. Find a hub, not a switch, that has multiple stations attached to it and LEDs that tell you the utilization rate and when collisions are taking place.

2. Observe the utilization and collision rates over a 5-minute period.

3. Initiate a large file transfer (16MB to 20MB) between two of the stations.

4. While the transfer is occurring, look again at the collision and utilization rates on the hub. Notice how both have climbed drastically?

It is easy to see how heavy usage on an overutilized LAN with many stations can affect connectivity and production. Eventually, a LAN can get so saturated that most of the traffic will need to be retransmitted because of excessive collisions causing all sorts of errors, from application timeouts to sporadic connections to file servers.

CSMA/CD Protocol

The CSMA/CD protocol is responsible for ensuring that a transmission is sent only when the transmission medium is free. Essentially, because Ethernet uses the concept of a shared transmission medium, stations must constantly monitor the wire to check whether or not stations are transmitting. A station that wants to send data must first ensure that no other station is using the medium at the time. Using a feature of the CSMA/CD protocol, it is able to "sense" whether or not the medium is free. If two stations decide to send data at the same time, a collision occurs. Both stations must then wait a random period of time as defined by the CSMA/CD protocol and then retransmit their data.

CSMA/CD: Binary Exponential Back-off Algorithm Operation

For a hypothetical network between two stations, A and B, utilizing Ethernet and the CSMA/CD protocol, a collision occurs during a data transfer. In that first collision, each station randomly selects a value of either 0 or 1. This value represents the back-off interval that the station must wait before retransmitting. If, in selecting one of these values, both stations happen to select the same value, another collision occurs. Of course, in the real world, this situation is highly unlikely between only two stations, but on a network with many nodes, it is entirely possible. In the second collision, stations randomly select values from the set of numbers 0, 1, 2, 3. This is double the number of choices in the first collision. After 10 successive collisions, the stations have reached the set of numbers 0...1023. The back-off algorithm keeps selecting from this set until 16 collisions have been reached. At this point, the algorithm gives up and a message that an error occurred is sent to a higher-layer protocol. A station that wins a collision debate is allowed to reset its back-off choices to 0 and 1 again.

Collision Detection

The functions of the CSMA/CD protocol include the responsibility that each station must also monitor its own transmissions to ensure that they are not corrupted by collisions. How does a station monitor its own transmission? When a station sends a frame, it is also scrutinizing data on its receiving wire path. It does this because the frame that is being sent is looped back on the receiving path. If no collisions occur, the transmission was successful. If a collision occurs, it is detected because the received data does not match the data that was sent. The station then sends a "jam" signal down the wire and waits a random period of time, as specified in the back-off algorithm of CSMA/CD, and then retransmits. The jam signal consists of 32–42 bits and is initiated long enough to ensure that other stations on the segment have detected the collision. Of course, this method of collision detection occurs only in the Ethernet 10BaseT specification for devices operating at half-duplex.

Late Collisions

A *late collision* is a collision that is detected only after a station places a complete frame of the network. By CSMA/CD definition, a collision must be detected within the first 64 bytes of a frame. Late collisions are therefore detected after 64 bytes of a frame have been sent on the wire. Typically, late collisions occur when one device is configured as half-duplex while the other is full-duplex. The half-duplex device tries to either send *or* receive, but the full-duplex one sends *and* receives. The late collisions occur on the half-duplex end because, while it is transmitting, the full-duplex end also decides to transmit. The full-duplex thinks that it is legal, but the half-duplex disagrees. This is somewhat similar to two trains traveling on the same rail (due to schedule conflicts) without anyone aware of the error. At some point, the two trains collide.

Ethernet has limitations on the length of a network segment. You might remember the famous 5-4-3 rule of Ethernet, which states that an Ethernet network can be made up of only five segments, of which four may contain repeaters and only three must contain nodes. Ethernet at half-duplex is limited by the fact that a collision must be detected with the first 64 bytes of a frame. In other words, round-trip delay in a collision domain must not exceed 512 bit times, or 51.2 microseconds. It is easy to see how having an excessively long segment will make the delay much greater than 51.2ms, thereby causing a "late collision."

With the advent of Fast Ethernet and full-duplex operation, times changed. In 10BaseT Ethernet with devices operating at half duplex, only one device can be transmitting or receiving at any one time. Please note that some vendors manufacture NICs that do support full-duplex operation at 10BaseT. This is not a standard, however, and this option must be set manually in the NIC software. With 100BaseT or Fast Ethernet, full-duplex operation was made possible. A station could now transmit and receive simultaneously because the transmit and receive paths were different. See Figure 3-8. Fast Ethernet devices can also run at half duplex to provide backward compatibility with older devices.

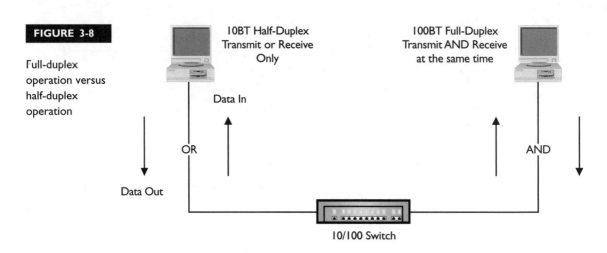

FIGURE 3-8

Full-duplex
operation versus
half-duplex
operation

The delay for Fast Ethernet also decreased by a factor of 10 down to 5.12ms, compared with 51.2ms for 10BaseT. Collisions must still be detected within the first 64 bytes of a frame.

exam

🐬 **a t c h**

Using 10/100 NICs and 10Mbps hubs and switches, and vice versa, can sometimes cause trouble with connectivity. Most equipment from major manufacturers of NICs and other vendors usually work well together. However, situations arise when a NIC just cannot negotiate the correct speed or duplex setting (half or full) with the hub or switch. In those cases, you're better off disabling autonegotiation and manually setting the speed and duplex setting on the NIC. (It's easier to set the NIC than the switch or hub.) This usually eliminates this kind of issue. On the exam, pay special attention to questions about duplex settings.

Ethernet Statistics for Troubleshooting

To properly troubleshoot Ethernet networks, you must understand a few basic characteristics of the standard. The following discussion includes a number of terms you need to know. Keep in mind that most if not all of these statistics can be viewed only with a protocol analyzer. Protocol analyzers can also help you detect malfunctioning equipment on your network. See the "Troubleshooting LANs" section of this chapter for more on this topic. Symptoms of malfunctions can be indicated by LEDs on network equipment. Get to know what the LEDs on your equipment mean. They can quickly help you pinpoint problems and enable you to determine proper operation. Collisions, for example, can cause CRC errors and runts on your network. The only indications of this situation, however, are collision LEDs being lit up on a hub, for example.

Frame Sizes for Ethernet Frames

There is a limit to the size of frames an Ethernet segment can transmit:

- Minimum: 64 bytes
- Maximum: 1518 bytes

Frames that are smaller than 64 bytes are called either *runts* or *fragments,* depending on the validity of the FCS. Frames over the maximum frame size are considered *giants* (oversized).

Frame Check Sequence

The *frame check sequence (FCS)* provides a mechanism for error detection. Each transmitter computes a CRC with the address fields, the type/length field, and the data field. The CRC is then placed in a 4-byte FCS field. Keep in mind that faulty NICs can also result in FCS errors.

Jabbers

Jabbers are long, continuous frames exceeding 1518 bytes that provide a self-interrupt functionality that prevents all stations on the network from transmitting data. Unlike the CSMA/CD access technique used in Ethernet, in which stations must listen before sending data, *jabbering* completely violates CSMA/CD implementation by prohibiting stations from transmitting data. Be aware of the fact that jabbering can be the result of defective NICs, which might need to be replaced immediately. A jabbering condition can result in poor network performance, ultimately causing workstation and server disconnects.

CRC Errors

As a rule of operation, a CRC on data fields is initialized before any Ethernet transmissions. The results are appended to the data frame in the FCS field, which are 4 bytes in length. A CRC is also conducted when the destination receives the frame. The CRC on the data field is then compared to the FCS field. If the results do not match, the frame is discarded and the CRC error count is incremented.

Runts

Runts are short frames that are less than 64 bytes long. They are usually the result of collisions. If a runt frame is well formed (that is, it has a valid FCS), however, it is usually the result of a faulty NIC or its driver.

Utilization

Ethernet has a typical sustained utilization percentage of 40 percent. You can find this information on the LED readout on most hubs and switches. A protocol analyzer also tells you how much of the bandwidth is being utilized on a particular segment. Sustained higher utilization rates lead to collisions on your network. Occasionally, the utilization rate bursts up to much higher values due to events such as large file transfers, but consistent rates above 40 percent lead to problems on your network.

The SHOW INTERFACES ETHERNET Command

When troubleshooting Ethernet problems, you can use the SHOW INTERFACES ETHERNET command to look at errors, collision rates, and so on. This command can be found in Cisco's *IOS Software Command Summary* reference manual for Release 11.2 and higher. Figure 3-9 illustrates the output from this command in Cisco routers.

In the highlighted section from the SHOW INTERFACES ETHERNET command output, you can see three different statistics:

- **Output errors**   The sum of all errors that prevented the final transmission of datagrams from the interface examined.

- **Collisions**   Number of messages retransmitted due to an Ethernet collision.

- **Interface resets**   Displays the number of times the interface has been reset. This can happen if packets queued for transmission have not been sent for several seconds.

FIGURE 3-9   Output from the SHOW INTERFACES ETHERNET command

```
RouterA#show interfaces ethernet 0/0
Ethernet0/0 is up, line protocol is up
  Hardware is AmdP2, address is 0050.3ef8.eb80 (bia 0050.3ef8.eb80)
  Internet address is 192.10.10.3/24
  MTU 1500 bytes, BW 10000 Kbit, DLY 1000 usec,
     reliability 255/255, txload 1/255, rxload 1/255
  Encapsulation ARPA, loopback not set
  Keepalive set (10 sec)
  ARP type: ARPA, ARP Timeout 04:00:00
  Last input 00:00:00, output 00:00:00, output hang never
  Last clearing of "show interface" counters never
  Queueing strategy: fifo
  Output queue 0/40, 0 drops; input queue 0/75, 0 drops
  5 minute input rate 15000 bits/sec, 15 packets/sec
  5 minute output rate 4000 bits/sec, 6 packets/sec
     15035461 packets input, 3681144254 bytes, 0 no buffer
     Received 3946808 broadcasts, 0 runts, 0 giants, 0 throttles
     2485 input errors, 2485 CRC, 1849 frame, 0 overrun, 0 ignored
     0 input packets with dribble condition detected
     653890 packets output, 72785320 bytes, 0 underruns
     10 output errors, 2693 collisions, 1 interface resets
     0 babbles, 0 late collision, 1712 deferred
     0 lost carrier, 0 no carrier
     0 output buffer failures, 0 output buffers swapped out
```

Table 3-1 provides a complete description of the statistics in the SHOW INTERFACES ETHERNET command. As you will see, many of the statistics are repeated for other types of interfaces such as Token Ring and FDDI.

exam
ⓦatch

The SHOW INTERFACES command is important to remember. It is a valuable asset in troubleshooting common problems. It can provide a great deal of information on collisions, interface resets, and other important statistics. Remember to track and monitor excessive collision rates. Keep in mind the utilization rate before collisions present serious problems on the network.

TABLE 3-1   SHOW INTERFACES ETHERNET command statistics

Statistic	Description
Ethernet 0/0 is up... is administratively down	Indicates the state of the hardware and if it has been shut down by an administrator. "Disabled" indicates that more than 5000 errors have occurred in a keepalive interval on the interface.
Line protocol is up|down|administratively down	Indicates whether there is a fault at Layer 2 or if it has been disabled by an administrator.
Hardware	Hardware specifications of the router.
Internet Address	Displays the configured IP address of the router and the subnet mask.
MTU	The maximum transmission unit of the interface—in other words, the largest packet size that the router will process.
BW	Bandwidth of the interface in kilobits per second
DLY	Delay of the interface in microseconds.
Rely	Reliability of the interface as calculated over a 5-minute average, displayed as a fraction of 255; 255/255 indicates 100 percent reliability.
Load	Load of the interface as calculated over a 5-minute average, also displayed as a fraction of 255; 255/255 indicates that the interface is completely saturated.
Encapsulation	Type of encapsulation active on the interface.
Loopback	Tells you whether a loopback has been configured.
Keepalive	Tells you whether the keepalive interval has been set.
ARP type	Type of ARP assigned.
Last input	Time elapsed in hours, minutes, and seconds since the interface last received a packet.
Output	Time elapsed in hours, minutes, and seconds since the interface last transmitted a packet.
Output hang	Time elapsed in hours, minutes, and seconds since the interface was reset because a transmission took too long.
Last clearing	Time when the counters for the SHOW INTERFACES command were reset to zero. Note that routing variables such as load and reliability are not reset.
Queuing strategy	Tells you what type of queuing has been implemented on the interface.
Output queue	Number of packets in each queue. Drops indicate packets dropped because a queue was full.

TABLE 3-1   SHOW INTERFACES ETHERNET command statistics *(continued)*

Statistic	Description
5-minute input rate and 5-minute output rate	Average number of bits and packets transmitted/received over a 5-minute period.
Packets input and bytes	Total number of packets received that were error free. Bytes tells you the total size of all the packets.
No buffers	Number of packets that were discarded because there was no buffer space in the router.
Received .... Broadcasts	Total number of broadcasts/multicasts received by the interface.
Runts ... Giants	Runts indicate the number of packets discarded because they did not meet the minimum size. Giants indicate the number of packets that were discarded because they exceeded the maximum size.
Throttles	Indicates the number of times the receiver on the interface has been disabled due to overload of the buffer or processor.
Input errors	Indicates the total number of errors for runts, giants, no buffer, CRC, frame overrun, and ignored counts. Might be different than individual sum of these errors because one error could generate more than one statistic.
CRC	CRC errors. Indicates noise or transmission problems on the interface. A high number of errors could be the result of a station sending bad data.
Frame	Number of packets received that have CRC errors and malformed sizes.
Overrun	Indicates how many times the interface receiver could not handle the amount of data being received.
Ignored	Number of packets that were ignored because there was no internal buffer available. Different from the "No buffers" statistic mentioned previously.
Dribble condition	Indicates how many packets were received that were just a bit too long. These packets are still processed.
Packets output ... bytes	Indicates the total number of packets transmitted out the interface. Bytes tells you how many total bytes of data have been sent out the interface.
Underruns	The number of times the transmitter has run faster that the router can handle.
Output errors	Sum of all errors that prevented the transmission of packets out the interface.
Collisions	Indicates the number of messages retransmitted due to Ethernet collisions.
Interface resets	Number of times an interface has been completely reset. This can occur if packets in queue have not been transmitted for several seconds. If the line protocol is down, interface resets will occur periodically in an attempt to bring it up.

| TABLE 3-1 | SHOW INTERFACES ETHERNET command statistics *(continued)* |

Statistic	Description
Babbles	Indicates packets where the transmit jabber time expired.
Late collisions	Indicates the number of packets retransmitted after a collision occurred after the first 64 bytes of a frame.
Deferred	Indicates the number of times the transmitter had to wait to transmit a packet because the carrier was reasserted.
Lost carrier	Indicates the number of times the carrier was lost during transmission.
No carrier	Indicates the number of times the carrier was not present during a transmission.

See if the following Scenario & Solution is clear to you. If not, go back and review the material to brush up on your weak areas.

SCENARIO & SOLUTION

Ethernet uses a _____-based method of access to the network.	Contention. All stations must listen, then transmit when free. The station that first determines when the media is free is allowed to transmit first.
What protocol do stations on an Ethernet LAN use to get access to the transmission medium?	CSMA/CD is the protocol that stations use to determine whether or not it is safe to transmit.
If you have excessively long segments in your network, what do you think the result could be?	Excessive segment lengths could lead to late collisions. Late collisions mean that the frame is completely placed onto the network before the collision is detected, instead of being detected within the first 64 bytes. Late collisions mean that the collision occurs after more than 64 bytes have been placed on the wire.
Can 10BaseT operate at full duplex?	Yes, 10BaseT can operate at full duplex, but it is not part of the standard. Only some NIC manufacturers support this option, which must be set manually in the NIC software.

Collision Domains and Broadcast Domains

By now you should be well aware of the difference between collision domains and broadcast domains. A collision domain and a broadcast domain are defined at the Data-Link Layer.

A *collision domain* is essentially the shared medium over which a group of stations must compete to gain access to transmit and receive data. For example, if one 12-port hub links 12 stations and that is the entire network, the collision domain is the diameter of the network that the stations cover.

A *broadcast domain* differs from a collision domain in that one broadcast domain can span multiple collision domains. One broadcast domain covers an entire LAN and refers to all stations that will receive broadcasts or transmissions that are meant for all stations. Broadcasts are addressed to the MAC address, FFFFFFFFFFFF.

Switches reduce the collision domain by giving each station dedicated access to its own segment. Instead of all stations competing for a chance to transmit, the medium between a station and its connection to the switch belongs to that station only. No other stations have access to that segment. The station can therefore make full use of the bandwidth offered by the segment. A transmission between Station A on a switch and Station B on a switch occurs because a switch associates the MAC address of Station A with the port to which Station A is connected and the MAC address of Station B with the port to which Station B is connected. If Station A wants to communicate with Station B, data meant for Station B has Station B's MAC address in the Data-Link Layer header. The switch examines the MAC address and determines which port is associated with it. Upon finding it, the switch forwards the frame out only that port.

If the switch did not know what port Station B's MAC address was on, it floods the frame out of all ports. Whichever station responds with an acceptance of the data, the switch associates that port with the MAC address of Station B. Thus, all stations receive broadcasts.

Bridges and switches reduce collision domains because they associate MAC addresses with specific ports. They "know" where a station is, so they do not waste bandwidth by letting all stations receive data meant for specific stations.

Routers, on the other hand, reduce broadcast domains because they filter out broadcasts. Routers, by default, do not forward broadcasts from one LAN to another LAN.

Using a combination of routers and switches or bridges can dramatically increase the performance of a network.

CERTIFICATION OBJECTIVE 3.04

Token Ring/IEEE 802.5

Stations on a Token Ring LAN behave differently than on Ethernet. The name of this LAN technology describes its operation very well. Access to the transmission medium on a Token Ring LAN is granted by means of a token, which continually circles around the ring. Only a station that possesses the token is allowed to transmit. Access is therefore deterministic instead of contention based, as with Ethernet. Each station on a Token Ring LAN has a NIC that has a ring-in port and a ring-out port. The stations are attached to a multistation access unit (MAU), sometimes referred to as an MSAU by way of lobe cables. A lobe cable is to the Token Ring world what a patch cable is to the Ethernet world. See Figure 3-10. In Token Ring, there is no minimum or maximum size for a frame.

| FIGURE 3-10 | Stations on a Token Ring LAN |

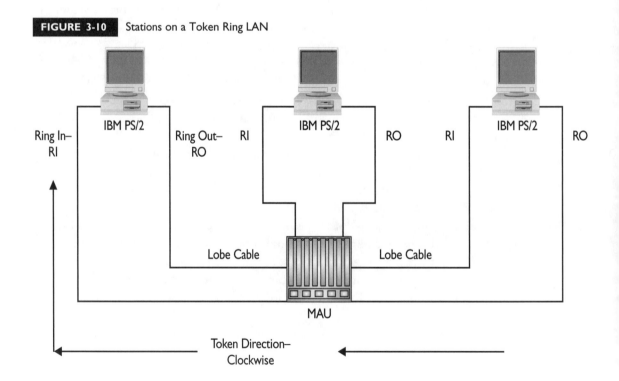

If a station wants to send data, it goes through the following steps:

- Listen for the passing token.

- Determine if the token is busy by looking at the "token" bit in the frame format.

- If the token is not busy, the station seizes the token, changes the "token" bit to indicate that it is now busy, adds its data, and transmits the data onto the ring.

- The frame circulates around the ring, reaches its destination, is processed, and continues around the ring until it reaches its source again. The source station then removes it from the ring due to the fact that the MAC address in the frame matches it.

- Depending on whether the station has more data or not, it can either create a new token and send it out, indicating it is free for use by another station, or it can send more data onto the ring.

Note: A station that has seized control of a token cannot monopolize that token if it has a lot of data to transmit. A timer called a *token holding timer,* or *THT,* has an interval of 9.1ms. Along with the THT, each station that has control of the token has a limit on the amount of data that it can transfer. If a station has the token and transfers data up to the specified amount or the THT expires, it must release the token for other stations to use. If a station does not have enough data to completely take up its allotted time and data limit, it performs an *early token release,* or *ETR.* So if a station has only one or two frames of a small amount of data, it releases the token as soon as it has finished sending its last frame onto the wire. This gives other stations quicker access to the transmission medium. As you can see, this means that every station on the ring gets a chance to use the token. This might seem a slow method of access, but in reality, the delay is unnoticeable.

Understanding MAC Communications

The key to troubleshooting and isolating the inherent problems of Token Ring networks is your ability to understand MAC communications. As mentioned, connecting token stations to a shared medium involves wiring stations to a central hub, commonly known as a MAU. The MAU can be used to interconnect other MAUs to expand the size of the ring. Typically, a MSAU connects up to eight

Token Ring stations. When interconnecting MSAUs, be sure that they are oriented in the ring. Otherwise, the Token Ring has a break and does not operate properly.

In order for new stations to enter the network, a ring-insertion routine must first be conducted. Initially, the station first conducts a media check to find the existing lobe connections (if any exist). After checking the lobe connections, the station then attaches the ring and searches the ring for an active monitor. If no active monitor is on the ring (in an 18-second lapse time), the station then initiates a claim-token process. Then the station transmits a duplicate address test (DAT) frame, which is checked by each active station to see that the new station address is unique. A flag in the frame is set to indicate an error if the station's address duplicates an existing station already on the ring. If no errors are detected, the new station continues with the initialization process.

Token Ring frames always travel in one direction, in a downstream motion. Stations relay frames in a logical ring fashion by repeating the frame, bit for bit. This puts a tremendous amount of dependency on the stations waiting to receive signals from their nearest active upstream neighbor (NAUN). These signals are then repeated to nearest active downstream neighbors (NADN). A station must always know the MAC address of its NAUN in case it receives incorrect data. A neighbor notification, which occurs every 7 seconds, allows stations to discover their MAC addresses.

On receiving data frames, an address recognized and frame copied bit, usually located in the frame status field, is set at the end of the frame. See Figure 3-11 of the Token Ring frame format and Figure 3-12 of the Frame Status field.

The term *frames* has been used in many instances to describe the data portion traversing the network ring. To fully understand exactly how this ring topology operates, you need to understand the frame format in Figure 3-11. In this format,

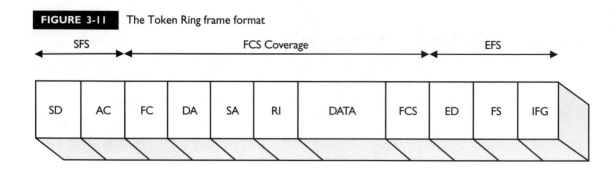

FIGURE 3-11   The Token Ring frame format

you have access to the setting information, which determines the ring operation. The following are the fields in the frame format:

- **Starting delimiter (SD)**   Indicates start of frame.
- **Access control (AC)**   Priority settings.
- **Frame control (FC)**   Indicates frame type as either MAC or LLC.
- **Destination address (DA)**   Specifies the address of destined station.
- **Source address (SA)**   Specifies the station address of originating frame.
- **Routing information (RI)**   Contains user data (LLC) or control information (MAC frame information).
- **Data**   User data.
- **Frame check sequence (FCS)**   CRC-32 error check on FC, DA, SA, and information fields.
- **Ending delimiter (ED)**   Indicates end of data or token frame.
- **Frame status (FS)**   Contains A and C bits indicating frame status:

  A   Address recognized bits.
  C   Frame copied bits.
  r   Reserved.

The frame then traverses the ring until the originator receives it. The originator checks the A and C bits to verify the frame was received. The frame is then stripped, and the token is released by the sender in order for the process to reinitialize. If a station receiving the token has no information to send, the token is forwarded to the next station. One bit of the frame, the T bit, is altered if the station possessing the token has information to receive. Unlike Ethernet, in Token Ring the frames proceed sequentially around the ring. Because a station must claim the token before transmitting, collisions do not occur in a Token Ring infrastructure.

For efficiency in this LAN architecture, a priority mechanism is used. This priority mechanism permits certain user-designated, high-priority stations to use the

FIGURE 3-12								
A	C	r	r	A	C	r	r

The Token Ring Frame Status field

network more frequently. Two Token Ring access fields control the priority mechanism: the *priority field* and the *reservation field*. See Figure 3-13 for a diagram of the Access Control field.

P   Priority bits
T   Token bit
M   Monitor bit
R   Reservation bits

Stations with a priority equal to or higher than the priority of a token can seize that token. Once the token is seized and changed to an information frame, the stations with priority higher than that of the transmitting station can possess the token for the next pass around the network. The new generated token includes the highest priority of the station seizing the token.

To effectively manage the ring, Token Ring stations frequently assume specific management functionality on the local ring. The *active monitor* is one of the leading management functions for the ring. One station on every ring is assigned to the active monitor role. The active monitor's sole purpose is to ensure integrity. The active monitor has seven main responsibilities:

■ Initiate the neighbor notification process

■ Monitor the neighbor notification process

■ Ensure data frames do not continually traverse the rings

■ Detect lost tokens and data frames

■ Purge the ring

■ Maintain the master clock

■ Ensure ring delay

Once a station has been designated the active monitor, it continues to perform the tasks until it leaves the ring or experiences extremely high numbers of physical errors. If for some reason the active monitor is unable to assume its responsibility,

FIGURE 3-13						

FIGURE 3-13

The Access Control field

the remaining stations (otherwise known as the *standby stations*) take over the role. The remaining stations contend for the designated active monitor role, called *token claiming*.

Ring error monitoring is another important and effective management tool. The purpose of the ring error monitor is to receive soft errors or beacons—MAC frames—that are transmitted from any Token Ring station. A MAC address table is maintained for those stations transmitting errors as well as active counts and error types. LAN administrators can use protocol analyzers to respond to the ring error monitor functional address. These analyzers capture beacon and soft-error MAC frames as well as insert them into a beaconing ring.

A *ring purge* is a normal method of resetting communications on a Token Ring network. This mechanism provides a means for issuing a new token. Ring purges are normal events and are typically encountered during ring insertion and ring de-insertion; however, as with Ethernet collisions, high numbers of ring purges cause network performance degradation.

When the active monitor enters the ring purge process, the purge timer starts and the active monitor transmits a ring purge MAC frame. The transmission occurs without waiting for a free token and without releasing a free token on completion. Continuous idles (0) are sent by the adapters. After the frame has traversed the ring, the active monitor receives the transmission and checks for transmission errors. Such errors could be code violation errors or check sequence (CRC) errors.

Any error detection triggers transmission of ring purge MAC frames until a frame is received with no transmission errors or until the expiration of the ring purge timer. This timer's function is to limit the number of retransmissions of ring purge MAC frames during this process. Once the ring purge MAC frame has traversed the ring without error, the active monitor sets a 1-second timer. After an error-free frame is received, the adapter transmits a free token of a priority equal to the reservation priority in the last ring purge MAC frame that was stripped by the adapter.

Troubleshooting Token Ring Networks

When troubleshooting Token Ring problems, you can use the SHOW INTERFACES TOKENRING command to look at errors, collision rates, and so on. Figure 3-14 illustrates the output from the SHOW INTERFACES TOKENRING command in Cisco routers. This command can be found in Cisco's *IOS Software Command Summary* reference manual for Release 11.2 and higher:

FIGURE 3-14

Output from the
SHOW
INTERFACES
TOKENRING
command

```
RouterA#show interfaces to 0/0
TokenRing0/0 is up, line protocol is up
  Hardware is cxBus, address is 0050.3ef8.eb80 (bia 0050.3ef8.eb80)
  Description: User ring SEG=F4
  Internet address is 192.10.10.3/24
  MTU 4464 bytes, BW 16000 Kbit, DLY 1000 usec,
     reliability 255/255, txload 1/255, rxload 1/255
  Encapsulation SNAP, ARP Timeout 04:00:00
  Ring speed: 16Mbps, early token release
  Single ring node, Source Route Transparent Bridge capable
  Source Bridging enabled, srn 3876 bn 1trn 3485 (ring group)
     proxy explorers disabled, spanning explorer disabled, NetBIOS
     cache disabled
  Group address: 0x00000000, Functional Address: 0x0880011A
  Ethernet Transit OUI: 0x000000
  Last Ring Status 4w4d <Error> (0x2000)
  Last input 00:00:00, output 00:00:00, output hang never
  Last clearing of "show interface" counters never
  Queueing strategy: fifo
  Output queue 0/40, 74 drops; input queue 0/75, 75537 drops
  5 minute input rate 247000 bits/sec, 96 packets/sec
  5 minute output rate 61000 bits/sec, 96 packets/sec
     15035461 packets input, 3681144254 bytes, 0 no buffer
     Received 3946808 broadcasts, 0 runts, 0 giants, 0 throttles
     2485 input errors, 0 CRC, 0 frame, 0 overrun, 0 ignored
     0 input packets with dribble condition detected
     653890 packets output, 72785320 bytes, 0 underruns
     10 output errors, 0 collisions, 0 interface resets
     0 output buffer failures, 0 output buffers swapped out
     0 transitions
```

Along with the statistics already explained in Table 3-1 on the SHOW INTERFACES ETHERNET command, Token Ring-specific information is provided by the SHOW INTERFACES TOKENRING command (see Table 3-2).

Being able to understand the ring processes is critical for effectively troubleshooting Token Ring networks. Many LAN administrators overlook such key processes. A good rule of thumb when troubleshooting is to try not to oversimplify the problem-resolution process. The obvious is not always the best indicator; a thorough approach is more realistic for isolating LAN performance problems.

The following are the most common ring processes:

■ **Ring insertion** A five-phase process through which every station must go to insert into the ring; described in detail earlier in this chapter.

TABLE 3-2   Statistics in the SHOW INTERFACES TOKENRING Command

Statistic	Description
Ring Speed	Speed of the Token Ring, 4Mbps or 16Mbps.
Single Ring node|multiring node	Indicates whether the node can collect and use source route bridging information in the routing information field (RIF).
Source Bridging enabled	Indicates whether this node is actively participating in source route bridging.
Group Address	The group address of the interface, if any. This is a multicast address; each interface can have only one group address. This address may be shared among other interfaces.
Ethernet Transit OUI	Tells the router the mode of translation to use when converting Ethernet frames to Token Ring frames and vice versa.
Last Ring Status	Status of the Token Ring interface.
Transitions	Number of times the ring made a transition from up to down or vice versa. A large number of transitions indicates a problem with the ring or interface.

- **Token claiming**   The process by which standby monitors contend with and elect a new active monitor.

- **Neighbor notification**   The process by which a station notifies a downstream neighbor of its MAC address.

- **Beaconing**   The process stations utilize in an attempt to remove bad segments.

- **Ring purge**   Instructs all NICs to reset. This process is an attempt to recover from a break in the Token Ring. Ring purges are normal reactions to the simple soft errors that occur when stations enter or leave the ring.

- **Protocol timers**   There are 14 timers on every Token Ring NIC. Each timer performs its own function.

The following key statistics and events are extremely helpful and necessary for proper baselining and troubleshooting of Token Ring networks:

- **Aborts**   If a station regularly reports that it is aborting transmissions, that station is usually in error. Transmissions are aborted when errors are detected—errors internal to a station or a token in which the third byte is not an ending delimiter.

- **Beacon**   If a beacon alert appears, chances are your ring is inoperable. This situation demands immediate attention. Some protocol analyzers indicate the beaconing station. Usually the fault occurs between the beaconing station and its upstream neighbor.

- **Beacon recovery**   An event is logged in the system when the ring recovers from a beacon event.

- **Claim token**   The presence of claim frames on the ring means that the ring is going through the monitoring contention process. You can determine what station initiated monitor contention by analyzing the events that precede the claim tokens.

- **Duplicate MAC address**   This event occurs when a Token Ring station that is trying to enter the ring has the same MAC address as an existing station on the ring. Be careful regarding the use of LAAs versus BIAs.

EXERCISE 3-4

Determining the Type of Address in Use

1. To determine whether a router is using an LAA or a BIA, issue the SHOW INTERFACES TOKENRING command on the router.

2. Look at the output from the command. You will see output similar to the following:

```
TokenRing 1 is up, line protocol is up
Hardware is 16/4 Token Ring,
address is 0000.0d00.fc77 (bia 0000.0c00.dc77)
```

3. In the output, you can see that this station is using an LAA. The BIA is different from the address in use. LAAs can be a cause of trouble if you are not careful, because a mistake could result in two stations having the same MAC address.

FDDI

Fiber Distributed Data Interface (FDDI) was developed for the transmission of data over fiber optic media at 100Mbps. FDDI is implemented using a dual-ring topology via single or multimode fiber and UTP. See Figure 3-15. FDDI's dual ring serves as a measure of redundancy in the network. A station in an FDDI network can be either a *dual-attached station (DAS)* or a single-attached station (SAS). DASs are connected to both rings. If a ring fails, the station can automatically fail-over to the other ring. SASs have only a single *physical medium-dependent (PMD)* connection to the primary ring.

Access to the network is granted by means of a token, just like Token Ring. Also like Token Ring, frame formats have no minimum or maximum size defined. However, typical FDDI frames are as large as 4500 bytes. Unlike Token Ring implementation, all

FIGURE 3-15

FDDI dual-ring topology

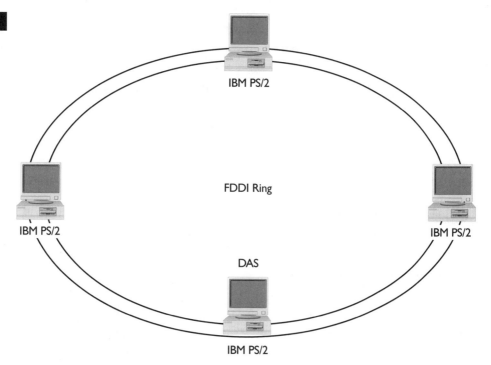

IBM PS/2

FDDI Ring

IBM PS/2

IBM PS/2

DAS

IBM PS/2

stations monitor the ring for invalid conditions such as lost tokens, persistent data frames, or a break in the ring. Beacon frames are cascaded throughout the FDDI network (identifying failures within the domain) if a node has determined that no tokens have been received from its NAUN during a predetermined time period.

Whenever a station receives its own beacon from an upstream station, it automatically assumes that the ring has been repaired. If beaconing exceeds its timer, DASs on both sides of the failure domain loop the primary ring with the secondary ring in order to maintain full network redundancy.

Token passing is a more sophisticated way for stations to get access to the medium. At high utilization levels, token technology surpasses the contention-based access of Ethernet. The support for larger frame sizes also means that FDDI is more efficient than Ethernet because each FDDI frame can contain much more data than the smaller Ethernet frames. When the two are compared, it is easy to see how header information in the smaller Ethernet packets results in greater overhead than the FDDI packet. The format of an FDDI frame is shown in Figure 3-16.

FDDI Specifications

FDDI is defined by four separate specifications:

- **MAC**   Defines how the medium is accessed, including frame format, token handling, addressing, and error recovery.

- **Physical Layer Protocol (PHY)**   Defines data encoding/decoding procedures, clocking requirements, framing, and other functions.

- **Physical Layer Medium (PMD)**   Defines Physical Layer characteristics such as clocking, bit rate, and so on.

FIGURE 3-16   FDDI frame format

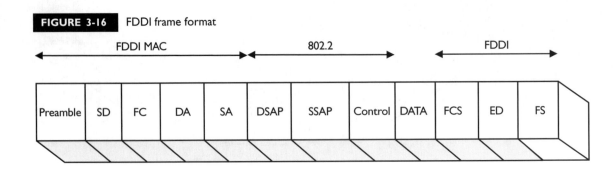

■ **Station Management (SMT)**   Defines FDDI station configuration, ring configuration, and control features.

FDDI Traffic Types

FDDI supports real-time allocation of network bandwidth so that it can provide support for a wide range of applications. This support is provided because FDDI defines two types of traffic: synchronous and asynchronous. *Synchronous traffic* gets a portion of the 100Mbps bandwidth; *asynchronous traffic* is allocated the other portion. Synchronous traffic originates from stations that require continuous transmission capability. This is very useful for voice-over-IP (VOIP) applications as well as video transmissions. FDDI SMT defines a method for allocating bandwidth.

Asynchronous bandwidth is allocated using an eight-level priority scheme. Each station is assigned an asynchronous priority level. The FDDI priority mechanism can lock out a station that cannot use synchronous bandwidth and have an asynchronous priority that is too low.

Because of the highly redundant nature of FDDI and the more expensive implementation of dual rings, it is often implemented as a backbone for networks. FDDI is seldom used as a transport for desktops. FDDI rings can also cover large distances of up to 200Km, making it ideal for campus networks, metropolitan area networks (MANs), and other networks that are spread over a large area.

EXERCISE 3-5

Examining the Status of Neighbors in an FDDI Network

1. Troubleshooting FDDI problems can be simplified if you understand the output from the SHOW INTERFACES FDDI command. Look at the following code listing and see if you can determine what the MAC addresses of the neighbors are telling you:

```
RouterA#show interfaces fddi 1/0
listing abbreviated for clarity
Upstream neighbor 0000.0c02.ba83, downstream neighbor
0000.f800.0000
```

2. If you've correctly interpreted the output, you will recognize that the MAC address of the upstream neighbor is a valid, unique MAC address. The MAC address of the downstream neighbor is something else entirely. In FDDI networks, an unknown MAC address is listed as 0000.f800.0000. This

means that the neighbor has not yet been identified, and it could indicate a problem on the FDDI ring.

CERTIFICATION OBJECTIVE 3.06

Troubleshooting LANs

The increasingly complex nature of LANs today means that troubleshooting their problems has become more difficult. Encountering widely differing technologies from company to company is guaranteed. All administrators and support staff have their own sets of applications and implementations with which they are most comfortable. It is up to the support personnel to keep track of all problems and solutions that they come across and to remember that they might have use for them in another situation. Support staff must understand a wide range of transmission standards—Ethernet, Token Ring, and FDDI. They must be able to quickly associate particular problems with each standard and implement solutions in a cost-effective and efficient manner.

This section covers common problems and solutions related to Ethernet, Token Ring, and FDDI that are prevalent in today's networks. You must be able to understand these three standards because they are the most common types of networks that exist today.

Baselining is extremely important in maintaining and troubleshooting a network. You must have a reference of a properly working network—or a starting point, at least—if you are to be able to successfully implement improvements and changes and have a record of the changes as well as their impact on your network. Always create a baseline before you start making changes. That way, you always have a reference point against which you can measure and see what, if any, improvements have been made.

This chapter discusses common problems that occur on each network and proposes possible courses of action. These actions aid in isolating the problem. Problem definition is a valuable step, since you must first isolate the problem before you can begin to solve it. Solutions can then be found using the tools provided by Cisco, coupled with other helpful troubleshooting tools, such as the PING and

TRACE commands and the protocol analyzers. The key to quick problem determination and resolution is to follow a sound troubleshooting method.

e x a m
🅦 a t c h

Remember to baseline before you do anything. Baselining helps you check to see whether or not your solutions are indeed correcting problems. With a baseline, you create a clear point of reference to look back on and determine if your solution has helped or created another set of problems. Your baseline can help you restore the network to its state before you applied your solution. Take note of any and all procedures that you implement; that way, if you do something wrong, you'll know where to correct the error. Thoroughly understand baselining for the CIT exam. It is crucial. Cisco has shown its importance by frequently mentioning the value of proper network baselining on the exam. You'll probably get at least one question on baselining.

FROM THE CLASSROOM

The SHOW Commands: Some of the Best Cisco IOS Troubleshooting Tools

SHOW commands can provide a wealth of information that can help you quickly diagnose problems within your network. However, to make full use of the SHOW commands, you must be able to understand the statistics presented in their output. You'll often find yourself troubleshooting with the SHOW commands; if you don't understand the output, you will be in for a very difficult time. It is a good idea to always have a Cisco IOS command reference manual at hand.

These manuals can provide you with the proper guidance in interpreting the output from the commands. It is also a good idea to have a manual that provides detailed information on how to go about troubleshooting different areas of your network. Cisco Press as well as a number of other publishers print a number of these books. Find one that you like and get to know it. You'll definitely need it at some point in your work.

—*Vijay Ramcharan,* CCNP, CCDA, MCSE

Ethernet

In addition to the discussion of Ethernet technologies earlier in this chapter, you should thoroughly review the following material.

Ethernet can run over different types of media. Only the most widely found types are discussed here:

- **10Base5, or ThickNet**   This is not a very common medium today. Characteristics include a half-inch diameter; it is heavy and very difficult to manage. "Vampire taps" are used to make connections to workstations. Vampire taps can easily become dislodged. Excessive segment lengths lead to collisions. Improper grounding leads to connectivity issues. Bending and flexing the cable could cause the copper conductor inside to break.

- **10Base2, or ThickNet**   Also not very common today. ThickNet is much ThickNet and lighter than ThickNet . In fact, it resembles coax TV cables. Like ThickNet , ThickNet segments need to be terminated and grounded properly. Drops to workstations are integrated into the NIC, unlike ThickNet, and they are attached to the NIC by means of an extended threaded connector. Excessive cable lengths are also something to watch out for.

Note: You usually find ThickNet and ThickNet in large old buildings such as hospitals, college campuses, and libraries. These were some of the first buildings that were wired when Ethernet technologies first became widely available.

- **UTP**   Unshielded twisted-pair wire, which includes 10BaseT, 100BaseT, 1000BaseT. UTP is by far the most common type of medium in use today. It is inexpensive, fast, and widely available and implemented. It is easy to work with and is a lot easier to troubleshoot than the two types of media previously mentioned.

Note: UTP cabling can be of different types. Category 3 and 5 are most common. Cat 3 cable is the older standard that was used for 10BaseT connections and can be found in most buildings. Cat 5 is used for 100BaseT and 1000BaseT speeds. Note that 10BaseT and 100BaseT use only two pairs of wires. A standard called 100Base-T4 uses all four pairs of wire. There is a 100-meter limit to the length of a segment (a desktop to a hub) for Ethernet UTP. Cat 5 cable is required for most 100Mbps and 1000Mbps speeds, so if you require those speeds and your cable is not up to spec, you need new cable installed by qualified personnel.

Common Ethernet Problems

Problem: Occurrence of collisions (jabbering—when an Ethernet NIC transmits data continuously).

Response: Check collision rate with the SHOW INTERFACES ETHERNET command. The ratio of the number of collisions to the number of output packets should be 1:10. Check for unterminated Ethernet cables with a time-domain reflectometer (TDR). TDRs are used to check for breaks in cables. Coaxial cabling is prone to breakage, and a TDR can help you locate a defective cable quickly. Check transceivers attached to stations; look for media problems.

Problem: Collisions, excessive number of repeaters.

Response: Check collision rate with the SHOW INTERFACES ETHERNET command. Networks with an excessive number of hubs (repeaters) create a very large collision domain. Packets collide on a frequent basis due to excessive network diameter. Try to segment the network using switches or bridges. This greatly decreases the size of the collision domain.

Problem: Occurrence of runt frames.

Response: There is a limit to the size of frames an Ethernet segment can transmit. The maximum is 1518 bytes and the minimum is 64 bytes. *Runt frames* are a violation of the minimum 64-byte frame size. Runt frames are a result of bad software on a NIC if the frame occurs with low collision rate or in a switched network. Use a protocol analyzer to find the source address of the bad frame. Runt frames can also result from excessive collisions when shared media networks exceed maximum length specifications.

Problem: Occurrence of noise on wire.

Response: Check the CRC errors and collision rate with the SHOW INTERFACES ETHERNET command. If numerous errors are occurring and there is a low collision rate, this usually indicates a high noise level. Check cabling for damage. Look for reflections being caused by bad taps spacing. Check to be sure that you are using the appropriate cabling (that is, Category 5 cabling when necessary).

Problem: Unusually high level of activity detected on a segment.

Response: A station could have a defective NIC that is randomly spewing out frames. Use a protocol analyzer to pinpoint the source of the trouble. Exercise 3-6 demonstrates this action.

EXERCISE 3-6

Identifying the Source of High Network Activity

1. Use Microsoft's Network Monitor to perform a capture of frames on the affected segment.

2. Stop the capture after a period of about 1 hour. Bring up the capture window and go to Tools | Experts. See Figure 3-17.

3. Bring up the Experts window and select Top Users. Click the Add to Run List button. Click Run Experts. See Figure 3-18.

4. The expert calculates the top sources of network activity and puts the results in an easy-to-understand list. See Figure 3-19.

Looking at the results of the Top Users expert, you can easily identify potential problem machines that are sending out an excessive number of frames.

FIGURE 3-17

Network
Monitor tools

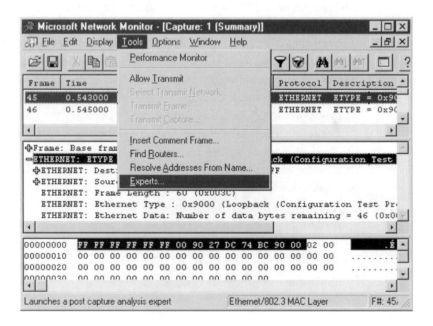

FIGURE 3-18

Network
Monitor experts

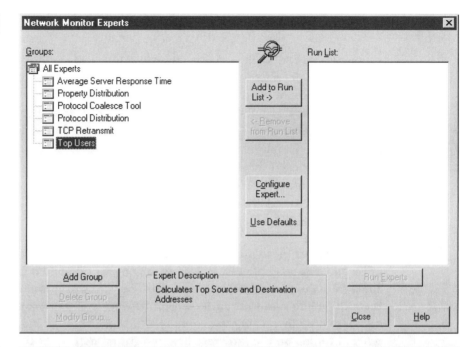

FIGURE 3-19

Results of the
Top Users tool

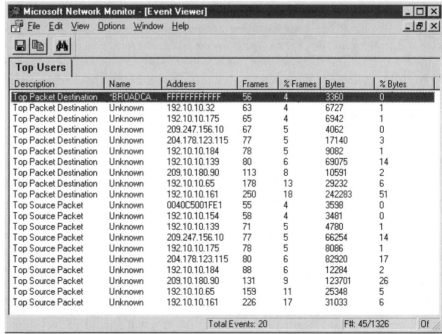

Problem: Desktop has no connectivity.

Response #1: Check the patch cable. On an Ethernet network using twisted-pair wiring, two types of cables can exist: straight through and crossover. Straight-through cables are for desktop-to-hub connectivity and for switch-to-switch (hub-to-hub) connectivity if the device has an uplink port. Crossover cables are used for switch-to-switch (hub-to-hub) connectivity in a case in which the device does not have an uplink port. Crossover cables can also be used to connect two PCs back to back. For more information on straight-through and crossover cable pin-outs, visit the following Web site: www.cisco.com/univercd/cc/td/doc/product/lan/cat3ks/c3ksug/cat3ksa.htm.

Response #2: Check the existence of link and status LEDs on the switch and on the PC. If either LED is off, it could indicate a break in the cable or an incorrect cable.

on the job

Don't underestimate the value of the information offered by status and link LEDs and a good cable tester. Not so long ago, I crimped a fresh new patch cable for an external HP JetDirect unit. The wire was brand new, straight off the roll. I made sure that both connectors were crimped properly. I spent 15 minutes carefully routing the wire under a table, through a duct, and over to a hub. I turned on the JetDirect box and got no activity LEDs. The status LED was on, but there was no activity. I double-checked the connectors to be sure that they were crimped properly. I finally decided to use a cable tester and found that there was a break somewhere inside the cable. It took all of 30 seconds to find that out. I had to remove the cable and install a new one. If you're making your own cables, use a cable tester to be sure that they're good before installing them. Don't assume that just because they're new, nothing could be physically wrong with them.

Response #3: Check the duplex settings on the NIC. Most of the time, for 10/100 networks, the speed on the NIC can be negotiated automatically with the repeater port. In some cases, however, there is a mismatch and the desktop will not get connectivity. Usually this occurs when you have an older 10BaseT repeater and a new 10/100 NIC. Manually adjust the speed of the NIC port in the NIC software (see Figure 3-20) to match that of the hub, and your problem should disappear.

Token Ring

Traffic on a Token Ring consists of data frames and token frames. The data frame contains information similar to information on an Ethernet frame (destination

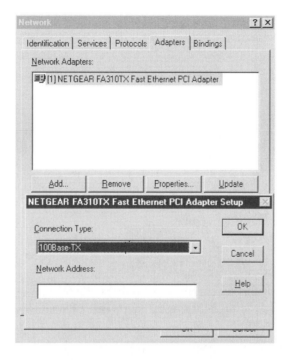

FIGURE 3-20

Adjusting the
port speed of the
NIC in Windows

address, source address, data field, and an FCS). The token frame is simply 3 bytes long, consisting of a start delimiter, an access control byte, and an end delimiter.

When troubleshooting a Token Ring network, use the SHOW INTERFACES TOKENRING command.

Note: If you don't provide additional parameters when you type the SHOW INTERFACES command, statistics are displayed for all network interfaces.

Common Token Ring Problems

Problem: Ring is congested.

Response: Check to see if installation of ring is successful during low-traffic periods. If it is, you might need to segment your network to distribute the traffic.

Note: Because a Token Ring network cannot have collisions, the Collisions field is always zero.

Problem: Ring is not functioning.

Response: Check Token Ring status via the SHOW INTERFACES TOKENRING command. If the status shows a line or protocol is down, check the physical cabling. If this is a new installation, verify that the MAU is initialized.

Problem: "Open Lobe Fault" message at console.

Response: This message indicates that a relay is open in the MAU. Check the cable to the MAU. Verify that the correct type of cabling has been used. Connections between a MAU and a station require a straight-through cable. Reset the interface using the CLEAR INTERFACE command. Verify the interface status using SHOW INTERFACES TOKENRING. The line protocol and interface should be in up/up status. If the problem persists, disconnect devices from MAU and reset the MAU. Reconnect the router and verify interface status using the SHOW command. If the problem persists, connect the router to a MAU you know is working correctly to help isolate the problem. Check Token Ring cards and cable wiring. If the problem continues, replace cabling and check status of the interface to verify it is functional.

Fiber Distributed Data Interface

This chapter covers FDDI only briefly because it is not as prevalent as Ethernet or Token Ring. FDDI is a token-passing technology that uses a dual ring. Networks with FDDI backbones do exist, but these network backbones are rapidly being replaced by technologies such as ATM, Fast Ethernet, and Gigabit Ethernet.

To troubleshoot an FDDI ring, continue to use your basic troubleshooting techniques. The Cisco IOS command SHOW INTERFACES FDDI is helpful in solving FDDI problems. This command is used in a manner that is very similar to the SHOW INTERFACES ETHERNET and SHOW INTERFACES TOKENRING commands.

Note: Because an FDDI ring cannot have collisions, the collisions field is always zero.

Common FDDI Problems

Problem: FDDI ring is not functioning.

Response: Check status of FDDI interfaces using the SHOW INTERFACES FDDI command. See Figure 3-21 for an example of the output from this command.

Additional FDDI-specific information from the SHOW INTERFACES FDDI command is explained in Table 3-3. Test connectivity between routers by pinging the gateway addresses. Verify that the MAC addresses of neighbors are correct. If you see all zeros in the address fields, check physical connectivity.

FIGURE 3-21

Output from the
SHOW
INTERFACES
FDDI command

```
RouterA#show interfaces fddi 0/0
TokenRing0/0 is up, line protocol is up
  Hardware is cxBus, address is 0050.4776.eb80 (bia 0050.3ef8.eb80)
  Description: Utility Server Ring SEG=6B
  Internet address is 192.10.10.3/24
  MTU 4470 bytes, BW 100000 Kbit, DLY 100 usec,
     reliability 255/255, load 1/255
  Encapsulation SNAP, loopback not set, keepalive not set
  ARP Type: SNAP, ARP Timeout 04:00:00
  Phy-A state is connect, neighbor is unk, cmt signal bits 008/000,
     status QLS
  Phy-B state is active, neighbor is M, cmt signal bits 20C/00E,
     status ILS
  ECM is in, CFM is c_wrap_b, RMT is ring_op
  Requested token rotation 5000 usec, negotiated 5000 usec
  Configured tvx is 2500 usec ring operational 1w2d
  Upstream neighbor 0000.1d23.21da, downstream neighbor 0004.c107.9240
  Last input 00:00:00, output 00:00:00, output hang never
  Last clearing of "show interface" counters never
  Queueing strategy: fifo
  Output queue 0/40, 74 drops; input queue 0/75, 75537 drops
  5 minute input rate 247000 bits/sec, 96 packets/sec
  5 minute output rate 61000 bits/sec, 96 packets/sec
     15035461 packets input, 3681144254 bytes, 0 no buffer
     Received 3946808 broadcasts, 0 runts, 0 giants, 0 throttles
     2485 input errors, 0 CRC, 0 frame, 0 overrun, 0 ignored
     0 input packets with dribble condition detected
     653890 packets output, 72785320 bytes, 0 underruns
     10 output errors, 0 collisions, 0 interface resets
     0 output buffer failures, 0 output buffers swapped out
     330 transitions, 0 traces, 799 claims, 0 beacon
```

TABLE 3-3   SHOW INTERFACES FDDI Command Statistics

Statistic	Description
Phy- {A|B}	State of the neighbors on the primary and secondary rings.
cmt signal bits	CMT or connection management shows the transmitted/received CMT bits. The transmitted bits are 0x008 for a Physical A type and 0x20C for Physical B type.
Status	Shows the actual status of the fiber.
ECM	This is the Entity Coordination Management feature of SMT, which oversees the operations of CFM and PCM.
CFM	Contains information about the current state of the MAC connection.

| TABLE 3-3 | SHOW INTERFACES FDDI Command Statistics *(continued)* |

Statistic	Description
RMT	Ring management is the SMT MAC-related status field.
Requested token rotation	Value that is used by all stations on the network for token rotation.
Negotiated	Actual negotiated token rotation time.
Configured tvx	Transmission timer.
Ring operational	Value for negotiated token rotation time for all stations in an operational ring. If the ring is nonoperational, the message "Ring not operational" is displayed.
Upstream... downstream neighbor	Displays the MAC addresses of the NAUN and NADN.
Transitions	Number of times the ring made a transition from operational to nonoperational and vice versa.
Traces	Indicates the number of times this interface started a trace.
Claims	Indicates the number of times this interface has been in a claim state.
Beacons	Indicates the number of times the interface has been in a beacon state.

By now you should have a clear idea of what it takes to successfully resolve problems at the Physical and Data-Link Layers of all the technologies discussed. See what answers you would come up with in the following Scenario & Solution.

SCENARIO & SOLUTION

What technologies use management functions on stations to prevent and correct faults and errors?	Token Ring and FDDI use management functions to implement error detection and correction.
Which is more efficient at higher utilization rates: Token Ring or Ethernet?	Token Ring is efficient at higher utilization rates because stations do not have to deal with collisions, so they can transmit up to the full bandwidth of the media and not suffer any problems. Ethernet, on the other hand, can use only up to about 40 percent of available bandwidth.
What command would you use to monitor Token Ring interface statistics on a Cisco router?	SHOW INTERFACES TOKEN RING. Remember the exact syntax for exam purposes. It is not INTERFACE but INTERFACES.

CERTIFICATION SUMMARY

Ethernet networks today most commonly use twisted-pair media for data transmission because it is both cheap and easy to install. Twisted-pair media have the advantages of being cheap and fairly easy to install and troubleshoot. The bandwidth available on twisted pair has also increased dramatically. From the old 10Mbps standard to the recently ratified gigabit over copper standard (802.3ab), twisted pair has become the medium of choice for most organizations. However, all LANs still face similar problems, whether they are 10Mbps LANs or 1000Mbps LANs. Token Ring LANs and FDDI have unique issues. By understanding the information presented in the previous sections, you will be able to apply more efficient problem-solving techniques to everyday issues.

Common issues such as sporadic workstation connectivity, an extremely high level of activity from a station that is running an application that generates only a minimal level of traffic, and a total lack of functionality when everything other parameter is correct all point to a problem at the Physical Layer. Check the Physical Layer first if you are not absolutely sure of the cause of a problem. Remember the SHOW INTERFACES command and learn to interpret its output. It will prove extremely valuable in troubleshooting Physical and Data-Link Layer problems. Create a baseline analysis of your network, and remember to document in detail all problems and solutions that you come across. This baseline will prove invaluable because you will routinely encounter similar types of problems on almost all networks. If you already have a record of the problem and the recommended solutions, it's very easy for you to refer to your documentation and quickly apply a solution that fits your needs.

When faced with a network problem of any scope, your most powerful weapon will be knowledge. You must know about the network for which you're responsible and understand how data flows throughout the network. This knowledge, coupled with a sound troubleshooting methodology and proper diagnostic tools, equips you with the necessary ammunition to effectively solve any network problem you encounter. Be very familiar with the tools that are available to you; that will make it easier to determine the root of the problem and naturally lead you to possible solutions.

Always be calm; do not panic. Take your time to analyze the symptoms and determine a logical course of action. Of course, it is hoped that your actions result in a solution. If your first action plan is unsuccessful, return the network to its original state and try action plan number two. Remember that Cisco does provide you with additional sources of help. Never rule out physical hardware or cabling problems. Often, physical failure is the cause and is very easy to fix. Remember to use the many resources around you—your coworkers, online technical assistance, documentation, and your own common sense.

✓ TWO-MINUTE DRILL

Here are some of the key points from each certification objective in Chapter 3.

Physical Layer Responsibilities

- ❑ The Physical Layer is Layer 1 of the OSI model.
- ❑ Characteristics include connectors, pin-outs, voltage, and signaling and clocking.
- ❑ The Physical Layer does not perform encapsulation.

Data-Link Layer Responsibilities

- ❑ The Data-Link Layer specifies how data is to be transferred across media.
- ❑ The Data-Link Layer is composed of the MAC and LLC sublayers.

Ethernet/IEEE 802.3

- ❑ Ethernet/IEEE 802.3 refers to the set of rules established by the IEEE for data transmission at the Physical and Data Link Layers.
- ❑ Ethernet is contention based and access is determined by the CSMA/CD protocol.
- ❑ Use the SHOW INTERFACES command for troubleshooting statistics.

Token Ring/IEEE 802.5

- ❑ Access is deterministic and is granted to whichever station is holding the token.
- ❑ Frames don't have preset maximum or minimum limits and they always travel in one direction—downstream.
- ❑ Special stations in the Token Ring network perform management functions.

FDDI

- ❑ Is also deterministic like Token Ring. Access is also granted by way of token.
- ❑ Uses dual, counter-rotating rings for a fault-tolerant network.

❑ Stations can be either DAS or SAS; all stations perform management functions.

Troubleshooting LANs

❑ Remember to create a network baseline for troubleshooting.

❑ Use tools such as cable testers and LEDs on equipment to verify proper operation at the Physical Layer.

❑ Check speed and duplex settings if all physical factors have been ruled out.

SELF TEST

The following questions will help you measure your understanding of the material presented in this chapter. Read all the choices carefully because there might be more than one correct answer. Choose all correct answers for each question.

Physical Layer Responsibilities

1. Which of the following are functions of the Physical Layer? Choose two.

   A. Clocking

   B. MAC addressing

   C. CSMA/CD

   D. Cabling specifications

2. What is the most common type of Physical Layer media in use today?

   A. Coax

   B. ThinNet

   C. UTP

   D. STP

3. Your network seems to slow as more users are added to it. Users need multimedia capabilities as well as large file transfer options. What first step would you take to determine whether or not the network could support 100Mbps speeds to increase available bandwidth?

   A. Check if cabling is Category 3.

   B. Check if hubs and switches are 100Mbps capable.

   C. Check if cabling is Category 5.

   D. Make sure that twisted-pair cabling is installed.

Data-Link Layer Responsibilities

4. What is a function of the Data-Link Layer?

   A. CSMA/CD

   B. IP addressing

   C. Bit rate

   D. FTP

5. What sublayers make up the Data-Link Layer? Choose two.

    A. TCP

    B. LLC2

    C. MAC

    D. LLC

6. Which of the following is connection oriented when we are speaking of the LLC sublayer?

    A. UDP

    B. TCP

    C. LLC1

    D. LLC2

7. You want to reduce the collision domain of your network by replacing hubs with switches. You know that this step will greatly decrease the number of collisions that you are seeing. You also think that the broadcasts will also be reduced. Are you correct in making this last assumption?

    A. Yes, collisions and broadcasts will be reduced by this method.

    B. Using switches will stop all collisions on your network and confine broadcasts to individual LANs.

    C. Broadcasts can be reduced at the expense of increasing collisions.

    D. No, switches do not prevent or decrease broadcasts.

Ethernet/IEEE 802.3

8. Which of the following is *not* a type of LAN technology?

    A. FDDI

    B. Ethernet

    C. TCP/IP

    D. Token Ring

9. What is the speed of Fast Ethernet?

    A. 10Mbps

    B. 16Mbps

    C. 1000Mbps

    D. 100Mbps

10. Choose the terms that refer to the MAC address of a NIC. Choose all that apply.

   A. BIA

   B. Unicast address

   C. Hardware address

   D. Network address

11. Suppose you have added a new computer to a bridged LAN. A user wants to send a message to the new computer across the bridge. How would the bridge handle the message sent to the new computer, assuming that it does not know where the destination of the message is located? Choose all correct answers.

   A. The bridge automatically knows out of which interface to forward the message.

   B. The new PC registers itself with the bridge by means of a three-way handshake.

   C. The message is flooded out through all interfaces of the bridge.

   D. The new PC acknowledges that the transmission is meant for it; the bridge then adds an entry to its MAC table so that it knows where to send messages that are destined for that MAC address.

Token Ring/IEEE 802.5

12. A Token Ring network works great during periods of low traffic, but at other times, it gets congested. Which of the following possible solutions would you recommend to correct this problem?

   A. Segment the network

   B. Switch to Ethernet

   C. Add additional nodes to your network

   D. Reboot all routers

13. What command would you use in Cisco's IOS to check the status of Token Ring interfaces on a router?

   A. SHOW INTERFACE TR

   B. SHOW INTERFACES TOKEN RING STATUS

   C. SHOW STATUS TOKEN RING

   D. SHOW INTERFACES TOKENRING

14. Stations on a Token Ring LAN use a _____-based method to gain access to the transmission medium.

    A. Contention

    B. Broadcast

    C. Beaconing

    D. Deterministic

FDDI

15. What command would you use to check the status of FDDI interfaces on a Cisco router?

    A. SHOW STATUS FDDI

    B. SHOW INTERFACES FDI

    C. SHOW INTERFACES FDDI

    D. SHOW FDDI INTERFACES

16. Which of the following specifications outlined in FDDI handles data link addressing?

    A. Wrap_a

    B. SMT

    C. Data-Link Layer

    D. MAC

17. You have just started working for a company that has an FDDI network. The previous network administrator was unable to get a remote location up within the FDDI network. You have logged in to the router at the main office, and you execute the SHOW INTERFACES FDDI command. You notice that the RMT output says the ring is "non_up_dup." What does this mean, and how would you correct it?

    A. RMT status does not apply in this situation. There is a problem with the router hardware. Notify the vendor and have them ship you another one.

    B. The remote router is not on. Call someone at the remote end and have them turn the router on.

    C. The interface is adminstratively down; you must log in to the remote router and enable it.

    D. A duplicate MAC address on the network is causing the ring to be nonoperational. Change the MAC address that's a duplicate.

Troubleshooting LANs

18. To use the Cisco IOS SHOW INTERFACES commands, you must be in which mode?

A. Line

B. Privileged

C. Telnet

D. Config

19. Which of the following is a command to check the collision rate?

A. SHOW INTERFACE RATES

B. SHOW ETHERNET COLLISIONS

C. SHOW INTERFACES ETHERNET

D. SHOW COLLISION RATE

20. What condition is indicated by lots of errors with a low collision rate?

A. Poor physical connection

B. Duplicate MAC addresses

C. Trouble with network monitoring software

D. Runt frames

21. As part of the network support group for a large company, you routinely handle calls from remote offices when there are connectivity problems. One day you get a call from an office and are told that there has been a loss of connectivity with your central location. The remote office uses a 64K Frame Relay circuit for connection to the central office. The remote office has a small LAN and dial-up connectivity available for remote access by roaming users via a Windows NT Server running the Remote Access Service. How would you check on the status of the Cisco router that the caller is reporting as down?

A. From your desktop in the central office, you initiate a Telnet session to the remote router and execute the SHOW INTERFACES command.

B. You tell the user to reboot the router and watch the output on the terminal as the router restarts.

C. You attempt to ping the remote router, hoping to get a reply.

D. You dial in to the remote office and check on the status of the router by Telnetting to it and issuing the SHOW INTERFACES command.

LAB QUESTION

As a consultant for a network integration firm, you have been called in to provide possible solutions for Parts, Inc. You have learned that the company has grown tremendously over the past two years and with that growth their network has increased in size. Parts, Inc., has a number of buildings that are concentrated over one geographical area. The company's current network administrators have used a large number of hubs that are cascaded off a few switches in the main building. Parts uses a client/server computing environment. Each station meets the distance requirements of Ethernet over UTP. Users report intermittent loss of communications all over the network throughout the day. The company has also started using computer-aided design (CAD) software, and its engineers want to collaborate over the network with other engineers who are in different buildings by sharing large CAD illustrations.

Parts, Inc., used fiber cabling and bridging to connect the other buildings to the main building. The company just won a major manufacturing contract with an auto parts supplier, and work on the contract will start in a few months. The company would like to improve and correct any errors in its network to reduce loss of productivity when work on the contract starts.

It is your job to baseline the current network and come up with a quick but effective solution to improve the network performance while making it redundant so that communications will stay up if something should happen to a link between the main buildings.

Assuming that this work has to be completed fairly quickly, what changes would you implement in the network of Parts, Inc., so that workers can be assured that their network will perform to their expectations?

SELF TEST ANSWERS

Physical Layer Responsibilities

1. ☑   **A** and **D.** Clocking and cabling specifications are correct because clocking and cabling are characteristics of the Physical Layer.
   ☒   **B** and **C** are incorrect because MAC addressing and CSMA/CD are functions of the Data-Link Layer.

2. ☑   **C.** UTP is the correct answer because unshielded twisted pair is most commonly in use today. Most LANs use twisted pair in one form or another.
   ☒   **A** and **B** are incorrect because coax and ThinNet were used in the days when Ethernet first became popular. Twisted pair was not used then. **D** is incorrect because STP refers to *shielded twisted pair,* a more expensive and less common form of twisted-pair cabling.

3. ☑   **C.** Check if cabling is Category 5. This is the correct answer because the very first step to take is to determine if the cabling can support higher speeds than the current speed. The other two factors in this increase of speed would be to check to see whether or not users stations could support the speed and whether or not the network equipment, such as hubs or switches, could run at this higher speed. The most important and potentially most troublesome aspect of this change is the cabling, though.
   ☒   **A** is incorrect because category 3 cabling cannot support 100Mbps. **B** is incorrect because this step comes after making sure that current cabling can support the speed. **D** is incorrect because it does not specify what type of twisted-pair cabling should be deemed as adequate for the upgrade.

Data-Link Layer Responsibilities

4. ☑   **A,** CSMA/CD is the correct answer because the CSMA/CD protocol is responsible for granting stations on an Ethernet network access to the transmission medium.
   ☒   **B** is incorrect because IP addressing is a function of the Network Layer. **C** is incorrect because bit rate is a function of the Physical Layer. **D** is incorrect because FTP is an Application Layer protocol or application.

5. ☑   **C** and **D.** MAC and LLC are correct because they are the two sublayers of the Data-Link Layer in the OSI model.
   ☒   **A** is incorrect because TCP is a Transport Layer protocol. **B** is incorrect because LLC2 is a function within the LLC sublayer itself and is not a sublayer by itself.

6. ☑ **D.** LLC2 is correct because LLC2 is the connection-oriented mode of LLC operation.

    ☒ **A** is incorrect because UDP is a Transport Layer protocol. **B** is incorrect because TCP is a Transport Layer protocol. **C** is incorrect because LLC1 is the nonconnection-oriented mode of LLC operation.

7. ☑ **D.** No, switches do not prevent or decrease broadcasts. Switches are responsible only for decreasing collisions. They cannot control broadcasts.

    ☒ **A** is incorrect because switches reduce only collisions, not broadcasts. **B** is incorrect because switches cannot stop all collisions on your network; they can only reduce them. The very nature of Ethernet is collision detection, and you will experience collisions even by using switches. **C** is simply ridiculous because switches don't affect broadcasts and they certainly can't offer the option of either decreasing broadcasts or increasing collisions.

Ethernet/IEEE 802.3

8. ☑ **C.** TCP/IP is a routed protocol, not a type of LAN technology.

    ☒ **A, B,** and **D** are incorrect because FDDI, Ethernet, and Token Ring are all types of LAN technology.

9. ☑ **D.** 100Mbps. Fast Ethernet, or 100BaseT, runs at 10 times the speed of 10BaseT.

    ☒ **A, B,** and **C** are all incorrect because they refer to the speed of other types of Ethernet technology.

10. ☑ **A** and **C.** BIA and hardware address are correct because these are common terms used to describe the MAC address.

    ☒ **B,** unicast address, is incorrect because a unicast address is used to describe a Layer 3 address or a Network Layer address. **D** is incorrect because network address is the term used to refer to addresses at Layer 3 of the OSI model.

11. ☑ **C** and **D.** These are the correct procedures that a bridge goes through if it does not know where a station is located. Bridges forward transmissions based on their MAC address table. Any MAC addresses of which the bridge is not aware are identified when a message destined for it is accepted and the bridge receives that acknowledgment.

    ☒ **A** is incorrect because a bridge does not know automatically where a station is located unless it receives a message that is intended for that station and it must find that station by broadcasting the message through all interfaces. **B** is incorrect because no three-way handshake is involved. The three-way handshake is used when referring to TCP/IP's method of establishing a session between two stations.

Token Ring/IEEE 802.5

12. ☑   **A**, segment the network. Token Ring uses a deterministic method of access to the transmission medium. Only stations that possess the token are permitted to transmit. If the network is slow during busy periods, it means that the token is not being passed around to the stations quickly enough because there are too many stations. If the network were segmented, each segment would be smaller and would have its own token, making it easier for stations to gain access to the token.

    ☒   **B**, switch to Ethernet, is incorrect; in fact, it would probably make the situation even worse because stations would compete for access to the network instead of waiting for a token. Token Ring usually works better than Ethernet at high loads, and if Token Ring is saturated, Ethernet under the same loads would be practically unusable. **C**, add additional nodes to the network, is incorrect because it would only add to the problem. **D**, reboot the routers, is incorrect because it has no relevance to this problem. Routers work at Layer 3 of the OSI model and are not concerned with how fast stations access the transmission medium.

13. ☑   **D.** SHOW INTERFACES TOKENRING displays the status of Token Ring interfaces on a Cisco router.

    ☒   **A, B,** and **C** are all incorrect because they do not correspond to commands recognized by the IOS.

14. ☑   **D.** Deterministic. Stations on a Token Ring LAN can transmit only if they possess the token. This method of access is deterministic.

    ☒   **A**, contention, is incorrect because it refers to Ethernet and its method of giving stations access to the transmission medium. **B** is incorrect because broadcast refers to a feature of all LANs, whether Token Ring, Ethernet, or FDDI. **C**, beaconing, is incorrect because it refers to a feature in Token Ring LANs whereby stations send out a "beacon" to let other stations know that there is a problem in the network.

FDDI

15. ☑   **C.** SHOW INTERFACES FDDI is the correct command to check the status of FDDI interfaces on a Cisco router.

    ☒   **A, B,** and **D** are all incorrect because they are unknown commands to the Cisco IOS. **B** might look correct, but there's a typo in FDDI.

16. ☑   **D.** MAC. Just as in Token Ring and Ethernet, the MAC sublayer is responsible for handling all Data-Link Layer addressing in FDDI.

    ☒   **A** and **B** are incorrect because Wrap_a and SMT refer to different aspects of FDDI operation in a network. **C** is also incorrect because the Data-Link Layer, although involved in addressing, is not the specification that defines addressing.

17. ☑ **D.** A duplicate MAC address on the network is causing the ring to be nonoperational. Change the MAC address that's a duplicate. The RMT field in the output of the SHOW INTERFACES FDDI command tells you the status of ring management in FDDI. Non_op_dup tells you that the ring is nonoperational because a duplicate MAC address is detected. To correct this, you have to change the duplicate MAC address.

☒ **A, B,** and **C** are incorrect because none of those actions addresses the core of the problem; they have no bearing on a real solution. **A** would probably work but it is not the correct solution.

Troubleshooting LANs

18. ☑ **B.** Privileged. The SHOW INTERFACES commands can be executed only in privileged exec mode.

☒ **A** and **D** are incorrect because line and config modes will not allow you to execute the SHOW INTERFACES command. **C** is incorrect because Telnet does not refer to any mode of operation.

19. ☑ **C.** SHOW INTERFACES ETHERNET. This command gives you the collision rate on the Ethernet interfaces of the router.

☒ **A, B,** and **D** are incorrect and will result in an "% Invalid input detected at '^' marker" message from the Cisco IOS.

20. ☑ **A.** A poor physical connection could be responsible for transmitting frames with errors onto the network. These would show up as errors.

☒ **B** and **C** are incorrect because duplicate MAC addresses and trouble with network monitoring software are not a cause of errors with low collision rate statistics. **D**, runt frames, is incorrect because runt frames are the result, not the cause, of collisions.

21. ☑ **D.** You dial in to the remote office and check on the status of the router by Telnetting to it and issuing the SHOW INTERFACES command. In this situation, direct Telnet to the remote router won't work, because the circuit itself appears to be down. By dialing in to the remote LAN, you gain access to the Ethernet interface of the router through your active dial-up connection that supports Telnet. You can monitor and check on the router in this manner.

☒ **A** is incorrect because the Frame Relay circuit appears to be dead; therefore, you will not be able to Telnet directly to the router. **B** is incorrect because the user has no idea what to look for on the output from the router. **C** is incorrect because trying to ping the router will not indicate what exactly is wrong with the router. The ping would not be successful because the Frame Relay circuit is not active.

LAB ANSWER

The first action that you should take is to create a baseline of the current network. Take note of statistics such as collisions, segment utilizations, heavy traffic areas, the number of broadcasts throughout the network, and the like.

Because Parts, Inc., is experiencing a large number of collisions and intermittent network outages; the most probable cause is overutilization of the LAN segments due to the fact that they're using too many hubs. Distance limitations have not been exceeded, because the company used fiber to interconnect the various buildings and Ethernet rules have not been broken.

To reduce the number of collisions, the most obvious thing to do is to reduce the size of the collision domain. You can use switches to virtually eliminate collisions. Replace all hubs with switches as necessary. With switches, the bandwidth available to each user increases dramatically. You have satisfied the requirements of decreasing collisions and network outages due to overutilization with this one step. Engineers can also communicate more effectively with the increased bandwidth.

To provide redundancy in the links between the various buildings, consider using an FDDI dual-ring topology. FDDI should provide the capacity and redundancy that this network needs.

To reduce excessive broadcasts, you can use routers between the buildings. Routing contains broadcasts crossing the different LANs to their individual LANs.

4

Identifying Troubleshooting Targets

Data link troubleshooting occurs at Layer 2 of the OSI model. Initial troubleshooting begins at Layer 1 of the OSI model. When troubleshooting problems at the data-link layer, you should have already eliminated the Physical Layer as the source of your trouble. As long as the Physical Layer has been determined to be operational, Layer 2 diagnostics must be performed. Layer 2 diagnostics involve examining software processes, which obviously depend on the hardware at Layer 1. On a Cisco router, software processes such as the correct encapsulation type are concerned mainly with proper configuration of the IOS. Software processes can also depend on external factors such as a provider's Frame Relay circuit equipment. For example, if the Frame Relay circuit was recently installed, and you are having problems bringing the link up, and you have verified that your equipment is correctly configured at both ends, then the problem could lie elsewhere—in the service provider's network.

on the **Job**

I remember an incident not long ago where I was moving a Frame Relay installation from one site to another. I had the equipment all set up and ready at the new location, and I called the service provider to have them turn the circuit up. I made sure the DLCI numbers were correct and all configuration details were double-checked. The customer service rep told me that the circuit had been turned up and it should be active. However, a SHOW INTERFACES command told me that on the serial port, Layer 1 was functional, but Layer 2 was down.

I put in a call to the service provider again, believing that the circuit still wasn't turned up. Their customer service rep told me that everything was supposed to be up. I hung up and re-examined the configuration on the router and CSU/DSU. Everything checked out. I put in another call to the service provider and got in touch with their tech support department. After a few minutes, the technician still couldn't figure out what was wrong with the circuit. He offered to check out the problem thoroughly and call me back. About a half-hour later, he called back and said that there shouldn't be any problems now. According to him, one of their Frame Relay switches was malfunctioning and had to be replaced.

The point of this? In cases in which you absolutely cannot figure out what's wrong with a circuit installation, it's best to call your service provider. More often than not, your provider will be able to give you some answers.

With proper usage of the tools provided by Cisco's IOS, you can quickly determine whether a problem is internal to your network or if it exists because of a fault outside your network. Understanding the information displayed from various SHOW commands is of great importance if you are to successfully isolate and correct any internetwork problems.

This chapter focuses on the use of IOS commands that can provide insight into Layer 2 problems. Please remember that before you troubleshoot at the data-link layer, you should first eliminate the Physical Layer as the possible cause of your trouble.

CERTIFICATION OBJECTIVE 4.01

Understanding Data Link Troubleshooting Targets

The discussion of identifying data link troubleshooting targets is one of the most important sections in this chapter. It focuses on how to troubleshoot Layer 2 problems and how they relate to the other layers of the OSI model, particularly Layer 3. The data-link layer of the OSI model involves encapsulations such as Frame Relay, HDLC, SDLC, PPP, FDDI, and Ethernet. These encapsulations ensure the proper framing of the Network Layer and the data sent to the Physical Layer.

In order for two devices to communicate effectively, the same encapsulation method must be specified on each device. Incorrect encapsulation types between devices will cause inconsistencies in your network. It can also disrupt communication between end stations as well as eliminate routing at the Network Layer because devices cannot communicate effectively. When two devices are using different encapsulation types, it is as though they are speaking different languages. One device cannot properly understand what the other device is trying to say, resulting in confusion of both devices.

Frame Relay

Frame Relay is based on a digital packet-switching technology that uses both permanent virtual circuits (PVCs) and switched virtual circuits (SVCs) to communicate between data terminal equipment (DTE). Frame Relay works by ensuring that a virtual connection is specified at both ends of the connection of the DTE. A Data Link Connection Identifier (DLCI) is used to identify endpoints in a Frame Relay network. A DLCI number is specified at both ends of the physical connection (the DTE), enabling a virtual connection to be established between the two DTE devices. Note that the DLCIs are locally significant only, so DLCIs can (and often are) different on each end of a circiut. DLCIs can be assigned to major interfaces for multipoint connections or subinterfaces for both multi-point and point-to-point connections.

HDLC and SDLC

Synchronous Data Link Control (SDLC) and High-Level Data Link Control (HDLC) are data link protocols that are responsible for encapsulation of data at Layer 2 of the OSI model. SDLC and HDLC encompass a group of communication protocols that are responsible for transferring data at Layer 2 between network nodes. SDLC is typically used in IBM mainframe environments, in which communications occurs between host mainframe computers, which are usually the primary stations. The client computers are normally referred to as *secondary stations.* SDLC is based on the HDLC protocol and is basically a different format of HDLC. SDLC can encapsulate data for synchronous connections, whereas HDLC can encapsulate data for both synchronous and asynchronous connections.

Point-to-Point Protocol

The Point-to-Point Protocol (PPP), a Layer 2 encapsulation protocol, is responsible for transmitting data between two nodes. PPP encapsulates data over a serial connection and is an enhancement over the Serial Line Internet Protocol (SLIP) because it can support multiple protocols and provide enhanced authentication features. SLIP can only support TCP/IP and password authentication in clear text. PPP can handle IPX/SPX, TCP/IP, NetBEUI, and other protocols and can support various types of authentication, including clear text and Challenge Handshake Authentication Protocol (CHAP). PPP is capable of handling asynchronous as well synchronous connections and thus can handle any Physical Layer specifics. PPP's function is to establish a connection over a point-to-point link via Link Control Protocol (LCP) frames, which test the Data-Link Layer. Once the Data-Link Layer has been verified as operational, a connection is established and the end stations are ready to send data via whatever Network Layer protocol has been specified, over the established PPP link.

PPP encapsulates data over a point-to-point link in a network, hence the name *point-to-point protocol.* Most network problems with PPP are usually a result of an improper encapsulation at one end of the PPP connection, different authentication schemes being specified, or different protocols being used.

Fiber Distributed Data Interface and Copper Distributed Data Interface

FDDI is very similar to the Token Ring protocol and uses pulses of light that travel through fiber optic strands as the physical medium for transferring data. Fiber optic interface cables, which are used to connect network equipment, use separate strands for sending and receiving data. That is, the receiving strand has its own connector, which is plugged into the receiving port on the network equipment, whereas the sending strand also has its own connector going to the sending port on the equipment.

on the
on the job

The first time I started working with fiber optic media was while doing a migration in a large hospital in the Bronx, New York. That was quite early in my networking career. I knew practically nothing about fiber optic cables and how it is supposed to be used. I was part of a team whose members were all existing employees of the facility. As part of the migration, we were supposed to swap out existing hubs with hubs that had been through flash ROM upgrades. We were also introducing fiber connections to the upgraded equipment.

I remember looking at the fiber cables and finding no marks that differentiated the receiving strand from the sending strand. We plugged in the fiber patch cables from the router to the hub, the sending strand from the router going to the sending strand of the hub, and the receiving strand from the router going to the receiving strand of the hub. Surprise! The hub refused to work.

I asked my co-worker (who was supposed to know how the equipment was interconnected because he had been working there for some time) whether the equipment was plugged in correctly. He said yes. Nevertheless, I couldn't help thinking that something was wrong. After all, if data is sent out through the LAN port of a router, the hub must receive that data. Following this thinking, I reversed the sending and receiving cables on the hub and it booted up correctly. My co-worker, needless to say, was quite embarrassed.

This was obviously a Layer 1 problem that was easily remedied. As usual, when troubleshooting, you should first make sure that Layer 1 is working properly before you move higher up the OSI model.

FDDI is defined by four specifications:

■ **Media Access Control (MAC)**   This specification describes how the medium is accessed by the use of token passing and frame format.

- **Physical Layer Protocol**   PHY is used to encode data as well as clocking and framing functions of the Physical Layer.

- **Physical medium-dependent (PMD)**   PMD details how the fiber optic cabling at the Physical Layer controls the bit rates and optical components.

- **Station management (SMT)**   The primary function is to ensure that the station is configured for FDDI standards such as ring control and configuration, fault recovery, and statistics.

CDDI is very much similar to FDDI in that it has all the data link specifications of FDDI except that its Physical Layer specification uses copper lines—hence the name Copper Distributed Data Interface. This specification was created as a result of the high cost of fiber optic lines as well the need to use copper lines in existing copper-based networks.

Ethernet

Ethernet is the most common LAN technology in use today. It can be used over a variety of types of copper media, such as thinnet, thicknet, and twisted pair. Although it is rare to find new installations that use either thinnet or thicknet, they are still an integral part of the large, long-standing networks in libraries, schools, and hospitals. Most new installations of Ethernet use twisted pair as the transport medium of choice. Twisted pair is cheap and easy to install and can now support Gigabit speeds. Coupled with industrywide vendor support, Ethernet is definitely the most popular type of network found today.

Ethernet stations use a contention-based method to gain access to the network, commonly referred to as Carrier Sense, Multiple Access with Collision Detection (CSMA/CD). This means that every station on a LAN "listens" on the wire to see if any stations are currently transmitting. If no station is transmitting, a station is free to transmit. This means that only one device may send or receive data at any one point in time.

The Possible Interfaces of a Cisco Router

Cisco routers are available in either fixed configurations, such as the 2500 and below series (except the 1601, 2523, and 2524 which are modular), or modular chassis, such as the 2600 and up series. A *fixed configuration* means that the equipment comes with factory-installed interfaces that cannot be removed or modified. Modular routers come with spare slots that can accept a variety of types of interfaces in the form of "cards." For example, a 2610 router can accept up to two WAN interface cards (WICs) and one network module for features such as voice over IP (VOIP).

Practically all routers come with a LAN interface such as Ethernet, WAN interfaces such as ISDN and DSL, and serial ports such as a 56K port with integrated CSU/DSU. In the case of the modular routers, WICs have to be purchased separately, and these fit into various slots on the router. In larger modular routers, such as the 3600 series, every interface is a separate purchase. The advantage of the modular routers is that, depending on the type of network for which you are provisioning, various interface cards can be purchased and installed on the router. So, for example, you could have one router with several different WICs, connecting multiple locations, each with a different type of WAN interface.

A Cisco router has a variety of interfaces, depending on the type of network that the router is supporting. Interface types can be categorized as either LAN or WAN.

The Ethernet interface is considered a LAN interface. This type of interface is used for Ethernet LAN connections to a private network or LAN. The Ethernet interface of a router normally represents the LAN side of a Cisco router, whereas the serial interface of a Cisco router usually represents the WAN side of the router. FDDI and Token Ring connections are other examples of LAN interfaces.

The serial interface of the router represents the interface of the router that it uses to connect to a remote network, usually via a WAN link such as a T1 or Frame Relay connection. Serial interfaces and interfaces such as ISDN BRI and PRI are considered WAN interfaces. ISDN PRI is used mainly for companies, which support a large number of remote access users or remote offices, whereas ISDN BRI is usually implemented in small branch and remote offices and home offices. Low-speed asynchronous interfaces would also be categorized as WAN. Most WAN interfaces are usually complemented by an external piece of equipment called a *channel service unit/data service unit (CSU/DSU)*. CSUs are used to connect the local network to the WAN connection that has been installed and provided by the telco. Cisco routers can also have WAN interfaces with built-in CSUs. In the ISDN world, the CSU/DSU is an NT1, where in the async world, it is simply called a modem.

Differentiating Between LAN and WAN Interfaces

The interfaces on a Cisco router can be categorized as either LAN or WAN. A LAN interface is used to connect the router to the private internal network of a company.

One of the most commonly used LAN interfaces is the Ethernet interface, which is used for routing information to the LAN.

A WAN interface is used to connect the router to an external network. A WAN interface is basically used to connect the router to the network of a telecommunications provider, which then provides a link to another branch of the company that is located in a geographically separate area. The network of the telco is used as a highway for transporting the company's data from one location to another remote location—hence the term *wide area network.*

CERTIFICATION OBJECTIVE 4.02

Troubleshooting Physical and Data Link Characteristics

Whenever you are troubleshooting a network, it is always important to start from the Physical Layer and work your way up the OSI model. Verification of the Physical Layer entails making sure that all the cables are connected correctly and that hardware of the router or switch is working correctly. Several tools can be used to test the Physical Layer and see if it is working correctly. These tools—cable testers, network monitors, and protocol analyzers—are discussed in the following subsections.

Cable Testers

One Physical Layer problem that you may encounter is problems with faulty cables. A faulty cable can be identified using cable-testing gear such as time-domain reflectometers (TDRs), optical time-domain reflectometers (OTDRs), multimeters, and oscilloscopes. These devices are able to find cable breaks and other cable problems. Sending a signal on the line and interpreting the response that the signal returns enables the tester to pinpoint where the problem occurs. The TDR measures the time for one of its signals to reflect to the point of origin. Some of the fields that these testers are able to measure are AC and DC voltage, current, resistance, capacitance, and cable continuity. These measurements are helpful in determining where a problem occurs in the cable.

Scanners or cable testers are able to test Layer 1 problems such as fiber breaks and Layer 2 problems where improper encapsulation could occur. Scanners and cable testers can report on cable conditions such as attenuation, noise, and wire map functions. They are also able to display Layer 2 information such as MAC addresses, which could be used to help solve encapsulation problems.

Network Monitors

Network monitors are able to track a variety of information on a network, such as the number of packets, the packet sizes, the number of hosts on a network, and the hosts' MAC addresses. These devices enable the network administrator to analyze and evaluate the information to see if there are problems in the network. This type of information becomes more important if the network is running multiple protocols and different encapsulations.

Protocol Analyzers

Data link troubleshooting tools can include the SHOW commands available in a Cisco router that enable the user to view Layer 2 information such as encapsulation and framing errors. For a more specific breakdown of network data, *protocol analyzers* provide indispensable tools for troubleshooting Layer 2 problems. Protocol analyzers collect information and interpret it, based on how a specific communication protocol works in a network. Protocol analyzers provide information such as the frame contents and which layer is involved in its production. They can provide information on which protocol is consuming the most bandwidth as well as which workstations are sending out the most data. Protocol analyzers can isolate workstations that have possibly defective network interface cards (NICs).

Exercise 4-1 takes you through the basics of using Microsoft's Network Monitor to capture bridge protocol data units (BDPUs) from all bridges on the network. Network Monitor is a protocol analyzer that is included with Windows NT Server.

Like most Microsoft products, Network Monitor is user friendly and, as a bonus, it's free with NT Server. Please note that the version included with NT Server is limited to capturing data that is being sent and received only on the machine on which it is installed. The full product is included when you purchase Microsoft's Systems Management Server.

EXERCISE 4-1

Using Network Monitor to Capture Bridge Traffic

1. Open Network Monitor and click the Capture option.

2. Click Filter. In the Filter window, double-click the SAP/ETYPE field. You are presented with a list of available protocols. Click the Disable All button to disable capture for all protocols.

3. Double-click the BPDU protocol type to enable capture for just that protocol. Click OK to save your choice. Click OK again to go back to the main capture window.

4. Click the Capture button to start capturing BPDUs. See Figure 4-1.

5. Stop and examine the captured frames by clicking the Eyeglass button. You will see a list of all BPDU frames captured.

FIGURE 4-1	

Network monitor main window

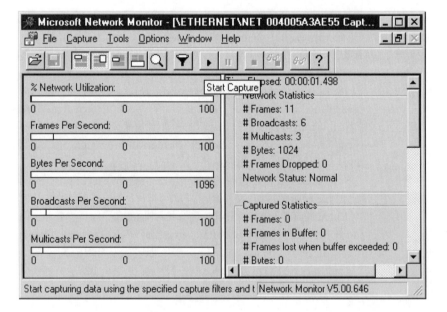

Breakout Boxes

Breakout boxes (also called *Fox boxes*) are used to troubleshoot cable pinouts of serial cables. Frequently, when interconnecting network hardware for WAN interfaces, you use external CSU/DSUs. These connections require cables of specific pinouts. If you are in a shop that is making its own cables, breakout boxes can tell you whether your pinouts are correct or not. Of course, incorrect pinouts result in nonoperational equipment.

Physical Checking

Verifying operation of the Physical Layer involves checking for problems such as loose, dirty, or incorrect cabling; cable breaks; and problems with your network hardware. Hardware problems could be related to improperly seated interface cards or failed hardware modules. Status light emitting diodes (LEDs) are usually a good indicator of the current condition of your hardware. Cable testers can tell you whether a cable is good or not.

The CLEAR COUNTERS Command

On a Cisco router, counters are kept based on packets that are sent and received by the router. The purpose of these counters is to let you know exactly how much traffic was sent and received by the router, errors encountered, and other statistics such as the number of collisions and broadcasts on the interface. There are a number of different counters, each providing specific types of data.

The CLEAR COUNTERS command is used to reset the traffic counters of the router interface. This means that all packet counters are reset to zero.

The CLEAR COUNTERS command first appeared in IOS version 10.0. This command is useful for troubleshooting problems related to packets that seem to be stuck in the router's interface. A problem such as this is readily evident if you perform a SHOW INTERFACES command and note the counter values of the interface that you suspect is having problems. Clear the interfaces using the CLEAR COUNTERS command and look at the interface counters again. If an interface is displaying steadily increasing input packet counters while the number of output packets is not increasing, there could be a problem with the output interface of the router.

The CLEAR COUNTERS command can be used on any interface in the Cisco router. The command syntax is: **clear counters <interface type> <interface number>**.

If you do not provide an optional interface/type, all interfaces are cleared. The interface counters can be displayed by issuing the SHOW INTERFACES command. The output from the SHOW INTERFACES command follows. This listing is from the Ethernet 0/0 interface of a router:

```
ROUTER_A# show interfaces Ethernet 0/0
  Ethernet0/0 is up, line protocol is up
  Hardware is AmdP2, address is 0050.3ef8.eb80 (bia 0050.3ef8.eb80)
  Internet address is 192.10.10.3/24
  MTU 1500 bytes, BW 10000 Kbit, DLY 1000 usec,
     reliability 255/255, txload 1/255, rxload 4/255
  Encapsulation ARPA, loopback not set
  Keepalive set (10 sec)
  ARP type: ARPA, ARP Timeout 04:00:00
  Last input 00:00:00, output 00:00:00, output hang never
  Last clearing of "show interface" counters never
  Queueing strategy: fifo
  Output queue 0/40, 0 drops; input queue 0/75, 1 drops
  5 minute input rate 161000 bits/sec, 44 packets/sec
  5 minute output rate 2000 bits/sec, 4 packets/sec
     62129712 packets input, 1326155552 bytes, 0 no buffer
     Received 15262964 broadcasts, 0 runts, 0 giants, 0 throttles
     1900 input errors, 1900 CRC, 68 frame, 0 overrun, 0 ignored
     0 input packets with dribble condition detected
     2419651 packets output, 266413055 bytes, 0 underruns
     66 output errors, 10566 collisions, 1 interface resets
     0 babbles, 0 late collision, 6796 deferred
     0 lost carrier, 0 no carrier
     0 output buffer failures, 0 output buffers swapped out
```

This command was issued on an Ethernet interface. If it was issued on any other interface, "ethernet" would be replaced by the specific router interface. The CLEAR COUNTERS command can be specifically used to reset the fields generated from a SHOW INTERFACES command. This command is a necessity when you are tracking statistics that are incrementing. Whenever a CLEAR COUNTERS command is performed, the fields that are highlighted in the code listing are reset to zero.

The SHOW INTERFACES Command

The SHOW INTERFACES command, with no additional parameters, is used to display physical and data link layer information on the status of all interfaces that are present in the router. From the output of this command, you are able to determine whether an interface is active, operational, or disabled. You can see statistics on the traffic that has been processed by the router and the errors encountered while processing that traffic.

For troubleshooting purposes, the SHOW INTERFACES command is extremely useful because it provides you with a quick way to determine the status of an interface and configuration details such as the encapsulation type configured, LMI type used (for Frame Relay networks), keepalive status, and traffic counters. The LMI type, for example, is extremely important because it determines whether the router is able to successfully bring up an interface that is being used for Frame Relay. LMI is used for sending circuit status messages between two DTEs.

The various statistics presented in the output of the SHOW INTERFACES command are covered in detail later in this chapter.

The SHOW CONTROLLERS Command

The SHOW CONTROLLERS command displays low-level memory management information and extremely detailed information on the hardware interfaces in the router. Information is not displayed for virtual interfaces such as the loopback interface or subinterfaces. The output from this command follows (*the listing is abbreviated for clarity*):

```
ROUTER_A#sh controllers
Interface Ethernet0/0
Hardware is AMD Presidio2
ADDR: 80B4C3B4, FASTSEND: 800279A0, MCI_INDEX: 0
DIST ROUTE ENABLED: 0
Route Cache Flag: 0
 LADRF=0x0400 0x0100 0x0420 0x0000
 CSR0  =0x00000072, CSR3  =0x00001044, CSR4  =0x00004B1D, CSR15 =0x00008000
 CSR80 =0x0000D900, CSR114=0x00000000, CRDA  =0x015175B0, CXDA  =0x015178E0
 BCR9 =0x00000000 (half-duplex)
 HW filtering information:
  Promiscuous Mode Enabled, PHY Addr Enabled, Broadcast Addr Enabled
  PHY Addr=0050.3EF8.EB80, Multicast Filter=0x0400 0x0100 0x0420 0x0000
 amdp2_instance=0x80B4DDFC, registers=0x40000000, ib=0x1517460
```

You can see that the listing contains detailed information regarding the interface type as well as how the interface interacts with the IOS. The hardware, for example, is manufactured by Advanced Micro Devices (AMD), and it is a Presidio 2 chipset.

This type of information is mostly used by Cisco's TAC personnel. They are able to use this information for troubleshooting.

The SHOW CDP NEIGHBORS Command

The SHOW CDP NEIGHBORS command is used to display information about directly connected devices that are running the Cisco Discovery Protocol (CDP). By default, CDP is enabled on all Cisco equipment. The output from the SHOW CDP NEIGHBORS command can tell you whether directly connected neighbors are Cisco devices or not (assuming that CDP has not been disabled) and the interface being used to connect to each device.

The SHOW CDP NEIGHBORS command is covered in detail in the CDP section of this chapter.

By now you should have a clear idea of characteristics to look at when troubleshooting the Data-Link Layer. Look at the following Scenario & Solution and see if you understand the solutions given.

SCENARIO & SOLUTION

Which command is used to show the status of Layer 1 and Layer 2 on a Cisco router?	The SHOW INTERFACES command is used to view Layer 1 and 2 status.
The CLEAR COUNTERS command is mostly used when troubleshooting what type of problem?	The CLEAR COUNTERS command is useful in determining whether an interface has problems forwarding traffic.
The pinouts of serial cables and devices can be verified using which tool?	A breakout box can show you details on how a serial cable or device is wired.

CERTIFICATION OBJECTIVE 4.03

Clearing the Interface Counters

Counters are maintained on a Cisco router for all traffic sent and received. All errors are indicated by the respective counter being incremented according to the number of errors encountered while the router is processing inbound and outbound packets. From a troubleshooting standpoint, packet counters can help you determine whether there are any faults in your network that need to be addressed. Excessive broadcasts, for example, point out a need for protocol tuning or removal. NetBEUI is one protocol that we can all get by without. NetBEUI should be removed as soon as possible from your network because it is entirely broadcast based. Excessive collisions could indicate that your LAN is overloaded and might require the use of switches.

Packet counters are useful in troubleshooting failed router operation; they can indicate whether packets are being sent out of the router or being rejected by an interface because the output packets counter is not increasing.

Defining the Interface Packet Counters

Interface packet counters are the packet statistics that are displayed when the SHOW INTERFACES command is issued on the router. The counters begin from zero if reset and increment according to the traffic processed by the router. A sample from the serial 0 interface of a router follows (*the listing is abbreviated for clarity*):

```
2420783 packets input, 251754803 bytes, 0 no buffer
    Received 530467 broadcasts, 0 runts, 0 giants, 0 throttles
    232 input errors, 50 CRC, 62 frame, 0 overrun, 0 ignored, 120 abort
    26205727 packets output, 2221912989 bytes, 0 underruns
    0 output errors, 0 collisions, 117 interface resets
    0 output buffer failures, 0 output buffers swapped out
```

The statistics displayed here are all counters that are incremented during normal router operation. If there were a problem with one of the interfaces, you would notice that the packet output counters for that interface would indicate this problem by remaining at one value, without incrementing. The CLEAR COUNTERS command described in the next section can provide a useful troubleshooting tool when used in conjunction with the SHOW INTERFACES command.

Table 4-1 provides a brief description of all the counters presented in the listing.

The CLEAR COUNTERS Command

The CLEAR COUNTERS command resets the counters that a router uses to keep track of such statistics as the number of packets sent and received, the total size in bytes of the packets sent and received, collisions, broadcasts, and a number of other statistics. It can be useful for troubleshooting transmission errors associated with an interface.

TABLE 4-1 Packet Counters in a SHOW INTERFACES Command Output

Counter	Description
Packets input/packets output	Number of packets the router received/sent that had no errors.
Bytes	Total of the size of all error-free packets received/sent, in bytes.
No buffer	Number of packets that were dropped because the input buffer was full. No buffer errors usually result from broadcast storms on an Ethernet LAN.
Received xx broadcasts	Number of broadcast packets received on the interface.
runts	Number of packets received with a runt condition. *Runts* are frames that do not meet the minimum size requirement of the interface. Runts are a result of collisions resulting in malformed packets or a defective NIC.
giants	*Giants* are packets that have exceeded the maximum packet size specified by the interface.
throttles	*Throttles* refer to the number of times a message was sent to the sender requesting that the rate of packets being sent should be decreased.
Input errors	*Input errors* are the total number of errors (CRC, frame, overrun, ignored) detected on packets received.
CRC	This counter represents the number of CRC errors on the interface. CRC errors are from collisions that have resulted in damaged packets. CRC errors in packets can also be generated from a malfunctioning NIC.
Frame	Frame errors indicate the number of packets received with an incorrect frame type. For Ethernet, the frame type should be ARPA.
Overrun	This counter represents the number of times the interface was unable to move received data to a buffer because the input rate was greater than the interface could handle.
Ignored	The number of packets that were ignored because there was not enough buffer space to accommodate the storage of those packets.
Abort	The router issues an abort after an excessive number of times that a station tries to retransmit packets due to collisions.
Underruns	The number of times the router's transmitter was operating faster than the router could handle.
Output errors	The total of all errors that prevented packets from being transmitted.
Collisions	The number of times that packets have collided on the interface, resulting in retransmittal of those packets.

TABLE 4-1	Packet Counters in a SHOW INTERFACES Command Output *(continued)*

Counter	Description
Interface resets	Interface resets occur when a packet could not be transmitted within a certain period. The router resets the interface in an attempt to fix whatever is preventing the transmission of packets.
Output buffer failures	The number of times that the buffer was filled to capacity, resulting in the reallocation of resources within the router.

FROM THE CLASSROOM

Understanding Collisions, Frame Errors, and CRC Errors

Collisions, frame errors, and CRC errors—these terms are quite common but frequently misunderstood. In the output from a SHOW INTERFACES command, they are presented as important enough to warrant separate counters.

The collisions counter is used to indicate the number of times that packets had to be retransmitted because a collision occurred. Collisions occur when two stations on an Ethernet LAN try to transmit at the same time. Collisions are termed *early* if they are detected within the first 64 bytes of the frame. *Late collisions* occur after the first 64 bytes of the frame. Collisions are a normal feature of Ethernet networks, but if they occur excessively, they indicate problems that need to be addressed. Excessive collisions reduce a network to about 35 to 40 percent of usable bandwidth. Collisions should consume no more than 5 percent of all traffic on a LAN.

Frame errors indicate the number of packets that have been received with incorrect frame types. For Ethernet, the frame type should be ARPA.

The CRC error counter tells you the total number of CRC errors discovered in all packets. The CRC is a value that allows the receiving station to determine whether the format of a packet conforms to the state in which it was originally sent and whether it meets Ethernet specifications.

—Vijay Ramcharan, CCNP, CCDP, MCSE

The output from this command follows. The first listing is the output from the Ethernet interface of a router that has not been cleared (*the listing is abbreviated for clarity*):

```
ROUTER_A# show interfaces ethernet 0/0
   5 minute input rate 161000 bits/sec, 44 packets/sec
   5 minute output rate 2000 bits/sec, 4 packets/sec
      62129712 packets input, 1326155552 bytes, 0 no buffer
      Received 15262964 broadcasts, 0 runts, 0 giants, 0 throttles
      1900 input errors, 1900 CRC, 68 frame, 0 overrun, 0 ignored
      0 input packets with dribble condition detected
      2419651 packets output, 266413055 bytes, 0 underruns
      66 output errors, 10566 collisions, 1 interface resets
      0 babbles, 0 late collision, 6796 deferred
      0 lost carrier, 0 no carrier
      0 output buffer failures, 0 output buffers swapped out
```

The following code listing is from the same Ethernet interface that has now had its counters cleared by the CLEAR COUNTERS ETHERNET 0/0 command (*the listing is abbreviated for clarity*):

```
ROUTER_A# clear counters ethernet 0/0
Clear "show interface" counters on this interface [confirm]y
ROUTER_A#
ROUTER_A#show interfaces ethernet 0/0

 Last clearing of "show interface" counters 00:00:09
  Queueing strategy: fifo
  Output queue 0/40, 0 drops; input queue 0/75, 0 drops
  5 minute input rate 61000 bits/sec, 13 packets/sec
  5 minute output rate 1000 bits/sec, 2 packets/sec
      250 packets input, 90636 bytes, 0 no buffer
      Received 27 broadcasts, 0 runts, 0 giants, 0 throttles
      0 input errors, 0 CRC, 0 frame, 0 overrun, 0 ignored
      0 input packets with dribble condition detected
      39 packets output, 3057 bytes, 0 underruns
      0 output errors, 0 collisions, 0 interface resets
      0 babbles, 0 late collision, 1 deferred
      0 lost carrier, 0 no carrier
      0 output buffer failures, 0 output buffers swapped out
```

From the highlighted portions of the listings, the effect of the CLEAR COUNTERS command on the interface is clearly shown. The number of input packets was reset to zero, the total number of bytes received was reset to zero, and input errors, CRC errors, frame errors were all reset to zero. The second listing doesn't show a zero value for these counters because the router was busy transmitting packets in the 9 seconds since the reset, but you can still see that the counters were reset.

The CLEAR COUNTERS command is used to aid in troubleshooting interface problems by helping you determine whether or not packets are leaving the router's interface. By clearing the current counters and recording the fields that are incrementing versus the fields that are remaining constant, you can pinpoint which interfaces are presenting a problem.

exam
ⓦatch

The CLEAR COUNTERS command is used to establish a baseline against which you can troubleshoot interface counters. Know and understand the command syntax of this extremely useful command.

Exercise 4-2 takes you through the steps required to establish a baseline for your interface counters.

EXERCISE 4-2

Using the CLEAR COUNTERS Command to Aid in Establishing a Baseline for Interface Counters

Please note that the logging described in this exercise is a simple way to achieve what might be better accomplished (and more complex to implement) by using a Syslog server:

1. Assuming that you are using Windows 95/98 or Windows NT, start your Telnet application by clicking Start | Run and typing in **Telnet**. Press Enter. Your Telnet window should now appear.

2. Click the Terminal option, and click Start Logging. You will be prompted for a filename to save your Telnet session commands and output to. A good name would probably include the name of the router and the date and time of capture.

3. Log in to your router and go into privileged mode. For the interface that you want to baseline (assuming the Ethernet interface), type in the command **clear counters ethernet 0**. This command resets all your Ethernet 0 interface counters to zero.

4. Type the command **show interfaces ethernet 0**. The output from this command enables you to see the counters at their minimum level of traffic statistics.

5. Assuming that you want to monitor the traffic in three-hour periods for one day, you would now log out of the router. In the Telnet window, click Terminal, and click Stop Logging. All commands as well as the command output from your session are now saved.

6. Three hours later, using the same Telnet application, you log in to the same router, choose the same logging options, including the filename, and do another SHOW INTERFACES ETHERNET 0 command. The traffic counters for the past 3 hours will now be added to the log file.

7. Repeat Steps 1 through 6 until you are satisfied that you have obtained an accurate analysis of the traffic trends on the Ethernet interface of the router.

CERTIFICATION OBJECTIVE 4.04

Troubleshooting Commands

The below sections describe troubleshooting commands.

The SHOW INTERFACES Command

The SHOW INTERFACES command is one of the most commonly used troubleshooting tools in a network. The SHOW INTERFACES command enables the network administrator to see status information for all interfaces on the router. It is here that you can detect Layer 1 and Layer 2 problems by examining the status of the interfaces as well as the counters of each interface. The SHOW

INTERFACES command provides a wealth of useful information for router interfaces. Each type of interface provides some different type of information. For example, a SHOW INTERFACES ATM <INTERFACE NUMBER> command displays virtual circuit status, whereas a SHOW INTERFACES command for an Ethernet interface displays no information on virtual circuits. However, all SHOW INTERFACES commands display the following similar types of information:

- **Physical interface characteristics** Interface name, physical status, data link status, hardware type, MAC address, BIA address (if appropriate—e.g.: serial lines do not have MAC addresses).

- **Interface traffic characteristics** MTU, bandwidth, delay, reliability, load, encapsulation, type.

- **Interface parameters** ARP type, ARP timeout, loopback, keepalives.

- **Interface traffic statistics and counters** Last input/output, last clearing, input/output queues, packets input/output, no buffer, broadcasts, runts, giants, input errors, CRC, frame, overrun, ignored, packets output, underruns, output errors, collisions, interface resets.

exam
ⓦatch *The SHOW INTERFACES command is quite common and is very useful for troubleshooting interface problems. It is reasonable to expect this command to appear in some form on the Support exam.*

A Basic Template for All SHOW INTERFACES Commands

The SHOW INTERFACES command provides a variety of statistical information for each interface type on the router. This command can be used to x display information on either a specific interface on the router or all interfaces on the router. Because a lot of information that is presented by the SHOW INTERFACES <INTERFACE TYPE> <INTERFACE NUMBER> command is repeated for each type of interface on the router, Table 4-2 lists the common fields along with an explanation of each.

exam
ⓦatch *You might notice that descriptions for the packet counter fields are not provided in Table 4-2. This is to prevent presentation of redundant information. Readers should refer to the earlier section of this chapter on Interface Packet Counters, which explains those fields in detail.*

TABLE 4-2   Common Fields in All SHOW INTERFACES Command Outputs

Field	Description
<Interface type> is <status>	Shows the most important information regarding the status of the interface. This is explained in the following section.
Hardware	The hardware type refers to the specific hardware used by the interface and the MAC address. This router is using the hardware type MCI, or Multiport Communications Interface card. The hardware type refers to the chipset that is being used by the interface.
Internet address	The IP address of the interface followed by the subnet mask.
MTU, BW, DLY, Reliability, txload, rxload	Used only by routing protocols that consider items such as bandwidth, delay, reliability, load, and MTU as metrics. IGRP and EIGRP use all these values, but OSPF uses only the bandwidth field. The reliability and load values should never really be used to determine how utilized the interface actually is. The input and output rates are used for this metric.
Encapsulation	The Encapsulation field indicates the acceptable frame type; since this an Ethernet interface, it is set to ARPA. If this were a serial interface, it could be set to PPP or HDLC encapsulation, for example.
Loopback	The loopback option indicates whether a loopback was set.
Keepalive	The keepalive option indicates whether the keepalive option is enabled; on this interface, it is currently set to 10 seconds.
ARP type	The encapsulation type used by frames on the interface. Valid types are ARPA, SNAP, Novell-ether, and SAP.
ARP timeout	The ARP timeout indicates the time period that ARP entries will be kept in the router's cache before they are automatically cleared out. By default, this value is set at 14,400 seconds, or 4 hours.
Last input/last output	The last input and last output values on an interface indicate when the last packets where received and sent by the router. This type of information is useful for troubleshooting whenever an interface is down on a router.
Last clearing of …	The last clearing specifies how long ago the interface counters were cleared. A value of 7w4d, for example, tells you that the interface was last cleared 7 weeks and 4 days ago.
5 minute input rate/ 5 minute output rate	The 5-minute input and output rates represent the number of bits and packets transmitted per second, averaged over the past 5 minutes. The time period can be modified to get a more exact utilization over a shorter period of time. Input and output rate calculation is explained later in this chapter.

The **SHOW INTERFACES ETHERNET** Command

The SHOW INTERFACES ETHERNET command is used for determining the status of Ethernet interfaces on the router. You can view the status of both the Physical and Data-Link Layers, encapsulation type, MAC addresses, traffic counters, and many other useful types of information. The encapsulation type, for example, is useful for troubleshooting IPX problems that could be related to an incorrect encapsulation configured on the router. The output from the SHOW INTERFACES ETHERNET command is:

```
ROUTER_A> sh in eth 0/0
Ethernet0/0 is up, line protocol is up
  Hardware is AmdP2, address is 0050.3ef8.eb80 (bia 0050.3ef8.eb80)
  Internet address is 192.10.10.3/24
  MTU 1500 bytes, BW 10000 Kbit, DLY 1000 usec,
     reliability 255/255, txload 1/255, rxload 1/255
  Encapsulation ARPA, loopback not set
  Keepalive set (10 sec)
  ARP type: ARPA, ARP Timeout 04:00:00
  Last input 00:00:00, output 00:00:00, output hang never
  Last clearing of "show interface" counters 1d00h
  Queueing strategy: fifo
  Output queue 0/40, 0 drops; input queue 0/75, 0 drops
  5 minute input rate 9000 bits/sec, 15 packets/sec
  5 minute output rate 0 bits/sec, 0 packets/sec
     1071692 packets input, 272065445 bytes, 0 no buffer
     Received 306409 broadcasts, 0 runts, 0 giants, 0 throttles
     23 input errors, 23 CRC, 0 frame, 0 overrun, 0 ignored
     0 input packets with dribble condition detected
     58456 packets output, 5421468 bytes, 0 underruns
     0 output errors, 247 collisions, 0 interface resets
     0 babbles, 0 late collision, 129 deferred
     0 lost carrier, 0 no carrier
     0 output buffer failures, 0 output buffers swapped out
```

The information provided by the SHOW INTERFACES ETHERNET command was explained in the preceding sections on interface packet counters and the SHOW INTERFACES template. *Note:* Most of the statistics described in this command are also generated for other SHOW INTERFACES commands. For example, like the SHOW INTERFACES ETHERNET command, the SHOW INTERFACES ATM command also has fields such as hardware type, IP address, and encapsulation.

Note: Information on packet counters can be found in the "Clearing the Interface Counters" section.

Line and Line Protocol Status

The line and line protocol status of the Ethernet interface is displayed on the second line of the output from the SHOW INTERFACES ETHERNET command. The line status tells you the state of the Ethernet hardware (Physical Layer); the line protocol status tells you the state of the Data-Link Layer on the interface. Possible status types are as follows:

- **Ethernet0 is up, line protocol is up**   This indicates that the Ethernet hardware initialized correctly and is operational, and Layer 2 is up and ready to pass traffic.

- **Ethernet0 is up, line protocol is down**   This tells you that the Ethernet hardware has correctly initialized but the Data-Link Layer is not operational, possibly due to misconfiguration or other connectivity issues.

- **Ethernet0 is administratively down, line protocol is down**   "Administratively down" occurs when the interface is taken down by an administrator who used the SHUTDOWN command. Naturally, if the Physical Layer has been taken down, the Data-Link Layer will not be able to initialize correctly.

- **Ethernet0 is down, line protocol is down**   This usually signifies a cable cut or a Physical Layer problem associated with the interface, such as disconnected or incorrect cabling.

exam
ⓦatch
The SHUTDOWN and NO SHUTDOWN commands are used for disabling interfaces.

exam
ⓦatch
You should know and understand the various states of the Physical and Data-Link Layers as listed in the SHOW INTERFACES command output and how they are related. For example, if the Physical Layer is listed as down, the Data-Link Layer will also be shown as down, because the Data-Link Layer depends on correct operation of the Physical Layer.

Now that you have a good understanding of the use of the SHOW INTERFACES command, see if you can determine what action to take in the circumstances shown in the following Scenario & Solution.

SCENARIO & SOLUTION

There appears to be a problem with your serial interface. How would you determine whether it is a hardware problem or a software configuration problem?	Issue the SHOW INTERFACES command. Look at the second line of the output and determine whether the hardware has correctly initialized by examining the status. If the hardware is not up, the line protocol or Layer 2 cannot initialize correctly.
You've recently added a serial interface card to your router, but when you perform a SHOW INTERFACES command, the interface is not present. What could be the cause of this problem?	Because this is a new addition to your router, the interface card might not be seated correctly. Turn off your router and remove, then reinsert, the card, making sure that it's firmly seated.
While troubleshooting a router, you notice that the Ethernet hardware is not coming up. The interface seems to be seated properly, and you've restarted the router, just to be sure that it is properly detected by the IOS. What could be the problem?	Any interface on the router must be connected to the requisite equipment before it can be brought up. In this case, the Ethernet interface must be connected to a hub or switch. Double-check your connections and make sure that your cable is good by either swapping it or checking it with a cable tester.

on the Job

I had a client one time perform their own migration from Token Ring to Ethernet. After a hectic weekend swapping TICs for NICs, they were stumped as to why the PCs could no longer access the network. Although the same wiring plant was in use (Category 5 cabling), they never bothered to examine the network closets. It is rather difficult for an Ethernet NIC to successfully terminate in a Token Ring MAU.—Neil Lovering, CCIE 1772.

Burned-In and RAM-Based MAC Addresses

Burned-in addresses (BIAs) are MAC addresses that have been factory assigned at the time of manufacture of the hardware. This address used to be encoded onto a read-only memory (ROM) chip on the hardware unit or router, in this case. In recent years, however, administrators got the option to manually assign MAC addresses to their equipment. This manual assignment is referred to as *RAM-based MAC addressing.* The SHOW INTERFACES command can tell you if a RAM-based or burned-in MAC address is being used on the router. Simply look at the second line of the command output, and you will be able to tell.

In the following line from a SHOW INTERFACES command, the MAC address in brackets is the BIA, whereas the MAC address listed for the AmdP2 hardware is the MAC address that is currently active on the router. They are the same in this case, so no change was made to the factory-assigned address (*the listing is abbreviated for clarity*):

```
Hardware is AmdP2, address is 0050.3ef8.eb80 (bia 0050.3ef8.eb80)
```

exam
ⓦatch   ***RAM-based MAC addresses are commonly used on Token Ring and FDDI networks. You should be able to recognize a locally administered address versus a BIA.***

Routing Metrics

Routing metrics are used by routing protocols to determine the shortest or best path to a destination network. Routing protocols such as RIP, EIGRP, and OSPF all use different types of routing metrics. RIP, for example, uses a metric based on hop count; OSPF uses a metric based on the cost of the interface. Routes from one routing protocol can be redistributed to other routing protocols. This is done automatically in the case of EIGRP-to-IGRP routes for interfaces which are in the same AS, whereas EIGRP-to-OSPF route redistribution needs to be manually configured. This redistribution of router is frequently a cause of problems associated with packets being routed through a less optimal path than is offered by the network because as the routes are redistributed, the metrics of those routes have to be manually redefined within the routing protocol that is receiving the redistributed routes. Incorrect configuration of the metrics will result in packets taking paths that they were never intended to take.

Routing protocols are assigned an administrative distance. The AD of a routing protocol determines which protocol the router would prefer for routing traffic. For example, a static route has a default AD of 1, while OSPF has a default distance of 110. Therefore, if a router has a static route to a destination network and it is also running OSPF, which also has a route to that same destination network, the router would prefer to use the static route because it has a lower administrative distance.

Input and Output Queues

Input and output queues are the buffers used for temporarily storing packets received and packets that have to be sent out. The following listing shows that the last packet was received 1 second ago, whereas the last packet was also sent 1 second ago. The output queue currently contains zero packets that have to be sent out, and it can hold a maximum of 40 packets. The input queue currently contains no packets, and it can hold a maximum of 75 packets. The drops indicate the number of packets that were dropped because the buffer limit was exceeded. In this case, there were no drops (*the listing is abbreviated for clarity*):

```
Last input 0:00:01, output 0:00:01, output hang never
     Output queue 0/40, 0 drops; input queue 0/75, 0 drops
```

Input and Output Rates

The input and output rates are measured in bits per second and packets per second. These rates give you an average of the all data sent (output) and all data received (input) within the last 5 minutes. The rates are calculated by a default in 5-minute time intervals. Therefore, for a 5-minute period, the output rate is measured by the total number of bits sent divided by 300 seconds, which yields the output rate in bits per second. The packet-per-second rate is calculated in the same manner. The time period can be adjusted with the **load-interval** interface configuration command.

This counter is useful in determining whether the bandwidth that has been given for an interface is adequate enough for the amount of data that the router has to process. For example, a 64Kbps link can handle approximately 64,000 bits per second.

exam
Watch

Be sure to remember that input and output rates are calculated over the 5-minute period and not from a single instance in time.

Input and Output Packet Errors

Input errors are the number of errors that occurred in packets received by the router. These include runts, giants, no buffer, CRC, frame, overrun, and ignored counts. Some packets can result in multiple types of errors, so the total of all input errors might not be the same as the individual error-type counts.

Output errors are the sum of all errors that prevented the transmission of packets out of the particular interface. Again, some packets can result in multiple types of errors, so the total of all output errors might not be the same as the individual error-type counts.

The SHOW INTERFACES TOKENRING Command

The information displayed by the SHOW INTERFACES TOKENRING command contains much of the same types of data as the SHOW INTERFACES ETHERNET command, but Token Ring-specific information is also provided. Important information listed in the output from this command includes ring speed, MAC address in use, and bridging capabilities.

The following listing is the output from the SHOW INTERFACES TOKENRING command. Use this command to determine the status of Token Ring interfaces on a router, the ring speed, and the MAC address in use. The ring speed is very important because Token Ring networks can operate at either 4Mbps or 16Mbps only. Stations cannot run at 16Mbps while the router runs at 4Mbps:

```
Router_A# show interfaces tokenring 0/0
TokenRing 0/0 is up, line protocol is up
Hardware is 16/4 Token Ring, address is 0040.05A3.AE55 (bia 0090.27df.55f6)
      Internet address is 192.10.10.203, subnet mask is 255.255.255.0
       MTU 8136 bytes, BW 16000 Kbit, DLY 630 usec, rely 255/255, load 1/255
       Encapsulation SNAP, loopback not set, keepalive set (10 sec)
   ARP type: SNAP, ARP Timeout 4:00:00
   Ring speed: 16 Mbps
   Single ring node, Source Route Bridge capable
       Group Address: 0x00000000, Functional Address: 0x60840000
     Last input 0:00:00, output 0:00:00, output hang never
     Output queue 0/40, 0 drops; input queue 0/75, 0 drops
     Five minute input rate 0 bits/sec, 0 packets/sec
     Five minute output rate 0 bits/sec, 0 packets/sec
        14561 packets input, 1357825 bytes, 0 no buffer
   Received 6875 broadcasts, 0 runts, 0 giants
   0 input errors, 0 CRC, 0 frame, 0 overrun, 0 ignored, 0 abort
     29664 packets output, 8635312 bytes, 0 underruns
     0 output errors, 0 collisions, 1 interface resets, 0 restarts
     2 transitions
```

A description of the fields shown in the output from the SHOW INTERFACES TOKENRING command is provided in Table 4-3. Please note that the table presents only additional information that was not already described in the SHOW INTERFACES ETHERNET command output.

exam
ⓦ*atch*

You should know by now why Token Ring networks do not experience collisions. The deterministic method of access by stations prevents collisions from occurring.

TABLE 4-3	Statistics in the SHOW INTERFACES TOKENRING Command

Field	Description
Token Ring 0/0 is up	This shows the status of the Physical Layer or the Token Ring hardware itself. *Up* means that the physical connection is fine. The following are the possible outputs for the first part of line 1 and explanations for each status type: **up ǀ down** The interface is either currently active and is part of the ring (up) or is not active and not inserted in the ring network (down). **Reset** This means that there is a hardware failure. A possible problem could be that a faulty MAU is connected to the Token Ring port of the router. **Initializing** The hardware is up and the router is about to be inserted into the ring. **Administratively down** This line means that the hardware is fine; however; an administrator intentionally took down this line. For example, if you want to troubleshoot interface problems, you can shut down the interface using the SHUTDOWN command.
Ring Speed	The Token Ring speed, which can use only 4Mbps or 16Mbps.
Single Ring ǀ multiring node	Indicates whether a node is configured to use source routing information (RIF) for routable Token Ring protocols.
Group Address	If any group address has been configured for the interface, it will be shown here. The group address is a multicast address. Any number of interfaces on the ring can share the same group address. Each interface can have a maximum of one group address.
Collisions	Since Token Ring does not have collisions, this statistic should be 0. Only in rare instances will you see a non-zero number here.
Resets	The number of times that the interface has been reset. Resets can occur due to an error within the router, or they can be initiated by a command on the router.
Restarts	*Restarts* refer to the number of times that the Token Ring interface has been shut down and then reinitialized by the IOS. This field should always be zero.
Transitions	Number of times the ring changed in status from up to down or down to up. A large number of transitions indicates a problem with the ring or the interface.

Ring Speed

The ring speed on a token ring network must be the same for all stations or else there are connectivity problems. As we've seen, Token Ring can operate at either 4Mbps or 16Mbps. Use the SHOW INTERFACES TOKENRING command to verify that the correct ring speed has been configured.

Resets, Restarts, and Transitions

Resets on an interface occur when the IOS encounters some internal processing errors. The IOS resets the interface in an attempt to correct those errors. The interface can also be reset by issuing the command CLEAR INTERFACE TOKENRING.

Restarts occur when the IOS has repeatedly attempted to transmit data, resulting in failure. The IOS restarts the interface in an attempt to correct the problem. On a Token Ring interface, the Restarts field should always be zero because the lack of errors on a Token Ring interface would never result in the router having to restart an interface.

Transitions occur when an interface changes status from up to down or down to up. This could be due to errors within the Token Ring LAN or an error on the router itself. A large number of transitions indicate that there is a serious problem that needs to be addressed.

The SHOW INTERFACES FDDI Command

The SHOW INTERFACES FDDI command displays information on FDDI interfaces in the router. You can view information on upstream and downstream neighbors, MAC addresses in use, ring management status, the time elapsed since the ring has been operational, and more. A lot of the information on packet counters is similar to that already discussed for Ethernet interfaces. The following listing shows the output for this command; the relevant fields are described in Table 4-4. *Note:* Only fields that are relevant to FDDI and that have not already been discussed in previous sections are described in the table.

```
ROUTER_A> show interfaces fddi 1/0
Fddi1/0 is up, line protocol is up
  Hardware is cxBus Fddi, address is 0020.affa.39f5 (bia 0000.0829.b85d)
  Internet address is 192.10.10.32/24
  MTU 4470 bytes, BW 100000 Kbit, DLY 100 usec, rely 255/255, load 1/255
  Encapsulation SNAP, loopback not set, keepalive not set
  ARP type: SNAP, ARP Timeout 4:00:00
  Phy-A state is  connect, neighbor is unk, cmt signal bits 008/20C, status QLS
  Phy-B state is  active, neighbor is  M, cmt signal bits 20C/008, status ILS
  ECM is in, CFM is c_wrap_b, rmt is ring_op
  Requested token rotation 5000 usec, negotiated 5000 usec
  Configured tvx is 2500 usec, ring operational 22:12:25
  Upstream neighbor 0000.0f02.ac93, downstream neighbor 0004.0f02.ca43
```

```
Last input 0:00:00, output 0:00:00, output hang never
Last clearing of "show interface" counters 0:48:12
Queueing strategy: fifo
Output queue 0/40, 0 drops; input queue 0/75, 0 drops
Five minute input rate 0 bits/sec, 0 packets/sec
Five minute output rate 0 bits/sec, 0 packets/sec
    223456 packets input, 31621592 bytes, 0 no buffer
    Received 205 broadcasts, 0 runts, 0 giants
    0 input errors, 0 CRC, 0 frame, 0 overrun, 0 ignored, 0 abort
    4520 packets output, 496406 bytes, 0 underruns
    0 output errors, 0 collisions, 1 interface resets, 0 restarts
    0 output buffer failures, 0 output buffers swapped out
    120 transitions, 0 traces, 305 claims, 0 beacons
```

TABLE 4-4   FDDI Statistics from the SHOW INTERFACES FDDI Command

Field	Description
Phy-A, Phy-B state	The state of the physical A/B ports. Valid states are off, active, trace, connect, next, signal, join, verify, break. These are described in detail in the following section.
Neighbor is	State of the directly connected neighbor. Valid states are described in detail in the "Upstream and Downstream Neighbors" section.
Cmt signal bits	The total in bits of connection management messages sent and received. An inactive connection will not have any CMT bits.
Status	Shows the current state of the fiber connection. Valid states are NLS, MLS, ILS, HLS, QLS, ALS, and LSU.
ECM	Entity coordination management is used to control the removal of a station from the ring and still keep the ring operational. Valid states are in, out, trace, leave, path_test, insert, check, deinsert.
CFM	Configuration management gives information about the MAC connection. Valid states are thru, wrap_a, c_wrap_b, wrap_s, isolated.
RMT	Ring management is responsible for MAC status. Valid states are isolated, non_op, ring_op, detect, non_op_dup, ring_op_dup, directed, trace.
Requested token rotation	Token rotation time can be autonegotiated. The default value is 5000 microsecs.
Ring operational	The total time in hours, minutes, and seconds since the ring has been operational.
Upstream/downstream neighbor	Displays the MAC addresses of neighbors. Unknown MAC addresses are denoted by the MAC address 0000.f800.0000.

Phy-a and Phy-b Status

Phy-a and *Phy-b status* refer to the connection types that a dual FDDI ring can accommodate. The Phy-a and Phy-b status of the physical FDDI A and B ports can be in the following states:

- **Off**   Indicates that connection management (CMT) is off. If the interface is seen as being up, this could mean that the DISCONNECT command was issued for either port.

- **Tra**   *Trace state* indicates that a problem occurred with a station, resulting in a beacon condition.

- **Brk**   *Break* is the first state that occurs when a physical management (PCM) connection is first started.

- **Con**   *Connect state* indicates that each end of the physical connections have passed initial synchronization.

- **Nxt**   When a MAC local loop is performed, the connection state is shown as Nxt.

- **Sig**   *Signal* is the next state and occurs when a bit is ready to be transmitted.

- **Join**   *Join* is the first of the last three states in establishing communication with a physical neighbor.

- **Vfy**   *Verify state* ensures that synchronization is complete before the neighbor becomes active.

- **Act**   This final state indicates that communication has been established with the neighbor.

Upstream and Downstream Neighbors

In an FDDI ring, each station has an upstream and a downstream neighbor. These neighbors are adjacent to the station. The MAC address of the neighbors, if known, is displayed in the output of the SHOW INTERFACES FDDI command. Neighbor states can be one of the following, and the state of each neighbor is shown in the "neighbor is …" field of the command output:

- **A**   Indicates that the neighbor is a Phy-A type DAS or concentrator that attaches to primary Ring In and secondary Ring Out.

- **B**   Indicates that the neighbor is a Phy-B type DAS or concentrator that attaches to primary Ring Out and secondary Ring In.

- **S**   Neighbor is a single-attached station (SAS).

- **M**   Neighbor is a Phy-M type concentrator that serves as master to an adjacent station.

- **Unk**   The router has not completed the CMT process and therefore doesn't know its neighbor.

Ring Operational Status

The ring operational status field shows you the total time in hours, minutes and seconds that has elapsed since the ring has been operational.

The SHOW INTERFACES ATM Command

The SHOW INTERFACES ATM command displays the status and interface details of ATM interfaces on the router. The module can have multiple subinterfaces, all of which have their very own individual thresholds of information. Each interface can have separate IP addresses but is still seen as part of one physical module. When you apply the SHOW INTERFACES ATM0/0/0 command, you are viewing information on an entire ATM module or port adapter residing on a Versatile Interface Processor (VIP) card or a module on that router.

The output from the SHOW INTERFACES ATM command is:

```
ROUTER_A# show interface atm10/0/0
ATM10/0/0 is up, line protocol is up
  Hardware is cyBus ENHANCED ATM PA
  MTU 4470 bytes, sub MTU 4470, BW 33920 Kbit, DLY 200 usec, rely 255/255, load 1/255
  Encapsulation ATM, loopback not set, keepalive set (10 sec)
  Encapsulation(s): AAL5 AAL3/4
  4096 maximum active VCs, 2 current VCCs
  VC idle disconnect time: 300 seconds
  Last input never, output 00:00:00, output hang never
  Last clearing of "show interface" counters 03:55:08
  Queueing strategy: fifo
  Output queue 0/40, 0 drops; input queue 0/75, 338 drops
  30 second input rate 4064000 bits/sec, 337 packets/sec
  30 second output rate 0 bits/sec, 1 packets/sec
     3496889 packets input, 979428910 bytes, 0 no buffer
     Received 0 broadcasts, 0 runts, 0 giants
     0 input errors, 0 CRC, 0 frame, 0 overrun, 0 ignored, 0 abort
```

```
9243 packets output, 641692 bytes, 0 underruns
0 output errors, 0 collisions, 0 interface resets
0 output buffers copied, 0 interrupts, 0 failures
```

In monitoring the ATM interface, highlight and observe the following specific areas in the listing:

■ Queuing drops are always a concern and often lead to poor service quality.

■ ATM input errors can occur due to AAL5 trailer CRC errors via dropped cells in the ATM network. This problem is known as *packet shredding*. The VC parameters should be adjusted to better shape the ATM VC contract.

Use the SHOW INTERFACES ATM command to obtain specific information for the following considerations:

■ Verifying framing encapsulation, whether PLCP or direct mapping

■ Verifying whether the clock source is being obtained internally or from the line

■ Verifying E3/DS3 scrambling

■ Viewing the packet loss

To identify observable problems on a specific interface, you can start by checking to see whether or not the interface is discarding packets or the interface is able to hold data sent to the input queue. You can check the number of drops in either the Output queue or the Input queue to see if the buffers are becoming overloaded. If you discover increasing drops, after clearing the interface counters, you can proceed to increase the hold queue of both the Output and Input queues.

You can also lessen the impact on input drops on an interface by reducing the input queue size, using the HOLD-QUEUE IN interface configuration command, to force input drops to become output drops. Output drops have less impact than input drops on the performance of the router.

Identifying common problems that might appear in a SHOW INTERFACE output is also the number of increasing CRC errors on a line. To accurately identify this number, you can repeatedly apply the SHOW INTERFACE ATM command over an interval period and observe the produced output.

TX and RX Buffers

A *buffer* is a storage area dedicated to handling data while it is in transit. Buffers are used to receive and store sporadic deliveries of data bursts usually received from faster devices.

Transmit (TX) buffers represent the storage area or queue for sending information out through a particular interface or backplane. A router can perform switching between the interface backplanes on routers that support fast switching and have buffers to send traffic in and out of various interfaces.

The TX buffer as related to ATM is used to indicate the maximum number of buffers that are available on the router for packet fragmentation. As you already know, ATM uses a fixed cell size of 53 bytes for sending and receiving data. All packets that are received by the ATM interface must be fragmented to the correct size before they can be sent. The TX buffer specifies how many packet fragmentations the ATM interface can process concurrently. The default value is 256, but it can go from 0 to 512.

Similarly, the *receive (RX) buffer* tells you the number of packet reassemblies that can take place concurrently. This value also has a default of 256.

Virtual Channels/Circuits and User-to-Network Interface

A virtual channel or circuit (VD) is derived from a virtual path. VCs are used to further divide each virtual path. A *virtual circuit* is a circuit or path between points in a network that appears to be a discrete, physical path but is actually a managed pool of circuits from a specific virtual path.

The term *User-to-Network Interface (UNI)* defines communication between ATM end stations (such as workstations and routers) and ATM switches in private ATM networks. A UNI is associated with a specific PVC to the ATM switch. Inside the ATM switch network exists an NNI architecture, defined as network-to-network peering, inside which exists a specific smart permanent virtual circuit (SPVC). SPVCs are run between switches inside an ATM network to find the fastest path within the network to route traffic going to and coming from PVC connections.

To view all the ATM VCs configured on the router, use the SHOW ATM VC command:

```
ROUTER_A# show atm vc
                                  AAL /          Peak  Avg.  Burst
   Interface    VCD   VPI   VCI Type  Encapsulation Kbps  Kbps  Cells Status
   ATM2/0.32     32     0    32  PVC   AAL5-SNAP     2000  2000    96 ACTIVE
```

```
ATM2/0.33        33     0    33   PVC   AAL5-SNAP        2000   2000    96 ACTIVE
ATM10/0/0.36     30     0    36   PVC   AAL5-SNAP         800    400    10 ACTIVE
ATM10/0/0.37     31     0    37   PVC   AAL5-SNAP         800    400    10 ACTIVE
```

When configuring multiple VCs on a Cisco router, it is important to get a snapshot view of all VCs in order to verify the following:

■ VCD is used for local VCC identification on the router

■ VPI/VCI

■ AAL5 encapsulation method as AAL5snap, AAL5nlpid, or AAL5mux

■ Peak, sustained, and burst rates

■ Interface is currently active

To look at an individual VC, display the information relevant to its VCD, as shown here:

```
ROUTER_A# show atm vc 31
ATM10/0/0.37: VCD: 31, VPI: 0, VCI: 37, etype:0x0, AAL5 - LLC/SNAP, Flags: 0x30
PeakRate: 800, Average Rate: 400, Burst Cells: 10, VCmode: 0x0
OAM DISABLED, InARP DISABLED
InPkts: 1776004, OutPkts: 3936, InBytes: 2671969328, OutBytes: 259230
InPRoc: 4395, OutPRoc: 23, Broadcasts: 3797
InFast: 0, OutFast: 0, InAS: 1771609, OutAS: 116
InPktDrops: 0, OutPktDrops: 0
CrcErrors: 0, SarTimeOuts: 0, OverSizedSDUs: 0
OAM F5 cells sent: 0, OAM cells received: 0
Status: ACTIVE
```

When using the SHOW ATM VC command to verify statistics and status for a particular VCC, use the output for the following checks:

■ Verifying that the packet counters are increasing

■ Looking at the packet drops

■ Looking at the CRC errors

■ Verifying whether OAM cells (if enabled) are being sent and received

CERTIFICATION OBJECTIVE 4.05

Cisco Discovery Protocol

Cisco Discovery Protocol, or CDP, is a Cisco proprietary data link protocol that is available only on Cisco devices. The function of CDP is to enable Cisco devices to discover directly connected neighbors. CDP devices use the multicast MAC address 0100.0ccc.cccc to send messages. CDP is enabled by default on all Cisco devices.

Devices using CDP periodically send messages to the multicast address mentioned previously and in turn listen for status messages from other CDP devices. This enables the devices to keep track of such instances as when an interface goes down.

CDP can also be used for SNMP information. The information sent between CDP devices includes IP and MAC addresses, device capabilities, versions of IOS in use, the platform type, and the ports used between directly connected neighbors.

CDP, currently in Version 2, provides a number of enhancements over the previous version, including new logging options as well as new output statistics that are generated by the SHOW CDP command.

The SHOW CDP NEIGHBORS Command

Directly connected neighbors that are Cisco devices and that also have the CDP protocol enabled can be shown using the SHOW CDP NEIGHBORS command. A sample output is provided here:

```
ROUTER_A>sh cdp nei
-------------------
Capability Codes: R - Router, T - Trans Bridge, B - Source Route Bridge
                  S - Switch, H - Host, I - IGMP, r - Repeater
Device ID      Local Intrfce    Holdtme   Capability  Platform  Port ID
Router_B       Ser 0/0.1        156          T         2610      Ser 0/0.1
Router_C       Ser 0/0.2        159          R         2610      Ser 0/0.2
```

In this listing, there are two directly connected neighbors, Router_B and Router_C. Router_B is a transparent bridge; Router_C is a router. The local interfaces are subinterfaces of the serial 0 interface, meaning that these devices are most likely on a Frame Relay network.

CDP is a great tool to use to verify that the Physical Layer is operational. If you see CDP neighbors, then there is no question about the Physical Layer. Unfortunately, the opposite statement is not true. If you do not see neighbors, it is not necessarily the Physical Layer's fault. CDP could have been disabled on the equipment.

The SHOW CDP NEIGHBORS command does displays no Layer 3 information about its directly connected neighbors. This information is obtained using the SHOW CDP NEIGHBORS DETAIL command. The output from the latter command is listed here:

```
ROUTER_A> show cdp nei det
-------------------------
Device ID: ROUTER_B
Entry address(es):
  IP address: 192.10.10.3
Platform: cisco 2610,  Capabilities: Trans-Bridge
Interface: Serial0/0.1,  Port ID (outgoing port): Serial0/0.1
Holdtime : 179 sec
Version :
Cisco Internetwork Operating System Software
IOS (tm) C2600 Software (C2600-I-M), Version 12.0(5)T1,  RELEASE SOFTWARE
(fc1)
Copyright (c) 1986-1999 by cisco Systems, Inc.
Compiled Tue 17-Aug-99 13:57 by cmong
advertisement version: 2
```

In this listing, the CDP neighbor has an IP address of 192.10.10.3, is a transparent bridge (not a router), and is running the 12.0(5) T1 version of the IOS. The holdtime of CDP advertisements is at the default of 179 seconds.

CERTIFICATION OBJECTIVE 4.06

Data-Link Layer Exercises

The Data-Link Layer is commonly referred to as Layer 2. Protocols such as FDDI, HDLC, and PPP are found at this layer. Data link problems are usually the result of misconfigured equipment, the ever-present Physical Layer problems, and—in the case of WAN links—problems with the provider's equipment or network.

ARP is responsible for resolving Layer 3 addresses or IP addresses to Layer 2 MAC or hardware addresses. As a result, ARP has often been considered a protocol that exists between Layer 2 and Layer 3 because it does work in both layers. Reverse ARP, or RARP, is a subprotocol of ARP. RARP is responsible for resolving MAC addresses to IP addresses.

Various Data-Link Sniffer Traces

Protocol analyzers can be invaluable tools in resolving troublesome networking problems. Sometimes faulty NICs can cause all sorts of troublesome issues, such as an inexplicably high rate of collisions, that can be really difficult to troubleshoot. A protocol analyzer can help you pinpoint a station which is sending frames out at a very high rate when there is no reason for it to be doing so. Protocol analyzers can also help you determine, which protocol or protocols are responsible for the highest utilization of your LAN. This could possibly result in redesigning your network architecture in terms of protocols to achieve more efficient utilization of bandwidth.

Examining the Contents of a CDP Packet Using Microsoft Network Monitor

CDP messages are multicast to the MAC address of 01000CCCCCCC. Cisco devices are part of this multicast group, and they receive these messages. The packet capture that follows is the detail from a CDP packet that has been sent to the CDP multicast MAC address.

From the information presented in the capture window shown in Figure 4-2, the following points are apparent:

■ The source MAC address of this CDP packet was 00503EF8EB80.

■ The destination MAC address was the multicast address of 01000CCCCCCC.

■ The CDP packet was an Ethernet 802.3 frame with a length of 324 bytes.

■ The length of the actual data was 310 bytes, so the header information in the frame was 14 bytes.

■ The DSAP and SSAP fields have a value of 0xAA, indicating that a SNAP header is also present in the frame. The SNAP header can either provide you with a length value or a protocol identifier. If the SNAP Etype (Ethertype) is a value greater than 0x05DC, then the Ethertype value will represent a protocol identifier. If the value is less than 0x05DC, the value represents the length of the packet. IP for example is represented by the Ethertype value of 0x0800.

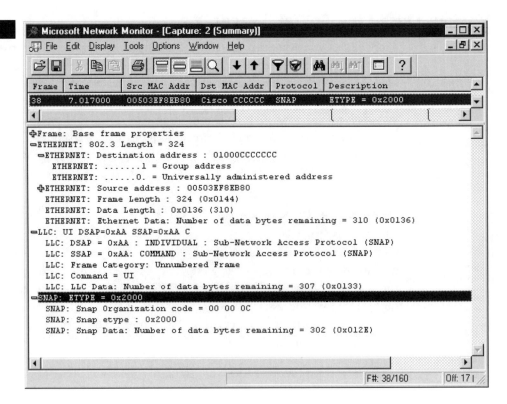

FIGURE 4-2

A CDP packet decoded in Network Monitor

CERTIFICATION SUMMARY

Cisco provides a feature-rich command set for troubleshooting LAN and WAN interfaces. Fluency with these commands and the ability to quickly scan through the displayed results are extremely important skills when you're troubleshooting real network events.

Interface signaling, packet loss, and errors are all indications of a misconfigured or overutilized network. It is important to detect these problems quickly. Although the exam does not specifically test for CPU or memory problems, these issues come up every day. When you're adding new features, expanding routing, or increasing utilization, these enhancements all begin to consume more of the routers' resources and must be continually monitored for performance.

The SHOW INTERFACES commands, along with some of the other tools mentioned in this chapter, will prove extremely useful to you when you are troubleshooting interface and traffic problems. Time after time, these commands can provide more than adequate information for diagnosing many common problems and issues occurring with your interface, CPU, memory, and routing.

✓ TWO-MINUTE DRILL

Here are some of the key points from each certification objective in Chapter 4.

Understanding Data Link Troubleshooting Targets

❑ Cisco routers have either LAN or WAN interfaces.

❑ Ethernet, FDDI, and Token Ring are common types of LAN interfaces.

Troubleshooting Physical and Data Link Characteristics

❑ Protocol analyzers can provide detailed information on Layer 2 and Layer 3 traffic.

❑ Cable testers are indispensable in identifying defective cables.

Clearing the Interface Counters

❑ Clearing the interface counters is useful when you are establishing a baseline for your network.

❑ The command used to clear the interface counters is: **clear counters <interface type> <interface number>.**

Troubleshooting Commands

❑ The **SHOW INTERFACES** command displays physical and data link the status of all interfaces on the router.

❑ Interface counters can be seen in the output of this command.

❑ The SHOW INTERFACES ETHERNET command is used to display the status of an Ethernet interface on the router.

❑ An interface that has been disabled manually by the shutdown command is listed as being administratively down.

❑ The SHOW INTERFACES TOKENRING command is used to view the status of Token Ring interfaces on the router.

❑ The Token Ring collisions field should always be zero.

❑ The SHOW INTERFACES FDDI command is used to display the status of FDDI interfaces in the router and can indicate the current status of the FDDI ring.

❑ The SHOW INTERFACES ATM command allows you to see the number of VCs configured as well as the configuration information and status of ATM interfaces on the router.

Cisco Discovery Protocol

❑ CDP is a Cisco proprietary data link protocol that is used to enable Cisco devices to discover directly connected neighbors.

❑ The SHOW CDP NEIGHBORS DETAIL command is used to display detailed information on directly connected neighbors.

Data-Link Layer Exercises

❑ The MAC multicast address that CDP uses is 01000CCCCCCC.

❑ The Data-Link Layer is commonly referred to as Layer 2. Protocols such as FDDI, HDLC, and PPP are found at this layer.

SELF TEST

The following questions will help you measure your understanding of the material presented in this chapter. Read all of the choices carefully because there might be more than one correct answer. Choose all correct answers for each question.

Understanding Data Link Troubleshooting Targets

1. Which of the following tools is used for finding cable breaks in a line?

    A. Time-domain reflectometer (TDR)

    B. Protocol analyzer

    C. Microsoft Network Monitor

    D. CiscoWorks 2000

2. What tool can be used to test physical connectivity in a network?

    A. Protocol analyzer

    B. CiscoWorks 2000

    C. Digital multimeter

    D. Sniffer

3. You are having problems with your network and want to view the frames sent out by router. What device can be used to display Layer 3 information on your network?

    A. Protocol analyzer

    B. Cable tester

    C. CiscoWorks

    D. CLEAR COUNTERS command

Troubleshooting Physical and Data Link Characteristics

4. PPP is a point-to-point protocol. On what interface would it be used?

    A. FDDI

    B. Ethernet

    C. Serial

    D. Token Ring

5. Which encapsulation method is usually found in an Ethernet interface?

A. Frame Relay

B. ARPA

C. FDDI

D. PPP

6. Which are the following is an example of token-passing network?

A. Token Ring and FDDI

B. Token Ring and Ethernet

C. Token Ring and AppleTalk

D. Token Ring and IEEE 802.3

Clearing the Interface Counters

7. What happens when the receive buffers of the destination interface of a router are filled to capacity?

A. The packets are dropped.

B. Nothing happens.

C. The router is rebooted.

D. The router crashes.

Troubleshooting Commands

8. The following is a result of a SHOW command. Which of the following command(s) would result in this output? Choose all that apply.

```
Ethernet 0 is up, line protocol is up
Hardware is MCI Ethernet, address is aa00.0400.0134 (via
000.0c00.4369)
Internet address is 131.108.1.1, subnet mask is 255.255.255.0
MTU 1500 bytes, BW 10000 Kbit, DLY 1000 usec, rely 255/255, load /255
```

A. SHOW CONTROLLERS ETHERNET 0

B. SHOW INTERFACES

C. SHOW INTERFACES ETHERNET 0

D. SHOW INT CONTROLLERS

9. Which of the following is not an example of a LAN interface?

    A. Ethernet

    B. Token Ring

    C. FDDI

    D. Serial

10. You have found out that since an upgrade of your router's IOS, the link to a remote office has not been reestablished. You perform a SHOW INTERFACES command on the router, and it displays the following:

    ```
    Serial0 is administratively down, line protocol is down
    ```

    How would you fix this problem?

    A. The router has to be reconfigured because the IOS upgrade wiped the old configuration clean.

    B. Do a SHUTDOWN command on the serial interface.

    C. Check the encapsulation type and reboot the router.

    D. Do a NO SHUTDOWN command on the serial0 interface.

11. A network administrator performs a SHOW INTERFACE ETHERNET0, and the first line shows an output of the following:

    ```
    Ethernet0 is administratively down, line protocol is down
    ```

    What is the most likely cause of the problem?

    A. The LAN is experiencing a broadcast storm.

    B. The cable is cut somewhere on the network.

    C. A network administrator disabled the interface.

    D. The IP address assigned to the interface is incorrect.

12. A SHOW INTERFACE ETHERNET0 command was performed on a Cisco router, and the following results were displayed. What is the hardware address of the router?

    ```
    Ethernet0/0 is up, line protocol is up
    Hardware is AmdP2, address is 0050.3ef8.eb80 (bia 0050.3ef8.eb80)
      Internet address is 192.10.10.3/24
      MTU 1500 bytes, BW 10000 Kbit, DLY 1000 usec,
        reliability 255/255, txload 1/255, rxload 1/255
      Encapsulation ARPA, loopback not set
    ```

```
Keepalive set (10 sec)
ARP type: ARPA, ARP Timeout 04:00:00
Last input 00:00:00, output 00:00:00, output hang never
Last clearing of "show interface" counters 1d06h
```

A. 143.10.21.1

B. 255.255.255.0

C. Aa00.0400.0127

D. 0050.3ef8.eb80

13. A previously working router, which is used to connect your network to the Internet, appears to have a problem. You log on to your router and the first line displays the following:

```
Ethernet0 is down, line protocol is down
```

What would a possible cause of this problem?

A. An administrator has taken down the interface.

B. There is Physical Layer problem such as a cable cut.

C. The router was not rebooted correctly.

D. None of the above.

14. From the output of a SHOW INTERFACES TOKENRING command, you notice the following line:

```
Phy-B state is active, neighbor is unk, cmt signal bits 20C/008, status
ILS
```

What does this tell you about the state of the neighbor?

A. The neighbor has a hostname of *unk*.

B. The neighbor is not active.

C. This line does not provide enough information. The neighbor is unknown.

D. A status of *unk* means that the neighbor is currently unknown.

15. Which of the following four specifications accurately define FDDI?

A. MAC, PHY, PMD, SMT

B. PMD, PAS, MAC, SMT

C. MAC, PAI, PAHY, SMT

D. MAC, PHY, PMC, SMG

16. You are performing a baseline of your FDDI network. You have logged in to the router and performed a SHOW INTERFACES FDDI command. The following line is part of the output:

```
ECM is in, CFM is c_wrap_b, rmt is ring_op
```

What does this mean, and does it indicate a problem?

A. This is a normal state of an FDDI interface but ring management is not working properly.

B. The FDDI ring is experiencing problems.

C. Nothing is wrong with the interface, and it is functioning properly.

D. A station has failed, causing the ring management process to wrap around the failed station and keep the network operational.

17. True or false: the SHOW INTERFACES ATM command displays information on the number of VCs configured on the interface.

A. True

B. False

Cisco Discovery Protocol

18. CDP is a data link protocol that runs on all _____ devices.

A. Network hardware

B. Network

C. Cisco

D. Routing

19. You are troubleshooting a network and want to see all the directly connected neighbors on a router. What command will you use?

A. SHOW ATTACHED DEVICES

B. SHOW CDP NEIGHBORS

C. SHOW NEIGHBORS

D. SHOW NEIGHBORS CDP

Data-Link Layer Exercises

20. If the Physical Layer is down on a Cisco router, could the Data-Link Layer be listed in an Up state?

    A. Yes. The Data-Link Layer is not dependent on the Physical Layer.

    B. No. The Data-Link Layer depends on the Physical Layer.

    C. The Physical Layer depends on the Data-Link Layer.

    D. The LAN interface of the router must be connected to a switch or hub in order to bring up the Physical Layer.

LAB QUESTION

As a network support consultant, you have been asked to verify the IOS versions of the Cisco routers on an IP network and obtain the configuration of each router in preparation for possible upgrades. You do not currently have a listing of any of the IP addresses of the routers. What steps would you take to get, or how would you go about getting, this information?

SELF TEST ANSWERS

Understanding Data Link Troubleshooting Targets

1. ☑ **A.** A TDR can find cable breaks in a line by sending a signal throughout the cable.
   ☒ **B** and **C** are incorrect because protocol analyzers display Layer 2 and up information on a network. **D** is incorrect because a network monitoring device cannot find cable breaks in a line.

2. ☑ **C.** A digital multimeter is used to test physical connectivity.
   ☒ **A** is incorrect because a protocol analyzer cannot test the Physical Layer. **B** is incorrect because CiscoWorks is a network monitoring application and is incapable of testing physical connectivity. **D** is incorrect because Sniffer is a protocol analyzer.

3. ☑ **A** is correct because a protocol analyzer is used to analyze communication protocols by examining Layer 2 and higher information.
   ☒ **B** is incorrect because a cable tester is used to test physical connectivity. **C** is incorrect because CiscoWorks is a network monitoring application and cannot analyze packets for Layer 3 information. **D** is incorrect because clearing the counters merely resets the statistics on an interface.

Troubleshooting Physical and Data Link Characteristics

4. ☑ **C.** PPP can be used to encapsulate data over serial interfaces.
   ☒ **A, B,** and **D** are incorrect because all are types of LAN technology.

5. ☑ **B.** ARPA is the correct encapsulation type for Ethernet.
   ☒ **A** and **D** are incorrect because Frame Relay and PPP are both WAN encapsulations. **C** is incorrect because FDDI is a type of LAN technology and is not an encapsulation method.

6. ☑ **A.** Token Ring and FDDI both use tokens to give stations access to the transmission medium.
   ☒ **B, C,** and **D** are incorrect because Ethernet, AppleTalk, and IEEE 802.3 are not token passing networks.

Clearing the Interface Counters

7. ☑ **A.** When the buffers are filled, the router drops any additional packets until buffer space is freed up.
   ☒ **B, C,** and **D** are all incorrect because none of these events is the result of full buffers.

Troubleshooting Commands

8. ☑ **B** and **C**. Both SHOW INTERFACES and SHOW INTERFACES ETHERNET 0 could result in the output given.

☒ **A** is incorrect because SHOW CONTROLLERS ETHERNET 0 would not result in the give display. **D** is incorrect because SHOW INT CONTROLLERS is not a valid IOS command.

9. ☑ **D**. Serial interfaces are exclusively used for WAN connections.

☒ **A, B,** and **C** are incorrect because Ethernet, Token Ring, and serial are all types of LAN interfaces that can be present on a Cisco router.

10. ☑ **D**. Do a NO SHUTDOWN command on the serial0 interface. An interface that is showing as administratively down has been disabled by the SHUTDOWN command. Performing a NO SHUTDOWN should bring the interface online.

☒ **A** is incorrect because IOS upgrades do not wipe out the existing configuration of the router. **B** is incorrect because the interface has already been disabled by the SHUTDOWN command. **C** is incorrect because the encapsulation type has nothing to do with an interface being administratively down.

11. ☑ **C**. A network administrator disabled the interface. "Ethernet 0 is administratively down" means that it was taken down by an administrator with a SHUTDOWN command.

☒ **A** is incorrect because a broadcast storm results in increased collisions, not a disabled interface. **B** is incorrect because it has no bearing on the question. **D** is incorrect because an incorrect IP address will not result in an administratively disabled interface.

12. ☑ **D**. 0050.3ef8.eb80 is correct because it matches the hardware address given in the second line of the display.

☒ **A** and **B** are incorrect because they represent Layer 3 information. **C** is incorrect because it is not the MAC address shown in the display.

13. ☑ **B**. There is Physical Layer problem such as a cable cut. This is the most correct answer because an interface showing the output will point to a Physical Layer problem such as cable cut or other hardware problem on the router.

☒ **A** is incorrect because if an administrator took down the interface, the display would say that Ethernet0 is administratively down. **C** is incorrect as well because rebooting the router does not resolve a problem with an interface. **D**, none of the above, is obviously incorrect.

14. ☑ **D**. A status of *unk* means that the neighbor is currently unknown.

☒ **A** is incorrect because *unk* does not refer to a hostname. **B** is incorrect because it is not a conclusion drawn from the listing. **C** is incorrect because the listing provides you with all the information you need to determine the status of the neighbor.

15. ☑ **A.** FDDI can be defined by four specifications: the Media Access Control (MAC), which is responsible for token passing and frame formatting; the Physical Layer Protocol (PHY), which is used to encode data as well as clocking functions to the Physical Layer; the (PMD) Physical Medium Dependent Layer, which entails how bit rates and the Physical Layer control optical components; and SMT, which stands for station management, which ensures that each station is configured to the standards that are specific to FDDI.
☒ **B, C,** and **D** are all incorrect because they do not represent the four FDDI specifications.

16. ☑ **C.** Nothing is wrong with the interface, and it is functioning properly. "The ECM is IN state" means that the router has been inserted correctly into the ring. The CFM state, c_wrap_b, means that data is being received and transmitted as normal on Phy-B. The RMT state is ring_op, which means that the ring is operational.
☒ **A** is incorrect because ring management is working properly. **B** is incorrect because this line from the output does not indicate that there is a problem. **D** is incorrect because, given the output, there are no indications that a station has failed.

17. ☑ **A.** The output from this command tells you the number of VCs that have been configured on the interface.
☒ **B** is incorrect because this command does in fact show the number of VCs configured.

Cisco Discovery Protocol

18. ☑ **C.** CDP is a Cisco proprietary protocol that runs on all Cisco devices.
☒ **A** is incorrect because CDP doesn't run on all network hardware, only on Cisco devices. **B** and **D** include devices that are not made by Cisco Systems, so they are also incorrect.

19. ☑ **B.** The SHOW CDP NEIGHBORS command displays all directly connected CDP devices.
☒ **A, C,** and **D** are all incorrect because SHOW ATTACHED DEVICES, SHOW NEIGHBORS, and SHOW NEIGHBORS CDP are not valid IOS commands.

Data-Link Layer Exercises

20. ☑ **B.** The Data-Link Layer depends on the Physical Layer being fully operational.
☒ **A** is incorrect because the Data-Link Layer is dependent on the Physical Layer. **C** is incorrect because the Physical Layer does not depend on the Data-Link Layer in order to initialize successfully. **D**, though correct as a fact by itself, is not applicable to the question.

LAB ANSWER

You have the following options when attempting to obtain the required information. You could:

1. Visit every router in the network and get the information.

2. Telnet to all the routers and obtain the required information.

3. Use the SHOW VERSION command to get this information.

4. Use the SHOW CDP NEIGHBORS DETAIL command to obtain a list of all directly connected neighbors. From the information obtained, Telnet to each successive router in turn and perform the same command to get a listing of each router's directly connected neighbors. Use this information to perform additional SHOW commands on each router.

Option 1 is not feasible because, even though it could provide you with the information, it would be extremely time consuming.

Option 2 would also provide you with the information, but you'd need IP addresses in order to Telnet. Since you don't have this information, you cannot Telnet in to the routers, so Option 2 has to be ruled out.

Option 3 would also provide you with the information, but you can only perform a SHOW version if you're at the router console or if you've Telnetted in to the router. Since neither of these methods is feasible given your current situation, Option 3 would not work for you.

Option 4 would give you the required information. Using the SHOW CDP NEIGHBORS DETAIL command on the closest available router console will provide you with enough information to discover all routers on the network. Because each router will display only information on directly connected neighbors, you will have to Telnet to each discovered router in turn and find out what neighbors they are connected to.

You would obtain the IP addresses to Telnet to the additional routers from the output of the SHOW CDP NEIGHBORS DETAIL command. You would perform the SHOW RUNNING-CONFIG command to get a listing of the configuration of each router. Alternatively and more effectively, you could also set up a TFTP server and use the COPY RUN TFTP command to send the configuration of each router to this machine.

You have now been able to not only gather the required information but also create a comprehensive map of the entire network.

CISCO® CERTIFIED NETWORK PROFESSIONAL

5

Applying Cisco Troubleshooting Tools

CERTIFICATION OBJECTIVES

I n troubleshooting a network problem, using the correct tool can mean the difference between a 10-minute fix and days of digging. Often, the correct tool pinpoints the problem in seconds; the only trick is in selecting that tool. The Cisco IOS provides a wide variety of monitoring and troubleshooting tools—so wide that sometimes the variety can be overwhelming. This chapter discusses these tools at length, with emphasis on learning to understand when to use which one.

First, the IOS SHOW and DEBUG commands are discussed and some of the more common commands examined in detail. Next, we cover the operation of the router. We examine its decision-making processes and its various switching processes as well as a trace of a packet path through a router. Then we study the interface buffers and RAM, including the various counters associated with them. Finally, we look at error logging and some of the different captures you might be asked to provide when calling the Cisco Technical Assistance Center (TAC).

CERTIFICATION OBJECTIVE 5.01

Cisco IOS Software Troubleshooting Tools

The most useful tools for troubleshooting Cisco environments are found right at the IOS command line. The following IOS commands should be enough to solve virtually any internetworking problem you come up against:

- **SHOW commands** Cisco provides hundreds of SHOW commands that can help you pinpoint exactly what is happening inside a router. Use SHOW commands to see the status of physical components such as interfaces, controllers, and buffers. You can also use SHOW to see configurations, protocols, and logical devices—even details about neighboring routers. Use SHOW ? to see all the possibilities; you should find just about everything covered.

- **DEBUG commands** DEBUG commands are used to display live protocol processes and state information as they happen. Although these commands can be very resource intensive, DEBUG mode can provide an abundance of information about what is happening inside the router as well as about the traffic passing through it. This information is often vital in solving deep networking issues. DEBUG ? shows you all the DEBUG commands that are available. Beware, though: DEBUG mode can cause as much harm as good. A set of DEBUG safety guidelines is presented later in the chapter.

■ **PING command**   PING is perhaps the most widely used diagnostic and troubleshooting command. It is used to test end-to-end connectivity between two stations on an internetwork. Originally devised for use in IP environments, PING has been extended to IPX, AppleTalk, and DECNET networks. PING basically consists of one station sending an Internet Control Message Protocol (ICMP) echo packet to a remote station. If the remote station successfully receives the packet, it responds with an ICMP echo-reply packet. When the originating station receives this response, the PING is said to be successful. Since PING tests end-to-end internetwork connectivity, it is considered an OSI Layer 3 test. A successful PING usually implies that OSI Layers 1, 2 and 3 are all functional. That is why PING is so useful; it only takes seconds and can quickly assess Layer 3 status.

■ **TRACEROUTE command**   Used in IP networks, TRACEROUTE tracks a packet's path as it travels from its source to its destination. Its exact mechanics are covered later, but suffice it to say that TRACEROUTE employs a clever use of the time to live (TTL) field in an IP packet to capture every Layer 3 hop it hits during its route.

exam
ⓦatch

Cisco's default IPX PING was developed before Novell developed a ping utility; therefore, the two are incompatible. A Novell server does not respond to a Cisco default IPX PING, and vice versa. However, in IOS Version 10.3, Cisco added a Novell-compliant IPX PING that can be issued to communicate with Novell servers. To switch from the Cisco default IPX PING to the Novell-compliant format, use the IPX PING-DEFAULT NOVELL global configuration command.

EXERCISE 5-1

Assessing the Status of an Ethernet Interface

A client calls you with a router problem. He just plugged an Ethernet cable into the Ethernet0/0 interface of a new 2601 router. However, he does not feel the router is responding to IP traffic. Give some ideas on how each of the following tools could be used to troubleshoot the situation:

■ SHOW commands

■ DEBUG commands

■ PING command

Solution: First, you might suggest he try SHOW INTERFACE E0/0. Suppose the output looked like this:

```
Router4#sh int e0/0
Ethernet0/0 is administratively down, line protocol is down
  Hardware is AmdP2, address is 0030.808a.a620 (bia 0030.808a.a620)
  Internet address is 172.16.0.25/16
  MTU 1500 bytes, BW 10000 Kbit, DLY 1000 usec, rely 255/255, load 1/255
  Encapsulation ARPA, loopback not set, keepalive set (10 sec)
  ARP type: ARPA, ARP Timeout 04:00:00
  Last input 00:01:07, output 00:00:57, output hang never
  Last clearing of "show interface" counters 00:00:05
  Queueing strategy: fifo
  Output queue 0/40, 0 drops; input queue 0/75, 0 drops
  5 minute input rate 0 bits/sec, 0 packets/sec
  5 minute output rate 0 bits/sec, 0 packets/sec
     0 packets input, 0 bytes, 0 no buffer
     Received 0 broadcasts, 0 runts, 0 giants, 0 throttles
     0 input errors, 0 CRC, 0 frame, 0 overrun, 0 ignored, 0 abort
     0 input packets with dribble condition detected
     0 packets output, 0 bytes, 0 underruns
     0 output errors, 0 collisions, 0 interface resets
     0 babbles, 0 late collision, 0 deferred
     0 lost carrier, 0 no carrier
     0 output buffer failures, 0 output buffers swapped out
```

Based on this output, you would tell him that the interface is disabled and suggest he use the NO SHUTDOWN interface configuration command.

If that still does not fix the problem, you might try DEBUG IP PACKET. If this command produces no output, IP packets are not being received by the router. You might suggest that he check the hub or switch to which the router is connected.

CERTIFICATION OBJECTIVE 5.02

Understanding the Output of Diagnostic Commands

Of course, for diagnostic commands to be useful, you must understand their output. This chapter briefly touches on SHOW INTERFACES (although it has been covered thoroughly elsewhere in this book), then moves to PING and TRACEROUTE. More SHOW and DEBUG commands come later in the chapter.

The SHOW INTERFACES Command

As explained in previous chapters, SHOW INTERFACES provides extensive Layer 2 information. Use it to examine interface status, counters, and configuration. The following is the output of SHOW INTERFACES ATM from a model 3600 series router:

```
Router6#sh int atm1
ATM1 is up, line protocol is up
  Hardware is ATM T1
  Internet address is 10.0.9.2/24
  MTU 4470 bytes, sub MTU 4470, BW 3000 Kbit, DLY 20000 usec,
      reliability 255/255, txload 16/255, rxload 36/255
  Encapsulation ATM, loopback not set
  Keepalive not supported
  Encapsulation(s): AAL5
  256 maximum active VCs, 1 current VCCs
  VC idle disconnect time: 300 seconds
  Last input 00:00:00, output 00:00:00, output hang never
  Last clearing of "show interface" counters never
  Input queue: 0/75/0 (size/max/drops); Total output drops: 386
  Queueing strategy: Per VC Queueing
  5 minute input rate 433000 bits/sec, 226 packets/sec
  5 minute output rate 195000 bits/sec, 215 packets/sec
     218889701 packets input, 2614216984 bytes, 0 no buffer
     Received 6365562 broadcasts, 0 runts, 0 giants, 0 throttles
     0 input errors, 444 CRC, 0 frame, 0 overrun, 0 ignored, 0 abort
     176783914 packets output, 4228526076 bytes, 0 underruns
     0 output errors, 0 collisions, 0 interface resets
     0 output buffer failures, 0 output buffers swapped out
```

Cisco keeps the output of its commands very consistent. Observe how similar and easy to understand this output is after mastering SHOW INTERFACES ETHERNET in an earlier chapter.

PING

PING tests end-to-end internetwork connectivity by sending an echo packet to a remote destination and (hopefully) receiving a response. A successful PING looks like this:

```
Router3>ping 10.1.1.1
Type escape sequence to abort.
Sending 5, 100-byte ICMP Echos to 10.1.1.1, timeout is 2 seconds:
!!!!!
Success rate is 100 percent (5/5), round-trip min/avg/max = 4/8/12 ms
By default, a Cisco device sends 5 echo packets.  Each "!" above represents a
successful response.  An unsuccessful ping would be represented by a different
symbol, such as in the following example:
Router3>ping 10.43.1.9
Type escape sequence to abort.
Sending 5, 100-byte ICMP Echos to 10.43.1.9, timeout is 2 seconds:
N.N.N
Success rate is 0 percent (0/5)
```

In the output, *N* represents destination network unreachable; a period (.) represents a timeout. Table 5-1 shows the most common response symbols for IP PINGs.

TABLE 5-1	Symbol	Meaning
Response Symbols for IP PINGs	!	A successful reply was received.
	.	The router timed out while waiting for a reply.
	U	Destination unreachable.
	A	Administratively prohibited (access list).
	N	Destination network unreachable.
	P	Destination protocol unreachable.
	Q	Source quench; destination host was being overwhelmed.

IPX PINGs respond exactly like IP PINGs:

```
Router3#ping ipx 1001.0000.0000.0001
Type escape sequence to abort.
Sending 5, 100-byte IPX Novell Echoes to 2222.0000.0000.0001, timeout 2
seconds:
!!!!!
Success rate is 100 percent (5/5), round-trip min/avg/max = 1/1/1 ms
```

Unsuccessful IPX PINGs, however, use different symbols. The most common ones are shown in Table 5-2.

exam
ⓦatch

Cisco's PING utility operates differently between exec mode and privileged exec mode. PING in privileged exec mode allows many customization options, such as packets sent, size, timeout, and type of service. These options are covered in more detail later in the book.

The TRACEROUTE Command

Cisco's TRACEROUTE utility traces the path a datagram takes across an internetwork. The output of a successful trace looks like this:

```
Router3>trace 10.0.90.12
Type escape sequence to abort.
Tracing the route to 10.0.90.12
  1 10.0.26.1 8 msec 8 msec 4 msec
  2 10.0.56.67 8 msec 8 msec 12 msec
  3 10.0.78.89 288 msec 280 msec 280 msec
  4 10.0.90.12 284 msec 284 msec 288 msec
```

The IP address (or DNS name, if resolved) of each hop along the way is displayed, along with the round-trip time of each packet.

TABLE 5-2	Symbol	Meaning
Response Symbols for IPX PINGs	!	A successful reply was received.
	.	The router timed out while waiting for a reply.
	U	Destination unreachable.
	C	Congestion error.
	?	Unknown packet type.

Unfortunately, TRACEROUTE is not always successful. Even worse, a failed TRACEROUTE does not always imply problems. Due to the way TRACEROUTE "manipulates" the TTL mechanism, some devices do not respond well to it. Therefore, failures are common in stable networks. Here is an example of a bad TRACEROUTE:

```
Router3>trace 10.0.90.12
Type escape sequence to abort.
Tracing the route to 10.0.90.12
  1 10.0.26.1 8 msec 8 msec 4 msec
  2 10.0.56.67 8 msec 8 msec 12 msec
  3 10.0.78.89 276 msec 288 msec 284 msec
  4  *  *  *
  5  *  *  *
(output deleted ...)
 29  *  *  *
 30  *  *  *
```

The asterisk (*) represents a timeout. The TRACE utility uses failure codes similar to those used by the PING utility; the more common ones are shown in Table 5-3.

Also like PING, the privileged exec TRACE command contains many customization options, such as packets sent, minimum and maximum TTL, and port. More details are covered in a later chapter.

TABLE 5-3	Symbol	Meaning
Response Symbols for IP TRACEROUTE	a.b.c.d nmsec	A successful reply was received in n milliseconds.
	*	The router timed out while waiting for a reply.
	U	Destination port unreachable.
	N	Destination network unreachable.
	H	Destination host unreachable.
	P	Destination protocol unreachable.
	Q	Source quench; destination host was being overwhelmed.

FROM THE CLASSROOM

Understanding TRACEROUTE

The TRACEROUTE program is interesting because, unlike other tools offered on the Internet, TRACEROUTE was not originally intended to be there. It actually works by cleverly taking advantage of the TTL mechanism in an IP packet. Recall that the TTL tracks how many hops an IP packet passes. The idea of the TTL is this: you can avoid an endless packet loop by allowing packets to live for only a designated period of hops. To accomplish this, pick an initial TTL, usually 255, and assign it to each packet when it is sent. Each router that passes the packet subtracts one from the TTL. If the TTL reaches 0, the packet is dropped. That way, if a loop occurs, the packet loops for a maximum of approximately 254 hops and is then discarded. The dropping router then sends an ICMP message to the source indicating "Time To Live exceeded in Transit," or ICMP Type 11.

The TRACEROUTE program simply sends a series of packets with set TTL values to the destination. The first has a TTL value of 1, the second has a TTL value of 2, and so on until the destination is reached. The first router responds with an ICMP Type 11 packet, and TRACEROUTE records its source address as the first hop. The second hop does the same, and so on until the complete route is traced.

Most UNIX operating systems and the Cisco IOS use UDP packets; the destination port number is usually somewhere in the 33,000 range. These port numbers do not mean anything in particular, because they are intended to expire anyway. The TRACEROUTE program that comes with Microsoft Windows (TRACERT.EXE) does something a little different, however: it uses ICMP packets instead of UDP. Specifically, it sends ICMP echo requests, or the first half of PING packets. Although the protocol used is not usually important, since it is the side effect that is desired, it might make a difference in certain situations. For example, when a firewall is being used, one type of TRACEROUTE might work while the other does not. If you have a Windows desktop computer, it could be useful to be able to execute UDP-style TRACEROUTE from your router. On the Cisco exam, be prepared to recognize which type of TRACEROUTE is sent by a particular operating system and how TRACEROUTE works in general.

—*Don Dettmore, CCNP, MCSE, CNE*

EXERCISE 5-2

Understanding PING Output

You try to PING a server on a remote network and receive the following results:

```
Router3>ping server6
Type escape sequence to abort.
Sending 5, 100-byte ICMP Echos to 10.22.1.2, timeout is 2 seconds:
U.U.U
Success rate is 0 percent (0/5)
```

What is most likely the problem?

A. The server is down.

B. The server's local router is down.

C. The server's local switch is down.

Solution: The answer is B. The server's local router is down. If the local router is down, a route to its network could still appear in the internetwork, but it would be reported as destination unreachable. Answers A and C would result in timeouts, not destination unreachable.

CERTIFICATION OBJECTIVE 5.03

The Routing Process

To understand the implications of Cisco troubleshooting tools, you must understand exactly what is happening inside the router. The next few sections focus on describing what happens from the time a frame enters a router until it leaves. Some of the explanations are a bit simplified (routers can be very complex), but you should gain an overall understanding of each part of the routing process.

Cisco makes a distinction between routing and switching, although the distinction can often get quite fuzzy. Put simply, *routing* consists of building and maintaining routing tables and determining the best path for a packet to take to get to its destination. *Switching* involves receiving a packet on one interface and moving it to the correct exit interface. We examine routing first.

Routing Protocols

Routing protocols perform the job of building and maintaining the routing table, which is contained in dynamic random access memory (DRAM). After the router boots and initializes its routing protocols, it sends neighboring routers information about its interfaces and networks. It then receives information about its neighbors and builds a routing table consisting of destinations and next hops. Some protocols (such as link-state) go further and build a topological map of the entire network to enhance performance and stability. Although the mechanics of the protocols differ, the basic process of building a table for next-hop determination remains relatively the same. Figure 5-1 exhibits the basic process of building a routing table.

FIGURE 5-1

Building a routing table

Network	Metric	Next Hop
123		
456		
	....	
	....	

Router B — Router A — Router C

Routing Updates — Routing Updates

Network 123 — Network 456

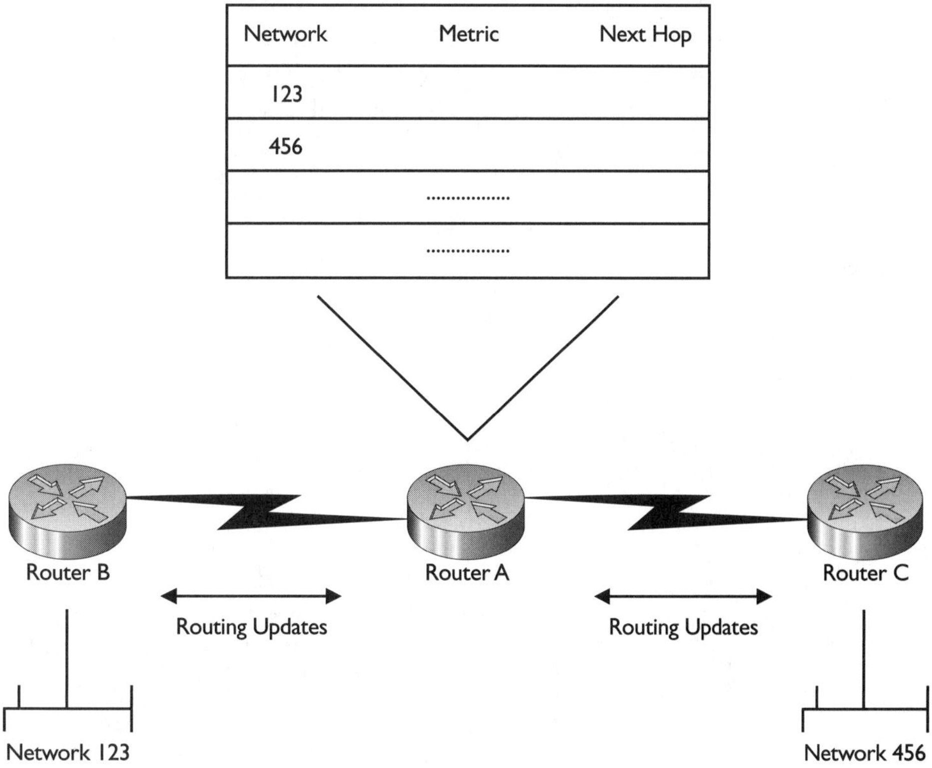

Note that each router builds and maintains its own routing table and can make decisions independent of the state of other routers.

The Route Processor and the Routing Table

The route processor (RP) builds the routing tables as well as the routing updates to be send to neighboring routers (the RP has other responsibilities as well; those are covered soon). Building the routing table can be a processor-intensive task, depending on the path determination mechanism of the routing protocol. For example, RIP uses a simple algorithm for determining the next hop to a destination—the one with the least number of hops. Therefore, RIP is not very processor-intensive. However, link-state protocols or advanced distance-vector protocols such as OSPF or EIGRP use more sophisticated processes and can include factors such as load balancing and failover. These protocols require more overhead. The routing table itself (as well as any topological databases) is stored in DRAM. All these facts are important because cumulatively, they make these components very busy. When switching methods are discussed, the chapter focuses on ways to avoid overburdening some of these central routing components.

An example of an IP routing table follows:

```
CAT6006R15>sh ip route
Codes: C - connected, S - static, I - IGRP, R - RIP, M - mobile, B - BGP
       D - EIGRP, EX - EIGRP external, O - OSPF, IA - OSPF inter area
       N1 - OSPF NSSA external type 1, N2 - OSPF NSSA external type 2
       E1 - OSPF external type 1, E2 - OSPF external type 2, E - EGP
       i - IS-IS, L1 - IS-IS level-1, L2 - IS-IS level-2, ia - IS-IS inter area
       * - candidate default, U - per-user static route, o - ODR
       P - periodic downloaded static route
Gateway of last resort is 10.1.2.3 to network 0.0.0.0
R       10.0.11.0/24 [120/4] via 10.0.2.2, 00:00:07, E20
R       10.0.0.0/24 [120/7] via 10.0.2.2, 00:00:07, E20
R       10.0.15.0/24 [120/6] via 10.1.2.2, 00:00:07, E20
C       10.1.2.23/24 is directly connected, E2
C       10.0.0.1/24 is directly connected, E1
     14.14.0.0/16 is variably subnetted, 4 subnets, 2 masks
D EX    14.14.0.0/16 [170/6026752] via 10.0.0.1, 00:17:44, E1
D EX    14.14.10.0/24 [170/5565952] via 10.1.2.23, 00:17:44, E2
D EX    14.14.8.0/24 [170/5565952] via 10.1.2.23, 00:17:44, E2
D EX    14.14.9.0/24 [170/5565952] via 10.1.2.23, 00:17:44, E2
     192.168.48.0/24 is variably subnetted, 2 subnets, 2 masks
D EX    192.168.48.0/25 [170/41001216] via 10.1.2.23, 00:17:44, E2
```

The table contains the vital information to be discussed: next hop and metric information. This is a very small table, so routing maintenance would be low. However, in large internetworks with hundreds or thousands of routers, routing table maintenance can become a significant burden for the RP.

EXERCISE 5-3

The Routing Process

Based on this chapter, which routing protocol do you think would have the most CPU overhead?

    A. RIP

    B. IGRP

    C. OSPF

    D. Static routing

Solution: The answer is C, OSPF. As discussed, computing the best path and maintaining the adjacency database is a CPU intensive process. Answers A and B are distance-vector protocols—they might be *network* intensive, due to the frequency of routing updates, but they are less CPU intensive. D is the simplest method of routing.

CERTIFICATION OBJECTIVE 5.04

The Switching Process

The switching process handles frames when they enter the router, using the foundation provided by the routing process. In this section, we examine the switching process at its most basic level; later we look at the Cisco bells and whistles.

Basically, switching involves receiving a frame, looking up its destination in the routing table, building a new data link header, and moving the frame it its exit interface or interfaces. Figure 5-2 shows this process in more detail.

FIGURE 5-2

The basic
switching process

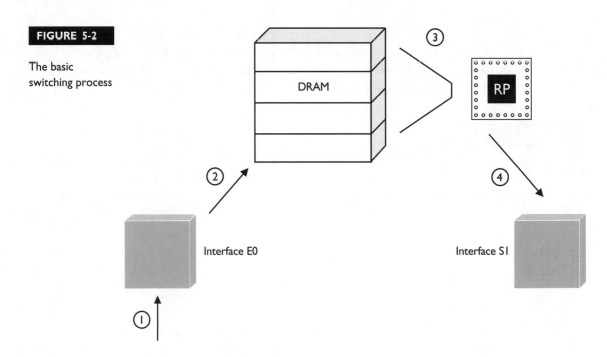

The process follows these steps:

1. When a frame is first received, it is placed in the interface buffer.

2. Next, the frame is copied to main DRAM, where it stays while the RP works on it.

3. The RP processes the packet, then performs the following tasks:

   A. It strips the old Layer 2 header from the packet.

   B. It extracts the Layer 3 destination address and looks it up in the routing table to determine the next hop.

   C. Based on the next hop learned from the routing table, the RP determines the exit interface(s) of the packet.

   D. It determines the Layer 2 address of the next destination (using the specific protocol's mechanism, such as ARP) and builds a new Layer 2 header for the frame. The RP also computes the CRC.

4. When the RP is finished, the frame is copied to the exit interface buffer to be sent out on the network.

The Switching Process

Before some of today's high-speed switching techniques, routers were frequently considered the bottleneck of internetworks. Which of the steps mentioned in this section can require the most time in an IP network?

Solution: In an IP network, the Layer 2 address determination stage—ARP—can take the longest time. In fact, it could take full seconds—an eternity for a router.

Switching Initialization

Unfortunately, the base switching process, called *process switching*, is not very efficient. The RP must perform several operations on every packet. Although useful in some WAN environments, this procedure can quickly become a bottleneck in high-speed LAN environments. So, for the past decade, Cisco has been introducing different technologies to make the routing process quicker. These technologies generally involve offloading some of the RP tasks to dedicated high-speed processors and memory. This section discusses the most widely deployed of these switching methods.

Process Switching

The base switching procedure, process switching, is extremely resource intensive—and therefore slow. Some of the more sophisticated switching processes described in this section can increase the traffic throughput on a router 500–2500 percent (and more). Every year, it seems, Cisco releases a new technology that improves on this even more, further emphasizing the weaknesses of process switching.

Despite its weak performance, process switching must be used at times. Later, this chapter elaborates on these circumstances. For now, know that the command to force a router to exclusively process-switch on an interface is NO *PROTOCOL*

ROUTE-CACHE (the interface configuration command). The *PROTOCOL* keyword tells which protocol you are configuring; different protocols might use different switching mechanisms.

Since process switching is basically the core switching method of a router, it is available on every Cisco model.

Fast Switching

Fast switching is the simplest upgrade from process switching and is available on every model router. It involves the use of a small section of memory to cache recently used next-hop and data link information. Fast switching works like this:

1. A frame comes into a router and is process switched, as described previously. However, during this process, the RP initializes the fast-cache section of memory with the following information from the frame: next hop, exit interface, and a copy of the new Layer 2 header.

2. When the next packet with the same destination address comes in, only the Layer 3 header is copied to DRAM. The RP then simply extracts the Layer 2 header from the fast cache and adds it to the packet. The packet is then copied to the exit interface (according to the fast cache), where the interface processor computes the CRC.

3. For every subsequent frame that arrives, the header is copied to DRAM. The RP then consults the fast cache to see if the destination address has an entry. If it does, the frame is fast switched. If it does not, the entire frame is copied to DRAM, the frame is process switched, and the fast cache is initialized.

Fast switching can significantly increase the performance of a router; a 500–1000 percent packet per second (PPS) increase is not unusual. Fast switching is typically enabled by default, although it varies, depending on the interface or media type. Fast switching can be manually enabled on a per-interface or per-protocol basis with the *PROTOCOL* ROUTE-CACHE interface configuration command. Fast switching is most popular on series 2500, 2600, 3500, and 4500 routers.

exam
Ⓦatch
Fast switching is most effective with connection-oriented protocols such as TCP. The first packet of a conversation is process switched, and the rest are fast switched. This series of packets is referred to as a flow.

Optimum Switching

Optimum switching is very similar to fast switching; it uses a portion of RAM to cache destination addresses and Layer 2 headers. The RP uses this cache as it does in fast switching. However, in optimum switching, the RP uses a more advanced lookup algorithm, making the cache interaction much faster. This results in a significant increase in PPS performance over fast switching.

Optimum switching is available on the route switch processor (RSP), which is the routing engine for the Cisco 7000 and Cisco 7500 series. It is enabled by default for the IP protocol.

Other Switching Methods

Cisco has devised numerous other variations of the fast-switching technique. Typically, they involve dedicated hardware to completely offload the cache-lookup process from the RP or DRAM:

- **Autonomous switching** Available on the older 7000 series routers, autonomous switching locates fast-cache memory on the CiscoBus processor itself—on the switch processor (SP) card. As in fast switching, the first packet of a flow is process switched, and the destination interface and header are cached in this memory. Subsequent packets in the flow are handled directly by the CiscoBus processor; they need never be touched by the RP.

- **Silicon switching** Also available on 7000 series routers, the silicon switching processor (SSP) is an add-on module that performs caching and lookup at high speed, completely independent of the RP. The SSP is about twice as fast as the SP, so the silicon switching process is faster than the autonomous switching process.

- **Distributed switching** Available on the Cisco 7500 series routers, distributed switching typically works hand in hand with optimum switching. It uses a Versatile Interface Processor (VIP) card at the interface level to copy the cache from DRAM and perform optimum switching. Distributed switching gets its name from the fact that the VIP is separate from the RP—and can take care of most of the switching.

- **NetFlow switching** Also available on 7500 series routers, NetFlow switching often works together with distributed switching. The NetFlow process collects the statistics on data flows for accounting and resource utilization purposes. Typically, service providers use this information to bill customers who are charged for usage.

SCENARIO & SOLUTION

Which switching processes cache pre-built Layer 2 headers in main system DRAM?	**Optimum and fast switching**
Which switching method uses a Virtual Interface Processor card?	**Distributed switching**
Which switching process can track resource utilization statistics?	**NetFlow switching**
Which switching method offers the lowest performance levels?	**Process switching**

EXERCISE 5-5

Switching Processes

Which form of switching might be most popular at your ISP?

    A. Process switching

    B. Fast switching

    C. NetFlow switching

Solution: C. NetFlow switching. Since the ISP must bill you for access, they probably use NetFlow to track your usage. Both Answers A and B would be inferior (slow) technologies for a large ISP.

CERTIFICATION OBJECTIVE 5.06

Tracing Packet Flow

Now that we have discussed the various switching methods used by high-end routers, the chapter examines a packet's path as it travels through a Cisco model 7000 router. This router is equipped with a silicon switch processor card and silicon cache with fast switching enabled. The packet is the first of an FTP flow headed to the ATM0 interface. Figure 5-3 illustrates.

FIGURE 5-3   Tracing a packet through a model 7000 router

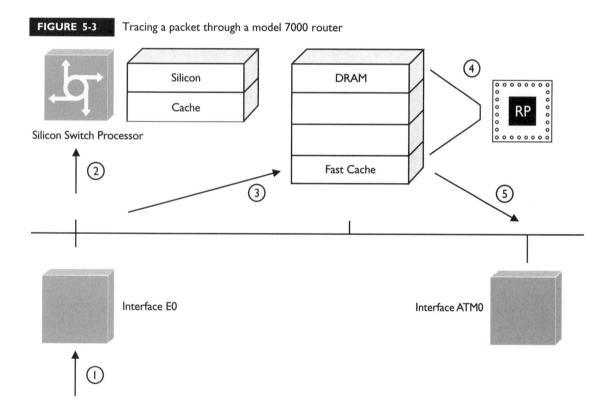

The process is as follows:

1. The frame arrives and is placed in the input buffer of the Ethernet0 interface.

2. When the packet's turn arrives, it is copied across the Cisco extended bus to an SSP buffer. The SSP extracts the destination Layer 3 address and checks the silicon cache for a match. It does not find one.

3. Since neither external cache found an entry, the Layer 3 header is copied to main system DRAM, where the RP checks the fast cache for a matching destination address. Again, since this is the first packet in a flow, no entry is found.

4. Finally, the entire packet is copied to DRAM, the RP does a route table lookup, and the destination address is determined.

5. The RP creates a new Layer 2 header and copies the frame to the exit interface, where it is placed on the wire.

6. The fast and silicon caches are all initialized with the new destination address and Layer 2 header.

7. All subsequent packets in the flow should be switched by the SSP. If they are not, they can be fast switched.

EXERCISE 5-6

Silicon Switching

Why do you think silicon switching would not work on an interface if you applied an access list to that interface?

Solution: Access lists require the CPU to examine every packet and determine if it is permitted or denied. This information would not be found in the silicon switching cache, so it would be useless in this situation.

CERTIFICATION OBJECTIVE 5.07

What the Route Processor Handles Directly

We have discussed a number of switching methods designed to reduce the load on the RP. Usually, they are turned on by default. As we mentioned, the performance of process switching tends to be pitiful compared to that of the other methods. However, numerous types of packets (or situations) require the RP to be hit directly, no matter what. Planning for these situations must go into any network design, purchasing, or troubleshooting decision you make. Here is a brief overview of those situations:

- **DEBUG** In DEBUG mode, the RP must examine every packet that is being debugged. That, combined with the process of writing output, can make DEBUG mode one of the most processor-intensive process you run. Before running DEBUG in a production environment, be absolutely sure you know the consequences and are prepared for the additional load. If you are not sure, call your TAC representatives; they are able to help.

- **Error logging** The RP generates error logs and writes them to output. If sent to a Syslog server, these packets are built by the RP and process switched.

- **SNMP** Like error logging, the RP is usually responsible for building and transmitting SNMP messages. Thus, these are also process switched.

- **Protocol translations** Translations such as terminal translations (such as LAT to Telnet), network address translations (NAT), and translational bridging are all handled by the RP and are process switched.

- **Tunneling** The endpoints of protocol tunneling mechanisms, such as data link switching (DLSw) and serial tunneling (STUN), must process switch the packets.

- **Special queuing** Custom and priority queuing are process switched.

- **Broadcasts** Data-Link Layer broadcasts, such as IP ARP and IPX SAP, must hit the RP. In addition, broadcasts sent by the router itself, such as routing updates and keepalives, are processed switched.

on the
job

Some processes conflict with the fast switching processes and require the switching processes to be turned off entirely! For example, you will experience problems if optimum switching is enabled while you are debugging.

EXERCISE 5-7

Process Switching

Do you think compression would require process switching?

Solution: Yes. The goal of every fast switching technology is to keep the entire packet out of DRAM and keep the CPU workload low. However, for the CPU to compress a packet, the whole packet must be copied into DRAM.

CERTIFICATION OBJECTIVE 5.08

The DEBUG Utility

Sometimes SHOW commands do not tell you everything that is happening within the router; when you troubleshoot, you need more. The DEBUG utility can dig deeper and provide a line-by-line account of what is going on (or not going on). DEBUG commands, which are entered at the privileged exec prompt, show traffic, errors, and processes as they happen on the router. For example, the following is the output of DEBUG RADIUS during an authentication of a user:

```
Router1#debug radius
Radius protocol debugging is on
Router1#
02:06:24: RADIUS: ustruct sharecount=1
02:06:24: RADIUS: added cisco VSA 2 len 4 "tty3"
02:06:24: RADIUS: Initial Transmit tty3 id 2 10.1.242.4:1645, Access-Request, len 90
02:06:24:       Attribute 4 6 0A01F2FE
02:06:24:       Attribute 5 6 00000003
02:06:24:       Attribute 26 12 0000000902067474
02:06:24:       Attribute 61 6 00000005
02:06:24:       Attribute 1 10 64657474
02:06:24:       Attribute 31 12 31302E31
```

```
02:06:24:          Attribute 2 18 A31A5F3B
02:06:24: RADIUS: Received from id 2 10.1.242.4:1645, Access-Accept, len 56
02:06:24:          Attribute 6 6 00000001
02:06:24:          Attribute 25 30 5342522D
02:06:24: RADIUS: saved authorization data for user 8D1BC at 8D374
```

You can see from the preceding output that the router built an access-request packet and sent it to 10.1.242.4 (Line 6). A response was received in Line 15; it appears that the user was successfully authenticated.

exam
ⓌⓐⓉ⓬ⓗ

By default, DEBUG output is written to the console terminal. If you are connected to a router via Telnet, you can write the output to your session with the TERMINAL MONITOR privileged exec command. In addition, writing output to the console is very processor intensive—if you are not using it, turn it off with the NO LOGGING CONSOLE global configuration command. Instead, you can adjust the level of output messages to the console with the LOGGING CONSOLE XXX command; select a level lower than DEBUG.

DEBUG Performance Considerations

Although the DEBUG utility is perhaps the most useful IOS tool, it has a tradeoff: it requires a significant amount of CPU time. Debugging is assigned a high CPU priority, which can cause disruption of normal service. In fact, careless use of DEBUG commands can completely overload a router and cause it to crash. For this reason, Cisco recommends that DEBUG be used only for troubleshooting and never during normal operational monitoring.

During debugging, the CPU must examine every packet it is looking at. This effectively places a router into process-switching mode, regardless of the fast-cache technologies loaded on the router. This mode worsens the impact on router performance and can slow a router considerably.

Due to these performance issues, try to follow this list of guidelines for planning a DEBUG session:

- **Do not use DEBUG ALL** DEBUG ALL enables all possible debugging options. As you can imagine, this command generates tons of output and can bring down any router that experiences a significant amount of traffic. In addition, there is so much output that sifting through all of it is a daunting task.

- **Narrow down your DEBUGs** Be as specific as possible when using DEBUG commands. For example, the command DEBUG IP RIP would generate output like this:

```
Router1#debug ip rip
RIP protocol debugging is on
Router1#
01:30:02: RIP: sending v1 update to 255.255.255.255 via
Ethernet0(10.1.242.254)
01:30:02:     default, metric 2
01:30:02:     network 172.16.0.0, metric 2
01:30:02:     network 192.168.0.0, metric 1
01:30:02:     network 192.168.254.0, metric 3
01:30:02:     network 192.168.1.0, metric 2
01:30:02: RIP: sending v1 update to 255.255.255.255 via Serial0
(192.168.0.2)
01:30:02:     network 10.0.0.0, metric 1
```

As you can see, the output displays the full contents of every RIP packet sent and received by the router. Although it's not a big deal in this example, if the routing table contained a few hundred entries, imagine the output you would be facing. If you only needed to know if an interface was sending RIP updates, you could try DEBUG IP RIP EVENTS to see the RIP transactions as they occurred:

```
Router1#debug ip rip event
RIP event debugging is on
Router1#
01:30:58: RIP: sending v1 update to 255.255.255.255 via Ethernet0
(10.1.242.254)
01:30:58: RIP: Update contains 5 routes
01:30:58: RIP: Update queued
```

As you can see, even if the routing table is much larger, the output is still concise. This presents a common theme among DEBUG commands: the distinction between *packet debugging* and *event debugging*. In general, DEBUG packet commands, such as DEBUG FRAME-RELAY PACKET, produce voluminous output—output for every packet that passes through the router. However, DEBUG event commands, such as DEBUG FRAME-RELAY EVENTS, notifies you only when certain events occur.

- **Use terminal sessions to debug** Debugging to virtual terminal sessions, such as Telnet, requires much less CPU overhead than debugging to the console (debugging to the console requires an interrupt per character). Whenever possible, use TERMINAL MONITOR to send output to the terminal and LOGGING CONSOLE XXX to disable DEBUG messages to the console.

- **Use access lists with DEBUG** You can further limit the packets your DEBUG captures by associating an access list with it. For example, look at the following command:

```
Router5#debug ip packet 5
```

The 5 associates access list 5 with the DEBUG command, restricting it to examine only packets that pass the access list. In other words, only packets that have a source IP address permitted through access list 5 are actually debugged by the RP. All other packets are switched at the higher speeds.

Service Time Stamps

The first part of each line of DEBUG output specifies the time that the event occurred. By default, this is displayed as the amount of time since the router was booted. See the following example:

```
01:18:31: IP: s=192.168.0.2 (local), d=10.1.242.4 (Ethernet0), len 56, sending
```

This was captured one hour, 18 minutes, and 31 seconds after boot.

Unfortunately, this is not always the most meaningful way to present the time. Fortunately, Cisco provides the service time-stamps facility to set exactly how you want the time displayed. In global configuration mode:

```
Router(config)# service timestamps type format
```

- *type* specifies the output to which the command applies—either debug or log.
- *format* allows you to set exactly how you want the time displayed—either *uptime* (default) or *datetime* (GMT). You can further refine *datetime* with options such as *localtime* (local time) and *msec* (add milliseconds).

DEBUG output now looks like this:

```
Jan  2 19:56:42 UTC: %LINEPROTO-5-UPDOWN: Line protocol on
Interface Serial4/0:0.1, changed state to down
```

Debug Restrictions

Do you think there is a difference between the output of a DEBUG command in exec mode and the output of the same command in privileged exec mode?

Solution: Yes. DEBUG is not permitted in normal exec mode, so there would be zero output. Debugging can seriously degrade the performance of a router—hence the need for privileged mode.

CERTIFICATION OBJECTIVE 5.09

Error Message Logging

When network errors occur, you need to know about them. In addition, this information needs to logged and stored somewhere, so it can be retrieved by an administrator. That is the function of the Cisco IOS logging facility. A router can take any error message or informational tidbit and log it to one or more configurable places.

An error message looks like the following:

```
%LINEPROTO-5-UPDOWN: Line protocol on Interface TokenRing0, changed state to down
```

Error messages are always preceded by a % sign, after which they are spilt into four distinct parts:

- **Facility** The first part of the error message tells the *facility* that is being affected. The facility can be hardware, software, protocols, or anything else inside the router. In this case, the line protocol is being reported on.

- **Error level** After the facility, the error level is reported. Error levels are detailed in the next section.

■ **Error code**   After the error level is a code that defines the error being reported. In this case, the UPDOWN code means that an interface or protocol has gone either up or down.

■ **Text description**   Following the error code is a text description that describes the error condition. This description usually contains specific details about protocols, interfaces, and the like. In this case, the line protocol on a Token Ring interface has gone down.

Logging Levels

Cisco devices assign one of eight error levels to each error message. They range from 0 to 7 and are based on the severity of the error condition. Table 5-4 details the error levels.

The following are some examples of error-level conditions:

```
%LINK-3-UPDOWN: Interface Serial2/0, changed state to up
```

Serial 2/0 has come up. Even though this is technically not an error, it is an important event and thus qualifies for level 3.

```
%SYS-4-SNMP_WRITENET: SNMP WriteNet request. Writing current
configuration to 10.1.1.1
```

The router has used SNMP to write information to 10.1.1.1. This is considered a warning.

TABLE 5-4	Level	Keyword	Description
IOS Logging Levels	0	Emergency	System unusable.
	1	Alert	Immediate action required.
	2	Critical	Critical condition.
	3	Error	Error condition.
	4	Warning	Warning condition.
	5	Notification	Normal but significant condition.
	6	Informational	Informational messages.
	7	Debug	Debug output.

```
%SYS-5-RESTART: System restarted
```

The system has been restarted. Note that this is only a notification.

```
%STANDBY-6-STATECHANGE: Standby: 1: Vlan1 state Standby -> Active
```

VLAN 1 has gone from standby mode to active mode. Cisco considers this message only informational. Not every logging method records all eight levels of error message (by default—though this can be modified). The various logging methods are covered in the following section.

Console

By default, error messages (all eight levels) are logged to the system console. However, console logging causes significant overhead—a large number of processor interrupts—and therefore is not always the recommended method. In fact, most organizations access their routers via Telnet, so console logging is not needed.

You can limit console logging in one of two ways: either turn it off or reduce the number of messages sent to it based on severity:

- To turn console logging off, use the NO LOGGING CONSOLE global configuration command.

- To reduce the console output, use the LOGGING CONSOLE *LEVEL* global configuration command. The *LEVEL* keyword corresponds with an error-level keyword; all messages at this specified error level *and lower* are logged to the console. All others are not. Possible keywords are as follows:

```
Router1(config)#logging console ?
  <0-7>          Logging severity level
  alerts         Immediate action needed        (severity=1)
  critical       Critical conditions            (severity=2)
  debugging      Debugging messages             (severity=7)
  emergencies    System is unusable             (severity=0)
  errors         Error conditions               (severity=3)
  guaranteed     Guarantee console messages
  informational  Informational messages         (severity=6)
  notifications  Normal but significant conditions (severity=5)
  warnings       Warning conditions             (severity=4)
  <cr>
```

Remember, the lower the level, the more important the information (in other words, the lower the number associated with the information).

Virtual Terminal

These days, Telnet is the preferred way of monitoring a Cisco router, so sometimes you want error messages directed there. This is particularly true in situations in which you need to see real-time data, as when you are using DEBUG mode. To enable logging to your virtual terminal session, use the TERMINAL MONITOR privileged exec command. Remember that this command turns on logging for only this specific session; if you disconnect and reconnect, you must enable it again.

Virtual terminal logging does not generate nearly the CPU overhead of console logging. However, as with console logging, you might limit the severity of messages sent to the terminal session. Use the LOGGING MONITOR *LEVEL* global configuration command—again, the *LEVEL* keyword specifies all messages of that level and lower are logged.

Buffered

Most of the time you are not looking at the console or terminal session when an error occurs. Therefore, you always want to capture error messages and save them for later examination. The most convenient way of doing this is logging to internal router memory, which is called *logging to a buffer*. Use the LOGGING BUFFERED *SIZE* global configuration command to set up this type of logging. *SIZE* specifies the number of bytes in memory to set aside for the log messages.

Remember the following three points about logging to a buffer:

- The buffer logs in a circular fashion. Once the buffer fills up, new entries overwrite the oldest ones.

- The buffer is in DRAM, so the log entries are lost when the router is powered off or rebooted.

- Logging to a buffer requires the least amount of CPU overhead of all logging methods. However, if you want to limit the severity of the entries, use the LOGGING BUFFERED *LEVEL* global configuration command.

Syslog

Sometimes you want to send log output to a more permanent location than the buffer in DRAM. Cisco also allows you to send to a host running a Syslog daemon or application. Use the LOGGING *IP-ADDRESS* global configuration command to send logs to the specified IP address. The Syslog daemon picks up the logs and store them in the file system. Remember the following notes about logging to a Syslog host:

- Logging to a Syslog server requires very little overhead (second only to buffered logging). However, you can restrict the severity of log messages sent with the LOGGING TRAP *LEVEL* global configuration command.

- You can customize to which process (daemon) on the Syslog server you send the log messages. The default is Syslog, but it can be changed with the LOGGING FACILITY *PROCESS* global configuration command.

- You can send log messages to multiple Syslog servers—just use the LOGGING *IPADDRESS* command for every server.

The **SHOW LOGGING** Command

The SHOW LOGGING exec command displays two sets of information. First, it shows the current logging setup—levels of each type of logging enabled and IP addresses of Syslog servers. Next, it shows the contents of the log buffer, if one is configured. The following is an example of SHOW LOGGING from a Cisco 3640 router:

```
R3640>sh log
Syslog logging: enabled (0 messages dropped, 0 flushes, 0 overruns)
    Console logging: level debugging, 473 messages logged
    Monitor logging: level debugging, 0 messages logged
    Buffer logging: level debugging, 473 messages logged
    Trap logging: level informational, 478 message lines logged
        Logging to 10.0.0.56, 478 message lines logged

Log Buffer (32768 bytes):
Jan 19 17:32:07 EST: %IMA-5-ACTIVE_LINK_CHANGE: ATM1 now has 1 active links,
 active link bitmap is 0x1.
```

```
Jan 19 17:32:08 EST: %IMA-5-ACTIVE_LINK_CHANGE: ATM1 now has 2 active links,
active link bitmap is 0x3.
Jan 19 17:32:08 EST: %LINEPROTO-5-UPDOWN: Line protocol on Interface ATM1,
changed state to up
Jan 19 17:32:08 EST: %IMA-5-ACTIVE_LINK_CHANGE: ATM1 now has 1 active links,
active link bitmap is 0x1.
Jan 19 17:32:10 EST: %LINEPROTO-5-UPDOWN: Line protocol on Interface ATM1,
changed state to down
Jan 26 14:22:38 EST: %TR-3-WIREFAULT: Unit 0, wire fault: check the lobe
cable MAU connection.
Jan 26 14:22:40 EST: %LINK-5-CHANGED: Interface TokenRing2/0, changed state
to initializing
Jan 26 14:22:41 EST: %LINEPROTO-5-UPDOWN: Line protocol on Interface TokenRing2/0,
changed state to down
Jan 26 14:22:42 EST: %TR-3-OPENFAIL: Unit 0, open failed: lobe media test,
function failure
Jan 26 14:22:44 EST: %LINK-3-UPDOWN: Interface TokenRing2/0, changed state to down
```

> **Note:** Like DEBUG output, each log entry is stamped with a time; *uptime* is the default format. Log time stamps can be customized exactly like DEBUG; see the previous section for details on the SERVICE TIMESTAMPS global configuration command.

SCENARIO & SOLUTION

What command logs error messages to an internal system buffer?	**Logging buffered**
What privileged EXEC command logs error messages to your Telnet session?	**Terminal monitor**
What command can be used to disable logging to the console?	**No logging console**
What command will log error messages to a Syslog server at 192.168.1.3?	**Logging 192.168.1.3**

Error Message Logging

A client calls about a troublesome router that crashed suddenly and without warning yesterday. Which of the following logs might give you a clue as to what happened?

A. Console log

B. Terminal log

C. Buffer log

D. Syslog server

Solution: D. The Syslog server might have caught error messages before the router was completely down. Answers A and B are incorrect because you would have had to be watching the router when the crash happened. C is incorrect because the DRAM was flushed when the router was brought down.

The SHOW VERSION Command

SHOW VERSION is the first command to use when you need to know what you have got. It shows a great deal of information about the software, firmware, and hardware of a Cisco device. The following SHOW VERSION output comes form a model 3660 modular router:

```
R3660#sh ver
Cisco Internetwork Operating System Software
IOS (tm) 3600 Software (C3660-DS-M), Version 12.0(7)
TAC:Home:SW:IOS:Specials for info
Copyright (c) 1986-2000 by cisco Systems, Inc.
Compiled Thu 16-Mar-00 17:38 by phanguye
Image text-base: 0x60008900, data-base: 0x61010000
ROM: System Bootstrap, Version 12.0(6r)T
ROM: 3600 Software (C3660-DS-M), Version 12.0(7)
R3660 uptime is 8 weeks, 20 hours, 21 minutes
System returned to ROM by power-on at 23:59:45 EST Tue FEB 6 2000
System image file is "flash:c3660-ds-mz_120-7"
cisco c3660 (R527x) processor with 55296K/9216K bytes of memory.
R527x CPU at 225Mhz, Implementation 40, Rev 10.0, 2048KB L2 Cache
Bridging software.
```

```
X.25 software, Version 3.0.0.
2 FastEthernet/IEEE 802.3 interface(s)
1 Token Ring/IEEE 802.5 interface(s)
4 ATM network interface(s)
2 Compression AIM(s)
DRAM configuration is 64 bits wide with parity disabled.
125K bytes of non-volatile configuration memory.
32768K bytes of processor board System flash (Read/Write)
8192K bytes of processor board PCMCIA Slot0 flash partition 1 (Read/Write)
8192K bytes of processor board PCMCIA Slot0 flash partition 2 (Read/Write)
Configuration register is 0x2102
```

■ **IOS version**   As expected, the first item displayed by the SHOW VERSION command is the current IOS version in use on the router.

■ **Bootstrap version**   The version of the bootstrap program is also displayed. Remember that the bootstrap program can help you isolate or rule out hardware problems that occur when installing your router.

■ **Uptime**   The router's *uptime* is shown, as is how it was started (powered on, in this case). SHOW VERSION provides a quick and easy way to find this information.

■ **IOS used**   The router displays where the IOS was loaded from, whether ROM, TFTP, or the like. In this case, the IOS was loaded from ROM, and the *filesystem:filename* is shown.

■ **Processor and RAM**   These are both displayed; the RAM shows total memory/IO memory. The I/O memory total correlates with the information given by the SHOW MEMORY command (discussed later in this chapter).

■ **Hardware and software options**   Hardware (such as installed modules) and software (optional packages) are shown next.

■ **Interfaces**   All interfaces on the router are displayed, including installed modules. This is a quick and easy method for finding out if a router is recognizing an interface.

■ **Flash/NVRAM**   Both flash and NVRAM amounts are displayed, including any provided by add-on cards.

■ **Configuration register**   The current configuration register is recorded here, in hexadecimal. Remember, the configuration register sets what the router does during the boot process. The default is 0x2102, which means "boot to the image specified by the boot command." However, you can change this value to cause the router to boot into ROM Monitor mode or boot from ROM.

Here is a common problem: you buy a new line card for your modular router. After installing and powering up, you try SHOW VERSION, and your router does not recognize the new card. Do you have defective hardware? More likely, your IOS version does not recognize the hardware. Newer router modules often require new versions of IOS to operate. Try updating the code, and your module will most likely appear.

EXERCISE 5-10

Using the SHOW VERSION Command

A client asks a question about upgrading the IOS on her model 3640 router. She would like to load the newest revision of IOS but would also like to keep the old version on the router for emergency purposes. SHOW VERSION on the router produces the following output:

```
R3640>sh ver
Cisco Internetwork Operating System Software
IOS (tm) 3600 Software (C3640-IK2S-M), Version 12.0(4)
Compiled Thu 29-Apr-99 18:12 by kpma
Image text-base: 0x600088F0, data-base: 0x60BFA000
ROM: System Bootstrap, Version 11.1(20)AA1
R3640 uptime is 7 weeks, 1 day, 5 hours, 38 minutes
System restarted by power-on at 10:19:47 edt Sun Jan 2 2000
System image file is "flash:c3640-ik2s-mz.120-4.T"
cisco 3640 (R4700) processor (revision 0x00) with 73728K bytes of memory.
R4700 CPU at 100Mhz, Implementation 33, Rev 1.0
Bridging software.
X.25 software, Version 3.0.0.
3 Ethernet/IEEE 802.3 interface(s)
4 Serial network interface(s)
DRAM configuration is 64 bits wide with parity disabled.
125K bytes of non-volatile configuration memory.
8192K bytes of processor board System flash (Read/Write)
8192K bytes of processor board PCMCIA Slot0 flash (Read/Write)
Configuration register is 0x2102
```

Both the new and old IOS code measure 5MB in size. Does the client have the room to do this?

Solution: Yes, she can do it. Remember, the IOS is placed in Flash. The client has 8MB in standard Flash, which we can see houses her current code. She also has 8MB of Flash in an add-on PCMCIA card. You can use this space to hold the new code and boot from that location.

CERTIFICATION OBJECTIVE 5.10

Buffers and Queues

Most of the action happens in memory—in buffers. Buffers are memory segments in which frames are stored as they proceed through the router. Two kinds of buffers—interface buffers and system buffers—are discussed here.

Interface buffers hold frames that have just arrived at an interface or are about to be sent out of an interface. Thus, they are divided into two sections: the input queue and the output queue. When a frame arrives, it is held in the input queue until its turn to be transferred to system buffers—usually in first-in, first-out (FIFO) order. Likewise, the output queue holds frames waiting to go back out on the wire. Together, their status can be examined with the SHOW INTERFACE command.

Note: On small routers, the interface buffers are contained in central DRAM. Larger routers have interface buffers built into the interface itself.

System buffers are contained in the router's central DRAM. They hold the frame while it is processed by the RP. The amount of memory set aside for system buffers is configurable with the BUFFER global configuration command. However, Cisco does not recommend changing the default values without assistance from the TAC.

I/O Buffer Error Conditions

Interface queue error conditions are examined with the SHOW INTERFACES command:

```
Ethernet1 is up, line protocol is up
  Hardware is AmdP2, address is 0020.5234.1454
  Internet address is 10.1.2.3
  MTU 1500 bytes, BW 10000 Kbit, DLY 1000 usec,
     reliability 255/255, txload 1/255, rxload 1/255
  Encapsulation ARPA, loopback not set
  Keepalive set (10 sec)
  ARP type: ARPA, ARP Timeout 04:00:00
  Last input 00:00:00, output 00:00:00, output hang never
  Last clearing of "show interface" counters never
  Queueing strategy: fifo
  Output queue 0/40, 218 drops; input queue 0/75, 183 drops
  5 minute input rate 73000 bits/sec, 73 packets/sec
  5 minute output rate 20000 bits/sec, 19 packets/sec
     226289598 packets input, 928256843 bytes, 0 no buffer
     Received 124442443 broadcasts, 0 runts, 0 giants, 0 throttles
     0 input errors, 0 CRC, 0 frame, 0 overrun, 0 ignored
     0 input packets with dribble condition detected
     102876216 packets output, 4092826669 bytes, 0 underruns
     28 output errors, 400403 collisions, 2 interface resets
     0 babbles, 0 late collision, 2228951 deferred
     27 lost carrier, 0 no carrier
```

Buffer statistics are in the bottom section.

- **Drops**   The number of times a packet was dropped from an I/O buffer while waiting to be transferred to DRAM.

- **Ignored**   The number of times an interface did not accept a packet because it lacked available I/O buffers.

- **No buffers**   The number of packets dropped because there was no available system memory (DRAM).

- **Overruns**   The number of times the receiving hardware was so overwhelmed it could not transfer incoming frames to the I/O buffers fast enough.

- **Underruns**   The number of times the interface transfers outgoing packets faster than the router can handle; it often results in a transmit abort. Typically, underruns result from an overburdened RP not being able to keep up with the transmitting interfaces.

The **SHOW BUFFERS** Command

SHOW BUFFERS gives the status of both the internal (DRAM) buffers and the interface buffers. Observe the following output from a Cisco 2501 router:

```
Router1#sh buf
Buffer elements:
     499 in free list (500 max allowed)
     10951 hits, 0 misses, 0 created

Public buffer pools:
Small buffers, 104 bytes (total 50, permanent 50):
     49 in free list (20 min, 150 max allowed)
     2080 hits, 0 misses, 0 trims, 0 created
     0 failures (0 no memory)
Middle buffers, 600 bytes (total 25, permanent 25):
     23 in free list (10 min, 150 max allowed)
     3053 hits, 0 misses, 0 trims, 0 created
     0 failures (0 no memory)
Big buffers, 1524 bytes (total 50, permanent 50):
     50 in free list (5 min, 150 max allowed)
     262 hits, 0 misses, 0 trims, 0 created
     0 failures (0 no memory)
VeryBig buffers, 4520 bytes (total 10, permanent 10):
     10 in free list (0 min, 100 max allowed)
     0 hits, 0 misses, 0 trims, 0 created
     0 failures (0 no memory)
Large buffers, 5024 bytes (total 0, permanent 0):
     0 in free list (0 min, 10 max allowed)
     0 hits, 0 misses, 0 trims, 0 created
     0 failures (0 no memory)
Huge buffers, 18024 bytes (total 0, permanent 0):
     0 in free list (0 min, 4 max allowed)
     0 hits, 0 misses, 0 trims, 0 created
     0 failures (0 no memory)

Interface buffer pools:
Ethernet0 buffers, 1524 bytes (total 32, permanent 32):
     9 in free list (0 min, 32 max allowed)
     33 hits, 2 fallbacks
     8 max cache size, 6 in cache
Serial0 buffers, 1524 bytes (total 32, permanent 32):
     7 in free list (0 min, 32 max allowed)
     294 hits, 0 fallbacks
     8 max cache size, 8 in cache
```

```
Serial1 buffers, 1524 bytes (total 32, permanent 32):
    7 in free list (0 min, 32 max allowed)
    25 hits, 0 fallbacks
    8 max cache size, 8 in cache
```

■ **Buffer sizes**   There are six classes of system buffers, broken down by size. When a frame arrives, it is placed in the appropriately sized buffer.

■ **Total**   The total number of buffers (of this type) currently allocated. This number includes the permanent buffers plus however many buffers have been dynamically allocated due to demand.

■ **Permanent**   The number of buffers permanently allocated to this size. These buffers are created when the router boots.

■ **Free list**   The number of buffers currently unallocated (empty).

■ **Minimum allowed**   The minimum number of buffers a router attempts to keep free (available) at any given time. When the number of free buffers drops below this minimum, the router attempts to create more buffers.

■ **Maximum allowed**   The maximum number of buffers a router attempts to keep free (available) at any given time. When the number of free buffers rises above this figure, the router attempts to trim some buffers.

■ **Hits**   The number of times a buffer was successfully allocated.

■ **Misses**   The number of times no buffer was available. If fast switching is enabled, the packet is dropped. Under process switching, a buffer is dynamically created.

■ **Created**   The number of buffers created due to the free list dropping below the minimum allowed.

■ **Trims**   The number of buffers removed due to the free list exceeding the maximum allowed.

■ **Failures**   The number of times the router requested a buffer to be created but was denied (usually due to a lack of memory).

The SHOW MEMORY Command

Memory usage can also be examined using the SHOW MEMORY command, which provides an overview of used and available memory, then a block-by-block listing of memory contents. Although not terribly useful to end users, SHOW MEMORY can provide interesting insight into what is actually happening. The Cisco TAC frequently asks you to run this command when troubleshooting difficult problems. Sample output from a model 2610 router is shown here:

```
Router4#sh mem
                Head     Total(b)    Used(b)    Free(b)   Lowest(b)  Largest(b)
Processor    808C26AC   11786580    3133076    8653504    8589180    8477020
       I/O   1400000     4194304    1722768    2471536    2453380    2470268
             Processor memory
Address    Bytes Prev.    Next      Ref  PrevF   NextF Alloc PC   What
808C26AC   1064  0        808C2B00   1                 80201514   List Elements
808C2B00   2864  808C26AC 808C365C   1                 80201514   List Headers
808C365C   9000  808C2B00 808C59B0   1                 80217418   Interrupt Sta
. . . . . . . . . . . .
             I/O memory
Address    Bytes Prev.    Next      Ref  PrevF   NextF Alloc PC   What
1400058     276  1400000  1400198    1                 801D6888   *Packet Data*
1400198     276  1400058  14002D8    1                 801D6888   *Packet Data*
14002D8     276  1400198  1400418    1                 801D6888   *Packet Data*
. . . . . . . . . . . .
```

- **Processor memory** This is DRAM. It reflects the amount of memory available to the router after the IOS has been loaded into RAM.
- **I/O Memory** These are the buffers.

Note that both processor and interface memory totals are further subdivided between free and used. Always make sure you install enough memory to leave at least 25 percent free to survive occasional spikes.

The SHOW PROCESSES Command

To see what processes are currently running in memory and how much CPU time they are burning, use the SHOW PROCESSES command:

```
Router4#sh proc
CPU utilization for five seconds: 1%/0%; one minute: 0%; five minutes: 1%
```

```
PID QTy        PC Runtime (ms)      Invoked    uSecs    Stacks TTY Process
  1 Csp 8021C448            0         28193        0 2664/3000   0 Load Meter
  2 M*         0         2736           879  311210140/12000    0 Exec
  3 Lst 80209E0C       114867         16698     6879 5760/6000   0 Check heaps
  4 Cwe 8020F524            0             1        0 5652/6000   0 Pool Manager
  5 Mst 801A2BA4            4             2     2000 5620/6000   0 Timers
(output deleted …)
 49 Hwe 803537EC           40           104      384 5644/6000   0 Multilink PPP
 50 Mwe 8035B108          230            11    20909 4184/6000   0 Multilink
 53 Mwe 803C908C       104100         10148    10258 8352/9000   0 RIP Router
 54 Hwe 803C87A0           28          5079        5 4836/6000   0 RIP Send
. . . . . . . . . . . . .
```

- **CPU Utilization** This is shown measured over the last 5 seconds, 1 minute, and 5 minutes.

- **PID** Process ID.

- **Runtime** Total CPU time a process has used, in milliseconds.

- **Invoked** Total number of times this process has been called.

- **USecs** Average number of milliseconds of CPU time used per invocation.

Use the SHOW PROCESSES command to troubleshoot high CPU utilization situations—it can pinpoint exactly which processes are causing problems.

In addition, to see the amount of memory allocated to each process, use SHOW PROCESSES MEMORY:

```
Router4#sh proc mem
Total: 11786580, Used: 3132944, Free: 8653636
 PID TTY  Allocated      Freed    Holding    Getbufs    Retbufs Process
   0   0      60028       1252    2545748          0          0 *Init*
   U   U        496     186060        496          0          0 *Sched*
   0   0    7600760    2927124       3636     178680          0 *Dead*
   1   0        268        268       3836          0          0 Load Meter
   2   0      20748      19540      13928          0          0 Exec
   3   0          0          0       6836          0          0 Check heaps
   4   0         96          0       6932          0          0 Pool Manager
   5   0        268        268       6836          0          0 Timers
   6   0        268        268       6836          0          0 Serial
(output deleted …)
  49   0        536        268       7104          0          0 Multilink PPP
  50   0      70932      41732      21608          0          0 Multilink
  53   0     456152          0      17176        780          0 RIP Router
  54   0         96     445608       6932          0          0 RIP Send
                                  3131624 Total
```

FROM THE CLASSROOM

CPU Utilization

In the SHOW PROCESSES output, notice that the 5-second utilization entry contains two values, in this case 1 percent and 0 percent. The first is total CPU utilization, and the second is the utilization by the interrupts. Interrupt utilization includes the following:

- Fast switching
- Console and auxiliary port output

Process (noninterrupt) utilization includes these:

- Anything that is process switched (DEBUG, SNMP, routing updates, etc.)
- Virtual terminal sessions

There is an interesting relationship between the two values. In a fast-switching environment, interrupt utilization should be the majority of total processor utilization. For example, if 5-second utilization reads 52 percent/48 percent, then fast switching is accounting for most of the router's workload. This is optimal under normal conditions. However, a reading of 52 percent/18 percent might indicate that much of the router's traffic is being process switched (for whatever reason). This information can be very helpful when troubleshooting high-utilization problems.

—Don Dettmore, CCNP, MCSE, CNE

The SHOW CONTROLLERS CXBUS Command

The CXBUS is the Cisco Extended Bus on a model 7000 router. It contains the SP, which arbitrates the bus between all the interfaces. Use the SHOW CONTROLLERS CXBUS command to display hardware information about the SP and all the connected interfaces:

```
router5> show controllers cxbus
Switch Processor 5, hardware version 11.1, microcode version 130.2
  Microcode loaded from system
  512 Kbytes of main memory, 128 Kbytes cache memory
  120 1520 byte buffers, 70 4484 byte buffers, 212 byte system buffer
  Restarts: 0 line down, 0 hung output, 0 controller error
 FIP 2, hardware version 6.2, microcode version 9.1.7
  Microcode loaded from system
  Interface 24 – Fddi2/0, station addr 0000.0c02.1234 (bia 0000.0c02.1234)
    70 buffer RX queue threshold, 71 buffer TX queue limit, buffer size 4484
    ift 0006, rql 66, tq 0000 0000, tql 70
```

```
EIP 4, hardware version 5.1, microcode version 128.10
  Interface 32 - Ethernet4/0, station addr 0000.0c02.1111 (bia
0000.0c02.1111)
     20 buffer RX queue threshold, 28 buffer TX queue limit, buffer size 1520
     ift 0000, rql 20, tq 0000 0000, tql 28
     Transmitter delay is 0 microseconds
  Interface 33 - Ethernet4/1, station addr 0000.0c02.2222 (bia
0000.0c02.2222)
     20 buffer RX queue threshold, 28 buffer TX queue limit, buffer size 1520
     ift 0000, rql 20, tq 0000 0000, tql 28
     Transmitter delay is 0 microseconds
```

You can see each line card that is installed. Line cards are given codes such as EIP, for Ethernet Interface Processor; FIP, for FDDI Interface Processor; and MIP, for Multichannel Interface Processor. Some of the information displayed about the line cards includes:

- Hardware and microcode versions
- Interfaces
- Interface buffers

The SHOW STACKS Command

SHOW STACKS is another command that is of little use to the end user but highly valuable to the TAC. It is used to display the stack usage of the processes and interrupts running on the router. It also displays a stack trace, if one has been taken. A *stack trace* is a brief snapshot of memory that is automatically taken when the router experiences abnormal conditions (such as a crash). Observe the following output from a model 3660 router:

```
Router4#sh stacks
Minimum process stacks:
 Free/Size    Name
 5344/6000    Router Init
10160/12000   Init
 5376/6000    RADIUS INITCONFIG
 5472/6000    DHCP Client
 9976/12000   Exec
23748/24000   VTEMPLATE Background Mgr
```

```
Interrupt level stacks:
Level    Called Unused/Size  Name
  1      183129   8436/9000  Network interfaces
  2           0   9000/9000  Timebase Reference Interrupt
  3          13   8760/9000  PA Management Int Handler
  6       84967   8892/9000  16552 Con/Aux Interrupt
  7    35226344   8932/9000  MPC860 TIMER INTERRUPT
```

Note that if a crash has occurred, the reason for the crash is displayed here.

Core Dumps

Sometimes a problem is so severe that the Cisco TAC instructs you to perform a core dump on the router. A *core dump* is basically a snapshot of the contents of the router's memory, placed in a binary file. It tends to be very large (it is exactly the size of your router's RAM), and generally it cannot be understood by non-Cisco engineers. However, Cisco TAC engineers know what to look for, and they can sometimes glean valuable insight from the core dump, particularly in instances of strange behavior or unexplained crashes.

Taking a core dump involves taking a snapshot of memory and sending it to a TFTP server in file format. There are two ways of doing this:

- You can take a core dump of a functioning (or malfunctioning) router via the WRITE CORE command. Simply enter enable mode and type **write core** *ip-address*, where *IP-ADDRESS* represents the address of the TFTP server.

- If a router is extremely unstable, you can use the EXCEPTION DUMP command to cause the router to take a core dump when a system crash occurs. This helps the TAC by giving them the exact state of the router at the time of the crash. EXCEPTION DUMP *IP-ADDRESS* is the command syntax, entered in global configuration mode. Again, *IP-ADDRESS* is the address of your TFTP server.

Core dumps are often unsuccessful. Remember, you are trying to copy a large amount of data with a (by definition) faulty router. However, if you do get a good one, it is written to the TFTP server under the name *HOSTNAME-CORE*. The next step is usually to FTP the file to Cisco, where it is closely examined. You can also examine it yourself, if you like; Cisco provides a free stack decoder at *www.cisco.com/stack/stackdecoder.shtml.*

Buffer Errors

You are experiencing problems with an interface. SHOW INTERFACE reveals a high ratio of ignores to drops. Someone suggests that a high number of drops means you need more system DRAM. Do you think that is the case?

Solution: No. If your ignores are almost as high as your drops, the interface is probably being flooded with more traffic than it can handle. Look to moving stations off that segment and reducing its workload.

CERTIFICATION SUMMARY

This chapter covered a lot of ground. Cisco provides a wealth of troubleshooting options, and we touched on many of them. First, the PING and TRACEROUTE commands were discussed and their output was examined. Next, we examined the inner processes of a router. The differences between the routing process and the switching process were discussed. Then we covered switching in detail, including the base process switching and many of the high-speed alternatives. We also traced a packet all the way through a high-end router.

Once we understood what was happening inside the router, it was time to dive into the technical stuff. The chapter covered DEBUG commands and stressed importance of preparation before trying them out. It then discussed logging, the importance of which should be obvious. Each of the four logging methods has its own unique advantages and disadvantages. Finally, buffers and queues were covered. Although the TAC usually handles problems in this area, it is important for a competent Cisco engineer to have a solid understanding of these topics.

✓ TWO-MINUTE DRILL

Here are some of the key points from each certification objective in Chapter 5.

Cisco IOS Software Troubleshooting Tools

❑ The Cisco IOS has a variety of built-in troubleshooting tools, such as SHOW, DEBUG, PING, and TRACEROUTE.

Understanding the Output of Diagnostic Commands

❑ PING and TRACEROUTE use special characters to provide detailed network feedback.

The Routing Process

❑ The routing process involves the building and maintenance of routing tables based on the best-path determination mechanism of the routing protocols.

The Switching Process

❑ The switching process receives a frame, looks up its destination in the routing table, builds a new data link header, and moves it to its exit interface or interfaces.

Switching Initialization

❑ Fast switching uses a cache in DRAM to store destination addresses and Layer 2 headers so that the RP doesn't have to process every single packet.

❑ Cisco provides several other mechanisms to move switching overhead away from the RP and onto dedicated hardware. Some of these include optimum switching, autonomous switching, silicon switching, and distributed switching.

Tracing Packet Flow

❑ The first packet in a flow is process switched. The appropriate caches are then initialized so that subsequent packets can be switched by faster mechanisms.

What the Route Processor Handles Directly

❑ Many situations require process switching. Some of these include debugging, error messages, SNMP, protocol translations, tunneling, and special queuing.

The DEBUG Utility

❑ One of the more powerful tools in Cisco's command set is DEBUG, which is used to view ongoing protocol processes and state information.

❑ When using the DEBUG command, be aware of the extra CPU and network overhead it imposes on the router and bandwidth.

Error Message Logging

❑ You can log error messages to up to four sources: console, virtual terminal, Syslog server, and internal buffer.

❑ If the router is configured with the SERVICE TIMESTAMP command, each event message in the log will be time-stamped.

❑ SHOW VERSION gives a great overview of the hardware and software running on a router.

Buffers and Queues

❑ System buffers are located in DRAM and can be examined via the SHOW BUFFERS command. Interface buffers (input queue and output queue) can also be examined with SHOW BUFFERS, though errors can be seen with SHOW INTERFACES.

❑ The TAC might require you to provide them with in-depth system information. This can include things such as the output from SHOW MEMORY, SHOW PROCESSES, SHOW STACKS, and a core dump.

SELF TEST

The following questions will help you measure your understanding of the material presented in this chapter. Read all the choices carefully because there might be more than one correct answer. Choose all correct answers for each question.

Cisco IOS Software Troubleshooting Tools

1. TRACEROUTE is possible because IP routers are required to send which of the following?

   A. ICMP echo replies

   B. ICMP TTL-exceeded messages

   C. SNMP traps

   D. TRACEROUTE response packets

2. A client calls with a routing problem. He is afraid his router is routing packets over low-speed serial links instead of high-speed ATM links. What tool should you use to determine if his suspicion is true?

   A. SHOW commands

   B. DEBUG commands

   C. PING command

   D. TRACEROUTE command

Understanding the Output of Diagnostic Commands

3. You try to PING a device on a remote network and receive the following result:

   ```
   Router3>ping 10.3.1.4
   Type escape sequence to abort.
   Sending 5, 100-byte ICMP Echos to 10.3.1.4, timeout is 2 seconds:
   .....
   Success rate is 0 percent (0/5)
   ```

   This points to a failure at which OSI layer?

   A. Layer 1

   B. Layer 2

   C. Layer 3

   D. Cannot tell

Routing Process

4. You have correctly configured EIGRP as your routing protocol, but your routing table is still empty. Which command would help you best troubleshoot the situation?

   A. SHOW INTERFACE

   B. SHOW EIGRP

   C. DEBUG IP EIGRP

   D. DEBUG IP PROTOCOL

Switching Process

5. A client wants to know which is the fastest switching method for his 4000 series router. Which do you tell him?

   A. Process switching

   B. Fast switching

   C. Distributed switching

   D. Silicon switching

Switching Initialization

6. A client is considering purchasing a Versatile Interface Processor (VIP) card for his 7500 series router. He asks you what the benefit would be over optimum switching. What do you tell him?

   A. The VIP card requires less memory.

   B. The VIP relieves the RP of some of its switching duty.

   C. The VIP card takes the routing duty from the RP.

   D. The VIP card handles DEBUG output.

7. Process switching includes a route table lookup. This route table is contained in:

   A. Autonomous cache

   B. Fast cache

   C. Optimum cache

   D. DRAM

Tracing Packet Flow

8. Which of the following does *not* describe an advantage of fast switching over process switching?

   A. Only the Layer 3 header is copied to DRAM.

   B. The next-hop information is cached.

   C. Layer 2 headers are pre-made.

   D. The RP is not involved in the switching transaction.

9. A client calls with a performance issue. While troubleshooting, they applied DEBUG IP PACKET to an Ethernet interface of a model 2600 series router. Now users are complaining that the network is slow. What do you do?

   A. Call Cisco—the Ethernet interface might have gone bad.

   B. Use DEBUG INTERFACE ETHERNET to try looking for the host that is causing the problem.

   C. Turn DEBUG off. DEBUG requires process switching; it tends to degrade performance.

   D. Use an Ethernet interface filter to restrict the DEBUG output.

What the Route Processor Handles Directly

10. Which of the following requires process switching? Choose all that apply.

   A. Tunneling

   B. Route redistribution

   C. ICMP echoes

   D. Protocol translation

The DEBUG Utility

11. Why is it preferable to watch DEBUG output in a Telnet session rather than on the console?

   A. The Telnet session requires much less processing overhead.

   B. The Telnet session requires less memory overhead.

   C. The Telnet session does not require a Syslog server.

   D. Actually, the console is preferable.

12. True or false: applying an access list to a DEBUG IP command is not a good idea because access lists require processing overhead.

   A. True

   B. False

13. Each line of DEBUG output contains a time stamp. By default, it is in "router uptime" format. How do you change this to standard date/time format?

   A. TIMESTAMP DATETIME

   B. SERVICE TIMESTAMPS

   C. SERVICE DATETIME

   D. DATETIME SERVICE

14. True or false: DEBUG IP RIP PACKET generates more output than DEBUG IP RIP EVENTS.

   A. True

   B. False

Error Message Logging

15. What command is used to configure a router to log system and error messages to a remote Syslog host?

   A. LOGGING *HOST*

   B. LOGGING BUFFERED

   C. LOGGING SYSLOG

   D. LOGGING REMOTE

16. You are troubleshooting a client router and use the SHOW VERSION command. It shows that the running IOS version is different from the version stored in ROM. Is this a concern?

   A. Yes

   B. No

17. Which element determines where the router gets its IOS when it boots?

   A. IOS version

   B. Configuration register

   C. NVRAM

   D. Processor type

18. You are at a new customer's site to troubleshoot a router you have never seen before. What command gives you the best overview of the software and hardware installed on the route?

A. SHOW IP INTERFACES

B. SHOW PROCESSES MEMORY

C. SHOW VERSION

D. WRITE CORE

Buffers and Queues

19. You are troubleshooting a router. When you execute SHOW BUFFERS, you see the following output:

```
(output deleted …)
Small buffers, 104 bytes (total 150, permanent 50):
    2 in free list (20 min, 150 max allowed)
    12230 hits, 3254 misses, 0 trims, 100 created
    545 failures (545 no memory)
(output deleted …)
```

What might be happening here? Choose all that apply.

A. You have an insufficient number of permanent small buffers for your traffic patterns.

B. You are being hit by a broadcast storm.

C. Your network has been infected by a virus.

D. You do not have enough input buffers for your traffic patterns.

20. Which of the following is *not* a system buffer size?

A. Little

B. Middle

C. Very big

D. Huge

LAB QUESTION

A customer would like you to construct a configuration that logs error messages according to the following guidelines:

- Since console logging is intensive, only log errors or worse are written to the console.

- They would like to view DEBUG output in Telnet sessions, so log all messages to virtual terminals.

- The Syslog server is central repository for error messages; log all but DEBUG output to 10.0.0.50.

- The internal buffer will be used as an emergency backup to the Syslog server. Set aside 32K of memory and log warnings or worse there.

Enter the configuration here:

```
(config)#_____
(config)#_____
(config)#_____
(config)#_____
(config)#_____
```

SELF TEST ANSWERS

Cisco IOS Software Troubleshooting Tools

1. ☑ **B.** ICMP TTL-exceeded messages. TRACEROUTE uses messages with the TTL about to expire.
   ☒ **A** is incorrect because ICMP echoes are not required. **C** is incorrect because SNMP traps have nothing to do with TRACEROUTE. **D** is incorrect because TRACEROUTE response packets do not exist.

2. ☑ **D.** TRACEROUTE tracks the path packets are taking.
   ☒ **A** and **B** are incorrect because you could possibly use a SHOW IP ROUTE or a DEBUG command, but it would be much more indirect than using TRACEROUTE. **C** is incorrect because PING would not help at all in determining a route.

Understanding the Output of Diagnostic Commands

3. ☑ **D.** You cannot tell at which OSI layer the failure occurred. Layer 1, 2, or 3 could be the problem. PING can tell you if Layer 3 is down, but it cannot tell you which layer is the culprit.
   ☒ **A, B,** and **C** are incorrect because any one of those could potentially be the problem. The answer is not clear from the information given.

Routing Process

4. ☑ **C.** DEBUG IP EIGRP. You would be able to see if EIGRP updates are actually being sent and received.
   ☒ **A** is incorrect because SHOW INTERFACE does not show any routing protocol information. **B** and **D** are incorrect because SHOW EIGRP and DEBUG IP PROTOCOL are not valid commands.

Switching Process

5. ☑ **B.** Fast switching is the fastest available method for the 4000 series.
   ☒ **A, C,** and **D** are incorrect because process switching is the slowest, and distributed and silicon switching are available only on 7000 series routers.

Switching Initialization

6. ☑ **B.** The VIP relieves the RP of some of its switching duty. The advantage of the VIP is that it performs the cache lookup for the RP.
☒ **A** is incorrect because VIP does not require less memory. **C** and **D** are incorrect because VIP does not help with routing duty or DEBUG output.

7. ☑ **D.** DRAM. Process switching is the most base switching and looks up destinations on the main system routing table in DRAM.
☒ **A, B,** and **C** are incorrect because they all contain route table caches of some sort, but they are not used by process switching.

Tracing Packet Flow

8. ☑ **D.** The RP is not involved in the switching transaction. This answer is correct because the RP *is* involved in manipulating the packet header and cache lookup.
☒ **A, B,** and **C** are incorrect because they all describe the primary advantages of fast switching.

9. ☑ **C.** Turn DEBUG off. DEBUG requires process switching; it tends to degrade performance. Process switching slows a high-speed interface.
☒ **A, B,** and **D** are incorrect because turning DEBUG off will increase network speed.

What the Route Processor Handles Directly

10. ☑ **A and D.** Both tunneling and protocol translation require process switching.
☒ **B and C** are incorrect because they can take advantage of any fast switching technique.

The DEBUG Utility

11. ☑ **A.** Telnet sessions are preferable because they require less processing overhead.
☒ **B and C** are incorrect because a Telnet session does not require extra memory or a Syslog server. **D** is incorrect because the console is *not* preferable.

12. ☑ **B.** False. Even though access lists require processing overhead, they reduce DEBUG output so much that they are well worth it.
☒ **A,** true, is incorrect because your overall processing overhead would be reduced.

13. ☑ **B.** SERVICE TIMESTAMPS. The syntax is SERVICE TIMESTAMPS *TYPE FORMAT.*
☒ **A, C,** and **D** are nonexistent commands.

14. ☑ **A.** True. Packet debugging almost always produces more output than event debugging. Packet debugging generates output for every single packet being examined, whereas event debugging produces output only when a significant event occurs.
    ☒ **B**, false, is incorrect because DEBUG IP RIP PACKET does generate more output than DEBUG IP RIP EVENTS.

Error Message Logging

15. ☑ **A.** LOGGING *HOST* (or *IPADDRESS*) configures logging to a Syslog server.
    ☒ **B** is incorrect because LOGGING BUFFERED logs to an internal buffer. **C** and **D** are incorrect because LOGGING SYSLOG and LOGGING REMOTE are not IOS commands.

16. ☑ **B.** No. The ROM contains the IOS version that came with router. It is not upgraded when you upgrade the Flash and is normally not used except in emergencies.
    ☒ **A**, yes, is incorrect because it is not a concern if the running IOS version is different from the version stored in ROM.

17. ☑ **B.** The configuration register determines whether the router boots from Flash or ROM or enters ROM monitor mode.
    ☒ **A**, **C**, and **D** are important but they do not determine any boot options.

18. ☑ **C.** SHOW VERSION displays IOS, interfaces, and hardware options, giving a good overview of the router.
    ☒ **A**, **B**, and **D** are incorrect because SHOW IP INTERFACES shows only IP interfaces, SHOW PROCESSES MEMORY shows only process information, and WRITE CORE does not really show anything useful.

Buffers and Queues

19. ☑ **A.** You have an insufficient number of permanent small buffers for your traffic patterns. You currently have 150 of 150 maximum buffers created. Only two are free, and you have numerous failures, so you do not have enough small buffers.
    ☒ **B** and **C** are incorrect because there is no proof that supports either of these hypotheses. **D** is incorrect because input buffers are not addresses in this snippet.

20. ☑ **A.** Little. There are no little buffers; they are called *small buffers* and are 104 bytes in size.
    ☒ **B**, **C**, and **D** are all system buffer sizes; middle buffers are 600 bytes, very big buffers are 4520 bytes, and huge buffers are 18,024 bytes.

LAB ANSWER

```
(config)# logging console error
(config)# logging monitor debugging
(config)# logging 10.0.0.50
(config)# logging trap informational
(config)# logging buffered 32768 warning
```

6

Common
Routing
Protocols

I n order to effectively troubleshoot a network, it is important to have an in-depth understanding of routing protocols and their impact on the network. This understanding comes from fundamental knowledge of how the routing protocol functions, the available tools for diagnosis, and an experience base in problem identification and resolution.

This chapter presents an in-depth discussion of the following periodic broadcast-based routing protocols: RIP v1 and v2, IGRP, IPX RIP/SAP, and AppleTalk RTMP. This chapter also presents an in-depth discussion of the following event-driven protocols: OSPF, EIGRP, BGP, and IPX/AppleTalk EIGRP. A number of troubleshooting techniques are also presented. It is important for the reader to experiment and become familiar with the various elements within the router tables, processes, and debugging information.

CERTIFICATION OBJECTIVE 6.01

Periodic Broadcast-Based Protocols

Routing protocols are generally subdivided into two categories: periodic broadcast protocols and event-driven protocols.

Periodic broadcast protocols send route updates at regular, timed intervals. Should a certain number of consecutive updates be missed over an extended interval, the routers in the network assume the route to be inaccessible and eventually remove the route altogether. This method of routing requires constant updating of the routes, whether there has been a routing table change or not.

Periodic broadcast protocols are considered to be of the "legacy" variety. Although periodic broadcast protocols are more antiquated, a considerable installed base of these protocols still exists, including the Routing Information Protocol (RIP) and Cisco's Interior Gateway Routing Protocol (IGRP). Since these protocols can be a little temperamental and sometimes have obscure effects on routing within large networks, they provide substantial input to the Cisco Certified Internetwork Expert (CCIE) troubleshooting section.

Periodic broadcast protocols such as RIP were used widely within the early ARPANET. As networks grew to scale, elements such as longer convergence times, multiple routing loops, and hierarchical models required more robust and scalable network routing protocols.

Periodic broadcast protocols consume bandwidth by continuously sending routing updates over a network, even if there have been no changes to the network topology. It is possible to control the interval of these updates; however, the unnecessary consumption of bandwidth is still unavoidable.

Event-driven protocols provide for this more scalable network architecture in that routing updates are generated only in the event of a network topology change. For instance, when a subnet is disconnected from a router, causing a change in the routing table, an event-driven protocol advertises the removal of the route. When the subnet reattaches, the route is advertised again.

Often periodic broadcast protocols and event-driven protocols are confused with *distance-vector* and *link-state protocols*. However, the correct association of these terms is that distance-vector protocols can be either periodic broadcast or event-driven. For example, BGP is a distance-vector, event-driven protocol; OSPF is a link-state, event-driven protocol; and IGRP is a distance-vector, periodic broadcast protocol.

Distance-vector protocols only maintain a database of the destination routes and the metric required to reach the network. Link-state protocols, on the other hand, maintain an entire network topology database and locally determine the best path to each destination network.

Routing Information Protocol

RIP is a periodic broadcast, distance-vector routing protocol that comes in two different versions. Version 1 is the original version, which has many limitations. Version 2 is an enhanced version based on the original version and alleviates many of the limitations of Version 1.

RIP Version 1

As previously mentioned, RIP v1 is one of the "legacy" periodic broadcast, Bellman-Ford (or distance-vector) algorithm-based routing protocols. It is defined in RFC 1058. RIP functions by broadcasting its full routing table to all its neighbors. Since broadcast packets are not forwarded by routers, it takes many stages of updates for the entire network to become aware of update information. All routers eventually receive the advertised routes and regularly update their forwarding tables. Before sending out route broadcasts, RIP edits its routing table based on split-horizon, metric limitations, and variable mask conflicts.

In the event that certain routes are no longer advertised, it is assumed that those routes are no longer active. Due to the complexity of large periodic broadcast networks using RIP, various convergence and synchronization issues regarding RIP broadcasts can exist.

RIP maintains a routing table with the criteria listed in Table 6-1.

The following are various timers associated with RIP:

- **Update timers** Frequency at which the entire routing table is broadcast. RIP defaults to 30 seconds for the update timer.

- **Invalid timers** Interval after which a route is determined to be no longer valid and is no longer advertised. RIP defaults to 180 seconds for the invalid timer.

- **Flush timers** Interval after which a route is removed from the IP routing table. RIP defaults to 240 seconds for the flush timer.

RIP (by default) requires route updates every 30 seconds via broadcasts in order to keep the routes fresh. After the 180-second invalid timer period, the routes are no longer accessible and are no longer advertised. After the 240-second flush timer period, the route originating from the neighbor router is removed. In large-scaled, meshed networks with up to 16 routers in a path, waiting 4 minutes for routing tables to reconverge can be intolerable.

TABLE 6-1		
RIP Version 1 Routing Table Criteria	Network destination	Represents the network or subnet for which this packet is destined.
	Next hop	Represents the IP address of the next router on the path to the destination network.
	Hop distance	Represents the number of router hops required to reach the actual destination network. RIP is restricted to a network diameter of fewer than 16 hops.
	Timers	Represent the update and expiration times associated with the routes.
	Flags	Represent the network state of a route.

In order to accommodate various routing loops that could occur within certain network topologies, RIP has implemented a number of features to reduce looping effects:

- **Holddown** While in holddown, a router does not believe updates about a suspicious network unless the incoming metric is better than the metric already known to the router. Without holddown, routers would believe any other update about any network, regardless of the metric.

- **Split horizon** Prevents a router from advertising a route back to its source. Split horizons prevent two-node routing loops, which can cause a "count to infinity" hop count problem. Split horizon is enabled for all RIP interfaces by default.

- **Poison reverse** Advertises an unreachable metric back to the source of the announcement (a temporary violation of split horizon). This way, RIP can quickly announce a down route, rather than wait for the invalid timer to expire.

Classful Routing RIP suffers from limitations of its IP addressing abilities. IP RIP is a *classful* routing protocol. In the earlier classful Internet routing networks, IP addresses were categorized based on their IP addressing range:

- **Class A** 1.0.0.1–126.255.255.254
- **Class B** 128.0.0.1–191.255.255.254
- **Class C** 192.0.0.1–223.255.255.254

In a classful subnetting environment, if one chooses to subdivide a particular class of address space (say, the Class A range 10.0.0.0, for instance) into further subnets (using a mask of 255.255.255.0), the entire address space for the address class must be subnetted with that same netmask, 255.255.255.0. This means that all LANs, as well as point-to-point serial interfaces, are required to use an entire /24 for each subnet. Allowing only one subnet mask of the classful IP address space for both LANs and point-to-point networks can be both limiting and wasteful within today's networking environments.

The term *classful* refers to a major network number of Class A, B, or C. Classful protocols share the characteristic that they do not transmit mask information along with destination network information. Instead, the receiving router infers a mask from the configured mask on the receiving interface, when the route is a subnet of the same major network number. Since the receiving router must guess at a mask, the sending router edits its routing updates. Updates about destination networks belonging to the same major network number are sent only if they match the network configured.

This scheme breaks down when a router must send an advertisement into an interface configured in a different major network number. Here the classful routing protocol creates a summary advertisement representing the entire major network number. When a router receives an advertisement of a network number not belonging to the same major network number as that configured on the receiving interface, that router examines only the network bits (8, 16, or 24 bits, respectively, for a Class A, B, or C network number). This advertisement is assumed to be a classful summary.

More recent protocols allow for variable-length subnet masking (VLSM), which allows for a nonclassful (or classless) IP addressing scheme. If a LAN has a subnet address of 10.1.1.0/24, for instance, and a Frame Relay point-to-point subinterface is assigned 10.1.2.0/30, RIP v1 cannot propagate the subnet mask information associated with the route. All subnets within the class must have only one netmask, which is associated with a connected interface on the router. Therefore, when using RIP v1 while subnetting, be sure to consistently use the same subnet mask within a network class. RIP v2 carries the subnet mask along with the network updates, so VLSM is possible.

It is important to remember that if a bunch of VLSM routes are being redistributed into a classful protocol such as RIP or IGRP, that protocol cannot possibly understand all the various masks in use. Thus, a summary route (typically pointing to the null interface) should be created that best summarizes the various subnets into a single entity.

exam
ⓦatch

When redistributing routing protocols with classless VLSM networks into RIP v1, be sure that subnetted static routes with a null next hop are redistributed as well.

Routing protocols such as EIGRP, OSPF, BGP, and others propagate subnet mask information along with routing updates. Routing protocols that allow for VLSM updates allow for "classless" routing where subnetting can be of different lengths.

RIP Version 2

RIP v2 is also a periodic, distance-vector routing protocol. It is defined in RFC 1388 and RFC 1389. RIP v2 functions similarly to RIP v1 by advertising its full routing table to all other routers in the network. All routers receive the advertised routes and regularly update their forwarding tables.

RIP v2 offers several advantages over RIP v1. RIP v2 makes better use of the header field included in each packet. RIP v2 also includes better information to handle subnetting and authentication.

The command, address family identifier, IP address, and metric are identical in RIP v1 and RIP v2. The Version field specifies version number 2 for RIP datagrams that use authentication or carry information in any of the newly defined fields.

In RIP v2, there is an optional authentication mechanism. When in use, this option consumes almost an entire RIP entry and leaves space for, at most, 24 RIP entries in the remainder of the packet. The most widespread authentication type is simple password, which is Type 2.

The Routing Domain field enables some routing domains to interwork on the same physical infrastructure while logically ignoring each other. This simply gives the ability to implement various kinds of policies. A default routing domain is assigned the value 0.

The Subnet Mask field contains the subnet mask, which is applied to the IP address to yield the nonhost portion of the address. If this field is zero, no subnet mask is included for this entry.

The Next Hop field is the immediate next-hop IP address to which packets to the destination specified by this route entry should be forwarded. The purpose of the Next Hop field is to eliminate packets being routed through extra hops in the system. It is particularly useful when RIP is not run on all the routers on a network.

Multicasting is an optional feature in RIP v2, using IP address 224.0.0.9. This feature reduces unnecessary load on those hosts that are not listening to RIP v2. The IP multicast address is used for periodic updates. The use of the multicast address is the default in a Cisco router.

RIP v2 is totally backward compatible with RIP v1. Its applications allow fine tuning for RIP v1 emulation, to be RIP v1 compatible or fully RIP v2.

exam
ⓦatch

Whenever redistributing routes with RIP v1 or RIP v2, always include the SUBNETS option.

When installing new or updating existing corporate networks, make sure you are using a routing protocol that is flexible enough to handle possible growth. Don't forget: both versions of RIP have a hop-count limitation of 15.

Troubleshooting RIP

When troubleshooting RIP, it is always best to start by looking in the routing table for "RIP." First determine if the routing entry exists, using the SHOW IP ROUTE RIP command. Then determine its hop count and the next hop. The two values in brackets, shown as [120/1], represent the route's administrative distance (AD) and metric, respectively.

Consider this router's IP RIP routing table:

```
Lab_Con# show ip route rip
     10.0.0.0/24 is subnetted, 4 subnets
R       10.3.1.0 [120/1] via 10.2.1.3, 00:00:16, Ethernet0
R       10.5.1.0 [120/1] via 10.2.1.2, 00:00:23, Ethernet0
R       10.4.1.0 [120/1] via 10.2.1.3, 00:00:16, Ethernet0
```

Although RIP might be advertising a specific route, due to RIP's high AD (120), another routing protocol with a lower AD, such as EIGRP, might also be advertising the same route and be populating the forwarding information base.

In the following example, EIGRP has a lower routing AD than RIP and therefore has preference over RIP in the routing table, as shown by the SHOW IP ROUTE command:

```
RouterA# sh ip route
Codes: C - connected, S - static, I - IGRP, R - RIP, M - mobile, B - BGP
       D - EIGRP, EX - EIGRP external, O - OSPF, IA - OSPF inter area
       E1 - OSPF external type 1, E2 - OSPF external type 2, E - EGP
       i - IS-IS, L1 - IS-IS level-1, L2 - IS-IS level-2, * - candidate default
       U - per-user static route

Gateway of last resort is not set

     10.0.0.0/24 is subnetted, 4 subnets
D       10.3.1.0 [90/409600] via 10.2.1.3, 00:04:17, Ethernet0/0
C       10.4.1.0 is directly connected, Ethernet0/0
C       10.5.1.0 is directly connected, Serial5/0/4
```

Some strange routing occurrences could exist where routes vanish and reappear due to competing routing protocols. Asynchronous updates in lower AD routing protocols supersede routes originated by higher AD protocols. This phenomenon can occur with RIP and IGRP originating the same routes. It is therefore important to verify the entry time associated with each route in the routing table.

Table 6-2 depicts the default ADs associated with each routing protocol.

exam
Ⓦⓐtⅽh

Running RIP with an instance of another periodic routing protocol, such as IGRP, can result in routing issues due to the asynchronous updates and administrative distances competing for insertion.

Resorting to DEBUG Mode

If all else fails and you cannot figure out what is going on in the network, it is time to get into DEBUG mode and start monitoring all RIP packets and updates traversing the network. Verify that the RIP routes are being advertised correctly and being originated from the appropriate routers. There are two forms of IP RIP debugging. EVENTS shows only the fact that updates are occurring.

TABLE 6-2	Route Source	Default Distance
Routing Protocol Administrative Distances	Connected interface	0
	Static route	1
	Enhanced IGRP summary route	5
	External BGP	20
	Internal enhanced IGRP	90
	IGRP	100
	OSPF	110
	IS-IS	115
	RIP	120
	EGP	140
	External enhanced IGRP	170
	Internal BGP	200
	Unknown	255

TRANSACTIONS (the default DEBUG) shows the contents of each RIP packet. Each method is shown here:

```
router2# deb ip rip events
RIP event debugging is on
router2#
RIP: received v1 update from 172.16.123.2 on Serial1
RIP: Update contains 4 routes
RIP: sending v1 update to 255.255.255.255 via Ethernet0 (172.16.21.1)
RIP: Update contains 10 routes
RIP: Update queued
RIP: Update sent via Ethernet0
RIP: sending v1 update to 255.255.255.255 via Serial0 (172.16.112.2)
RIP: Update contains 5 routes
RIP: Update queued
RIP: Update sent via Serial0
RIP: sending v1 update to 255.255.255.255 via Serial1 (172.16.123.1)
RIP: Update contains 7 routes
RIP: Update queued
RIP: Update sent via Serial1
RIP: received v1 update from 172.16.112.1 on Serial0
RIP: Update contains 6 routes
router2#
```

In this DEBUG capture, you can see that updates are being received and sent out both the serial 0 and serial 1 interfaces. The DEBUG tells you how many routes are contained in each update but no specifics about the routes. The generic DEBUG screen that follows fills in the gaps:

```
router2#deb ip rip
RIP protocol debugging is on
router2#
RIP: received v1 update from 172.16.123.2 on Serial1
      172.16.31.0 in 1 hops
      172.16.113.0 in 2 hops
      172.4.0.0 in 2 hops
      172.3.0.0 in 1 hops
RIP: sending v1 update to 255.255.255.255 via Ethernet0 (172.16.21.1)
      subnet  172.16.31.0, metric 2
      subnet  172.16.11.0, metric 2
```

```
      subnet  172.16.123.0, metric 1
      subnet  172.16.112.0, metric 1
      subnet  172.16.113.0, metric 2
      network 172.10.0.0, metric 3
      network 172.4.0.0, metric 3
      network 172.1.0.0, metric 2
      network 172.2.0.0, metric 1
      network 172.3.0.0, metric 2
RIP: sending v1 update to 255.255.255.255 via Serial0 (172.16.112.2)
      subnet  172.16.31.0, metric 2
      subnet  172.16.21.0, metric 1
      subnet  172.16.123.0, metric 1
      network 172.2.0.0, metric 1
      network 172.3.0.0, metric 2
RIP: sending v1 update to 255.255.255.255 via Serial1 (172.16.123.1)
      subnet  172.16.21.0, metric 1
      subnet  172.16.11.0, metric 2
      subnet  172.16.112.0, metric 1
      subnet  172.16.113.0, metric 2
      network 172.10.0.0, metric 3
      network 172.1.0.0, metric 2
      network 172.2.0.0, metric 1
RIP: received v1 update from 172.16.112.1 on Serial0
      172.16.31.0 in 2 hops
      172.16.11.0 in 1 hops
      172.16.113.0 in 1 hops
      172.10.0.0 in 2 hops
      172.4.0.0 in 2 hops
      172.1.0.0 in 1 hops
router2#
```

This time, you can see the same count of inbound and outbound RIP updates. However, you can also see the exact networks or subnetworks that are being advertised or learned. You can also see the individual metrics associates with each route. With these two DEBUG screens, you can see which routes are being learned on each interface and whether they are being propagated to neighbor routers out other interfaces.

Now that you have a better idea of RIP v1 and v2, take a look at the following Scenario & Solution.

298 Chapter 6: Common Routing Protocols

What IOS commands are necessary to enable RIP routing on a Cisco router?	ROUTER RIP NETWORK *X.X.X.X (where X.X.X.X* is a connected network).
What IOS command under ROUTER RIP must be typed to enable RIP v2?	Version 2.
What is the default frequency of broadcasts that RIP uses to send its entire routing table?	Thirty seconds.
What happens to a router that is 16 hops away from a router on a RIP network?	It is unreachable.

Cisco's Interior Gateway Routing Protocol

Cisco's *Interior Gateway Routing Protocol (IGRP)* is also a periodic broadcast protocol, with stronger decision-making criteria based on real-time network events and congestion states. IGRP allows for more dynamic routing decisions based on real-time network states, including the following:

- Load
- Reliability
- Bandwidth
- Delay
- MTU

In addition, IGRP has the ability to balance traffic, even within unequal, multipath networks. For instance, if two neighboring routers have a T1 and a 512K circuit between them, IGRP can balance the traffic by proportionally routing traffic to destinations on each circuit.

IGRP contains three types of routes: interior, system, and exterior. *Interior routes* reference the directly connected interfaces of a router. *System routes* are routes within IGRP's autonomous system (AS). *Exterior routes* are learned outside IGRP's AS.

An *autonomous system* is a routing domain that contains all routers within an IGRP network, as shown in Figure 6-1. Any external routes to the AS must be learned via redistribution from another routing protocol or reached via a default route.

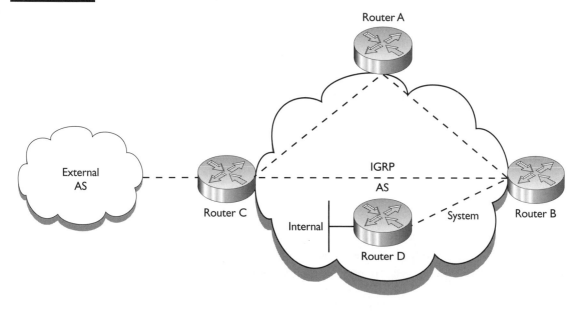

FIGURE 6-1   An IGRP autonomous system

The following timers are associated with IGRP:

- **Update timer**   Frequency at which the entire routing table is broadcast. IGRP defaults to 90 seconds.

- **Invalid timer**   Interval after which a route is determined to be valid no longer. IGRP defaults to 270 seconds.

- **Holddown timer**   The interval in which updates with worse metrics are ignored. Better metrics are always welcome, but while in holddown, the chances of receiving one is rather slight. The default is 280 seconds.

- **Flush timer**   The interval after which a route is removed from the RIP table. IGRP defaults to 630 seconds.

Like RIP, IGRP is a periodic broadcast-based routing protocol. IGRP, however, updates routes at 90-second intervals, designates a route as inaccessible after 270 seconds, and removes the route entirely after 630 seconds. IGRP also uses Flash updates for sending immediate update messages as well as poison reverse updates to reduce the possibility of routing loops. Poison reverse is enabled by default and has the same effect as described for RIP.

IGRP is also a classful IP routing protocol and follows the same IP subnetting rules as RIP.

exam
ⓦatch

When redistributing routing protocols with classless VLSM networks into IGRP, be sure that classful static routes with a null next hop are redistributed as well.

Troubleshooting IGRP

When troubleshooting an IGRP network, always start with the IGRP routing table. The two values in the brackets, shown as [100/1600], represent the route's AD and metric, respectively. Make sure that the route exists within the IGRP routing table. If it exists, verify that it is in the routing table via the SHOW IP ROUTE IGRP command, which follows. In addition, ensure that the route's entry time shows that it is stable. Any value greater than 90 seconds indicates that a recent update has not been received for the network in question.

```
Lab_Con# show ip route igrp
     10.0.0.0/24 is subnetted, 4 subnets
I       10.3.1.0 [100/1600] via 10.2.1.3, 00:00:38, Ethernet0
I       10.5.1.0 [100/1600] via 10.2.1.2, 00:00:48, Ethernet0
I       10.4.1.0 [100/1200] via 10.2.1.3, 00:00:38, Ethernet0
```

In the event that the IGRP routes do not appear in the IGRP table, you should consider debugging IGRP. Look to see that routes containing the routing updates are being received. If they are not being received, the neighbor router that should be advertising the routes most likely has a filter, has an access list, or is down. Use the DEBUG IP IGRP EVENTS or DEBUG IP IGRP TRANSACTIONS command to enable IGRP debugging. As with RIP, EVENTS simply shows that something is happening, whereas TRANSACTIONS shows the details of each inbound and outbound update packet. Patience is also important during IGRP debug sessions, since the updates only occur every 90 seconds by default:

```
router2#deb ip igrp events
IGRP event debugging is on
router2#
IGRP: received update from 172.16.112.1 on Serial0
```

```
IGRP: Update contains 3 interior, 4 system, and 0 exterior routes.
IGRP: Total routes in update: 7
IGRP: received update from 172.16.123.2 on Serial1
IGRP: Update contains 3 interior, 4 system, and 0 exterior routes.
IGRP: Total routes in update: 7
IGRP: sending update to 255.255.255.255 via Ethernet0 (172.16.21.1)
IGRP: Update contains 5 interior, 5 system, and 0 exterior routes.
IGRP: Total routes in update: 10
IGRP: sending update to 255.255.255.255 via Loopback1 (172.2.1.1)
IGRP: Update contains 4 interior, 5 system, and 0 exterior routes.
IGRP: Total routes in update: 9
IGRP: sending update to 255.255.255.255 via Loopback2 (172.2.2.1)
IGRP: Update contains 4 interior, 5 system, and 0 exterior routes.
IGRP: Total routes in update: 9
IGRP: sending update to 255.255.255.255 via Loopback3 (172.2.3.1)
IGRP: Update contains 4 interior, 5 system, and 0 exterior routes.
IGRP: Total routes in update: 9
IGRP: sending update to 255.255.255.255 via Loopback4 (172.2.4.1)
IGRP: Update contains 4 interior, 5 system, and 0 exterior routes.
IGRP: Total routes in update: 9
IGRP: sending update to 255.255.255.255 via Loopback5 (172.2.5.1)
IGRP: Update contains 4 interior, 5 system, and 0 exterior routes.
IGRP: Total routes in update: 9
IGRP: sending update to 255.255.255.255 via Serial0 (172.16.112.2)
IGRP: Update contains 3 interior, 3 system, and 0 exterior routes.
IGRP: Total routes in update: 6
IGRP: sending update to 255.255.255.255 via Serial1 (172.16.123.1)
IGRP: Update contains 4 interior, 3 system, and 0 exterior routes.
IGRP: Total routes in update: 7
router2#
```

As seen here, IGRP updates are arriving from and being sent out both serial 0 and serial 1. The total number of routes in each package, as well as the count for each type of route, is shown. No details on the actual contents are seen here. However, the following TRANSACTIONS DEBUG capture corrects that:

```
router2#deb ip igrp transactions
IGRP protocol debugging is on
router2#
IGRP: sending update to 255.255.255.255 via Ethernet0 (172.16.21.1)
      subnet 172.16.31.0, metric=8576
      subnet 172.16.11.0, metric=8576
      subnet 172.16.123.0, metric=8476
      subnet 172.16.112.0, metric=8476
```

```
       subnet 172.16.113.0, metric=10476
       network 172.10.0.0, metric=10002002
       network 172.4.0.0, metric=9076
       network 172.1.0.0, metric=8976
       network 172.2.0.0, metric=501
       network 172.3.0.0, metric=8976
IGRP: sending update to 255.255.255.255 via Serial0 (172.16.112.2)
       subnet 172.16.31.0, metric=8576
       subnet 172.16.21.0, metric=1100
       subnet 172.16.123.0, metric=8476
       network 172.4.0.0, metric=9076
       network 172.2.0.0, metric=501
       network 172.3.0.0, metric=8976
IGRP: sending update to 255.255.255.255 via Serial1 (172.16.123.1)
       subnet 172.16.21.0, metric=1100
       subnet 172.16.11.0, metric=8576
       subnet 172.16.112.0, metric=8476
       subnet 172.16.113.0, metric=10476
       network 172.10.0.0, metric=10002002
       network 172.1.0.0, metric=8976
       network 172.2.0.0, metric=501
router2#
IGRP: received update from 172.16.123.2 on Serial1
       subnet 172.16.31.0, metric 8576 (neighbor 1100)
       subnet 172.16.11.0, metric 10676 (neighbor 8676)
       subnet 172.16.113.0, metric 10576 (neighbor 8576)
       network 172.10.0.0, metric 10004102 (neighbor 10002102)
       network 172.4.0.0, metric 9076 (neighbor 1600)
       network 172.1.0.0, metric 11076 (neighbor 9076)
       network 172.3.0.0, metric 8976 (neighbor 501)
router2#
```

This time, not only can you see the fact that IGRP updates are happening, you can see the detailed information contained in each update packet. Each individual network is shown, along with the new metric that is displayed in this router's routing table. The NEIGHBOR statement shows the metric from the neighbor's perspective—in other words, the metric represented in the neighbor's routing table.

IPX RIP and Service Advertisement Protocol

Although IP has made significant progress as the common communications protocol within the last few years, there is still a significant installed base of Internetwork Packet Exchange (IPX) equipment and networks. Service Advertisement Protocol

(SAP) is an enterprise network services protocol used to advertise information regarding file servers, print servers, job servers, and so on. IPX can be routed via IPX RIP, IPX EIGRP, or NLSP.

Cisco IPX routing is a packet-based routing protocol; SAP is a services advertising protocol. *Networking* and *services* can be regarded as somewhat different entities within IPX. IPX networks are represented by an eight-digit hexadecimal number uniquely identifying the network segment. There can be multiple network numbers on a single physical cable.

Cisco allows for filtering both IPX networks and services based on the following:

- Standard source and destination network numbers, access list numbers 800–899

- Extended IPX protocol type, access list numbers 900–999

- SAP and GNS, access list numbers 1000–1099

- NetBIOS, access list numbers 1000–1099

Filters can be applied to both interfaces and routing updates.

Troubleshooting IPX RIP

When troubleshooting an IPX network, always start with the IPX routing table. Identify each network and make sure that the routing table is complete. Use the SHOW IPX ROUTE command to look at the IPX forwarding table. Make sure that each IPX network and next-hop interface are accurate:

```
router2> show ipx route
Codes: C - Connected primary network,   c - Connected secondary network
       S - Static, F - Floating static, L - Local (internal), W - IPXWAN
       R - RIP, E - EIGRP, N - NLSP, X - External, A - Aggregate
       s - seconds, u - uses

26 Total IPX routes. Up to 1 parallel paths and 16 hops allowed.

No default route known.

C          2A (UNKNOWN),       Lo1
C          2B (UNKNOWN),       Lo2
C          2C (UNKNOWN),       Lo3
C          2D (UNKNOWN),       Lo4
```

```
C          2E (UNKNOWN),        Lo5
C          B1 (NOVELL-ETHER),   Et0
C        1122 (HDLC),           Se0
C        2233 (HDLC),           Se1
R          1A [07/01] via       1122.0010.7b39.dacb,     1s, Se0
R          1B [07/01] via       1122.0010.7b39.dacb,     1s, Se0
R          1C [07/01] via       1122.0010.7b39.dacb,     1s, Se0
R          1D [07/01] via       1122.0010.7b39.dacb,     1s, Se0
R          1E [07/01] via       1122.0010.7b39.dacb,     1s, Se0
R          3A [07/01] via       2233.0010.7b39.d91d,     3s, Se1
R          3B [07/01] via       2233.0010.7b39.d91d,     5s, Se1
R          3C [07/01] via       2233.0010.7b39.d91d,     5s, Se1
R          3D [07/01] via       2233.0010.7b39.d91d,     5s, Se1
R          3E [07/01] via       2233.0010.7b39.d91d,     5s, Se1
R          4A [08/02] via       2233.0010.7b39.d91d,     5s, Se1
R          4B [08/02] via       2233.0010.7b39.d91d,     5s, Se1
R          4C [08/02] via       2233.0010.7b39.d91d,     5s, Se1
R          4D [08/02] via       2233.0010.7b39.d91d,     5s, Se1
R          4E [08/02] via       2233.0010.7b39.d91d,     5s, Se1
R          A1 [07/01] via       1122.0010.7b39.dacb,     4s, Se0
R          C1 [07/01] via       2233.0010.7b39.d91d,     5s, Se1
R        1133 [07/01] via       1122.0010.7b39.dacb,     4s, Se0
router2>
```

In this IPX routing table, you can see various routes learned from two different serial interfaces. Each route is displayed with the appropriate [ticks/hops], which are the IPX metrics. Ticks are assigned for either a WAN interface (6 ticks) or a LAN interface (1 tick). Thus, for route 1133 shown at the bottom of the IPX routing table, it is 1 hop from this router and has a cost of 7 ticks (6 for crossing the serial interface from where it was learned and 1 for simply being advertised). Note that the ticks do not take into account the actual bandwidth of the WAN interface, which can be virtually any speed imaginable.

To verify that an IPX host is available, use the PING IPX command to verify reachability:

```
RouterB# ping ipx AAAA.0060.8388.bb00

Type escape sequence to abort.
Sending 5, 100-byte IPX cisco Echoes to AAAA.0060.8388.bb00, timeout is 2 seconds:
!!!!!
Success rate is 100 percent (5/5), round-trip min/avg/max = 1/3/4 ms
```

This output shows a successful PING, as evidenced by the bang (!) characters. If dots (.) were displayed, the PING would be unsuccessful. It is quite easy to mistype an IPX network address since it can be very long and is represented in hexadecimal. If only every other or every third ping packet succeeds (!), there are probably parallel paths in the routing table but only one of the paths is currently active (thus in the process of route convergence).

To verify that a Novell server is being advertised throughout the network, use the SHOW IPX SERVERS command. This command not only verifies that a service is available in the network, it also shows how this router would reach the service in question:

```
router2>show ipx servers
Codes: S - Static, P - Periodic, E - EIGRP, N - NLSP, H - Holddown, + = detail
4 Total IPX Servers

Table ordering is based on routing and server info

   Type Name                      Net      Address    Port     Route Hops Itf
P     4 server-1A                 1A.0000.0000.0001:1000       7/01     4 Se0
P     4 server-1B                 1B.0000.0000.0001:1000       7/01     3 Se0
P     7 4A-printer                4A.0000.0000.0001:1050       8/02     6 Se1
P     7 4B-printer                4B.0000.0000.0001:1050       8/02     5 Se1
router2>
```

In this display, the SAPs shown were learned via the periodic SAP broadcasts (P). The respective tick/hop metric values are shown in the Route column. The actual number of hops that the resource is from this router is represented in the Hops column. The fact that the hop values are different in this display indicates that the SAPs have been manually (or statically) introduced into this network. This is normally done to avoid the SAP overhead in various network locations, such as slow serial lines. The hop counts in the Route and Hops columns would usually be identical.

It is usually a good idea to DEBUG various routers and verify correct IPX operation. Look for network updates at regular intervals. If certain networks are not being advertised, a neighbor router could be route filtering, have access lists, or be down. IPX allows for EVENTS and ACTIVITY debugs. Similar to IP RIP and IGRP, EVENTS shows that something is happening. Unfortunately, EVENTS shows only that updates are being sent out, not received. ACTIVITY displays the actual routing updates:

```
router2#debug ipx routing events
IPX routing events debugging is on
IPXRIP: positing full update to 2233.ffff.ffff.ffff via Serial1 (broadcast)
IPXRIP: positing full update to B1.ffff.ffff.ffff via Ethernet0 (broadcast)
IPXRIP: positing full update to 1122.ffff.ffff.ffff via Serial0 (broadcast)
router2#
```

Here you can see that updates are being broadcast out the appropriate IPX interfaces, but no information is provided about the contents of the updates, nor is anything mentioned about incoming updates:

```
router2# deb ipx routing activity
IPX routing debugging is on
router2#
IPXRIP: positing full update to 1122.ffff.ffff.ffff via Serial0 (broadcast)
IPXRIP: src=1122.0010.7b39.da2b, dst=1122.ffff.ffff.ffff, packet sent
    network C1, hops 2,  delay 13
    network 3A, hops 2,  delay 13
    network 3B, hops 2,  delay 13
    network 3C, hops 2,  delay 13
    network 3D, hops 2,  delay 13
    network 3E, hops 2,  delay 13
    network 4E, hops 3,  delay 14
    network 4D, hops 3,  delay 14
    network 4C, hops 3,  delay 14
    network 4B, hops 3,  delay 14
    network 4A, hops 3,  delay 14
    network 2233, hops 1,  delay 7
    network B1, hops 1,  delay 7
    network 2E, hops 1,  delay 7
    network 2D, hops 1,  delay 7
    network 2C, hops 1,  delay 7
    network 2B, hops 1,  delay 7
    network 2A, hops 1,  delay 7
IPXRIP: positing full update to 2233.ffff.ffff.ffff via Serial1 (broadcast)
IPXRIP: src=2233.0010.7b39.da2b, dst=2233.ffff.ffff.ffff, packet sent
    network A1, hops 2,  delay 13
    network 1A, hops 2,  delay 13
    network 1B, hops 2,  delay 13
    network 1C, hops 2,  delay 13
    network 1D, hops 2,  delay 13
    network 1E, hops 2,  delay 13
    network 1133, hops 2,  delay 13
    network 1122, hops 1,  delay 7
```

```
    network B1, hops 1,  delay 7
    network 2E, hops 1,  delay 7
    network 2D, hops 1,  delay 7
    network 2C, hops 1,  delay 7
    network 2B, hops 1,  delay 7
    network 2A, hops 1,  delay 7
IPXRIP: positing full update to B1.ffff.ffff.ffff via Ethernet0 (broadcast)
IPXRIP: src=B1.0010.7b39.da2b, dst=B1.ffff.ffff.ffff, packet sent
    network C1, hops 2,  delay 8
    network 3A, hops 2,  delay 8
    network 3B, hops 2,  delay 8
    network 3C, hops 2,  delay 8
    network 3D, hops 2,  delay 8
    network 3E, hops 2,  delay 8
    network 4E, hops 3,  delay 9
    network 4D, hops 3,  delay 9
    network 4C, hops 3,  delay 9
    network 4B, hops 3,  delay 9
    network 4A, hops 3,  delay 9
    network A1, hops 2,  delay 8
    network 1A, hops 2,  delay 8
    network 1B, hops 2,  delay 8
    network 1C, hops 2,  delay 8
    network 1D, hops 2,  delay 8
    network 1E, hops 2,  delay 8
    network 1133, hops 2,  delay 8
    network 2233, hops 1,  delay 2
    network 1122, hops 1,  delay 2
    network 2E, hops 1,  delay 2
    network 2D, hops 1,  delay 2
    network 2C, hops 1,  delay 2
    network 2B, hops 1,  delay 2
    network 2A, hops 1,  delay 2
router2#
```

In this much larger DEBUG display, the actual route updates are seen, as are the metrics applied to each route in the IPX routing table. In this screen, the term DELAY refers to tick value, which we discussed earlier.

You can also view incremental SAP updates for regular activity. As with routing updates, you can examine EVENTS (short form) or ACTIVITY (long form). Remember that EVENTS shows only that updates are being sent:

```
router2#debug ipx sap events
IPX service events debugging is on
```

```
router2#
IPXSAP: positing update to 1122.ffff.ffff.ffff via Serial0 (broadcast) (full)
IPXSAP: positing update to 2233.ffff.ffff.ffff via Serial1 (broadcast) (full)
IPXSAP: positing update to B1.ffff.ffff.ffff via Ethernet0 (broadcast) (full)
router2#
```

Here, only the fact that SAP updates are sent is displayed. This is useful if a possible problem is that no SAPs are being propagated at all. However, if you need to see exactly which SAPs are being advertised, you must use the ACTIVITY DEBUG:

```
router2#deb ipx sap activity
IPX service debugging is on
router2#
IPXSAP: Response (in) type 0x2 len 288 src:1122.0010.7b39.dacb dest:1122.ffff.ff
ff.ffff(452)
 type 0x7, "4B-printer", 4B.0000.0000.0001(1050), 5 hops
 type 0x7, "4A-printer", 4A.0000.0000.0001(1050), 6 hops
 type 0x4, "server-1B", 1B.0000.0000.0001(1000), 3 hops
 type 0x4, "server-1A", 1A.0000.0000.0001(1000), 4 hops
IPXSAP: Response (in) type 0x2 len 288 src:2233.0010.7b39.d91d dest:2233.ffff.ff
ff.ffff(452)
 type 0x7, "4B-printer", 4B.0000.0000.0001(1050), 5 hops
 type 0x7, "4A-printer", 4A.0000.0000.0001(1050), 6 hops
 type 0x4, "server-1B", 1B.0000.0000.0001(1000), 5 hops
 type 0x4, "server-1A", 1A.0000.0000.0001(1000), 6 hops
IPXSAP: positing update to 1122.ffff.ffff.ffff via Serial0 (broadcast) (full)
IPXSAP: Update type 0x2 len 160 src:1122.0010.7b39.da2b dest:1122.ffff.ffff.ffff
(452)
 type 0x7, "4A-printer", 4A.0000.0000.0001(1050), 7 hops
 type 0x7, "4B-printer", 4B.0000.0000.0001(1050), 6 hops
IPXSAP: positing update to 2233.ffff.ffff.ffff via Serial1 (broadcast) (full)
IPXSAP: Update type 0x2 len 160 src:2233.0010.7b39.da2b dest:2233.ffff.ffff.ffff
(452)
 type 0x4, "server-1A", 1A.0000.0000.0001(1000), 5 hops
 type 0x4, "server-1B", 1B.0000.0000.0001(1000), 4 hops
IPXSAP: positing update to B1.ffff.ffff.ffff via Ethernet0 (broadcast) (full)
IPXSAP: Update type 0x2 len 288 src:B1.0010.7b39.da2b dest:B1.ffff.ffff.ffff
(452)
 type 0x4, "server-1A", 1A.0000.0000.0001(1000), 5 hops
 type 0x4, "server-1B", 1B.0000.0000.0001(1000), 4 hops
 type 0x7, "4A-printer", 4A.0000.0000.0001(1050), 7 hops
 type 0x7, "4B-printer", 4B.0000.0000.0001(1050), 6 hops
 type 0x4, "server-1A", 1A.0000.0000.0001(1000), 5 hops
```

```
type 0x4, "server-1B", 1B.0000.0000.0001(1000), 4 hops
type 0x7, "4A-printer", 4A.0000.0000.0001(1050), 7 hops
type 0x7, "4B-printer", 4B.0000.0000.0001(1050), 6 hops
router2#
```

This time you can see the exact SAPs that are advertised out each IPX interface of the router. Remember that split horizon is also in effect for SAP updates, so services learned on one interface are not advertised back out the same interface. The hops are also reported, whether it is an inbound or outbound update. For inbound updates, the reported hop value is that of the neighbor router. For outbound, the hops are the current metric from this router.

AppleTalk Routing Table Maintenance Protocol

The AppleTalk *Routing Table Maintenance Protocol (RTMP)* is another distance-vector, periodic broadcast, RIP-based protocol. Cisco's support of AppleTalk includes the following:

- Phase 1 and Phase 2 AppleTalk (even though they are incompatible)
- Extended and nonextended networks
- AppleTalk Address Resolution Protocol (AARP)
- AppleTalk Port Group
- Datagram Delivery Protocol
- Name Binding Protocol
- Zone Information Protocol
- AppleTalk Echo Protocol
- AppleTalk Transaction Protocol

AppleTalk Phase 1 allows for 254 devices, with 127 end nodes and 127 servers and only one zone per network. AppleTalk Phase 2 allows for 253 node devices per network, with multiple zones per network.

AppleTalk uses a 16-bit decimal, cable number addressing scheme concatenated with a node address. It employs a media-dependent address selection protocol to dynamically assign node addresses. An extended network cable range can be represented as a single network number or a start/end contiguous network-numbering sequence. A typical cable range assignment can be represented in the form *4-8*. An AppleTalk node would be represented as *4.53*.

Each AppleTalk network can be a member of one or more zones, but a node is part of only one zone. A *zone* contains a logical group of networks. A single AppleTalk enterprise network can contain up to 255 zones. The various zones localize the nodes (printers, hosts, servers) within a large-scale enterprise network.

Large AppleTalk networks may contain an inordinate number of zones and networks requiring filtering of certain information. Cisco allows for filtering AppleTalk information based on the following:

■ Zones

■ Network numbers

■ Get zone list requests/replies

■ Routing table updates

■ Zone Information Protocol (ZIP) replies

■ Name Binding Protocol (NBP)

Cisco allows for outbound access lists to apply interface filters on AppleTalk datagram packets based on packets' source network, cable range, or zone. Routing table update filters can also be used to limit advertised AppleTalk zones and networks.

With get zone list (GZL) reply/request filters, Cisco routers can also limit the zone information permitted in the Macintosh Chooser. All routers on the attached network must have the same GZL filters or the Chooser receives conflicting information and zones appear and disappear. ZIP filters are applied to routing table updates so that zones are not advertised to unauthorized routers.

Troubleshooting AppleTalk Networks

In troubleshooting AppleTalk networks, always start with the routing table. Make sure that the router has all the correct information for forwarding AppleTalk packets. Try using a big whiteboard with lots of color markers; this technique is often invaluable when trying to localize problems and identify the nature of a problem. By drawing the local network and verifying where packets are being routed, you can more easily verify correct routing.

Here is output from the SHOW APPLETALK ROUTE command:

```
router2#show appletalk route
Codes: R - RTMP derived, E - EIGRP derived, C - connected, A - AURP
       S - static  P - proxy
6 routes in internet

The first zone listed for each entry is its default (primary) zone.

R Net 11-15 [1/G] via 112.237, 3 sec, Serial0, zone site1
C Net 21-25 directly connected, Ethernet0, zone site2
R Net 31-35 [1/G] via 123.42, 9 sec, Serial1, zone site3
C Net 112-112 directly connected, Serial0, zone serial
R Net 113-113 [1/G] via 112.237, 3 sec, Serial0, zone serial
C Net 123-123 directly connected, Serial1, zone serial
router2#
```

If the router does not appear to have a complete set of routes or is missing particular zones, you need to verify routing neighbors, filters, and access lists, as discussed later in this section. If the router *does* have full routes, use the SHOW APPLETALK ARP command to verify that the local LAN segments also have connectivity and that all nodes are reachable:

```
RouterB#show appletalk arp
Address      Age (min)  Type      Hardware Addr        Encap   Interface
2.223             12   Dynamic   0060.5cf4.1554.0000  SNAP    Ethernet10/0
2.241              -   Hardware  0060.8394.e940.0000  SNAP    Ethernet10/0
9.210             12   Dynamic   0060.8388.bb00.0000  SNAP    Ethernet10/0
```

In this AppleTalk ARP table, each AppleTalk address that has been learned by this router is displayed. The logical AppleTalk address as well as the hardware-derived MAC address are shown. AppleTalk always uses the SNAP encapsulation type. AppleTalk ARPs also occur only on LAN interfaces. A dynamic address refers to LAN neighbor; a hardware address is the local AppleTalk address. The MAC addresses shown always include an additional "0000" field.

AppleTalk also supports the PING command. You must know the destination AppleTalk address before you attempt to reach it with the PING utility. Normally, if a device is in the AppleTalk ARP cache, there is no need to PING it. However, you can verify network reachability by attempting to PING AppleTalk addresses of distant devices or router ports. You need to capture the appropriate AppleTalk addresses from the AppleTalk ARP cache or with the SHOW APPLETALK INTERFACE BRIEF command:

```
RouterA#ping AppleTalk 2.223

Type escape sequence to abort.
Sending 5, 100-byte AppleTalk Echoes to 2.223, timeout is 2 seconds:
!!!!!
Success rate is 100 percent (5/5), round-trip min/avg/max = 4/5/8 ms
```

If the AppleTalk node is unreachable, according to the PING command, it could be a cabling problem, an interface problem, or a problem with either the AppleTalk routing table or zone table. AppleTalk interfaces can be reset with the CLEAR APPLETALK INTERFACE command.

If you cannot identify any local problems on the router, you must begin looking upstream, at the network. Verify that all AppleTalk RTMP neighbors are established and have been available for a considerable period of time. Make sure that the neighbors are not resetting themselves or having intermittent connectivity problems:

```
router1# sh apple neighbor
AppleTalk neighbors:
  112.190       Serial0, uptime 00:21:25, 2 secs
        Neighbor has restarted 1 time in 00:22:25.
        Neighbor is reachable as a RTMP peer
  113.90        Serial1, uptime 00:19:26, 6 secs
        Neighbor has restarted 1 time in 00:20:28.
        Neighbor is reachable as a RTMP peer
router1#
```

In this display, each AppleTalk neighbor of router1 has reset itself approximately 20 minutes ago. This is not really any cause for alarm. If the reset had been more recent, you should monitor multiple screens of the SHOW APPLE NEIGHBOR command to ensure that the neighbors are not continually resetting the connections. If they are, it could indicate either faulty media connecting the neighbors or bad interfaces.

Sometimes an end user might not see particular zones within the enterprise network. In order to verify that all zones are available, use the SHOW APPLETALK command to view the zones that are known by the router:

```
router2#show apple zone
Name                                    Network(s)
```

```
serial                          113-113 123-123 112-112
site1                           11-15
site2                           21-25
site3                           31-35
Total of 4 zones
router2#
```

If a particular zone is not shown on the router, it is either down or filtered by an upstream router. You should verify any access lists being applied on the interface connecting the two routers. You can verify access lists with the SHOW APPLE ACCESS-LISTS command:

```
RouterB#show appletalk access-lists
AppleTalk access list 600:
  permit cable-range 1-10
  deny other-access
AppleTalk access list 601:
  permit zone A
  deny additional-zones
  deny other-access
```

If the router is aware of the zone but a particular cable segment is unable to access that particular zone, it might be that an access list applied to that cable segment's interface is blocking that particular zone's advertisement. To verify the access list applied to the interface, use the SHOW APPLETALK INTERFACES command:

```
router2#sh app int e 0
Ethernet0 is up, line protocol is up
  AppleTalk cable range is 21-25
  AppleTalk address is 24.74, Valid
  AppleTalk zone is "site2"
  AppleTalk address gleaning is disabled
  AppleTalk route cache is disabled, port has access control
  AppleTalk access-group is 600
router2#
```

Here you can see that AppleTalk access list 600 is applied to interface Ethernet 0. AppleTalk access lists can be applied in only the outbound direction. If you are having connectivity problems through the Ethernet 0 interface, this access list could be the source.

Putting DEBUG to Work

Finally, if you cannot determine the nature of the problem or if you want to verify protocol behavior, look at the individual DEBUG information and make sure that updates are occurring at regular intervals.

For instance, DEBUG is also helpful to ensure that ZIP broadcast storms are not congesting the network. A *ZIP broadcast storm* occurs when a route advertisement without a corresponding zone triggers the network with a flood of ZIP requests. This behavior is typical of non-Cisco networks; Cisco routers have software mechanisms in place that prevent such ZIP storms from occurring.

To verify routing operations such as update intervals and routing update notifications, use the DEBUG APPLETALK RTMP command:

```
router2#deb app rtmp
AppleTalk RTMP routing debugging is on
router2#
AT: RTMP from 123.42 (new 0,old 2,bad 0,ign 0, dwn 0)
AT: RTMP from 112.237 (new 0,old 3,bad 0,ign 0, dwn 0)
AT: src=Ethernet0:24.74, dst=21-25, size=40, 5 rtes, RTMP pkt sent
AT: src=Serial0:112.190, dst=112-112, size=28, 3 rtes, RTMP pkt sent
AT: src=Serial1:123.230, dst=123-123, size=34, 4 rtes, RTMP pkt sent
AT: Route ager starting on Main AT RoutingTable (6 active nodes)
AT: Route ager finished on Main AT RoutingTable (6 active nodes)
AT: RTMP from 123.42 (new 0,old 2,bad 0,ign 0, dwn 0)
AT: RTMP from 112.237 (new 0,old 3,bad 0,ign 0, dwn 0)
router2#
```

In this display, you can see RTMP packets being sent and received. The actual data inside the RTMP updates cannot be seen during a DEBUG session. You can view the results only by examining the routing table.

CERTIFICATION OBJECTIVE 6.02

Event-Driven Protocols

With the emergence of large-scale networks within both the enterprise and on the Internet, robust, less "chatty" routing protocols are required. Three such powerful protocols are Open Shortest Path First (OSPF), Enhanced Interior Gateway Routing Protocol (EIGRP), and Border Gateway Protocol (BGP).

OSPF is purely an IP-based routing protocol intended for hierarchical, large-scale networks. EIGRP is a multiservice routing protocol that supports IP, IPX, and AppleTalk. BGP is used for interconnecting huge IP networks and defining strict routing policies.

All three of these routing protocols usually provide only state-change information rather than regularly sending the entire network. OSPF and EIGRP have periodic (30 minutes to a few hours) refresh cycles to ensure that the routing information is fresh. BGP never updates or refreshes the routing table. Depending on the routing environment, each one of these protocols is appropriate for certain network architectures.

Open Shortest Path First

OSPF is an IETF standards-based, event-driven, link-state protocol based on RFC 1583. OSPF is intended for enterprise hierarchical networks with a centralized backbone supporting various subordinate networks. An OSPF network architecture (see Figure 6-2) contains a backbone area 0 with other attached network areas. All areas must attach to at least one portion of the backbone area 0 and must be contiguous.

Each network interface that is to run OSPF on a router must be associated with an area. A router that has interfaces in various areas is called an *area border router (ABR)*. The ABR maintains a separate link-state network topology for each attached area. The main features of OSPF include the following:

- Supporting cost metric
- Allows multipath/equal path
- Type-of-service routing
- Variable-length subnet mask
- Route summarization
- Stub areas

OSPF uses cost as its metric. In a Cisco router, the interface cost is in direct relation to the bandwidth of that interface. All links and their states are maintained

FIGURE 6-2   The OSPF hierarchical topology

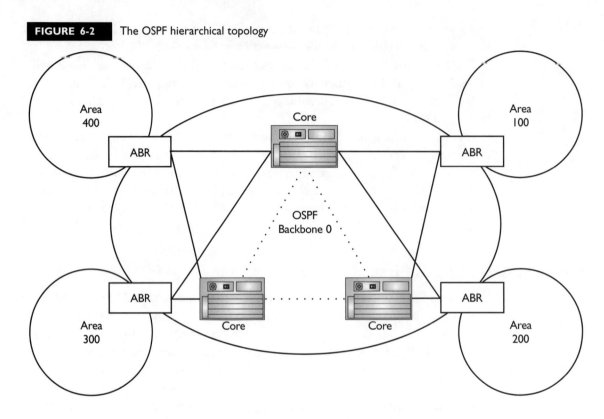

in a link-state database. OSPF uses the Dijkstra link-state algorithm to compute the shortest path to any destination based on the additive assigned metrics. Each network connection is either up or down. In the event of a link-state change, OSPF floods a link-state advertisement to all OSPF routers, which then recompute the shortest path to all known destinations; then routing reconverges.

exam

Watch

Understand how to use OSPF in point-to-point, point-to-multipoint, and broadcast media.

OSPF supports five packet types:

- **Hello**   Periodic (default: 10 seconds) messages that help determine what other OSPF routers are in the area as well as help elect the designated router on each broadcast segment.

- **Database description** The first type of routing update packets sent between OSPF neighbors en route to adjacency. The database description (DD) packets give a short summary of all known routes to the new neighbor. The neighbor then decides which ones need further detail.

- **Link-state request** A request for complete information for some or all routes advertised with the DD packets.

- **Link-state update** A response containing detailed information about specific routes. This information is used to populate the link-state database.

- **Link-state acknowledge** OSPF routers acknowledge the receipt of routing information. Designated routers never send acknowledgment packets. After the acknowledgment packets are received by each router, the two routers are said to be fully adjacent.

In addition, there are seven types of link-state advertisement:

- **Router link advertisements** Advertisements from each OSPF router about local routes. Router links remain within an area.

- **Network link advertisements** Advertisements forwarded from each designated router about broadcast links. Network links stay within an area.

- **Summary link advertisements** Advertisements forwarded between areas. Summary links are not necessarily summarized.

- **Default route summary link advertisements** Advertisements about any default route created in another area.

- **AS external advertisements** Detailed information about routes redistributed into OSPF from another routing protocol.

- **Multicast** Routing information for the Multicast OSPF (MOSPF) protocol.

- **Not so stubby area (NSSA)** Advertisements passed through an NSSA are redistributed routes, yet the area maintains the characteristics of a stub area. By definition, a stub area cannot perform redistribution. NSSA allows for much better control of the Type 5 external advertisements.

exam
ⓦatch
Be sure to design an OSPF network and assign IP addresses so that they summarize. In addition, beware of summarizing routes and then redistributing them into classful routing protocols.

Corporate OSPF networks can become complex and an administrative nightmare. Make sure you have a good network diagram detailing the OSPF aspects of the network before you attempt troubleshooting.

Troubleshooting OSPF

OSPF has a number of design-related issues that can cause networkwide problems. For instance, a large OSPF network with unstable links can generate a considerable amount of LSA flooding. In designing a hierarchical OSPF network, it is important to try to contain most of these LSAs within the areas. Route summarization is the way the LSAs are contained within each area. You can see evidence of an OSPF network that is too large and has too many unstable links by looking at the CPU usage of the routers (SHOW PROCESSES CPU). Recomputation of a large SPF database can consume substantial CPU resources.

A general rule of thumb is for an area to contain fewer than 100 routers. In addition, an OSPF domain should be no larger than 30 areas. Although successful larger OSPF networks do exist, and some smaller ones have design problems, other protocols (such as Border Gateway Protocol) are designed for larger, well-meshed networks.

When troubleshooting OSPF networks, start with the OSPF routing process itself, using SHOW IP OSPF. Verify redistribution of selected routes and make sure that the SPF algorithm is not continually recomputing. The SPF ALGORITHM EXECUTED line shows the network stability. Successive executions of the SHOW IP OSPF command show how often the network is reconverging:

```
router2>show ip ospf
Routing Process "ospf 1" with ID 172.2.5.1
 Supports only single TOS(TOS0) routes
 It is an area border and autonomous system boundary router
 Summary Link update interval is 00:30:00 and the update due in 00:09:07
 External Link update interval is 00:30:00 and the update due in 00:09:38
 Redistributing External Routes from,
 SPF schedule delay 5 secs, Hold time between two SPFs 10 secs
 Number of DCbitless external LSA 0
 Number of DoNotAge external LSA 0
 Number of areas in this router is 2. 2 normal 0 stub 0 nssa
    Area BACKBONE(0)
        Number of interfaces in this area is 2
        Area has no authentication
        SPF algorithm executed 10 times
        Area ranges are
```

```
        Link State Update Interval is 00:30:00 and due in 00:09:07
        Link State Age Interval is 00:20:00 and due in 00:19:07
        Number of DCbitless LSA 0
        Number of indication LSA 0
        Number of DoNotAge LSA 0
    Area 2
        Number of interfaces in this area is 6
        It is a stub area
          generates stub default route with cost 1
        Area has no authentication
        SPF algorithm executed 6 times
        Area ranges are
           172.2.0.0/16 Active(1)
        Link State Update Interval is 00:30:00 and due in 00:08:45
        Link State Age Interval is 00:20:00 and due in 00:18:45
        Number of DCbitless LSA 0
        Number of indication LSA 0
        Number of DoNotAge LSA 0
router2>
```

This capture shows an ABR. It has two interfaces in Area 0 and six in Area 2. Area 2 is also summarizing all the 172.2.0.0 subnets into a single update before they are advertised into Area 0. The SPF algorithm has executed 10 and 6 times, respectively, for Areas 0 and 2. These numbers are alarming only if they are increasing rapidly, as demonstrated with multiple SHOW IP OSPF screens in succession. Such appearance of these screens indicates network instability.

Area 2 is configured as a stub area. This means that all routers in the area must agree with this setting. The stub area information is carried in the hello packets every 10 seconds.

After verifying the OSPF process, use the SHOW IP ROUTE command to make sure that the selected routes in the forwarding table are based on OSPF. Verify that each route learned also has the appropriate routing code: O for learned via OSPF within this area, IA for learned by OSPF from another area, E1 or E2 for learned from another routing process, or N1 or N2 for redistributed from another routing process and currently inside a not so stubby area. Consider the following output:

```
router2#sh ip ro
Codes: C - connected, S - static, I - IGRP, R - RIP, M - mobile, B - BGP
       D - EIGRP, EX - EIGRP external, O - OSPF, IA - OSPF inter area
       N1 - OSPF NSSA external type 1, N2 - OSPF NSSA external type 2
       E1 - OSPF external type 1, E2 - OSPF external type 2, E - EGP
       i - IS-IS, L1 - IS-IS level-1, L2 - IS-IS level-2, * - candidate default
       U - per-user static route, o - ODR
```

```
Gateway of last resort is not set

O E2 172.10.0.0/16 [110/10] via 172.16.112.1, 00:05:26, Serial0
O IA 172.4.0.0/16 [110/75] via 172.16.123.2, 00:05:26, Serial1
O IA 172.1.0.0/16 [110/65] via 172.16.112.1, 00:05:26, Serial0
     172.2.0.0/24 is subnetted, 5 subnets
C       172.2.4.0 is directly connected, Loopback4
C       172.2.5.0 is directly connected, Loopback5
C       172.2.2.0 is directly connected, Loopback2
C       172.2.3.0 is directly connected, Loopback3
C       172.2.1.0 is directly connected, Loopback1
O IA 172.3.0.0/16 [110/65] via 172.16.123.2, 00:05:26, Serial1
     172.16.0.0/24 is subnetted, 6 subnets
O IA    172.16.31.0 [110/74] via 172.16.123.2, 00:05:26, Serial1
C       172.16.21.0 is directly connected, Ethernet0
O IA    172.16.11.0 [110/74] via 172.16.112.1, 00:05:26, Serial0
C       172.16.123.0 is directly connected, Serial1
C       172.16.112.0 is directly connected, Serial0
O       172.16.113.0 [110/128] via 172.16.112.1, 00:05:28, Serial0
router2#
```

Here are various networks that are directly connected, learned from within this area (O), learned from another area (IA), and learned via some redistribution (E2). It is not possible to know the actual routing source of the redistributed route.

In the event that certain routes are not being advertised, a very common mistake occurs in the masking of the wildcard bits in the NETWORK statement. In addition, make sure that the correct area is assigned to the networks:

```
router2#show running-config
(output deleted …)
router ospf 1
 network 172.16.21.0 0.0.0.255 area 2
 network 172.2.0.0 0.0.255.255 area 2
 network 172.16.112.0 0.0.0.255 area 0
 network 172.16.123.0 0.0.0.255 area 0
 default-metric 10
 area 2 stub
 area 2 range 172.2.0.0 255.255.0.0
--More--
```

Here you can see various NETWORK commands used to create the OSPF process. Furthermore, you can see the summarization of Area 2. Note that the summarization process uses a normal subnet mask, whereas the definition of NETWORK statements uses a wildcard mask (another common mistake).

A virtual link can be used to extend Area 0 out to some area that does not have its own personal link to Area 0. Although this is not a good design, it is often used as a temporary patch to a network when waiting for equipment or circuits to arrive. Ensure that the virtual link does not attempt to cross a stub area. If it does, the virtual link fails, and the area without its own personal link to Area 0 cannot access other areas within the OSPF network.

exam
ⓦatch   *Understand how and where to use virtual links for extending a backbone area.*

After verifying correct configuration and local routing, look toward your upstream routers and verify that you have established adjacent neighbor relationships. If an OSPF neighbor is not being established, it might be that the link between the routers is down or an access list could be misconfigured.

```
router3>show ip ospf nei
Neighbor ID     Pri   State          Dead Time    Address         Interface
172.4.5.1        1    FULL/BDR       00:00:35     172.16.31.2     Ethernet0
172.2.5.1        1    FULL/  -       00:00:34     172.16.123.1    Serial1
router3>
```

In this capture, router3 has two OSPF neighbors. Both are fully adjacent. This router is the backup designated router (BDR) on the Ethernet 0 interface. A DR is never elected on point-to-point serial lines or circuits. In the routing table, these two neighbor routers can be the only sources of routing updates.

It might also be necessary to view the entire OSPF database and verify that all links are showing up. Inside the database, you can see the various link-state packets that have been exchanged between this router and its neighbor(s):

```
router2#show ip ospf database
OSPF Router with ID (172.2.5.1) (Process ID 1)
            Router Link States (Area 0)
Link ID         ADV Router      Age        Seq#         Checksum Link count
172.1.5.1       172.1.5.1       1186       0x80000009   0x2946   4
172.2.5.1       172.2.5.1       1020       0x80000006   0x6EEE   4
172.3.5.1       172.3.5.1       638        0x80000004   0x8687   2
172.4.5.1       172.4.5.1       513        0x80000003   0x170B   2
            Summary Net Link States (Area 0)
Link ID         ADV Router      Age        Seq#         Checksum
172.1.0.0       172.1.5.1       1186       0x80000002   0x7D5C
172.2.0.0       172.2.5.1       1020       0x80000002   0x696E
172.3.0.0       172.3.5.1       638        0x80000004   0x5182
172.3.0.0       172.4.5.1       513        0x80000004   0xAD1B
172.4.0.0       172.3.5.1       638        0x80000002   0xAD1D
```

```
172.4.0.0        172.4.5.1       513        0x80000002 0x4192
172.16.11.0      172.1.5.1       1186       0x80000002 0xA90D
172.16.21.0      172.2.5.1       1020       0x80000002 0x3378
172.16.31.0      172.3.5.1       638        0x80000004 0xB8E5
172.16.31.0      172.4.5.1       515        0x80000002 0xB4EA
                 Router Link States (Area 2)
Link ID          ADV Router      Age        Seq#       Checksum Link count
172.2.5.1        172.2.5.1       1043       0x80000006 0x2AEA   6
                 Summary Net Link States (Area 2)
Link ID          ADV Router      Age        Seq#       Checksum
0.0.0.0          172.2.5.1       1022       0x80000002 0x6424
172.1.0.0        172.2.5.1       1022       0x80000003 0x1485
172.3.0.0        172.2.5.1       1022       0x80000004 0xF99C
172.4.0.0        172.2.5.1       1022       0x80000004 0x5239
172.16.11.0      172.2.5.1       1022       0x80000003 0x4036
172.16.31.0      172.2.5.1       1022       0x80000005 0x5F01
172.16.112.0     172.2.5.1       1022       0x80000003 0x809A
172.16.113.0     172.2.5.1       1022       0x80000003 0xF7E1
172.16.123.0     172.2.5.1       1022       0x80000003 0x709
                 Type-5 AS External Link States
Link ID          ADV Router      Age        Seq#       Checksum Tag
172.10.0.0       172.1.5.1       1168       0x80000004 0xC6AD   0
router2#
```

Here router and summary link-state updates can be seen for both Areas 0 and 2 on this ABR. A report of external (redistributed) routes is also shown as Type 5 links. The age is in seconds. Since each route is refreshed every 30 minutes, this number should not climb any larger than 1800. If it does, it typically means that the route has gone bad and is waiting to be flushed at 3600 seconds.

FROM THE CLASSROOM

Troubleshooting OSPF Virtual Links

When setting up virtual links in OSPF, make sure you use the OSPF router IDs. If you use the next-hop IP addresses instead of the OSPF router IDs, your virtual link cannot function properly. Make sure you verify both OSPF router IDs before configuring your virtual link.

—*Brad Ellis, CCIE#5796, MCNE, MCSE, CCDP*

Cisco's Enhanced IGRP

EIGRP is a comprehensive, event-driven enterprise routing protocol created by Cisco. It effectively routes IP, IPX, and AppleTalk within a single routing protocol architecture. However, each routed protocol uses a different instance of EIGRP. EIGRP is a renovated version of IGRP, with the following added features:

- Variable-length subnet masking (VLSM)
- More robust routing
- Faster convergence times
- Partial event-driven updates
- Multiple Network Layer support
- Full compatibility with IGRP

The stronger routing protocol delivered by EIGRP is the result of the following features:

- Distributed Update Algorithm (DUAL)
- Reliable Transport Protocol
- Neighbor discovery
- Protocol-dependent modules

At the heart of EIGRP is the DUAL finite state machine, which uses a concept called *feasible successors* to select a loop-free balanced routing topology. The topology table maintains a set of minimum-cost downstream routers as feasible successors for each network destination. DUAL uses feasible successors in selecting a least-cost path through the network that is guaranteed not to be part of a routing loop. During a network topology change, DUAL checks for feasible successors (or queries its neighbors, if no successors are found) and then reconverges routing.

EIGRP uses both unicast and multicast messages to more efficiently communicate with its neighbors within the EIGRP network. In addition, routing updates are encapsulated within a reliable transport protocol to guarantee delivery, while common hellos for keepalive purposes are unacknowledged.

EIGRP's strength comes from the breadth of network protocol communication with its neighbors, exchanging routing and real-time network state information only when network events change. EIGRP provides for such a robust routing architecture using various packet types, neighbor tables, topology tables, routing states, and routing tags:

- In attaining real-time network state information, EIGRP uses a variety of packet protocol types, including hello/acknowledgment, update (unicast and multicast), queries, replies, and requests.

- In providing valuable neighbor information, EIGRP neighbor tables include the neighbor's address, the neighbor's connected interface, and Reliable Transport Protocol information.

- In providing valuable network topology information, EIGRP topology tables include the destination, the neighbor, and the metric.

- EIGRP maintains one of two routing states per network: active (recomputing) and passive (stable). One of two routing tags is maintained per network: internal or external.

on the
ὑob   *EIGRP is a very easy protocol to configure and implement in a corporate network. If a company is using all Cisco routers, EIGRP is probably the routing protocol of choice.*

Troubleshooting EIGRP

In troubleshooting EIGRP, start by looking locally on the router on which the problem exists. Use the SHOW IP EIGRP INTERFACES command to verify all the interfaces on which EIGRP is currently enabled.

```
router2>show ip eigrp int
IP-EIGRP interfaces for process 1
                    Xmit Queue    Mean    Pacing Time   Multicast     Pending
Interface   Peers   Un/Reliable   SRTT    Un/Reliable   Flow Timer    Routes
Et0          0         0/0          0         0/10           0            0
Se0          1         0/0         809        0/15         4043           0
Se1          1         0/0         36         0/15          175           0
router2>
```

Look at the number of EIGRP peers to verify the correct number of neighbors. In this case, EIGRP is configured on the Ethernet 0 interface, yet no neighbors are established there. This might indicate a physical or configuration problem. It might also mean that there are no Cisco routers out this interface. In this case, EIGRP should be configured to *not* send updates out that interface.

Sometimes, low-bandwidth congested links can cause routing update problems. Since hello packets are sent to each neighbor, a slow link might cause some of the hellos to be lost. Since EIGRP sends hello packets every 5 seconds and considers a neighbor "dead" after only 15 seconds (or three successive lost hello packets), routing problems can occur. Such challenges can be found on heavily populated, multilink Frame Relay interfaces.

If certain routes are not being received by a router, but all local configuration and connectivity elements seem to be operating at the IP level, begin looking upstream at the neighboring routers. Start by using the SHOW IP EIGRP NEIGHBOR command to verify that all neighbors are established:

```
router2>show ip eigrp neigh
IP-EIGRP neighbors for process 1
H    Address                   Interface     Hold Uptime     SRTT    RTO   Q  Seq
                                             (sec)           (ms)          Cnt Num
1    172.16.123.2              Se1             12 00:08:09     36    216   0  6
0    172.16.112.1              Se0             11 00:08:27    809   4854   0  9
router2>
```

Look at each neighbor and make sure it is established on the appropriate WAN and LAN links. Here, two EIGRP neighbors have been established. Compared to the previous SHOW IP EIGRP INTERFACES screen, the two peers have been validated here. However, if an expected peer/neighbor is missing, these two screens cannot tell why.

The Hold column indicates the holddown timer. This value should never dip below 10 seconds. If it does, it is possible that the neighbor shown has failed and is about to be aged out of the table (when this counter reaches zero). The Uptime column shows how long the neighbor session has been established. If multiple successive SHOW IP EIGRP NEIGHBOR screens continue to show this value as rather small, the neighbor in question is not very stable.

Furthermore, use the SHOW IP EIGRP TOPOLOGY command to make sure that all routes are part of the topology table and that the feasible successors are accurate:

```
router2>sh ip ei top
IP-EIGRP Topology Table for process 1

Codes: P - Passive, A - Active, U - Update, Q - Query, R - Reply,
       r - Reply status

P 172.16.31.0/24, 1 successors, FD is 2195456
         via 172.16.123.2 (2195456/281600), Serial1
P 172.4.0.0/16, 1 successors, FD is 2323456
         via 172.16.123.2 (2323456/409600), Serial1
         via 172.16.112.1 (2809856/2297856), Serial0
P 172.16.21.0/24, 1 successors, FD is 281600
         via Connected, Ethernet0
P 172.1.0.0/16, 1 successors, FD is 2297856
         via 172.16.112.1 (2297856/128256), Serial0
P 172.2.0.0/16, 1 successors, FD is 128256
         via Summary (128256/0), Null0
P 172.3.0.0/16, 1 successors, FD is 2297856
         via 172.16.123.2 (2297856/128256), Serial1
P 172.16.11.0/24, 1 successors, FD is 2195456
         via 172.16.112.1 (2195456/281600), Serial0
P 172.16.0.0/16, 1 successors, FD is 281600
         via Summary (281600/0), Null0
P 172.16.123.0/24, 1 successors, FD is 2169856
         via Connected, Serial1
P 172.16.112.0/24, 1 successors, FD is 2169856
         via Connected, Serial0
P 172.16.113.0/24, 1 successors, FD is 2681856
         via 172.16.112.1 (2681856/2169856), Serial0
         via 172.16.123.2 (2707456/2195456), Serial1
router2>
```

The topology table lists all practical ways of getting to each destination network or subnet. FD indicates the feasible distance. This is the best metric that this router has for each route shown. In fact, the "successor" is actually the current best path, not the "next in line." The FD (best metric) is then compared to each metric that is advertised to this router from each neighbor. Only those metrics (from neighbors) that are better than the metric from this router are kept as alternate routes, should the primary fail.

In the code listing shown, subnet 172.16.113.0 /24 has one primary route via 172.16.112.1 and one alternate via 172.16.123.2. Note that the metric from the neighbor (2195456) is less than the metric used in this router (2681856). If you examine subnet 172.16.11.0 /24, only one path is shown. All alternates have been thrown out because their advertised metrics are worse than the metric used by this router (2195456).

If all neighbors are established and the feasible-successor topology table is accurate, verify that the routes in the routing table are being advertised via EIGRP. Sometimes there are other routing protocols with lower ADs whose routes get selected in the routing table. Use the SHOW IP ROUTE command to verify the routes in the routing table and the protocols that made the entry:

```
router2>sh ip ro
Codes: C - connected, S - static, I - IGRP, R - RIP, M - mobile, B - BGP
       D - EIGRP, EX - EIGRP external, O - OSPF, IA - OSPF inter area
       N1 - OSPF NSSA external type 1, N2 - OSPF NSSA external type 2
       E1 - OSPF external type 1, E2 - OSPF external type 2, E - EGP
       i - IS-IS, L1 - IS-IS level-1, L2 - IS-IS level-2, * - candidate default
       U - per-user static route, o - ODR

Gateway of last resort is not set

D    172.4.0.0/16 [90/2323456] via 172.16.123.2, 00:24:03, Serial1
D    172.1.0.0/16 [90/2297856] via 172.16.112.1, 00:24:03, Serial0
     172.2.0.0/16 is variably subnetted, 6 subnets, 2 masks
C       172.2.4.0/24 is directly connected, Loopback4
C       172.2.5.0/24 is directly connected, Loopback5
C       172.2.2.0/24 is directly connected, Loopback2
C       172.2.3.0/24 is directly connected, Loopback3
D       172.2.0.0/16 is a summary, 00:24:03, Null0
C       172.2.1.0/24 is directly connected, Loopback1
D    172.3.0.0/16 [90/2297856] via 172.16.123.2, 00:24:03, Serial1
     172.16.0.0/16 is variably subnetted, 7 subnets, 2 masks
D       172.16.31.0/24 [90/2195456] via 172.16.123.2, 00:24:03, Serial1
C       172.16.21.0/24 is directly connected, Ethernet0
D       172.16.11.0/24 [90/2195456] via 172.16.112.1, 00:24:03, Serial0
D       172.16.0.0/16 is a summary, 00:24:04, Null0
C       172.16.123.0/24 is directly connected, Serial1
C       172.16.112.0/24 is directly connected, Serial0
D       172.16.113.0/24 [90/2681856] via 172.16.112.1, 00:24:04, Serial0
router2>
```

In this routing table, the EIGRP metrics (as well as those shown in the neighbor table) are quite large. The composite metric that EIGRP uses is 256 times larger than the same IGRP metric. You can also see that EIGRP automatically summarizes subnets of a major network number before advertising them out a different network number. In this case, the 172.16.0.0 subnets have been summarized (null 0) automatically. Also note that the routing table shows only the best path, whereas the topology shows all "feasible" routes.

In troubleshooting IPX EIGRP, verify that the routes in the routing table are being advertised via EIGRP and not via IPX RIP or NLSP, as shown here:

```
router2#sh ipx ro
Codes: C - Connected primary network,    c - Connected secondary network
       S - Static, F - Floating static, L - Local (internal), W - IPXWAN
       R - RIP, E - EIGRP, N - NLSP, X - External, A - Aggregate
       s - seconds, u - uses
26 Total IPX routes. Up to 1 parallel paths and 16 hops allowed.
No default route known.
C        B1 (NOVELL-ETHER),  Et0
C      1122 (HDLC),          Se0
C      2233 (HDLC),          Se1
E        1A [2297856/0] via      1122.0010.7b39.dacb, age 00:05:56,
                          7u, Se0
E        1B [2297856/0] via      1122.0010.7b39.dacb, age 00:05:56,
                          7u, Se0
E        1C [2297856/0] via      1122.0010.7b39.dacb, age 00:05:56,
                          1u, Se0
E        1D [2297856/0] via      1122.0010.7b39.dacb, age 00:05:58,
                          1u, Se0
E        1E [2297856/0] via      1122.0010.7b39.dacb, age 00:05:58,
                          1u, Se0
(output delctcd …)
E        A1 [2195456/0] via      1122.0010.7b39.dacb, age 00:05:59,
                          1u, Se0
E        C1 [2195456/0] via      2233.0010.7b39.d91d, age 00:06:14,
                          1u, Se1
E      1133 [2681856/0] via      1122.0010.7b39.dacb, age 00:06:16,
                          1u, Se0
router2#
```

EIGRP uses the same metrics to determine best path, whether for IP, IPX, or AppleTalk. As shown in this routing table, the best path to each IPX network is shown with a rather large-looking metric. The age shown indicates how long ago that route was advertised to this router. If the age remains low on successive routing table displays, it indicates that the route in question is constantly changing state.

For IPX EIGRP, also verify the IPX EIGRP topology for feasible successors:

```
router2#sh ipx eigrp top
IPX EIGRP Topology Table for process 1
Codes: P - Passive, A - Active, U - Update, Q - Query, R - Reply,
       r - Reply status
P 2233, 1 successors, FD is 2169856
        via Connected, Serial1
P 1A, 1 successors, FD is 2297856
        via 1122.0010.7b39.dacb (2297856/128256), Serial0
P 1B, 1 successors, FD is 2297856
        via 1122.0010.7b39.dacb (2297856/128256), Serial0
P 1C, 1 successors, FD is 2297856
        via 1122.0010.7b39.dacb (2297856/128256), Serial0
P 1D, 1 successors, FD is 2297856
        via 1122.0010.7b39.dacb (2297856/128256), Serial0
P 1E, 1 successors, FD is 2297856
        via 1122.0010.7b39.dacb (2297856/128256), Serial0
P 1133, 1 successors, FD is 2681856
        via 1122.0010.7b39.dacb (2681856/2169856), Serial0
        via 2233.0010.7b39.d91d (2707456/2195456), Serial1
P 1122, 1 successors, FD is 2169856
        via Connected, Serial0
(output deleted …)
P A1, 1 successors, FD is 2195456
        via 1122.0010.7b39.dacb (2195456/281600), Serial0
P B1, 1 successors, FD is 281600
        via Connected, Ethernet0
P C1, 1 successors, FD is 2195456
        via 2233.0010.7b39.d91d (2195456/281600), Serial1
router2#
```

The FD is used the same for IPX as it was for IP. Only those routes that have an advertised metric better than the metric of this router are allowed to stay in the topology table. In fact, the metric values used for IPX are identical to those used for IP. Of the entire table shown, only network 1133 has a feasible backup path. All others must be queried from neighbors, should they fail.

For IPX EIGRP, verify that all EIGRP neighbors are established:

```
router2#sh ipx eig neighbors

IPX EIGRP Neighbors for process 1
H   Address                  Interface   Hold Uptime    SRTT   RTO  Q  Seq
                                         (sec)          (ms)      Cnt Num
1   2233.0010.7b39.d91d      Se1          12 00:12:31    37    222  0  22
0   1122.0010.7b39.dacb      Se0          12 00:12:55    31    200  0  31
router2#
```

Here the IPX EIGRP neighbors are the same physical routers as were in the SHOW IP EIGRP NEIGHBORS screen, only this time their IPX addresses are shown. The table is read the exact same way as the IP table.

For AppleTalk EIGRP, verify that all EIGRP neighbors are established:

```
router2#sh app nei
AppleTalk neighbors:
  112.237        Serial0, uptime 01:10:32, 3 secs
        Neighbor has restarted 1 time in 01:11:32.
        Neighbor is reachable as a EIGRP peer
  123.42         Serial1, uptime 01:11:00, 1 sec
        Neighbor is reachable as a EIGRP peer
router2#
```

Note that only EIGRP is configured on the two serial interfaces shown. Between routers (typical of a serial connection), it makes no sense to also run the very chatty RTMP routing protocol. Although this router does have an Ethernet interface, no AppleTalk neighbor appears there. This could indicate that either no other AppleTalk routers are out there or that the interface is down.

The SHOW APPLETALK EIGRP NEIGHBORS command is very similar to its IP and EIGRP cousins:

```
router2#sh appletalk eigrp neighbors
AT/EIGRP Neighbors for process 1, router id 1
H   Address                  Interface   Hold Uptime    SRTT   RTO  Q  Seq
                                         (sec)          (ms)      Cnt Num
1   123.42                   Se1          13 00:05:15    24    200  0  15
0   112.237                  Se0          13 00:05:30   423   2538  0  10
router2#
```

Since the EIGRP protocol operates identically whether transporting IP, IPX, or AppleTalk, the various SHOW screens and their interpretations are virtually identical.

Using Debugging

You should become comfortable with debugging EIGRP routing for IP, IPX, and AppleTalk EIGRP networks. Since EIGRP is a robust protocol, it can also be fairly complex. Start with the DEBUG IP EIGRP command and watch the routing updates or network errors:

```
router2# debug ip eigrp
IP-EIGRP: Processing incoming UPDATE packet
IP-EIGRP: Int 172.16.113.0/24 M 2681856 - 1657856 1024000 SM 2169856 - 1657856 5
12000
IP-EIGRP: Int 172.16.31.0/24 M 2707456 - 1657856 1049600 SM 2195456 - 1657856 53
7600
IP-EIGRP: 172.16.31.0/24 routing table not updated
```

This is a sample output from the DEBUG IP EIGRP command. Remember that EIGRP generates updates only when necessary, so this DEBUG output occurs only when something happens on the network. Furthermore, this DEBUG command can generate a severe amount of data, so be careful about using it on a large or busy network.

The first column shows that the advertised routes are "int," meaning internal, or within this AS. The other possible value is "ext," which indicates that the route is redistributed from another AS or routing protocol and is flagged as external by EIGRP.

The two values reported for each network or subnet are the metric (M) and the source metric (SM). The metric is calculated by this router, whereas the source metric is the metric reported by the neighbor router to this router. Both metrics are a sum of the inverse bandwidth and the delay (the two numbers after the M and SM, respectively). Since EIGRP tracks its feasible successors by comparing the metric used by the neighbor, both values are necessary.

For the first subnet, 172.16.113.0 /24, the SM is 2169856 and the local metric is 2681856. The local metric is always larger than the advertised metric, since at least one more delay value is added. For this subnet, it can be seen that the bandwidth is the same for both the neighbor and the local router, so the only difference is the delay value. The calculated delay between the neighbor and this router is approximately 500,000 (which is directly related to the bandwidth of the receiving interface).

Since the SM is less than or equal to the M, this update is a feasible successor. A SHOW IP EIGRP TOPOLOGY command would verify this. For the second subnet, 172.16.31.0 /24, the SM is also a feasible successor, since it is less than the M. However, the statement that the routing table was not updated indicates that this route has probably already been received, and this iteration is no revelation to the routing table.

IPX EIGRP DEBUG allows for you to watch all routing updates from each neighbor and verify that all reachability information is being received:

```
RouterA#debug ipx eigrp events
IPX EIGRP events debugging is on

IPXEIGRP: External CCCC metric 45842176 hop 1 delay 1
IPXEIGRP: External BBBB metric 269312000 hop 2 delay 2
IPXEIGRP: External DDDD metric 269312000 hop 2 delay 2
IPXEIGRP: Received update from AAAA.0060.8394.e940 for net BBBB
IPXEIGRP: Received update from AAAA.0060.8394.e940 for net BBBB
IPXEIGRP: External BBBB metric 4294967295 hop 1 delay 1
IPXEIGRP: DDDD via AAAA.0060.5cf4.1554 metric 45867776
IPXEIGRP: Received update from AAAA.0060.5cf4.1554 for net DDDD
IPXEIGRP: better [0/0/45867776] route for DDDD from AAAA.0060.5cf4.1554,
        flushing old [2/1/0] route/paths
        external hop count in table 1, in update 1
IPXEIGRP: Received update from AAAA.0060.5cf4.1554 for net DDDD
IPXEIGRP: Received update from AAAA.0060.5cf4.1554 for net DDDD
```

Here you can see that a better route for network DDDD has been received, and the old "best" path is flushed. There is no EVENTS option with the IP version of this command.

Now that you have a better idea of EIGRP, take a look at the following Scenario & Solution.

SCENARIO & SOLUTION

What IOS commands are necessary to enable EIGRP routing on a Cisco router?	ROUTER EIGRP Y NETWORK X.X.X.X (where X.X.X.X is a connected network and Y is an autonomous system number).
What protocols does EIGRP support?	IP, IPX, and AppleTalk.
What brand of routers can run EIGRP?	Only Cisco. EIGRP is a Cisco proprietary routing protocol.

EXERCISE 6-1

Configuring EIGRP

When configuring EIGRP, you need to follow several steps:

1. Log in to the router and go into configuration mode by typing **config terminal**.

2. Enable EIGRP routing on the router with the global command **router EIGRP 10**.

3. Inside the EIGRP configuration interface, enter the network portion of the interface that will participate in sending and receiving updates: **network 10.0.0.0**.

4. Enter any other network portions of interfaces that will participate in the EIGRP updates.

5. Exit out of configuration mode: **exit**.

6. Save the changes to the router's NVRAM: **copy run start**.

7. Follow the same procedure on another connected router.

8. Verify that routes are being received by typing the command **show ip route**.

Border Gateway Protocol

Border Gateway Protocol (BGP) is the routing protocol of the Internet. Logically, there are two portions to BGP: External BGP (EBGP) and Internal BGP (IBGP).

EBGP exchanges routing information with other ASs. IBGP exchanges routing information within an AS. Within an AS, there are also Interior Gateway Protocols (IGPs) such as RIP (v1 and v2), IGRP, EIGRP, and OSPF. An IGP is needed within an AS to advertise all routes to all routers of the AS. IBGP rides on top of the IGP. EBGP connects autonomous systems, where no IGP runs.

Within an AS, BGP must be fully meshed. In other words, all BGP speakers must have a TCP session to every other BGP speaker. IBGP routers are not allowed to send IBGP updates to another IBGP neighbor. Due to this rule, a large BGP AS can have a tremendous number of IBGP neighbors for each BGP router. This adds configuration overhead for the administrators, as well as memory and processing overhead within each router.

BGP allows *route reflectors* and *BGP confederations* to reduce IBGP routing meshing. With route reflectors, one router is elected as the "reflector." All other IBGP neighbors send their IBGP updates to that one router, and it reflects the routes to every other IBGP router. Backup reflectors can be configured for redundancy within the AS. Confederations are a way of breaking a large AS into groups of smaller autonomous systems. Each smaller AS is fully meshed (because that is the rule), and each small AS is fully meshed to every other AS. By breaking up the large AS, the number of BGP neighbors is greatly reduced.

When you use either route reflectors or confederations, you must take great care to ensure that all routers speak to the reflector or all routers are fully meshed within the new, smaller autonomous systems. There are very few (if any) error statements when BGP is not fully and properly configured; there are only empty routing tables.

Sometimes a stub IBGP neighbor is used within an AS for remote sites that are not multihomed or for some larger, hierarchical type ASs trying to reduce the size of an IBGP mesh. The route reflector is an IBGP router that allows for a peer not to be part of the full IBGP mesh. To verify whether a neighbor is a route reflector, use the SHOW IP BGP NEIGHBOR command, and the third line should identify whether it is a route reflector or not:

```
RouterA#show ip bgp neighbor 10.2.2.1
BGP neighbor is 10.2.2.1, remote AS 65000, internal link
Index 34, Offset 4, Mask 0x4
 Route-Reflector Client
```

The topology illustrated in Figure 6-3 shows the relations between EBGP, IBGP, and an IGP.

BGP gathers and advertises routes from network external boundaries. Due to the enormous wealth of routes within the Internet, it makes sense that BGP is an event-driven protocol.

BGP does not make per-hop routing decisions; rather, it functions under an entire network cloud called an AS. When any two BGP routers connect and exchange routes, this process is called *peering*. When two such routers are in different autonomous systems, it is called EBGP. Such peering within a common AS is an example of IBGP. BGP allows for specific peering policies to be defined on any BGP router so that routes can be filtered, deterred, or preferred based on AS numbers, community tags, metrics, and other criteria.

FIGURE 6-3 The BGP internetwork topology

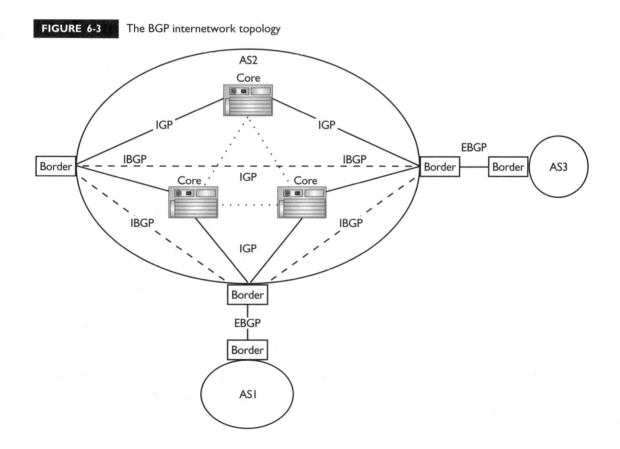

When a BGP router receives updates from multiple ASs that describe different paths to the same destination, it selects only the single best path for reaching that destination. However, BGP propagates all known paths to a destination to its neighbors. As with any routing protocol, each BGP router is responsible for making the decision as to best path. The decision is based on the value of attributes such as administrative weight (Cisco proprietary, local preference) used within an AS, the origin of the route (BGP or non-BGP) and AS path length (number of autonomous systems that must be passed through) that the update contains and other BGP-configurable factors.

Some IGPs run inside the AS. The IGP provides for intra-AS routing and does not carry external routing information (BGP attributes or metrics). Common IGPs within an Internet routing environment are OSPF and EIGRP.

As shown in the BGP internetwork topology in Figure 6-3, packets from AS 1 transit AS 2 to reach AS 3. Routes from AS 1 are not originated by the IGP of AS 2 (they are learned externally via EBGP from AS 1). Thus, the routes from AS 1 must be carried via IBGP across AS 2 to reach AS 3.

Unfortunately, IBGP does not advertise routes to other IBGP routers if the IGP is not already aware of the routes. This concept, known as *synchronization*, ensures that unwanted BGP routes are not carried through an AS unless specifically desired. Since synchronization is on by default, AS 2 is considered a stub AS. Since the routes from AS 1 are intended to be advertised to AS 3, AS 2 must become a transit AS. To do this, AS 2 must disable synchronization with the IGP in order to advertise the routes to AS 3.

exam
ⓦatch

IGP synchronization is disabled with the NO SYNCHRONIZATION router configuration command.

BGP peers must be manually configured and individually identified to exchange updates. This peering establishment must be performed for all BGP peers, IBGP as well as EBGP. In the event that an IBGP peer is not included in the configuration, that router cannot learn any EBGP routes from that particular BGP peer. Remember that IBGP must be a full mesh within the AS, either logically or through the use of route reflectors or confederations.

exam
ⓦatch

When originating a BGP route using the NETWORK router command, make sure that the route is already in the IGP routing table. If it is not, the network number specified is not added to the BGP updates.

Cisco provides for a peer-group feature in which a bundle of peers can be identified by a string. In configuring IBGP or EBGP peering, it is helpful to bundle all peers into a common group to ease in the configuration of additional optional properties.

Cisco also provides support for extensive BGP routing policy definitions using regular expressions, access lists, community tags, and route maps.

Troubleshooting BGP

When troubleshooting BGP, especially with a full Internet routing table, it is best to start with a summary snapshot of BGP. Ensure that all neighbors are established and that all BGP table versions are synchronized for each neighbor. In addition, it is important to see how long the BGP session with each neighbor has been up and established. Use the SHOW IP BGP SUMMARY command to give an overview of the BGP state:

```
RouterA> show ip bgp summary
BGP table version is 159505, main routing table version 159505
1299 network entries (2502/3897 paths) using 274900 bytes of memory
504 BGP path attribute entries using 69380 bytes of memory
142 BGP route-map cache entries using 2272 bytes of memory
0 BGP filter-list cache entries using 0 bytes of memory

Neighbor       V    AS MsgRcvd MsgSent   TblVer  InQ OutQ Up/Down   State/PfxRcd
10.2.1.1       4     1   81106   45150   159505    0    0 4w3d              1059
10.3.1.1       4     2 5128660  173273   159505    0    0 2w2d               146
10.4.1.1       4     1   86799   45155   159505    0    0 2w3d              1296
```

This is a small BGP table. The actual Internet BGP table would contain close to 80,000 network entries. Verify that the number of routing entries is about what is expected. If the number is dramatically smaller than expected, it might be that some routes are being filtered out.

All of the BGP table versions ("TblVer") should be the same on the router. The up/down state, which gives you an idea of how long the BGP session has been active, suggests stability. In this case, the neighbors have been established for four weeks and two weeks, respectively. If the up/down state shows "Active," BGP is attempting to establish a TCP session with the neighbor IP address indicated.

If a particular session appears to be in a hung state or continues initializing, it sometimes helps to clear the BGP session with the CLEAR IP BGP privileged mode command and see if it comes active:

```
RouterA#clear ip bgp 10.2.1.1
```

If you are searching for a particular route, use the SHOW IP BGP X.X.X.X. command to locate the route. Viewing an entire Internet BGP table can take considerable time. Here is an example:

```
RouterA#sh ip bgp 192.31.7.130
BGP routing table entry for 192.31.7.0/24, version 34967033
Paths: (2 available, best #1, advertised over EBGP)
 65001 65002
   10.2.1.1 (metric 4) from 10.2.1.1 (10.2.1.1)
     Origin IGP, localpref 90, valid, internal, best
     Community: 1:1
     Originator : 10.2.1.1, Cluster list: 10.2.1.1
```

In the SHOW IP BGP X.X.X.X. output, verify that the proper AS path is shown for the particular route. Also look at the "Originator" to verify that the appropriate BGP router or routers are originating and advertising the route via IBGP.

If routing communities are being used with BGP routes, it could be important to check the route maps associated with the community tags. Communities are used to define routing attributes as routes enter an AS. Routes could be allowed to exit the AS, remain in the AS, remain in the receiving router only, or have specific values set that can be read later on in the routing journey with route maps. Route maps can get rather complex, especially with Internet routing. Use the SHOW ROUTE-MAP command to view route maps associated with community routing tags, as shown here:

```
Router> show route-map peer-out
route-map peer-out, permit, sequence 10
  Match clauses:
    community (community-list filter): 53
  Set clauses:
    as-path prepend 1000
  Policy routing matches: 0 packets, 0 bytes
route-map peer-out, permit, sequence 20
  Match clauses:
    community (community-list filter): 20
  Set clauses:
  Policy routing matches: 0 packets, 0 bytes
```

In this example, the route map named "peer-out" has two lines (10 and 20). The first line says that if the community attribute is set to the value of 53, prepend the number 1000 to the AS path of the route and permit the route. The second line says that if the community attribute is set to 20, simply permit the route. All other routes would be filtered (discarded) if sent through this route map. This alone could be a major (and unexpected) loss of routes in the network.

Route maps allow for modifying BGP routing metrics, local preferences, communities, AS path, and influencing other BGP parameters in order to manage BGP routing policies. Although route maps can be very powerful, they can also be confusing and should be structured accordingly.

A typical BGP configuration shown by the SHOW RUNNING-CONFIG command might look like this:

```
show running-config
(output deleted …)
router bgp 1
neighbor test peer-group
neighbor test remote-as 65000
neighbor test version 4
neighbor test distribute-list 110 in
neighbor test distribute-list 111 out
neighbor test route-map peer-in in
neighbor test route-map peer-out out
neighbor test filter-list 50 in
neighbor test filter-list 51 out
```

This sample configuration shows a peer group named *test*. All the members of this peer group are in AS 65000. Thus, it is assumed that this is an IBGP peer group. All members of this group also use an inbound distribution list of 110 and an outbound list of 111. In addition, each member has the same inbound route map as well as the same outbound route map. The same is true for inbound and outbound filter lists. If certain BGP routers are experiencing routing problems, it could be that they should not be members of this peer group. Some of the policies shown could be detrimental if not fully understood.

To view a particular peer-group peering session, use the SHOW IP BGP PEER-GROUP command:

```
RouterA#sh ip bgp peer-group test

BGP neighbor is test, peer-group leader,  remote AS 65001
Index 2, Offset 0, Mask 0x4
```

```
BGP version 4
Minimum time between advertisement runs is 5 seconds
Incoming update network filter list is 110
Outgoing update network filter list is 111
Route map for incoming advertisements is peer-in
Route map for outgoing advertisements is peer-out
```

In viewing the SHOW IP BGP PEER-GROUP output, verify that the appropriate AS number is being applied, if this is an IBGP peer group.

By default, all BGP advertises all originated routes to all neighbors. EBGP advertises every BGP route to every configured peer, IBGP or EBGP. IBGP routers advertise only either originated routes or EBGP routes to other IBGP neighbors. As mentioned earlier, IBGP neighbors do not forward IBGP information to other IBGP routers. Due to the complexity and quantity of neighbors necessary to accomplish an IBGP full mesh, route reflectors are used.

In the event that you want to filter routing advertisements either in or out based on a certain IP address block, you should create access lists specifying the particular IP address range you want to deny or permit. Extended IP access lists are used to specify both the range of network numbers and the range of subnet masks used with the network numbers. Although quite powerful, the syntax of the extended access lists used to filter both network numbers and masks quickly becomes confusing. In IOS Version 12.x, prefix lists are used to filter ranges of networks with a much more user-friendly syntax.

An access list can be applied to a BGP peering session via a route map or a distribute list in the BGP peering statement, as shown in the following configuration display. The numbers shown here are IP extended access lists being used to filter routes learned from or sent to particular BGP neighbors. An extended access list can also be used to match routing entries as part of a route map:

```
neighbor test distribute-list 110 in
neighbor test distribute-list 111 out
```

or

```
route-map peer-in permit 10
match ip address 110
```

If there are particular autonomous systems that must be filtered, an as-path access list can be used:

```
ip as-path access-list 50 deny _65002_
```

> This example says that any route that is learned via a path that includes AS 65002 is denied. Of course, as with any Cisco filter, you must specify something to be permitted; otherwise, all routes are denied. The as-path filter can be applied via a filter list or within a route map:

```
neighbor test filter-list 50 in
neighbor test filter-list 51 out
```

> or

```
route-map peer-in permit 10
match as-path 50
```

> Finally, BGP can often be very processor-intensive; it should be checked periodically to see if it is sustaining high CPU utilization. If you are maintaining a number of BGP peering sessions on a single router, clearing BGP can cause CPU spikes when processing an inordinate amount of information. Here is a sample of the SHOW PROC CPU command:

```
RouterA#show proc cpu
CPU utilization for five seconds: 96%/90%; one minute: 92%; five minutes: 85%
(output deleted …)
```

CERTIFICATION SUMMARY

Although newer networks are generally not built with periodic broadcast protocols, there still exists a substantial base of legacy networks supporting these routing protocols. These protocols are often used in multivendor routing environments because periodic broadcast protocols are somewhat simpler and more interoperable. For this reason, it is important to be able to troubleshoot and debug various routing protocols at the lowest level.

RIP is found at the core of many protocols such as IPX and RTMP. Only in exclusive Cisco environments does one have the advantage of bundling IP, IPX, and AppleTalk into a robust event-driven enterprise routing protocol such as EIGRP.

Event-driven protocols are much more scalable and more applicable within larger networks than periodic broadcast protocols. OSPF and EIGRP both have their own advantages and disadvantages, and each is intended for specific types of network architectures. BGP, the routing protocol of the Internet, can be very complex, with extremely cryptic and nonintuitive routing policies.

Regardless of the routing environment, protocols, or architecture, it is important that a system administrator have a solid base of troubleshooting skills and tools for understanding and diagnosing the nature of certain anomalies. Cisco provides a wide range of commands, views, and features to assist in determining where a problem might exist so that a solution can be found.

✓ TWO-MINUTE DRILL

Here are some of the key points from each certification objective in Chapter 6.

Periodic Broadcast-Based Protocols

❑ Periodic broadcast protocols send route updates at regular, timed intervals.

❑ RIP functions by broadcasting its full routing table to all other routers in the network. All routers receive the advertised routes and regularly update their forwarding tables.

❑ RIP generally requires route updates every 30 seconds via broadcasts in order to keep the routes fresh.

❑ In order to accommodate various routing loops that could occur within certain network topologies, RIP has implemented a number of features to reduce looping effects:

  ❑ Holddown

  ❑ Split-horizon

  ❑ Poison reverse

❑ When redistributing routing protocols with classless VLSM networks into RIP, be sure that subnetted static routes with a null next hop are redistributed as well.

❑ Whenever redistributing routes, always include subnets.

❑ When you are troubleshooting RIP, it is always best to start by looking in the routing table for RIP.

❑ Running RIP with an instance of another periodic broadcast routing protocol, such as IGRP, can result in routing issues due to the asynchronous updates and administrative distances competing for inserting routes into the forwarding table.

❑ Cisco's Interior Gateway Routing Protocol (IGRP) is also a periodic broadcast protocol, with stronger decision-making criteria based on real-time network events and congestion states.

❑ The following timers are associated with IGRP:

❑ Update timer

❑ Invalid timer

❑ Holddown timer

❑ Flush timer

❑ When redistributing routing protocols with classless VLSM networks into IGRP, be sure that classful static routes with a null next hop are redistributed as well.

❑ When you are troubleshooting an IGRP network, always start with the IGRP routing table.

❑ Although IP has made significant progress within the last few years as the common communications protocol, there is still a significant installed base of Internetwork Packet Exchange (IPX) equipment and networks.

❑ Service Advertising Protocol (SAP) is an enterprise network services protocol used to advertise information regarding file servers, print servers, job servers, and so on.

❑ When you are troubleshooting an IPX network, always start with the IPX routing table.

❑ AppleTalk Routing Table Maintenance Protocol (RTMP) is another distance-vector, periodic broadcast, RIP-based protocol.

❑ In troubleshooting AppleTalk networks, always start with the routing table.

Event-Driven Protocols

❑ *Event-driven protocols* provide for a more scalable network architecture in that routing updates are generated only in the event of a network topology change.

❑ Three powerful event-driven protocols are Open Shortest Path First (OSPF), Enhanced IGRP (EIGRP), and Border Gateway Protocol (BGP).

❑ OSPF is purely an IP-based routing protocol intended for hierarchical large-scale networks.

❑ EIGRP is a multiservice routing protocol supporting IPX, AppleTalk, and IP.

❑ BGP is used for interconnecting networks and defining strict routing policies.

❏ Understand how to use OSPF in point-to-point, point-to- multipoint, and broadcast media.

❏ OSPF has a number of design-related issues that can cause networkwide problems.

❏ When redistributing OSPF routes, be sure to include External 1, External 2, *and* subnets.

❏ Understand how and where to use virtual links for extending a backbone area.

❏ In troubleshooting EIGRP, start by looking locally on the router on which the problem exists.

❏ Synchronization should almost always be disabled.

❏ When generating an EBGP route using the NETWORK command, make sure that the route is already in the IGP routing table.

❏ When you are troubleshooting BGP, especially with a full Internet routing table, it is best to start with a summary snapshot of BGP.

SELF TEST

The following questions will help you measure your understanding of the material presented in this chapter. Read all of the choices carefully because there might be more than one correct answer. Choose all correct answers for each question.

Periodic Broadcast-Based Protocols

1. What causes a router running RIP to broadcast its entire routing table?

    A.   It receives an update from another router and must immediately update its neighbors.

    B.   RIP never sends its entire routing table; it sends only updates.

    C.   Thirty seconds has passed since it last broadcast its entire routing table.

    D.   Thirty seconds has passed since it last received an updated route from a neighbor router.

2. Which of the following are valid Class A address(es)? Choose all that apply.

    A.   10.5.256.1

    B.   51.52.254.254

    C.   128.5.1.1

    D.   14.0.0.1

3. Which of the following is the correct command to view the RIP routes in an IP routing table?

    A.   SHOW IP ROUTE RIP

    B.   SHOW ROUTER RIP

    C.   SHOW IP ROUTER RIP

    D.   SHOW IP ROUTE

4. When is it necessary to use a virtual link?

    A.   For RIP to maintain a path to a router greater than 15 hops away

    B.   To connect an OSPF area to Area 0 through another area

    C.   For EIGRP to redistribute routes with BGP external neighbors

    D.   To connect a remote IGRP area border router with the backbone router

5. EIGRP supports which of the following protocols? Choose all that apply.

   A. IP

   B. SNA

   C. IPX

   D. AppleTalk

6. ACME Electric needs a routing protocol that will support IP and IPX. Which routing protocol(s) could you recommend to ACME Electric? Choose all that apply.

   A. EIGRP

   B. BGP

   C. RIP

   D. IGRP

7. ACME Fusion Inc. needs a routing protocol that will support IP and AppleTalk. Which of the following protocol(s) could you recommend? Choose all that apply.

   A. RIP

   B. EIGRP

   C. OSPF

   D. BGP

8. What protocol(s) does RTMP support?

   A. IP

   B. IPX

   C. SNA

   D. AppleTalk

9. OSPF support what kinds of media? Choose all that apply.

   A. Broadcast

   B. Multipoint-to-multipoint

   C. Point-to-point

   D. Point-to-multipoint

10. Two connected routers running BGP are not exchanging BGP routes. The two routers can PING each other. Which of the following could be the cause of the problem?

    A. One or both of the routers have missing or incorrect neighbor statements.

    B. One of the routers has all its interfaces shut down.

    C. The routers are not exchanging IGP routes with each other.

    D. BGP routers cannot be directly connected.

11. An IPX address is a concatenation of which of the following?

    A. A 16-bit XNS address with a 32-bit network-assigned address

    B. A 32-bit network-assigned address and a 48-bit MAC address

    C. A 32-bit 802.2 address and a 32-bit MAC address

    D. A 48-bit NetBIOS address and a 32-bit MAC address

Event-Driven Protocols

12. What is the first step in troubleshooting an AppleTalk network?

    A. Clear all AppleTalk Zones.

    B. Reboot the router.

    C. Check the AppleTalk routing table.

    D. Reinitialize the AppleTalk routing process.

13. Which of the following is an enterprise network services protocol used to advertise information regarding file servers, print servers, and job servers?

    A. TCP

    B. SAP

    C. DDR

    D. OSPF

14. EBGP advertises what routes to its neighbors (assuming no filtering has been applied)?

    A. Internal routes to its IBGP neighbors only

    B. Some routes to its EBGP neighbors and all routes to its IGBP neighbors

    C. No routes to its IBGP neighbors and all routes to its EBGP neighbors

    D. All routes to all neighbors

15. What are some advantages of EIGRP? Choose all that apply.

    A. Neighbor discovery

    B. Partial compatibility with IGRP

    C. Variable-length subnet masking (VLSM)

    D. No redistribution is necessary with OSPF

16. What are some advantages of OSPF? Choose all that apply.

    A. Variable-length subnet masking (VLSM)

    B. Route summarization

    C. Stub areas

    D. Automatic virtual links to Area 0

17. What interface filters does Cisco allow for AppleTalk datagram packets? Choose all that apply.

    A. Source network

    B. Source cable range

    C. Source IP address

    D. Source zone

18. How many devices does AppleTalk Phase 1 allow?

    A. 127

    B. 254

    C. 1023

    D. 16

19. Which of the following timers are associated with IGRP?

    A. Invalid timer

    B. Valid timer

    C. Not-connected timer

    D. Flush timer

LAB QUESTION

When troubleshooting a network, you must consider many things. It is necessary to have an organized and well thought out plan of attack. The first part of resolving any network issue is to understand the problem. Once the problem is understood, you can begin the actual troubleshooting process. The best approach to troubleshooting a problem is to start close to the source of the problem. The following exercise provides some of the necessary steps involved in troubleshooting a routed network:

1. Get as many people as you can together to assist you in this test. Not everyone needs to test at the same time or place, but they need network connectivity to the routers that you are using for the test.

2. Connect three Cisco 25xx routers together using two back-to-back serial cables, as shown below:
   R1-R2-R3
   Serial port 0 of R1 should connect to serial port 0 of R2. Serial port 1 of R2 should connect to serial port 0 on R3. For this exercise, make sure to put the DCE end of the cables on R2's serial ports.

3. Design an appropriate IP network, and configure all three routers for RIP v2. Do not forget to put the CLOCK RATE command on R2's serial interfaces.

4. Create two loopback interfaces, one on R1 and one on R3. Make sure that these routes are advertised through RIP.

5. Verify that all routes are showing up in each router's routing table.

6. Have one person "break" your configuration (in other words, remove a cable, change a router's configuration, remove a loopback interface, etc.).

7. Try to troubleshoot the problem using a methodical approach.

8. What were the results? Could you get the network back up and functioning?

SELF TEST ANSWERS

Periodic Broadcast-Based Protocols

1. ☑ **C.** Thirty seconds has passed since it last broadcast its entire routing table. RIP is a periodic broadcast-based routing protocol that sends its entire routing table to its neighbors every 30 seconds.
☒ **A** is incorrect because that is a property of an event-driven routing protocol. **B** is incorrect because RIP sends only its entire routing table. **D** is incorrect because the broadcast frequency is not dependent on updated routes it receives from neighbors.

2. ☑ **B** and **D** are correct because the first octet is between 1 and 127 (inclusive) and the remaining octets are also valid (between 0 and 255).
☒ **A** is incorrect because the third octet is 256 (and it should not be greater than 255). **C** is incorrect because the first octet is 128, which is a Class B network address.

3. ☑ **A.** SHOW IP ROUTE RIP. This command is an extension of the SHOW IP ROUTE command.
☒ **B, C,** and **D** are incorrect because SHOW ROUTER RIP, SHOW IP ROUTER RIP, and SHOW IP ROUTE are invalid commands.

4. ☑ **B.** To connect an OSPF area to Area 0 through another area is the correct answer because OSPF uses virtual links to connect remote areas (areas that are not directly connected to area 0) to area 0.
☒ **A, C,** and **D** are incorrect because RIP, EIGRP, and IGRP do not use virtual links.

5. ☑ **A, C,** and **D.** EIGRP is a multiservice routing protocol that supports IPX, AppleTalk, and IP.
☒ **B** is incorrect because EIGRP does not support SNA.

6. ☑ **A** and **C.** EIGRP and RIP are the correct answers because both protocols support IP and IPX.
☒ **B** and **D** are incorrect because BGP and IGRP support only IP, not IPX.

7. ☑ **B.** EIGRP is the correct answer because it supports IP, IPX, and AppleTalk.
☒ **A, C,** and **D** are incorrect because RIP, OSPF, and BGP do not support AppleTalk.

8. ☑ **D.** AppleTalk is the correct answer because RTMP is used only with AppleTalk networks.
☒ **A, B,** and **C** are incorrect because RTMP does not support IP, IPX, or SNA.

9. ☑ **A, C, and D.** Broadcast, point-to-point, and point-to-multipoint are the correct answers because OSPF supports these media.

   ☒ **B** is incorrect because multipoint-to-multipoint is not supported OSPF media.

10. ☑ **A.** One or both of the routers have missing or incorrect neighbor statements. If BGP neighbors are missing or do not have the correct peering statements, BGP routes will not be exchanged.

    ☒ **B** is incorrect because the routers can PING each other. **C** is incorrect because the exchange of IGP routes is not a contributing factor. **D** is incorrect because BGP neighbors can be directly connected.

11. ☑ **B.** An IPX packet address is a 32-bit network-assigned address and a 48-bit MAC address. An IPX address is formed by concatenating a 32-bit network-assigned network address with the device's 48-bit MAC address.

    ☒ **A, C, and D** are incorrect because they are nonexistent frame types.

Event-Driven Protocols

12. ☑ **C.** Check the AppleTalk routing table. When troubleshooting AppleTalk networks, always start with the routing table.

    ☒ **A, B, and D** are incorrect because they are not the initial step involved in troubleshooting an AppleTalk network.

13. ☑ **B.** SAP is the enterprise network services protocol that is used to advertise information regarding file servers, print servers, and job servers.

    ☒ **A, C, and D** are incorrect because TCP, DDR, and OSPF are used in other aspects of networking.

14. ☑ **D.** All routes to all neighbors is the correct answer because EBGP advertises all routes to all neighbors.

    ☒ **A, B, and C** are incorrect because they do not completely encompass the entire answer.

15. ☑ **A and C.** Neighbor discovery and VLSM are two advantages of EIGRP.

    ☒ **B** is incorrect because EIGRP provides *full* compatibility with IGRP. **D** is incorrect because it is necessary to redistribute between EIGRP and OSPF.

16. ☑ **A, B, and C.** OSPF provides features for VLSM, route summarization, and stub areas.

    ☒ **D** is incorrect because it is necessary to manually create virtual links to Area 0.

17. ☑ **A, B,** and **D.** Cisco allows for access lists to apply interface filters on AppleTalk datagram packets based on packets' source network, cable range, and zone.

    ☒ **C** is incorrect because you cannot apply an AppleTalk access list to an IP address (they are different Layer 3 protocols).

18. ☑ **B.** AppleTalk Phase 1 allows for 254 devices, with 127 end-nodes, 127 servers, and only one zone.

    ☒ **A, C,** and **D** are incorrect. AppleTalk Phase 2 allows for 253 node devices per network, with multiple zones per network.

19. ☑ **A** and **D.** Invalid and flush timers. IGRP uses the following timers: update, invalid, holddown, and flush.

    ☒ **B** and **C** are incorrect because valid timers and not-connected timers are not actual timers used by IGRP or any other routing protocol.

LAB ANSWER

The first steps in this exercise should have been to create a small test network. After verifying all routes are present in all routers, someone should have "broken" the network. The troubleshooting steps used should have involved verifying correct cabling (check the DTE/DCE ends and cable connection orientation). After your Physical Layer was verified, routing tables and configurations should have been checked. If you were unable to fix the network and bring it back to its original configuration, you should have worked with the person who broke the network to determine what other possible troubleshooting steps you could have done.

CISCO® CERTIFIED NETWORK PROFESSIONAL

7

Diagnosing and Correcting IP Problems

CERTIFICATION OBJECTIVES

T he most popular network protocol family in existence today is the Transmission Control Protocol/Internet Protocol, commonly abbreviated as TCP/IP. TCP/IP is the fundamental Internet protocol, and its use has increased dramatically in the last several years, due in large part to the popularity of the Internet—although the protocol itself has been around in various forms for over 20 years.

Because of this popularity, many organizations have a connection to the Internet. For simplicity's sake, they could also use TCP/IP as the primary protocol on their internal networks (intranets). Most of the network operating system vendors that for years favored a more proprietary network protocol, such as IPX or AppleTalk, can now operate exclusively over TCP/IP without using any of the other protocols. For example, Novell now supports TCP/IP in its NetWare 5 operating system. Network engineers who want to stay current must develop a good understanding of TCP/IP.

This chapter covers the details of how TCP/IP works. It also covers a selection of application protocols that depend on TCP/IP and are in wide use on the Internet and private networks. In addition to preparing you for passing the TCP/IP portions of the support test, this chapter takes you beyond minimum knowledge of the protocol, giving you a look at the way TCP/IP works and why.

ISO Layer 3, IP

The description of TCP/IP starts at Layer 3, the Network Layer; for the TCP/IP protocol suite, Layer 3 is called "Internet." Easily the most distinguishable feature of the Internet layer is the IP address. Generally speaking, for devices to communicate over an IP network, each device must have a unique IP address.

IP Version 6, now in the works, changes the number of bytes used for IP addresses as well as a great many other things about IP. IPv6 looks to be still a few years off, and the standard is not firm yet. It will likely require that most networking professionals be retrained and recertified.

OSI Layer 4, TCP and UDP

The Transport Layer of the OSI model maps to the "Transport" Layer of the TCP/IP model. For TCP/IP, this usually means either the TCP or UDP protocols.

FROM THE CLASSROOM

Understanding How IP Addressing Works

In many instances, you need to have detailed, in-depth knowledge of IP addressing to successfully solve problems. One such case could be where you are called on to troubleshoot routing failures involving network summarization. If you do not have a firm grasp of IP addressing, you might find this a difficult task indeed. Before you go any further, make sure that you know IP addressing basics such as subnets, VLSM, and CIDR. Although this book does not cover IP addressing, you are expected to know about it. For a quick refresher on IP addressing, visit *www.cisco.com/warp/public/701/3.html.*

The 3Com Web site also has a very detailed coverage of IP addressing at *www.3com.com/nsc/501302s.html.* The paper presented on that site is quite lengthy but very clear and easy to understand.

—Vijay Ramcharan, CCNP, CCDP, MCSE

Other protocols live at the Transport Layer, such as IGRP, EIGRP, OSPF and ICMP, the latter of which is discussed later. Although IP is an open standard, and other Layer 4 IP protocols do exist and will doubtless be added in the future, their use is negligible compared with TCP and UDP. These two transport protocols provide nearly all the functionality a protocol designer could want for a transport protocol.

UDP is sometimes nicknamed the "Unreliable" Datagram Protocol. Part of the reason behind this misleading term is that TCP is considered to be a *reliable protocol.* The word *reliable* in this case means that the protocol has specific characteristics of which higher-level protocols can take advantage. It does *not* mean that communications are 100 percent reliable, and it certainly does not mean that TCP can overcome a network outage.

on the **Job**

At a company where it was my job to manage the routers for the network, I once received a call from a user in a remote field office. His network response time was very poor. I tried to Telnet to the router for his office, and my Telnet program would simply hang for a few minutes and then finally report that it was unable to connect. This was a little puzzling because I was able to PING the router, so it appeared to be up. I loaded an SNMP management program (SNMP uses UDP for transport) and was able to query the router, so I knew for sure it was up. Still, I couldn't Telnet to it. I looked at a number of the available statistics from the SNMP (UDP) management program and found that the router had run out of memory. It turns out that when you Telnet to a router, it has to allocate memory for buffers and so forth. This router had 0 bytes free, so it was unable to allocate even the small amount needed to establish a TCP connection. Given this information, I was able to determine that the best course of action was to reboot the router, which fixed the problem temporarily, and then schedule a software upgrade after hours. The router's current software version had a memory leak, and if I had simply rebooted the router without investigating the cause of the problem, the same problem would likely have occurred a few more times until I did figure it out. In this case, the lightweight nature of UDP was a huge advantage because the router didn't need to allocate any memory to reply to my query, and I was able to communicate with the router to determine the problem.

CERTIFICATION OBJECTIVE 7.01

TCP Connection Sequence

The TCP connection sequence occurs between two stations that want to establish communications. For example, suppose Client A wants to connect to Server B, most often as a result of a command given by a user on Client A. See Figure 7-1.

Based on information in the client's software, the IP address of the server and the port number of the desired service are known. Because TCP needs a sequence number and a port number, the client's operating system supplies one of each. The client now has all the information it needs to send the first packet.

Because this is a new connection, the client sends a special type of packet called a SYN (short for *synchronize*) packet. The server responds with a SYN + ACK (short for *acknowledgment*) packet. Finally, the client sends an ACK packet to acknowledge

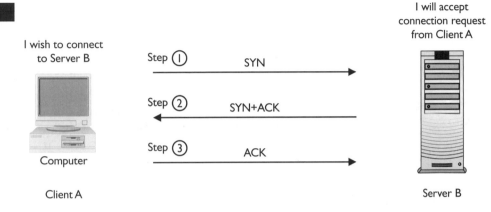

FIGURE 7-1

The TCP connection sequence

I wish to connect to Server B

Computer

Client A

Step ①   SYN

Step ②   SYN+ACK

Step ③   ACK

I will accept connection request from Client A

Server B

the SYN + ACK packet. This is called the *three-way TCP handshake*. At this point, the client and server are said to have a TCP connection and can exchange data.

We now know how TCP goes about establishing a connection. The rest of the connection continues in this manner, with the sequence and acknowledgment numbers incrementing and the hosts ACKing each other's packets.

on the ❗ **o b**

NFS has a much simpler retry mechanism than TCP. NFS attempts to retransmit the request at fixed intervals but gives up in a relatively short period of time. Here's an example: at the company where I work, we have a standing policy with the systems administrators that we do not officially support NFS mounts across our WAN, and we do not guarantee they will work reliably. Between two of our offices that are fairly close geographically, we had a full DS3 45MB link—in other words, a WAN line that had many of the performance characteristics of a LAN. The systems administrators had done some independent testing, decided they were satisfied with the performance and reliability of the link, and set up a number of more or less permanent NFS mounts across the link. One day, the DS3 CSU/DSU failed at the far end. Our network had redundant links, but the backup link was only a fractional DS1 Frame Relay link that was good for about 512KB. Of course, the NFS mounts all failed; IP traffic had to be rerouted across a link, with a lot more delay and not nearly as much bandwidth. The link did not fill up entirely, but it would fill at peaks due to the burst nature of NFS. Meanwhile, the other, mostly TCP-based traffic, such as HTTP, mail, FTP, and Telnet, limped along rather sluggishly but fully functionally. (Unfortunately, saying "I told you so" would not have helped the engineers who could not work.)

Routing Protocol Traffic

At this stage in your studies, you should be familiar with the traffic-related aspects of major routing protocols such as RIP, EIGRP, and OSPF. You should know the various methods that each protocol uses to keep its neighbors notified of changes in the internetwork and the methods used to make sure that all information in routing tables is accurate. You should also know how often these protocols notify neighbors of changes or send acknowledgments and the size of those updates and acknowledgments.

Routers, which run dynamic routing protocols such IGRP, RIP, RIPv2, EIGRP, and OSPF, all send updates and acknowledgments to neighboring routers. Some routing protocols send more routing table and acknowledgment traffic than others. RIP for example, sends routing updates every 30 seconds by default, and those updates are the complete routing table that resides on the router.

Address Resolution Protocol

So far, we have discussed Layer 3 and above protocols. Most of the work within IP takes place at those levels. At least one protocol that does not fall into that category, however, deserves discussion: ARP. *ARP, Address Resolution Protocol,* is used for mapping IP addresses to Layer 2 addresses. You can think of ARP as being both Layer 2 and Layer 3, or as a binding between the two.

For an IP stack to deliver an IP packet to the IP stack on another host, it has to determine the other host's Layer 2 address so that delivery can happen at Layer 2. The mechanism chosen for this determination is automatic mapping of IP addresses to Layer 2 addresses. This is where ARP comes in.

Somewhat like the PING exchanges of echoes and replies, ARP exchanges consist of an ARP request and an ARP reply. The ARP request contains the IP address for which the Layer 2 address (MAC address) is desired, and the reply contains both the requested IP address and Layer 2 address. The requester caches the response to avoid having to ask for it for each message sent to that host. This cached reply has an attached timer, so that it does not stick around forever. ARP is strictly a local network protocol. This means that a host never tries to resolve an IP address for a host on a different subnet, but rather ARPs for the address of the router (default gateway) the host uses to reach that subnet.

When one host wants the MAC address that corresponds to an IP address, the host broadcasts an ARP request packet. All hosts on the LAN segment process the broadcast. Usually, the IP stack of each host processes the packet and determines whether its own IP address is the one being requested. If so, the requester's IP address is added into the processing host's own ARP cache. Each processing host then builds an ARP reply and sends it back to the requesting host.

The host receiving the ARP request caches the requester's IP address because if it did not, it would have to ARP for the requester's IP in order to reply, resulting in an *ARP loop*. Although the replying host could broadcast the reply, that host has enough information to send it directly, and broadcasts are expensive in terms of network resources. Broadcast packets have to go to all hosts and be processed by all hosts.

ARP Problems

So, ARP seems pretty simple and fairly well defined. What could go wrong? Recall the caching mechanism. It exists so that a host does not have to ARP every time it wants to talk to another host. But if one host is going to send one packet, chances are good that it wants to send more, and probably soon; thus the caching is also the main problem area with ARP. If two hosts have communicated via IP recently, they each have an entry for the other in their ARP caches. They have finished their current communication, but the ARP cache entry is still there, waiting in case they need to communicate again. Often these entries stay for 15 minutes or more (sometimes hours).

Perhaps something changes about one of the IP addresses. Maybe a host is removed and a new host is given the old host's IP address. Maybe a network card is swapped out, so that IP address now has a different MAC address. The host that has changed knows it has a new address, and whatever caused the change is also likely to have caused the other host's ARP entry to be removed, probably because of a reboot. The host that *has not* changed, however, still has the ARP entry for the old MAC address. If this host tries to make a connection to the now-incorrect cached MAC address, the packet is sent to the wrong MAC address and the other host does not receive it.

How is this situation corrected? One choice is to simply wait. Eventually the bad ARP entry times out, and the host ARPs again and gets the right information. ARP entries time out when they are supposed to (minutes to hours). Another solution is to go to the changed host and cause it to contact the confused host. This should cause the changed host to ARP for the confused host; at that point the confused host is supposed to update its ARP table, and all should be well. Unfortunately, although most OSes are perfectly willing to cache a new ARP entry for a host that ARPed for them, they are not always willing to replace an existing one.

The final solution is to manually flush the ARP table on any confused hosts. This is covered later in the "Cisco IOS Software Tools and Commands" section of this chapter.

Proxy ARP

Before we leave the subject of ARP, we need to touch on another aspect: *proxy ARP*. Proxy ARP is the process of one host using its own MAC address to answer an ARP request for another host on a remote network. Normally a router would answer the request in this manner. Proxy ARP is not required functionality for IP, but it can be a useful extra under the right circumstances. On Cisco routers, proxy ARP is on by default.

Hosts determine whether another host is on their same subnet using the subnet mask with which they are configured. If the other host is within the range indicated by the subnet mask, that host must be on the same subnet, and it can be ARPed for directly. When that host is on a different subnet, the MAC address of the default gateway is used instead, and the packet is sent to that MAC address.

What if the host has the wrong subnet mask? If the mask is incorrect, the host determines that other hosts that are actually on remote subnets are local. The host tries to ARP for the supposedly local host instead of forwarding packets to the router, as it should. Since the ARP would not normally work under those circumstances (hosts can only ARP for other hosts in the same broadcast domain), communications fail. However, if proxy ARP is turned on at the router, the router answers for the remote host, and the host with the wrong subnet mask ends up adding the router's MAC address to its ARP table and forwarding the packet to the router. The proxy ARP feature is useful in cases in which a host has a less specific mask than the router—for example, if a host has a /16 and the router has a /24. The router will obviously have a more specific path or route to a network that the host might believe to be local. The router will therefore proxy ARP in response to a host's ARP queries and forward packets to the correct subnet.

Three-Way Handshake

The *three-way handshake* refers to the TCP connection sequence. If a client wants to start a TCP session with another machine, it sends a SYN packet to the client. If the request is valid, the destination host responds with a SYN + ACK packet. On receipt of this packet, the client issues an ACK packet to tell the destination host that it is ready to begin the connection.

Now that you have a clear idea of the various "helper" protocols within the TCP/IP stack, review the following Scenario & Solution.

SCENARIO & SOLUTION

Why do you think TCP is referred to as *connection oriented*?	TCP is connection-oriented because transmissions are acknowledged.
UDP is connectionless and unreliable. Why?	UDP does not use acknowledgments for transmissions between stations. It makes a "best effort" to transmit the packets, with no knowledge of whether they are successfully received or not.
What is the function of ARP, and why is it so necessary?	ARP provides IP-to-MAC address mapping. MAC addresses are used in Ethernet to identify for which stations data is meant.
The three-way handshake is used in TCP. What is the packet sequence?	TCP uses the SYN, SYN + ACK and ACK packets to establish a connection.

CERTIFICATION OBJECTIVE 7.02

Cisco IOS Software Tools and Commands

The Cisco IOS provides a number of extremely useful troubleshooting tools and commands for troubleshooting TCP/IP. This section reviews those tools and commands and presents common TCP/IP problems and techniques to solve those problems. Since TCP/IP works at the Transport and Network Layers, most tools you use for troubleshooting are used on your router. These tools include the SHOW and DEBUG commands.

The SHOW commands display pertinent information about the status of the interface and protocol as well as traffic and routes. Table 7-1 lists the SHOW commands that are covered in this chapter. A brief explanation of each command is provided beside each command. These commands are covered in greater detail later in this chapter.

exam
ⓦatch

To view output in a Telnet session that is normally displayed through the router's console, use the TERMINAL MONITOR command. This command copies the output sent to the router console to your Telnet application window.

TABLE 7-1   SHOW Commands for Troubleshooting TCP/IP

Command	Description
SHOW IP INTERFACE	Provides information on configured IP interfaces on the router.
SHOW IP PROTOCOLS	Shows current status and configuration information of routing protocols and processes on the router.
SHOW IP ROUTE	Displays the IP routing table on the router.
SHOW IP TRAFFIC	Shows IP protocol statistics such as TCP packets, UDP packets received, and so on.
SHOW IP ACCESS-LISTS	Displays all configured IP access lists on the router.
SHOW IP OSPF	Shows configured OSPF routing processes on the router.
SHOW IP OSPF DATABASE	Displays information on the OSPF link-state database.
SHOW IP OSPF INTERFACE	Lists information on routing configuration specifics for IP interfaces related to OSPF processes.
SHOW IP OSPF NEIGHBOR	Displays OSPF neighbor information.
SHOW IP OSPF VIRTUAL-LINKS	Displays the status of any configured OSPF virtual links on the router.
SHOW IP EIGRP INTERFACES	Shows details of interfaces configured with the EIGRP routing protocol.
SHOW IP EIGRP NEIGHBORS	Shows the status of EIGRP neighbors.
SHOW IP EIGRP TRAFFIC	Shows EIGRP traffic received and sent by the router.
SHOW IP EIGRP TOPOLOGY	Shows the EIGRP topology table and the status of DUAL and the state of successors.

The PING and TRACE commands are also very valuable in troubleshooting. The PING command sends an Internet Control Message Protocol (ICMP) echo request to a host. If a station receives the request, a reply is sent to the source host. The TRACE command uses the error message generated by routers when a datagram exceeds its TTL. With TRACE, you can view the path taken to reach a specified destination. TRACE commands allow you to see messages that help determine if your protocols are performing correctly.

Both the PING and TRACE commands are covered in greater detail later in this chapter.

Use the following Scenario & Solution to determine whether you understand which commands will provide the correct information.

SCENARIO & SOLUTION

Which command displays the IP routing table?	SHOW IP ROUTE
How would you know which interfaces on the router are using TCP/IP?	SHOW IP INTERFACE [BRIEF]
Which command tells you what IP routing protocols are configured on the router?	SHOW IP PROTOCOLS
How would you get details on IP access list configuration?	SHOW IP ACCESS-LIST

Table 7-2 lists the DEBUG commands commonly used for troubleshooting TCP/IP. These commands are covered in greater detail later in this chapter. *Note:* Be careful when using DEBUG commands; some of them generate a lot of output for each processed packet. Debugging can even halt an overutilized router, resulting in angry users breathing down your neck and causing grief for you. Try to use DEBUG during off-peak hours.

TABLE 7-2 DEBUG Commands Used for Troubleshooting TCP/IP

Command	Description
DEBUG IP ICMP	Displays information about ICMP messages.
DEBUG IP RIP	Shows information on RIP routing protocol activity.
DEBUG IP IGRP EVENTS	Turns on debugging for IP IGRP and shows information on the source and destination of routing updates as well as the number of routes in each update.
DEBUG IP EIGRP	Shows information on the activity of IP EIGRP.
DEBUG ARP	Displays information on ARP protocol transactions.
DEBUG IP PACKET	Displays information on IP packets traversing the router.
DEBUG IP PACKET [ACCESS-LIST-NUMBER]	Displays information on all IP packets that are permitted by the access list number specified. Any packet information for packets not matching the access list is not displayed.
DEBUG IP OSPF EVENTS	Displays OSPF event information for operations such as SPF calculations, adjacencies, and flooding information.
DEBUG IP OSPF ADJACENCIES	Shows information for OSPF activity related to neighbors.
DEBUG IP OSPF PACKET	Shows information on every OSPF packet that is received by the router.

DEBUG commands can be executed only at the privileged exec prompt. DEBUG commands can overwhelm a router, depending on how they are used. After debugging, use the command NO DEBUG ALL or UNDEBUG ALL to turn off all debugging on a router. You may also use the command UNDEBUG <DEBUG OPTION> to turn off debugging for a specific DEBUG command.

Exercise 7-1 demonstrates debugging the operation of ARP on a Cisco router. This is a very simple exercise, but remember to use caution when executing any DEBUG command, because they can bring your router to a stop. In addition, remember to use the UNDEBUG command to turn off debugging after you are finished.

EXERCISE 7-1

Watching ARP in Operation

Log in to your router and go into privileged mode. Remember, if you are Telnetting into the router, you must use the TERMINAL MONITOR command to see DEBUG messages on your Telnet application screen; this is because DEBUG messages are not sent to Telnet sessions by default. Now do the following:

1. Type the command **debug arp**. If your router is not actively running any ARP operations, you will not see any output. Initiate an ARP operation by pinging an IP address on your network.

2. You should now be able to see messages similar to these:

```
ROUTER_A#dcbug arp
ARP packet debugging is on
ROUTER_A#terminal monitor
ROUTER_A#ping 192.10.10.64
Type escape sequence to abort.
Sending 5, 100-byte ICMP Echos to 192.10.10.64, timeout is 2 seconds:
!!!!!
Success rate is 100 percent (5/5), round-trip min/avg/max = 1/202/1005 ms
ROUTER_A#
3w1d: IP ARP: creating incomplete entry for IP address: 192.10.10.64 interface
Ethernet0/0
3w1d: IP ARP: sent req src 192.10.10.3 0050.3ef8.eb80,
              dst 192.10.10.64 0000.0000.0000 Ethernet0/0
```

```
3w1d: IP ARP: sent req src 192.10.10.3 0,
              dst 192.10.10.64 0 Serial0/0.1
3w1d: IP ARP: sent req src 192.10.10.3 0050.3ef8.eb80,
              dst 192.10.10.64 0000.0000.0000 Serial0/0.1
3w1d: IP ARP: rcvd rep src 192.10.10.64 0020.affa.39f5,
              dst 192.10.10.3 Ethernet0/0
ROUTER_A#no debug all
```

3. Turn off debugging using the command NO DEBUG ALL.

The following section covers the previously introduced SHOW and DEBUG commands in detail as well as the CLEAR ARP-CACHE command. Learn to use them and to interpret the output that each command displays.

The CLEAR ARP-CACHE Command

The ARP cache is populated dynamically when the router issues an ARP request for an IP address. ARP resolution entries are entered into the ARP cache as the router learns of them and are dynamically removed after they time out. Cisco routers provide a 4-hour time limit on dynamic ARP cache entries, after which they time out and are removed.

The CLEAR ARP-CACHE command deletes all dynamic entries from the ARP cache, clears the fast-switching cache, and clears the IP route cache. Static ARP entries that have been entered into the ARP cache using the ARP *IP-ADDRESS HARDWARE-ADDRESS TYPE* [ALIAS] command must be manually removed using the NO form of this command.

The CLEAR ARP-CACHE command is useful in cases in which the hardware address of a host has changed, due to either manual configuration or a change of the hardware (NIC) itself.

The SHOW IP INTERFACE Command

The SHOW IP INTERFACE command is used to show the status of IP-enabled interfaces on the router. IP-specific information is displayed about these interfaces. It shows statistics such as helper addresses, access lists, split-horizon status, switching type used, and compression used. This command is very useful in determining what IP specific features have been enabled on the router and can help in pinpointing

problems that you might be experiencing. The types of information shown, such as
helper addresses and access lists, are the same for each interface:

```
ROUTER_A>show ip interface
Ethernet0/0 is up, line protocol is up
  Internet address is 192.10.10.3/24
  Broadcast address is 255.255.255.255
  Address determined by non-volatile memory
  MTU is 1500 bytes
  Helper address is not set
  Directed broadcast forwarding is disabled
  Outgoing access list is not set
  Inbound  access list is not set
  Proxy ARP is enabled
  Security level is default
  Split horizon is enabled
  ICMP redirects are always sent
  ICMP unreachables are always sent
  ICMP mask replies are never sent
  IP fast switching is disabled
  IP fast switching on the same interface is disabled
  IP Flow switching is disabled
  IP Null turbo vector
  IP multicast fast switching is disabled
  IP multicast distributed fast switching is disabled
  Router Discovery is disabled
  IP output packet accounting is disabled
  IP access violation accounting is disabled
  TCP/IP header compression is disabled
  RTP/IP header compression is disabled
  Probe proxy name replies are disabled
  Policy routing is disabled
  Network address translation is disabled
  WCCP Redirect outbound is disabled
  WCCP Redirect exclude is disabled
  BGP Policy Mapping is disabled
Serial0/0 is up, line protocol is up
  Internet protocol processing disabled
Serial0/0.1 is up, line protocol is up
  Internet address is 192.10.10.3/24
  Broadcast address is 255.255.255.255
  Address determined by non-volatile memory
  ...LISTING ABBREVIATED FOR CLARITY...
  BGP Policy Mapping is disabled
ROUTER_A>
```

Important types of information presented in this code are explained in Table 7-3.

Network Address Translation (NAT) is a feature that is similar to proxy ARP in the sense that it provides connectivity to subnets or hosts that would otherwise be unreachable. NAT can also be used a rudimentary security measure because it hides the IP address of the source host by changing the source address field in the packet's IP header. NAT can help in situations in which corporations or companies have merged and they are using the same address space. Using NAT, instead of a total lack of connectivity due to duplicate addresses within the companies, the IP addresses of one company can be translated to provide temporary connectivity until a permanent solution can be implemented.

TABLE 7-3   Variables Shown by the SHOW IP INTERFACE Command

Code Listing	Description
Internet address	IP address of the interface.
Broadcast address	Broadcast address that is being used by the interface.
Helper-address	Shows whether any helper addresses have been configured so that the router can forward specific types of broadcasts to the specified hosts.
Directed broadcast forwarding	Tells you whether an all-hosts broadcast is allowed or not. This option is usually disabled so that someone cannot issue a PING command to all hosts on the network, potentially causing a broadcast storm.
Inbound/outbound access list	Tells you what access lists, if any, have been set on the router.
Proxy ARP	Enables the router to provide connectivity for subnets/hosts that are actually remote but are believed to be local by a specific host(s). *Enabled* means that support is on.
Split horizon	Shows whether split horizon is on or off. If split horizon is off, a routing loop can occur on your network.
ICMP unreachables	*Always sent* means that if a PING command is issued to an unknown host, a "host unreachable" message will be sent to the source of the PING.
IP _____ switching	Type of switching enabled on the interface.
Router discovery	Shows if the ICMP router discovery protocol (IRDP) is running.

The **SHOW IP PROTOCOLS** Command

The SHOW IP PROTOCOLS command tells you the routing IP protocols that have been enabled on the router and gives a summary of useful information about each protocol—information such as access lists that have been applied to filter routing updates, adjacent neighbors, routing timers, and the administrative distance of each protocol. The code output from the SHOW IP PROTOCOLS command is as follows:

```
ROUTER_A>show ip protocols
Routing Protocol is "eigrp 10"
  Outgoing update filter list for all interfaces is
  Incoming update filter list for all interfaces is
  Default networks flagged in outgoing updates
  Default networks accepted from incoming updates
  EIGRP metric weight K1=1, K2=0, K3=1, K4=0, K5=0
  EIGRP maximum hopcount 100
  EIGRP maximum metric variance 1
  Redistributing: eigrp 10
  Automatic network summarization is in effect
  Routing for Networks:
    192.166.133.0
  Routing Information Sources:
    Gateway         Distance       Last Update
    192.166.133.1   90             1w4d
  Distance: internal 90 external 170
  Routing Protocol is "rip"
  Sending updates every 30 seconds, next due in 2 seconds
  Invalid after 90 seconds, hold down 180, flushed after 240
  Outgoing update filter list for all interfaces is
  Incoming update filter list for all interfaces is
  Redistributing: rip
  Default version control: send version 1, receive any version
  Routing for Networks:
    172.16.0.0
  Routing Information Sources:
    Gateway         Distance       Last Update
    172.16.1.1      255            00:00:10
Distance: (default is 120)
ROUTER_A>
```

Important information to consider from this output is described in Table 7-4.

TABLE 7-4   Variables in the SHOW IP PROTOCOLS Command

Code Listing	Description
Routing for networks	Shows you the networks being serviced by the routing protocol.
Routing information sources	Tells you where updates are being received from, the administrative distance of the update, and the time of the last update.
Routing protocol	Displays the routing protocol in use on the router as well as the process ID, if applicable. In the preceding listing, you can see that EIGRP is using a process ID of 10, whereas RIP does not have one.
Outgoing/incoming update filter	Tells you whether a filter has been applied to routing updates. The filter is an access list that has been configured on the router and applied to the routing process or protocol by the DISTRIBUTE-LIST command.
Redistributing	Indicates the routing process that is being redistributed into another routing process or protocol.
Automatic network summarization	Indicates whether networks are being automatically summarized at the classful boundary.
Routing information sources	Displays the sources of routing updates—in other words, the routing neighbors that this router has with this routing protocol.
Distance	Displays the administrative distance of the protocol.
Sending updates	The default timer, indicating the period at which routing updates are sent.
Default version control	For RIP, indicating which version of RIP is being used to send and receive routing updates.

RIP timers are used to determine when routing updates are sent, declared invalid, put into holddown, and then flushed. All RIP routers must have the same settings for timers, because routing inconsistencies result if there are misconfigured timers. The default timer settings are:

- Updates sent every 30 seconds
- Routes declared invalid after 90 seconds
- Routes are in holddown for 180 seconds
- Routes are flushed after 240 seconds

Inconsistent timer settings result in missing routes or routing tables, which undergo frequent changes. This results in intermittent connectivity between networks, at worst. Be sure that routers are configured with identical timers if you should decide to change the default timer periods.

The SHOW IP ROUTE Command

The SHOW IP ROUTE command is used to show the IP routing table of all configured IP routing processes on the router. This command can also be used to show what routes were obtained from a particular routing protocol, administrative distance of the routing protocol, time since the last update, and the default gateway of the router:

```
ROUTER_A>show ip ro
Codes: C - connected, S - static, I - IGRP, R - RIP, M - mobile, B - BGP
       D - EIGRP, EX - EIGRP external, O - OSPF, IA - OSPF inter area
       N1 - OSPF NSSA external type 1, N2 - OSPF NSSA external type 2
       E1 - OSPF external type 1, E2 - OSPF external type 2, E - EGP
       i - IS-IS, L1 - IS-IS level-1, L2 - IS-IS level-2, * - candidate default
       U - per-user static route, o - ODR
Gateway of last resort is 192.168.240.1 to network 0.0.0.0
     192.168.240.0/24 is variably subnetted, 2 subnets, 2 masks
C       192.168.240.0/24 is directly connected, Ethernet0
C       192.168.240.96/27 is directly connected, Ethernet0
S*   0.0.0.0/0 [1/0] via 192.168.240.1
```

The information given by SHOW IP ROUTE is easy to understand by looking at the output. You can see from the preceding listing, for example, that the default gateway is 192.168.240.1. The 0.0.0.0 network tells you that any traffic that is destined for an unknown destination should be routed out through 192.168.240.1. The default gateway does not appear unless it has been specifically configured on the router.

The static route, denoted by an S, tells you that this is a manually configured route, which also happens to be the default gateway.

exam
ⓦatch

The SHOW IP ROUTE command is one of the most useful SHOW commands for troubleshooting missing routes. Know its output and situations in which its use is applicable.

The SHOW IP TRAFFIC Command

The SHOW IP TRAFFIC command displays extensive statistics on all IP traffic traversing the router. Statistics from protocols such as ICMP, UDP, and ARP are included. Useful information on format and CRC errors can be shown using this command. Excessive broadcasts and multicasts can be easily identified:

```
ROUTER_A>show ip traffic
IP statistics:
  Rcvd:  1970 total, 1936 local destination
         0 format errors, 0 checksum errors, 0 bad hop count
         0 unknown protocol, 0 not a gateway
         0 security failures, 0 bad options, 0 with options
  Opts:  0 end, 0 nop, 0 basic security, 0 loose source route
         0 timestamp, 0 extended security, 0 record route
         0 stream ID, 0 strict source route, 0 alert, 0 cipso
         0 other
  Frags: 0 reassembled, 0 timeouts, 0 couldn't reassemble
         0 fragmented, 0 couldn't fragment
  Bcast: 17 received, 36 sent
  Mcast: 0 received, 0 sent
  Sent:  1652 generated, 32 forwarded
  Drop:  11 encapsulation failed, 0 unresolved, 0 no adjacency
         0 no route, 0 unicast RPF, 0 forced drop
ICMP statistics:
  Rcvd: 0 format errors, 0 checksum errors, 0 redirects, 0 unreachable
        2 echo, 15 echo reply, 0 mask requests, 0 mask replies, 0 quench
        0 parameter, 0 timestamp, 0 info request, 0 other
        0 irdp solicitations, 0 irdp advertisements
  Sent: 11 redirects, 29 unreachable, 15 echo, 2 echo reply
        0 mask requests, 0 mask replies, 0 quench, 0 timestamp
        0 info reply, 0 time exceeded, 0 parameter problem
        0 irdp solicitations, 0 irdp advertisements
UDP statistics:
  Rcvd: 91 total, 0 checksum errors, 78 no port
  Sent: 36 total, 0 forwarded broadcasts
TCP statistics:
  Rcvd: 1816 total, 12 checksum errors, 2 no port
  Sent: 1567 total
...LISTING ABBREVIATED FOR CLARITY...
ARP statistics:
  Rcvd: 648 requests, 229 replies, 7 reverse, 0 other
  Sent: 259 requests, 47 replies (5 proxy), 0 reverse
ROUTER_A>
```

Table 7-5 lists the most important statistics obtained from the SHOW IP TRAFFIC command. Only statistics for IP variables are shown because most of the information is repeated for the other protocols, such as TCP, UDP, and ARP.

The SHOW IP ACCESS-LISTS Command

The SHOW IP ACCESS-LISTS command shows you all the configured IP access lists on the router. Use this command to troubleshoot host connectivity issues, problems with routing updates not being received, and issues that point to filtering of IP packets. For example, a misconfigured access list could prevent a host or group of hosts from connecting to a server:

```
ROUTER_A#show ip access-lists
Standard IP access list 12
    deny   192.168.0.0, wildcard bits 0.0.255.255
    permit any
Standard IP access list 19
    permit 131.108.19.0
    deny   0.0.0.0, wildcard bits 255.255.255.255
Standard IP access list 49
    permit 131.108.31.0, wildcard bits 0.0.0.255
    permit 131.108.194.0, wildcard bits 0.0.0.255
    permit 131.108.195.0, wildcard bits 0.0.0.255
    permit 131.108.196.0, wildcard bits 0.0.0.255
    permit 131.108.197.0, wildcard bits 0.0.0.255
Extended IP access list 101
    permit tcp 0.0.0.0 255.255.255.255 0.0.0.0 255.255.255.255 eq 23
ROUTER_A#
```

In this listing, you can see that the standard IP access list 12 is denying connectivity for all IP hosts in the 192.168.0.0 network. All other networks are permitted. Standard IP access list 19 is permitting IP traffic from the 131.108.19.0 network. All other networks are denied. To see the access lists that have been applied to an interface, use the command SHOW IP INTERFACE, covered earlier in this chapter.

exam
ⓦatch

You should know basic access list functionality, the usage of PERMIT and DENY statements, the presence of the implicit DENY statement, the fact that every access list must have at least one permit statement, and so on. Also know that standard IP access lists are numbered from 1–99, while extended access lists are numbered from 100–199. Standard IP access lists filter only by source address.

TABLE 7-5   Variables in the Output from the SHOW IP TRAFFIC Command

Code Listing	Description
RCVD	Total number of IP packets received.
Local destination	Total number of packets bound for a directly connected network.
Format errors	Number of errors in the packet format, such as an impossible Internet header length.
Bad hop count	Indicates the number of packets that had an expired TTL field.
Frags-reassembled	Number of packets that had to be reassembled by the router.
Frags-fragmented	Indicates the total number of packets that had to be fragmented because they exceeded the maximum transmission unit (MTU) size.
Sent	Number of IP packets that were generated by the router.
Drop-encapsulation failed	Counted when the router discards a datagram it did not know how to route.

The SHOW IP OSPF Command

The SHOW IP OSPF command displays information for all configured OSPF processes on the router. More than one OSPF process can be active on the router:

```
ROUTER_A#show ip ospf
Routing Process "ospf 200" with ID 192.10.10.3
Supports only single TOS(TOS0) route
It is an area border and autonomous system boundary router
Summary Link update interval is 0:30:00 and the update due in 0:13:20
External Link update interval is 0:30:00 and the update due in 0:20:17
Redistributing External Routes from,
     igrp 200 with metric mapped to 2, includes subnets in redistribution
     rip with metric mapped to 2
Number of areas in this router is 3
Area 192.42.110.0
    Number of interfaces in this area is 1
    Area has simple password authentication
    SPF algorithm executed 8 times
    Area ranges are
    Link State Update Interval is 0:30:00 and due in 0:09:47
    Link State Age Interval is 0:20:00 and due in 0:08:24
ROUTER_A#
```

Relevant variables in the SHOW IP OSPF command output are displayed in Table 7-6.

TABLE 7-6   Variables in the SHOW IP OSPF Command Output

Code Listing	Description
Routing Process	Indicates the process ID of the OSPF process and the router ID used by the OSPF process for the router.
Type of router	Shows the type of OSPF router this is. In the output, this router is both an ABR and an ASBR, meaning that this router sits between OSPF areas and performs redistribution between routing protocols.
Summary link update interval	Specifies the interval for Summary Link updates and the time to the next update.
External Link update interval	Specifies the interval for External Link updates and the time to the next update.
Redistributing External Routes	Shows the routing protocols that are being used to receive redistributed routing updates.
Number of areas	The number of areas that this router is connected to. Addresses of the areas are also displayed.
Link-State Update Interval	Specifies the router and network link-state update interval in hours: minutes: seconds as well as time to the next update.
Link-State Age Interval	Specifies max-aged update deletion interval and time until next database cleanup in hours: minutes: seconds.

Update and Age intervals are very important due to the simple fact that they tell the router when it is time to update its link-state table. It is easy to see that if one router has a different timer than the other, the two cannot communicate properly, because their messages are sent at different times. If you must change the timers for some reason, be sure to make all timers on your network the same.

In the preceding listing, the router is redistributing routes from IGRP and RIP. This indicates that the router is also running these other routing protocols. Routes obtained from RIP and IGRP are being redistributed into the OSPF routing process to enable a consistent link-state table of the entire network. When redistributing IGRP and RIP, you must use the SUBNETS keyword; otherwise, only major networks, not subnets, are advertised.

You might have also noticed that authentication has been enabled on the router. What this means is that the OSPF process on this router can only communicate with other OSPF processes on other routers that have the same authentication settings. If the password does not match, there is no communication with the other router. All OSPF routers within the same network (same interface) should have the same authentication settings. Each interface can have a unique password. OSPF can support simple password authentication as well as Message Digest 5 (MD5) authentication.

The "Area ranges" statement tells you what networks have been summarized. In this listing, notice that no summarization has been configured. On small networks, this is not a problem, because there are not a lot of changes going on, links going down, and so on. On large networks, however, this option should be configured because frequent link-state changes can cause routers to constantly run the SPF algorithm, which is processor intensive. This results in overutilization of the router's CPU and could bring the router to a stop. Link-state changes also mean that updates are being sent back and forth across the network, wasting valuable bandwidth on a WAN link.

The SHOW IP OSPF DATABASE Command

The SHOW IP OSPF DATABASE command lists the OSPF link-state database for all OSPF routing processes. This command is used to troubleshoot inconsistencies in the OSPF processes and possible old or duplicate link-state advertisements (LSAs):

```
ROUTER_A#show ip ospf database
OSPF Router with id(192.10.10.32) (Autonomous system 300)
Displaying Router Link States(Area 0.0.0.0)
Link ID         ADV Router      Age     Seq#         Checksum    Link count
155.187.21.6    155.187.21.6    1731    0x80002CFB   0x69BC      8
155.187.21.5    155.187.21.5    1112    0x800009D2   0xA2B8      5
155.187.1.2     155.187.1.2     1662    0x80000A98   0x4CB6      9
155.187.1.1     155.187.1.1     1115    0x800009B6   0x5F2C      1
155.187.1.5     155.187.1.5     1691    0x80002BC    0x2A1A      5
155.187.65.6    155.187.65.6    1395    0x80001947   0xEEE1      4
155.187.241.5   155.187.241.5   1161    0x8000007C   0x7C70      1
155.187.27.6    155.187.27.6    1723    0x80000548   0x8641      4
155.187.70.6    155.187.70.6    1485    0x80000B97   0xEB84      6
Displaying Net Link States(Area 0.0.0.0)
Link ID         ADV Router      Age     Seq#         Checksum
155.187.1.3     192.20.239.66   1245    0x800000EC   0x82E
Displaying Summary Net Link States(Area 0.0.0.0)
Link ID         ADV Router      Age     Seq#         Checksum
155.187.240.0   155.187.241.5   1152    0x80000077   0x7A05
155.187.241.0   155.187.241.5   1152    0x80000070   0xAEB7
155.187.244.0   155.187.241.5   1152    0x80000071   0x95CB
```

TABLE 7-7	Code Listing	Description
Variables in the SHOW IP OSPF DATABASE Command Output	Link ID	Router ID number or ID number assigned by the OSPF process.
	ADV router	The router ID of the advertising router.
	Age	The age in seconds of the link shown. Maximum age is 1800 seconds.
	Seq#	The sequence number of the link state. Old or duplicate LSAs can be identified.
	Link count	The number of router interfaces that are participating in the OSPF process.

Relevant fields in the output of the SHOW IP OSPF DATABASE command are listed in Table 7-7.

The Link ID can be confusing if you do not recognize the information this field is giving you. Use the information in Table 7-8 to determine the information that is provided.

The Age field tells you how many seconds have passed since the link was last heard from. The maximum age is defined as 30 minutes, or 1800 seconds, which is the time period for OSPF routers to send out the link-state tables.

The sequence number is used to detect old or duplicate LSAs. Subsequent LSAs that are sent between the two routers are assigned sequence numbers that are incremented and referenced against the existing sequence number in the topological database and whose currency is determined.

LSAs are broken into five types:

■ *Router links (RLs)* are generated by all routers. These links describe the state of the router interfaces inside a particular area. These links are flooded only inside the interface's area.

TABLE 7-8	Code Listing	Description
Link ID Field Variables	Link type	Link ID.
	Point-to-point	Neighbor Router ID.
	Link to transit network	Interface address of DR.
	Link to stub network	Network/subnet number.
	Virtual link	Neighbor Router ID.

- *Network links (NLs)* are generated by a DR of a particular segment; these are an indication of the routers connected to that segment.

- *Summary links (SLs)* are the inter-area links (Type 3); these links list the networks inside other areas but still belonging to the autonomous system. Summary links are injected by the ABR from the backbone into other areas and from other areas into the backbone. These links are used for aggregation between areas.

- *ASBR-Summary links* are another type of summary link. These are Type 4 links that point to the ASBR to make sure that all routers know the way to exit the autonomous system.

- *External links (ELs)* are Type 5 links. These are injected by the ASBR into the domain.

The SHOW IP OSPF INTERFACE Command

The SHOW IP OSPF INTERFACE command can be used to verify the configuration of OSPF on an interface. By issuing the command SHOW IP OSPF INTERFACE without specifying an interface type and number, the output returned by the router shows configuration details for all interfaces that are configured for the OSPF protocol. This command is useful in situations in which you are troubleshooting adjacencies that have not been established due to misconfigured timer intervals and network types:

```
ROUTER_A# show ip ospf interface
Ethernet 0 is up, line protocol is up
    Internet Address 131.119.254.202, Mask 255.255.255.0, Area 0.0.0.0
    Process ID 201, Router ID 192.77.99.1, Network Type BROADCAST, Cost: 10
    Transmit Delay is 1 sec, StateFull, Priority 1
    Designated Router (ID) 131.119.254.10, Interface address 131.119.254.10
    Backup Designated router (ID) 131.119.254.28, Interface addr 131.119.254.28
    Timer intervals configured, Hello 10, Dead 60, Wait 40, Retransmit 5
    Hello due in 0:00:05
    Neighbor Count is 2, Adjacent neighbor count is 2
  Adjacent with neighbor 131.119.254.28  (Backup Designated Router)
  Adjacent with neighbor 131.119.254.10  (Designated Router)
```

Relevant information displayed by the SHOW IP OSPF INTERFACE command is shown in Table 7-9.

TABLE 7-9   Variables in the SHOW IP OSPF INTERFACE Command Output

Code Listing	Description
Internet Address	The IP address, subnet mask, and area of the interface.
AS	The autonomous system that this router belongs to.
Router ID	The router ID that the OSPF process is using for this router.
Network Type	The network type that is used by this router. Networks can be NBMA, point-to-point, point-to-multipoint, etc.
Transmit Delay	The interval used to transmit link-state changes.
Priority	The OSPF priority of the router; 1 specifies the default priority assigned by the OSPF protocol, meaning that the router with the highest ID will become the designated router.
Designated Router	The router ID of the designated router and its IP address.
Backup Designated router	The router ID of the BDR and its IP address.
Timer intervals configured	The intervals configured on the router for the OSPF process. Intervals are *hello, dead, wait*, and *retransmit.*
Hello	The hello interval configured on the router. Misconfigured hello intervals can result in inconsistencies in adjacencies and missing updates and routes.
Neighbor count	The number of neighbor relationships established as well as the list of adjacent neighbors.

In the listing, possible states of a router are as follows:

- **DOWN**   Heard from no one.
- **ATTEMPT**   Sent a hello on an NBMA but haven't heard a reply.
- **INIT**   Heard a hello but haven't yet reached neighbor status.
- **TWO-WAY**   Full neighbor relationship.
- **EXSTART**   Starting up a link for exchanging DDPs.
- **LOADING**   Building the database and LSAs from the DDPs.
- **FULL**   Adjacency.
- **DR**   The designated router for this LAN.

The timers and hello intervals must be the same on OSPF routers in an area in order for adjacency to be established. This is one of the rules of the OSPF specification and it must be followed. If the timers or hello intervals are different on some routers, formation of adjacencies is prevented.

The **SHOW IP OSPF NEIGHBOR** Command

The SHOW IP OSPF NEIGHBOR command displays a summary of all neighbors known to the router. Remember that all routers form an adjacency with both the DR and BDR on an OSPF network:

```
ROUTER_A# show ip ospf neighbor
   ID          Pri   State          Dead Time    Address         Interface
199.199.199.137 1   FULL/DR        0:00:31      160.89.80.37     Ethernet0
192.31.48.1     1   FULL/DROTHER   0:00:33      192.31.48.1      Fddi0
192.31.48.200   1   FULL/DROTHER   0:00:33      192.31.48.200    Fddi0
199.199.199.137 5   FULL/DR        0:00:33      192.31.48.189    Fddi0
```

Table 7-10 provides a description of the information provided by this command. The Priority field tells you the OSPF priority that has been configured for the router. The priority is used to determine whether a router will be selected as DR or BDR. A value of 1 is used by default. If this value is left at 1, the DR and BDR are elected based on the highest IP address of the routers participating in the OSPF process.

TABLE 7-10   Information Provided by the SHOW IP OSPF NEIGHBOR Command

Code Listing	Description
ID	The router ID of the neighbor OSPF router.
PRI	The priority of the router. A priority of 1 is the default value for OSPF processes.
State	The status of the router. Possible states are: DR: Designated router. BDR: Backup designated router. DROTHER: Router was not chosen as the DR or BDR. If the priority was set to zero on this router, the state would always be DROTHER because it could not participate in elections to become a DR or BDR.
Dead Time	The interval before a neighbor is declared dead.
Address	The IP address of the interface used in the OSPF process.
Interface	The interface that is participating in the OSPF process.

The router ID might be different from the IP address of the router's interface for one simple reason: it can be used to determine the eligibility of the router to become a DR or BDR. It is configured using the loopback interface of the router and assigning a high IP address to this interface. This influences the DR or BDR election process if the priority of the router is left at the default of 1.

The SHOW IP OSPF VIRTUAL-LINKS Command

One rule that all OSFP routers must follow is that they must connect to area 0. In instances in which this is not feasible, a router can use a "virtual link" to connect to area 0 by means of a tunnel that is created through another router that has a connection to area 0. The SHOW IP OSPF VIRTUAL-LINKS command shows all such tunnels that have been configured on the router. The output from this command is useful in troubleshooting OSPF operations that occur through virtual links:

```
ROUTER_A# show ip ospf virtual-links
Virtual Link to router 192.10.10.32 is up
Transit area 0.0.0.1, via interface Ethernet0, Cost of using 10
Transmit Delay is 1 sec, State POINT_TO_POINT
Timer intervals configured, Hello 10, Dead 40, Wait 40, Retransmit 5
Hello due in 0:00:08
Adjacency State FULL
```

Table 7-11 provides a description of the relevant fields shown in the listing.

All virtual links are considered point-to-point links. In the preceding listing, the virtual link would be pointing to the router ID of the router at the other end of the link, which is now seen as a neighbor.

exam
ⓦatch

The concept of the virtual link in OSPF areas is a critical issue that must be understood. Virtual links should be used only as a temporary measure until a more permanent solution can be reached. You should know the purpose of a virtual link as well as the SHOW command for troubleshooting it.

The SHOW IP EIGRP INTERFACES Command

To display EIGRP-related information on interfaces that have been configured to use the EIGRP routing protocol, use the SHOW IP EIGRP INTERFACES

TABLE 7-11	Information in the SHOW IP OSPF VIRTUAL-LINKS Command
Code Listing	**Description**
Virtual Link	The OSPF neighbor and the status of the virtual link.
Transit area	The transit area in which the virtual link tunnel is configured.
Via interface	The interface through which the virtual link is formed.
Cost of using	The cost of reaching the neighbor through the virtual link tunnel.
Transmit delay	The transmit delay of updates through the virtual link.
Adjacency State	The adjacency state of the OSPF router. Possible states are: DOWN: Heard from no one. ATTEMPT: Sent a hello on an NBMA but have not heard a reply. INIT: Heard a hello but have not yet reached neighbor status. TWO-WAY: Full neighbor relationship. EXSTART: Starting up a link for exchanging DDPs. LOADING: Building the database and LSAs from the DDPs. FULL: Adjacency. DR: The designated router for this LAN.

command. Optionally, you can specify an interface type and number to obtain information about a particular interface:

```
ROUTER_A> show ip eigrp interfaces
IP EIGRP interfaces for process 109
                    Xmit Queue   Mean    Pacing Time   Multicast    Pending
Interface   Peers   Un/Reliable  SRTT    Un/Reliable   Flow Timer   Routes
Di0         0       0/0          0       11/434        0            0
Et0         1       0/0          337     0/10          0            0
SE0:1.16    1       0/0          10      1/63          103          0
Tu0         1       0/0          330     0/16          0            0
```

Information displayed by the SHOW IP EIGRP INTERFACES command is described in Table 7-12.

The SHOW IP EIGRP NEIGHBORS Command

The SHOW IP EIGRP NEIGHBORS command is used to determine peers that have established relationships with the router that is running EIGRP. It is useful in

TABLE 7-12 Information Provided by the SHOW IP EIGRP INTERFACES Command

Code Listing	Description
Interface	The interface on which EIGRP is configured.
Peers	Number of directly connected neighbors.
Xmit Queue Un/Reliable	The number of packets in the unreliable and reliable queues that are awaiting transmittal.
Mean SRTT	The average smooth round-trip time (SRTT) in milliseconds. The mean SRTT is the interval elapsed between the time an EIGRP packet is sent to a neighbor and an acknowledgment is returned.
Pacing Time Un/Reliable	The interval at which EIGRP packets should be sent.
Pending Routes	The number of routes that are awaiting transmittal in the transmit queue.

determining when neighbors become active or inactive and can help in debugging various transport problems:

```
Router# show ip eigrp neighbors
IP-EIGRP Neighbors for process 77
Address                Interface    Holdtime Uptime     Q       Seq   SRTT  RTO
                                    (secs)   (h:m:s)    Count   Num   (ms)  (ms)
192.168.81.30          Ethernet1    13       0:00:41    0       11    4     20
192.168.80.30          Ethernet0    14       0:02:01    0       10    12    24
192.168.80.31          Ethernet0    12       0:02:02    0       4     5     20
```

A description of the output generated by the SHOW IP EIGRP NEIGHBORS command appears in Table 7-13.

The **SHOW IP EIGRP TRAFFIC** Command

The SHOW IP EIGRP TRAFFICE command shows the number of EIGRP packets that were sent and received on the router:

```
ROUTER_A# show ip eigrp traffic
IP-EIGRP Traffic Statistics for process 60
  Hellos sent/received: 210/205
  Updates sent/received: 10/23
  Queries sent/received: 3/0
  Replies sent/received: 0/2
  Acks sent/received: 18/14
```

| TABLE 7-13 | Variables Provided by the SHOW IP EIGRP NEIGHBORS Command |

Code Listing	Description
Process	AS number that is being used by the EIGRP protocol.
Address	IP address of the EIGRP neighbor.
Interface	The interface through which EIGRP hello packets are being received from the neighbor.
Holdtime	The number of seconds that must elapse before the neighbor is determined to be down. The default holdtime is 15 seconds.
Uptime	The time elapsed in hours, minutes, and seconds since this router first established a relationship with the neighbor.
Q Count	The Q Count shows the number of EIGRP update, query, and reply packets that are awaiting transmittal by the router.
Seq Num	The number of the last EIGRP packet that was received from the neighbor.
SRTT	The time in milliseconds that it takes for the router to send an EIGRP packet and receive an acknowledgment from the neighbor.
RTO	The Retransmission Timeout is used to determine the time in milliseconds before a packet in the retransmission queue is resent.

Table 7-14 provides a description of the information provided by this command.

| TABLE 7-14 | Information in the SHOW IP EIGRP TRAFFIC Command Output |

Code Listing	Description
Process	AS number that is being used by the EIGRP process.
Hellos sent/received	Number of hello packets that were sent and received by the router.
Updates sent/received	Number of update packets that were sent and received by the router.
Queries sent/received	Number of reply packets that were sent and received.
ACKS sent/received	Number of acknowledgment packets sent in reply to neighbor queries and number of replies received from neighbors for hello packets.

The SHOW IP EIGRP TOPOLOGY Command

The SHOW IP EIGRP TOPOLOGY command lists the status of DUAL and is used to debug possible problems with the diffusing update algorithm:

```
ROUTER_A# show ip eigrp topology
IP-EIGRP Topology Table for process 75
Codes: P - Passive, A - Active, U - Update, Q - Query, R - Reply,
       r - Reply status
P 192.168.80.0 255.255.255.0, 2 successors, FD is 0
          via 192.168.80.28 (46251776/46226176), Ethernet0
          via 192.168.81.28 (46251776/46226176), Ethernet1
          via 192.168.80.31 (46277376/46251776), Ethernet0
P 192.168.81.0 255.255.255.0, 1 successors, FD is 307200
          via Connected, Ethernet1
          via 192.168.81.28 (307200/281600), Ethernet1
          via 192.168.80.28 (307200/281600), Ethernet0
          via 192.168.80.31 (332800/307200), Ethernet0
```

The types of information given by this command are described in Table 7-15.

SHOW Command Summary

The SHOW commands that have been covered so far are all used to troubleshoot TCP/IP. The routing protocol commands that were reviewed might seem to have

| **TABLE 7-15** | Information Displayed by the SHOW IP EIGRP TOPOLOGY Command |

Code Listing	Description
Codes	State of the topology entry. *Passive* and *Active* refer to the status of EIGRP; *Query* and *Update* describe the type of packet that is sent.
Successors	Number of successors. This corresponds to the number of parallel successors in the routing table.
FD	Feasible distance. The feasible distance is used to calculate successors to a route in the event that the primary route is no longer usable.
Via	IP address of the peer who told the EIGRP process about this destination—the first N of these entries, where N is the number of successors. The remaining entries on the list are feasible successors.
(46251776/46226176)	These numbers represent metrics of the EIGRP routing protocol. The first number is the Enhanced IGRP metric that represents the cost to the destination. The second number is the Enhanced IGRP metric that this peer advertised.

no bearing on TCP/IP, but remember that these routing protocols are routing TCP/IP and you must understand the different methods of routing TCP/IP from one location to another. You are not expected to remember all the finer details of these commands, but you should at least know the general objective and type of information that you can obtain from them.

exam
⒲atch *Common commands such as SHOW IP ACCESS-LISTS, SHOW IP ROUTE, SHOW IP INTERFACE, and SHOW IP PROTOCOLS are commands with which you should be very familiar. Most likely, the exam will not try to pull a "fast one" on you by asking you to interpret the output from an obscure, uncommon command. Try to examine the output from these commands and become familiar with the types of information they present.*

DEBUG Commands

This section covers the DEBUG commands with which you should be familiar. Always remember to be cautious when using DEBUG commands. They can be powerful tools to aid you in troubleshooting, but they can also be a source of trouble if you are not careful. If possible, try to Telnet into your router when you are debugging, and send the output normally seen on the console during your Telnet session using the TERMINAL MONITOR command. Output that is sent to the router's console generates a processor interrupt for each character sent to the screen.

Note: You should know by now which commands turn off all debugging on your router. NO DEBUG ALL or UNDEBUG ALL turns off all debugging on your router. In addition, remember that DEBUG commands can be executed only at the privileged exec prompt.

The DEBUG IP RIP Command

The DEBUG IP RIP command is used to troubleshoot RIP. You can see status messages as updates are being received and sent out. The source of updates and the interface receiving those updates can be easily determined:

```
ROUTER_A#debug ip rip
RIP: received update from 192.10.80.1 on Ethernet1
   192.10.95.0 in 1 hops
   192.10.81.0 in 1 hops
   192.10.66.0 in 2 hops
   0.0.0.0 in 6 hops
```

```
RIP: sending update to 255.255.255.255 via Ethernet1 (160.10.80.2)
  subnet 192.10.94.0, metric 1
  131.108.0.0 in 16 hops (inaccessible)
RIP: sending update to 255.255.255.255 via Serial1 (192.10.81.10)
  subnet 192.10.64.0, metric 1
  subnet 192.10.66.0, metric 3
  131.10.0.0 in 16 hops (inaccessible)
  default 0.0.0.0, metric 8
```

In this listing, you can see that networks 131.108.0.0 and 131.10.0.0 are currently inaccessible because they have a hop count of 16. RIP has a maximum hop count of 15; the sixteenth hop means that the route is not reachable. You can also see that the default route of 0.0.0.0 has a metric of 8. In RIP, the metric refers to the number of hops (routers) by which a route is reachable.

The DEBUG IP IGRP EVENTS Command

The DEBUG IP IGRP EVENTS command displays summary information about IGRP routing, including the source and destination of routing updates, number of routes in the update, and the types of route. Route types can be interior, exterior, or system. The following listing presents a sample output. A description of the output follows:

```
ROUTER_A#debug ip igrp events
IGRP: sending update to 255.255.255.255 via Ethernet1 (192.10.10.8)
  IGRP: Update contains 20 interior, 35 system, and 5 exterior routes.
  IGRP: Total routes in update: 60
  IGRP: sending update to 255.255.255.255 via Ethernet0 (192.10.11.8)
  IGRP: Total routes in update: 1
  IGRP: Received update from 192.10.10.11.10 on Ethernet0
  IGRP: Update contains 15 interior, 1 system, and 3 exterior routes.
  IGRP: Total routes in update: 19
  IGRP: Received update from 192.10.10.11.11 on Ethernet0
  IGRP: Update contains 6 interior, 0 system, and 0 exterior routes.
  IGRP: Total routes in update: 6
```

The information listed is in summary form. The listing shows that the router has sent broadcast updates out interfaces Ethernet0 and Ethernet1. The router also received two separate updates from two different routers out the Ethernet0 interface.

The first line indicates whether the router sent or received the update packet, the source or destination address, and the interface through which the update was sent or received. If the update was sent, the IP address assigned to this interface is shown (in parentheses):

```
IGRP: sending update to 255.255.255.255 via Ethernet1 (192.10.10.8)
```

The second line summarizes the number and types of routes described in the update:

```
IGRP: Update contains 20 interior, 35 system, and 5 exterior routes.
```

The third line indicates the total number of routes described in the update:

```
IGRP: Total routes in update: 60
```

The DEBUG IP IGRP TRANSACTIONS Command

The DEBUG IP IGRP TRANSACTIONS command displays information similar to that of the DEBUG IP RIP command. Information is displayed concerning metrics, neighbors, and source of updates:

```
ROUTER_A# debug ip igrp transactions
IGRP: received update from 192.10.10.200 on Ethernet0
  subnet 192.10.11.0, metric 1300 (neighbor 1200)
  subnet 192.10.12.0, metric 8676 (neighbor 8576)
  subnet 192.10.13.0, metric 1300 (neighbor 1200)
  subnet 192.10.14.0, metric 1200 (neighbor 1100)
  subnet 192.10.15.0, metric 8676 (neighbor 8576)
network 192.50.10.0, metric 158550 (neighbor 158450)
network 150.136.0.0, metric 16777215 (inaccessible)
exterior network 140.222.0.0, metric 9676 (neighbor 9576)
IGRP: sending update to 255.255.255.255 via Ethernet0 (160.89.64.31)
  subnet 160.89.80.0, metric-16777215
  subnet 160.89.64.0, metric-1100
```

The listing shows that the router has received updates from one other router on the network. Router 192.10.10.200 sent information about five destinations in the update. This router sent a broadcast update out the Ethernet0 interface.

On the second line of the listing, the first field refers to the type of destination information. The second field is the IP address of the destination network. The third field is the metric stored in the routing table and the metric advertised by the neighbor sending the information. The message "Metric... inaccessible" usually means that the neighbor router has put the destination in holddown mode.

The DEBUG IP EIGRP Command

The DEBUG IP EIGRP command helps you analyze the packets that are sent and received via an interface. Be careful because this command generates large amounts of output, so try to use it when the router is not heavily loaded. You can use this command to troubleshoot problems related to routing updates, metrics, and so on. The following is sample listing of the output from this command:

```
ROUTER_A# debug ip eigrp
IP-EIGRP: Processing incoming UPDATE packet
IP-EIGRP: Ext 192.168.3.0 255.255.255.0 M 386560 - 256000 130560 SM 360960 -
256000 104960
IP-EIGRP: Ext 192.168.0.0 255.255.255.0 M 386560 - 256000 130560 SM 360960 -
256000 104960
IP-EIGRP: Ext 192.168.3.0 255.255.255.0 M 386560 - 256000 130560 SM 360960 -
256000 104960
IP-EIGRP: 172.24.43.0 255.255.255.0, - do advertise out Ethernet0/1
IP-EIGRP: Ext 172.24.43.0 255.255.255.0 metric 371200 - 256000 115200
IP-EIGRP: 192.135.246.0 255.255.255.0, - do advertise out Ethernet0/1
IP-EIGRP: Ext 192.135.246.0 255.255.255.0 metric 46310656 - 45714176 596480
IP-EIGRP: 172.24.40.0 255.255.255.0, - do advertise out Ethernet0/1
IP-EIGRP: Ext 172.24.40.0 255.255.255.0 metric 2272256 - 1657856 614400
IP-EIGRP: 192.135.245.0 255.255.255.0, - do advertise out Ethernet0/1
IP-EIGRP: Ext 192.135.245.0 255.255.255.0 metric 40622080 - 40000000 622080
IP-EIGRP: 192.135.244.0 255.255.255.0, - do advertise out Ethernet0/1
```

Table 7-16 lists the relevant fields in the output that need explanation.

The DEBUG ARP Command

ARP debugging can be used to monitor ARP events on a router. This command is useful in troubleshooting hosts that are experiencing connectivity issues that are

TABLE 7-16	Code Listing	Description
Variables in the Output for the SHOW IP EIGRP Command	IP-EIGRP	Indicates that this packet is an EIGRP packet.
	Ext	Shows that this destination is exterior.
	M	Shows the computed metric. The computed metric includes the metric between the router and the neighboring router. The first number is the composite metric; the other two numbers are the inverse bandwidth and the delay, respectively.

related to possible duplicate IP addresses due to misconfiguration. The DEBUG output tells you which host is responding to the ARP request for IP-to-MAC address resolution:

```
ROUTER_A#debug arp
ARP packet debugging is on
ROUTER_A #terminal monitor
ROUTER_A #ping 192.10.10.64
Type escape sequence to abort.
Sending 5, 100-byte ICMP Echos to 192.10.10.64, timeout is 2 seconds:
!!!!!
Success rate is 100 percent (5/5), round-trip min/avg/max = 1/202/1005 ms
ROUTER_A #
3w1d: IP ARP: creating incomplete entry for IP address: 192.10.10.64 interface
 Ethernet0/0
3w1d: IP ARP: sent req src 192.10.10.3 0050.3ef8.eb80,
            dst 192.10.10.64 0000.0000.0000 Ethernet0/0
3w1d: IP ARP: sent req src 192.10.10.3 0,
            dst 192.10.10.64 0 Serial0/0.1
3w1d: IP ARP: sent req src 192.10.10.3 0050.3ef8.eb80,
            dst 192.10.10.64 0000.0000.0000 Serial0/0.1
3w1d: IP ARP: rcvd rep src 192.10.10.64 0020.affa.39f5,
            dst 192.10.10.3 Ethernet0/0
```

In the code listing, you can see that the PING to host 192.10.10.64 resulted in an ARP request because the IP-to-MAC address mapping is being verified. The PING was successful, meaning that the MAC address for IP address 192.10.10.64 was already in the router's ARP cache. In the first ARP message line, the destination MAC address appears to be unknown because of the presence of the all-zeros MAC address. On the last line of the ARP DEBUG output, a reply was received from 192.10.10.64, confirming that the MAC address is indeed 0020.affa.39f5.

The DEBUG IP PACKET <ACCESS-LIST-NUMBER> Command

The DEBUG IP PACKET <ACCESS-LIST-NUMBER> command specifies an optional argument to the DEBUG IP PACKET command. Because the DEBUG IP PACKET command examines each and every IP packet that is entering and leaving the router, the load placed on the router could be tremendous. On a production router, this command could very well bring the router to a halt. By specifying an access list number, only packets that are permitted by the access list are examined, which decreases the impact on the router.

The **DEBUG IP OSPF EVENTS** Command

The DEBUG IP OSPF EVENTS command generates information concerning OSPF-related events, such as adjacencies, flooding information, designated router selection, and SPF calculations. Possible uses for this command include troubleshooting connectivity issues related to the following situations:

- The IP subnet masks for routers on the same network do not match.

- The OSPF hello interval for the router does not match that configured for a neighbor.

- The OSPF dead interval for the router does not match that configured for a neighbor.

A sample output from this command is as follows:

```
ROUTER_A#debug ip ospf events
OSPF events debugging is on
OSPF: Rcv hello from 192.10.10.199 area 200
      from Ethernet0/0 192.10.13.12
OSPF: End of hello processing
OSPF: hello with invalid timers on interface Ethernet0
      hello interval received 10 configured 10
      net mask received 255.255.255.0 configured 255.255.255.0
      dead interval received 40 configured 30
```

In the preceding output, the OSPF process received a hello packet from host 192.10.10.199, which is in area 200, via the Ethernet0/0 interface. There is a message indicating that the hello packet was received with invalid timers. In this case, the dead interval configured on the interface is 30, but the dead interval received from the packet is 40. This is one of many reasons that two OSPF routers do not become neighbors.

The **DEBUG IP OSPF ADJACENCY** Command

An *adjacency* is a relationship formed between selected neighboring routers for the purpose of exchanging routing information. Not every pair of neighboring routers becomes adjacent. Instead, adjacencies are established with some subset of the router's neighbors. Routers connected by point-to-point networks and virtual links always become adjacent. On multiaccess networks, all routers become adjacent to both the *designated router* and the *backup designated router.*

The DEBUG IP OSPF ADJACENCY command can be used to check for misconfigured hello and dead intervals, area IDs, stub area E bits (E bits identify stub area routers), and network masks:

```
ROUTER_A#debug ip ospf adj
OSPF: Mismatched hello parameters from 141.108.10.3
      Dead R 40 C 40, Hello R 10 C 10 Mask R 255.255.255.0 C 255.255.255.252
```

In the listing, there is a network mask mismatch. The mask received from router 141.108.10.3 is 255.255.255.0, and the mask configured on ROUTER_A is 255.255.255.252.

The DEBUG IP OSPF PACKET Command

The DEBUG IP OSPF PACKET command displays information on every OSPF packet that is received on the router. A description of the variables provided in the following output appears in Table 7-17:

```
Router# debug ip ospf packet
OSPF: rcv. v:2 t:1 l:48 rid:200.0.0.116
      aid:0.0.0.0 chk:0 aut:2 keyid:1 seq:0x0
```

CERTIFICATION OBJECTIVE 7.03

PING and TRACE

PING and TRACE are two of the most common and frequently used tools in a troubleshooter's arsenal. They can be found not only on Cisco routers but on virtually all equipment that support a user interface for management purposes. Every operating system has these two tools. Every piece of equipment that supports the TCP/IP protocol can help you in providing PING responses; every router can support TRACE requests.

PING uses the ICMP protocol for generating echo requests and replies. Echo requests and replies are encapsulated in IP packets, meaning that Layer 3 connectivity can be tested.

TABLE 7-17

Information in
the DEBUG IP
OSPF PACKET
Command
Output

Code Listing	Description
V:	OSPF version.
T:	Type of OSPF packet. Possible packet types are: 1: Hello 2: Data description 3: Link-state request 4: Link-state update 5: Link-state acknowledgment
L	Length of the OSPF packet in bytes.
Rid	OSPF router ID.
Aid	OSPF area ID.
Chk	OSPF checksum.
Aut	OSPF authentication type. Possible authentication types are: 0: No authentication 1: Simple password 2: MD-5
Keyid	MD5 key ID.

The function of TRACE is to discover the path that a packet takes to a destination. Every router or hop that the packet crosses is reported back to the station running the trace. Traces to destinations over the Internet usually result in the DNS name of the router in addition to the IP address also being displayed.

The Standard IP PING Command

The PING command followed with an IP address is used to send ICMP *echo messages* to check host reachability and network connectivity. If an IP device receives an ICMP echo message destined for it, it sends an ICMP echo reply message back to the source of the ICMP echo message.

The PING command in a Cisco router supports not only IP but IPX and AppleTalk PINGs as well.

Multicast and broadcast PINGs are fully supported. When you PING the broadcast address of 255.255.255.255, the router sends the broadcast PING out every IP interface. Since it is a broadcast, it stays on the local segments. All devices that respond are listed. If the router's interface is configured with the NO IP

DIRECTED-BROADCAST command, you cannot send PINGs to a broadcast address.

The PING command is as follows:

```
ping [protocol] {host | address}
```

A sample of the output from a PING to a host is:

```
ROUTER_A>ping 192.10.10.32
Type escape sequence to abort.
Sending 5, 100-byte ICMP Echos to 192.10.10.32, timeout is 2 seconds:
!!!!!
Success rate is 100 percent (5/5), round-trip min/avg/max = 1/2/4 ms
ROUTER_A>
```

Table 7-18 lists the variables in the PING command output.

The Extended IP PING Command

The extended IP PING command can be used only in privileged exec mode. It offers additional parameters that can enhance the function of the PING command. You can specify the number of packets to send, packet size, source address, timeout period, whether or not the "Do not fragment" bit is set to On, and other parameters. The extended IP PING is useful for checking connectivity between LAN technologies such as Ethernet and Token Ring. As you already know, Ethernet imposes a 1500-byte limit on packet size. Token Ring has a much higher limit. If

TABLE 7-18	Symbol	Description
Symbols That Represent PING Reply Types	!	Indicates a successful reply.
	.	Indicates that a timeout occurred while waiting for a reply.
	U	Means that the destination is unreachable.
	N	Means that the network is unreachable.
	P	Means that the protocol is unreachable.
	Q	Means that a source quench message was received.
	M	Means that the packet could not be fragmented.
	?	Means that the packet type is unknown.

you are experiencing problems between the two, you can use the extended IP PING to check whether the Ethernet stations are able to fragment the larger packets received from the Token Ring segment.

Exercise 7-2 shows some of the functionality of the extended IP PING command.

EXERCISE 7-2

Using Extended PING

1. Log in to your router and go into privileged mode.

2. Type **ping** and press Enter.

3. You will be presented with a listing that looks like the following:

```
ROUTER_A#ping
Protocol [ip]:
Target IP address: 192.10.10.64
Repeat count [5]:
Datagram size [100]:
Timeout in seconds [2]:
Extended commands [n]: y
Source address or interface:
Type of service [0]:
Set DF bit in IP header? [no]:
Validate reply data? [no]:
Data pattern [0xABCD]:
Loose, Strict, Record, Timestamp, Verbose[none]:
Sweep range of sizes [n]:
Type escape sequence to abort.
Sending 5, 100-byte ICMP Echos to 192.10.10.64, timeout is 2 seconds:
!!!!!
Success rate is 100 percent (5/5), round-trip min/avg/max = 1/2/4 ms
ROUTER_A#
```

4. You may specify different options, such as a larger packet size, an increased timeout interval, or whether to send a range of packet sizes.

You can see that numerous options are available with the PING command. The options become available when you answer "Yes" to the Extended Options question.

A possible use for the extended PING command is testing connectivity problems between Ethernet and Token Ring or FDDI LANs. The larger packet size that is used in Token Ring and FDDI LANs can cause problems with Ethernet stations if those stations have the "Do not fragment" (DF) bit set. Using extended PING, you can specify a range of sizes for the packets, up to and greater than the Ethernet MTU of 1600 bytes. By verifying whether connectivity stops at an MTU that is greater than 1600 bytes, you are able to determine whether the workstation is able to fragment packets larger than 1600 bytes.

The **STANDARD IP TRACE** Command

The standard TRACE command on a Cisco router is used to discover the IP path the packets from the router actually take when traveling to their destination. The TRACE command works by taking advantage of the error messages generated by routers when a datagram exceeds its TTL value.

The TRACE command starts by sending probe datagrams, one at a time, with a TTL value of 1. This causes the first router to discard the probe datagram and send back an error message. The TRACE command sends several probes with increasing TTL values and displays the round-trip time for each. Each outgoing packet can result in one or two error messages. A "Time exceeded" error message indicates that an intermediate router has seen and discarded the probe. A "Destination unreachable" error message indicates that the destination node has received the probe and discarded it because it could not deliver the packet. If the timer goes off before a response comes in, trace prints an asterisk (*).

The trace terminates when the destination responds, when the maximum TTL is exceeded, or when the user interrupts the trace with the escape sequence.

The syntax of the TRACE command is:

```
trace <ip-destination>
```

The IP-DESTINATION refers to the IP address or the host name of the trace destination. The default parameters for the appropriate protocol are assumed and the tracing action begins.

The following code display shows a sample of the IP TRACE output when a destination host name has been specified:

```
ROUTER_A>trace www.yahoo.com
Type escape sequence to abort.
Tracing route to www.yahoo.akadns.net (216.32.74.52)
  1  192.10.10.119  160 ms    140 ms    141 ms
  2  192.10.10.1  160 ms    180 ms    161 ms
  3  142-065.cosmoweb.net [63.78.142.65]  220 ms    191 ms    180 ms
  4  DS3-RT-NY.medialoginc.com [208.223.112.12]    200 ms    170 ms       *
  5  500.Serial3-9.GW10.NYC4.ALTER.NET [157.130.19.177]    200 ms    170 ms
200 ms
```

Table 7-19 describes the fields shown in the display.

The Extended IP TRACE Command

Similar to the standard TRACE, the extended TRACE is used to discover the path that the router's packets actually take when traveling to their destination. To use nondefault parameters and invoke an extended TRACE test, enter the command without a destination argument. You will be stepped through a dialog box sequence

TABLE 7-19	Code Listing	Description
Trace Output Variables	nn ms	For each node, the round-trip time in milliseconds for the specified number of probes.
	*	The probe timed out.
	?	Unknown packet type.
	Q	Source quench.
	P	Protocol unreachable.
	N	Network unreachable.
	U	Port unreachable.
	H	Host unreachable.

to select the desired parameters. The following code display shows a sample TRACE command involving the extended dialog of the TRACE privileged exec command:

```
ROUTER_A#trace
Protocol [ip]:
Target IP address: www.yahoo.com
Source address:
Numeric display [n]:
Timeout in seconds [3]:
Probe count [3]:
Minimum Time to Live [1]:
Maximum Time to Live [30]:
Port Number [33434]:
Loose, Strict, Record, Timestamp, Verbose[none]:
Type escape sequence to abort.
Tracing the route to www.yahoo.akadns.net (216.32.74.52)
  1  192.10.10.119  160 ms    140 ms    141 ms
  2  192.10.10.1  160 ms    180 ms    161 ms
  3  142-065.cosmoweb.net [63.78.142.65]  220 ms    191 ms    180 ms
  4  DS3-RT-NY.medialoginc.com [208.223.112.12]    200 ms    170 ms       *
  5  500.Serial3-9.GW10.NYC4.ALTER.NET [157.130.19.177]    200 ms    170 ms
200 ms
```

Table 7-20 describes the fields that are unique to the extended TRACE sequence, as shown in the display.

CERTIFICATION OBJECTIVE 7.04

Problem Isolation in IP Networks

Finding the source of problems in TCP/IP-based networks is best solved by applying a model to all problems.

First you must gather facts about the problem. That means that you must document the symptoms of the problem along with such facts as whether this is an ongoing problem or a new one. Maybe something has changed on the network that could be the possible source of the trouble. It is up to you to find out what, if anything, has been changed. You must then come up with possible solutions to the problem.

TABLE 7-20   Extended TRACE Command Options

Code Listing	Description
Target IP address	You must enter a host name or an IP address. There is no default.
Target IP address	Source address. One of the interface addresses of the router to use as a source address for the probes.
Numeric display	The default is to have both a symbolic and numeric display; however, you can suppress the symbolic display.
Timeout in seconds	The number of seconds to wait for a response to a probe packet. The default is 3 seconds.
Probe count	The number of probes to be sent at each TTL level. The default count is 3.
Minimum Time to Live [1]	The TTL value for the first probes. The default is 1, but it can be set to a higher value to suppress the display of known hops.
Maximum Time to Live [30]	The largest TTL value that can be used. The default is 30. The TRACE command terminates when the destination is reached or when this value is reached.
Port Number	The destination port used by the UDP probe messages. The default is 33434.
Loose, Strict, Record, Timestamp, Verbose	IP header options. You can specify any combination. The TRACE command issues prompts for the required fields. Note that TRACE places the requested options in each probe; however, there is no guarantee that all routers (or end nodes) will process the options.
Loose Source Routing	Allows you to specify a list of nodes that must be traversed when going to the destination.
Strict Source Routing	Allows you to specify a list of nodes that must be the only nodes traversed when going to the destination.
Record	Allows you to specify the number of hops to leave room for.
Timestamp	Allows you to specify the number of time stamps to leave room for.
Verbose	If you select any option, the verbose mode is automatically selected and trace prints the contents of the option field in any incoming packets. You can prevent verbose mode by selecting it again, toggling its current setting.

Then you implement those solutions and observe the results. If the problem is not solved, you must undo your changes, rethink your solutions, and then implement those solutions and observe the results.

Following a well-documented process of problem isolation greatly speeds up the process of problem elimination. You must always remember to document every change that you implement so that in case things get worse, you can always revert to the earlier situation with the original problem.

This section of the chapter deals with common issues that affect devices on a TCP/IP network. Try to relate these issues to problems that you have already faced and see if you can come up with a similar or even better solution.

The Local Host

The *local host* refers to the station or device that you are troubleshooting locally. *Locally* means that you are at the device itself. *Local host* in this case refers to a station or device (other than a router) that you are troubleshooting.

NIC Failure

The failure of the network interface card on the host results in the loss of all connectivity through that interface. NIC failure is attributed to hardware failure itself due to a possible manufacturing defect or mishandling of the unit. You can tell if there is a NIC failure if you have checked the cabling and drivers (if applicable) on a host and there is still no connectivity. If the NIC is not connected to a hub or switch, it cannot show a Link Active LED lit up. In such rare cases of NIC failure, it is best to replace the card itself and see if your problem clears up.

Cabling

Cabling issues can result in anything from a total loss of connectivity to intermittent loss of connectivity. Cabling issues involve connectivity as related to network usage. Straight-through cables are used to connect a host to a switch or a hub. A crossover cable results in zero connectivity. (See Chapter 3 for a detailed description of crossover and straight-through cables.) Cabling can also go bad over time. Check the condition of the cables using a cable tester. A cable tester tests for end-to-end connectivity on all four wire pairs and can also tell you if a cable is straight through or crossover, simply by letting you know if the wires are connected in order.

IP Address, Network Mask, and Default Gateway

Most hosts should have a default route set if they expect to be able to communicate with hosts on other networks. When discussing routers, routing, and network paths, we usually call this route a *default router*, but many hosts refer to it as a *default gateway.*

In terms of Layer 3 protocols, *gateway* is usually synonymous with *router*, but *gateway* is another one of those networking terms that means many things to many people, and so its context must be clear. The default gateway must be on the same subnet as the host, or the host cannot use it.

Most of what can go wrong with default gateways on hosts has to do with misconfiguration. The gateway address might be wrong, it might not be on the same subnet as the host, or the gateway might not be functional in some way. To troubleshoot, you should check to see that the host has a default gateway listed, that it is correct, and that the host is able to ARP for it. If a host cannot communicate with hosts on other subnets but can communicate with hosts on its own subnet, all other problems aside, the problem is likely to be a missing or incorrect default gateway.

The Local Gateway

The *local gateway* refers to the router that is on the same subnet as the host or device that you are troubleshooting. The failure of the NIC on the local gateway results in the loss of all connectivity through that interface. NIC failure is attributed to hardware failure itself due to a possible manufacturing defect or mishandling of the unit. You can tell if there is a NIC failure if you perform a SHOW INTERFACES command on the router and discover that the Ethernet interface is in a down/down state, even though it is connected to a hub or switch. If the NIC is not connected to a hub or switch, it cannot come up. In such rare cases of NIC failure, it is wise to contact the network equipment reseller where you purchased your equipment. If you purchased directly from Cisco, you can reach the Cisco Technical Assistance Center (TAC) either by submitting a problem online at *www.cisco.com* or by calling the Cisco support number. Current support numbers are available at the CCO Web site (*www.cisco.com*).

Port Failure

Port failure on a router is indicated by a loss of connectivity with the respective network to which the port is connected or a console that is not displaying correctly. Port failure can be caused by any of the following:

- **Disconnected or improperly plugged in interface cable**   The LED on the network interface indicates any of these.
- **Improperly seated NIC**   Turn off the router, reseat the card, and power on the router. Check the status of the interface on the router by issuing the SHOW INTERFACES command. The interface should be listed as present and in an up/up state.

If the console port appears to be malfunctioning, make sure that you are using the right cable and connector to connect the terminal screen and the console port. Console cables are usually referred to as "rollover" cables. If connecting a console to a PC, you must also make sure that you have the correct serial port adapter.

Cabling

Cabling issues regarding a router involve three things:

- Incorrect cable type (crossover or straight through)
- Incorrect cabling pinout used for the console
- Damaged cable

The presence of any of these three issues results in problems. Remember that a console port uses a rollover cable. Router-to-hub connectivity is achieved by means of a straight-through cable. Damaged cabling can be checked using a cable tester.

IP Address, Network Mask, and Default Gateway

Default routes on routers can be a little more complicated. Unlike most hosts, a router does not always have a default route. It is quite common for a router connected to multiple subnets to learn a default route via a routing protocol rather than having it statically entered so that the network can reroute during a failure. When a router or host has a default route, that router or host is deferring to a router that presumably has a more complete routing table. Often this is done for simplicity's sake. For a host that can reach only one router, why should it have anything more than a default route?

Imagine a corporate network that has one Internet connection. All the corporate routers inform each other of the subnets they control. Therefore, those routers have a complete list of the corporate nets. When one of the routers receives a packet, the packet is destined for either a corporate net or something else. The router can consult its own complete table to determine if the packet is for the corporate net. If it is not, it must be destined for the Internet, because there really is no other choice. So, all the corporate routers would have a default route pointing to the router that connects to the Internet. Furthermore, the easiest way to accomplish this task is to manually add a default route on the Internet-connected router and let it advertise that default (typically via route redistribution) to all the other internal routers. This saves configuration time and allows the other routers to know if that path goes away.

Routing Protocol

Misconfigured routing protocols can lead to routes missing from the routing table, intermittent connectivity, and generally inconsistent behavior from routers. Make sure that routers have been correctly configured with the correct routing protocols by issuing the SHOW IP PROTOCOLS command. This command lists all currently configured IP routing protocols on the router. (See a description of this command earlier in this chapter.) Issue the SHOW IP ROUTE command to see the routes that are missing.

Remember also that OSPF uses specific timers for different routing events. Misconfigured timers will be a source of trouble. Issue the DEBUG IP OSPF EVENTS command that was covered earlier in this chapter to see if there are any invalid timers.

exam
ⓦatch

The DEBUG IP OSPF EVENTS command can tell you if invalid OSPF timers are configured on the router.

A source of missing routes could be due to incorrectly configured or missing DISTRIBUTE-LIST commands. Issue the SHOW IP PROTOCOLS command to see if you have correctly configured the redistribute commands for the routing protocol in question. Redistribute commands are usually filtered by an access list. The SHOW IP ACCESS-LISTS command displays the access lists that are configured on the router.

Access Lists

Access lists are used to filter incoming and outgoing traffic. Traffic can be either user data or routing data. Incorrectly configured access lists can lead to clients not being able to connect to a particular network segment or LAN. A router that is filtering routing updates by means of an access list could be advertising the wrong routes, or it might not be advertising the necessary routes. Use the SHOW ACCESS-LISTS command to see the access lists that are configured on the router, and use the SHOW IP PROTOCOLS command to view if any routing protocols are using access lists to filter routing updates. Look for DISTRIBUTE-LIST commands to see what protocols are filtering updates and if the filtering is being done for inbound routes or outbound advertisements.

exam
ⓌatchWatch

Questions on access lists will definitely be on the support exam simply because access list use is so common. You should know the options that can be used with standard and extended IP access lists, the access list numbers that are used for standard and extended lists, and the commands used to apply, edit, and remove them from a router.

Review the following Scenario & Solution and see if you understand the solutions.

Remote Routers

Remote routers are those that are over a WAN link such as leased line or circuit-switched service such as ISDN. Problems with remote routers can be difficult

SCENARIO & SOLUTION	
What command applies outbound access list 12 on a Cisco router?	IP ACCESS-GROUP 12 OUT.
Is access list 12 a standard or extended access list?	Access list 12 is a standard IP access list.
What method of filtering is permitted when using access list 12?	Access list 12 is standard access list, so it can filter only by source IP address.
How would you remove outbound access list 12 from an interface?	ROUTER_A(CONFIG-IF)# NO IP ACCESS-GROUP 12 OUT.

to troubleshoot because often the very link that they are using to connect to your location is the one that is needed to log in to the router and check its configuration. If you do not know which remote router is causing the trouble, you can issue the TRACE command to find out. The TRACE command, covered earlier in this chapter, sends out packets and generates messages for each router that the packets cross. Traces that result in timeout, host unreachable, and network unreachable messages are useful in determining the router that is a possible source of trouble. After you have determined the source of trouble, you can then take measures to rectify the problem.

Port Failure

Port failures on remote routers can result in a very difficult situation. If the port failure is related to an Ethernet port that is connected to a local LAN, you can still access the router over the WAN link and determine the possible cause of failure using the SHOW INTERFACES command. If the port failure is related to a WAN port, you have an issue that is a bit more complicated. The WAN port supports your Telnet requests to log in and check the status of the interfaces, but if it is down, you cannot establish a connection to the router. In such a case, if there is no redundant path to the remote router, you must find some other way to gain access to the router—possibly physically visiting the location.

Another very important issue to consider is that most, if not all, remote troubleshooting requires eventual Telnet access to the router. In this case, you need a valid IP address to Telnet to. If the IP address that was assigned to the failed port is the IP address that you are going to Telnet to, you cannot establish a connection. It is usually a good idea to assign an IP address to the loopback interface because the loopback interface is a virtual interface and never goes down. Again, if you are troubleshooting a WAN port, in any case the port probably is unavailable for Telnet. It is usually a good idea to provide a POTS dial-up connection of some sort, which would enable you to connect to a failed router at a remote location. This could be done by connecting a modem to the AUX port of the router or an async interface, if available, or even connecting a modem to a computer at the remote location that can provide a remote control application that you can access from wherever you are located.

Cabling

Cabling issues involving remote routers usually stem from damaged cabling or connectors on the cables that have come loose. Check for damaged cabling using a cable tester. Remove the cable from the router and reinsert it to make sure that it is properly seated. Dust can also accumulate on the cable connectors over time. Make sure that they are clean before you reinsert them.

Circuit Failure

Circuit failures can be detected by error LEDs on your CSU/DSU in the case of fractional T1, T1, Frame Relay, ISDN PRI, and so on. Before you assume anything, check the basics such as cabling for damaged or loose connectors, and make sure your equipment is properly connected.

Using a CSU/DSU, you can configure a manual loopback on the circuit itself to test if there is connectivity to the local telco switch. If the loopback does not run successfully, you can be sure that there is a problem with the circuit itself. Notify your carrier of the problem. Be prepared with specifics such as the circuit ID number, circuit location, contact reach number, and the nature of the problem.

If you do not have a CSU/DSU, as in the case of ISDN BRI, you can issue the SHOW INTERFACES command. If you notice a message on your output indicating that the line protocol is down for a previously working WAN port, this most likely means that either there is a problem with the circuit itself or the cable from the telco wall jack to your equipment could be damaged or loose. First check the cabling; once you are sure that nothing is wrong with it, contact your carrier and ask them to check your line.

IP Address, Network Mask, and Default Gateway

Problems occur when two routers on the same major network have different subnet masks configured. Packets are not routed correctly. To check if interfaces have the correct IP address and subnet mask, use the SHOW IP INTERFACES command. This command shows you the IP information for each interface of the router. Make sure that the IP address and subnet mask are correctly configured. If either is incorrect, enter interface configuration mode and correct the error.

A default gateway is used to route packets that are destined for an unknown network. If the default gateway is not present or configured, the router does not know where to route packets that have destinations the router does not know about. These packets are dropped. The SHOW IP ROUTE command shows if the default gateway statement is missing or incorrect. Default gateway statements can be identified because they are similar to the last line in the following listing and are denoted by an "S," meaning that they are static:

```
ROUTER_A#show ip route
Codes: C - connected, S - static, I - IGRP, R - RIP, M - mobile, B - BGP
       D - EIGRP, EX - EIGRP external, O   OSPF, IA - OSPF inter area
       N1 - OSPF NSSA external type 1, N2 - OSPF NSSA external type 2
       E1 - OSPF external type 1, E2 - OSPF external type 2, E - EGP
       i - IS-IS, L1 - IS-IS level-1, L2 - IS-IS level-2, * - candidate default
       U - per-user static route, o - ODR

Gateway of last resort is 192.168.240.1 to network 0.0.0.0
     192.168.240.0/24 is variably subnetted, 2 subnets, 2 masks
C        192.168.240.0/24 is directly connected, Ethernet0
C        192.168.240.96/27 is directly connected, Ethernet0
S*   0.0.0.0/0 [1/0] via 192.168.240.1
```

Routing Protocol

Misconfigured routing protocols can lead to routes missing from the routing table, intermittent connectivity, and generally inconsistent behavior from routers. Make sure that routers have been correctly configured with the correct routing protocols by issuing the SHOW IP PROTOCOLS command. This command lists all currently configured IP routing protocols on the router. (See a description of this command earlier in this chapter.) Issue the SHOW IP ROUTE command and see what routes are missing. Remember also that OSPF uses specific timers for different routing events. Misconfigured timers will be a source of trouble. Issue the DEBUG IP OSPF EVENTS command that was covered earlier in this chapter to see if there are any invalid timers.

A source of missing routes could be due to incorrectly configured or missing DISTRIBUTE-LIST commands. Issue the SHOW IP PROTOCOLS command to see if you have correctly configured the redistribute commands or if they are present in the router. Redistribute commands are usually filtered by an access list. The SHOW IP ACCESS-LISTS command displays the access lists that are configured on the router.

Discontiguous Subnets with Classful Protocols

Discontiguous subnets refer to subnets that cross class boundaries, through either variable length subnet masking (VLSM) or supernetting.

Classful routing protocols such as RIP and IGRP do not advertise the subnet mask with the network address when they send updates. They automatically summarize to the classful network boundary of the network. Since RIP and IGRP behave this way, they could summarize too much and actual subnets become unreachable.

As a result, there could be a lack of connectivity in parts of the network. If you must use classful routing protocols, you must make sure that you do not use discontiguous subnets. Conversely, if you must use discontiguous subnets, you must use a classless routing protocol such as RIPv2, EIGRP, or OSPF.

Remote Hosts

Issues involving remote hosts usually fall into three categories: those caused by NIC failures, those caused by cabling issues, and those due to IP misconfiguration. These three categories are discussed in this section.

NIC Failure

Host NIC failures can result from manufacturing defects or mishandling. NIC failures usually take the longest to pinpoint because a NIC can appear to be working when it actually isn't. You would have to go through your entire set of IP troubleshooting tools before concluding that there is a problem with the card itself. Usual methods of troubleshooting NIC failures are:

- Checking link LEDs. If the NIC is correctly wired to the network and the link LED is still not lit, you can safely conclude that the NIC should be replaced.

- Checking whether the hub or switch port that it is connected shows an active connection.

- Attempting to PING the IP address of the host to verify connectivity.

Cabling

Cabling a host to the network is usually accomplished by the use of a straight-through cable. (If you have doubts about what exactly a straight-through cable should look like, refer to Chapter 3.) A straight-through cable can be easily verified—not only for pinouts but for continuity—using a cable tester.

Damaged cabling that is used to connect the host to a wall jack is easy enough to identify. What about cabling that runs from the wall jack to the patch panel? In this case, because the cable is most likely going through the wall or up in the ceiling, you need a cable tester that can do remote verification of cable continuity. This means that one end of the unit plugs into the wall jack and the other end is used at the patch panel to find and check the cable that is suspect. A variety of vendors, including Black Box and Paladin, manufacture these tools.

IP Address, Network Mask, Default Gateway

Misconfigured IP addresses or subnet masks and default gateways are usually not too difficult to pinpoint. In these cases, most likely you already know what the correct settings should be, and you should be able to correct these easily.

IP address issues arise when hosts are configured with static IP addresses. If careful record is not kept of manual IP addressing, it is quite conceivable that two stations could end up with the same IP address, resulting in intermittent loss of connectivity in the network. Of course, once you find one station that has the duplicate IP address, you can take that station off the network and discover the other station by the use of the PING command. You also need to clear the ARP cache of the router from which you are issuing the PING command by typing the command CLEAR ARP CACHE. This command forces the router to rediscover the MAC-to-IP address mapping that you suspect.

Network mask and default gateway issues are easily checked by looking at the IP configuration of the host. You already know that all hosts on the same network must have the same subnet mask and default gateway information. You can verify whether the host has the correct configuration by checking the configuration of another host that is functioning properly.

CERTIFICATION OBJECTIVE 7.05

Problem Isolation in Windows 95 and 98 Networks

Problems in Windows-based networks are usually simple to troubleshoot because working with Windows-based machines is a task with which most support personnel are familiar. When working with Windows, you can gain access to configuration information easily, and making changes is also not a particularly difficult. The user interface of Windows is very friendly; most of the time, problems can be quickly pinpointed. For example, on Windows NT and Windows 2000, you can see all IP configuration information for a machine by running one simple command at the command line. This command is IPCONFIG /A::. On Windows 98, a similar command is entered at the Start | Run command option. This command, the WINIPCFG command, provides a comprehensive listing of the entire IP configuration on that machine. Tools such as the PING and TRACE utilities are also available for command-line use on all Windows machines.

A sample screen for the IPCONFIG /ALL command on Windows 2000 is shown in Figure 7-2.

From Figure 7-2, it is easy to determine the exact configuration specifics for this machine. You can see, for example, that this machine does not have DHCP enabled, so it probably has a static IP address configuration. If you look closer, however, you'll also notice that the information provided is for a PPP adapter, meaning that the configuration details apply to a dial-up connection.

The following section covers various TCP/IP issues that can occur in Windows-based networks. Although by no means exhaustive, the points presented represent the most common sources of problems in these networks.

FIGURE 7-2

Output of the IPCONFIG /ALL command on Windows 2000

```
C:\WINNT\System32\command.com                              _ □ ✕
Microsoft(R) Windows DOS
(C)Copyright Microsoft Corp 1990-1999.

C:\>ipconfig /all

Windows 2000 IP Configuration

        Host Name . . . . . . . . . . . . : g6-500
        Primary DNS Suffix  . . . . . . . :
        Node Type . . . . . . . . . . . . : Hybrid
        IP Routing Enabled. . . . . . . . : No
        WINS Proxy Enabled. . . . . . . . : No

PPP adapter DD98-2128699182:

        Connection-specific DNS Suffix  . :
        Description . . . . . . . . . . . : WAN (PPP/SLIP) Interface
        Physical Address. . . . . . . . . : 00-53-45-00-00-00
        DHCP Enabled. . . . . . . . . . . : No
        IP Address. . . . . . . . . . . . : 192.10.10.118
        Subnet Mask . . . . . . . . . . . : 255.255.255.255
        Default Gateway . . . . . . . . . : 192.10.10.118
        DNS Servers . . . . . . . . . . . : 208.223.112.3
                                            208.223.112.2
        Primary WINS Server . . . . . . . : 192.10.10.65

C:\>_
```

The Local Host

Local host refers to the Windows PC or server that you are troubleshooting. In Windows networks, the terms *client* and *server* can refer to the same machine. Peer-to-peer Windows 98 workgroup machines, for example, can all act as both client and server.

In the Windows domain model, a Windows NT server is commonly used as a dedicated server, providing a centralized user database and other services that distinguish it from a peer-to-peer type of network. Peer-to-peer workgroups have no such centralized database of users and services.

NIC Failure

The failure of the NIC on a Windows machine is identified by a lack of connectivity and access to common services such as shared or network printing, failure to authenticate with a domain controller, or a nonfunctional e-mail program. To isolate the problem to a NIC failure, you must first verify whether this problem occurred on a previously working machine or this is a newly installed machine. If it's a newly installed machine, the problem would seem to be misconfiguration of the TCP/IP settings; therefore, you should check the settings to make sure that they are correct. Use Exercise 7-3 to practice isolation of NIC failures on a Windows-based machine.

EXERCISE 7-3

Isolating NIC Failures in Windows 95 and 98

If the machine was previously fully operational, you must first make sure that the NIC is cabled correctly to the wall jack or hub. If the NIC is cabled to a wall jack, make sure that the connection is correct from the patch panel to the hub or switch port. Check that the link and activity LEDs are active on the NIC.

Verify that the user has not mistakenly removed the drivers for the NIC. To check this, reboot the PC. Go to Control Panel and double-click System Properties. Go to the Device Manager tab. Refer to the screen shown in Figure 7-3.

Expand the Network Adapters field by clicking the + symbol. Verify that the correct network adapter is listed. If the adapter is not listed, you must reinstall the drivers for the NIC. To do this, you must first obtain the model and manufacturer information for the NIC and obtain the correct drivers. If the adapter is listed but it

FIGURE 7-3

Device Manager
in Windows 95
and 98

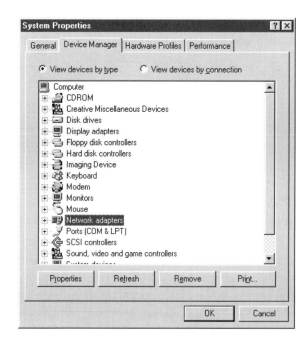

has a yellow exclamation (!) symbol next to it, that indicates that there is either a conflict with the network adapter resources and another device or the drivers are missing.

Reinstall the drivers and reboot the PC. When Windows is up again, make sure that there are no errors listed in Device Manager. Change all TCP/IP information to correct settings and perform another reboot. If everything worked out, the machine should now have full network connectivity.

If there are no errors, all configuration settings have been checked, and there is still no connectivity with the network, you should replace the faulty card with a new one.

Cabling

Cabling problems in Windows 95 and 98 networks revolve around four main issues:

- **Correct cabling being used**   Connecting a PC to a hub or switch port must be done by means of a straight-through cable. Verify that the correct cabling is used.

- **Damaged cabling** Use a cable tester to check the cable for breaks or loose wires.

- **Loose connections** Check the NIC, the wall jack, and the patch panel connections to be sure that the cable is securely connected. For an extra measure of safety, disconnect and reconnect all cables.

- **Dirty connectors** An amazing amount of dust can accumulate around electronic equipment. Make sure that the connectors and ports are clean and free from dust and dirt.

IP Address, Network Mask, and Default Gateway

IP configuration issues usually occur when stations are configured with static information. On any network with 20 or more stations all accessing a Windows NT server, manual IP configuration becomes a real chore. There is no reason that you should not use the free DHCP service that is provided with Windows NT Server. You configure the service once with all settings, and user machines obtain their IP address, subnet mask, default gateway, WINS server information, DNS server information, and other types of information from a centrally administered database.

If the machine's IP information is statically configured, use the WINIPCFG utility to determine current configuration. Check all settings to make sure that they are correct. If you need to change anything, you can go to the Control Panel | Network applet and make changes. Reboot the machine for the settings to take effect.

Dynamic Host Configuration Protocol

Dynamic Host Configuration Protocol (DHCP) is used to dynamically allocate IP addresses to machines as they are started up. Machines will broadcast a request for an IP address, and the DHCP server responds with a unique IP address as well as a subnet mask and default gateway information, if configured to do so.

DHCP is a free service that is provided with Windows NT Server. Of course, you can also use another DHCP service from another vendor. Cisco, for example, sells a product called Cisco Network Registrar that can provide DHCP service, among other things.

On your DHCP server, you must make sure that all settings are correct. One common issue that arises in DHCP server configuration is the allocation of IP addresses that could cause conflicts with another station on the network. This usually happens in an environment that uses a combination of static and dynamic address assignment. As a matter of fact, most environments use a combination of static and dynamic addressing.

The key to getting a properly working DHCP server is to make sure that your static IP address assignments and your dynamic IP addresses do not overlap. On a DHCP server, IP addresses are allocated from a configured pool of addresses. If the addresses in the pool overlap with static assignments, eventually a machine will receive an IP address that another station already possesses through static configuration.

Multiple Local Browse Masters

Windows clients maintain a list of machines that can provide the location of resources on the LAN. These machines that provide this list are called *browse masters*. Browse masters provide clients that are browsing Network Neighborhood for resources, a complete list of those resources, and the machines that provide them. Each machine that is starting Windows broadcasts a message to other machines querying the presence of a browse master. If there is no designated browse master, the Windows machine itself becomes a browse master if it is sharing any resources.

Windows NT Server becomes the browse master by default on Windows domain-based networks because it has priority over Windows 95 and 98 clients for maintaining a browse list.

Multiple browse masters result from a failure of the primary browse master. This can happen if the browse master loses connectivity with the rest of the network due to misconfiguration or failure of the network components, such as the NIC of the browse master. When this happens, an election is held to determine the succeeding master. This election can result in multiple masters being chosen if another NT server is not present. Multiple masters can result in inconsistent browsing lists, causing resources that can appear and disappear on the LAN.

Workgroup Name

The workgroup name in Windows 95 and 98 networks is the primary means by which resources are grouped. If you belong to a particular workgroup and you open up Network Neighborhood to browse for resources, you will see machines for the workgroup that you belong to that are providing resources first (see Figure 7-4).

In Figure 7-4, the list of machines that are sharing resources belong to the workgroup called Workgroup. This is the default workgroup name for machines on a peer-to-peer Windows 95 or 98 network.

FIGURE 7-4	
Workgroup resources in Windows	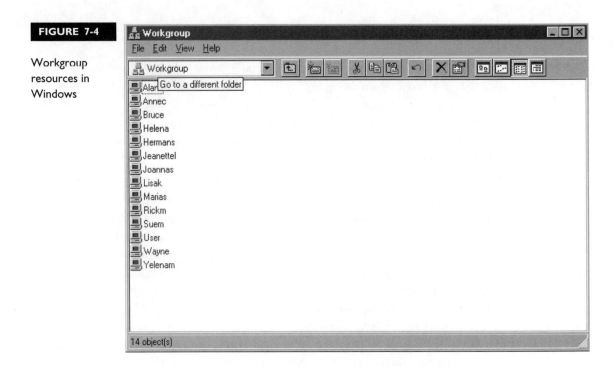

If the workgroup name is incorrect for a machine, the user will find no resources listed when he or she opens up Network Neighborhood to browse for resources. Instead, the user will find the names of the other workgroups and then must browse those other lists in an attempt to find the correct resource.

The Local Gateway

The *local gateway* refers to the router that clients contact when they need resources that are not located on the LAN. The local gateway could be a router that is providing a path to other LANs as well as the Internet. In today's networks, more and more users require access to the Internet for business use, such as research. The local gateway is therefore an essential component of the LAN because it provides access to critical business resources.

Port Failure

Port failure on the local gateway could be related to either a WAN port or an Ethernet port. Either way, the failure of one of them will result in lost connectivity to outside resources for the local LAN.

Ethernet port failure can be detected if it doesn't respond to Telnet requests or PINGs. If you cannot Telnet into the router, you must go to it and work at the console. Issue the SHOW INTERFACES command to see the nature of the trouble. The Ethernet port should be listed in an up/up status. If the Ethernet interface is listed as down, there is an issue with connectivity related to hardware or incorrect cabling. If the line protocol is down, there is a misconfiguration of the TCP/IP protocol. If the interface is shown as administratively down, it was disabled by the SHUTDOWN privileged exec command. Issue the NO SHUT command to re-enable the interface.

Cabling

Again, cabling issues involving the router follow four basic procedures:

- **Check the cable type**   Router-to-hub connections require a straight-through cable.

- **Check for damaged cabling**   Use a cable tester to check for breaks or loose wires.

- **Check for loose connectors**   Unplug and reinsert the connectors into the router and hub ports. Someone might have inadvertently knocked them loose.

- **Check for dirt and dust**   Dirt and dust can prevent successful connections. Make sure that the connectors and ports are clean.

IP Address, Network Mask, and Default Gateway

Misconfiguration of these three parameters will most certainly lead to routing failures. If the IP address of the router is misconfigured, clients will not be able to send packets to the correct gateway, simply because they will be sending the packets to a different IP address. If the network mask is incorrect, the router will behave as though it is on a different network than the local hosts. Again, clients will not be able to contact the default gateway.

If the default gateway on the router is incorrect, packets that are bound for unknown networks, such as Web sites on the Internet, will be dropped. Remember that the default gateway on the router is used to route packets with unknown destination IP addresses to a destination that supposedly has a better "idea" of where these packets should go.

To check the configured IP address and network mask of the router's interfaces, issue the SHOW RUNNING-CONFIG command on the router to see what IP addresses have been assigned to which interfaces.

To verify that the default gateway is correct, issue the SHOW IP ROUTE command. The entry that has a 0.0.0.0 statement pointing to an IP address of an interface on the router will be the default gateway configuration statement. The following listing provides an example:

```
ROUTER_A#sh ip ro
Codes: C - connected, S - static, I - IGRP, R - RIP, M - mobile, B - BGP
       D - EIGRP, EX - EIGRP external, O - OSPF, IA - OSPF inter area
       N1 - OSPF NSSA external type 1, N2 - OSPF NSSA external type 2
       E1 - OSPF external type 1, E2 - OSPF external type 2, E - EGP
       i - IS-IS, L1 - IS-IS level-1, L2 - IS-IS level-2, * - candidate default
       U - per-user static route, o - ODR
Gateway of last resort is 192.168.240.1 to network 0.0.0.0
S*   0.0.0.0/0 [1/0] via 192.168.240.1
```

Routing Protocol

Routing protocols are responsible for learning or knowing what routes packets should take to get to their destinations. Obviously, if routing protocols are misconfigured, packets will not be correctly routed to their destinations. Routes could appear and disappear from routing tables. Loops could be formed in the network, causing packets to circulate around the network until they time out. If the split-horizon feature on the router is disabled, routes could be learned from the wrong interface or protocol. Using the SHOW IP INTERFACE command can check split-horizon functionality. To check routing protocol configuration on a router, use the SHOW IP PROTOCOLS command. (This command is covered in detail earlier in this chapter.) A sample display is provided here.

```
Router# show ip protocols
Routing Protocol is "igrp 109"
     Sending updates every 90 seconds, next due in 88 seconds
     Invalid after 270 seconds, hold down for 280, flushed after 630
     Outgoing update filter list for all routes is not set
```

```
     Incoming update filter list for all routes is not set
     Default networks flagged in outgoing updates
     Default networks accepted from incoming updates
     IGRP metric weight K1=1, K2=0, K3=1, K4=0, K5=0
     IGRP maximum hopcount 100
     Redistributing: igrp 109
     Routing for Networks:
     131.108.0.0
     192.31.7.0
Routing Information Sources:
     Gateway            Distance         Last Update
     131.108.2.201         100             0:00:08
     131.108.200.2         100             5d15
     131.108.2.200         100             0:00:09
     131.108.2.203         100             0:00:11
```

You will be able to check the routing protocols that are present on the router and see if their parameters are correct.

Access Lists

A symptom of misconfigured access lists is that some applications could be able to function correctly while others cannot. For example, you might be able to PING a host, but a Telnet connection could fail. Certain parts of the network could also be inaccessible. If this is what you are experiencing, issue the SHOW ACCESS-LISTS command to see the access lists that are present on the router. Determine what each line of the access list does and see if the functions could be the cause of the trouble. To determine which interface has an access list applied; use the SHOW IP INTERFACE command. In the following listing, for example, a standard access list is permitting all traffic from the 131.108.19 network. All other networks are denied access. Remember that there is an implicit DENY any at the end of every access list:

```
ROUTER_A#show access-lists
Standard IP access list 19
     permit 131.108.19.0
     deny   0.0.0.0, wildcard bits 255.255.255.255
```

Forward Protocols

Routers by default do not forward broadcasts. However, in certain situations—such as when remote hosts need to contact a DHCP server—these types of broadcasts must be able to cross the router. In this case, you would use a helper address on the router. A helper address tells the router that specific types of broadcasts that it receives should be forwarded to a specific IP address. A helper address therefore allows the router to convert broadcast messages into a unicast message. To find out if a helper address is configured on the router, you could use the SHOW IP INTERFACE command.

When you specify a helper address on the router using the IP HELPER-ADDRESS <IP-ADDRESS> command, you are enabling default broadcast types such as DHCP requests to be forwarded. In some cases, you would need other broadcast types, such as DNS for example, to also cross the router.

To fine-tune the IP HELPER-ADDRESS command, you would use the IP FORWARD-PROTOCOL command. The command syntax is as follows:

```
ROUTER_A(Config)#ip forward-protocol <keyword>
```

Keywords can be UDP, ND, SDNS, DOMAIN, and so on.

IP Configuration

IP configuration on a router is checked using the SHOW IP INTERFACE command. This command provides a summary output of all interfaces configured to use the TCP/IP protocol. You will be able to check for accuracy in the configuration in terms of statistics such as switching type used on the interface, MTU size, helper address, and so on.

IP Addressing and Subnet Selection

Every host on a major network must be configured to use the same subnet mask. The subnet mask allows TCP/IP to distinguish between hosts on the local subnet and hosts on a remote network. Subnet selection is usually done so that the network has a hierarchical structure. This entails the use of subnets that are contiguous, meaning that they are on clearly defined bit boundaries. Classful selection of subnet masks are done using the three address classes, A, B, and C:

- **Class A** subnet masks are of the form 255.0.0.0.
- **Class B** subnet masks are of the form 255.255.0.0.
- **Class C** subnet masks are of the form 255.255.255.0.

You can see that the use of these classful masks will result in a tremendous waste of IP addresses. Today's hierarchical networks use VLSM to make more efficient use of the IP address space. Having a hierarchy means that the routing tables of routers can also be much more efficient. Individual routers will need to advertise only routes that are representative of the areas for which they provide service. For example, if a company has numerous remote offices, it needs individual network numbers for each of those offices. If those networks are chosen in a logical, contiguous manner, the backbone router needs to advertise only the summary network that represents those remote offices to another backbone router. There would be no need to advertise every single route to every single remote office. The routing table is therefore much smaller and more efficient.

Discontiguous Subnets and Classful/Classless Routing Protocols

Classful routing protocols automatically assume that a network is identified by class boundaries and they therefore do not send subnet mask information along with the network. This means that advertisements that are sent out are automatically summarized at the class boundary, with no regard to the subnet mask that is identifying the actual network number. That's why they are called *classful*. RIPv1 and IGRP are examples of classful routing protocols.

Classless routing protocols, on the other hand, not only advertise the network number, but they also send subnet mask information with the network number. This allows routers to know specifically where networks are located based on the network number and subnet mask combination.

Discontiguous subnets refer to subnets that do not follow a hierarchical addressing scheme. This can mean that Subnet A, for example, uses 20 bits for the network number, whereas Subnet B uses 26. To support these nonsequential allocations of network numbers, a router must be able to identify networks not by class but by bit boundary. A routing protocol that supports the advertisement of subnet mask information is therefore necessary. Classless routing protocols support this requirement.

NT Server

Troubleshooting TCP/IP on Windows NT Server necessitates having some familiarity with the operating system. Because NT is such a popular network operating system, it has been included in a number of Cisco's exams. The support

exam will test your knowledge of some basic aspects of Windows NT operation. It is
in your best interest as a support engineer that you at least become familiar, if not
expert, with it.

The LMHOSTS File

The LMHOSTS file helps distribute the browsing information and service client
requests. You can also use WINS to collect the browse lists and service client requests.

In the LMHOSTS file, the LM stands for LAN Manager; HOSTS is for the host
computer. Its job is to resolve NetBIOS names to the corresponding IP address of
remote hosts on different subnets. The purpose is to allow for communication
between master browsers on remote subnets and the domain master browser. This
sets up direct communication, enabling an updated list to be developed across a
subnet. The one thing to remember about an LMHOSTS file is that it is your
responsibility to create and maintain the file. A WINS service can dynamically
provide this resolution for you.

Using an LMHOSTS file is a workable solution, but be aware of some
considerations. The LMHOSTS file must be on each and every subnet's master
browser with an entry to the domain master browser to work. It must also be updated
manually any time there are changes to the LMHOSTS list. The LMHOSTS file
needs to be placed in the WINNTROOT\SYSTEM32\DRIVERS\ETC directory.
There are sample TCP/IP files that you can use to reference. The LMHOSTS file is
just a regular text file that can be created using any text editor. There is no file
extension, and Windows NT will look and reference the file in this location
whenever it needs to do so.

on the
job

*Maintaining LMHOSTS files can be a really distressing issue. Imagine having a
small 20-user network. Now imagine that every time an IP configuration
needs to be updated, you have to manually update all the LMHOSTS files on
your network. After you've done this a few times, you'll begin to wish for an
easier, better solution. Here's an idea: use WINS to handle client requests. If
you have DHCP on your network, you can configure your DHCP server to
give clients the IP address of the WINS server. Configuration changes are now
made virtually automatically. If the IP address of the WINS server changes,
all you need to do is update the DHCP server with the new address, and
you're all set.*

Address Resolution Protocol

ARP was covered in detail earlier in this chapter. ARP provides IP-to-MAC address mapping for TCP/IP hosts. There is virtually no difference in functionality in the ARP functions and features on a Cisco router and ARP on Windows NT. You can add and remove static mappings and display the ARP cache.

If an ARP entry in Windows NT becomes incorrect due to a misconfiguration issue—such as an entry for a host that has changed its NIC, thereby changing the hardware address—connectivity would not occur to that host. In such a case, you can remove the incorrect ARP entry by clearing the entire cache or by specifying the IP address to remove.

You can clear the ARP cache on NT by issuing the command ARP –D *. The * represents all ARP entries. Alternatively, you could specify the IP address to remove instead of the asterisk to remove just the problem entry. On a Cisco router, you would use the command CLEAR ARP-CACHE.

Windows Internet Naming Service

The *Windows Internet Naming Service (WINS)* maintains a dynamic database linking NetBIOS names to IP addresses. The database is dynamic because each name registration has a TTL value—after its TTL has expired, the record is discarded from the database. The WINS server receives registration, renewal, and release requests from WINS clients and updates its database based on this information. Name resolution queries from WINS clients are resolved using this database.

Using the WINS server for name registration, renewal, release, and resolution services provides a marked improvement over using broadcast messages or static mappings for these services. In the case of broadcast messages, rather than each computer sending a broadcast to all clients on its subnet for every name registration, each computer sends a unicast message to the WINS server.

The same applies for name queries: rather than sending a broadcast message to all clients on its subnet, a WINS client sends a unicast message directly to the WINS server. For networks using static mappings such as an LMHOSTS file, each computer has a fixed list of NetBIOS names and IP addresses, which can become difficult to manage—and impossible to manage when using dynamic IP address assignments such as environments using DHCP.

With the advent of Windows 2000, Microsoft has been touting its new Dynamic DNS (DDNS) feature. This is supposed to replace the aging WINS solution. However, WINS will be around for a very long time, due to the proliferation of Windows NT Server 4 networks. Be sure that you know the function of WINS in the Microsoft environment for the support exam.

Domain Name System

The Domain Name System (DNS) is one way to resolve host names in a TCP/IP environment. In non-Microsoft environments, host names are typically resolved through HOSTS files as used in UNIX, or DNS. In a Microsoft environment, WINS and broadcasts are also used. DNS is the primary system used to resolve host names on the Internet. With DNS, the host names reside in a database that can be distributed among multiple servers, decreasing the load on any one server and allowing more than one point of administration for this naming system. The name system is based on hierarchical names in a tree-type directory structure. DNS allows more types of registration than the simple host-name-to-TCP/IP-address mapping used in HOSTS files and allows room for future defined types. Because the database is distributed, it can support a much larger database than can be stored in a single HOSTS file. In fact, the database size is virtually unlimited because more servers can be added to handle additional parts of the database.

CERTIFICATION OBJECTIVE 7.06

IP Symptoms, Problems, and Action Plans

This section covers common problems and resolutions that you will experience in TCP/IP networks. Problems are presented, and the most common answers to those problems are given and explained. Take note of the issues covered in this section, because eventually you'll be asked to solve the same or a similar problem on your job.

Host Cannot Access Other Hosts on Different Subnets

Problem: A client that is on a local subnet cannot access hosts that are on remote subnets. Subnets are separated by WAN links and have one or more routers between them. You have attempted to PING remote hosts and have not been successful. Possible answers to this issue are:

- **No default gateway** No default gateway is configured on the client. If the client is Windows based, use the WINIPCFG utility for Windows 95 and 98 or IPCONFIG utility for NT to determine the presence of a default gateway configuration. If the client is UNIX based, use the NETSTAT-RN command to get a possible gateway list specification. If the default gateway is missing in either case, correct the problem by adding the default gateway statement. For UNIX, use the ROUTE ADD command to add the default gateway. For Windows, add the default gateway using the Control Panel | Network applet.

- **Misconfigured subnet mask** A misconfigured subnet mask makes the client behave as though it were on a different network than the other hosts that are on the same network. When this happens, the client will be unable to contact the default gateway because it will try to reach the default gateway using an incorrect subnet mask and will fail because it will believe that the gateway is on a remote network. Verify that the subnet mask is correct. Change it if it is incorrect and reboot the client.

- **Local gateway down** If the local gateway is down, all clients will be unable to access remote networks. Use the PING utility on the client to check whether or not the gateway is active. If the PING utility fails, the gateway might be off or disabled due to configuration error. You must go to the gateway and determine the cause of the trouble.

Host Cannot Access Other Subnets

Problem: The client cannot access remote networks. Subnets are separated by WAN links and have one or more routers between them. You have attempted to PING remote hosts and have not been successful. Possible answers to this issue are:

- **No default gateway** There is no default gateway configured on the client. If the client is Windows based, use the WINIPCFG utility for Windows 95 and 98 or IPCONFIG utility for NT to determine the presence of a default gateway configuration. If the clients is UNIX based, use the NETSTAT-RN command to get a possible gateway list specification. If the default gateway is missing in either case, correct the problem by adding the default gateway statement. For Unix, use the ROUTE ADD command to add the default gateway. For Windows, add the default gateway using the Control Panel | Network applet.

■ **Misconfigured access list**   Access list misconfiguration is often a source of reachability errors such as this. Determine what subnets are inaccessible. Determine the exit interface being used to access those subnets by issuing the SHOW IP ROUTE command on the router. Issue the SHOW IP INTERFACE command to see the access lists that have been applied to the interface. Issue the SHOW IP ACCESS-LISTS command to see the configuration of the access lists. Check for the presence of DENY statements that might be blocking access to those inaccessible subnets. Check for the presence of PERMIT statements that should give the clients access to the remote subnets. Remember that access lists must have at least one PERMIT statement.

■ **Bad network design with discontiguous subnets**   If there are discontiguous subnets on the network and automatic default network summarization is in effect (as in the case of EIGRP) or routing protocols do not support discontiguous subnets, there will be no connectivity between the local and remote subnets. Either turn off automatic network summarization using the NO AUTO-SUMMARY command if EIGRP is being used or, if a classful routing protocol is being used, now would be a good time to do that upgrade you've been planning to take care of this problem once and for all.

Host Can Access Some Hosts But Not Others

Problem: The host can access certain hosts while attempts to connect to other hosts fail.

■ **IP misconfiguration (IP address, subnet mask, default gateway)**   Check the IP configuration on the client by using the appropriate utility or command. Make sure that the IP address, subnet mask and default gateway are correct and correspond to what other hosts on the same subnet are using. Correct the errors if applicable and reboot the client.

■ **Misconfigured access list**   Check the router for any access list statement that may be restricting this client from making the connections that have been failing. Use the SHOW ACCESS-LISTS command to accomplish this task. If you suspect that the access list is causing the trouble, remove the access list from the interface by using the command NO IP ACCESS-GROUP <ACCESS-LIST-NUMBER> {IN | OUT}. See if the client is now able to connect. If the connection is successful, that means that the access list needs to be modified. Make the necessary changes and reapply the access list.

Host Can Access Some Services But Not Others

Problem: The host can access other hosts on remote subnet using certain applications while other applications fail. An example of this situation is an access list that is restricting Web access by denying connections through TCP port 80:

- **Misconfigured access list**   Check the router for any access list statement that could be restricting this client from making the connections that have been failing. Use the SHOW ACCESS-LISTS command to accomplish this task. If you suspect that the access list is causing the trouble, remove the access list from the interface using the command NO IP ACCESS-GROUP <ACCESS-LIST-NUMBER> {IN | OUT}. See if the client is now able to connect. If the connection is successful, that means that the access list needs to be modified. Make the necessary changes and reapply the access list.

Host Cannot Access Remote Hosts via Redundant Path

Problem: The redundant path to a remote network is not operational. Attempts to route traffic through the redundant path result in failure:

- **Discontiguous subnets**   If discontiguous subnets are present on the network, the redundant routers might have no knowledge of how to get to those remote subnets. Use the SHOW IP ROUTE command to check for the presence of the routes. If the routes are missing, review your routing protocol configuration to make sure that no automatic network summarization is occurring. Use the SHOW RUNNING-CONFIG command to check the configuration of the routers.

- **Routing convergence**   Routing convergence might not be occurring when the primary route fails. Use the SHOW IP INTERFACE command to check to make sure that split horizon is not disabled. Split horizon prevents routing loops from occurring. Use the DEBUG IP OSPF EVENTS command to verify timer configuration that might be preventing the route failure from being recognized.

■ **Misconfigured access list**   Check the router for any access list statement that might be restricting this client from making the connections that have been failing. Use the SHOW ACCESS-LISTS command to accomplish this task. If you suspect that the access list is causing the trouble, remove the access list from the interface using the command NO IP ACCESS-GROUP <ACCESS-LIST-NUMBER> {IN | OUT}. See if the client is now able to connect. If the connection is successful, that means that the access list needs to be modified. Make the necessary changes and reapply the access list. Issue the SHOW RUNNING-CONFIG command to check for the presence of a DISTRIBUTE-LIST statement. These indicate that access lists are being used to filter routing updates. Make sure that routing updates are not being blocked because this could prevent the redundant router from learning that the primary route has failed.

Router Sees Duplicate Routing Updates

Problem: The router is receiving routing updates that appear to be duplicated.

■ **Segments connected together via a hub, bridge, or switch**   Split horizon prevents the sending of routing updates back through the interface they learned. If split horizon is disabled, routing updates might get duplicated back on to the path they were received, resulting in routing loops. Use the SHOW IP INTERFACE command to determine whether split horizon is disabled. If disabled, re-enable using the IP SPLIT-HORIZON command. You should understand the consequences of having split horizon enabled or disabled.

Certain Protocols Routed While Others Are Not

Problem: Protocols appear to be going through a filter because some are working properly while others are not operational. This points to access list misconfiguration:

■ **Misconfigured access list**   Check the router for any access list statement that might be restricting this client from making the connections that have been failing. Use the SHOW ACCESS-LISTS command to accomplish this task. Look for statements in the access list that permit only specific protocols. Look for statements that deny those protocols that you are having trouble with. Look for the absence of statements that permit those protocols you are having trouble with.

Remove the access list from the interface using the command NO IP ACCESS-GROUP <ACCESS-LIST-NUMBER> {IN | OUT}. See if the client is now able to connect. If the connection is successful, that means that the access list needs to be modified. Make the necessary changes and reapply the access list.

Host/Router Cannot Reach Certain Subnets

Problem: Certain subnets appear to be inaccessible from specific hosts or routers.

■ **IP misconfiguration**   Remember that discontiguous subnets are accessible if you are running a routing protocol that supports discontiguous subnets. If not, those subnets would be unreachable.

Determine if any local interfaces are configured with incorrect IP information. This could cause the remote subnets to appear to be local, negating the use of a router. Correct any errors and determine whether this fixes the problem.

■ **Misconfigured access list**   Check the router for any access list statement that might be restricting this client from making the connections that have been failing. Use the SHOW ACCESS-LISTS command to accomplish this task. If you suspect that the access list is causing the trouble, remove the access list from the interface using the command NO IP ACCESS-GROUP <ACCESS-LIST-NUMBER> {IN | OUT}. See if the client is now able to connect. If the connection is successful, that means that the access list needs to be modified. Make the necessary changes and reapply the access list. Issue the SHOW RUNNING-CONFIG command to check for the presence of a DISTRIBUTE-LIST statement. These indicate that access lists are being used to filter routing updates. Make sure that routing updates are not being blocked, because this could prevent the redundant router from learning that the primary route has failed.

No Routing with Redistribution

Problem: Redistribution has been configured on the router. Routing updates are therefore being filtered according to criteria specified in an access list on the router. Misconfiguration of the access list is now preventing routing from occurring because the appropriate routes are not known to the router:

- **Configuration error (redistribute or default metric)** The DISTRIBUTE-LIST <ACCESS-LIST-NUMBER> {IN | OUT} command is used for filtering incoming or outgoing routes. If the access list is misconfigured, it might block routes that are supposed to be received or sent by the router. This will result in routing failures.
  To troubleshoot access list problems, use the following methods:
  Issue the SHOW RUNNING-CONFIG command to check for the presence of a DISTRIBUTE-LIST statement. These indicate that access lists are being used to filter routing updates. Make sure that necessary routing updates are not being blocked, because this could prevent the router from learning of route failure or updates. Use the SHOW ACCESS-LISTS command to see the configuration of the access lists on the router. If default metrics are changed on the router, some less desirable routes might be used to route packets. Issue the SHOW RUNNING-CONFIG command on problem routers and look for default-metric commands. These will change the metrics that have been assigned by default to routes. If you suspect that the default metric statement is incorrect, remove it using the NO DEFAULT-METRIC command.

- **Administrative distance** *Administrative distance* refers to the preference assigned to routing protocols and their routes. Lower values indicate higher preference for the router to use over another route with a higher administrative distance. For example, static routes have an administrative distance of 1, while RIP routes have a distance of 120. If the administrative distance has been misconfigured for a route, it might have a higher or lower administrative distance than required, causing routing problems. Use the SHOW RUNNING-CONFIG command to view distances that have been assigned to different routing processes. If necessary, enter protocol configuration mode and remove the DISTANCE statement. Reapply with the correct distance.

Windows 95 and 98 Symptoms, Problems, and Action Plans

Problems with Windows-based machines are usually related to issues such as DHCP failure over a WAN link, "Web site not found" errors, misconfigured subnet mask, and so on. The following issues are the most common problems when working with Windows.

Host Unable to Reach Target Address

Problem: Errors occur when the host tries to run specific applications or services. The station appears to freeze up while timeout operations are occurring. Attempts to access certain applications such as a Web browser result in error messages:

- **IP misconfiguration (IP address, subnet mask, default gateway)**   If the host has an incorrect IP configuration, it will be unable to perform certain tasks. If it has no default gateway or the default gateway address is incorrect, it will fail to access remote subnets or services over a WAN link. Use the WINIPCFG utility to find out the what the client is configured to use for an IP address and default gateway as well as other information such as what DNS servers it can query, if it is using DHCP or not, the WINS server, and so on.

- **IP helper address**   Whenever you get an error such as logon failures or an inability to renew an IP address lease, they can be narrowed down to specific problem areas. The most common of these issues is the DHCP problem. Hosts on a remote subnet that need to contact a DHCP server over a WAN link need the ability to send DHCP broadcasts over the link. The IP HELPER-ADDRESS <IP-ADDRESS> is used to convert these broadcasts into unicast messages over the WAN link. Multiple helper addresses can be specified. The helper address can also be used to forward other types of requests such as DNS or BOOTP broadcasts.

■ **Workgroup name** The workgroup name in Windows 95 and 98 is used to group clients together so that a common list of resources in that workgroup can be created and listed in Network Neighborhood. If a client has an incorrect workgroup, it will not see what resources are immediately available. It would have to manually browse the workgroups looking for resources.

■ **WINS** WINS is used to provide NetBIOS machine name to IP address mappings. WINS reduces the amount of name query broadcasts on a network by providing a central database of that information that is accessible to all clients. WINS server IP address information is usually sent to clients when they request DHCP addresses.

■ **DNS** DNS provides Internet domain name to IP address mapping. Commonly used for Web access, DNS is gaining popularity in use for replacing WINS. DNS requests or domain lookups need to be forwarded over a WAN link. This is done with the use of helper addresses and the IP FORWARD-PROTOCOL DOMAIN command.

CERTIFICATION OBJECTIVE 7.08

Data-Link and Network Layer Exercises

This section is used to provide some insight into the operations that go on in the background on a TCP/IP-based network. It uses a protocol analyzer to provide this look "behind the scenes."

These background operations are visible only when a DEBUG command is used on a Cisco router or a packet capture is performed using a protocol analyzer. The DEBUG commands give only an overhead view on the operation of the process being examined, but a protocol analyzer goes into greater detail by providing details on the actual contents of each packet that is being sent and received. A protocol analyzer is invaluable if you want to understand the operation of not only TCP/IP but other protocols such as IPX and AppleTalk as well. The amount of information that is in the packets of a simple TCP connection sequence is simply astounding. The first packet capture in the following section contains information of the three-way handshake and provides a breakdown of each packet in this sequence.

Various Data Link and IP Network Layer Sniffer Traces

In this section, a couple of packet captures are performed and analyzed. Packet captures and analysis is an integral part of troubleshooting because they can provide you with behind-the-scenes detail of protocol operation. Sometimes performing a packet capture is the only way to isolate a problem.

The Three-Way Handshake

Suppose that a client wants to connect to a server—most often as a result of a command given by a user on the client. The client figures out the IP address of the server and the port number of the desired service, based on information supplied by the user. Because TCP needs a sequence number and a port number, the client's operating system supplies one of each. The client now has all the information it needs to send the first packet.

Because this is a new connection, the client sends a special type of packet called a SYN (short for *synchronize*) packet. The server responds with a SYN + ACK (short for *acknowledgment*) packet. Finally, the client sends an ACK packet to acknowledge the SYN + ACK packet. This is called the *three-way TCP handshake*. At this point, the client and server are said to have a TCP connection and can exchange data.

Several things happened during this three-packet exchange. Let's take a look at an example, captured using Snoop on a Sparc 5 running Solaris 2.5.1. Snoop is a packet-capture program for Solaris. We have included only the TCP portions here. Normally, Snoop displays the entire frame, including Layer 2 and Layer 3 information.

First, here is the TCP SYN packet. We can tell this because SYN is the only flag bit that is on in the flags section. This is just the TCP portion of the packet, with the Layer 2 and IP headers and trailers stripped off. This type of packet always marks the beginning of a TCP connection:

```
TCP:  ----- TCP Header -----
TCP:
TCP:  Source port = 65445
TCP:  Destination port = 25 (SMTP)
TCP:  Sequence number = 16927230
TCP:  Acknowledgement number = 0
TCP:  Data offset = 28 bytes
TCP:  Flags = 0x02
TCP:        ..0. .... = No urgent pointer
TCP:        ...0 .... = No acknowledgement
```

```
TCP:             .... 0... = No push
TCP:             .... .0.. = No reset
TCP:             .... ..1. = Syn
TCP:             .... ...0 = No Fin
TCP:  Window = 8192
TCP:  Checksum = 0x1ef2
TCP:  Urgent pointer = 0
TCP:  Options: (8 bytes)
TCP:     - Maximum segment size = 1460 bytes
TCP:     - No operation
TCP:     - No operation
TCP:     - Option 4 (unknown - 0 bytes)
TCP:
```

Next is a SYN + ACK packet. The server returns this packet to the client that sent the SYN packet. By doing so, the server acknowledges that it has received the SYN packet and is listening on the port requested:

```
TCP:  ----- TCP Header -----
TCP:
TCP:  Source port = 25
TCP:  Destination port = 65445
TCP:  Sequence number = 1094177019
TCP:  Acknowledgement number = 16927231
TCP:  Data offset = 24 bytes
TCP:  Flags = 0x12
TCP:             ..0. .... = No urgent pointer
TCP:             ...1 .... = Acknowledgement
TCP:             .... 0... = No push
TCP:             .... .0.. = No reset
TCP:             .... ..1. = Syn
TCP:             .... ...0 = No Fin
TCP:  Window - 8760
TCP:  Checksum = 0x1f7d
TCP:  Urgent pointer = 0
TCP:  Options: (4 bytes)
TCP:     - Maximum segment size = 1460 bytes
TCP:
```

Finally, the client sends an ACK packet. In this case, looking at the flags alone doesn't tell us that this ACK packet is part of a TCP handshake instead of just a regular ACK. At this point, the client and server have verified each other's port numbers and agreed to exchange data using those ports:

```
TCP:   ----- TCP Header -----
TCP:
TCP:   Source port = 65445
TCP:   Destination port = 25 (SMTP)
TCP:   Sequence number = 16927231
TCP:   Acknowledgement number = 1094177020
TCP:   Data offset = 20 bytes
TCP:   Flags = 0x10
TCP:         ..0. .... = No urgent pointer
TCP:         ...1 .... = Acknowledgement
TCP:         .... 0... = No push
TCP:         .... .0.. = No reset
TCP:         .... ..0. = No Syn
TCP:         .... ...0 = No Fin
TCP:   Window = 8760
TCP:   Checksum = 0x373a
TCP:   Urgent pointer = 0
TCP:   No options
TCP:
```

exam

ⓦatch

Try to get comfortable with examining packet captures. You'll find that a number of questions on the exam will be presented in the form of a frame or packet capture, and you'll be asked to identify individual parts of the capture or identify the purpose of the packet overall. These won't be limited to IP, and the question could involve things that are covered in other sections of this book, such as Token Ring and IP together.

Examine the preceding listing carefully. The key fields there are source port, destination port, sequence number, acknowledgment number, and flags. Flags is a group of bits, and the bits are listed individually as follows. In this example, we're connecting to a mail server, so:

- The *destination port* is 25 (SMTP).

- The *source port* was assigned by the OS. These port numbers stay fixed during the life of the connection and, along with the IP addresses, represent this connection for both hosts.

- The client gets a *sequence number* from the OS (16927230) and sends it in a SYN packet. We know it's a SYN packet because the only flag set is SYN.

- The server responds from port 25 to port 65445 (reversed from the client's point of view) with its own sequence number (1094177019) and with an *acknowledgment number* of 16927231, which is one more than the sequence number the client originally sent.

- The server also sets both the SYN and ACK *flags,* signifying that it's both synchronizing (sending the sequence number it will be using) and acknowledging the first packet.

- Finally, the client sends an ACK to tell the server it got the reply. Notice that the acknowledgment number has increased by one (the server's sequence number previously).

We now know how TCP goes about establishing a connection. The rest of the connection continues in this manner, with the sequence and acknowledgment numbers incrementing and the hosts ACKing each other's packets.

ARP Caching

Most of the work within IP takes place at Layer 3 and above. At least one protocol that doesn't fall into that category, however, deserves discussion: ARP. ARP is used for mapping IP addresses to Layer 2 addresses. As such, you can think of it as being both Layer 2 and Layer 3 or as a binding between the two.

Recall from previous study in this chapter that for IP packets to be delivered, the addressing at Layer 2 has to be correct. So, for an IP stack to deliver an IP packet to the IP stack on another host, it has to determine the other host's Layer 2 address so that delivery can happen at Layer 2. The mechanism chosen for this determination is automatic mapping of IP addresses to Layer 2 addresses. This is where ARP comes in.

Somewhat like the PING exchanges, ARP exchanges consist of an ARP request and an ARP reply. The ARP request contains the IP address for which the Layer 2 address is desired, and the reply contains both the requested IP address and Layer 2 address. The requestor caches the response to avoid having to ask for it for each message sent to that host. This cached reply has an attached timer so that it doesn't stick around forever (the reasons for which will become apparent shortly). ARP is strictly a local network protocol. A host never ARPs for an address of another host on a different subnet, but rather ARPs for the address of the router the host will be using to reach that subnet.

We'll use Ethernet for our ARP caching example. Ethernet uses 6-byte, Layer 2 addresses, usually called MAC addresses. These MAC addresses are supposed to be globally unique; that is, no two Ethernet cards in the world should have the same MAC address. ARP relies on there being a broadcast mechanism in the Layer 2 network. When one host wants the MAC address that corresponds to an IP address, the host broadcasts an ARP request packet. (This is a Layer 2 broadcast, not an IP broadcast, as discussed earlier.) All hosts on the LAN segment process the broadcast. Usually, the IP stack of each host will process the packet and determine whether its own IP address is the one being requested. If so, the requestor host's IP address is added into the processing host's own ARP cache (the reason is explained in a moment). Each processing host then builds an ARP reply and sends it back to the requesting host.

Why does the host receiving the ARP request cache the requestor's IP address? Because if it didn't, it would have to ARP for the requestor's IP in order to reply, resulting in an *ARP loop*. (Although the replying host could broadcast the reply, that host has enough information to send it directly, and broadcasts are expensive in terms of network resources. Broadcast packets have to go to all hosts and be processed by all hosts.)

Let's look at a capture of an ARP exchange. The following packet is an ARP request, indicated by the opcode number 1:

```
ETHER:    ----- Ether Header -----
ETHER:
ETHER:    Packet 4 arrived at 23:45:41.30
ETHER:    Packet size = 60 bytes
ETHER:    Destination = ff:ff:ff:ff:ff:ff, (broadcast)
ETHER:    Source     = 8:0:20:78:29:f0, Sun
ETHER:    Ethertype = 0806 (ARP)
ETHER:
ARP:    ----- ARP/RARP Frame -----
ARP:
ARP:    Hardware type = 1
ARP:    Protocol type = 0800 (IP)
ARP:    Length of hardware address = 6 bytes
ARP:    Length of protocol address = 4 bytes
ARP:    Opcode 1 (ARP Request)
ARP:    Sender's hardware address = 8:0:20:78:29:f0
ARP:    Sender's protocol address = 10.1.1.33
ARP:    Target hardware address = ?
ARP:    Target protocol address = 10.1.1.34
ARP:
```

This is an ARP reply, indicated by opcode 2:

```
ETHER:  ----- Ether Header -----
ETHER:
ETHER:  Packet 5 arrived at 23:45:41.30
ETHER:  Packet size = 42 bytes
ETHER:  Destination = 8:0:20:78:29:f0, Sun
ETHER:  Source      = 8:0:20:21:37:c3, Sun
ETHER:  Ethertype = 0806 (ARP)
ETHER:
ARP:  ----- ARP/RARP Frame -----
ARP:
ARP:  Hardware type = 1
ARP:  Protocol type = 0800 (IP)
ARP:  Length of hardware address = 6 bytes
ARP:  Length of protocol address = 4 bytes
ARP:  Opcode 2 (ARP Reply)
ARP:  Sender's hardware address = 8:0:20:21:37:c3
ARP:  Sender's protocol address = 10.1.1.34
ARP:  Target hardware address = 8:0:20:78:29:f0
ARP:  Target protocol address = 10.1.1.33
ARP:
```

There are a few interesting things to see in this ARP exchange. As mentioned, the Layer 2 destination address on the first packet is the broadcast address. You'll also notice that the IP address and MAC addresses are in the Ethernet header as well as in the body of the packet. This is due to the protocol stack mechanism on most operating systems. Usually, lower-layer information is stripped off before it gets passed on to higher-layer handlers. This information is in the body of the ARP packet because ARPs and replies are normally handled by the IP protocol stack on an OS, and by the time the IP stack gets the body of the ARP packet, the Ethernet headers are gone.

You'll also notice that the reply is almost exactly the same as the request, except that the type has been changed from request to reply, the sender and target have been reversed, and the missing MAC address has been filled in. In addition, the reply is sent directly back to the requestor's MAC address rather than broadcast.

We've said that the ARP requestor's information must be cached so that the replying host doesn't have to ARP for the requester in order to reply. Strictly speaking, an ARP packet isn't an IP packet. It has a different Ethertype, for one thing, and no IP header, for another. However, ARP replies are built in much the same way as a regular IP packet in that there is apparently duplicate information within the body of the ARP packet. For example, the Ethernet MAC address is in the frame header as well as the data portion. When a packet exists in the memory of a host, there is no Layer 2 frame. Likewise, after a packet has been read from the wire, all Layer 2 information is removed and is unavailable; hence the need for the information to be repeated in the IP (or ARP) packet. The IP stack building the ARP reply relies on the ARP cache much as it does when sending a regular IP packet. This gives us a peek into the internals of IP stack management.

CERTIFICATION SUMMARY

We have covered a lot of information in this chapter. The most common issues that occur when working with TCP/IP networks were presented. Commands and utilities, which help in troubleshooting those issues, were also covered. Although being armed with information is a very good way of preparing to solve a problem, experience will allow you to arrive at quicker conclusions and solutions to everyday support problems.

The goal of this chapter was to give you general information on solving problems that you could encounter in your network. You might have noticed that most of the solutions do not go into detailed, step-by-step instructions for solving these problems. This is because such an approach could very well cover multiple volumes because of the diversity in networks today. No two networks are the same, and although we can give you detailed instructions for solving issues, they wouldn't be of much help, because you will need to use different approaches to solving these same issues in other networks. If you came away with a general troubleshooting strategy that you can adapt to your needs, this chapter was successful. Do not expect to memorize and learn every single command presented, because the information will not be useful to you that way. You should be able to identify a problem and tackle it in steps that gradually eliminate possible sources of trouble. Only then will you really understand what troubleshooting is all about.

TWO-MINUTE DRILL

Here are some of the key points from each certification objective in Chapter 7.

TCP Connection Sequence

❑ TCP is connection oriented. Acknowledgments are required between stations.

❑ TCP uses the three-way handshake, which is the SYN, SYN + ACK, and ACK sequence.

Cisco IOS Software Tools and Commands

❑ SHOW commands are used for listing information on router configuration.

❑ DEBUG commands are used to troubleshoot router operation by examining event by event operation of routing processes.

PING and TRACE

❑ PING is used to send ICMP echo requests to stations to verify Network Layer connectivity.

❑ TRACE is used to discover the path that a packet takes to a specified destination.

Problem Isolation in IP Networks

❑ Problem isolation in IP networks is usually first started with the PING and TRACE commands.

❑ From information obtained by PING and TRACE, various SHOW and DEBUG commands can be used to pinpoint the cause of problems.

Problem Isolation in Windows 95 and 98 Networks

❑ Windows 95 and 98 IP configuration information is viewed by using the WINIPCFG utility.

❑ WINS provides NetBIOS name to IP address mapping in Windows NT Server.

IP Symptoms, Problems, and Action Plans

❑ Misconfigured access lists can not only block the wrong hosts and applications but also restrict routing updates.

❑ The split-horizon feature prevents routing loops from occurring by preventing routing updates from being sent out back through the interface from which they were learned.

Windows 95 and 98 Symptoms, Problems, and Action Plans

❑ IP helper addresses are used to forward specific broadcasts through a router.

❑ DHCP may require IP helper address configuration on the router.

Data-Link and Network Layer Exercises

❑ A protocol analyzer can be used to provide a detailed analysis of packets that have been captured.

SELF TEST

The following questions will help you measure your understanding of the material presented in this chapter. Read all the choices carefully because there might be more than one correct answer. Choose all correct answers for each question.

TCP Connection Sequence

1. What is the TCP three-way handshake packet connection sequence?

   A. SYN, ACK, SYN

   B. SYN, SYNACK, SYN

   C. SYN, SYN, ACK

   D. SYN, SYN + ACK, SYN

2. TCP is connection oriented; UDP is connectionless. Which type of connection do you think will incur the most overhead in terms of packets sent between hosts?

   A. TCP will incur the most overhead.

   B. UDP will incur the most overhead.

   C. Both TCP and UDP incur the same overhead.

   D. There is no overhead when using these two protocols.

Cisco IOS Software Tools and Commands

3. Which SHOW command will provide a listing of the routing table?

   A. SHOW IP INTERFACE

   B. SHOW RUNNING-CONFIG

   C. SHOW IP ROUTE-TABLE

   D. SHOW IP ROUTE

4. You have an OSPF network in which a couple of routers are using software tunneling to establish connectivity to Area0. Which IOS command would tell you what tunnels have been configured on the router to support this type of OSPF connectivity?

   A. SHOW IP OSPF TUNNELS

   B. SHOW IP OSPF VIRTUAL-LINKS

C. SHOW IP OSPF VIRTUAL-TUNNELS

D. SHOW IP TUNNELING

5. You have been experiencing problems with your OSPF network. Neighbor relationships have not been established correctly, and routers are constantly updating their routing tables. You've determined that all WAN links are up and functioning correctly. What would be the most likely cause of these problems?

A. Misconfigured timers are the cause of the route instabilities.

B. The routers are defective.

C. Hardware failure is forcing routers to run the SPF algorithm constantly.

D. There is no IP address configured on one of the routers.

PING and TRACE

6. Which protocol does PING make use of when generating echoes and replies?

A. TCP/IP

B. UDP

C. IGMP

D. ICMP

7. TRACE is used in troubleshooting IP networks. What functions does the TRACE command provide? Choose all that apply.

A. Provides information on each hop crossed to a destination network

B. Provides IP address to NetBIOS name mapping

C. Provides IP-to-MAC address resolution

D. Provides a round-trip time of each packet sent

8. Extended PING can be used only in _____ exec mode, whereas standard TRACE can be used in _____ exec mode.

A. User, user

B. User, privileged

C. Config, privileged

D. Privileged, user

9. Your network consists of Token Ring and Ethernet segments. You notice that your users are experiencing a high number of errors when they communicate across the two topologies. Which tool can you use to determine what's happening when you try to communicate between the Token Ring LAN and the Ethernet LAN?

   A. Extended TRACE

   B. DEBUG IP ARP

   C. PING

   D. Extended PING

Problem Isolation in IP Networks

10. Router-to-hub connections require _____ cabling, whereas host-to-hub connections require _____ cabling.

    A. Straight-through, straight-through

    B. Crossover, straight-through

    C. Straight-through, crossover

    D. Crossover, crossover

11. Which of the following commands shows you the status of the interfaces on the router?

    A. SHOW IP INTERFACE

    B. SHOW INTERFACES ETHERNET

    C. SHOW INTERFACES

    D. SHOW INTERFACE STATUS

12. Users report that they are experiencing problems reaching remote networks. You've used the SHOW IP ROUTE command to view the routing table on the problem router. You've discovered that routes, which are supposed to be present, are missing from the router, thereby preventing connectivity to the remote networks. What would be your next step in isolating and solving the problem?

    A. Use the SHOW IP ROUTE command to check again on the missing routes.

    B. Add static routes to the router to provide a path to the remote networks.

    C. Use the SHOW RUNNING-CONFIG command to see what routes are being filtered with the DISTRIBUTE-LIST command.

    D. Remove all access lists from the router.

Problem Isolation in Windows 95 and 98 Networks

13. Which command can be used on Windows 95 and 98 to determine IP configuration?

    A. IPCFG

    B. WINIPCONFIG

    C. IPCFG /ALL

    D. WINIPCFG

14. DHCP can be used to provide all except which of the following? Choose all that apply.

    A. Workgroup name

    B. IP address

    C. Domain name

    D. MAC address

15. Using WINS for managing IP address to NetBIOS name mapping has a number of advantages over using a static LMHOSTS file. Select some of these advantages from the answers given.

    A. Dynamic mappings

    B. Centralized database

    C. Configuration changes are made at the WINS server only

    D. Workstation names can be changed at any time without affecting the functionality of WINS.

IP Symptoms, Problems, and Action Plans

16. Which command shows you what access lists have been configured on a router?

    A. SHOW ACL

    B. SHOW IP INTERFACE

    C. SHOW ACCESSLISTS

    D. SHOW ACCESS-LISTS

17. Users have reported that they are able to use certain applications, but when they attempt to access the Internet, they are unable to browse any Web sites. You have found out that over the weekend an access list was configured on the router to block certain users from accessing the Internet. However, now all users cannot access the Internet. Which of the following ACCESS-LIST statements would be the cause of this problem?

    A. ACCESS-LIST 100 DENY IP 192.10.10.0 0.0.0.255 EQ 23

   B. ACCESS-LIST 100 DENY IP 192.10.10.0 255.255.255.255 EQ 80

   C. ACCESS-LIST 100 DENY IP 192.10.10.0 0.0.0.255 EQ SMTP

   D. ACCESS-LIST 100 PERMIT IP 192.10.10.0 0.0.0.255 EQ DOMAIN

18. Which routing protocols can support discontiguous subnets? Choose all that apply.

   A. EIGRP

   B. IGRP

   C. RIP

   D. OSPF

Windows 95 and 98 Symptoms, Problems, and Action Plans

19. The IP HELPER-ADDRESS command is used most commonly to support which service?

   A. DNS

   B. Browsing

   C. Broadcasts

   D. DHCP

20. The workgroup name in Windows 95 and 98 is used to do which of the following?

   A. Group resources that belong to the same workgroup

   B. Give each machine a unique group

   C. Specify the domain name

   D. Assign specific functions to machines

Data-Link and Network Layer Exercises

21. True or false: Packet analysis can be performed on a Cisco router.

   A. True

   B. False

LAB QUESTION

Recall from your study of this chapter that discontiguous networks are those that cause routing problems because they result in the same route to two different networks. In other words, automatic summarization of those networks results in one route being advertised for both networks when there should really be two separate routes, one for each network.

Figure 7-5 represents the network of ABC Inc. ABC Inc. is about to add another remote office and they want to know if there are any issues that they should know about before they start the setup of the new office. As the senior support engineer, you have been asked to prepare a list of any possible issues that could hinder the setup of the new office.

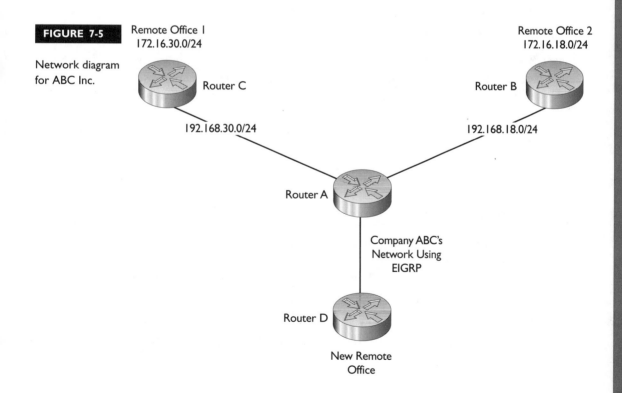

FIGURE 7-5

Network diagram for ABC Inc.

Remote Office 1
172.16.30.0/24

Router C

192.168.30.0/24

Remote Office 2
172.16.18.0/24

Router B

192.168.18.0/24

Router A

Company ABC's
Network Using
EIGRP

Router D

New Remote
Office

SELF TEST ANSWERS

TCP Connection Sequence

1. ☑ **D.** SYN, SYN + ACK, and SYN is the correct packet sequence for establishing TCP connections.
   ☒ **A, B,** and **C** are incorrect because they are not accurate in their depiction of the TCP connection establishment process.

2. ☑ **A.** TCP will incur the most overhead. The acknowledgments that are sent back and forth between two stations that have established a TCP connection will incur overhead.
   ☒ **B** is incorrect because UDP makes no attempt to send or receive any acknowledgment. **C** is incorrect because TCP and UDP operation do not result in the same overhead. **D** is incorrect because both TCP and UDP incur overhead.

Cisco IOS Software Tools and Commands

3. ☑ **D.** Show ip route will display the routing table of the router.
   ☒ **A, B,** and **C** are all incorrect because they provide other types of information.

4. ☑ **B.** SHOW IP OSPF VIRTUAL-LINKS. OSPF can use virtual links to provide software tunnels through which connectivity to Area0 can be established.
   ☒ **A, C,** and **D** are all incorrect because they are not valid IOS commands.

5. ☑ **A.** Misconfigured timers are the cause of the route instabilities. Timers can cause these types of problems.
   ☒ **B** and **C** are incorrect because they are not applicable to these issues. **D** is incorrect because an IP address must be present on the router in order to configure the OSPF protocol.

PING and TRACE

6. ☑ **D.** ICMP. PING uses ICMP echo requests and replies to generate reachability messages.
   ☒ **A** is incorrect because although TCP/IP is the transport protocol used, ICMP is the subprotocol that is part of the TCP/IP stack. **B** and **C** are incorrect because neither UDP nor IGMP are used for generating echoes and replies.

7. ☑ **A** and **D.** TRACE sends packets with incrementing TTL timers and provides information on each router crossed as well as the time taken to reach that router.

☒   **B** is incorrect because it refers to the function of WINS. **C** is incorrect because it refers to the function of ARP.

8. ☑   **D.** Privileged, user. Extended PING commands can be used only in privileged exec mode. TRACE can be used in user exec mode.
☒   **A, B,** and **C** are all incorrect because they do not refer to modes in which extended PING commands can be issued.

9. ☑   **D.** With extended PING, you can specify a packet size that will allow you to check whether hosts on the Ethernet LAN are able to fragment the larger Token Ring packets.
☒   **A, B,** and **C** are incorrect because they will not help you in troubleshooting dissimilar topology issues.

Problem Isolation in IP Networks

10. ☑   **A.** Straight-through connections are required when connecting dissimilar devices such as a router and a hub or a host and a hub.
☒   **B, C,** and **D** are all incorrect because they will not work with the connections required by the question.

11. ☑   **C.** SHOW INTERFACES. This command provides you with the current status of all interfaces on the router.
☒   **A** is incorrect because it displays IP configuration of all interfaces. **B** is incorrect because it shows you only the status of the Ethernet interfaces. **D** is incorrect because it is not a valid IOS command.

12. ☑   **C.** Use the SHOW RUNNING-CONFIG command to see what routes are being filtered with the DISTRIBUTE-LIST command. The output of the SHOW RUNNING-CONFIG command tells you if any routes are being filtered with access lists.
☒   **A** is incorrect because it will not help you isolate the problem if you run the same command again. **B** is incorrect because although it might work, you would not have addressed the core of the problem. **D** is a drastic measure that might solve your problem, but at what cost? You will have defeated the purpose of the access lists.

Problem Isolation in Windows 95 and 98 Networks

13. ☑   **D.** The WINIPCFG utility is used to provide IP configuration information on Windows 95 and 98 machines.
☒   **A, B,** and **C** are incorrect because they will result in a "File Not Found" message.

14. ☑ A, C, and D are the correct answers. None of these can be provided by a DHCP server.
    ☒ B is incorrect because an IP address can be provided by a DHCP server.

15. ☑ A, B, C, and D. WINS provides all these functions. None of them is applicable towards LMHOSTS files.
    ☒ There are no incorrect choices.

IP Symptoms, Problems, and Action Plans

16. ☑ D. SHOW ACCESS-LISTS. This is the correct syntax to show all configured access lists on the router.
    ☒ A and C are incorrect because they are not valid IOS commands. B shows you the access lists that have been applied to the router's interfaces.

17. ☑ B. ACCESS-LIST 100 DENY IP 192.10.10.0 255.255.255.255 EQ 80. Web browsers use TCP port 80 to access the Internet. By denying hosts from using port 80 all Web access is blocked.
    ☒ A and C are incorrect because they are blocking other types of traffic. D is incorrect because it is a PERMIT statement.

18. ☑ A an D. EIGRP and OSPF. They can both support discontiguous subnets because they advertise subnet mask information along with the route.
    ☒ B and C are incorrect because neither IGRP nor RIP advertise subnet mask information with routes so they cannot support discontiguous subnets.

Windows 95 and 98 Symptoms, Problems, and Action Plans

19. ☑ D. DHCP is the common service that requires the use of a helper address.
    ☒ A, B, and C, although all true in some degree, are not the most popular use of the helper address function.

20. ☑ A. Group resources that belong to the same workgroup. Workgroups are used to group resources together by workgroup name so that browsing for resources is made easier.
    ☒ B and D are incorrect because these are not functions of workgroups. C is incorrect because the domain name must be specified elsewhere.

Data-Link and Network Layer Exercises

21. ☑ **B.** False. Packet analysis cannot be performed on a Cisco router.

☒ **A** is incorrect because a Cisco router has no way of capturing packets, nor can it analyze any packets to provide any information.

LAB ANSWER

In Figure 7-5, you'll notice immediately that the routing protocol used is EIGRP. You'll also notice that Remote Office 1 and Remote Office 2 have discontiguous subnets.

EIGRP automatically summarizes at default network boundaries, so Router A will summarize the networks for Routers B and C into 172.16.0.0. This will result in the new remote office being unable to access the networks off Routers B and C.

To correct this problem, you should use the NO AUTO-SUMMARY command on the company's routers. This would prevent automatic summarization on the routers, and the result would be that the networks off Routers B and C would now be advertised as individual routes.

8

Diagnosing and Correcting IPX Problems

D espite its popularity, TCP/IP has not only not eliminated a number of protocols, but some, such as Internetwork Packet Exchange (IPX), have become more popular. Some parallels can be drawn between the two protocols. Both TCP and Sequenced Packet Exchange (SPX) are connection oriented; both IP and IPX are connectionless. TCP/IP uses port numbers at the Transport Layer; IPX/SPX uses socket numbers at the Transport Layer. The number of protocols associated with IPX/SPX is relatively limited compared to TCP/IP. See Table 8-1.

TCP/IP addresses are expressed in dotted-decimal format (192.168.1.1); IPX addresses are expressed in hexadecimal *network node* format (AA235A1E.0090.2784.c28a). Much like TCP/IP, IPX addresses consist of both a network component (AA235A1E) and a host component (0090.2784.c28a), although in IPX the host is referred to as a *node*. The network number is a 4-byte (32-bit) number that identifies a logical network. Unlike TCP/IP, IPX does not employ the concept of variable-length subnets; the portion before the first period is always the complete network number. Novell servers are inherently routers; therefore, each server has an internal network number that is contained and advertised from the file server to uniquely identify the server. A separate external network number is configured and bound to the network card. A Novell server (or client) may have

TABLE 8-1   IPX Protocols

Protocol	Description
IPX	Transmits each data unit as an independent entity without establishing a logical connection between the two end stations. Uses the IEEE 802.3 frame format without the LLC Layer. Operates at the Network Layer.
SPX	Is a connection-oriented protocol used for reliable peer-to-peer (client/server) communications based on the XNS Sequenced Packet Protocol. Reliable, guaranteeing sequenced packet delivery. Operates at the Transport Layer.
NetWare Core Protocol (NCP)	Provides connection services and is used as an OS director for supporting various network services. Operates at the Transport Layer.
Service Advertisement Protocol (SAP)	Active service advertisement of each network server. Operates at the Session and Application Layers.

multiple IPX logical networks associated with a single network card, one for each frame type available. The *frame type*, also referred to as *encapsulation*, refers to the IPX packet structure.

There are several versions of the Novell operating system, typically referred to by the major version number, with *x* referring to all flavors of the major version. There are still a few companies with servers on Version 3.x. Novell's 4.x, which is still widely deployed, was the first version with inherent TCP/IP functionality, although it was not entirely standards compliant. Prior to Version 4.x, TCP/IP NetWare Loadable Modules (NLMs) were available for direct IP connectivity. Version 5.x has been installed in a number of companies, although many companies have chosen to stay with 4.x because it is stable and meets their needs at the present time. Due to the differences in network functionality, it is important to know which version(s) are in your environment.

CERTIFICATION OBJECTIVE 8.01

IPX Connection Sequence

There is no requirement for an IPX client to be preconfigured with the local network number, nor is there a requirement for the client to be configured with a specific frame type. During initialization, the workstation sends a get nearest server (GNS) broadcast on each of the available frame types, listens for a response, and sets the frame type based on the GNS response. Once the frame type is determined, the nearest server is identified, the path to the server is identified, and the workstation issues the NCP logon request. Let's take a look at each component of this process in detail.

Routing Protocol Traffic

There are three IPX routing protocols: RIP, NLSP, and EIGRP. *Routing Information Protocol (RIP)* was the first and is still widely deployed in spite of its limitations in terms of scalability. Novell introduced *NetWare Link Services Protocol (NLSP)* to address RIP's limitations. NLSP is often compared to OSPF. To conserve bandwidth and allow for more advanced routing decisions, Cisco introduced

Enhanced Interior Gateway Router Protocol (EIGRP) in January of 1994 with IOS Release 9.21. Until the release of NetWare 4.x and NLSP, though, RIP was still the only protocol choice for communicating with a NetWare server or client. Since EIGRP is a proprietary protocol, EIGRP can only be used between Cisco routers, not to communicate with IPX devices.

IPX RIP

There is only one version of IPX RIP, essentially the same as RIPv1 for TCP/IP. In a Cisco router, if you want to use RIP for both TCP/IP and Novell IPX, you are executing two separate processes: *ROUTER RIP* and *IPX ROUTER RIP*. Routers running IPX RIP transport a maximum of 50 network destinations per packet (compared to the 25 for its IP cousin). As a distance-vector protocol, IPX RIP supports a maximum of 15 hops. Therefore, if a routing update is received from another router with a hop count of 15, the receiving router discards the packet without adding the route to its routing table. RIP is not scalable for extremely large networks because of the 15 hop-count limit. From a bandwidth standpoint, it is often the number of routing packets and the frequency of those updates (every 60 seconds) that forces network administrators to implement NLSP or IPX EIGRP.

IPX RIP maintains a forwarding table with all the known routes. Routes are learned from RIP broadcasts. When an IPX RIP router is first configured, and each time the interface is changed to an up status, the router issues a RIP routes request. When an IPX RIP interface is brought down, it issues RIP broadcasts to poison any routes it has advertised.

IPX EIGRP

In small companies, IPX RIP is widely deployed due to ease of implementation. In larger organizations, you are more to likely find IPX EIGRP in the WAN. It is very easy to configure, easily redistributes to and from RIP (to communicate with servers), is more scalable (up to 224 hops), and is less "chatty." EIGRP establishes a neighbor relationship before sharing routing updates with another EIGRP router. The neighbor router must be using the same *autonomous system (AS)* number and must be a member of the same IPX network before it is added to the neighbor list.

FROM THE CLASSROOM

EIGRP Stuck-in-Active State

EIGRP routes are transmitted reliably, meaning that an acknowledgment must be received from each neighbor router. The routing process keeps track of the state of each route. A stable route is in the *passive state*, meaning that all routing activities are complete and this route is considered reliable. When a neighbor relationship is lost, the routing process examines each route associated with the neighbor to see if a feasible successor exists. A *feasible successor* is a different route that is statistically guaranteed to be loop-free. If no feasible successor exists, the route is placed in the *active state*.

The router sends a *query* to all neighboring routers asking for a new route. All neighbors must *reply* before a new route can be installed. If one or more neighbors do not reply, the router waits until the active timer has expired. At that point, the router removes any neighbors that did not reply from its neighbor table, enters the active mode again, and issues an error message to the console that looks something like this:

```
%DUAL-3-SIA:  Route 1003. 00d0.baa2.ea60 Stuck-In-Active
```

It is normal that this message appears only occasionally on the console; it means that EIGRP is performing its job properly. If the message appears regularly, though, it is indicative of a problem that should be investigated and resolved.

— *Michelle Famiglietti, CCNP, CCDA*

NLSP

NLSP is a link-state routing protocol. Like OSPF, it is more complex to configure than either IPX RIP or IPX EIGRP, and it shares the same advantages (reliability, lower bandwidth overhead in stable networks) and limitations (high bandwidth overhead in unstable networks) as OSPF. Unlike EIGRP, NLSP can also be implemented at the server level for a single enterprisewide IPX routing protocol. NLSP must do a complete topology update every two hours, even when there are no changes at all. NLSP advertises a SAP only when it changes, instead of periodically, as RIP does. In addition, more than seven services may be advertised in a single update, reducing the number of packets required. When implemented on a NetWare server, NLSP is often configured to use *RIP/SAP compatibility* for backward compatibility with older servers as well as with routers still running RIP.

One unique requirement of NLSP is that every server and router must be configured with two network numbers. The external network number is the same in all routers or servers on the same physical segment using the same IPX frame type. The internal network number is unique to each and is somewhat analogous to a loopback address. For that reason, every Cisco router must have an internal IPX network address configured when using NLSP. NLSP is available on all 4.x and 5.x servers as well as the NetWare 3.2 Enhancement Pack.

NLSP Version 1.1 routers, like Cisco, support a feature known as *route aggregation*. Route aggregation is similar to using a TCP/IP subnet mask to group multiple networks together into a single network, except that the mask is created in hex because the network address format is hex. NLSP Version 1.0 routers do not support this feature. When a router interconnects multiple NLSP areas, the router must be configured to support multiple processes. This is done by *tagging* each process. Area summarization must be manually configured, if desired.

NLSP uses a special multicast MAC address to send out routing updates on LAN segments. When there are multiple NLSP routers on a LAN segment, one router assumes the responsibility for managing the table and broadcasts that table out to the other routers. The *pseudonode* is the managing router. Used in conjunction with NLSP, IPXWAN applies IPX header compression on the WAN links as specified in RFC 1533. IPXWAN can also compress NCP request and reply headers.

Multiple Routing Protocols

RIP is enabled by default as soon as *IPX ROUTING* is configured in the router. As a default, it does not appear in the configuration unless you modify it in some way. You can disable RIP entirely, using the NO IPX ROUTER RIP command. Alternatively, you can disable RIP on specific networks using the NO NETWORK *NETWORK* subcommand under the *IPX ROUTER RIP* portion of the configuration. Enabling either the EIGRP or NLSP protocols on the router does not eliminate RIP traffic, even if the routing statements show that the route is learned via NLSP or EIGRP. This is a common source of unnecessary routing traffic, which can be especially devastating to WANs. Even more important, failure to disable RIP on networks where it is not needed or desired can result in unanticipated routing table changes and network instability.

EIGRP, like NLSP, automatically redistributes IPX RIP routes. If you want to redistribute routes between EIGRP and NLSP, you must manually configure the redistribution. Cisco routers also automatically redistribute routes between multiple NLSP Version 1.0 areas, multiple NLSP Version 1.0 areas, and between NLSP Version 1.1 and Version 1.0 areas. All routes are redistributed as individual (not summarized) routes, by default. The router must be manually configured to take advantage of NLSP Version 1.1's summarization capabilities.

If the router receives a route to the same network through multiple protocols, it uses the *administrative distance (AD)* to decide which is the preferred route. The AD is a predefined number assigned to each routing protocol. For IPX, it cannot be configured, except in the case of static routes. A lower AD refers to a better route source. The AD for EIGRP is 90 for internal routes and 170 for external routes. Therefore, if there are two EIGRP routes to a destination, one originating within the EIGRP process and the other originating outside the EIGRP process, the EIGRP route will be preferred. A Cisco router receiving two updates from the same router prefers the EIGRP route over the RIP route, and any RIP route with a hop count of 2 or greater is not preferred over the EIGRP route.

exam
ⓌatcH

Contrary to the AD theory, Cisco routers always prefer a RIP route with a hop count of 1 over an EIGRP route with a hop count of 1. This preference ensures that a Novell server SAP is always preferred over the EIGRP route when hop counts are the same.

Service Advertisement Traffic

The operational difference between TCP/IP and IPX lies in the client-to-server communications. With TCP/IP, the client is expected to find the server. Novell's NetWare Core Protocol (NCP) is the upper-layer protocol for connection-oriented transmissions in IPX. This protocol provides the framework that facilitates interaction between workstations and servers (the client/server relationship). The server is expected to announce itself to the client using Service Advertising Protocol

(SAP) to advertise available services. SAP advertisements make service available dynamically. Although SAPs are broadcasts, only SAP agents, typically Novell servers and routers, store this information. Clients ignore unsolicited SAPs.

exam
ⓦatch

By default, SAPs are broadcast every 60 seconds; you can increase this window to effectively manage SAP broadcasts, but every SAP agent on the network must be configured with the larger window size or the SAP tables will become unstable. The benefits of reduced SAP traffic must be weighed against the cost of a delay in network convergence.

As with TCP/IP ports, the most common SAP types are those that are used routinely in access lists. Unlike TCP/IP, no official document lists all the SAPs available. Cisco provides a relatively long list of "unverified" SAPs in its *Troubleshooting Novell IPX* document on CCO. You can also search the Knowledgebase on Novell for its list. When dealing with a new SAP type, it is often easier to ask the server administrator what services are installed on the server, eliminate those you know, and make an assumption that what remains must belong to the new service.

Table 8-2 lists some of the more common SAP types. Of these, the most important is probably SAP Type 4, since this SAP is necessary for a client to log in to a server.

TABLE 8-2	Hex	SAP Description
Common Novell SAP Types	0003	Print Queue
	0004	File Server
	0007	Print Server
	0107	Remote Console (RCONSOLE)
	023F	Novell SMDR, SMS Testing and Development
	026B	Time Synchronization
	0278	Directory Services (NDS)
	030C	Intel Netport 2, HP JetDirect, or HP Quicksilver

EXERCISE 8-1

SAP Identification

For this lab, you need a Cisco router and a Novell server. Configure the router to use IPX RIP on the LAN segment. The external network address for the server should be the IPX network address configured on the router's LAN interface. The server should be configured to use NLSP with RIP/SAP compatibility. Use the SHOW IPX SERVERS command to display the SAPs being advertised by the Novell server. Identify the SAP types and the purpose of each.

Solution: The router configuration you use should include the following components. Naturally, the MAC address of your router will be different, and you might have chosen a different IPX network address as well as a different frame encapsulation.

```
ipx routing 00d0.baa2.ea60
interface FastEthernet0/0.1
 ipx network 10010 encapsulation SAP
```

The SHOW IPX SERVERS output might differ slightly depending on the version of Novell server used as well as the services provided on the server. The output should include several of these components:

```
Router#sh ipx ser
Codes: S - Static, P - Periodic, E - EIGRP, N - NLSP, H - Holddown, + = detail
U - Per-user static
7 Total IPX Servers
Table ordering is based on routing and server info
Type Name                       Net     Address    Port    Route Hops Itf
P     4 FAB-FAM                  10011.0000.0000.0001:0451    2/01   1  Fa0/0.1
P   107 FAB-FAM                  10011.0000.0000.0001:8104    2/01   1  Fa0/0.1
P   26B FAM_____            10011.0000.0000.0001:000A    2/01   1  Fa0/0.1
P   278 FAM_____            10011.0000.0000.0001:0640    2/01   1  Fa0/0.1
```

The following SAP types are visible from the Novell 5 server used in this lab: File Server (4), RCONSOLE (107), Time Synchronization (26B), NDS (278).

Get Nearest Server

A client cannot initiate a session with a file server without first having that server's address. *Get nearest server,* or *GNS* (SAP Type 4) is a SAP broadcast by the client at bootup to find the nearest login server. Alternatively, a client may issue a *get nearest directory server,* or *GNDS* (SAP Type 278). SAP Type 4 is used for Bindery mode, and SAP Type 278 is used with NDS.

The nearest NetWare file server responds with a SAP. If there is no server on the local segment, a Cisco router responds in place of a server. In this way, a client GNS broadcast serves a function similar to that of ARP in TCP/IP. It differs in that it is a request for the address of a specific *type* of device. At that point, the client can log in to the server, make a connection, set the packet size, and use the server's resources.

Note: With the release of NetWare 5 and NCP over IP, NetWare clients can locate a NetWare service through host files, SLP, or DNS and in some circumstances using DHCP. Since these are TCP/IP-based services, they are not addressed in this chapter.

NCP Request/Response

Next, the workstation sends a request for an NCP server. The NCP request and response are key parts of the logon process. NCP allows servers to provide services to clients. When the server picks up the client's NCP request, the server replies. The workstation now knows the name of the server, along with the network address and MAC address of the server.

Next, the client must find a route to the network, so it sends another broadcast, this time for a RIP route. The server responds with a RIP route. Once a client has found the name of a server, obtained the route to the server, and is ready to log in, an NCP connection request is issued to begin the actual logon process.

During session establishment, two performance-enhancement parameters can be set for the session. These are *Large Internet Packets (LIP)* and *Packet Burst,* sometimes called *PBurst.* LIP is supposed to allow the client and the server to negotiate the maximum packet size for all communications during the session. Prior to NetWare 5, the server examined the number of hops to the client and, if the number of hops was greater than 1, the server assumed that the stated packet size might not be reliable and set the maximum packet size to 512K. With smaller packet sizes, a higher number of packets must be sent through the network to transfer the same amount of data. In NetWare 5, support for LIP is automatically set to *On* and the negotiation works properly across multiple hops. The client workstation must also have the VLMs or the 32-bit NetWare client software appropriately configured.

Packet Burst is similar to TCP Window sizes. It must be enabled in earlier versions, but it is automatically supported in NetWare 5. Again, the client workstation must also have the VLMs or the 32-bit NetWare client software appropriate configured. If Packet Burst is not enabled, every packet must be acknowledged before the next one is sent. Across a WAN link, the delay is often noticeable.

To function properly, neither LIP nor Packet Burst requires any special configuration on the router or switch. However, when you are troubleshooting performance problems, signs of average packet sizes less than or equal to 512K are a clue that LIP is not enabled. *Sniffer traces* can help identify whether or not Packet Burst is enabled.

CERTIFICATION OBJECTIVE 8.02

Cisco IOS Software Tools and Commands

When troubleshooting a problem, you do not have the luxury of time, so knowing the appropriate commands to obtain the relevant information is critical to the troubleshooting process. This section looks at a number of SHOW commands, which are summarized in Table 8-3. In addition to these IPX protocol-specific commands, you will frequently want to use the SHOW INTERFACE command to ensure that the reported problem is not due to a network failure, traffic demand exceeding available bandwidth, or broadcast drops on the serial interface. Broadcast drops are particularly devastating in an IPX network because all SAP packets fall into this category and can frequently be the cause of problems.

Sometimes the SHOW commands do not provide sufficient information to identify the source of the problem. The DEBUG commands available through the IOS allow you to see deeper into the process. When you use DEBUG, the router records far more detail than is typically required. This process is much more processor intensive. Many engineers refuse to use DEBUG in a production environment, preferring instead to use other ways of gathering the information, such as sniffer traces. The difference is that the sniffer traces record the packets but cannot analyze the reason that a device does not respond. The DEBUG output from a Cisco router often gives a reason that a packet was discarded. It can save a lot of time to have the router "tell" you that it is discarding a SAP packet because there is no route in the routing tables for the SAP. Table 8-4 is a quick reference of the IPX-related DEBUG commands discussed in this chapter.

TABLE 8-3 IPX SHOW Commands

Command	When to Use
SHOW IPX INTERFACE	To see all the IPX characteristics of an interface
SHOW IPX ROUTE	To see a list of all IPX routes known to the router
SHOW IPX TRAFFIC	To see a summary of IPX packets sent and received
SHOW IPX ACCESS-LIST	To see all IPX access lists, sorted by type of list
SHOW IPX NLSP DATABASE	To see the NLSP link-state database
SHOW IPX NLSP NEIGHBORS	To see a list of NLSP neighbors
SHOW IPX EIGRP INTERFACES	To see a list of interfaces associated with IPX EIGRP
SHOW IPX EIGRP NEIGHBORS	To see a list of IPX EIGRP neighbors
SHOW IPX EIGRP TRAFFIC	To see a summary of IPX EIGRP traffic
SHOW IPX EIGRP TOPOLOGY	To see a topology table for IPX EIGRP, similar to an IPX routing table
SHOW IPX SERVERS	To see a list of IPX SAPs known to the router

TABLE 8-4 IPX DEBUG Commands

Command	When to Use
DEBUG IPX ROUTING	Displays every routing packet sent or received by the router
DEBUG IPX EIGRP	Displays every IPX EIGRP-related packet sent or received by the router
DEBUG IPX EIGRP EVENTS	Displays every event that triggers the IPX EIGRP process
DEBUG IPX EIGRP NEIGHBOR	Helps identify why a neighbor relationship is not being established or maintained
DEBUG IPX PACKET	Displays information about IPX packets received, transmitted, or forwarded through the router
DEBUG IPX SAP	Helps determine why a SAP is not appearing in the SAP tables
DEBUG IPX NLSP EVENTS	Displays every event that triggers the IPX NLSP process
DEBUG IPX IPXWAN	Helps verify or troubleshoot the IPXWAN startup negotiation process

The SHOW IPX INTERFACE Command

The output from the SHOW IPX INTERFACE command tells you almost everything you want to know about how the interface is configured. However, it cannot tell you whether or not GNS-ROUND-ROBIN is configured on the interface. That information can be determined only by examining the configuration itself.

```
1. Ethernet0/1 is up, line protocol is up
2. IPX address is A585A4E.0010.79ce.6801, SAP [up]
3. Delay of this IPX network, in ticks is 1 throughput 0 link delay 0
4. IPXWAN processing not enabled on this interface.
5. IPX SAP update interval is 60 seconds
6. IPX type 20 propagation packet forwarding is disabled
7. Incoming access list is not set
8. Outgoing access list is not set
9. IPX helper access list is not set
10. SAP GNS processing enabled, delay 500 ms, output filter list is not set
11. SAP Input filter list is not set
12. SAP Output filter list is not set
13. SAP Router filter list is not set
14. Input filter list is not set
15. Output filter list is not set
16. Router filter list is not set
17. Netbios Input host access list is not set
18. Netbios Input bytes access list is not set
19. Netbios Output host access list is not set
20. Netbios Output bytes access list is not set
21. Updates each 60 seconds aging multiples RIP: 3 SAP: 3
22. SAP interpacket delay is 55 ms, maximum size is 480 bytes
23. RIP interpacket delay is 55 ms, maximum size is 432 bytes
24. RIP response delay is not set
25. IPX accounting is disabled
26. IPX fast switching is configured (enabled)
27. RIP packets received 474044, RIP packets sent 4288493
28. SAP packets received 2049424, SAP packets sent 27848718
```

The Ethernet interface in the preceding output has had some minor adjustments to the defaults. As with all SHOW INTERFACE commands, Line 1 tells whether or not the interface is administratively up, whether or not it is electrically up, and whether or not the line protocol is up. Line 2 shows both the IPX network number assigned to the interface (A585A4E) and the router's node address (0010.79ce.6801). This information is followed by the IPX encapsulation—in this case, Novell's Ethernet 802.2, which Cisco refers to as SAP. Line 10 shows that the GNS response of the router has been delayed by 500ms to allow time for the local server to respond. Line 27 shows that clearly, the router is both sending and receiving RIP updates; Line 28 shows that the router is both sending and receiving SAP updates.

If a server SAP is not both sending and receiving updates, you need to check Line 12 to see whether or not a filter has been applied. Line 22 shows the SAP interpacket delay. If this delay does not match the one on the other end of a WAN link, the most common symptom will be instability of the SAP tables. Line 28 shows whether or not RIP packets are being sent or received on this interface. It is obvious that routing is taking place on this segment, because Line 29 shows that the router is both sending and receiving SAP updates.

The SHOW IPX ROUTE Command

The SHOW IPX ROUTE command provides a listing of all known IPX routes, the associated routing protocol, metrics, and the route itself. This list contains seven routes:

```
1. Router#sh ipx route
2. Codes: C - Connected primary network,    c - Connected secondary network
3. S - Static, F - Floating static, L - Local (internal), W - IPXWAN
4. R - RIP, E - EIGRP, N - NLSP, X - External, A - Aggregate
5. s - seconds, u - uses, U - Per-user static
6.
7. Total IPX routes. Up to 1 parallel paths and 16 hops allowed.
8.
9. No default route known.
10.
11. L       1004 is the internal network
12. C       1001 (SAP),         Fa0/0.1
13. C       2005 (NOVELL-ETHER), Fa0/0.2
14. C    B585A1E (UNKNOWN),      Lo0
15. N       2011 [20][01/00] via      1001.00e0.1eb9.11b3,  286s, Fa0/0.1
16. NX   9B23663 [20][01/01][01/01] via      1001.00e0.1eb9.11b3,  286s, Fa0/0.1
17. N    DD001DD [20][00/00]        via      1001.00e0.1eb9.11b3,  286s, Fa0/0.1
```

As with TCP/IP, it is possible to set a default route, although in this case none has been defined (Line 9). Of the seven total routes, three are directly connected (Lines 12 through 14), one is internal (Line 11), two are internal to the NLSP process (Lines 15 and 17), and one is an external route inserted into NLSP by another router (Line 16).

The SHOW IPX TRAFFIC Command

The SHOW IPX TRAFFIC command provides an overview of the IPX packets handled by the router:

```
1.  System Traffic for 0.0000.0000.0001 System-Name: IPX-RTR
2.  Rcvd:   2060785957 total, 1775627 format errors, 0 checksum errors, 634 bad
    hop count, 4386896 packets pitched, 218544049 local destination, 0 multicast
3.  Bcast: 188593821 received, 294977231 sent
4.  Sent:   427856194 generated, 1837850867 forwarded
5.  1 encapsulation failed, 11844 no route
6.  SAP:    1755112 Total SAP requests, 17605586 Total SAP replies, 1030 servers
7.  1370966 SAP general requests, 4334 ignored, 17603135 replies
8.  310994 SAP Get Nearest Server requests, 2451 replies
9.  73152 SAP Nearest Name requests, 0 replies
10. 0 SAP General Name requests, 0 replies
11. 20796873 SAP advertisements received, 127297677 sent
12. 731011 SAP flash updates sent, 2887 SAP format errors, last seen from
    A585A1E.0060.97a1.a919
13. RIP:    5049461 RIP requests, 4841 ignored, 2768777 RIP replies, 1061 routes
14. 4648992 RIP advertisements received, 16354961 sent
15. 426263 RIP flash updates sent, 0 RIP format errors
16. Echo:   Rcvd 0 requests, 5 replies
17. Sent 5 requests, 0 replies
18. 0 unknown: 0 no socket, 0 filtered, 0 no helper
19. 0 SAPs throttled, freed NDB len 0
20. Watchdog: 0 packets received, 0 replies spoofed
21. Queue lengths: IPX input: 0, SAP 0, RIP 0, GNS 0
22. SAP throttling length: 0/(no limit), 0 nets pending lost route reply
23. Delayed process creation: 0
24. EIGRP:   Total received 175017885, sent 176407891
25. Updates received 4907282, sent 4222433
26. Queries received 4074373, sent 4737292
27. Replies received 5255472, sent 4071153
28. SAPs received 1774094, sent 2325490
```

In a large, active network, SHOW IPX TRAFFIC is not very revealing, because these counters apply to all interfaces. It is very difficult to extrapolate whether or not errors such as those in Line 5 really mean anything. However, the overall information can provide some insight into the health of the IPX routing processes. For a remote, stub router, this information can be more informative and can help identify what kinds of problems are occurring in the network. For example, Line 5 might show that the traffic is failing because of a missing route. If no local servers are attached to the LAN segments of the router, Line 9 might be cause for concern, since the router is receiving GNS requests but not responding to them. The presence of SAP format errors (Line 12) points to encapsulation discrepancies between the router and the server, but it could also indicate that the server is configured to support multiple frame types while the router can support only one frame type. SHOW IPX TRAFFIC can be a good place to get an idea of where to focus an investigation.

Note: These counters are set when the router is loaded, when the IPX process is stopped and restarted, or using the CLEAR IPX TRAFFIC command. This last command is relatively new; it was introduced in 12.0(1)T.

The SHOW IPX ACCESS-LIST Command

This command is a variation of the SHOW ACCESS-LIST command. In this case, only IPX access lists are displayed:

```
Router#sh ipx access-li
IPX extended access list 900
    permit any A000658A
    deny any A000000A.0000.0000.0000 FFFFFF0.ffff.ffff.ffff
    permit any any
IPX sap access list 1010
    permit FFFFFFFF 0 IBID-ELG
    permit FFFFFFFF 0 IBID-COMM1
    permit FFFFFFFF 0 IBID-COMM2
    permit FFFFFFFF 0 IBID-REMOTE1
IPX sap access list 1011
    permit FFFFFFFF 0 IBID-ELG
    permit FFFFFFFF 0 IBID-COMM1
    permit FFFFFFFF 0 IBID-COMM2
    permit FFFFFFFF 0 IBID-COMM4
    permit FFFFFFFF 0 IBID-REMOTE1
    permit FFFFFFFF 0 IBID-VTMPNSA1
IPX sap access list 1052
    deny 9B23663 3E1
```

As with an IP access list, there are only two ways to tell whether or not an IPX access list is applied. You can use the SHOW IPX INTERFACE command, or you can use the SHOW RUNNING-CONFIG (or SHOW STARTUP-CONFIG) command to read through the active (or saved) configuration. The most common type of access list is an IPX SAP access list, numbered 1000–1099. When using NLSP, you might see an IPX summary address access list, numbered 1200–1299. The standard IPX access list (numbered 800–899) filters on both source and destination addresses. This is somewhat different from a standard IP access list, which can filter on either source or destination, but not both. Table 8-5 shows the extended access list (numbered 900–999) protocol type options. Table 8-6 shows the socket filter options.

The router must evaluate every SAP against each access list applied to each interface before generating the SAP itself. This process is processor intensive. A poorly written SAP filter can cause CPU utilization to spike, which can result in complaints that the network is slow. Alternatively, the router might not filter enough SAPs, so too many SAPs can be advertised through the network, again resulting in complaints that the network is slow. It is not always possible to consolidate access list entries, and to do so requires a thorough knowledge of the SAPs present in the network to begin with. The tendency with existing access lists is to simply add new servers or services to the end of the list. However, the entire list must be processed before that one server is admitted. When servers or services are removed from the network, the filters applied to the routers usually remain in place. Failure to periodically review and update SAP filters ultimately impacts router performance.

IPX access lists can be used on LAN segments, although most commonly they are used on WAN segments. They are particularly important in a dial-on-demand

TABLE 8-5	Option	Description
IPX Extended Access List Protocol Options	0–255	Protocol type number (DECIMAL)
	ANY	Any IPX protocol type
	NCP	NetWare Core Protocol
	NETBIOS	IPX NetBIOS
	RIP	IPX Routing Information Protocol
	SAP	Service Advertising Protocol
	SPX	Sequenced Packet Exchange

TABLE 8-6		IPX Extended Access List Socket Filter Options

Option	Hex	Description
0-FFFFFFFF	0-FFFFFFFF	Source Socket HEXIDECIMAL
ALL	0	All sockets
CPING	2	Cisco IPX ping
DIAGNOSTIC	456	Diagnostic packet
EIGRP	85BE	IPX Enhanced Interior Gateway Routing Protocol
LOG		Log matches against this entry
NCP	451	NetWare Core Protocol
NETBIOS	455	IPX NetBIOS
NLSP	9001	NetWare Link State Protocol
NPING	9086	Standard IPX ping
RIP	453	IPX Routing Information Protocol
SAP	452	Service Advertising Protocol
TIME-RANGE		Specify a time range
TRACE	456	Trace route packet

environment. An access list that has been created but not applied to any interface or process in the router is performing no function other than using memory resources in the router.

What happens if an access list is applied but does not exist? It depends on the version of IOS. Prior to 11.x, the implicit deny all would be applied. This created a lot of problems, and based on popular demand, the default behavior of the router was changed in Version 11.x to allow all traffic to pass through if an access list was applied to an interface but the access list did not exist.

The SHOW IPX NLSP DATABASE Command

NLSP is a link-state routing protocol. Like OSPF, it maintains a table of the link-state packet database. By default, this command provides a summary of the entries in the link-state packet (LSP) database:

```
1. Router#sh ipx nlsp database
2. NLSP Level-1 Link State Database: Tag Identifier = notag
3. LSPID              LSP Seq Num  LSP Checksum  LSP Holdtime    ATT/P/OL
4. Router.00-00      * 0x00000002  0x91F9        7216            0/0/0
5. Router.01-00      * 0x00000001  0xD2A0        7206            0/0/0
6. Router.02-00      * 0x00000001  0xF6A1        7206            0/0/0
7. Router.03-00      * 0x00000003  0x80B9        7444            0/0/0
8. Router.04-00      * 0x00000004  0xB966        7449            0/0/0
9. NLSP Level-1 Link State Database: Tag Identifier = myarea
10. LSPID             LSP Seq Num  LSP Checksum  LSP Holdtime    ATT/P/OL
11. Router.00-00     * 0x00000004  0xA3D2        7416            0/0/0
12. Router.01-00     * 0x00000001  0xD2A0        7206            0/0/0
13. Router.02-00     * 0x00000001  0xF6A1        7206            0/0/0
14. Router.03-00     * 0x00000003  0x80B9        7444            0/0/0
15. Router.04-00     * 0x00000001  0x730D        0 (7416)        0/0/0
16. Test.00-00         0x00000001  0xB275        7187            0/0/0
17. Test.02-00         0x00000001  0xE7C3        7188            0/0/0
18. Test.03-00         0x00000003  0x0167        7412            0/0/0
```

This router is running two separate NLSP processes. One has no tag associated with it (Line 2), and the other is tagged *myarea* (Line 9). This means that the router is connected to multiple NLSP areas. In the first column, the link-state packet ID (LSPID) is displayed. This field displays the system ID (the network number), pseudonode circuit identifier, and fragment number. The format is *xxxx.xxxx.xxxx.yy-zz*, where *xxxx.xxxx.xxxx* is the system identifier, *yy* is the pseudo identifier, and *zz* is the LSP number. The example demonstrates that the output of the system identifier can be replaced by the router name. On Line 8, for example, the system identifier is Test, the pseudo-identifier is 03, and the LSP number is 00.

The next column is the LSP Sequence number, which is used by the NLSP routers to verify that the database is current. The LSP Checksum is used by the NLSP routers to verify the integrity of the data. The LSP Holdtime refers to the time until the LSP expires. The last column is used to identify whether specific bits are set. These bits include ATT, which is the L2 attached bit; OL, the overload bit; and P, the partition repair bit. The partition repair bit is not used in NLSP, so it is always 0.

Optionally, you may append the key word DETAIL to the command to obtain more detailed information. When you are troubleshooting a particularly difficult NSLP routing problem, the detailed option provides more IPX management information than is shown in the summary. The detailed display is the complete list of all links on all known routers. Each link has an ID associated with it:

```
1. Router#sh ipx nlsp data det
2. NLSP Level-1 Link State Database: Tag Identifier = notag
3. LSPID                  LSP Seq Num  LSP Checksum  LSP Holdtime       ATT/P/OL
4. Router.00-00         * 0x00000002  0x91F9           7062             0/0/0
5. IPX Area Address: 00001000 FFFFF000
6. IPX Mgmt Info 1010.0000.0000.0001  Ver 1   Name Router
7. Metric: 20          Lnk Router.01            MTU 1500  Dly 1000  Thru 10000K
   Generic LAN
8. Metric: 6           Lnk Router.02            MTU 1514  Dly 5000  Thru 3705032K
   Generic LAN
9. Metric: 20          Lnk Router.03            MTU 1497  Dly 1000  Thru 10000K
   802.3/LLC
10. Metric: 20          Lnk Router.04            MTU 1500  Dly 1000  Thru 10000K
    802.3 Raw
```

The detailed output provides information about the metrics associated with each connection, including IPX management information. Here you can see the version of NLSP (Line 6) is Version 1. From the address on this same line (1010.0000.0000.0001), it is possible to determine whether or not this router is acting as the pseudonode. A nonpseudonode router advertises the internal network number, whereas a pseudonode router advertises the network number of the interface. In addition, a pseudonode LSP always reflects an MTU of 0. Looking at the previous output, one can tell that it was not generated by a pseudonode router.

The SHOW IPX NLSP NEIGHBORS Command

Since NLSP is a link-state protocol, it maintains a neighbor relationship with other routers. This is one of the fastest ways to identify whether or not your NLSP router is communicating with another NLSP router. A variation of this command is SHOW IPX NLSP NEIGHBORS DETAIL, which provides more detail about the neighbor router:

```
Router#sho ipx nlsp nei
NLSP Level-1 Neighbors: Tag Identifier = myarea
System Id        Interface    State  Holdtime  Priority  Cir Adj  Circuit Id
FAB-FAM          Fa0/0        Up     28        64        bc  bc   FAB-FAM.01
```

In this case, the system ID of the neighbor is a Novell server, FAB-FAM. The server is reachable through interface FastEthernet0/0 (Fa0/0), and the connection state is up. The hold time (28) is the remaining time in seconds before the neighbor relationship is assumed to have failed. The priority (64) is the designated router priority.

The **SHOW IPX EIGRP INTERFACES** Command

This command is a quick way to see which interfaces are active and associated with the EIGRP process. It is also useful for determining the smooth round-trip time (SRTT). If the Routes column has anything in it, routes that have not yet been transmitted are queued for transmission. This column can be very helpful to check when route updates are not being propagated through the network properly. For purposes of brevity, the following is a partial listing of the IPX EIGRP interfaces in a 7500 series router:

```
IPX EIGRP Interfaces for process 1

                      Xmit Queue   Mean    Pacing Time   Multicast     Pending
Interface    Peers    Un/Reliable  SRTT    Un/Reliable   Flow Timer    Routes
Se5/2          1        0/0         20        0/15           99            0
Se5/3          1        0/0         47       14/434         626            0
Se5/6          0        0/0          0        0/10            0            0
Se5/7          1        0/0          2        0/15           50            0
Se6/0/0.135    1        0/0         52       12/380         600            0
Se6/0/0.200    1        0/0        107       12/380         832            0
Se6/0/0.195    1        0/0        111       25/760        1212            0
Se6/0/0.215    1        0/0         99       25/760        1164            0
```

Listing the IPX EIGRP interfaces can be a quick way to verify that EIGRP is configured and running on the appropriate interfaces. For each interface, the following information is provided:

- **Peers** The number of peers reachable through the interface.

- **Xmit Queue Un/reliable** The number of unreliable packets and the number of reliable packets queued for transmission.

- **SRTT** The smooth round-trip time for all neighbors on the interface.

- **Pacing Time Un/reliable** The pacing of transmissions, in milliseconds, for unreliable and reliable transmissions.

- **Multicast Flow Timer** The length of time the router will wait for an acknowledgment of a multicast packet from a neighbor before transmitting the next packet.

- **Pending Routes** The number of routes waiting to be advertised through this connection.

When a connection is unreliable, the forwarding tables could become unstable because routes are not being transmitted. By checking the Pending Routes column, it is possible to determine whether all routes have been transmitted and, if not, how many remain. If the SRTT is high compared to other neighbors, this can be an indication that the link is saturated or unreliable. If packets are queued for transmission, the link is saturated or unreachable.

The SHOW IPX EIGRP NEIGHBORS Command

Like NLSP, EIGRP maintains a neighbor relationship with peer EIGRP neighbors. To verify that the router is properly communicating with another IPX EIGRP router, check the neighbor tables. This command is similar to the previous command, but instead of relating the information to a link where there can be multiple neighbors, the output is specific to each individual neighbor. This is also a good command to use to see whether or not the neighbor relationship is stable. A stable relationship results in extremely long uptimes and a queue count (Q) of zero. Watch for the queue count to increase, which means that the router has packets to transmit but is unable to do so because the hello packets are not being returned by the remote router.

```
1. IPX EIGRP Neighbors for process 1
2. H    Address                 Interface      Hold Uptime    SRTT   RTO   Q  Seq
3. (sec)           (ms)        Cnt Num
4. 51   F585581.0000.0c3e.a189  Se6/0/1.945     14 04:02:39    70   1140   0  90436
5. 42   F585240.0000.0c3e.9109  Se6/0/1.900     13 10:06:38    69   4560   0  3341
6. 9    F585567.00d0.baf3.c741  Se6/0/1.170     13 12:59:44    63   2280   0  89013
7. 4    D585D07.0000.0c3e.91d9  Se6/0/1.580     11 14:20:46    84   1140   0  77109
8. 14   F585555.0000.0c3e.9860  Se6/0/0.465     10 19:01:50   137   5000   0  417716
9. 50   F585519.0000.0c3e.80c7  Se6/0/0.240     10 19:22:26   143   4560   0  934403
10. 43   D585D230.0000.0c09.ac0b Se6/0/0.505     14 19:23:49   123   2280   0  817657
11. 22   F585518.0000.0c4a.1a20  Se6/0/1.295     13 19:25:39   131   4560   0  21698
```

The connection on Serial 6/0/0.240 above has a relatively high SRTT (143). This could be a factor of the distance to the remote location (perhaps it is on another continent), due to the low speed of the connection (perhaps it is a 56K port with a 32K PVC), or due to the volume of traffic currently passing through the link (maybe a main link failed and traffic is being rerouted through this smaller link). The number is not particularly meaningful unless it can be compared to a baseline.

If the baseline SRTT is 60 and users are complaining about performance, the current SRTT of 143 is one confirmation that the link is slower than normal.

About 4 hours ago, something caused the neighbor relationship to re-establish on Serial 6/0/1.945. If this number is consistently low, it could be an indication that the routes are flapping or that EIGRP hello packets are not making it through the network. If the neighbor status is stable, it is reasonable to conclude that the network connection itself is stable.

The hold time is the length of time that the router will wait to hear from a neighbor before declaring it to be inaccessible. This number is generally less than 15 seconds. Since the EIGRP process will wait for three missed hello packets before declaring a neighbor unreachable, it is possible to see a neighbor in this list and associated routes in the forwarding tables, even though no packets are actually reaching the remote end. When the hold time expires, all the routes associated with the neighbor are discarded. If a feasible successor exists, the router will update the forwarding table with the feasible successor route. All other routes are placed in the active state.

The SHOW IPX EIGRP TRAFFIC Command

This command is useful for determining whether or not EIGRP hellos are going in both directions as well as for gaining an idea of the traffic volume being generated by the routing protocol. Note that this command is specific to the IPX EIGRP traffic activity, even though the title reflected in the output from the router is *IP-EIGRP*.

```
Router#sh ipx eigrp traff
IP-EIGRP Traffic Statistics for process 1
  Hellos sent/received: 364/362
  Updates sent/received: 24/20
  Queries sent/received: 5/10
  Replies sent/received: 9/5
  Acks sent/received: 26/28
  Input queue high water mark 1, 0 drops
```

The SHOW IPX EIGRP TOPOLOGY Command

Ideally, each route should be in a passive state when you use the SHOW IPX EIGRP TOPOLOGY command. Although similar to the SHOW IPX ROUTE command, this command provides information specific to the IPX EIGRP routing process:

```
1. IPX EIGRP Topology Table for process 1
2. Codes: P - Passive, A - Active, U - Update, Q - Query, R - Reply,
3. r - Reply status
4. P 404, 1 successors, FD is 269824000
5. via D585D07.0000.0c3e.91d9 (269824000/269312000), Serial6/0/1.580
6. P F0F0F0F, 1 successors, FD is 269824000
7. via D585D02.0000.0c09.a6c7 (269824000/269312000), Serial6/0/0.475
8. P D230D230, 1 successors, FD is 41024000
9. via D585D230.0000.0c09.ac0b (41024000/10511872), Serial6/0/0.505
10. P F585502, 1 successors, FD is 40512000
```

In this example, the IPX EIGRP AS number is 1 (Line 1). Each of the four routes displayed is in a passive state, which is a positive indication. Network 404 has a feasible distance of 269824000 and is reachable through D585D07.0000.0c3e.91d9. This destination, reachable through serial 6/0/1.580, is a fully qualified address, including both the network and the MAC address. There is a single feasible successor whose distance is 269312000. If you need more detail about a specific network, including the network at the end of the SHOW command, SHOW IPX EIGRP TOPOLOGY 404 will provide a more detailed listing of the metrics, how and where the route was learned, and so on.

The SHOW IPX SERVERS Command

Cisco has added a number of filter options to the SHOW IPX SERVERS command in Version 12.x. Until Version 12.x, choices were limited. Here are the options now available:

```
Router#sh ipx ser ?
  detailed   Comprehensive display including path detail
  network    Display Services on a particular network
  regexp     Display server list elements whose name matches a regular expression
  sorted     Display server list in sorted order
  type       Display Services of a specific type
  unsorted   Display server list in internal order
```

By default, the SHOW IPX SERVERS command results in output sorted by SAP type. If you are looking for a file server (SAP Type 0004), you can do a search for all servers with SAP Type 4 by entering SHOW IPX SERVERS TYPE 4. More often, you will be looking for all specific SAPs for a given server, so you would use the SHOW IPX SERVERS SERVERNAME command ROUTER#SHOW IPX SER REG FAB:

```
Codes: S - Static, P - Periodic, E - EIGRP, N - NLSP, H - Holddown, + = detail
U - Per-user static
6 Total IPX Servers
```

Table ordering is based on routing and server information:

```
Type Name                    Net      Address    Port    Route Hops Itf
N     4 FAB-FAM              9B23663.0000.0000.0001:0451    1/00    0  Fa0/0
N   107 FAB-FAM              9B23663.0000.0000.0001:8104    1/00    0  Fa0/0
N   3E1 FAB-FAM              9B23663.0000.0000.0001:9056    1/00    0  Fa0/0
N  8202 FAB-FAM_BROKER       9B23663.0000.0000.0001:90B4    1/00    0  Fa0/0
```

The DEBUG IPX ROUTING Command

DEBUG IPX PACKET can be a useful tool when you need to see every packet, but if you are troubleshooting a routing problem, DEBUG IPX ROUTING is a better choice. This command shows every routing packet sent or received by the router. In the following example, the routing process is RIP. This command supplies the same information, regardless of which routing protocol is in use, although the header of the output changes to inform you of which routing process generated or received the packet:

```
1. Router#debug ipx routing act
2. IPX routing debugging is on
3. Router#clear ipx ro *
4. Router#
5. 02:25:46: IPXRIP: Deleting network DD001DD FFFFFFFF in table-wide purge
6. 02:25:46: IPXRIP: Deleting network 9B23663 FFFFFFFF in table-wide purge
7. 02:25:46: IPXRIP: Deleting network AB0101AB FFFFFFFF in table-wide purge
8. 02:25:46: IPXRIP: Marking network AB0101AB FFFFFFFF for Flash Update
9. 02:25:46: IPXRIP: Marking network DD001DD FFFFFFFF for Flash Update
10. 02:25:47: IPXRIP: General Query src=A0000003.0000.0000.0001,
    dst=A0000003.ffff.ffff.ffff, packet sent (via Internal)
11. 02:25:47: IPXRIP: General Query src=B585A1E.00d0.baa2.ea60,
    dst=B585A1E.ffff.ffff.ffff, packet sent (via Loopback0)
12. 02:25:47: IPXRIP: General Query src=A585A1E.00d0.baa2.ea60,
    dst=A585A1E.ffff.ffff.ffff, packet sent (via FastEthernet0/0.1)
13. 02:25:54: IPXRIP: Marking network 9B23663 FFFFFFFF for Flash Update
14. 02:25:54: IPXRIP: positing flash update to B585A1E.ffff.ffff.ffff via
    Loopback0
15. (broadcast)
16. 02:25:54: IPXRIP: RIP compatibility mode off, skip positing update to
    FastEthernet0/0.1
```

```
17. 02:25:54: IPXRIP: RIP turned off, skip positing update to FastEthernet0/0.2
18. 02:25:54: IPXRIP: Update len 56 src=B585A1E.00d0.baa2.ea60,
    dst=B585A1E.ffff.ffff.ffff(453)
19. 02:25:54:     network 9B23663, hops 1,  delay 3
20. 02:25:54:     network DD001DD, hops 2,  delay 4
21. 02:25:54:     network AB0101AB, hops 2,  delay 4
22. 02:25:56: IPXRIP: RIP compatibility mode off, skip positing update to
    FastEthernet0/0.1
23. 02:26:13: IPXRIP: update from BB001BB.00e0.1eb9.11b3
24. 02:26:13: IPXRIP: RIP turned off, discarding RIP packet from
    BB001BB.00e0.1eb9.11b3 (Fa0/0.2)
```

In order to force a routing change, all IPX routes are cleared in Line 3. In a real network, it is better to remove individual routes than to remove the entire routing table. The effects differ depending on the routing protocol(s) in use, but as a general rule you should never remove the entire routing table except in dire circumstances. Lines 5–7 reflect the router removing all routes in the table. This is an internal process in the router and would not be reported in a DEBUG IPX PACKETS output.

Next, the router marks two routes for flash updates, according to the protocol (Lines 8 and 9). It does not mark the third route for a flash update until Line 13. This is not an indication of a problem. Many changes internal to the routing process must be made. These changes are queued up as soon as they are ready. The linear process the human brain is conditioned to expect does not reflect the way the router functions.

When an IPX RIP router is initialized and when all routes are cleared, the router sends out a general broadcast requesting RIP routes. This broadcast speeds up the process of populating the routing table, as shown in Lines 10–12. Once all the routes are marked for flash updates, the router can begin to broadcast the routing tables. Lines 14 and 15 show the router broadcasting RIP routes to the loopback interface but not to the Fast Ethernet subinterfaces (Lines 16 and 17), because RIP has been turned off for those interfaces.

Following the router through each decision can be very helpful when you are uncertain as to the reason a route is not appearing in the forwarding tables. If routes are being received on the Fast Ethernet interfaces but the router is discarding them because RIP is disabled, it could be a clue that RIP needs to be enabled on those interfaces.

The DEBUG IPX EIGRP Command

If you need to see every packet sent and received by the router related to the EIGRP routing process, DEBUG IPX EIGRP is the command of choice. In a stable network, the volume of output should be relatively low. In an unstable network, the lines scroll by so fast you will not be able to read them. DEBUG IPX EIGRP is the most reliable way to determine whether or not a routing update was received from or sent to a neighbor router:

```
1. Test#debug ipx eigrp
2. IPX EIGRP debugging is on
3. 01:49:47: IPXEIGRP: Received update from BB001BB.00d0.baa2.ea60 for net A585A1E
4. 01:49:47: IPXEIGRP: create route to A585A1E via BB001BB.00d0.baa2.ea60, metric
   307200
5. 01:49:47: IPXEIGRP: Received update from BB001BB.00d0.baa2.ea60 for net CC001BB
6. 01:49:47: IPXEIGRP: create route to CC001BB via BB001BB.00d0.baa2.ea60, metric
   266521600
7. 01:49:47: IPXEIGRP: Received update from BB001BB.00d0.baa2.ea60 for net A0000003
8. 01:49:47: IPXEIGRP: create route to A0000003 via BB001BB.00d0.baa2.ea60, metric
   45867776
9. 01:49:47: IPXEIGRP: Received update from BB001BB.00d0.baa2.ea60 for net A0000003
10. 01:49:47: IPXEIGRP: Received update from BB001BB.00d0.baa2.ea60 for net CC001BB
11. 01:49:47: IPXEIGRP: Received update from BB001BB.00d0.baa2.ea60 for net A585A1E
12. 01:49:47: IPXEIGRP: External AB0101AB metric 4294967295 hop 1 delay 1
13. 01:49:47: IPXEIGRP: External DD001DD metric 4294967295 hop 1 delay 1
14. 01:49:47: IPXEIGRP: AB0101AB via BB001BB.00d0.baa2.ea60 metric 4294967295
15. 01:49:47: IPXEIGRP: DD001DD via BB001BB.00d0.baa2.ea60 metric 4294967295
16. 01:49:47: IPXEIGRP: External AB0101AB metric 45842176 hop 1 delay 1
17. 01:49:47: IPXEIGRP: External DD001DD metric 128256 hop 1 delay 1
18. 01:49:47: IPXEIGRP: AB0101AB via BB001BB.00d0.baa2.ea60 metric 4294967295
19. 01:49:47: IPXEIGRP: DD001DD via BB001BB.00d0.baa2.ea60 metric 4294967295
20. 01:49:47: IPXEIGRP: External AB0101AB metric 45842176 hop 1 delay 1
21. 01:49:47: IPXEIGRP: External DD001DD metric 128256 hop 1 delay 1
```

In this example, the router received an update about network A585A1E (Line 3) and created a route in the forwarding table to A585A1E via BB001BB (Line 4). The router then received an update for network CC001BB, also from BB001BB (Line 5), and created a route (Line 6). In Line 12, it is evident that the router is processing an external route to AB0101AB with a metric of 4294967295. Subsequently, the same external route is processed with a different metric, 45842176 (Line 16). This could be an indication of a routing loop.

The DEBUG IPX EIGRP EVENTS Command

When an EIGRP neighbor relationship is cleared, whether IP or IPX, all routes known through the connection are destroyed on both sides. In this case, the IPX EIGRP neighbor tables are cleared to force activity. In a large network, this situation can generate quite a bit of traffic, as demonstrated in a small test network with two routers. A brief excerpt is shown here:

```
Test#clear ipx eigrp nei
01:50:32: IPXEIGRP: External AB0101AB metric 45842176 hop 1 delay 1
01:50:32: IPXEIGRP: External DD001DD metric 128256 hop 1 delay 1
01:50:34: IPXEIGRP: External AB0101AB metric 45842176 hop 1 delay 1
01:50:34: IPXEIGRP: External DD001DD metric 128256 hop 1 delay 1
01:50:35: IPXEIGRP: A585A1E via BB001BB.00d0.baa2.ea60 metric 307200
01:50:35: IPXEIGRP: Received update from BB001BB.00d0.baa2.ea60 for net A585A1E
01:50:35: IPXEIGRP: better [0/0/307200] route for A585A1E from
          BB001BB.00d0.baa2.ea60, flushing old [65535/255/307200] route/paths
01:50:35:          external hop count in table 16, in update 1
01:50:35: IPXEIGRP: Received update from BB001BB.00d0.baa2.ea60 for net A585A1E
01:50:35: IPXEIGRP: create route to A585A1E via BB001BB.00d0.baa2.ea60, metric
          307200
01:50:35: IPXEIGRP: A0000003 via BB001BB.00d0.baa2.ea60 metric 45867776
01:50:35: IPXEIGRP: Received update from BB001BB.00d0.baa2.ea60 for net A0000003
01:50:35: IPXEIGRP: better [0/0/45867776] route for A0000003 from
          BB001BB.00d0.baa2.ea60, flushing old [65535/255/45867776] route/paths
01:50:35:          external hop count in table 16, in update 1
```

You might want to use the SHOW IPX EIGRP EVENTS command instead. It shows all the same information in a much more legible format and does not consume any additional CPU (in other words, this command will not crash the router). Whether to use one or the other depends on what you need to accomplish. If you know that there was a problem just a minute or two previously, SHOW IPX EIGRP EVENTS provides a snapshot of what was going on at the time. A limited buffer space is available for historical review and in active networks could cover only a span of a few minutes. In that case, the DEBUG command would be necessary. Debug is also more useful when troubleshooting an intermittent problem, since you can monitor the activity as it occurs and you can send the output to a SYSLOG server for further analysis:

```
Event information for AS 1:
1    00:36:27.143 Change queue emptied, entries: 4
2    00:36:27.139 Metric set: DD001DD 128256
3    00:36:27.139 Update reason, delay: new if 4294967295
4    00:36:27.139 Update sent, RD: DD001DD 4294967295
5    00:36:27.139 Update reason, delay: metric chg 4294967295
6    00:36:27.139 Update sent, RD: DD001DD 4294967295
7    00:36:27.139 Route install: DD001DD 0.0000.0000.0000
8    00:36:27.139 Find FS: DD001DD 4294967295
9    00:36:27.139 Rcv update met/succmet: 128256 0
10   00:36:27.139 Rcv update dest/orig: DD001DD Redistributed
```

The DEBUG IPX EIGRP NEIGHBOR Command

Unlike many other DEBUG commands, the DEBUG IPX EIGRP NEIGHBOR command requires a specific EIGRP neighbor as part of the command. This information is obtained from the SHOW IPX EIGRP NEIGHBOR command. The following is the output from a test router running Version 11.3(11)a software:

```
Test#debug ipx eigrp nei 1 BB001BB.00d0.baa2.ea60
IPX Neighbor target enabled on AS 1 for BB001BB.00d0.baa2.ea60
Test#clear ipx eigrp nei
02:06:47: IPXEIGRP: External AB0101AB metric 45842176 hop 1 delay 1
02:06:47: IPXEIGRP: External DD001DD metric 128256 hop 1 delay 1
02:06:48: IPXEIGRP: B585A1E via BB001BB.00d0.baa2.ea60 metric 409600
02:06:48: IPXEIGRP: Received update from BB001BB.00d0.baa2.ea60 for net B585A1E
02:06:48: IPXEIGRP: better [0/0/409600] route for B585A1E from
         BB001BB.00d0.baa2.ea60, flushing old [65535/255/409600] route/paths
02:06:48:        external hop count in table 16, in update 1
02:06:48: IPXEIGRP: Received update from BB001BB.00d0.baa2.ea60 for net B585A1E
02:06:48: IPXEIGRP: create route to B585A1E via BB001BB.00d0.baa2.ea60, metric
         409600
02:06:48: IPXEIGRP: A585A1E via BB001BB.00d0.baa2.ea60 metric 307200
02:06:48: IPXEIGRP: Received update from BB001BB.00d0.baa2.ea60 for net A585A1E
02:06:48: IPXEIGRP: better [0/0/307200] route for A585A1E from
         BB001BB.00d0.baa2.ea60, flushing old [65535/255/307200] route/paths
02:06:48:        external hop count in table 16, in update 1
```

The **DEBUG IPX PACKET** Command

The DEBUG IPX PACKET command can be used to determine whether or not IPX packets are crossing through the router. It displays information about packets received, transmitted, or forwarded through the router. Although you can issue this command without turning on IPX routing in the router, there is no output until you do. In addition, IPX ROUTE-CACHE must be disabled by using the NO IPX ROUTE-CACHE command on all interfaces on which you want to see traffic. If the route cache function is not disabled, only the first packet to a destination will show up in the output. Table 8-7 lists each component.

```
1. Router#debug ipx packet
2. IPX packet debugging is on
3. 00:07:29: IPX: Fa0/0:A585A1E.0020.7819.8644->0.ffff.ffff.ffff ln= 81 tc=00
pt=00 ds=9001 ss=9001, rcvd
4. 00:07:29: IPX: Fa0/0:A585A1E.0020.7819.8644->0.ffff.ffff.ffff ln= 81 tc=00
pt=00 ds=9001 ss=9001, local
5. 00:07:31: IPX: Fa0/0:A585A1E.0020.7819.8644->A585A1E.ffff.ffff.ffff ln= 40
tc=00 pt=01 ds=0453 ss=0453, rcvd
6. 00:07:31: IPX: Fa0/0:A585A1E.0020.7819.8644->A585A1E.ffff.ffff.ffff ln= 40
tc=00 pt=01 ds=0453 ss=0453, local
7. 00:07:31: IPX: Fa0/0:A585A1E.0020.7819.8644->A585A1E.ffff.ffff.ffff ln=416
tc=00 pt=04 ds=0452 ss=0452, rcvd
8. 00:07:31: IPX: Fa0/0:A585A1E.0020.7819.8644->A585A1E.ffff.ffff.ffff ln=416
tc=00 pt=04 ds=0452 ss=0452, local
9. 00:07:31: IPX: Fa0/0:A585A1E.0020.7819.8644->0.ffff.ffff.ffff ln=129 tc=00
pt=00 ds=9001 ss=9001, rcvd
```

| **TABLE 8-7** | DEBUG IPX Packet Components |

Component	Description
Header	The header is always IPX
Source	The source address and interface of the packet
Destination	The destination address of the packet
ln=	Length
ds=	Destination socket
ss=	Source socket
Action	The action describes whether the packet was received, forwarded, or locally generated

From the preceding DEBUG, it is possible to conclude that both RIP (Socket 453) and NLSP (Socket 9001) are active on the Fast Ethernet segment. Lines 3, 4, and 9 are NLSP related, whereas Lines 5 and 6 are RIP. The remaining two lines (Lines 7 and 8) are SAP packets (Socket 452). Also recorded with the packet are the source and destination addresses. This information can be helpful when you are troubleshooting a routing loop, identifying updates coming in from the wrong interface. If you are not using NLSP on the router and the only routing packets you see are NLSP, it is possible to conclude that the router might be misconfigured.

The DEBUG IPX SAP Command

When a server is known to exist on a segment, but the router shows no SAPs for the server, the DEBUG IPX SAP command can be helpful in determining the cause of the omission. There are two options for this command. First is DEBUG IPX SAP ACTIVITY. SAP activity occurs regularly on an Ethernet segment running RIP due to the protocol requirements to advertise every 60 seconds (by default). The DEBUG IPX SAP ACTIVITY command provides a detailed output, including displays of services in SAP packets:

```
1. Router#debug ipx sap act
2. IPX service debugging is on
3. 01:47:55: IPXSAP: Response (in) type 0x2 len 480 src:BB001BB.00d0.baa2.ea60
dest:BB001BB.ffff.ffff.ffff(452)
4. 01:47:55:   type 0x4, "FAKE", CC001BB.0123.4567.8901(451), 3 hops
5. 01:47:55:   type 0x8202, "FAB-FAM_BROKER", 9B23663.0000.0000.0001(90B4), 1 hops
6. 01:47:55:   type 0x3E1, "FAB-FAM", 9B23663.0000.0000.0001(9056), 1 hops
7. 01:47:55:   type 0x26B, "FAM_____I_UYF@@@@DPJ",
9B23663. 0000.0000.0001(A), 1 hops
8. 01:47:55:   type 0x107, "FAB-FAM", 9B23663.0000.0000.0001(8104), 1 hops
9. 01:47:55:   type 0x278, "FAM_____I_UYF@@@@DPJ",
9B23663. 0000.0000.0001(640), 1 hops
10. 01:47:55:  type 0x4, "FAB-FAM", 9B23663.0000.0000.0001(451), 1 hops
11. 01:47:55: IPXSAP: FAB-FAM_BROKER rejected, route 9B23663 not in table
12. 01:47:55: IPXSAP: FAB-FAM rejected, route 9B23663 not in table
13. 01:47:55: IPXSAP: FAM_____I_UYF@@@@DPJ rejected,
route 9B23663 not in table
14. 01:47:55: IPXSAP: FAB-FAM rejected, route 9B23663 not in table
15. 01:47:55: IPXSAP: FAM_____I_UYF@@@@DPJ rejected,
route 9B23663 not in table
16. 01:47:55: IPXSAP: FAB-FAM rejected, route 9B23663 not in table
```

In the DEBUG output, the router is receiving SAP updates for the server FAB-FAM (Lines 6–10). Instead of adding the SAPs to the SAP table, the router has checked the forwarding table, found no route to the source network (9B23663), and rejected the SAPs (Line 13–15). Within a few minutes of enabling DEBUG IPX SAP ACTIVITY, you can identify the reason a SAP is not being added to the SAP table: Either the SAP is not being received or no route to the network is associated with the SAP.

The second command is DEBUG IPX SAP EVENTS. This command limits the amount of output to a subset of "interesting" packets. In this case, an event is forced to occur by shutting down the interface and bringing it back up again to show what happens when a route disappears. This is not necessary, since SAP updates are routinely propagated through the network:

```
1. Router#debug ipx sap eve
2. IPX service events debugging is on
3. Router#conf t
4. Enter configuration commands, one per line.  End with CNTL/Z.
5. Router(config)#in f0/0
6. Router(config-if)#shut
7. 00:33:02: IPXSAP: positing update to A585A1E.ffff.ffff.ffff via FastEthernet0/0
8. (broadcast) (full)
9. 00:33:02: IPX: Poisoning A585A1E/FastEthernet0/0 because interface down
10. 00:33:02: IPX: State of itf:net Fa0/0:A585A1E is [down]:[up]
11. 00:33:02: IPX: Bringdown FastEthernet0/0:A585A1E
12. 00:33:04: %LINK-5-CHANGED: Interface FastEthernet0/0, changed state to
administratively down
13. 00:33:05: %LINEPROTO-5-UPDOWN: Line protocol on Interface FastEthernet0/0,
changed state to down
14. Router(config-if)#no shut
15. 00:33:10: %SYS-5-CONFIG_I: Configured from console by console
16. 00:33:11: %LINK-3-UPDOWN: Interface FastEthernet0/0, changed state to up
17. 00:33:13: %LINEPROTO-5-UPDOWN: Line protocol on Interface FastEthernet0/0,
changed state to up
18. 00:33:13: IPXSAP: General Query src=A585A1E.00d0.baa2.ea60,
dst=A585A1E.ffff.ffff.ffff, packet sent (via FastEthernet0/0)
19. 00:33:15: IPXSAP: positing update to A585A1E.ffff.ffff.ffff via
FastEthernet0/0 (broadcast) (full)
```

As you can see, the ACTIVITY output displays very limited information regarding the routing process. The EVENTS output displays more information about the routing process, so, if you are interested in routing-related activity, you should use DEBUG IPX SAP EVENTS, whereas you would use DEBUG IPX SAP ACTIVITY if you are looking for SAP updates on specific SAPs.

EXERCISE 8-2

SAP DEBUGs

Using the same router and server from the previous lab, add the following access list to the router:

```
access-list 1000 deny FFFFFFFF 4
access-list 1000 permit FFFFFFFF 0
```

Apply this access list to the LAN interface using the following statement:

```
ipx input-sap-filter 1000
```

Use the SHOW IPX SERVERS command. Which SAP is missing? Try to log in to the server. Use the DEBUG IPX SAP ACTIVITY command to see how the router handles the incoming SAPs. Can you tell from this information whether or not the router has accepted the SAP and added it to its SAP table? Use the DEBUG IPX SAP EVENTS command to see how the router handles the incoming SAPs. Can you tell from this information whether or not the router has accepted the SAP and added it to its SAP table?

Solution: The File Server SAP Type (4) should no longer be listed. With the File Server SAP Type 4 missing, it is not possible to successfully log in to a server.

Line 3 clearly shows that the SAP Type 4 was received by the router. This is followed by several other SAPs (Lines 4–8). The router processes the SAPs through the access list and records all SAPs that are added to the SAP table (Lines 9–13). From the DEBUG IPX SAP ACTIVITY, it is possible to tell that a SAP was rejected by the absence of a line with the phrase "new entry accepted," but it is not possible to discern the reason for its rejection:

```
1. 00:52:06: IPXSAP: General Query src=10010.00d0.baa2.ea60,
dst=10010.ffff.ffff.ffff, packet sent (via FastEthernet0/0.1)
2. 00:52:06: IPXSAP: Response (in) type 0x2 len 416 src:10010.0200.0000.1011
dest:10010.00d0.baa2.ea60(452)
3. 00:52:06:   type 0x4, "FAB-FAM", 10011.0000.0000.0001(451), 1 hops
4. 00:52:06:   type 0x28A, "IAMGFFFFF000Y00010011", 10011.0000.0000.0001(90B0), 1
hops
5. 00:52:06:   type 0x278, "FAM_____@B@HA@@@@@DPJ",
10011.0000.0000.0001(C40), 1 hops
6. 00:52:06:   type 0x107, "FAB-FAM", 10011.0000.0000.0001(8104), 1 hops
7. 00:52:06:   type 0x26B, "FAM_____@B@HA@@@@@DPJ",
10011.0000.0000.0001(A), 1 hops
```

```
8. 00:52:06:  type 0x3E1, "FAB-FAM", 10011.0000.0000.0001(9056), 1 hops
9. 00:52:06: IPXSAP: type 0x28A server "IAMGFFFFF000Y00010011" distance lowered;
new entry accepted [1/1/2]
10. 00:52:06: IPXSAP: type 0x278 server
"FAM_____@B@HA@@@@DPJ" distance lowered; new entry
accepted [1/1/2]
11. 00:52:06: IPXSAP: type 0x107 server "FAB-FAM" distance lowered; new entry
accepted [1/1/2]
12. 00:52:06: IPXSAP: type 0x26B server
 "FAM_____@B@HA@@@@DPJ" distance lowered; new entry
accepted [1/1/2]
13. 00:52:06: IPXSAP: type 0x3E1 server "FAB-FAM" distance lowered; new entry
accepted [1/1/2]
14. 00:52:06: IPXSAP: positing update to 10010.ffff.ffff.ffff via
FastEthernet0/0.1 (broadcast) (flash)
15. 00:52:06: IPXSAP: suppressing null update to 10010.ffff.ffff.ffff
```

You cannot tell from DEBUG IPX SAP EVENTS whether or not the router has accepted the SAP and added it to its SAP table. You can see when a flash update is sent as a result of a change in the routing table. You can see when a SAP is accepted but not if a SAP has been rejected. Lines 2–6 correspond to Lines 9–13 of the previous output:

```
1. 00:48:42: IPXSAP: General Query src=10010.00d0.baa2.ea60,
dst=10010.ffff.ffff.ffff, packet sent (via FastEthernet0/0.1)
2. 00:48:42: IPXSAP: type 0x28A server "IAMGFFFFF000Y00010011" distance lowered;
new entry accepted [1/1/2]
3. 00:48:42: IPXSAP: type 0x278 server
FAM_____@B@HA@@@@DPJ" distance lowered; new entry
accepted [1/1/2]
4. 00:48:42: IPXSAP: type 0x107 server "FAB-FAM" distance lowered; new entry
accepted [1/1/2]
5. 00:48:42: IPXSAP: type 0x26B server
"FAM_____@B@HA@@@@DPJ" distance lowered; new entry
accepted [1/1/2]
6. 00:48:42: IPXSAP: type 0x3E1 server "FAB-FAM" distance lowered; new entry
accepted [1/1/2]
7. 00:48:42: IPXSAP: positing update to 10010.ffff.ffff.ffff via FastEthernet0/0.1
(broadcast) (flash)
8. 00:48:42: IPXSAP: suppressing null update to 10010.ffff.ffff.ffff
9. 00:48:48: IPXSAP: positing update to 10010.ffff.ffff.ffff via FastEthernet0/0.1
(broadcast) (full)
10. 00:48:48: IPXSAP: suppressing null update to 10010.ffff.ffff.ffff
```

The DEBUG IPX NLSP EVENTS Command

Like the DEBUG IPX EIGRP EVENTS command, the DEBUG IPX NLSP EVENTS command should be used to see every packet that triggers an NLSP event. This includes adjacency changes, LSP activity, and other NLSP-related traffic:

```
1. 01:02:35: %CLNS-5-ADJCHANGE: NLSP: Adjacency to FAB-FAM (FastEthernet0/0) Up,
new adjacency
2. 01:02:35: %CLNS-5-MULTICAST: NLSP: Broadcast address in use on FastEthernet0/0
3. 01:02:35: %LINEPROTO-5-UPDOWN: Line protocol on Interface FastEthernet0/0,
changed state to up
4. 01:02:35: NLSP: Age routes, lsp {1/8}
5. 01:02:35: NLSP: Age routes, lsp {1/8} (Exit)
6. 01:02:35: NLSP: Age srvces, lsp {1/8}
7. 01:02:35: NLSP: Age srvces, lsp {1/8} (Exit)
8. 01:02:35: NLSP: Age routes, lsp {2/10}
9. 01:02:35: NLSP: Age routes, lsp {2/10} (Exit)
10. 01:02:35: NLSP: Age srvces, lsp {2/10}
11. 01:02:35: NLSP: Age srvces, lsp {2/10} (Exit)
```

As the Fast Ethernet interface comes up, the router establishes an adjacency to the Novell server FAB-FAM (Line 1). The router notes that multicast is in use on this interface (Line 2). Interestingly, the adjacency is established *before* the interface is completely up (Line 3). The router proceeds to age out all previous LSPs for both the routes and the services (SAPs).

CERTIFICATION OBJECTIVE 8.03

PING

As is the case with TCP/IP, the IPX PING is one of the simplest and most useful troubleshooting tools available. There are two versions. The standard version does not allow you to set any special options. The extended IPX PING allows you to specify several different parameters.

The Standard IPX PING Command

There are several ways to send an IPX PING. The correct syntax is:

```
ping ipx network.node
```

When pinging a client or another router, the network is the external network address assigned to the wire, and the node is the MAC address associated with the device you want to ping. More often, you will need to ping a Novell server, in which case the network is the internal network address of the IPX server and the node is the address as it appears in the SAP tables (which is always 0000.0000.0001). Note that this is not the MAC address of the server. Here the server is pinged:

```
Router#ping ipx 9b23663.0000.0000.0001

Type escape sequence to abort.
Sending 5, 100-byte IPX Novell Echoes to 9B23663.0000.0000.0001, timeout is
2 seconds:
!!!!!
Success rate is 100 percent (5/5), round-trip min/avg/max = 1/2/4 ms
```

You can also send an IPX PING to a Novell server by skipping the IPX and simply specifying the network and node, using the format PING *NETWORK.NODE*. Just be aware that this is not the technically correct way to do it. If DOMAIN-LOOKUP is enabled, the router first tries to resolve the name using DNS. Otherwise, it skips the name translation, first trying to identify the address as an IP device. Once it realizes that this is not a valid IP address, the router switches to the IPX protocol:

```
Router#ping 9b23663.0000.0000.0001
Translating "9b23663.0000.0000.0001"

Type escape sequence to abort.
Sending 5, 100-byte IPX Novell Echoes to 9B23663.0000.0000.0001, timeout is
2 seconds:
!!!!!
Success rate is 100 percent (5/5), round-trip min/avg/max = 1/1/1 ms
```

Now the PING is directed at the client. Note that the network is the same as that configured on the router. The node address is the MAC address of the client workstation:

```
Router#ping ipx A585A1E.00a0.cc25.949f

Type escape sequence to abort.
Sending 5, 100-byte IPX Novell Echoes to A585A1E.00a0.cc25.949f, timeout is
2 seconds:
!!!!!
Success rate is 100 percent (5/5), round-trip min/avg/max = 1/2/4 ms
```

EXERCISE 8-3

IPX PING

For this lab, you need an IPX client workstation configured to use the 802.2 frame type on network 10010 and a router configured to use the same frame type and network addressing on the Ethernet interface. From the router, use the IPX PING option to test connectivity to the client workstation.

Solution: The router configuration should include this component on the appropriate LAN interface:

```
ipx network 10010 encapsulation SAP
```

Obtaining the MAC address of the workstation might have been slightly more challenging. Even if a client workstation is not using the TCP/IP protocol on the network interface card, as long as the software is on the workstation, it is possible to use the WINIPCFG (or IPCONFIG /ALL) command to obtain the MAC address. If TCP/IP is not loaded on the workstation at all, you might have had to use the diagnostic software that came with the NIC card itself or use a DEBUG command while the workstation attempts to browse the network.

The correct syntax to ping the workstation should be PING IPX *<<NETWORK.NODE>>*. Note that the router is very specific about the syntax of the node address, which must be in the format of FFFF.FFFF.FFFF.

The EXTENDED IPX PING Command

Sometimes you need to verify not only connectivity to the server but also that various types of packets are reliably delivered. Perhaps you suspect that the server is not responding to larger packet sizes or that the server is responding to only a limited number of packets. Some of the same options with the extended IPX PING exist as with the extended IP PING. The datagram size must be between 48 and 4096. You may specify a VERBOSE option or a Novell Standard Echo:

```
Router#ping
Protocol [ip]: ipx
Target IPX address: 9b23663.0000.0000.0001
Repeat count [5]:
Datagram size [100]: 1400
Timeout in seconds [2]:
Verbose [n]:
Type escape sequence to abort.
Sending 5, 1400-byte IPX Novell Echoes to 9B23663.0000.0000.0001, timeout is
2 seconds:
!!!!!
Success rate is 100 percent (5/5), round-trip min/avg/max = 4/4/4 ms
```

The VERBOSE option provides slightly more information about the response times:

```
Test#ping
Protocol [ip]: ipx
Target IPX address: 1004.4000.baa2.ea60
Repeat count [5]: 5
Datagram size [100]: 100
Timeout in seconds [2]: 2
Verbose [n]: y
Novell Standard Echo [n]:
Type escape sequence to abort.
Sending 5, 100-byte IPX cisco Echoes to 1004.4000.baa2.ea60, timeout is 2 seconds:
0 in 36 ms
1 in 36 ms
2 in 36 ms
3 in 36 ms
4 in 32 ms
Success rate is 100 percent (5/5), round-trip min/avg/max = 32/35/36 ms
```

The IPX TRACEROUTE Command

As of 12.0 IOS versions, Cisco supports the Novell TRACEROUTE and PING diagnostic capabilities. If both the source and end devices support these diagnostic options, an IPX TRACEROUTE, similar to an IP TRACEROUTE, can be a valuable tool. There are two options: a standard TRACEROUTE with the syntax TRACEROUTE IPX <<*NETWORK.NODE*>> and an extended TRACEROUTE with syntax as shown in the example that follows. Here the remote device is not responding:

```
Router#trace
Protocol [ip]: ipx
Target IPX address: 10011.0000.0000.0001
Numeric display [n]: y
Timeout in seconds [3]:
Probe count [3]:
Minimum Time to Live [0]:
Maximum Time to Live [1]:
Verbose [n]: y
Type escape sequence to abort.
Tracing the route to 10011.0000.0000.0001

  0  *  *  *
  1  *  *  *

... tracing the route using Diagnostic Requests
 2 10011.0000.0000.0001 0 msec 0 msec 4 msec
```

CERTIFICATION OBJECTIVE 8.04

Problem Isolation in IPX Networks

There are network components common to all networks, regardless of the Network Layer protocol. These components include basic hardware such as network interface cards (NICs), physical cable infrastructure (Ethernet, Token Ring, FDDI, fiber), network equipment (hubs, switches, and routers), and the associated network protocol-specific configuration software. In addition to these common components, Novell IPX includes NetWare-specific components (SAPs in particular), along with a choice of frame types or encapsulation. This section looks at specific types of commonly encountered problems.

The Client

The typical call comes in on Monday morning and goes something like this: "Everything was fine when I left on Friday, but this morning my computer says it can't find the server." Starting with the client workstation and working your way into the network is the best direction to take. Check to see whether or not other users at the same location are affected.

Can you ping the client? If you work in an environment with both TCP/IP and IPX, you have the opportunity to verify twice. Since we know that many IPX network problems have to do with frame type mismatches, if you can ping the client using TCP/IP but not using IPX, this would be the best place to start.

Do the encapsulation types on the server and on the client match? If the client is configured for autoframe type detection and if there are multiple frame types on the Ethernet segment, each time the client workstation is powered on, the possibility of grabbing the wrong frame type is very real.

NIC Failure

If you cannot ping the client using either the TCP/IP or IPX protocol, you need to verify that the network cable is properly connected. Verify the Physical Layer and resolve any problems there before troubleshooting the Network Layer.

Cabling

If you have connected another workstation to the same cable and the problem is still occurring, the most likely cause of the performance problem is the cable itself. There are three cable segments that must be tested: from the user's workstation to the wall, from the wall to the switch or hub, and from the data center to the user's office. It is a common mistake to replace the patch cables, find the same problem exists, and assume that there is no cable issue. Unless all three segments have been verified, the potential cable problem has not been eliminated.

Encapsulation

One of the most common problems in an IPX network is the use of different encapsulations. Four frame types can be used on an Ethernet network, two in Token Ring, and three in FDDI. To further confuse matters, Cisco and Novell have different names for the frame types. Table 8-8 lists each frame type by nomenclature.

Novell-ether is also known as *802.3 raw*. Sap, called *Ethernet_802.2* or *Novell_802.2*, is the IEEE standard 802.3 frame format. Cisco routers default to what *used* to be the default frame type on a Novell server. Ethernet defaults to *novell-ether*. Token Ring defaults to *sap*, and FDDI defaults to *snap*. If you have newer servers or if the server is not using the default frame type (from Novell 3.x days), you must manually specify the frame type.

	Network	Cisco Nomenclature	Novell Nomenclature
TABLE 8-8 IPX Frame Types	Token Ring	Sap	Token-Ring
		Snap	Token-Ring_Snap
	Ethernet	Novell-ether	Ethernet_802.3
		Sap	Ethernet_802.2
		Snap	Ethernet_Snap
		Arpa	Ethernet_II
	FDDI	Snap	Fddi_Snap
		Novell-fddi	Fddi-Raw
		Sap	Fddi-802.2

In earlier Novell client software implementations (and their corresponding Microsoft clients for Novell networks), the frame type had to be manually specified. Today, the client software allows the workstation to "autosense" the frame type, in a way that is similar to the autosense of the network speed and duplex. Autosensing works well when only a single frame type is in use on the wire. With multiple frame types in use, the client should be manually configured for the correct encapsulation.

Bridges and Switches

Although both bridges and switches operate at Layer 2 of the OSI model, you need to watch out for a couple of potential pitfalls. Not too many companies have bridges connecting network segments anymore, but there are still some.

Bridging Between Media Types

There are frame encapsulation issues with IPX when bridging between FDDI and Ethernet. The FDDI module, by default, converts Ethernet 802.2 to FDDI 802.2 frame format. For the remaining frame types (Ethernet II, 802.3, and snap), FDDI translates all of these to FDDI SNAP. The FDDI module reads the incoming packets and makes a decision regarding the incoming frame type. If you are running multiple frame types on the Ethernet segment, the FDDI module will not always pick the correct frame type. Therefore, it is critical to specify the frame type conversions.

SPANNING TREE

With Layer 2 switches, it is not uncommon to see switches installed that have not been customized. Since every port can potentially lead to a loop, by default all switches come with SPANNING TREE enabled on every port. The SPANNING TREE algorithm goes through the listening, learning, forwarding stages in order every time a device activates on the line. If a NetWare workstation is connected to a port with SPANNING TREE enabled, the workstation might not be able to discover the IPX frame type, and the workstation cannot find the Novell tree because the workstation times out before the SPANNING TREE process is completed. The solution is to place have the switch place the port into the forwarding mode immediately. This is accomplished with the command SPANNING-TREE PORTFAST.

Trunking

Trunking works in conjunction with VLANs to allow multiple VLANs to use the same wire. Trunking is normally used between switches or between switches and routers, although it can be used to communicate with some servers. When connected to a typical workstation or server, trunking should be disabled. This is because the frame type used across a trunk port is not a typical Ethernet frame. Thus, the typical NIC has no chance of decoding it.

EtherChannel

EtherChannel, also called Fast EtherChannel (FEC) or Gigabit EtherChannel (GEC), allows multiple fast ethernet or gigabit cables to be bonded together to appear as a single cable. Typically, EtherChannel is used to aggregate bandwidth between switches. As they do trunking, some servers support FEC. When connected to a typical workstation or server, EtherChannel should be disabled. Since both ends of an EtherChannel link coordinate on the configuration, a misconfiguration causes the link to fail.

Port Failure

What appears to be a port failure might actually be a configuration error. First, verify that the port speed and duplex settings match. Switch port failures are difficult to detect. Sometimes the port is not active, but in many cases, it is active but does not function properly. Here are a few telltale clues to watch for:

■ Multiple users report similar problems within a short time period, and all users are physically connected to the same switch blade.

■ Connectivity is immediately established by moving to a different switch port, with an identical configuration (including VLANs).

■ A workstation that is not having problems is connected to the switch port and is unable to communicate.

CASE STUDY

Switch Port Failure

An end user called during the day in the middle of the week to complain that he was not able to see any of the IPX servers on the network. The end user reported that he was able to access the NT servers without any problems. Using a standard PING over TCP/IP to check the connectivity to the workstation, the network administrator verified what the end user said. The ping was successful. Physical connectivity having been verified, the network administrator proceeded to verify logical connectivity.

The workstation configuration was checked for the proper frame type and network address. Network Neighborhood displayed only NT servers. None of the Novell servers were visible. IPX was properly loaded and bound to the NIC. Unable to find any obvious problems, the network administrator checked to see whether or not the server was accessible from other workstations, which it was. The network administrator decided to eliminate the cable and the switch as the source of the trouble. He unplugged the cable from the back of the workstation and connected the cable from the back of the neighboring workstation (which was functioning properly) to the problem workstation. For reasons no one could explain, everything started working. He connected the cable from the problem workstation to the neighboring workstation, and it began to exhibit similar problems.

By this time, he knew that it was either a problem with the cable or a problem on the switch. The counters on the switch indicated that packets were being received at a normal rate, but the number of packets going out to the workstation was relatively low. No Physical Layer errors were reported by the switch. By moving the cable at the switch end, he was able to confirm that there was a problem with the port on the switch. The port was marked as bad, and a note was made that when there was time, the blade needed to be replaced.

The next day, a different user contacted the Network Group for assistance. This user was able to access the Novell servers but was unable to access the NT servers. About an hour later, a third user contacted the Network Group for assistance, indicating that although everything was working, everything was slow. By the time the fourth user called in, it was determined that each user who called was connected to the same blade. Moving each cable to a spare port on another blade resolved the problem.

This is an example of a cascading port failure problem that was particularly difficult to detect because the symptoms appeared to be protocol related.

The Local Gateway

The local gateway is usually the router. In this case, you have an advantage because most of the time you know about any changes that have been made to the router. If you are not sure, assuming that SERVICE TIMESTAMP is enabled, you can use the SHOW RUN command to see how long it has been since the configuration was last modified. If the configuration has been modified, check for the following:

■ Does the interface have the correct external network number configured? Especially in new installations with new servers, there is the possibility that the internal network number was configured instead of the external network number. With existing installations, if the server administrator made any changes without notifying the network administrator, checking the basics is well worth the few minutes invested.

■ Are any IPX access lists configured? The fastest way to eliminate an IPX access list as the source of a problem is to remove it from the interface in question, as long as you can do so without the risk of causing other problems. If eliminating the IPX access list is not an option, append a line to the access list to deny all traffic and to log the denials. Check the logs for errors. When you're finished, remember to remove the log keyword from the end of the access list. If you are using the named access list feature, you can remove just the individual line entry; if you are using a typical standard or extended access list, you must remove the access list and recreate it in the router.

- Is the global command IPX ROUTING enabled? It should be obvious if it is missing, because all of the associated IPX commands in the router will have vanished as well. One of the advantages of working with the Cisco IOS is the ability to abbreviate commands. If you are not careful, you can inadvertently issue a command without realizing it. Perhaps someone was trying to remove a static route or take out IPX ROUTER RIP.

- Verify that the MAC address appearing after the IPX ROUTING command is not a duplicate (this can happen if you copy and paste the configuration from one router to another). If this is the case, you want to be careful how you fix this problem. The obvious way is to remove the IPX ROUTING statement and reenter it, allowing the router to select its own MAC address. However, doing so will require you to reconfigure IPX in the router. A way to avoid this is to obtain the MAC address of the router and re-enter the command using the correct MAC address.

Port Failure

Port failures on routers are usually easy to spot. Generally, the line protocol is down and down, or up and down. Although not an everyday occurrence, port failures do occur on Cisco routers. If you have eliminated the cable, the switch or hub, the IOS version, and the configuration, there is a very strong likelihood that you are dealing with a hardware problem on your router. Consider a couple of real-life examples.

CASE STUDY

Token Ring Port Failure

The Token Ring interface on a 2500 series router was up and the state was "initializing." In other words, the router was trying desperately to insert itself into the ring, but the insertion never completed. The network administrator tried replacing the cable. Then she shut down a workstation that was functioning fine and connected the router to that workstation's port on the MAU. Then she shut down every workstation on the ring, so only the router was powered up. Still, the router never got past the initialization process. While the router was trying to insert itself into the ring, the ring was essentially not operational. The only resolution to this problem was to replace the router itself.

CASE STUDY

Ethernet Port Failure

In another case, a company had six 2610 routers installed at small branch offices. The router was powered up, configured, and functioning properly. Devices on the Ethernet segment were able to see and communicate with Novell servers at remote locations.

For several days, everything was fine. One morning the network administrator received a call from one of the branches indicating that they could not see any of the Novell servers. Checking the router revealed that the remote servers were all visible to the router at the remote branch. The administrator could send an IPX PING to the workstations on the local segment. The only unusual thing he noticed was that there was absolutely no indication that any packets were crossing the Ethernet interface. Every time the administrator checked the counters, there were zero bytes received. Shutting down the interface and bringing it back up did not resolve the problem.

In desperation, the administrator reloaded the router. Everything came back to life. Several days later, the administrator received the same complaint from the same branches. This process repeated two or three times. A check of the IOS bugs revealed nothing. They had the same version of IOS running in almost 200 other 2610 routers but were not having any problems with them. Ultimately, a call to the Cisco TAC revealed that a hardware bug was associated with the motherboard of the 2610 routers, causing the Ethernet port to stop passing any traffic.

Cabling

Cable problems can masquerade as performance problems. With workstations, the problem can be difficult to identify. Fortunately, routers and switches provide us with adequate tools to identify the potential for a cable problem. First, look for CRC errors on the interface. This is a sure sign of a Physical Layer problem and is almost always caused by the cable. Expensive tools are available to test the quality of cables, but these are rarely used in the real world to resolve problems. It is far simpler to replace or reterminate the cable.

Unless you are using known good cable (cable that has been used on another device that does not have problems with CRC and other Physical Layer errors) from end to end, you have not eliminated the cable as the source of the trouble.

Particularly when installing new devices, check to make certain the *right* cable has been used. A patch cable used for T1 circuits could look like a Category 5 cable, but it does not work. A crossover cable might look like a Category 5 cable, but it does not work. An RJ11 cable will fit in the jack, but it does not work, either. Similarly, the wrong transceiver can be used, preventing the line from becoming active.

Encapsulation

Once you have verified that the problem is not with the client or with the server, the next step is to check the router itself. If no IPX traffic is getting past the router, first check to see whether or not the router can see any IPX devices on the local segment. If there is a server on the segment, use the SHOW IPX SERVERS command. If you see no servers listed, chances are either the frame type or the network address is invalid. Due to differences in nomenclature, encapsulation discrepancies are not an uncommon problem with new installations. With existing installations, this situation generally occurs when servers are upgraded to newer versions with a different default frame type.

Routing Protocol

On the LAN segment, the potential for routing protocol problems is relatively low when you are using RIP. Routing protocol issues come up when someone decides to experiment with the settings on the server or on the router. This troubleshooting tactic usually falls under the "What changed?" category. More insidious are the NetWare servers acting as RIP routers with multiple NICs. What can happen in this case is a routing loop.

Because of the additional configuration elements, NLSP has more potential than RIP for routing protocol issues. Knowing how to read and understand the diagnostic commands available in the router will be your most valuable resource. If you have access to the server(s), you can also use the Novell console command LOAD IPXCON, which allows you to see the network from the server's perspective. Comparing the router and the server will help you target your investigation.

When you suspect a problem associated with the routing protocol itself, use the SHOW commands and the DEBUG commands discussed earlier in the chapter. You can develop a checklist customized to your environment by mixing and matching these commands to the types of problems you encounter most frequently. For example, if you do not use NLSP in your environment, your checklist would not include any of the NLSP commands but would include RIP for the LAN segment and either RIP or EIGRP for the WAN segment. If you use NLSP and IPXWAN exclusively, your checklist would include those commands alone.

Access Lists

Access lists can be the source of many problems, whether applied to the LAN segment or the WAN segment. The kind of access list and where it is applied needs to be taken into account when you are troubleshooting a problem. When dealing with a LAN issue, use the SHOW IPX INTERFACE command to check whether or not an access list is applied. If it is, use the SHOW IPX ACCESS-LIST command to review the access list to see if it could be causing the problem.

Usually the problem is that a local client cannot access a remote server. Use the SHOW IPX SERVERS command to check the router closest to the server to see whether or not it can see the server. If it can and the router closest to the client cannot, you might be dealing with an access list issue. Have the client use the SLIST command at the DOS prompt to list all the NetWare servers visible to it. If the server is not in the list, check to see whether or not you are filtering the route to the server's network or whether you are filtering the SAP itself.

Remote Routers

All the same principles apply to troubleshooting remote routers as apply to troubleshooting local routers. The only real difference is that with remote routers, you must troubleshoot the connections between the two routers. Here we look primarily at the connections from router to router.

Port Failure

Because port failures are relatively rare, the tendency is to dismiss the possibility entirely. Following good troubleshooting procedure, however, it is clear that every individual component must be considered and evaluated. There is no easy way to eliminate the port as the source of a problem when no other connection can be established on the port. With a WAN connection, you rarely have multiple circuits available so that you can move one circuit over to the port just to verify that the port is functioning properly. You need to rely on the commands available in the router to determine whether the port is functioning properly. Pay particular attention to any counters associated with Physical Layer errors, such as CRCs, runts, and so on. You can also watch the counters to see if traffic is flowing in both directions.

Cabling

WAN cabling problems are mostly encountered in new installations or upgrades. Usually the circuit appears to be down, when actually the wrong cable was used or it was connected to the wrong interface. Use the SHOW CONTROLLERS command to verify that the right cable is connected to the interface.

Other than the difficulty of working over the telephone with someone who is often not familiar with the equipment, troubleshooting remote routers suffers from the same cable problems as local routers. If you have checked the physical cable connections, identified potential cable problems (usually using the CRC counters as an indicator), and replaced the cable when appropriate and you are *still* having problems, you could be dealing with a circuit failure, a port failure, or hardware failure of the device connected to the router.

Circuit Failures

Circuit failures are one of the most common causes of problems associated with a remote client attempting to access a server. Check to make sure that the link is stable. You should not see CRC errors or interface resets. Flapping circuits can cause instability throughout the network. Depending on the routing protocol in use, a flapping circuit can force the router to broadcast new route and SAP updates to all routers in the network, resulting in high traffic.

IPX Network Numbers

If you have access to RCONSOLE to the server or have a server administrator who can work with you, from the System Console have the administrator LOAD IPXCON, select Services, and display Entire Services Table. If the server can see the rest of the network, the IPX network configurations of the router and the server are probably not the issue. Access lists to the server are probably not the issue, either, if the server can see the rest of the network.

Routing Protocols

A number of problems can be encountered with relation to routing protocols. IPX routing protocols are often tuned to reduce the frequency and quantity of broadcasts. Many different timers can be adjusted. In many companies, two groups are responsible for the network as a whole; one group handles the servers, and the other handles the infrastructure. It is not uncommon to find that one group has adjusted the timers, whereas the other group has not. Maintaining good communications between the two groups will result in fewer problems. Some timers are specific to the IPX protocol suite as well as the routing protocol.

RIP routes can be lost during heavy bandwidth utilization. RIP can actually cause heavy bandwidth utilization because, by default, RIP advertises the full routing table every 30 seconds.

In a large network, the routes might never fully converge if there are frequent changes. RIP-specific parameters that may be configured at the interface level are listed in Table 8-9.

Although the timers can be different for each interface, every device connected to that interface needs to have the same timers configured. In other words, if a RIP timer is set on an Ethernet interface, all the servers and all other routers on that Ethernet network must use the same timers.

If you are using the NLSP routing protocol, check to make sure that the server supports it as well. Using SHOW IPX NLSP NEIGHBOR, verify that you have an NLSP neighbor relationship. Check the link-state database using SHOW IPX NLSP DATABASE. If you are using the NLSP routing protocol, check to make sure that

TABLE 8-9   RIP-Specific Interface Timers

Command	Description
OUTPUT-RIP-DELAY	Interpacket delay for RIP updates
RIP-MAX-PACKETSIZE	Maximum size of RIP packets being sent on interface
RIP-MULTIPLIER	Multiple of RIP update interval for aging of RIP routes
RIP-RESPONSE-DELAY	Delay in answering RIP on this interface
TRIGGERED-RIP-DELAY	Interpacket delay for triggered RIP updates (overrides OUTPUT-RIP-delay for triggered updates only)
TRIGGERED-RIP-HOLDDOWN	Initial HOLDDOWN for triggered RIP updates

IPX RIP is disabled on the WAN segments and on any other interfaces on which it is not needed. By default, IPX RIP will be active. You must manually disable it. You should see an entry in the configuration that looks something like this:

```
ipx router rip
no network 1001
```

NLSP-specific timers can be set at the interface level. These are detailed in Table 8-10. As with RIP, the timers must match on all devices connected to the same segment.

NLSP may also be customized with a link metric. Since the link metric is used in calculating the shortest path, improperly configured metrics can cause traffic to take a less than optimal path. By default, Cisco's implementation of NLSP operates in multicast mode on multiaccess networks. Multicast is the recommended mode, but it can be disabled. Note that NetWare 5 servers default to using broadcast instead of multicast.

On a multiaccess network with a number of routers, it is better to specify the priority of each router rather than to allow the protocol to select a priority for you. For example, if you have three 2500 Series routers on a LAN segment along with a 4700 router, you probably want the 4700 router to control the NLSP database. In that case, you want to make sure that the priority of the 4700 router is set to be better than that of the 2500 routers. Otherwise, the priority negotiation process might result in one of the 2500 routers being responsible for the SPF calculations, adversely affecting that router's performance.

Finally, it is possible to manually specify, as you can with a server, whether to use RIP and/or SAP compatibility mode for backward compatibility with non-NLSP devices. Table 8-11 lists the syntax for each command.

TABLE 8-10	Command	Description
NLSP-Specific Interface Timers	CSNP-INTERVAL	Sets CSNP transmission interval
	HELLO-INTERVAL	Sets hello transmission interval
	HELLO-MULTIPLIER	Sets hello holding time multiplier
	LSP-INTERVAL	Sets LSP transmission (pacing) interval
	RETRANSMIT-INTERVAL	Sets LSP retransmission interval

TABLE 8-11	**Command**	**Description**
NLSP-Specific Interface Options	IPX NLSP METRIC	Sets link metric
	IPX NLSP MULTICAST	Selects multicast or broadcast addressing on LANs
	IPX NLSP PRIORITY	Sets designated router election priority
	IPX NLSP RIP	RIP compatibility mode
	IPX NLSP SAP	SAP compatibility mode

If you are using the IPX EIGRP routing protocol, check to make sure that IPX RIP is disabled on the WAN segments and on any other interfaces on which it is not needed. By default, IPX RIP is active. You must manually disable it as described in the previous section.

Use the SHOW IPX EIGRP NEIGHBOR command to verify that you have established an IPX EIGRP neighbor relationship. EIGRP will not transmit routes until a neighbor relationship is established. If the neighbor relationship is established and there are still no routes, use the SHOW IPX EIGRP TOPOLOGY command to check the routes.

EIGRP-specific timers may be set at the interface level. These are detailed in Table 8-12. As with RIP and NLSP, the timers must match on all devices connected to the same segment. Note that the EIGRP commands do not require the keyword EIGRP as part of the interface command.

TABLE 8-12	**Command**	**Description**
IPX EIGRP-Specific Interface Timers	HELLO-INTERVAL	Configures IPX EIGRP hello interval
	HOLD-DOWN	Configures IPX EIGRP route hold-down time
	HOLD-TIME	Configures IPX EIGRP hold time

EXERCISE 8-4

Timer Mismatch

For this exercise, you need a Novell server (SERVER) attached to a hub. To this same hub, connect a router (ROUTERA). Connect a V.35 DCE cable to a serial port on ROUTERA, and connect the other end of the cable to a V.35 DTE cable, which is then connected to another router (ROUTERB).

Configure SERVER to use IPX RIP to communicate on network 10010 using the 802.2 frame type.

Set ROUTERA to use network 10010 with the 802.2 frame type on the LAN segment. Configure the serial port to communicate using HDLC encapsulation, with IPX network BADBAD. Use IPX RIP for network 10010 and IPX EIGRP 1 for network BADBAD.

Set ROUTERB to use HDLC encapsulation on the serial port, with IPX network BADBAD. Use IPX EIGRP 1 for network BADBAD.

Check to make sure that all the appropriate server SAPs are visible in both ROUTERA and ROUTER B. Once you have verified this, add the following statement to the serial interface on ROUTERA:

```
ipx hello-interval eigrp 1 10
```

Observe what happens to the neighbor status on each router by continuously observing the output of the SHOW IPX EIGRP NEIGHBORS command. What happened to the IPX routes? What happened to the IPX SAPs? Explain why you observed these results. Remove the previous statement and add the following statement to the same interface:

```
ipx hold-time eigrp 1 60
```

Disable IPX EIGRP on ROUTERB by entering the following command:

```
ipx down BADBAD
```

Observe what happens to the neighbor status on each router by continuously observing the output of the SHOW IPX EIGRP NEIGHBORS command. Explain why you observed these results.

Solution: The configuration of ROUTERA should include the following statements:

```
ipx routing 00d0.baa2.ea60
interface FastEthernet0/0.1
 ipx network 10010 encapsulation SAP
interface Serial1/0
ipx network BADBAD
ipx router eigrp 1
 network BADBAD
ipx router rip
 no network BADBAD
```

The configuration of ROUTERB should include the following statements:

```
ipx routing 00e0.1eb9.11b3
interface Serial1/0
ipx network BADBAD
ipx router eigrp 1
 network BADBAD
ipx router rip
 no network BADBAD
```

Setting the hello interval on only one router results in differing timers on each router. Therefore, one router continues to believe that a neighbor relationship is established, while the other removes the neighbor status until the next hello is received. Because EIGRP ties routes to neighbor relationships, and SAPs are tied to routes, all the routes and SAPs associated with the neighbor disappear.

Setting the IPX EIGRP hold time on a router causes the router to hold open a neighbor relationship unless it is otherwise closed. In the lab, the IPX network was properly brought down by ROUTERB, so ROUTERA received notice that the neighbor relationship was no longer active. For this reason, ROUTERA terminated the neighbor relationship immediately instead of waiting 60 seconds. This command takes effect only if ROUTERA hears nothing from ROUTERB. The most likely cause would be a circuit failure.

The Server

Any time you deal with a server issue, ask yourself whether or not clients on the same segment as the server are having difficulty reaching the server. If you can eliminate the router and all its associated processes as the source of the problem, you have saved yourself a lot of work.

Next ask yourself what could go wrong. As with a workstation, you could be dealing with a NIC failure, cabling problems, network numbering issues, and the ever-present encapsulation questions. Do not overlook the obvious questions. Check to make sure the server is powered on and that the server has been loaded. Unlike an NT server, a Novell server can be configured to wait for a command to be entered to load the server before making itself available. If you are unable to see the server in the local router's SAP tables and if users are able to access remote servers, the problem is likely to be with the server itself. If you are unable to see the server in the local router's SAP tables and if users are unable to access remote servers, the problem is more likely to be related to the connection from the router to the LAN, the IPX network addressing, or the IPX frame type.

NIC Failure

When a server NIC fails, you usually know pretty quickly. The Help Desk is deluged with a flood of calls saying that the server is not available. A quick check in the router shows that the server is no longer listed in the SAP tables. If you have excellent documentation and know to which port the server is physically connected, you can check the switch to see if there is a valid link on the port. The absence of a link is a sure indication that there is a problem, but it might still be a cable issue. Before concluding that the problem is with the NIC, check the cabling, since cable problems are responsible for the majority of LAN problems.

Cabling

Clean cable terminations are more important with 100BaseT connections than with 10BaseT. The faster connections are less tolerant of electrical errors and are more likely to fail. You can tell whether or not there are errors by checking the switch statistics; look for CRC errors in particular, but runts and malformed frames are also indications of cable problems.

NetWare servers do not happily tolerate being disconnected from the network. They begin to beep constantly, and a message like the one shown in Figure 8-1 is displayed on the screen. If you receive a call from an end user who states that the server has started beeping regularly, either the cable has been disconnected or the server is receiving route advertisements for a different network address on its own frame type.

FIGURE 8-1

Disconnected
cable reported by
a Novell server

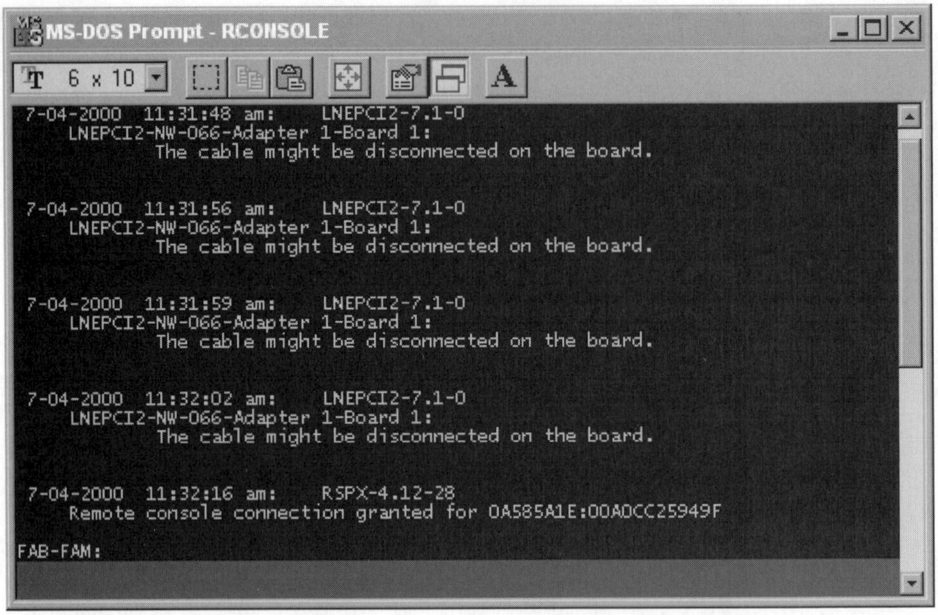

```
MS-DOS Prompt - RCONSOLE                                    _ □ ×

T  6 x 10 ▼   [] 🗎 🗐 🔲 🗐 🗗   A

7-04-2000  11:31:48 am:      LNEPCI2-7.1-0
    LNEPCI2-NW-066-Adapter 1-Board 1:
          The cable might be disconnected on the board.

7-04-2000  11:31:56 am:      LNEPCI2-7.1-0
    LNEPCI2-NW-066-Adapter 1-Board 1:
          The cable might be disconnected on the board.

7-04-2000  11:31:59 am:      LNEPCI2-7.1-0
    LNEPCI2-NW-066-Adapter 1-Board 1:
          The cable might be disconnected on the board.

7-04-2000  11:32:02 am:      LNEPCI2-7.1-0
    LNEPCI2-NW-066-Adapter 1-Board 1:
          The cable might be disconnected on the board.

7-04-2000  11:32:16 am:      RSPX-4.12-28
    Remote console connection granted for 0A585A1E:00A0CC25949F

FAB-FAM:
```

Network Numbers

IPX servers have two network numbers: one internal and the other external. The external network number must be shared by all other devices on the network. The internal number must be unique. If the router is configured with a different number from the server, the server begins reporting errors, both audibly (a loud beep occurring at regular intervals) and visibly (a message on the console screen that repeats itself regularly). If this occurs, you should have the server administrator use the LOAD INETCFG command to open the network configuration screen for the server.

Next, the server administrator should open the bindings for the NIC for the IPX protocol, and you can compare what the administrator has to what is programmed in the router. Someone has to change his or her configuration to resolve the problem. The decision about who that "someone" is resides at the political layer of the organization.

Encapsulations

An IPX server can have multiple frame types, each with its own network number, bound to a single interface card. In order to support this structure, a Cisco router can also have multiple frame types, each with its own network number, applied to a single interface. Cisco is phasing out the use of secondary addressing. If you are using secondary addressing, before upgrading to a new version of IOS check to make sure that the version you will be using supports secondary addressing. If it does not, change your configurations to use subinterfaces before the upgrade.

exam
ⓦatch

You can configure only a single network for each frame type per interface. You may have one network for each frame type, but you may not have multiple networks with the same frame type. If you are using NLSP, you must use subinterfaces to configure the separate frame types.

CERTIFICATION OBJECTIVE 8.05

IPX Symptoms, Problems, and Action Plans

Throughout the chapter, we have seen examples of symptoms, problems, and potential remedies for those problems. This section is intended to be a quick reference revolving around specific types of problems. We can't cover every possible scenario, so the most common problems are addressed in this section. You can consider this a list of reminders to point you in the right direction when you run into trouble.

Before troubleshooting the IPX implementation, you must first eliminate Layers 1 and 2 as the source of the trouble. Refer to the appropriate chapter in this book for specifics on how to troubleshoot those layers. A firm understanding of the IPX protocol suite will bear more fruit than memorizing a list of symptoms and resolutions. As you read through the following tips, challenge yourself to explain the reason that a specific action will resolve the problem.

Two of the most common problems encountered in an IPX network are encapsulation mismatch and improperly written access lists. Of course, port failures and circuit failures are just as common in an IPX network as they are in an IP network. If yours is a new installation, check with the server administrator to ensure that the router is configured correctly. If it is an existing installation that was previously stable, verify that the connection to the LAN is stable, then check with the server administrator to see if any changes have been made to the server. In all cases, check to see if any router configuration changes have been made recently, and ensure that these changes are not contributing to the problem at hand.

Client Cannot Access Local Server

As a general rule, if an individual client cannot access a local server, the router is not the source of the problem. Even if all the clients on a segment cannot access a server, the router might still not be the source of the problem. Even so, there is always the possibility that a network component is contributing to or is the source of the local problem. For this reason, it is important to understand the complete connection process.

A Physical Problem

When a client on a local segment is unable to access a server on a local segment, the cause is often physical. You might want to use a standard IPX PING to verify that the router can see the workstation. If you are in a mixed server environment, check to see if the client can see any other servers (NT, UNIX) or workstations. If it cannot, verify physical connectivity before troubleshooting the Network Layer.

SCENARIO & SOLUTION

Are you able to successfully IPX PING the client?	**Yes:** Physical connectivity and encapsulation are correct. IPX PING the server. **No:** Check to see if other protocols are working.
Are you able to successfully IPX PING the server?	**Yes:** Physical connectivity and encapsulation are correct. Check the router for the server's SAPs. **No:** Gather information, verify server configuration.
Is TCP/IP or another protocol working?	**Yes:** This is not a Physical Layer problem. Check the Logical Layer. **No:** Troubleshoot the Physical Layer.
Are clients on the local segment able to connect to a local server?	**Yes:** This is not a Physical Layer problem. Check the Logical Layer. **No:** Troubleshoot the Physical Layer.
Do the network and frame types on the server match what is configured in the router?	**Yes:** Troubleshoot the Physical Layer. **No:** Correct the configuration and check again.

o n t h e
(j) o b

Always remember that there are three cables you need to check. The first is the patch cable from the hub or switch to the patch panel. The second is from the patch panel to the wall in the client's office. The third is the from the wall in the client's office to the client's workstation. It is not sufficient to replace the patch cables on either end to eliminate a potential cable problem.

Encapsulation

Once you have verified that the cable is not at fault, check the configuration of the workstation. The default IPX frame type on Novell servers changed from 802.3 to 802.2, whereas the default Novell client installation changed from specifying a frame type to "auto" as an option. In an environment in which multiple frame types are used, the client workstation must be configured to use a specific frame type. Automatic frame type detection from the client workstation depends on the client seeing the proper frame type at initialization.

Server Issues

You might encounter a situation in which some clients can log in to the server some of the time, but there is no consistency. Check to see if there have been any upgrades or changes to the server. On occasion, a well-intentioned server administrator will have made changes to the server's network configuration without realizing that those changes have to be coordinated with the router.

Client Cannot Access Remote Server

When a client is unable to access a remote server, it is often easier to start with the remote router (the router closest to the client) than to start with the client

SCENARIO & SOLUTION	
Is IPX installed on the workstation?	**No:** Install IPX and configure it.
Does the client have the correct frame type?	**No:** Correct the frame type.
Is the client configured with the correct network address?	**No:** Correct the network address.

SCENARIO & SOLUTION

Use LOAD IPXCON at the Server Console to see the server configuration. Is the frame type correct?	**No:** Change the frame type on the server and reinitialize the server.
Use LOAD IPXCON at the Server Console to see the server configuration. Is the network address correct?	**No:** Change the network address on the server and reinitialize the server.
Have the number of client licenses been exceeded?	**Yes:** Buy more client licenses and install them on the server.
Is the server configured to send out SAPs?	**No:** Configure the server to advertise SAPs.
Is the server using the correct routing protocol?	**No:** Configure the server to use the correct routing protocol.
Use the SHOW IPX SERVERS command to list the SAPs visible to the router. Are all the SAPs visible? Does the number of SAPs change?	**Server SAPs not visible:** Verify server configuration; Monitor Track On.
Use the TRACK ON console command on the Novell server. Is the server sending and receiving all SAPs?	**No:** Verify Server configuration and check router access-lists.
Use the SHOW IPX ROUTE *NETWORK* command. Is there a route to both the external and the internal network for the server?	**No:** Check the router configuration, then check the routing process.

workstation itself for purposes of troubleshooting. This process eliminates the need to follow the same procedures detailed previously to eliminate local wiring and client workstation configuration issues. A time saving step is to first check the remote router to see if the server SAPs are visible and pointed to the correct interface. If they are, start with the client workstation. If they are not, resolve this problem first, then check to see if the client problem is resolved as well.

Gateway Router Issues

The list of potential problems related to the router includes, among other things, IPX configuration issues, problems with forwarding tables, Physical Layer problems such as port failures, and network problems such as frame relay or PPP.

In the IPX implementation, serial interfaces use the default Novell address—usually the first address of an active interface. The IPX routing process uses the default Novell address as well, unless otherwise manually configured using the IPX ROUTING <<*NODE*>> command. When you are configuring a router, it is best to allow the router to assign the node number. With a manual configuration, there is a risk of duplicate node numbers, which will prevent the router from functioning properly.

If you are using NLSP on the Ethernet segment, it is possible that the wrong router won the NLSP election. You might want to set the NLSP priority on the Ethernet segment to ensure that the optimal path is set. Another potential problem, and one that is more likely, is that the server has enabled packet forwarding. The server will keep track of all IPX routes and attempt to act as a router. This generates unnecessary traffic on the LAN segment. Worse, the client traffic might be directed through the server. At best, the throughput is affected; at worst, the traffic is never directed to the right interface, and the connection fails. These problems can be difficult to isolate, especially on a LAN segment with a high number of servers.

SCENARIO & SOLUTION

Is the LAN interface experiencing high drop rates on the input or output queues?	**Yes:** Check the SAP tables.
Do all the SAPs appear in the SHOW IPX SERVERS output?	**No:** High drops can cause the SAP tables to be unstable.
Does IPX TRACEROUTE take the correct path?	**No:** Check the routing tables.
Do you see routes through the wrong interface(s)?	**Yes:** Look for the source of the routing loop, duplicate network numbers, or duplicate node numbers.
Are any servers configured to act as routers?	**Yes:** Disable routing on the server(s), clear the bad routes, and check the routing tables.
Are any routers redistributing routes from one protocol into another?	Check the router configurations for possible errors.

Duplicate Network Numbers

As with TCP/IP, IPX does not support duplicate network numbers. If you have a router in Dallas that has IPX network address A00001 on the Ethernet segment and another router in Houston that has an IPX network address A00001 on its Ethernet segment, only one of these two networks will be able to reach any other remote location. Because routing tables discard the duplicate network, you see only one entry for the A00001 network in the routing tables.

To identify a duplicate network number problem without going to every router in the network, use the SHOW IPX ROUTE command to follow the trail. For example, if a user from Dallas calls saying she cannot reach a server in Gaithersburg, starting with the router closest to the user in Dallas, type **show ipx route A00001** and observe the output. You should see the network appear on the Ethernet interface. Next, go to the Gaithersburg router and enter the same command, **show ipx route A00001**. If you see the route appearing to come from interface s0.2, Telnet to the router at the other end of the connection. Repeat the command in that router. If the route appears on interface s0.5, Telnet to that router and repeat the command. Let's assume this is Houston. Aha—A00001 appears on the Ethernet

SCENARIO & SOLUTION

In SHOW IPX SERVERS, are SAPs with the same network number coming from a remote segment?	**Yes:** Follow the trail. **No:** Look for duplicate network numbers: SHOW IPX ROUTE.
In SHOW IPX ROUTE, is a route to the same network number coming from a remote segment?	**Yes:** Follow the trail. **No:** Check a different router.
Use the SHOW IPX SERVERS and the SHOW IPX ROUTE commands as detailed previously in a different router. Does the route come from the right location?	**Yes:** This is probably not a duplicate network number problem. **No:** Follow the trail.
Follow the trail: Go to the next-hop router for the source of the bad route. Does the source of the route point back to the correct router?	**Yes:** You might have a routing loop. Check the configuration, paying particular attention to redistribution. **No:** Continue to follow the trail until you find the source of the route.

interface! Now we know that we have a routing problem. We still need to verify that this is a duplicate network problem instead of a routing loop through a backdoor bridge. A quick check of SHOW IPX INTERFACE BRIEF reveals that the Houston router is configured to use A00001, and the same command in Dallas reveals that the Dallas router is configured to use A00001. To fix the problem, one of the two routers must be changed to use a different network address.

EXERCISE 8-5

Duplicate Network Problem

For this exercise, you need a Novell server (SERVER) attached to a hub. To this same hub, connect a router (ROUTERA). Connect a V.35 DCE cable to a serial port on ROUTERA, and connect the other end of the cable to a V.35 DTE cable, which is then connected to another router (ROUTERB).

Configure SERVER to use IPX RIP to communicate on network 10010 using the 802.2 frame type. Make sure that SERVER is using 10011 as the internal network number.

Set ROUTERA to use network 10010 with the 802.2 frame type on the LAN segment. Configure the serial port to communicate using HDLC encapsulation, with IPX network BADBAD. Use IPX RIP for network 10010 and IPX EIGRP 1 for network BADBAD.

Set ROUTERB to use HDLC encapsulation on the serial port, with IPX network BADBAD. Use IPX EIGRP 1 for network BADBAD.

Check to make sure that all the appropriate server SAPs are visible in both ROUTERA and ROUTERB. Once you have verified this, add the following statement to the loopback interface on ROUTERB:

```
ipx network 10011
```

What happened to the IPX routes? What happened to the IPX SAPs? Explain why you observed these results. Add this additional statement under the IPX ROUTER EIGRP 1 heading in ROUTERB:

```
ipx network 10011
```

What happened to the IPX routes? What happened to the IPX SAPs? Explain why you observed these results. If a remote user were connected through another serial interface coming in to ROUTERA, where would the router forward the packet? How could you track down the source of the problem?

Solution: The configuration of ROUTERA should include the following statements:

```
ipx routing 00d0.baa2.ea60
interface FastEthernet0/0.1
 ipx network 10010 encapsulation SAP
interface Serial1/0
ipx network BADBAD
ipx router eigrp 1
 network BADBAD
ipx router rip
 no network BADBAD
```

The configuration of ROUTERB should include the following statements:

```
ipx routing 00e0.1eb9.11b3
interface Loopback 0
ipx network 10011
interface Serial1/0
ipx network BADBAD
ipx router eigrp 1
 network BADBAD
ipx router rip
 no network BADBAD
```

Once the loopback address has been configured with the same IPX network number as the internal address of the server, ROUTERB no longer has a valid route to SERVER, so all associated SAPs are rejected and removed from the SAP table. ROUTERA is not affected because ROUTERB is not advertising the 10011 route via EIGRP. Since RIP uses hop counts, ROUTERA continues to use the correct path to reach SERVER. Any routers behind ROUTERB are not so fortunate.

As soon as ROUTERB begins to advertise 10011 through EIGRP, the administrative distance for 10011 appears to be better than the RIP advertisement, so ROUTERA looks to ROUTERB for all connections to network 10011. ROUTERB receives SAPs for SERVER via the Ethernet interface, checks the routing table for a valid route, finds one, and installs the SAP into the SAP table. Note that the SAP is visible through the correct interface when you execute the

SHOW IPX SERVERS command. However, since the forwarding table reflects a route to ROUTERB, ROUTERA dutifully forwards any packets for SERVER to ROUTERB. ROUTERB receives them but has nowhere to deliver them. A "black hole" has developed in the network.

Knowing what changed is an important first step in troubleshooting. Assuming that we are unaware of any changes made to the routers and have not followed good network management procedures by maintaining regular backup copies of the configurations, we must rely on the tools available through the Cisco IOS to identify the source of the trouble. If we know that SERVER should be reachable through the Ethernet interface of ROUTERA and have checked the SAP table, we know that the SAP is visible through the correct interface. The next step is to use the SHOW IPX ROUTE command to check the forwarding tables. We see the route to 10011 via the serial interface, so we connect to the router on the other side, in this case ROUTERB. Again using the SHOW IPX ROUTE command, we see that the route appears to terminate on the loopback interface. Since 10011 can appear in only one network, either the server is wrong or the router is misconfigured.

Encapsulation

In order for a client to communicate to a server through a router, the client and the server must both have encapsulation types that match the router. It is not necessary for the client and server to use the *same* encapsulation type, since the router converts the packet at the remote end. In other words, it is perfectly acceptable for the client and the remote router to use the 802.3 frame type while the local router and server use the 802.2 frame type. If the client and the server are using the 802.2 frame type while one or both routers are using the 802.3 frame type, there is a communications failure.

The number of potential reasons for a communication failure is too extensive to provide a complete list. The bottom line always seems to come down to a few basic questions. These questions can save a tremendous amount of time and energy. At the beginning of every list there should really be one question: "What changed?" The following On the Job illustrates this point well.

SCENARIO & SOLUTION

Does the encapsulation type on the router match that being used by clients?	**No:** Correct the encapsulation type. **Yes:** Check the server frame type.
Does the encapsulation type on the server match that being used by the client?	**No:** Correct the encapsulation type. **Yes:** Check the remote router SAP table.
Can the remote router see all the SAPs for the server?	**No:** Check the local router SAP table. **Yes:** IPX PING the client.
Can the local router see all the SAPs for the server?	**No:** Check the local server. **Yes:** Check the remote router route table.
Is the local server accessible to local clients?	**Yes:** Check the local router's network number. **No:** Troubleshoot the local server.
Can the remote router see all interim IPX networks and the destination network?	**Yes:** IPX PING the client. **No:** A routing problem could be preventing the SAPs from being added to the table. Troubleshoot the routing problem first.
Can you IPX PING the client from the remote router (closest to the client)?	**Yes:** IPX PING the client from the local router. **No:** Troubleshoot the local client connectivity.
Can you IPX PING the client from the local router (closest to the server)?	**Yes:** IPX PING the server from the remote router. **No:** Check the local router route table.
Does the local router have a route to the remote network?	**Yes:** IPX PING the remote router. **No:** Troubleshoot the routing problem first.

on the job

One morning I received a call from an administrator who said that his server could no longer see any of the other servers. The server wasn't visible to the local router. We spent about an hour checking cables and checking the switch. He verified that he could log in to the server locally. It didn't occur to either of us to find out whether or not the server had been touched over the weekend. I finally asked the administrator if he had changed anything on the server. Oh yes, he said; he had been in over the weekend, upgraded the server to 4.1, and changed the server to use the 802.2 frame type. It never occurred to him to mention this change. Here was a simple fix to the problem; always ask, "What changed?"

Access Lists

Several types of access lists are available for filtering IPX traffic in a Cisco router. Any one of these can cause a problem for a client as well as for a server.

Access lists can be used for many purposes. Some of these include filtering which servers can be included in a GNS response, which SAPs can be advertised through an interface, which routes can be advertised by a routing protocol or through a specific interface, and so on. Certain types of filters must use certain types of access lists. Either a standard (numbered 800–899) or an extended (numbered 900–999) access list can be applied as the following types of access lists on an interface: incoming access lists or outgoing access lists. A standard access list (numbered 800–899) can be applied as the following type of access list on an interface: IPX helper access list. A SAP access list (numbered 1000–1099) can be applied as the following types of access list on an interface, input filter, output filter, and router filter: SAP input filter, SAP output filter, and SAP router filter. An IPX summary address access list (numbered 1200–1299) can be applied as a distribution list.

The following steps need to be followed in every router in the path from the client to the server.

exam ⓦatch

Unless a default route is defined and all IPX routers in the network support NLSP 1.1, a valid route must exist for a SAP to be added to the SAP table in the router.

The Back-Door Bridge

The *back-door bridge* is usually a Novell server with two frame types bound to the same interface card and having the *forwarding* option enabled on the server. Essentially, this bridge turns the server into a router. A variation of this bridge is a

SCENARIO & SOLUTION

Are any access lists applied to the associated interfaces or to the routing process?	**Yes:** Display the access list(s). **No:** Access lists are not causing the problem.
Does the access list applied to the interface or routing process permit the route or SAP?	**Yes:** Use the SHOW RUN command. **No:** Modify the access list.

Novell server with two NICs on two different IPX networks that has the forwarding option enabled on the server. Alternatively, you might find an NT workstation or server with the routing option enabled. Finally, you might find someone who sneaked a hub into his or her office and has multiple cables connected back to different switches, with spanning tree disabled on those ports.

At various times, I have found each of these variations in every network. This can be one of the most difficult problems to track down. You can use TRACEROUTE to see the path the packet will take, but the end device must support the Novell diagnostic options or the TRACEROUTE will fail. With a spanning-tree problem, you must check the spanning-tree status in the switch(es) and then check the MAC address table in the switches to see if the address appears through more than one port.

SAP Updates Not Propagated by the Router

If the router has established an IPX connection with a remote router or is communicating properly with a LAN segment, there are four possible reasons that a router might not send SAP updates. First, the router might not be receiving the SAP

SCENARIO & SOLUTION

Is the bad hop-count field in the SHOW IPX TRAFFIC output incrementing?	**Yes:** Use a sniffer to look for packet loops on suspect segments. Look for RIP and SAP updates and hop counts that increment to 16. **No:** A back-door bridge is not likely to be the problem.
Are routes from remote networks appearing on local interfaces?	**Yes:** Use IPX TRACEROUTE to follow the bad path. Use a protocol analyzer to determine the source of the bad routing entry. **No:** A back-door bridge is not likely to be the problem.
Are packets whose source address is the MAC address of a remote node instead of that of the router?	**Yes:** Find the source MAC address and review the device's configuration. **No:** A back-door bridge is not likely to be the problem.

update, in which case it obviously will not propagate them. Second, the router might be receiving the SAP update but rejecting it because it is missing the route associated with the SAP. Third, the router might be prevented from forwarding a known SAP by a SAP filter. Fourth, the router might be prevented from issuing SAP updates due to a routing protocol issue. For example, IPX RIP could be disabled on the LAN segment, or an IPX EIGRP neighbor adjacency cannot be established. From these four reasons, a number of symptoms can be observed. Because a problem is rarely reported by its cause, here we examine the various symptoms.

Router Is Not Receiving SAP Updates from the Server

In this case, the cause might also be the symptom. If the router does not receive a SAP update from the server, it cannot propagate the SAP. However, it could appear that the router is not receiving the SAP updates when in reality the router is rejecting the updates it does receive. Start by checking the basics. Check the frame encapsulation configured on the router. Check to make sure the server is connected to the network and is operational. If the router is using NLSP on the LAN segment, check to make sure that the server is participating in the NLSP process and that both the router and the server are members of the same area.

If there is a mismatch between the local node(s) and the router, configure the proper encapsulation type using the command ENCAPSULATION <<*ENCAPSULATION TYPE*>>. Verify the new setting with the SHOW IPX INTERFACES command.

You might find that you have the opposite problem: there might be so many SAP updates going through the network that client traffic is put on hold while all the SAPs are transmitted. In that case, you will want to use the IPX UPDATE INTERVAL <<*#OF MILLISECONDS*>> command to make sure you insert a delay between each packet. By default, both NLSP and IPX EIGRP reduce the frequency of SAP updates, which also frees up bandwidth for client traffic.

While Booting Up, the Host Connects to a Remote Server Instead of the Local Server

The server might not respond to the GNS request as quickly as the router. If the GNS-RESPONSE-DELAY parameter is not set, the default delay is set to zero milliseconds. For IOS Versions 9.1(13) or earlier, you might have to manually decrease the GNS response delay to improve response time, although the recommended solution would be to upgrade to a more current version of software.

SCENARIO & SOLUTION

Does the frame encapsulation on the router match the server's encapsulation?	**No:** Correct the encapsulation. **Yes:** Check the IPX network address on the router.
Does the network address on the router match the server's external network address?	**No:** Correct the network address. **Yes:** Check the router's IPX forwarding table.
Does the router have a route to the server's *internal* network?	**No:** Determine why the route is missing and correct the problem. **Yes:** Check the NLSP or the IPX RIP process; check the server configuration.
Are the router and the server members of the same NLSP area?	**No:** Ensure that both are members of the same IPX NLSP area by changing the network addressing or the masking. **Yes:** Check the server configuration.
Use the SHOW IPX INTERFACES command. Are the RIP packets received and RIP packets sent counters incrementing?	**No:** If you are using IPX RIP, check the router configuration. If you are using NLSP or EIGRP, use the DEBUG IPX SAP ACTIVITY command. **Yes:** If you are using IPX RIP, use the DEBUG IPX SAP ACTIVITY command. If you are using NLSP, check the router configuration.
Is the server configured to use RIP/SAP compatibility?	**No:** Turn on RIP/SAP compatibility. **Yes:** Use the DEBUG IPX SAP ACTIVITY command.
Use the DEBUG IPX SAP ACTIVITY command. Is the router receiving SAPs but rejecting them?	**No:** IPX PING the server. **Yes:** Identify the reason the SAP is rejected and correct it.
Is the router able to IPX PING the server?	**No:** Troubleshoot connectivity to the server. **Yes:** Troubleshoot the server itself.

If you are using Cisco IOS 9.1(13) or later, you might have to manually increase the GNS response delay if a host has a slow processor or NIC. The command to set GNS response delay is IPX GNS-RESPONSE-DELAY *<<# OF MILLISECONDS>>*.

Alternatively, if multiple frame types are in use on the same wire, the client might not be on the same network as the server, and the router does not check the SAP tables for a local server when responding to a GNS request. This situation is more common in older Novell client environments. More recent Novell clients allow the user to specify the name of the server, alleviating the problem. A GNS filter can be configured to force the router to respond to GNS requests from a limited list of servers. Although not commonly implemented, this solution resolves the problem. A SAP access list must be defined to include the servers with which the router may respond. Once defined, the access list is applied to the appropriate interface using the command IPX OUTPUT-GNS-FILTER <<*1000-1999*>>.

If the router should never respond to a GNS request, it can be disabled entirely via the command IPX GNS-REPLY-DISABLE.

exam
Ⓦatⓒh
If you are using multiple LAN interfaces and the server(s) are connected to only one of those LAN interfaces, a GNS output filter needs to be applied to the router. The router will not distinguish between local and remote servers when responding to a GNS request.

SCENARIO & SOLUTION

Is the GNS response count incrementing in the SHOW IPX TRAFFIC output when it should not be?	**Yes:** Increase the delay using the IPX GNS-RESPONSE-DELAY command on the LAN interface. No or you cannot tell: use the SHOW IPX SERVERS command.
Are all of the local server's SAPs visible in the router?	**Yes:** Check for multiple frame types. **No:** Check the local server to make sure it is operational. Use the TRACK ON command to monitor SAPs.
Are you using multiple frame types on a single LAN interface(s) or are you using different frame types on multiple LAN interface(s)?	**Yes:** Increase the GNS response delay; consider implementing a GNS output filter. **No:** Check the client workstation.
Is the client specifying a server when attempting to connect?	**Yes:** Ensure that the correct server is specified. **No:** Increase the GNS response delay.

Server Misconfiguration

If the server is incorrectly configured, the router cannot see SAP updates from the server and therefore cannot propagate the SAP updates. If there is only one server on the LAN segment, the argument could be raised as to whether it is the router or the server that is misconfigured. It is assumed in this case that the server is misconfigured.

Consider the following scenario. All servers are supposed to be configured to use NLSP with RIP/SAP compatibility. In a remote location, the server was configured to use only RIP, and the router was configured to use only NLSP. The server does not see any of the other servers in the network. The router does not see the local server. Turning on DEBUG IPX PACKET in the router reveals the following:

```
01:26:04: IPX: Fa0/0:A585A1E.0020.7819.8644->0.ffff.ffff.ffff ln= 81 tc=00 pt=00
ds=9001 ss=9001, rcvd
01:26:04: IPX: Fa0/0:A585A1E.0020.7819.8644->0.ffff.ffff.ffff ln= 81 tc=00 pt=00
ds=9001 ss=9001, local
```

Using the NetWare server command LOAD INETCFG, you select Bindings, IPX, Expert Bind Options, and NLSP Bind Options, and you see that NLSP is turned off. Changing the NLSP State to On, saving the changes, and reinitializing the system results in the following DEBUG output on the router:

```
01:26:04: %CLNS-5-ADJCHANGE: NLSP: Adjacency to FAB-FAM (FastEthernet0/0) Up, new
adjacency
01:26:04: %CLNS-5-MULTICAST: NLSP: Broadcast address in use on FastEthernet0/0
```

Is it possible, without using DEBUG, to tell whether or not this is the problem? With a little detective work, yes, it is possible. First, you can use the SHOW IPX INTERFACE command to see if RIP packets are being received on the Ethernet interface:

```
RIP packets received 86, RIP packets sent 8, 0 Throttled
```

Second, you can enable RIP in the router to see if you now see the server. Finally, you can ask the server administrator responsible for the server to review the server settings with you.

The problem with each of these approaches is that you might miss important information. The DEBUG output will always give you exactly what crossed through the router and help you understand what the router did with the information it received. If you check to see whether or not RIP packets are being received on the interface, this information does not tell you *which* RIP packets were received or where they were from. If you turn RIP on in the router but have the wrong network address on the interface, you still do not see the server. Sometimes the person responsible for configuring the server is not available. Sometimes for political reasons you cannot contact the server administrator. It is important for you to understand the benefits and risks of each so that you know when it is appropriate to use each.

SCENARIO & SOLUTION

Do you see all the SAPs for the server in the local router (the router closest to the server)?	**Yes:** The server is properly communicating with the network. Check for other problems with the server. The local router might not be propagating SAP updates. **No:** IPX PING the server.
Can you IPX PING the server?	**Yes:** Use DEBUG IPX SAP ACTIVITY. **No:** Check the frame type.
Use the DEBUG IPX SAP ACTIVITY command. Is the router receiving SAP updates from the server?	**Yes:** The router might not be propagating the SAP updates. Follow the troubleshooting steps in that section. **No:** Use the DEBUG IPX PACKET command.
Use the DEBUG IPX PACKET command. Do you see any packets coming from the server?	**No:** The server might be configured with the wrong network address or frame type. **Yes:** From the output of the DEBUG IPX PACKET command, identify the possible cause of the problem and address it.
Are there enough client licenses? Does the user have an account on the server? Are other local users able to connect to the server?	**No to any of these questions:** Correct the identified problem with the server. **Yes to all of these questions:** The server appears to be properly configured. Check the router for other potential causes of the problem.

Access Lists

Because of the broadcast traffic associated with IPX, it is much more common to see access-lists in an IPX environment than in an IP environment. For this reason, access lists are one of the most common reasons a local server is not visible to the router.

on the Job

We've all heard the rule "Apply the access list as close to the source of the traffic as possible." This is a good rule when you want to limit traffic, but it does not help with troubleshooting. For example, if my traffic rules state that I will allow only the WILDFIRE server to be advertised, and I deny everything else from being received from the LAN segment, I cannot easily troubleshoot LAN problems. I must have access to a device on the LAN segment that can see what other devices on the LAN segment are able to see. Likewise, if I need to add something to an access list to allow new traffic through the filter, I might not have access to the information I need to build the new filter. Officially, the filter should be applied as an inbound filter on the Ethernet interface. Unofficially, I strongly recommend that filters be applied as outbound filters on the WAN segments. This practice allows you to see everything in the local router without saturating the WAN links with unnecessary traffic.

The list of questions in the following Scenario & Solution needs to be followed in every router in the path from the client to the server.

SCENARIO & SOLUTION

Are any access lists applied to the associated interfaces?	**Yes:** Use the SHOW IPX ACCESS-LISTS command to review the access list(s). **No:** Use the SHOW RUN command.
Does the access list applied to the interface permit the route or SAP?	**Yes:** Use the SHOW RUN command. **No:** Modify the access list.
Is a distribution list applied to the routing process?	**Yes:** Use the SHOW IPX ACCESS-LISTS command to review the access list(s). **No:** If no access lists are applied to any of the interfaces involved or to the routing process, access lists are not causing the problem.

Encapsulation

Fortunately, IPX encapsulation is only an issue on LAN segments. The router will not accept LAN encapsulations on a WAN interface. Therefore, when dealing with an IPX encapsulation issue the question of encapsulation is reduced to a LAN issue.

SCENARIO & SOLUTION

Does the encapsulation type on the server match that being used by the server?	**No:** Correct the encapsulation type. **Yes:** Check the remote router SAP table.
Can the remote router see all the SAPs for the server?	**No:** Check the local router SAP table. **Yes:** IPX PING the client.
Can the local router see all the SAPs for the server?	**No:** Check the local server. **Yes:** Check the remote router route table.
Is the local server accessible to local clients?	**Yes:** Check the local router's network number. **No:** Troubleshoot the local server.
Can the remote router see all interim IPX networks and the destination network?	**Yes:** IPX PING the client. **No:** Look for and resolve routing problems.
Can you IPX PING the client from the local router (closest to the server)?	**Yes:** IPX PING the server from the remote router. **No:** Check the local router route table.
Does the local router have a route to the remote network?	**Yes:** IPX PING the remote router. **No:** Look for an resolve routing problems.

Duplicate Network Numbers

If the server address is identical to the router address, the router does not establish an NLSP adjacency. Instead, the following type of message will appear in the log:

```
01:38:37: %CLNS-3-BADPACKET: NLSP: L1 LSP, Internal net matches ours, ID
0200.09B2.3663.00-00, seq 49, ht 7499 from 0020.7819.8644 (FastEthernet0/0)
```

SCENARIO & SOLUTION	
Do you see SAPs with the same network number coming from a remote segment?	**Yes:** Follow the trail. **No:** SHOW IPX ROUTE.
Is a route to the same network number coming from a remote segment?	**Yes:** Follow the trail. **No:** Check a different router.
Use the SHOW IPX SERVERS and the SHOW IPX ROUTE commands as detailed above in a different router. Does the route come from the right location?	**Yes:** This is probably not a duplicate network number problem. **No:** Follow the trail.
Follow the trail: go to the next-hop router for the source of the bad route. Does the source of the route point back to the correct router?	**Yes:** You might have a routing loop. Check the configuration, paying particular attention to redistribution. **No:** Continue to follow the trail until you find the source of the route.

Timer Mismatches

A timer mismatch generally occurs under one of two circumstances. The server administrator might have changed these times in an effort to reduce LAN traffic. Typically, this situation occurs only in settings with a large number of users. More likely, a well-meaning network administrator might have changed the settings on the router in an attempt to reduce WAN traffic inadvertently affecting the router's ability to communicate with the server.

Before changing any timer settings on the router, first verify whether or not the default settings for the servers should be used. On a severely congested LAN segment, the timers might be set to larger values to reduce broadcast traffic. Although it is not necessary to have the same settings on every LAN, this is usually the case. In most cases, the WAN segment will have longer intervals, whereas the LAN segment will use the NetWare defaults. If the LAN settings are modified on the router, every server on that segment must be modified.

The typical symptom of a timer mismatch is that the SAP tables are not stable. Each time you use the SHOW IPX SERVERS command, a different number of devices will appear in the list. The following Scenario & Solution could help you identify this condition.

SCENARIO & SOLUTION

Does the RIP timer configured on the router match what is configured on the Novell servers?	**No:** Reconfigure the router timer to match the servers. No access to the server to compare: use the DEBUG IPX ROUTING command.
Time the interval between RIP updates in DEBUG IPX ROUTING from the server. Does the interval match what is configured on the router?	**No:** Reconfigure the router timer to match the servers. **Yes:** Check the SAP update interval.
Using the SHOW IPX INTERFACES command compares the SAP update interval on the router to what is configured on the server. Do they match?	**No:** Correct the IPX SAP-INTERVAL. **Yes:** Check the routing protocol timers.
Use the SHOW RUNNING-CONFIG command to check the hello interval and hold-time intervals. Do they match on both routers?	**No:** Change the configuration of one router to match the other. **Yes:** A timer issue is not likely to be the cause of the problem. If SAPs and/or routes are being dropped, it could be due to congestion.

Slow Server Cannot Keep Up with Fast Router

In this case, the router maintains consistent SAP and route tables, but the server is not able to reliably maintain the same tables. Since the client must communicate with a local server to find available services, this situation can result in support calls in which the end user claims that the server is not available. Alternatively, if a server is heavily utilized and some of the traffic is coming from a remote location, the server might not be able to respond to all the client requests in a timely manner. This can result in higher bandwidth utilization as client requests are retransmitted and the delay inherent in crossing a WAN segment is exacerbated by the response-time issues with the server itself.

You can use the DEBUG RIP option on a router to monitor the RIP activity. The problem with doing so is that you will see all RIP activity for both the LAN segment and the WAN segment(s). You can use the TRACK ON command on a Novell server to monitor the RIP activity on the LAN segment.

In a small network, you might be able to read the output of the TRACK ON screen. In a large network, the information scrolls by so fast there is no reasonable way to read everything. TRACK ON tells you whether or not the server is receiving updates.

To tell whether or not the server is receiving all the updates, use the DISPLAY SERVERS command on the Server Console. At the bottom of the listing is a total count of servers. Check the output of the DISPLAY SERVERS command several times to see whether or not the total count changes. If it does, the router is not sending the updates, there is a loop in the network, or the server is unable to keep up. You can compare this to the total SAPs visible in the router via the SHOW IPX SERVERS command in the router. Use the IPX OUTPUT-SAP-DELAY *DELAY* command to insert a small delay between SAP packets. This command is useful, too, on saturated WAN links with high numbers of SAPs to allow actual data traffic to pass between the SAP packets.

SCENARIO & SOLUTION

Does the router show output drops on the interfaces involved?	**No:** Use the SHOW IPX SERVERS command. **Yes:** Increase the output queue or decrease the traffic.
Does the router show output drops after increasing the output queue using the HOLD-QUEUE command*?	**No:** Use the SHOW IPX SERVERS command. **Yes:** Decrease the traffic or increase available bandwidth.
Does the router still show output drops after applying filters to reduce the traffic?	**No:** Use the SHOW IPX SERVERS command. Yes: Check for routing loops or evaluate the network design.
Does the number of SAPs listed in the router match what is shown on the server?	**No:** Use the SHOW IPX ROUTE command.
Does the router have the same number of IPX routes listed when compared to the Novell server?	**No:** Use the IPX OUTPUT-RIP-DELAY command to increase the delay between RIP packets. Repeat the previous step. **Yes:** Use the IPX OUTPUT-SAP-DELAY command to increase the delay between SAP packets. Repeat the previous step.

*If you must do so, increase the hold queue in small increments only. If the hold queue is too large, it will take too long for the packet to be delivered, in which case the route or SAP will time out anyway. If you find that you must increase the hold queue by more than twice the default, it might be more appropriate to find a way to increase available bandwidth.

Data Link and Network Layer Traces

Some problems defy simple explanation. Even after using the many powerful tools provided in the Cisco IOS, it might not be possible to clearly define the problem. In these cases, it might be necessary to use a protocol analyzer to capture the traffic crossing the network. A number of well-known (and expensive) protocol analyzers are available today. There are also a number of lesser-known (and less expensive) protocol analyzers. The format of the output from each could vary slightly, and some protocol analyzers do a better job of identifying and explaining what has been captured, but the content is what counts.

In this section, various types of packets are presented, along with a limited description of some of the key components of those packets. A number of excellent texts provide more detailed explanations. This chapter is not intended to provide a thorough presentation of every component of the IPX protocol suite, but it should have covered enough salient points for you to read the basic components. When you need to know more, spend a few minutes reading before looking at the capture. The time spent preparing to look at the capture will ultimately save you much time and prevent you from making time-consuming mistakes.

Although it might help, it is not necessary to be able to fully understand every single line of a sniffer capture as long as you can follow the basic thread and understand the key components. It is important to be careful drawing conclusions under those circumstances. When reading a capture, regardless of the protocol, you must first know what you should see. Otherwise, you will not recognize when a critical step is missing. Knowing what is normal allows you to spend your energy looking for what is missing or for something that is present but should not be.

For example, if you never see a GNS request from the client, that would be an indication that the client is not communicating on Layer 3 at all and that you should check the Layer 2 connectivity first. If you never see an NLSP packet from a server but you do see RIP packets, you might conclude that perhaps the server was not configured to use NLSP, in spite of what you were told. If clients are unable to log on to a server, it would be surprising to see an NCP response from the server to the client.

Client Broadcast GNS Request

A client must issue a GNS request in order to locate a server. The GNS request is a broadcast (Line 6) SAP packet (Line 8) of the type Nearest Service Query Line 13 and specifies the server type as a File Server (Line 15):

```
1.  IPX: SAP Packet - 0.00A0CC25949F.4002 -> 0.FFFFFFFFFFFF.452 - 0 Hops
2.  IPX: Checksum = 65535 (0xFFFF)
3.  IPX: IDP Length = 34 (0x22)
4.  IPX: Transport control = 0 (0x0)
5.  IPX: Packet type = IPX
6.  IPX: Destination Address Summary 0.FFFFFFFFFFFF.452
7.  IPX: IPX Address = 00000000.FFFFFFFFFFFF
8.  IPX: Socket Number = SAP
9.  IPX: Source Address Summary 0.00A0CC25949F.4002
10. IPX: IPX Address = 00000000.00A0CC25949F
11. IPX: Socket Number = 0x4002
12. IPX: Data: Number of data bytes remaining = 4 (0x0004)
13. SAP: Nearest Svc Query [Nearest Service Query]
14. SAP: Packet Type = Nearest Service Query
15. SAP: Server Type = File Server
```

Server GNS Response

A local server should respond to a client GNS request. In the absence of a local server, the router might respond as a proxy. The response will be a Nearest Service Response (Line 2) and will include the Server Name (Line 4), Server Type (Line 5), and the Server Address (Line 7), plus the socket type (Line 8).

```
1.  SAP: Nearest Svc Resp  [FAB-FAM - File Server]
2.  SAP: Packet Type = Nearest Service Response
3.  SAP: [FAB-FAM - File Server]
4.  SAP: Server Name = FAB-FAM
5.  SAP: Server Type = File Server
6.  SAP: Server Address 9B23663.000000000001.451
7.  SAP: IPX Network Address = 09B23663.000000000001
8.  SAP: Well known socket = NCP
9.  SAP: Intermediate Networks = 1 (0x1)
```

Client RIP Route Request

Once the client has the name of the server and the address of the server, it will issue a RIP route request. This is a broadcast packet of a RIPX packet type request (Line 2) for network 09B23663 (Line 1):

```
1. RIPX: RIP Request   [Net 0x09B23663]
2. RIPX: Packet Type = Request
3. RIPX: Network Number = 162674275 (0x9B23663)
4. RIPX: Hop Count = 65535 (0xFFFF)
5. RIPX: RIP Time = 0xFFFF Ticks (Request)
6. RIPX: Padding
```

Server RIP Route Response

The server or router will respond with a RIPX Packet Type response (Line 2). Since the route is on the local segment, the hop count is 1 (Line 4). Note the tick information provided to the client (Line 5):

```
1. RIPX: RIP Response [Net 0x09B23663: 1 Hops]
2. RIPX: Packet Type = Response
3. RIPX: Network Number = 162674275 (0x9B23663)
4. RIPX: Hop Count = 1 (0x1)
5. RIPX: RIP Time = 2 Ticks (110 milliseconds)
6. RIPX: Padding
```

Client NCP Request

Armed with the name and type of the nearest server along with the route to that server, the client next issues an NCP request. Now the packet type is an NCP packet (Line 5). Note that the packet is once again a broadcast (Line 6):

```
1. IPX: SAP Packet - A585A1E.00A0CC25949F.4003 -> A585A1E.FFFFFFFFFFFF.452 - 0
Hops
2. IPX: Checksum = 65535 (0xFFFF)
3. IPX: IDP Length = 90 (0x5A)
4. IPX: Transport control = 0 (0x0)
5. IPX: Packet type = NCP
6. IPX: Destination Address Summary A585A1E.FFFFFFFFFFFF.452
7. IPX: IPX Address = 0A585A1E.FFFFFFFFFFFF
8. IPX: Socket Number = SAP
9. IPX: Source Address Summary A585A1E.00A0CC25949F.4003
10. IPX: IPX Address = 0A585A1E.00A0CC25949F
```

```
11. IPX: Socket Number = 0x4003
12. IPX: Data: Number of data bytes remaining = 60 (0x003C)
13. SAP: Summary = N/A
14. SAP: Packet Type = 0x000E
```

Server NCP Response

The NCP response is returned as an IPX packet type IPX (Line 5) and is a directed packet specifically addressed to the client (Line 6). Once again, the server name and type are provided (Lines 16 and 17), along with the SAP server address (Line 18):

```
1. IPX: SAP Packet - A585A1E.002078198644.452 -> A585A1E.00A0CC25949F.4003 - 0
Hops
2. IPX: Checksum = 65535 (0xFFFF)
3. IPX: IDP Length = 96 (0x60)
4. IPX: Transport control = 0 (0x0)
5. IPX: Packet type = IPX
6. IPX: Destination Address Summary A585A1E.00A0CC25949F.4003
7. IPX: IPX Address = 0A585A1E.00A0CC25949F
8. IPX: Socket Number = 0x4003
9. IPX: Source Address Summary A585A1E.002078198644.452
10. IPX: IPX Address = 0A585A1E.002078198644
11. IPX: Socket Number = SAP
12. IPX: Data: Number of data bytes remaining = 66 (0x0042)
13. SAP: Summary = N/A
14. SAP: Packet Type = 0x000F
15. SAP: [FAB-FAM - File Server]
16. SAP: Server Name = FAB-FAM
17. SAP: Server Type = File Server
18. SAP: Server Address 9B23663.000000000001.451
19. SAP: IPX Network Address = 09B23663.000000000001
20. SAP: Well known socket = NCP
21. SAP: Intermediate Networks = 1 (0x1)
```

Client NCP Connection Request

Finally, the client can issue the NCP connection request, which establishes the real data connection to the server. This packet is addressed specifically to the server (Line 2). It is an NCP packet type (Line 21) on the NCP socket (Line 24), and we can see that this is a connect request (Line 31):

```
1. ETHERNET: 802.3 Length = 60
2. THERNET: Destination address : 002078198644
3. ETHERNET: .......0 = Individual address
```

4. ETHERNET: ......0. = Universally administered address
5. ETHERNET: Source address : 00A0CC25949F
6. ETHERNET: ....0 = No routing information present
7. ETHERNET: ......0. = Universally administered address
8. ETHERNET: Frame Length : 60 (0x003C)
9. ETHERNET: Data Length : 0x0028 (40)
10. ETHERNET: Ethernet Data: Number of data bytes remaining = 46 (0x002E)
11. LLC: UI DSAP=0xE0 SSAP=0xE0 C
12. LLC: DSAP = 0xE0 : INDIVIDUAL : Novell IPX/SPX
13. LLC: SSAP = 0xE0: COMMAND : Novell IPX/SPX
14. LLC: Frame Category: Unnumbered Frame
15. LLC: Command = UI
16. LLC: LLC Data: Number of data bytes remaining = 43 (0x002B)
17. IPX: NCP Packet - A585A1E.00A0CC25949F.4004 -> 9B23663.000000000001.451 - 0
Hops
18. IPX: Checksum = 65535 (0xFFFF)
19. IPX: IDP Length = 37 (0x25)
20. IPX: Transport control = 0 (0x0)
21. IPX: Packet type = NCP
22. IPX: Destination Address Summary 9B23663.000000000001.451
23. IPX: IPX Address = 09B23663.000000000001
24. IPX: Socket Number = NCP
25. IPX: Source Address Summary A585A1E.00A0CC25949F.4004
26. IPX: IPX Address = 0A585A1E.00A0CC25949F
27. IPX: Socket Number = 0x4004
28. IPX: Data: Number of data bytes remaining = 7 (0x0007)
29. NCP: Connect
30. NCP: NCP Request Header = 11 11 00 FF 3A FF 00
31. NCP: Request Type = Connect
32. NCP: Sequence Number = 0 (0x0)
33. NCP: Connection Number Low = 255 (0xFF)
34. NCP: Header Task Number = 58 (0x3A)
35. NCP: Connection Number High = 255 (0xFF)
36. NCP: Padding

EXERCISE 8-6

Protocol Analyzer

For this exercise, you need two routers connected to the same LAN hub. Attached to the LAN hub, you need a workstation with a protocol analyzer.

Configure the routers to use IPX RIP on the LAN segment to communicate. Add an IPX NETWORK statement to the loopback interface of each router. Using the protocol analyzer, capture the packets on the LAN segment. Locate an IPX RIP packet. What socket number does it use? Do you see any acknowledgment packets returned to the router?

Solution: The IPX RIP packet uses socket 453 for communications and the packet is a broadcast packet. There is no acknowledgment packet because RIP does not establish a neighbor relationship.

CERTIFICATION SUMMARY

The IPX protocol is similar to the IP protocol suite. Like IP, IPX is connectionless. Like TCP, SPX is connection oriented. Novell added Service Advertising Protocol (SAP) to identify services available through the network. One of the unique features of IPX is the choice of encapsulation, called *frame types*. A difference in encapsulation, or frame type, is also one of the most common problems in an IPX network.

Three routing protocols are associated with IPX: IPX RIP, NLSP, and IPX EIGRP. IPX RIP is a distance-vector protocol, NLSP is a link-state protocol, and IPX EIGRP is a hybrid protocol. RIP and NLSP are the only two choices for communicating with Novell servers. IPX EIGRP is a proprietary protocol used on WAN segments.

Both NLSP and IPX EIGRP maintain neighbor relationships, and you can check the neighbor tables to verify that the relationship has been established. Both use hellos to maintain neighbor status. You can check the NLSP database to verify the status of the network if you are using NLSP, and you can check the EIGRP topology tables to verify the status of the network if you are using EIGRP. With all three, you can check the routing tables.

When an IPX client boots up, if it has not been configured for a specific frame type, it will listen for the frame type in use. Next, a GNS broadcast will be sent by the client, and it will listen for a GNS response. Having the name of the server and its address, it will then send a RIP broadcast and listen for a RIP response to find the route to the server. The next step is the NCP connection request, followed by the NCP connection acknowledgment from the server, to actually initiate the logon process.

TWO-MINUTE DRILL

Here are some of the key points from each certification objective in Chapter 8.

IPX Connection Sequence

❑ A NetWare client issues a get nearest server (GNS) SAP to begin the connection sequence.

❑ A Cisco router can respond to a GNS request as a proxy.

❑ SAP broadcasts are sent out every 60 seconds in an IPX RIP network, but only servers listen for them. IPX clients listen only for directed SAPs.

❑ RIP broadcasts are sent out every 30 seconds in an IPX RIP network, but only servers and routers listen for them. After the IPX client receives a GNS response, it issues a RIP route broadcast.

❑ After the IPX client receives a RIP route response it can begin the logon request using NCP.

❑ NLSP sends out a complete update every two hours, using incremental updates instead of full updates in the interim.

Cisco IOS Software Tools and Commands

❑ The SHOW IPX INTERFACE command provides a detailed listing of the IPX configuration for an interface.

❑ The GNS-ROUND-ROBIN command cannot be verified using the SHOW IPX INTERFACE command.

❑ If a default route is configured in the router or if the default route is propagated by another router, it can be verified using the SHOW IPX ROUTE command.

❑ The SHOW IPX TRAFFIC command provides a summary of the various types of IPX packets seen by the router.

❑ The CLEAR COUNTERS command will not clear the counters associated with the SHOW IPX TRAFFIC command; these counters are cleared only by using the CLEAR IPX TRAFFIC command.

❑ If you want to know what interfaces and in what direction an IPX access list is applied, you must use either the SHOW IPX INTERFACE or the SHOW RUNNING-CONFIG command.

❑ The SHOW IPX NLSP DATABASE command provides a summary of the link-state database maintained by the NLSP process.

❑ Both NLSP and EIGRP maintain neighbor relationships, so the two have similar commands to view the neighbor tables, whereas RIP does not maintain a neighbor relationship with other routers.

❑ Use the SHOW IPX NLSP NEIGHBOR command to verify that the NLSP neighbor relationship has been established.

❑ Use the SHOW IPX EIGRP NEIGHBOR command to verify that the EIGRP neighbor relationship has been established.

❑ The SHOW IPX EIGRP INTERFACES command allows you to identify all interfaces associated with the EIGRP process.

❑ The SHOW IPX EIGRP TRAFFIC can be used to see the number of hellos, updates, queries, replies, and acknowledgments sent for the EIGRP process.

❑ The SHOW IPX EIGRP TOPOLOGY is similar to the IPX routing table but includes more detailed information about the feasible distance and feasible successors.

❑ The SHOW IPX SERVERS is one of the most useful IPX commands and is applicable regardless of the IPX routing process. This command is used to list all the SAPs known to the router.

❑ The DEBUG IPX ROUTING ACTIVITY command shows all the activity associated with the IPX routing tables, regardless of protocol.

❑ The DEBUG IPX EIGRP command shows all the activity associated with the EIGRP routing process.

❑ The DEBUG IPX EIGRP EVENTS command shows any routing table maintenance associated with the EIGRP process.

❑ The DEBUG IPX EIGRP NEIGHBOR command requires that you specify a neighbor and is used to monitor neighbor status changes.

❑ The DEBUG IPX PACKET command consumes a considerable number of CPU cycles since it identifies every IPX packet processed by the router.

❑ The DEBUG IPX SAP command is used to monitor activity associated with the SAP tables.

❑ The DEBUG IPX NLSP EVENTS command is similar to the DEBUG IPX EIGRP EVENTS command, specific to the NLSP process.

❑ The DEBUG IPX IPXWAN command is used to troubleshoot the startup negotiations between two routers running IPX through a WAN link.

PING

❑ To send an IPX PING to a client, use the PING IPX NETWORK.NODE format, where NETWORK is the network segment programmed on the router's interface and NODE is the client's MAC address.

❑ To send an IPX PING to a server, you must use the NETWORK.NODE address as shown in the SAP tables. This is not the server's MAC address but an internal address used by the server.

❑ To trace the route to an IPX endpoint, use the new command TRACEROUTE IPX NETWORK.NODE, where NETWORK is the network segment programmed on the router's interface, and NODE is the endpoint's MAC address.

Problem Isolation in IPX Networks

❑ If you are unable to ping the client, check the client's IPX frame type to make sure it is configured correctly.

❑ If you are unable to ping the client, check to make sure the cable is properly secured and that the client has a link light.

❑ If you are able to ping the client but the client cannot see the server, verify that you can see all the server's SAPs in the router using the SHOW IPX SERVER command.

❑ If the client is connected to a switch, check to make sure that portfast is disabled on the interface.

❑ If there are no servers on the local segment, check to make sure that the router does not have an access list, preventing it from responding to a GNS request.

❑ If there are no servers on the local segment, check to make sure that IPX RIP has not been disabled on the local segment.

❏ There are four frame types for Ethernet, two for Token Ring, and three in FDDI.

❏ Novell-ether is known as 802.3 raw, but SAP, also called Ethernet_802.2 or Novell 802.2, is the IEEE standard 802.3 frame format.

IPX Symptoms, Problems, and Action Plans

❏ With new installations, compare the router to the server to ensure that the router is configured with the correct encapsulation and network address.

❏ With existing installations, check the Layer 2 connectivity before checking for Layer 3.

❏ With existing installations, ask whether anything has changed with the router, the switch, the server, or the client.

❏ Check the SAP tables to make sure all required SAPs are visible through the correct interfaces.

❏ Check the forwarding tables to make sure all required routes are visible through the correct interfaces.

❏ Check each interface for access lists that might be preventing traffic, routes, GNS responses, or SAPs from crossing through the router.

❏ Be careful when setting timers associated with the IPX process or with the IPX routing protocol, since these must match on all routers connected to the affected interface.

Data Link and Network Layer Exercises

❏ When reading a trace from a protocol analyzer, look for the unexpected packets. This will help you identify a device that might be misconfigured.

❏ When reading a trace from a protocol analyzer, look for missing steps in the connection sequence. This will help you identify at what point in the process the connection is failing.

❏ It is not necessary to understand every line of a sniffer capture. As long as you know what to expect and can understand the basic components, you can still use a capture to help find the source of a problem.

SELF TEST

The following questions will help you measure your understanding of the material presented in this chapter. Read all the choices carefully because there might be more than one correct answer. Choose all correct answers for each question.

IPX Connection Sequence

1. The Novell server is configured to use the 802.3 SAP encapsulation for network AA001BB. Which of the following is a correct configuration for the router?

    A. NETWORK ENCAPSULATION SAP AA001BB

    B. IPX ENCAPSULATION 8023 NETWORK AA001BB

    C. NETWORK AA001BB ENCAPSULATION NOVELL-ETHER

    D. IPX NETWORK AA001BB ENCAPSULATION SNAP

    E. IPX NETWORK AA001BB

2. What is the purpose of a SAP?

    A. To tell the client of all available services in the network

    B. To tell all servers in the network of all available services in the network

    C. To tell all servers in the network how to get to other servers

    D. Both B and C

3. Place in the proper order the following steps that must happen before an IPX client can issue a logon request to a Novell server, eliminating any that do not apply.

    A. The client issues an IPX RIP route broadcast request.

    B. The client issues an NCP connection request.

    C. The server issues a GNS directed broadcast reply.

    D. The router issues a SAP broadcast of all SAPs in the network.

    E. The client issues a GNS broadcast request.

    F. The router issues an IPX RIP route reply.

4. Which IPX routing protocols must be manually configured to redistribute into each other?

    A. EIGRP and RIP

    B. RIP and NLSP

C. RIP and OSPF

D. EIGRP and NLSP

5. When you are connecting a Cisco router to another vendor's router, what IPX routing protocol cannot be used, and why?

A. IPX IPXWAN, because it is a Cisco proprietary solution.

B. IPX EIGRP, because it is a Cisco proprietary solution.

C. IPXWAN, because it must be redistributed into EIGRP.

D. IPX RIP, because it can be used only on the LAN segments.

Cisco IOS Software Tools and Commands

6. You see the following output from the router when you use the SHOW IPX ROUTE command. What can you tell from this information?

```
L        1004   is the internal network
```

A. The IPX EIGRP routing process is probably being used.

B. The 1004 network is applied to the loopback interface.

C. The internal network is on the line interface.

D. The NLSP routing process is probably being used.

7. You have received a call from a user complaining that she is unable to access the Novell server. The server is located in a different office. While troubleshooting, you use the SHOW INTERFACE command and obtain the following output (only portions of which are shown here):

```
Serial4/0/0 is up, line protocol is up
MTU 1500 bytes, BW 1544 Kbit, DLY 20000 usec,
Broadcast queue 0/64, broadcasts sent/dropped 26046027/12833017,
interface broadcasts 38879044
Last clearing of "show interface" counters never
Output queue 0/40, 69850 drops; input queue 0/75, 19 drops
5 minute input rate 73000 bits/sec, 40 packets/sec
5 minute output rate 92000 bits/sec, 46 packets/sec
```

What is one possible cause of the problem?

A. There is no way to tell from this limited information.

B. The circuit is up, but there is no routing protocol.

C. Too much traffic is on the network.

D. Too many IPX route and SAP packets are being dropped, resulting in unstable forwarding tables and SAP tables.

8. Which DEBUG command provides information about all IPX packets received, transmitted, or forwarded through the router?

    A. DEBUG IPX PACKET ACTIVITY

    B. DEBUG IPX PACKET

    C. DEBUG IPX ALL

    D. DEBUG IPX TRAFFIC

9. Which command causes the router to report when a SAP is rejected due to missing routes?

    A. DEBUG IPX SAP EVENTS

    B. DEBUG IPX SERVER EVENTS

    C. DEBUG IPX SAP REJECT

    D. DEBUG IPX SAP ACTIVITY

10. What is a quick way to find all the active NLSP routers directly reachable from a specific router?

    A. SHOW IPX NLSP NEIGHBORS

    B. SHOW IPX NLSP DATABASE

    C. SHOW IPX NLSP TOPOLOGY

    D. SHOW IPX NLSP ROUTE

PING

11. What are the two options available for an extended IPX PING?

    A. Source address

    B. Novell Standard Echo

    C. Data pattern

    D. Novell Standard Ping

    E. Verbose

12. Which of the following combinations allows the TRACEROUTE IPX command to function properly? Choose all that apply.

    A. ROUTERA on IOS version 11.3.17 to ROUTERB on IOS version 12.1.1

    B. ROUTERA on IOS version 12.1.0 to ROUTERB on IOS version 11.2.19

    C. ROUTERA on IOS version 12.1.1 to ROUTERB on IOS version 12.0.3

    D. ROUTERA on IOS version 12.0.3 to ROUTERB on IOS version 12.1.1

Problem Isolation in IPX Networks

13. When using the IPX RIP routing protocol with default timers, which of the following might cause a problem?

    A. RIP route advertisements every 10 seconds

    B. RIP neighbor status updates every 30 seconds

    C. RIP route advertisements every 30 seconds

    D. SAP route advertisements every 30 seconds

14. In a switched network, what interface-level statement should be set to resolve problems with Novell clients that are unable to get a response to the GNS request?

    A. SPEED AUTO

    B. DUPLEX AUTO

    C. SPANNING-TREE PORTFAST

    D. A and B

    E. A and C

15. What are two of the most common problems encountered in an IPX network, compared with a TCP/IP network?

    A. Encapsulation mismatch

    B. Improperly configured routing protocols

    C. Improperly written access lists

    D. Circuit failures

IPX Symptoms, Problems, and Action Plans

16. What is the proper command to reduce the frequency of SAP advertisements?

    A. IPX UPDATE INTERVAL SAP 70

    B. IPX OUTPUT-SAP-DELAY 70

    C. IPX UPDATE-INTERVAL-SAP 60

    D. IPX OUTPUT SAP INTERVAL 50

17. What are two ways to reduce the frequency of SAP advertisements on a WAN link?

   A. Implement SAP filters.

   B. Use the RIP routing protocol.

   C. Use the NLSP routing protocol.

   D. Use the IPX EIGRP routing protocol.

18. On a Monday morning, you receive a call from an end user in a remote office in California. The user states that he can no longer access the server WILDFIRE. The server is located in the same office as the user. What should you check? Choose all that apply.

   A. The routing tables in the core router.

   B. The port status on the switch in California.

   C. The LED status on the end user's workstation.

   D. The SAP table in the router in California.

19. What does the following statement accomplish?

```
ipx output-sap-delay 90
```

   A. It prevents the router from responding to SAP requests for 90 milliseconds.

   B. It prevents the router from sending any SAP broadcasts for 90 milliseconds after the last broadcast is sent.

   C. It prevents the router from responding to any SAP requests if it cannot respond in the first 90 milliseconds.

   D. It prevents the router from delaying more than 90 milliseconds between SAP updates.

20. A user is unable to log in to the server TGIF, which is on network BADBAD. When you check the SAP table in the local router, you can see a SAP Type 23F. What should you do next?

   A. Use the DEBUG IPX ROUTING command.

   B. Clear the route to BADBAD.

   C. Find out why SAP Type 4 is not visible in the router.

   D. IPX PING the client.

Data Link and Network Layer Exercises

21. Read the output from the following protocol analyzer:

```
IPX: Destination Address Summary 0.FFFFFFFFFFFF.9001
IPX: IPX Address = 00000000.FFFFFFFFFFFF
        IPX: Socket Number = 0x9001
    IPX: Source Address Summary A585A1E.002078198644.9001
        IPX: IPX Address = 0A585A1E.002078198644
        IPX: Socket Number = 0x9001
```

What can you tell from this information?

A. It is from a client workstation.

B. It is from a server.

C. It is from a router.

D. There is no way to know the type of device that generated this packet.

22. From the network capture in the previous question, identify the socket.

A. 9001 is the NLSP socket.

B. 9001 is the EIGRP socket.

C. 9001 is the diagnostic PING socket.

D. 9001 is the NCP socket.

23. You have used a protocol analyzer on the LAN segment with the server named WILDFIRE. You are able to successfully IPX PING the server, but clients are unable to log in to the server, either locally or remotely. Which of the following would you be surprised to see in the trace results? Choose all that apply.

A. An NCP response from the server

B. An IPX RIP route response from the server

C. An IPX RIP route request from the server

D. A GNS response from the server

LAB QUESTION

This lab requires one Ethernet router, an Ethernet hub, and one Novell server. Configure the router with IPX frame encapsulation 802.2, using network 10010, with the IPX internal network address 10011001. Set up the Novell server to use only NLSP with RIP/SAP compatibility, and disable RIP on both routers. The server should use 10010 for the external network address and 10011 for the internal network address. Use the area address 10011000 with a mask of FFFFF000 for the NLSP process. Verify that you can see the server in the router.

In the router, remove the area address statement and change it so that the area is 20011000 with a mask of FFFFF000. Change the internal network address of the router to 2011001. Use the SHOW IPX NLSP NEIGHBORS command to see whether or not you still have connectivity with the server. Explain why you do or do not still have connectivity.

Leaving the internal network address as 2011001, add a second area address statement for NLSP as 10011000 with a mask of FFFFF000. Use the SHOW IPX NLSP NEIGHBORS command to see whether or not you still have connectivity with the server. Explain why you do or do not still have connectivity.

SELF TEST ANSWERS

IPX Connection Sequence

1. ☑ **E.** IPX NETWORK AA001BB. Cisco uses the 802.3 (Novell-ether) encapsulation by default if no encapsulation is specified. To configure an IPX network, the correct syntax is IPX NETWORK <<*NETWORK*>> [*ENCAPSULATION*].

   ☒ **A** is incorrect because the syntax is incorrect and the statements are out of order. **B** is incorrect because the statements are out of order and the encapsulation type is wrong. **C** is incorrect because the statement is missing the key word IPX at the beginning. **D** is incorrect because the snap encapsulation on the router does not correspond to the 802.3 frame type on the Novell server.

2. ☑ **B.** To tell all servers in the network of all available services in the network. Only servers and routers listen for SAP updates.

   ☒ **A** is incorrect because a client ignores SAPs unless the client has issued a SAP request, in which case a client will listen for a SAP response only. **C** is incorrect because although a route must generally be present for a SAP to be accepted by a server or router, a SAP includes no routing information. That is the purpose of the RIP or NLSP or EIGRP routing updates. **D** is incorrect because C is incorrect.

3. ☑ **E, C, A, F, B.** This is the correct sequence. First the client issues a GNS broadcast request. The server (or router) issues a GNS directed broadcast reply. The client then issues an IPX RIP route broadcast request, which is answered by the router. Finally, the client issues an NCP connection request.

   ☒ **D** is not included in the sequence because a client ignores general SAP broadcasts. If the steps occurred in any other order, the connection would not be properly established.

4. ☑ **D.** EIGRP and NLSP must be manually configured to redistribute into each other; redistribution is turned off by default.

   ☒ **A** is incorrect because EIGRP and RIP automatically redistribute into each other. **B** is incorrect because RIP and NLSP automatically redistribute into each other. **C** is incorrect because OSPF is not an IPX routing protocol.

5. ☑ **B.** EIGRP is a Cisco proprietary solution and can be used only between Cisco routers.

   ☒ **A** is incorrect because IPX IPXWAN is not a Cisco proprietary solution. It is a standards-based solution associated with NLSP and can be used on non-Cisco routers. **C** is incorrect because IPX IPXWAN must be associated with the NLSP process, which is a standards-based solution that can be used on non-Cisco routers. **D** is incorrect because IPX RIP can be used on both LAN and WAN segments as a single enterprise routing protocol, albeit limited to 15 hops.

Cisco IOS Software Tools and Commands

6. ☑ **D.** *L* stands for *local*, or internal. Since NLSP is the only IPX routing protocol that requires an internal network, the router is probably running NLSP.
   ☒ **A** is incorrect because the IPX EIGRP routing process in not associated with using an internal network. **B** is incorrect because the 1004 network is not on the loopback interface. **C** is incorrect because an internal network is not applied to any interfaces and because the line interface does not exist.

7. ☑ **D.** The router generates the SAP packets and IPX routes, sending them out as broadcasts. High numbers of broadcast drops result in unstable SAP and route tables, potentially preventing users from accessing servers.
   ☒ **A** is incorrect because this information is sufficient to begin to draw some conclusions about the rate of traffic on the interface, even if the counters have not been reset. **B** is incorrect because it is not possible to tell from the SHOW INTERFACE command the routing protocol that is in use or if the interface is associated with any routing protocol. **C** is on the right track, but is incorrect because it is not specific. A diagnosis must include a specific explanation. In addition, the quantity of traffic on the network is not the issue; it is the quantity of SAP and IPX route broadcasts being dropped that are at issue.

8. ☑ **B.** The DEBUG IPX PACKET command provides information about all packets received, transmitted, or forwarded through the router if IPX cache is disabled.
   ☒ **A** is incorrect because there is no such command as DEBUG IPX PACKET ACTIVITY. **C** is incorrect because although DEBUG IPX ALL will certainly provide this information, it provides much more than the information required in this case. **D** is incorrect because there is no such command as DEBUG IPX TRAFFIC.

9. ☑ **D.** When you use the DEBUG IPX SAP ACTIVITY command, if the router receives a SAP and finds no route to the destination network, a log entry is generated with the key phrase "no route" as the reason for rejection.
   ☒ **A** is incorrect because the DEBUG IPX SAP EVENTS command causes the router to generate log entries for all SAPs received and for all SAPs added to the SAP table, but rejected SAPs are only conspicuous by their absence from the log entries. **B** and **C** are incorrect because DEBUG IPX SERVER EVENTS it and DEBUG IPX SAP REJECT are not valid commands.

10. ☑ **A.** NLSP establishes a neighbor relationship to other NLSP routers. The forwarding table (SHOW IPX ROUTE) shows all the links, but it is up to you to filter out those that are not associated with the NLSP process.

    ☒ **B** is incorrect because in a large network, SHOW IPX NLSP DATABASE is not really a quick way to see all the connections to other routers. The NLSP database (SHOW IPX NLSP DATABASE) shows the LSP information but will not filter out duplicate links, so it is up to you to identify the unique connections. **C** and **D** are incorrect because SHOW IPX NLSP TOPOLOGY and SHOW IPX NLSP ROUTE are not valid commands.

PING

11. ☑ **B** and **E.** The Novell Standard Echo specifies that the router should use the Novell IPX Ping format, which is used for communicating with Novell devices. Verbose provides one line of output for each PING request, and on that line the response time is recorded.

    ☒ **A** is incorrect because source address is an option with the extended IP PING, but there is no such option with IPX. **C** is incorrect because data pattern is an option with the extended IP PING, but there is no such option with IPX. **D** is incorrect because the concept is the same, but the terminology is slightly different (Ping instead of Echo).

12. ☑ **C** and **D.** Both are correct, since both ROUTERA and ROUTERB are using IOS Versions 12.0 or higher. Both the sending and the receiving device must support the Novell diagnostic sockets in order for the trace to successfully complete.

    ☒ **A** is incorrect because ROUTERA is not using Version 12.0 or higher and therefore does not support the Novell diagnostic sockets. The command is not an option in this version of software, so A cannot generate a TRACEROUTE request. **B** is incorrect because ROUTERB is not using Version 12.0 or higher and therefore does not support the Novell diagnostic sockets. ROUTERA can generate the request, but the trace will fail because ROUTERB does not know how to respond.

Problem Isolation in IPX Networks

13. ☑ **C.** RIP routes are advertised every 30 seconds by default. This generates a lot of traffic on small WAN links and as a result is often the source of trouble.

    ☒ **A** is incorrect because RIP routes are not advertised every 10 seconds. If the timers are adjusted to advertise more frequently, this could be the source of problems. **B** is incorrect because RIP routers do not establish a neighbor relationship. Therefore, there are no neighbor status updates. **D** is incorrect. First, SAP is not related to RIP; SAP updates are propagated regardless of the routing protocol. Second, the default SAP update interval is 60 seconds, not 30. Finally, SAPs are not route advertisements and they do not generate route advertisements.

14. ☑ **C.** SPANNING-TREE PORTFAST. When the workstation first boots up, SPANNING-TREE places the port into the listening and learning modes before placing the port into forwarding mode. Because of the delay associated with SPANNING-TREE, Cisco recommends that client workstations be connected to ports with SPANNING-TREE disabled.
  ☒ **A** and **B** are incorrect because a failure of port speed and duplex negotiation will result in more than a problem with GNS requests. The client will not be able to sense the frame encapsulation or find the network at all. In most cases, using the autonegotiation features of the switch to sense the port speed and the duplex settings works properly. In those cases in which the NIC does not properly implement the negotiation standards, these default commands should be overridden by manually specifying the port speed and duplex settings. **D** is incorrect because both **A** and **B** are incorrect. **E** is incorrect because **A** is incorrect.

15. ☑ **A** and **C.** Because of the many choices for frame encapsulation on the LAN segments and the difference between Cisco and Novell (not to mention IEEE) in terms of nomenclature for those frame types, encapsulation mismatches are among the most common problems encountered in an IPX network. Due to the broadcast nature of an IPX network, you are more likely to find access lists applied in an IPX network. Thanks to the rich IOS feature set that allows filtering for many different parameters, the opportunity for errors abounds in this area.
  ☒ **B** might appear to be correct at first glance, but the protocol itself is usually properly configured. RIP and EIGRP are very simple to configure, as is IPXWAN. NLSP is more complex but still does not account for a high percentage of problems encountered on a regular basis in the network. **D** is incorrect because an IPX network suffers from no more circuit failures than does a TCP/IP network.

IPX Symptoms, Problems, and Action Plans

16. ☑ **A.** The default advertisement interval is 60, and the correct command to modify this is IPX UPDATE INTERVAL SAP <<*SECONDS*>>.
  ☒ **B** is incorrect because the command IPX OUTPUT-SAP-DELAY affects the timing between SAP updates, not the frequency of the updates. **C** is incorrect because the syntax of IPX UPDATE-INTERVAL-SAP 60 is incorrect (there should be no hyphens). In addition, since the default is 60, the frequency would not be affected by this command. **D** is incorrect because the default interval of 60 results in a lower frequency of updates than an interval of 50.

17. ☑ **C** and **D.** Both are correct because they use incremental updates unless there has been a change in the network, in which case flash updates are used. Since regular updates are not issued, the frequency of SAP advertisements is lower with these protocols.

    ☒ **A** is incorrect because although SAP filters will reduce the number of advertisements, the frequency of those advertisements will remain the same. **B** is incorrect because the RIP routing protocol uses regular advertisements. The frequency of the updates may be manually configured, but using the RIP protocol alone will not reduce the frequency.

18. ☑ **B, C,** and **D.** These answers are correct because they all involve checking the local network connections. When troubleshooting a problem between a client and a server on a local network segment, the first things to check involve local connectivity.

    ☒ **A** is incorrect because whether or not the core router has visibility to the end user's network is irrelevant when you are dealing with a LAN problem.

19. ☑ **B.** The IPX OUTPUT-SAP-DELAY <<*MILLISECONDS*>> command is designed to provide a brief interval between SAP updates, both to allow real traffic through and to provide the server time to process the updates.

    ☒ **A** is incorrect because a router does not generally respond to SAP requests except for GNS requests. The command to change the interval related to GNS responses is IPX GNS-RESPONSE-DELAY <<*MILLISECONDS*>>. **C** is incorrect because there is no command that tells the router to ignore a request that cannot be responded to within a certain interval. **D** is incorrect because there is no command that prevents the router from delaying more than 90 milliseconds between SAP updates.

20. ☑ **C.** Find out why SAP Type 4 is not visible in the router. A user will be unable to access a server if the file server SAP type is not reachable.

    ☒ **A** is incorrect because the 23F SAP would not have been installed in the SAP tables without a valid route. Therefore, the route is not at issue. **B** is incorrect because, from the information available, there is no problem with the route. If a route problem were suspected, you would first check the routing table. **D** is incorrect because until SAP Type 4 is visible from the server, there is no need to troubleshoot the client. If all required SAPs were visible and the client still could not reach the server, using IPX PING would then be appropriate.

Data Link and Network Layer Exercises

21. There is no way to know the type of device that generated this packet.

    ☑ **D.** There is no way to know the type of device that generated this packet. This packet could be generated by a router or a server.

☒ **A** is incorrect because it is impossible to tell the source of the packet, but it is possible to determine that it must have been generated by a server or a router because of the socket. **B** and **C** could be correct, but there is no way to tell for certain without knowing if the MAC address corresponds to that of a server. Therefore, this answer is incorrect.

22. ☑ **A.** 9001 is the NLSP socket.
    ☒ **B** is incorrect because EIGRP uses IPX socket 85BE. **C** is incorrect because a diagnostic PING uses IPX socket 9086. **D** is incorrect because NCP uses IPX socket 451.

23. ☑ **A.** If the client is unable to log on to the server, the client will never reach the stage of issuing an NCP request to the server. Therefore, an NCP response from the server should not be in the trace results.
    ☒ **B** is incorrect because the server could be functioning properly as a router and still not responding to logon requests. **C** is incorrect because the server could be functioning properly as a router and TimeSync could still be functioning properly, and the server might still not respond to logon requests. **D** is incorrect because the server might respond to GNS requests, providing the name of a different server for the client to log on to.

LAB ANSWER

The router configuration should include the following key statements to begin with:

```
ipx routing 00e0.1eb9.11b3
ipx internal-network 10011001
interface Loopback0
ipx network DD001DD
interface Ethernet0.2
 ipx network 10010 encapsulation SAP
ipx nlsp enable
ipx router nlsp
 area-address 10011000 FFFFF000
ipx router rip
 no network 10010
```

The configuration statements for the first set of changes should be as follows:

```
ipx router nlsp
no area-address 10011000 FFFFF000
area-address 20011000 FFFFF000
ipx internal-network 20011001
```

The neighbor relationship will be lost after these changes are made. NLSP uses the concept of an area mask to identify multiple networks. In this case, both the 10010 and the 10011 networks must be covered by the same statement. Furthermore, the network portion of the address is 10011 (covered by the mask FFFFF), whereas the local address is the remaining three digits (the part of the mask that reads 000). The internal network does not need to be covered by the mask. However, the mask must cover the network connecting the router to the next NLSP device. In other words, you must have an area address that covers the LAN segment in this case.

The configuration statements for the second set of changes should be as follows:

```
ipx router nlsp
area-address 10011000 FFFFF000
```

The neighbor relationship will be re-established because the area address covers the shared LAN segment.

9

Diagnosing and Correcting AppleTalk Problems

CERTIFICATION OBJECTIVES

Fans of Apple computers might be familiar with what is sometimes referred to as "The Macintosh Way." Entire books have been written on exactly what The Macintosh Way is, so this chapter will not even try to come close to a complete definition and will limit the discussion here to AppleTalk—Apple Computer Inc.'s networking environment—and its related protocols. For the purposes of this chapter, The Macintosh Way means "making things easy and seamless for the Macintosh user."

Apple has succeeded admirably in its goal of making things easy and seamless for the Macintosh user. However, the company's goal did not necessarily include making things easy for the AppleTalk network manager.

Most of the time, the Mac is very easy to use, is intuitive, and runs free of trouble, just as Apple says it does. When a failure occurs, however, solving the problem can be maddeningly complex. The process of AppleTalk networking closely parallels the way the Macintosh operating system works. Most of the time, things work well, but when problems occur, they can be difficult to solve.

That is not intended to imply that there is something inherently wrong with AppleTalk. On the contrary—Apple was years ahead of other network systems with some of the features available in AppleTalk and related protocols, just as the company led the industry with the Mac OS. Sometimes, though, all the things that are supposed to work together automatically do not. When that happens, you as an AppleTalk network manager must know what is happening behind the scenes. You also must know all the little details that the users are not supposed to have to worry about.

This chapter concerns the details of AppleTalk and how to use your understanding of those details to troubleshoot AppleTalk networks. This chapter covers how the AppleTalk protocol works and how to troubleshoot it from desktop computers as well as Cisco routers. Typically, the only reason that you have an AppleTalk network is that you have Apple Macintoshes. Therefore, most of the desktop computer examples in this chapter are done with a Mac.

CERTIFICATION OBJECTIVE 9.01

The Evolution of AppleTalk

The chapter starts by examining the history of AppleTalk. A form of the AppleTalk protocol was first introduced with the Apple LaserWriter, Apple's first laser printer and the first laser printer with PostScript. This printer was one of the major factors in Apple's dominance of the desktop publishing market and has much to do with the Mac being as popular as it is. Unfortunately, in the mid-1980s, all these technical innovations came at a fairly steep price—several thousand dollars. Apple realized that these printers would have to be sharable in order to help justify their purchase prices.

Actually, early versions of AppleTalk existed *before* the LaserWriter, but the printer's marketing is what really drove the need for Mac networking. Apple built AppleTalk into the ROMs of the LaserWriter and—with an OS update for the Macs and some cables and connectors supplied by Apple—helped users create small, serviceable networks that allowed sharing of the expensive printers.

LocalTalk

This LaserWriter-generated networking technology, originally called AppleBus, eventually became known as LocalTalk. LocalTalk was a relatively slow (230Kbps) serial networking technology. Nonetheless, it had one massive advantage: it was already built into nearly every Mac and laser printer that Apple sold—even some of the dot-matrix printers. LocalTalk's cost dropped even more when third parties such as Farallon (now Netopia) sold versions of the connectors that would function over standard telephone line.

In contrast to Ethernet and Token Ring networks, on which the work is shared partly by the NIC and partly by the host, LocalTalk devices were strictly dumb. They contained no networking logic to speak of—just some electronics for signal conversion and noise prevention. This meant that the software on the Macs (and printers) were responsible for everything from OSI Layer 2 up. It also meant that there were no built-in networking addresses to take advantage of. Apple could have required users or administrators to program an address into each device, but that would have been contrary to Apple's goal of simplicity. Besides, it would have been somewhat difficult on the printers, since there was no keypad of any sort to do so.

What Apple decided to do was, in simple terms, have AppleTalk devices simply pick an address at random. If you have ever had to track down a duplicate-address problem on some other type of network, this approach might sound a little dangerous. Apple took this factor into account, giving AppleTalk a mechanism to ensure that a duplicate address is not picked. When the AppleTalk device picks an address, it does an AppleTalk Address Resolution Protocol (AARP) broadcast, discussed later in this chapter, to see if that address is in use. If it is, another one is picked. As long as most of the addresses are not already in use, this system works fine.

As you'll see later in the chapter, some of these mechanisms designed to make things automatic on small, local networks occasionally do not work in larger networks.

Bootup and Address Assignment

Like nearly all networking protocols, AppleTalk uses a numbering scheme to differentiate nodes. Unlike other protocols that are typically hardcoded (IP, DECNet) or automatically assigned according to MAC address (IPX), AppleTalk uses a dynamic addressing scheme.

AppleTalk Phase I

Back when LocalTalk was all there was, the version of AppleTalk that would have been in use is now known as *AppleTalk Phase I*. The current version of AppleTalk is *AppleTalk Phase II*. The biggest change is that Phase II supports multiple networks. In Phase I, only a single network of 254 addresses was permitted. In Phase II, 65,535 networks (give or take; see next section) of 254 addresses each are permitted. Multiple network numbers (also called *cable ranges*) can be assigned to a single broadcast domain, except on LocalTalk networks, which are limited to one network number.

Phase I AppleTalk is, for all intents and purposes, obsolete. AppleTalk Phase II was released in 1989, and Apple has been slowly removing Phase I support since that time. Recent AppleTalk devices and Mac OSs might not include the option to use Phase I at all.

on the
job

If Phase I devices do exist, support is usually provided with a LocalTalk-to-EtherTalk (AppleTalk over Ethernet) router or a converter of some sort. One option is to use an EtherWave adapter from Netopia (under the Farall on brand name). These adapters can be a little expensive, but their cost might be preferable to maintaining LocalTalk-to-EtherTalk routers, depending on how many LocalTalk devices you have to support. You can find information about the EtherWave adapters on the Web at www.farallon.com/products/ether/adapters/ewmprad.html.

The rest of this chapter focuses on AppleTalk Phase II, unless otherwise noted, and LocalTalk is ignored. Cisco does not produce any LocalTalk equipment, and Cisco routers have long been Phase II compatible.

CERTIFICATION OBJECTIVE 9.02

AppleTalk Connection Sequence

When discussing how any protocol works in a network, it is always a good idea to look at how that protocol uses the OSI model. Table 9-1 shows the Apple protocol stack compared with the OSI model.

The Physical and Data-Link Layers provide connectivity. The Physical Layer comprises hardware or transport media and device drivers. The physical hardware provides the nodes on a network with a data transmission medium called a *link*. AppleTalk supports various types of networking hardware, such as:

- LocalTalk
- Ethernet
- Token Ring
- FDDI
- ATM

A protocol used on the Data-Link Layer specifies the physical aspects of the data link and the link access protocol. The job of sending the data packet over the transport medium is handled here. AppleTalk was designed with the idea of being

TABLE 9-1	OSI Model Layer	AppleTalk Protocol Stack
	Application	AppleTalk Filing Protocol (AFP) Postscript
AppleTalk vs. the OSI Model	Presentation	AppleTalk Data Stream (ADSP) Zone Information Protocol (ZIP) AppleTalk Session Protocol (ASP)
	Session	Printer Access Protocol (PAP)
	Transport	Routing Table Maintenance Protocol (RTMP) AppleTalk Echo Protocol (AEP) AppleTalk Transaction Protocol (ATP) Name Binding Protocol (NBP)
	Network	Datagram Delivery Protocol (DDP)
	Data Link	TokenTalk, EtherTalk, LocalTalk
	Physical	Ethernet, Token Bus, Token Ring, Sonet Local Talk, ISDN, FDDI

data link independent, thus allowing various types of hardware and link access protocols. A user can select between various networks to be used, providing the machine has the proper hardware and software installed for the various link types. AppleTalk supports link access protocols for the following:

- LocalTalk
- EtherTalk
- TokenTalk
- ATM
- FDDITalk

To differentiate between the links, AppleTalk relies on the Link Access Protocol (LAP) manager. The LAP manager is a set of operating-system utilities, not an AppleTalk protocol. There are two functions of the LAP manager. First, the LAP manager must connect the LAP for the link type (typically the one the user selects, such as EtherTalk) to the lower-level hardware device driver for that link. Second, the LAP manager must connect the higher-level AppleTalk protocols. This functionality is similar to that of Microsoft's NDIS Link Layer device drivers.

AppleTalk Phase II

If you are familiar with TCP/IP, you might have noticed a parallel between AppleTalk addresses and IP addresses. AppleTalk uses an addressing scheme with an 8-bit network number followed by a 16-bit node number. When a packet is transmitted, addresses are usually represented in decimal notation, like this: 1000.10. In IP terms, this is equivalent to a 24-bit address space, with a fixed subnet mask of 255.255.0. The network number range is 0 through 65,535, and the node number range is 0 through 255. Of course, there are some reserved addresses in those ranges, which we cover later. These addresses operate at OSI Layer 3, much as IP addresses do.

AppleTalk Address Resolution Protocol

The parallels between TCP/IP and AppleTalk do not end there. As was mentioned briefly, Apple has a protocol called the *AppleTalk Address Resolution Protocol,* or *AARP.* AARP is much like IP ARP and is used to map Layer 3 AppleTalk addresses to Layer 2 addresses. When Macintoshes boot, they dynamically learn their AppleTalk addresses. One of the jobs of AARP is to ensure that each workstation has a unique address. On successful bootup, the workstation stores the address in parameter RAM (PRAM) and attempts to use that same address the next time the workstation boots.

AARP is also used for AppleTalk node to MAC address translation on link layer networks such as Ethernet, Token Ring, and FDDI. The AARP resides between the LAP manager and the LAP. AARP also maintains an address-mapping table (AMT) within each node on the network. For example, when you use EtherTalk, the AMT contains a list of AppleTalk addresses along with the corresponding Ethernet hardware address. AARP maps between these two sets of addresses.

exam
ⓦatch
Try to get used to identifying the various parts of AppleTalk packets. You might be asked to identify the protocol of a packet, its purpose, and so forth.

The AMT is also commonly called an *ARP table* or, for purposes of Cisco commands, the *Apple ARP table.* Following is an example output from a Cisco router for the SHOW APPLETALK ARP command:

```
Router> show apple arp
Address         Age (min)   Type       Hardware Addr        Encap   Interface
2249.129                6   Dynamic    0800.097e.ce90.0000  SNAP    Ethernet0/0
2249.131                4   Dynamic    0800.0977.721d.0000  SNAP    Ethernet0/0
2249.155                -   Hardware   0000.0c39.cc04.0000  SNAP    Ethernet0/0
2204.180                -   Hardware   0000.0c39.cc09.0000  SNAP    Ethernet0/5
2225.13               169   Dynamic    00c0.4900.5634.0000  SNAP    Ethernet1/0
2225.30               169   Dynamic    00c0.4900.ba19.0000  SNAP    Ethernet1/0
2225.32               173   Dynamic    00c0.4900.563f.0000  SNAP    Ethernet1/0
2225.168                -   Hardware   0000.0c39.cc0c.0000  SNAP    Ethernet1/0
281.43                  -   Hardware   0000.0c39.cc0d.0000  SNAP    Ethernet1/1
280.30                 12   Dynamic    0800.2012.e4f3.0000  SNAP    Ethernet1/2
280.36                 37   Dynamic    0800.0796.740e.0000  SNAP    Ethernet1/2
280.41                177   Dynamic    0000.c51a.1544.0000  SNAP    Ethernet1/2
280.59                 55   Dynamic    0800.0726.37ae.0000  SNAP    Ethernet1/2
280.87                160   Dynamic    0800.076f.f6c4.0000  SNAP    Ethernet1/2
280.108               132   Dynamic    0800.079c.51f8.0000  SNAP    Ethernet1/2
280.116                37   Dynamic    0000.9423.05f0.0000  SNAP    Ethernet1/2
280.128               110   Dynamic    0800.09c1.a109.0000  SNAP    Ethernet1/2
280.129               109   Dynamic    0800.097d.b57c.0000  SNAP    Ethernet1/2
280.130               109   Dynamic    0800.0997.a171.0000  SNAP    Ethernet1/2
280.131               108   Dynamic    0800.092d.1396.0000  SNAP    Ethernet1/2
280.132                74   Dynamic    0800.0999.563d.0000  SNAP    Ethernet1/2
280.134               109   Dynamic    0800.092d.53ea.0000  SNAP    Ethernet1/2
```

The left-hand column shows the network.node address that AppleTalk uses. The age, in minutes, is shown next. The hyphen (-) in this column means that this address belongs to the router (also indicated by a "hardware" type). The MAC address, encapsulation type (always SNAP), and interface finish out the table. This is a good way to see how many AppleTalk devices are active on any given router interface.

Routing Protocol Traffic

The communication between networks along with the routing of data packets between nodes is specified on the Network Layer. AppleTalk uses the Datagram Delivery Protocol (DDP) as the Network Layer protocol. DDP is a connectionless, socket-to-socket protocol that delivers AppleTalk packets across an AppleTalk network. AppleTalk packets are routed by DDP from a source socket within one node to a destination socket within another node. The AppleTalk data encapsulated within a DDP packet is a *datagram*. Furthermore, as in IP, the sequencing, retransmissions, and other features to ensure reliability are the responsibility of higher-layer protocols. The following describes the fields of the DDP portion of an AppleTalk packet:

■ **Hop count**   This is the number of router hops a DDP packet has made while traveling to its destination. Hop count is analogous to the IP TTL counter, but hop count is fixed at a maximum of 15. If the count reaches 15 and the router that currently "has" the packet cannot deliver it to a directly attached node, the packet must be discarded.

■ **Length**   This is the number of bytes of DDP information—that is, the DDP header and data portions. Apple has defined the maximum length as 599 bytes (13 for the header and up to 586 for data).

■ **Checksum**   This is a 16-bit checksum for the DDP packet, covering all DDP bytes following the Checksum field. This feature is intended to provide a simple check for packet corruption. If the checksum does not match the data, the packet must be discarded. According to the protocol specification, the checksum is optional. A checksum of 0 implies that the checksum was not calculated and receiving nodes should not perform a checksum calculation.

■ **Destination network number**   This is the network number for which the packet is destined. AppleTalk routers make forwarding decisions based on the destination network, just as IP routers do. This number is also used by nodes to determine if a packet is destined for them. The Destination Network Number field is equivalent to a network or subnetwork number in IP.

■ **Source network number**   This is the network number of the transmitting node.

■ **Destination node**   This is the node (station) on the destination network that is to receive this packet. This field is equivalent to the host portion of an address in IP. Host number 255 is the broadcast address. Node 0 is used to represent any router for the indicated network number. Node 254 is reserved and should not be used.

■ **Source node**   This is the sending node (station) on the source network.

■ **Source socket**   AppleTalk, like IP, uses socket numbers to differentiate among multiple processes running on various nodes. (On IP, sockets are more commonly called *ports*, but the concept is the same.) Unlike IP, AppleTalk socket numbers are defined at Layer 3, not Layer 4. Apple uses 8 bits to hold a socket number, so the possible range of values is 0 through 255. Numbers 0 and 255 are reserved:

- Socket numbers 1 through 127 are the Statically Assigned Sockets (SASs). Apple has reserved use of sockets 1 through 63. Sockets 64 through 127 are available for development use and should *only* be used by developers for experimental purposes, *not* in production software.

- Sockets 128 through 254 are the Dynamically Assigned Sockets (DASs) and should be used for user-installed services. The DASs are assigned by the OS via a system call.

- **Destination socket**   This field contains the socket number of the receiving node (or nodes).

- **DDP type**   This field indicates the transport type. AppleTalk tends to use more transport types than does IP, and AppleTalk's are more application specific.

Workstations on an AppleTalk network are uniquely identified with a network number, a node number, and a socket number. If you were looking for a location in a city, the network number would be the street name, the node number would be the building number, and the socket number would be the room inside the building.

Earlier we stated that an AppleTalk address consists of a 16-bit network number and an 8-bit node identifier. Phase I of AppleTalk provided support for only one 16-bit network that supported 254 nodes. Each of these nodes was dynamically assigned using DDP addressing: an 8-bit network number along with a 16-bit node number. Phase I supported only on AppleTalk zone.

In Phase II of AppleTalk, each device has a unique range of network numbers. Each of these network numbers in the specified range can be associated with 253 available node IDs, so the number of devices the network can support would be 253 multiplied by the number of network numbers. Phase II removed the single network limitation and replaced it with a cable range. This enables multiple networks per LAN segment. Each of these multiple networks support 253 nodes per network number, not per LAN segment.

Network numbers are still dynamically assigned using the 24-bit network node pair from DDP. The maximum number of zones is now 255. An advantage to using multiple zones is the flexibility offered to administrators. For example, you can place multiple servers on a high-speed backbone, but users will see only the devices they need in their local networks. The LAN and LocalTalk zone names are maintained on the router. Each route contains a Zone Information Table (ZIT). This table contains all known networks it can reach and is used by the router to maintain the integrity of the network.

The job of the AARP software to pick a nonconflicting node ID. It does so by picking an ID at random and sending an AARP request for that address to see if there are any responses.

In addition to the node ID, the AppleTalk device also has to pick a network number. Apple decided to accomplish this task by reserving a particular range of network numbers for this purpose. The range is FF00 through FFFE in hex, or 65.280 through 65.534 in decimal. This range is the startup range. When a Mac boots up on an AppleTalk network for the first time, it acquires a node ID in one of the networks listed in this startup range. The primary purpose of this address is for communication with an AppleTalk router to determine the correct network number(s) to use. This communication is done via the *Zone Information Protocol (ZIP)*.

ZIP Queries and Replies

A new AppleTalk device sends a particular type of ZIP packet, a GetNetInfo request, using the startup address it has chosen. If any AppleTalk routers are on that network, they see the request and reply with a ZIP packet that contains a GetNetInfo reply message. This message contains, among other fields, a starting network number, an ending network number, and the zone name. (Read more about zone names in the "GETZONELIST Request and Replies" section of this chapter.) This is enough information for the node to choose an address in the proper network number range using the same process it used to choose an address in the startup range.

If no router is present, the AppleTalk device keeps its startup address and uses that to communicate. This facilitates small ad hoc networks without a router, useful for simple file sharing and printing. A Mac retains its previous address and zone name on the local hard drive and attempts to use that information next time it boots. Other AppleTalk devices might or might not have nonvolatile storage for the same purpose, but they can always utilize the dynamic process. Storing the previous information is merely a time-saver.

exam
ⓦatch

A Mac stores the previous network address and zone on its hard drive, but it keeps other kinds of information in a special, small section of memory called Parameter RAM (PRAM). PRAM stores special settings about the Mac, mostly hardware information (about the hard drive, video card, and so on). If you are familiar with PC hardware, think of PRAM as similar to the CMOS. PRAM also stores information about the network card. On occasion, PRAM becomes corrupt or miss-set and needs to be cleared. You might need to perform the following procedure if a Mac does not seem to be recognizing its network card properly.

To clear the PRAM on a Mac, you restart it and, while it is restarting (before the "happy Mac" picture appears), press and hold down Command-Option-P-R. Yes, indeed, that is four keys, all pressed at the same time, while restarting the Mac. When the PRAM has been cleared, the boot process may be different while the Mac rediscovers its hardware.

The process of an AppleTalk device obtaining an address is one of the common failure points on the network. The details of this process are important and are discussed in detail in the "Cisco IOS Software Tools and Commands" section.

GETZONELIST Request and Replies

The *zone list* is one of the defining characteristics of AppleTalk. A *zone* is simply a name for a logical grouping of AppleTalk devices. Zones are for the benefit of people, not computers, and are commonly named according to function, location, department, and so on—for example, "Houston, San Francisco, Boston…" or perhaps "Legal, HR, Engineering…." The names chosen are not important, as long as they make sense to the people they represent.

Mac users normally access the zone list by accessing the Chooser from the Apple menu in the upper-left corner of the screen.

Where does the Mac get the zone list? It gets the list from an AppleTalk router. The ZIT, discussed earlier, comes into play here. Just as routers keep address tables, AppleTalk routers also maintain a list of zone names and their associated cable ranges. To view the table on a Cisco router, use the SHOW APPLE ZONE command. Here is an example of the output:

```
Router> show apple zone
Name                              Network(s)
Chicago                           2236-2236 2243-2243 210-210
```

```
Atlanta                            52 252-252
Madrid                             268-268 68 1013
New York                           18 218-218
Maarssen                           45 245-245
El Segundo                         207-207
Atrium                             270-270 275-275 2208-2208
Tokyo                              295-295 94 95 97 2209-2209 2269-2269
                                   2258-2258
Btrium                             243-243
Frankfurt                          257-257 57 157
Boulder                            1002-1002 1001-1001 1007-1007
Nagoya                             27 297-297
North American Twilight Zone       8017-8017 8006-8006 8005-8005 4011-4011
                                   8035-8035 8000-8000 8032-8032 8002-8002
```

As you can see, several of the zones have multiple associated cable ranges. This allows AppleTalk devices in those areas to be logically grouped together, even if they are on different networks. In addition, notice that upper- and lowercase are maintained in zone names, and spaces are permitted. It is very important that you take care not to add extra spaces or type the names slightly wrong in some way. If you do, you can end up with two similarly named zones in the Chooser. If an error occurs because of an extra space at the end of a zone name, you might not be able to tell why the "duplication" is occurring.

At this point, you might be wondering what exactly is the relationship between a zone name and a cable range. As is demonstrated in the output shown previously, a zone can consist of more than one cable range. The cable ranges do not have to be contiguous or related in any way, except that you want them to be in the same zone.

You can also have more than zone per cable range—useful when you want to make more than one logical grouping on one network segment. This creates an interesting situation for AppleTalk devices, since they now have a choice as to what zone they are "in."

NBP Broadcast Requests and Propagation

Name Binding Protocol (NBP) is an AppleTalk distributed name service that operates on the Transport Layer of the OSI model. The idea here is that each network station acts as a name server. The NBP maps the logical name of an entity to an Internet socket address. Table 9.2 shows the four types and levels of services provided by NBP.

TABLE 9-2

NBP Services

Service	Description
Name registration	Registers its name for name-to-address mapping.
Name deletion	Deletes the name-to-address mapping to terminate operation.
Name lookup	Responds to a name registration.
Name confirmation	Confirms name mapping.

Some types of file services include things such as printing, file sharing, and mail service and can be made available through the Chooser. The service request process is the same for other services as it is for AFPServer. The requesting workstation simply requests the appropriate service name, which is typically hardcoded into both the server process and client driver. Independent developers can create whatever sort of service they like; they just have to develop the client and server processes and choose a name.

Macs do not keep a complete network-to-zone map, so they have to rely on the routers for that. The Mac builds an NBP packet that contains that Mac's own network number, node ID, and the socket with which it wants to communicate NBP information. The packet also contains two strings—one for the zone desired and one for the type of service. This information makes up an NBP *broadcast request* packet. The Mac forwards this packet to a local router, requesting that the router broadcast the packet. The local router converts this packet into a *forward* request, consults its zone-to-network table, and forwards a copy of the packet to all the networks in that zone.

NBP Lookup and Response

NBP broadcast requests received by a router are changed into NBP lookup packets. The router forwards normal lookup packets as DDP data packets. Each AppleTalk host has a name directory that maps all entity names in the host to their Internet socket addresses. NBP implementation has several responsibilities, such as:

- Searching for names
- Registering names in the directory
- Deleting names in the directory

Names are registered in the directory each time the host is started. Hosts use NBP to learn the addresses of resources in other nodes. A host has an NBP process that transmits an NBP broadcast request packet to a router on the network. This packet requests information about resources in specified zones. The router then forwards the packet to other routers on the paths to networks associated with specified zones. When this request finally reaches the destination network (actually a router directly connected to the destination network), the router broadcasts the request to the network. Responses are returned through the network to the requesting host.

ATP Request and Reply

AppleTalk Transaction Protocol (ATP) is a transaction-based protocol that is used to guarantee reliability between nodes. A process in one host requests services from a process in another host. Next, the process in the responding host reports back on the outcome of the request. This communication between the two hosts is called a *transaction*. The ATP request is numbered to provide a link between the request and the response.

ATP also notifies the responding device of how many packets it can hold in memory for the answer (a maximum of eight). The response packets are sent until the requesting host's memory is full or until the answer is complete. If the entire answer is too big, the requester initiates a new transport request to receive the remaining portion of the answer. ATP uses the services of DDP to deliver data and provides transport for session protocols such as AppleTalk Session Protocol (ASP) and AppleTalk Filing Protocol (AFP). When you send an AppleTalk packet, ATP has the job of guaranteeing delivery from the source socket to a destination socket. Remember that both the request and the response carry data.

CERTIFICATION OBJECTIVE 9.03

Cisco IOS Software Tools and Commands

The following section discusses various SHOW and DEBUG commands available with the Cisco IOS. When you use the DEBUG commands, you should exercise the usual cautioning actions that affect the network and lead to excessive output on the screen.

The SHOW APPLETALK INTERFACE Command

The SHOW APPLETALK INTERFACE command is used to display the status and the parameters configured on each interface that has AppleTalk configured. This command displays the interface cable range and zone as well as the line protocol status. In the following example, the word *valid* is shown after the AppleTalk address. This confirms that there are no conflicts with other addresses on the network. If the command is used with no specification for an interface, all interfaces that have AppleTalk configured are displayed:

```
Router1# show appletalk interface ethernet 0
Ethernet 0 is up, line protocol is up
   AppleTalk address is 123.126, Valid
   AppleTalk zone is Sydney
   AppleTalk routing protocols enabled are RTMP
      AppleTalk address gleaning is enabled
      AppleTalk route cache is not initialized
```

Normally, the router acquires its AppleTalk address dynamically. Whether the address is dynamic or static, this screen verifies that it has been validated (as being unique on the network) by one of the AppleTalk neighbors. In addition, each interface must be associated with at least one AppleTalk zone ("Sydney," in this case). There is no need for an interface to run a routing protocol for the sake of being "up," but if there are other routers out there, a routing protocol must be selected. It is possible for more than one routing protocol to be active at one time, which typically causes unnecessary traffic (since only one routing protocol can win the "battle").

The SHOW APPLETALK ROUTE Command

The SHOW APPLETALK ROUTE command displays all the entries in the AppleTalk routing table. In the following example, the router has two routes that are directly connected, two routes that have been learned via RTMP and are one hop away, and one static route that has been configured by the administrator. Notice that all routes (except for the static one, at this point) are in different zones:

```
Router1# show appletalk route
Codes: R - RTMP derived, E - EIGRP derived, C - connected, A - AURP
P - proxy, S - static
5 routes in internet
```

```
C Net 258 directly connected, 1431 uses, Ethernet0, zone Sydney
R Net 6 [1/G] via 123.128, 7 sec, 0 uses, Ethernet0, zone Tokyo
C Net 11 directly connected, 342 uses, Ethernet1, zone Paris
R Net 2154 [1/G] via 123.128, 7 sec, 3482 uses, Ethernet0, zone Athens
S Net 1111 via 123.128, 0 uses, Ethernet0, no zone set
```

The AppleTalk routing table shows all routes of which this router is aware. They can be directly connected, statically configured, or dynamically learned. This table shows all three types. RTMP uses hop count as a metric. The metric is shown within the brackets ([ ]). The letter codes shown are all G, which indicates that these routes are good (in other words, updates have been received within the last 10 seconds). In this table, it has been 7 seconds since the last batch of updates was received. Other codes include S for *suspect* (an update has not been received for 10 seconds, but no more than 20 seconds have elapsed) and "B" for *bad* (more than 20 seconds have passed since an update was received about this route). After 60 seconds, RTMP flushes bad routes from the routing table.

The **SHOW APPLETALK ZONE** Command

The SHOW APPLETALK ZONE command displays all the entries in the ZIT. The zones here can be associated with cable ranges that were learned or locally connected networks. RTMP is used here to exchange zone information. An issue to consider in this area is that routers could take several hours to clear a zone or cable range that is no longer in use. It is an option with this command to specify a zone name:

```
Router1# show appletalk zone
Name                        network(s)
Athens                      4012-4012
Boise City                  21-21
Amarillo                    4023-4023  4025-4025  4026-4026
```

This screen lists the AppleTalk zones and the cable ranges associated with each. Each zone must have at least one cable range. Those that do not are called *ghost zones*. They typically appear as a result of a ZIP storm. This is a good screen to examine in an attempt to find overlapping cable ranges. There are very rarely any configuration error statements that indicate overlapping cable ranges if they occur on different routers. However, they are collected and can be shown here. Symptoms of an overlapping cable range include periodic (almost random) lack of connectivity.

Often overlaps are not discovered, since the resources that reside on the common logical segments never connect to each other.

The SHOW APPLETALK TRAFFIC Command

The SHOW APPLETALK TRAFFIC command displays the statistics of AppleTalk traffic. A display of packets (transmitted and received) and error information for all protocols, including routing protocols, is shown here. It is an option to specify a zone name here:

```
Router1# show appletalk traffic
AppleTalk statistics:
    Rcvd:    388471 total, 0 checksum errors, 124 bad hop count
             338406 local destination, 0 access denied
             0 for MacIP, 0 bad MacIP, 0 no client
             12210 port disabled, 2567 no listener
             0 ignored, 0 martians
    Bcast:   191181 received, 278906 sent
    Sent:    367293 generated, 38795 forwarded, 1090 fast forwarded, 0 loopback
             0 forwarded from MacIP, 0 MacIP failures
             436 encapsulation failed, 0 no route, 0 no source
    DDP:     399965 long, 0 short, 0 macip, 0 bad size
    NBP:     304758 received, 0 invalid, 0 proxies
             48905 replies sent, 56787 forwards, 897674 lookups, 422 failures
    RTMP:    145654 received, 0 requests, 0 invalid, 49089 ignored
             95670 sent, 0 replies
    EIGRP: 0 received, 0 hellos, 0 updates, 0 replies, 0 queries
           0 sent,    0 hellos, 0 updates, 0 replies, 0 queries
           0 invalid, 0 ignored
    AURP: 0 Open Requests, 0 Router Downs
          0 Routing Information sent, 0 Routing Information received
          0 Zone Information sent, 0 Zone Information received
          0 Get Zone Nets sent, 0 Get Zone Nets received
          0 Get Domain Zone List sent, 0 Get Domain Zone List received
```

This screen provides a snapshot of all types of AppleTalk packets sent and received up to a particular moment in time. This is a great screen to use to find if certain protocols or events have been occurring without looking into any more complicated tables. In addition, this screen breaks out each type of AppleTalk packet, something that the simple packet counts on the interfaces fail to do.

The SHOW APPLETALK ACCESS-LIST Command

The SHOW APPLETALK ACCESS-LIST command displays all the current access lists. This command is useful when you are checking for the type of filters the list contains and the interfaces the list has applied:

```
Router1# show appletalk access-list
AppleTalk access list 604:
      permit zone Sydney
      permit zone Tokyo
      deny additional-zones
      permit network 123
```

AppleTalk access lists (600–699) can filter both AppleTalk cable ranges (numerical) and zones (names). If a zone is blocked, all cables in that zone are unreachable. Normally, it is difficult to block one particular AppleTalk machine by its network.node address (since they are dynamically acquired), so AppleTalk access lists allow you to filter by a device's NBP name.

The SHOW APPLETALK ARP Command

The SHOW APPLETALK ARP command displays the AppleTalk Address Resolution Protocol (AARP) cache. ARP establishes the mapping between network addresses and hardware (MAC) addresses. This information is contained in the router's ARP cache. In the following example, the addresses that have "hardware" listed as the type are router interfaces:

```
Router> show apple arp
Address      Age (min)  Type      Hardware Addr        Encap   Interface
2249.129             6  Dynamic   0800.097e.ce90.0000  SNAP    Ethernet0/0
2249.131             4  Dynamic   0800.0977.721d.0000  SNAP    Ethernet0/0
2249.155             -  Hardware  0000.0c39.cc04.0000  SNAP    Ethernet0/0
2204.180             -  Hardware  0000.0c39.cc09.0000  SNAP    Ethernet0/5
2225.13            169  Dynamic   00c0.4900.5634.0000  SNAP    Ethernet1/0
2225.30            169  Dynamic   00c0.4900.ba19.0000  SNAP    Ethernet1/0
2225.32            173  Dynamic   00c0.4900.563f.0000  SNAP    Ethernet1/0
```

The SHOW APPLETALK GLOBALS Command

The SHOW APPLETALK GLOBALS command shows information about settings and parameters for the router's configuration. Basic timer information is shown, such as the 10-second update interval for AppleTalk's ZIP and RTMP:

```
Router1# show appletalk globals
AppleTalk global information:
        The router is a domain router.
        Internet is compatible with older, AT Phase1, routers.
        There are 12 routes in the internet.
        There are 7 zones defined.
        All significant events will be logged.
        ZIP resends queries every 10 seconds.
    RTMP updates are sent every 10 seconds.
```

The SHOW APPLETALK NAME-CACHE Command

The SHOW APPLETALK NAME-CACHE command shows the router's cache of local names and services:

```
Router# show appletalk name-cache
AppleTalk Name Cache:
Net         Adr   Skt   Name                Type           Zone
2345        17    8     secure              SNMP Agent     outside
2345        18    123   secure.Ether0       ciscoRouter    outside
2345        22    8   . guymon              SNMP Agent     outside
```

The SHOW APPLETALK NBP Command

The SHOW APPLETALK NBP command identifies NBP services registered by the router. The router learns the names of AppleTalk NBP objects. Some of the information displayed is the host address, zone, and interface where the object was learned. In the following example, the router is running AppleTalk on two Ethernet interfaces. In addition, the only object the router knows about is itself:

```
Router1# show appletalk nbp
Net  Adr Skt Name                 Type           Zone
1234 345 254 Router1.Ethernet0    ciscoRouter    Sydney
1234 234 254 Router1.Ethernet1    ciscoRouter    Sydney
```

The SHOW APPLETALK EIGRP INTERFACES Command

The SHOW APPLETALK EIGRP INTERFACES command determines on which interfaces EIGRP is active and displays information about EIGRP:

```
Router1# show appletalk eigrp interfaces

AT/EIGRP interfaces for process 1, router id 24096
                    Xmit    Queue  Mean  Pacing Time   Multicast  Pending
Interface  Peers  Un/Reliable  SRTT  Un/Reliable  Flow Timer  Routes
Et0          0        0    0/0        0          11/434   0           0
Et1          1        0    0/0      337           0/10                0
```

In this screen, only the Ethernet0 and Ethernet1 interfaces are configured for EIGRP.

The SHOW APPLETALK EIGRP NEIGHBORS Command

The SHOW APPLETALK EIGRP NEIGHBORS command displays the neighbors discovered by EIGRP:

```
Router# show appletalk eigrp neighbors
AT/EIGRP Neighbors for process 1, router id 83
Address         Interface   Holdtime  Uptime   Q      Seq  SRTT  RTO
                            (secs)    (h:m:s)  Count  Num  (ms)  (ms)
2345.27         Ethernet0   49        0:06:47  0      277  4     20
2348.128        Ethernet1   43        1:14:22  0      233  4     20
```

The SHOW APPLETALK EIGRP TOPOLOGY Command

The SHOW APPLETALK EIGRP TOPOLOGY command displays the AppleTalk EIGRP table:

```
Router1# show appletalk eigrp topology
IPX EIGRP Topology Table for process 1, router id 1
Codes: P - Passive, A - Active, U - Update, Q - Query, R - Reply,
          r - Reply status
P 2166-0, 1 successors, FD is 0
                 via Redistributed (28801/0),
                 via 100.1 (2496016/2195456), Fddi0
                 via 4220.67 (2496016/53760), Serial1
P 2166-0, 1 successors, FD is 365470
                 via Redistributed (1049750/0),
```

```
      via 100.1 (2199356/2195456), Fddi0
      via 4220.77 (2163416/1028410), Serial1
```

This screen shows the feasible and advertised distances (FD/AD) used by the EIGRP protocol.

The DEBUG APPLETALK ROUTING Command

The DEBUG APPLETALK ROUTING command displays output from the RTMP and EIGRP routines. This command is useful for monitoring acquisition of routes, advertising of routes, and aging routing table entries and if there is a concern of conflicting network numbers:

```
Router1# debug apple routing
AT: src=Ethernet0:4234.33, dst=16-16, size=17, 2 rtes, RTMP pkt sent
AT: src=Ethernet1:43947.12, dst=42947, size=237, 37 rtes, RTMP pkt sent
AT: src=Ethernet2:4391.29, dst=16-16, size=427, 93 rtes, RTMP pkt sent
AT: Route ager starting (2 routes)
AT: Route ager finished (37 routes)
```

The DEBUG APPLETALK NBP Command

The DEBUG APPLETALK NBP command displays debugging output from the NBP routines. This command is useful for determining if a router is receiving NBP lookups from a host on the network:

```
Router1# debug apple nbp
AT: NBP ctrl = LkUp, ntuples = 1, id = 45
AT: 2345.2, skt 2, enum 0, name: =:Router2@Sydney
AT: LkUp =:Router2r@Sydney
```

The DEBUG APPLETALK ZIP Command

The DEBUG APPLETALK ZIP command displays debugging output from the ZIP and GZL routines. This command is useful when there is a need to see events such as new zones and zone list inquires or to determine if a ZIP storm is occurring on your network. This command can be used per interface or as a general command on the router, as shown in the following example:

```
Router1# debug apple zip
AT: Sent GetNetInfo request broadcast on Ether0
AT: Recvd ZIP cmd 3 from 2345.2-4
```

```
AT: 3 query packets sent to neighbor 2345.2
AT: 1 zones for 31902, ZIP XReply, src 2345.2
AT: net 23875, zonelen 33, name Tokyo
```

The DEBUG APPLETALK PACKET Command

The DEBUG APPLETALK PACKET command displays debugging output on a per-packet basis. One line of debugging output is displayed for each AppleTalk packet processed, so, due to the large amount of output generated, you should be cautious when using this command. You can identify packet-level errors such as encapsulation errors when using this command:

```
Router1# debug apple packet
Ether1: AppleTalk packet: enctype SNAP, size 50, encaps00000000000000000000000000
AT: src=Ethernet1:2345.2, dst=2345-2345, size=20, 2 rtes, RTMP pkt sent
AT: ZIP Extended reply rcvd from 2345-2
AT: ZIP Extended reply rcvd from 2345-2
AT: src=Ethernet1:2345-2, dst=2345-2345, size=20, 2 rtes, RTMP pkt sent
Ether1: AppleTalk packet: enctype SNAP, size 50, encaps00000000000000000000000000
Ether0: AppleTalk packet: enctype SNAP, size 50, encaps00000000000000000000000000
```

The DEBUG APPLETALK ARP Command

The DEBUG APPLETALK PACKET command displays debugging output of AARP. This command is useful for determining if the router is receiving ARP probes if there is a problem connecting to a particular host on the local network:

```
Route1r# debug apple arp
Ether0: AARP: Sent resolve for 2345.33
Ether0: AARP: Reply from 2345.33(0000.0c00.0463) for 2345.134(0000.0c00.e349)
Ether0: AARP: Resolved waiting request for 2345.33(0000.0c00.0463)
Ether0: AARP: Reply from 2345.22(0000.0c00.0345) for 2345.134(0000.0c00.e349)
Ether0: AARP: Resolved waiting request for 2345.22(0000.0c00.0345)
Ether0: AARP: Reply from 2345.19(0000.0c00.0345) for 2345.134(0000.0c00.e349)
```

The DEBUG APPLETALK ERRORS Command

The DEBUG APPLETALK ERRORS command displays debugging output of AppleTalk errors on the network. If the network is configured properly, this command shows very little output:

```
Router1# debug apple errors
%AT-3-ZONEDISAGREES: Ethernet2: AppleTalk port disabled; zone list incompatible
 with 2345.22
```

```
%AT-3-ZONEDISAGREES: Ethernet2: AppleTalk port disabled; zone list incompatible
  with 2345.22
%AT-3-ZONEDISAGREES: Ethernet2: AppleTalk port disabled; zone list incompatible
  with 2345.22
```

The DEBUG APPLETALK EVENTS Command

The DEBUG APPLETALK EVENTS command displays debugging output about special events, unstable interfaces, and neighbors becoming reachable and unreachable. If the network is configured properly, this command shows very little output:

```
Router1# debug appletalk events
E2: AT: Resetting interface address filters
%AT-5-INTRESTART: E2: AppleTalk port restarting; protocol restarted
E2: AppleTalk state changed; restarting -> probing
%AT-6-ADDRUSED: E2: AppleTalk node up; using address 2345.22
E2: AppleTalk state changed; probing -> verifying
AT: Sent GetNetInfo request broadcast on Ethernet2
%AT-3-ZONEDISAGREES: E0: AT port disabled; zone list incompatible with 2345.22
AT: Config error for E2, primary zone invalid
E2: AppleTalk state changed; verifying -> config mismatch
```

CERTIFICATION OBJECTIVE 9.04

PING and TRACE

This section discusses the PING and TRACE commands. The PING command is useful for testing connectivity from one host to another. The PING command generates five (by default) ICMP echo messages to send to the destination host. The corresponding host sends five echo-reply messages, indicating successful connectivity. The TRACE command is useful for seeing the actual route the packet takes from one host to another. The TRACE command works with the error messages generated by routers when a datagram exceeds its TTL value. TRACE sends a datagram starting with a TTL value of 1, which increments for each set of packets. Each router decrements the TTL value. When the TTL reaches 0, it is sent back to the source, indicating the TTL exceeded error. The round-trip time for each datagram is displayed.

The Standard AppleTalk PING Command

The PING command is useful for testing connectivity from one host on the network to another or for verifying connectivity between a router interface and particular host. In a standard AppleTalk PING, five ICMP messages are generated. In addition, the minimum, average, and maximum round-trip times of the packet are displayed. For example:

```
Router1# ping appletalk 2345.19
Type escape sequence to abort.
Sending 5, 100-byte AppleTalk Echoes to 2345.19, timeout is 2 seconds:
!!!!!
Success rate is 100 percent, round-trip min/avg/max = 4/4/4 ms
```

The Extended AppleTalk PING Command

With the extended AppleTalk PING command, the same idea of the standard AppleTalk PING is used, with added features. In the extended AppleTalk PING, we can specify the number of requests to send, the datagram size, and the timeout. For example:

```
Router1# ping
Protocol [ip]: appletalk
Target AppleTalk address: 2345.19
Repeat count [5]:
Datagram size [100]:
Timeout in seconds [2]:
Verbose [n]:
Sweep range of sizes [n]:
Type escape sequence to abort.
Sending 5, 100-byte AppleTalk Echos to 2345.19, timeout is 2 seconds:
!!!!!
Success rate is 100 percent, round-trip min/avg/max = 4/4/4 ms
```

The Standard AppleTalk TRACE Command

The TRACE command is useful for verifying a route from one host to another. Another possibility is to check the route to verify that your routing protocols are working properly. A potential problem might be when all your data is routed across a 128k link and there is a T-1 available. For example:

```
Router1# trace appletalk 1295.22
Type escape sequence to abort.
```

```
Tracing the route to 1295.22
     1 4621.22 1000 msec 8 msec 4 msec
     2 2398.11 8 msec 8 msec 8 msec
     3 1233.22 8 msec 4 msec 4 msec
     4 1295.22 8 msec 8 msec 8 msec
```

The Extended AppleTalk TRACE Command

As with the standard and extended AppleTalk PING, several more options are available with the extended TRACE. For example, the router sends three probes (datagrams) by default. You can configure the router to send several probes along with the timeout, maximum TTL, minimum TTL, and port number. For example:

```
Router1# trace
Protocol [ip]: appletalk
Target AppleTalk address: 1295.22
Source address:
Numeric display [n]:
Timeout in seconds [3]:
Probe count [3]:
Minimum Time to Live [1]:
Maximum Time to Live [30]:
Port Number [33434]:
Loose, Strict, Record, Timestamp, Verbose[none]:
Type escape sequence to abort.
Tracing the route to 1295.22
     1 4621.22 1000 msec 8 msec 4 msec
     2 2398.11 8 msec 8 msec 8 msec
     3 1233.22 8 msec 4 msec 4 msec
     4 1295.22 8 msec 8 msec 8 msec
```

CERTIFICATION OBJECTIVE 9.05

AppleTalk Symptoms, Problems, and Action Plans

The following section describes various AppleTalk symptoms and problems. Following each symptom or problem is an idea of an action plan the administrator might use to alleviate the problem.

Host Cannot See Zones or Remote Services

One problem that you might run into is an inability to access zones or services that appear in your Chooser window. Users on your network might or might not be able to access various services. Some of the errors could be as described in the following subsections.

Configuration Mismatch

The first step in determining a configuration mismatch is to use the SHOW APPLETALK INTERFACE command. The error here would be a configuration mismatch message. This message tells you that there is a difference in the router and the listed neighbor configurations.

If there is no error message here, the next step is to use the CLEAR APPLE INTERFACE command. Occasionally, the interface will become operational, indicating that there is no mismatch on the interface. If there is still a problem, check the router configuration, specifically looking to ensure that all configurations agree on network number, cable range, zone, and zone list. To avoid mismatch problems, a router can be configured as either nonseed or soft seed. A *nonseed router* has the cable range of 0-0 and must learn the cable range from another router. A *soft seed router* includes the cable range; however, if the router discovers a different cable range, the interface is disabled.

Phase I/Phase II Incompatibility

When using Phase I and Phase II routers on the same network, you must follow two rules. First, no cable range can span more that a single network number. For example, the cable range of 23–25 would not be acceptable, but 34–34 would be fine. In addition, multiple zones cannot be assigned to a single cable range. It is possible for services located on networks running Phase I to not be visible on the other side of the network.

Another issue when using Phase I and Phase II is that Phase I AppleTalk has three types of NBP packets and Phase II has four types of NBP packets. This fact can lead to communication errors between the two phases.

Services Are Not Available Outside the Local Network

Another problem that you might run into is an inability to locate services outside of the local network. Some of the possible errors that can cause this are described in the following subsections.

Duplicate Cable Range Numbers

Problems such as packets not being routed to the proper destination can occur if duplicate network numbers exist within an internetwork. Remember, network numbers must be unique within an internetwork. When services do not appear in the Chooser, there is a good chance of duplicate network numbers. One option is to change the cable range or network number to a different value. Next, view the routing to see if the network number or cable range is still listed. If it is, you have found the duplicate; if the network or cable range is gone after 40 seconds, you have not found the duplicate.

Phase I/Phase II Incompatibility

When using Phase I and Phase II routers on the same network, you must follow two rules. First, no cable range can span more that a single network number. For example, the cable range of 23–25 would not be acceptable, but 34–34 would be fine. In addition, multiple zones cannot be assigned to a single cable range. It is possible for services located on networks running Phase I to not be visible on the other side of the network.

Another issue when using Phase I and Phase II is that Phase I AppleTalk has three types of NBP packets and Phase II has four types of NBP packets. This fact can lead to communication errors between the two phases.

Configuration Mismatch

The first step in determining a configuration mismatch is to use the SHOW APPLETALK INTERFACE command. The error here would be a configuration mismatch message. This message tells you that there is a difference in the router and the listed neighbor configurations. If there is no error message here, the next step is to use the CLEAR APPLE INTERFACE command. Occasionally, the interface will become operational, indicating that there is no mismatch on the interface. If there is still a problem, check the router configuration, specifically looking to ensure that all configurations agree on network number, cable range, zone, and zone list. To avoid mismatch problems, a router can be configured as either nonseed or soft seed. A *nonseed router* has the cable range of 0–0 and must learn the cable range from another router. A *soft seed router* includes the cable range; however, if the router discovers a different cable range, the interface is disabled.

Access Lists

The first step is to see if any distribution lists, filters, or access lists are configured on the router. If there are, disable the access list on the interface in question. Once the access lists are disabled, check for the zones and services availability. If the zones and services are now available, one of the access lists was the problem. Now enable the access lists one at a time until the error occurs again.

Zones Are Missing from Chooser

A fairly common problem is the inability to locate zones that are missing from the Chooser. Some of the possible errors that can cause this are described in the following subsections.

Access Lists

The first step is to see if any distribution lists, filters, or access lists are configured on the router. If there are, disable the access list on the interface in question. Once the access lists are disabled, check for the zones and services availability. If the zones and services are now available, one of the access lists was the problem. Now enable the access lists one at a time until the error occurs again.

Configuration Mismatch

The first step in determining a configuration mismatch is to use the SHOW APPLETALK INTERFACE command. The error here would be a configuration mismatch message. This message tells you that there is a difference in the router and the listed neighbor configurations.

If there is no error message here, the next step is to use the CLEAR APPLE INTERFACE command. Occasionally, the interface will become operational, indicating that there is no mismatch on the interface. If there is still a problem, check the router configuration, specifically looking to ensure that all configurations agree on network number, cable range, zone, and zone list. To avoid mismatch problems, a router can be configured as either nonseed or soft seed. A *nonseed router* has the cable range of 0–0 and must learn the cable range from another router. A *soft seed router* includes the cable range; however, if the router discovers a different cable range, the interface is disabled.

ZIP Storms

ZIP storms occur when a router tells its neighbors about a router for which it has no zone name; the route is then passed to other neighbors. To identify a ZIP storm, use the SHOW APPLETALK TRAFFIC command and note the number of ZIP requests. Use the same command 30 seconds later and note the new number of ZIP requests. If the number of ZIP requests increases by more than 10, there is a good chance that a ZIP storm is occurring.

Using the DEBUG APPLE ZIP command, you can identify the network for which the zone is requested. Now you can identify the router that is injecting the network number causing the excessive ZIP traffic. If a network is found for which no zone is set, a host on that network is probably not responding to ZIP requests, resulting in the ZIP storm.

Unstable Routers or Convergence

Unstable routers or convergence problems can occur if the network traffic load is excessive. The excessive traffic load can prevent routers from sending RTMP updates every 10 seconds. At this point, routers age out routes after missing RTMP updates. In addition, inconsistent RTMP updates can result in frequent route changes. Check the traffic load for each interface by viewing the field displayed in the SHOW APPLE INTERFACES command. An idea here is to reconfigure the RTMP timer values, allowing fewer updates if the load is less than 50 percent.

Services Are Not Always Available

The below subsections describe possible errors that can cause services to not always be available.

Duplicate Network Numbers

Problems such as packets not being routed to the proper destination can occur if duplicate network numbers exist within an internetwork. Remember, network numbers must be unique within an internetwork. When services do not appear in the Chooser, there's a good chance there are duplicate network numbers. One option is to change the cable range or network number to a different value. Next, view the routing to see if the network number or cable range is still listed. If it is, you have found the duplicate; if the network or cable range is gone after 40 seconds, you have not found the duplicate.

ZIP Storms

ZIP storms occur when a router tells its neighbors about a router for which it has no zone name; the route is then passed to other neighbors. To identify a ZIP storm, use the SHOW APPLETALK TRAFFIC command and note the number of ZIP requests. Use the same command 30 seconds later and note the new number of ZIP requests. If the number of ZIP requests increases by more than 10, there is a good chance that a ZIP storm is occurring.

Using the DEBUG APPLE ZIP command, you can identify the network for which the zone is requested. Now you can identify the router that is injecting the network number causing the excessive ZIP traffic. If a network is found for which no zone is set, a host on that network is probably not responding to ZIP requests, resulting in the ZIP storm.

Unstable Routers or Convergence

Unstable routers or convergence problems can occur if the network traffic load is excessive. The excessive traffic load can prevent routers from sending RTMP updates every 10 seconds. At this point, routers age out routes after missing RTMP updates. In addition, inconsistent RTMP updates can result in frequent route changes. Check the traffic load for each interface by viewing the field displayed in the SHOW APPLE INTERFACES command. An idea here is to reconfigure the RTMP timer values, allowing fewer updates if the load is less than 50 percent.

Overloaded Network

An overloaded network can result in several problems. As discussed in the previous section, excessive traffic can affect routing updates. Another issue here is the possibility of zones fading in and out of the Chooser, connections being dropped, and route flapping.

Services Visible But Not Usable

The subsections below describe possible errors that can cause services to be visible but not usable.

Duplicate Network Numbers

Problems such as packets not being routed to the proper destination can occur if duplicate network numbers exist within an internetwork. Remember, network numbers must be unique within an internetwork. When services do not appear in the Chooser, there's a good chance there are duplicate network numbers. One option is to change the cable range or network number to a different value. Next, view the routing to see if the network number or cable range is still listed. If it is, you have found the duplicate; if the network or cable range is gone after 40 seconds, you have not found the duplicate.

ZIP Storms

ZIP storms occur when a router tells its neighbors about a router for which it has no zone name; the route is then passed to other neighbors. To identify a ZIP storm, use the SHOW APPLETALK TRAFFIC command and note the number of ZIP requests. Use the same command 30 seconds later and note the new number of ZIP requests. If the number of ZIP requests increases by more than 10, there is a good chance that a ZIP storm is occurring.

Using the DEBUG APPLE ZIP command, you can identify the network for which the zone is requested. Now you can identify the router that is injecting the network number causing the excessive ZIP traffic. If a network is found for which no zone is set, a host on that network is probably not responding to ZIP requests, resulting in the ZIP storm.

Access Lists

The first step is to see if any distribution lists, filters, or access lists are configured on the router. If there are, disable the access list on the interface in question. Once the access lists are disabled, check for the zones and services availability. If the zones and services are now available, one of the access lists was the problem. Now enable the access lists one at a time until the error occurs again.

Zone List Changes Each Time Chooser Is Opened

The subsections below describe possible errors that can cause zone list changes each time the Chooser is opened.

Unstable Routers or Convergence

Unstable routers or convergence problems can occur if the network traffic load is excessive. The excessive traffic load can prevent routers from sending RTMP updates every 10 seconds. At this point, routers age out routes after missing RTMP updates. In addition, inconsistent RTMP updates can result in frequent route changes. Check the traffic load for each interface by viewing the field displayed in the SHOW APPLE INTERFACES command. An idea here is to reconfigure the RTMP timer values, allowing fewer updates if the load is less than 50 percent.

Configuration Mismatch

The first step in determining a configuration mismatch is to use the SHOW APPLETALK INTERFACE command. The error here would be a configuration mismatch message. This message tells you that there is a difference in the router and the listed neighbor configurations.

If there is no error message here, the next step is to use the CLEAR APPLE INTERFACE command. Occasionally, the interface will become operational, indicating that there is no mismatch on the interface. If there is still a problem, check the router configuration, specifically looking to ensure that all configurations agree on network number, cable range, zone, and zone list. To avoid mismatch problems, a router can be configured as either nonseed or soft seed. A *nonseed router* has the cable range of 0–0 and must learn the cable range from another router. A *soft seed router* includes the cable range; however, if the router discovers a different cable range, the interface is disabled.

Connection to Services Drops

Another problem that you may encounter is when the connection to services drops. Some of the possible errors that can cause this are described in the subsections below.

Unstable Routers or Convergence

Unstable routers or convergence problems can occur when the network traffic load is excessive. The excessive traffic load can prevent routers from sending RTMP updates every 10 seconds. At this point, routers age out routes after missing RTMP updates. In addition, inconsistent RTMP updates can result in frequent route changes. Check the traffic load for each interface by viewing the field displayed in the SHOW APPLE INTERFACES command. An idea here is to reconfigure the RTMP timer values, allowing fewer updates if the load is less than 50 percent.

ZIP Storms

ZIP storms occur when a router tells its neighbors about a router for which it has no zone name; the route is then passed to other neighbors. To identify a ZIP storm, use the SHOW APPLETALK TRAFFIC command and note the number of ZIP requests. Use the same command 30 seconds later and note the new number of ZIP requests. If the number of ZIP requests increases by more than 10, there is a good chance that a ZIP storm is occurring.

Using the DEBUG APPLE ZIP command, you can identify the network for which the zone is requested. Now you can identify the router that is injecting the network number causing the excessive ZIP traffic. If a network is found for which no zone is set, a host on that network is probably not responding to ZIP requests, resulting in the ZIP storm.

Router Ports Stuck Restarting or Acquiring

A router port can become stuck when trying to acquire its dynamic AppleTalk address. Normally, there are two reasons for this: a configuration mismatch or the lack of a seed router. The subsections below describe these errors.

Configuration Mismatch

The first step in determining a configuration mismatch is to use the SHOW APPLETALK INTERFACE command. The error here would be a configuration mismatch message. This message tells you that there is a difference in the router and the listed neighbor configurations.

If there is no error message here, the next step is to use the CLEAR APPLE INTERFACE command. Occasionally, the interface will become operational, indicating that there is no mismatch on the interface. If there is still a problem, check the router configuration, specifically looking to ensure that all configurations agree on network number, cable range, zone, and zone list. To avoid mismatch problems, a router can be configured as either nonseed or soft seed. A *nonseed router* has the cable range of 0–0 and must learn the cable range from another router. A *soft seed router* includes the cable range; however, if the router discovers a different cable range, the interface is disabled.

No Seed Router

It is possible to configure a Cisco router to simply "discover" the appropriate network information out a LAN interface. However, this discovery assumes that there is at least one router that is willing to actually provide this information (cable range and zone[s]) when prompted. If all routers are attempting to discover the network information about an interface, all will fail.

Old Zone Names (Ghost Zones) Appear in Chooser

When old zone names or "ghost zones" appear in the Chooser, they can be caused either by crossed wires or an improper process that was used to change the zone name. The subsections below describe these errors.

Crossed Wires

Very few wiring closets actually have wires that are labeled. If some fall out or are temporarily removed for whatever reason, it is quite easy to replace them in the wrong ports. If this happens, an inappropriate zone gets injected onto a wire. The other devices do not agree with the configuration but they have no means of stopping it. Thus, a ghost zone starts. Since the zone information that is being propagated onto the network is configured on the router, this ghost does not simply float away.

Improper Process Used to Change Zone Names

AppleTalk does not like sudden change. If you change a zone name on one router, you must change it on all others on that segment. However, if routers are in discovery mode, they tend to "discover" the old and new zones, and it is very difficult to convince a router to lose this information. The best means of changing a zone name is to first remove the zone entirely and then install the new zone where the old one once lived.

CERTIFICATION SUMMARY

AppleTalk originally gained popularity as a way to share expensive printers among multiple Macintosh computers and because it came built into each of those printers and Macintoshes. AppleTalk was designed after TCP/IP was created, and AppleTalk's creators used some of the IP designs. AppleTalk addressing uses 24 bits: 16 for a network number and 8 for a node ID. This type of AppleTalk is called *AppleTalk Phase II*. AppleTalk Phase I was originally used on LocalTalk networks and was limited to 253 devices.

When an AppleTalk device first boots, it must choose an address. This is done by first randomly picking a node ID and network number from the startup network number range. The device verifies that the address it has picked is not already in use by requesting its own address via an AARP request. If the device receives no reply, it knows it can use the address it has chosen. Once it has picked a startup address, the device can use that to communicate with a local AppleTalk router to determine if there is a cable range assigned to the network segment that the router is on. If so, the device picks another node ID within that range and sends an AARP request for that address as well.

The protocol AppleTalk uses at Layer 3 is called DDP. DDP is a connectionless, unreliable protocol. Reliability features must be implemented at higher layers.

Mac users typically access network resources through the Chooser. In the Chooser, the user sees a list of service types and a list of zones from which to choose the services. When the Chooser is first launched, it requests a list of zone names from a local router via the Zone Information Protocol (ZIP). The Mac might need to make more than one request because all the zones might not fit in one packet.

✓ TWO-MINUTE DRILL

Here are some of the key points from each certification objective in Chapter 9.

The Evolution of AppleTalk

❑ A form of the AppleTalk protocol was first introduced with the Apple LaserWriter—Apple's first laser printer and the first laser printer with PostScript.

❑ Unlike other protocols that are typically hardcoded (IP and DECNet) or automatically assigned according to MAC address (IPX), AppleTalk uses a dynamic addressing scheme.

AppleTalk Connection Sequence

❑ To differentiate between links, AppleTalk relies on the Link Access Protocol (LAP) manager. The LAP manager is a set of operating system utilities, not an AppleTalk protocol.

❑ AARP is much like IP ARP and is used to map Layer 3 AppleTalk addresses to Layer 2 addresses.

❑ Name Binding Protocol (NBP) does a couple of things, depending on how it's used, but its main function is to map a named service to its network number, its node ID, and its socket number.

❑ When a Mac boots up on to an AppleTalk network for the first time, it acquires a node ID in one of the networks listed in the startup range. The primary purpose of this address is for communication with an AppleTalk router to determine the correct network number(s) to use. This communication is done via ZIP.

Cisco IOS Software Tools and Commands

❑ By default, using this form of the command, APPLETALK ROUTING, turns on Routing Table Maintenance Protocol (RTMP) routing.

❑ The DEBUG APPLETALK PACKET command displays debugging output on a per-packet basis.

❑ The Mac stores the previous network address and zone on its hard drive, but it keeps other kinds of information in a special, small section of memory called Parameter RAM (PRAM).

PING and TRACE

❑ The PING command is available for testing connectivity on the network.

❑ The TRACE command is available for determining the path of the packet from the source to the destination.

AppleTalk Symptoms, Problems, and Action Plans

❑ The first step in determining a configuration mismatch is to use the SHOW APPLETALK INTERFACE command.

❑ ZIP storms occur when a router tells its neighbors about a router for which it has no zone name; the route is then passed to other neighbors. To identify a ZIP storm, use the SHOW APPLETALK TRAFFIC command.

SELF TEST

The following questions will help you measure your understanding of the material presented in this chapter. Read all of the choices carefully because there might be more than one correct answer. Choose all correct answers for each question.

The Evolution of AppleTalk

1. AppleTalk devices dynamically select their Network Layer address using which of the following protocols?

    A. NCP

    B. ARP

    C. AARP

    D. AppleTalk addresses are statically assigned

2. Your company has been using the Mac OS for many years. Recently, certain connectivity issues have been raised throughout the AppleTalk portion of the network. What could be the problem?

    A. AppleTalk is slowly becoming obsolete.

    B. AppleTalk Phase I and Phase II can cause problems in the routers.

    C. AppleTalk and IP are incompatible.

    D. AppleTalk must run on network segments without any other Network Layer protocols.

3. Which protocol was built into nearly every Mac and Apple laser printer?

    A. IP

    B. Netopia

    C. EtherTalk

    D. LocalTalk

AppleTalk Connection Sequence

4. Which of the following is not a true AppleTalk media format?

    A. EtherTalk

B. TVTalk

C. TokenTalk

D. FDDITalk

5. While troubleshooting an AppleTalk problem on the network, a user reports that the AppleTalk address of his machine is 172.16.10.1. What can you conclude from this report?

A. The user has not properly found the AppleTalk address, since 172.16.10.1 is the IP address.

B. AppleTalk is misbehaving and reporting the incorrect address.

C. More information is needed.

D. You also need the subnet mask to determine the proper AppleTalk subnet.

6. What does AppleTalk use the AMT for?

A. The AMT maps IP addresses to AppleTalk addresses.

B. The AMT tracks which interface the packet is destined for.

C. The AMT determines how long each device has been operational.

D. The AMT tracks each AppleTalk address and MAC address on a segment.

7. Which of the following commands can you use to track the AMT in the Cisco router?

A. SHOW APPLE AMT

B. SHOW APPLE ARP

C. SHOW APPLE AARP

D. SHOW APPLE ARP-TABLE

8. AppleTalk users in your network report that they are unable to access any of the AppleTalk services on the network. You have traced the problems to one 300-user segment in your network. Each day, it appears that a random assortment of users reports the same problem. What could be causing the problem?

A. The network is configured with Phase I, which supports a total of only 254 users.

B. The network is configured with Phase II, which supports a total of only 254 users.

C. There are sporadic bad ports on the local Ethernet switch.

D. The Cisco router is fast aging its AMT table.

9. Based on a report of hackers in your AppleTalk network, you have configured an access list to block the AppleTalk cable range 65,280 through 65,534. The next morning, no AppleTalk users can access the network. What might be the problem?

   A. The hacker managed to destroy the network that night.

   B. All AppleTalk users must use cable range 65,280 through 65,534 for all network applications.

   C. There is no network problem, so it must be a user thing.

   D. The cable range that has been blocked is used by AppleTalk clients to acquire an address.

10. When would an AppleTalk client actually use a network number in the range of 65,280 through 65,534?

   A. Never

   B. Always

   C. Only if this range is applied to a router interface

   D. When there is no router present on the segment

11. AppleTalk users in your network report problems reaching some of the resources in the Engineering zone of the network. These problems have been present only since a new router was introduced to segment traffic. You have verified that the new router is correctly configured with the engineering zone. What is the problem?

   A. There is a bad port on the new router.

   B. The two zones do not match (Engineering vs. engineering).

   C. The cable ranges are not configured correctly.

   D. More information is necessary to resolve this problem.

12. Which of the following is not a function of NBP?

   A. Searching for names

   B. Creating new names

   C. Registering names in the directory

   D. Deleting names in the directory

Cisco IOS Software Tools and Commands

13. Examine the following AppleTalk routing table. Why is network 6 not showing G for *good*?

```
Router1# show appletalk route
Codes: R - RTMP derived, E - EIGRP derived, C - connected, A - AURP
P - proxy, S - static
5 routes in internet
C Net 258 directly connected, 1431 uses, Ethernet0, zone Sydney
R Net 6 [1/S] via 123.128, 17 sec, 0 uses, Ethernet0, zone Tokyo
C Net 11 directly connected, 342 uses, Ethernet1, zone Paris
R Net 2154 [1/G] via 123.128, 7 sec, 3482 uses, Ethernet0, zone Athens
S Net 1111 via 123.128, 0 uses, Ethernet0, no zone set
```

A. The zone associated with it is incorrect.

B. The network is unreachable.

C. More than 10 seconds have elapsed since an update was received about this network.

D. The metric is unreachable.

14. Users in your network report that they are unable to access AppleTalk services in the Boston zone. They claim that the zone appears in their Chooser, yet no services appear on request. Based on the following SHOW APPLE ZONE display, what is the problem?

```
Router1# show appletalk zone
Name                                    network(s)
Athens                                  4012-4012
Boston
Amarillo                                4023-4023 4025-4025 4026-4026
```

A. There are overlapping cable ranges.

B. Boston is spelled wrong.

C. There are too many zones in the table.

D. There is no cable range associated with the zone.

15. Users in the Sydney zone report problems reaching services in the Boston zone. From the following SHOW APPLE ACCESS-LIST display, what could be the problem?

```
Router1# show appletalk access-list
AppleTalk access list 604:
        permit zone Sydney
        permit zone Tokyo
        deny additional-zones
        permit network 123
```

A. The Boston zone is not permitted.

B. The access list is applied to the wrong interface.

C. Boston is spelled wrong.

D. Cable range 123 is not part of the Boston zone.

16. A junior network administrator in your company has been assigned to correct an AppleTalk problem in the building. He comes to you with the following AARP table from one of the routers and swears that he has found the problem (no age reported for two AppleTalk addresses) but cannot solve it. What do you tell him?

```
Router> show apple arp
Address       Age (min)  Type      Hardware Addr       Encap   Interface
2249.131             4   Dynamic   0800.0977.721d.0000 SNAP    Ethernet0/0
2249.155             -   Hardware  0000.0c39.cc04.0000 SNAP    Ethernet0/0
2204.180             -   Hardware  0000.0c39.cc09.0000 SNAP    Ethernet0/5
2225.13            169   Dynamic   00c0.4900.5634.0000 SNAP    Ethernet1/0
```

A. This is a serious problem, but it will take additional information before a solution can be implemented.

B. There is no problem here, since these represent the router interfaces.

C. This shows duplicate AppleTalk addresses.

D. This shows that a user has statically configured incorrect addresses on the network.

17. There are reports of sporadic connectivity problems throughout your AppleTalk network. A view of the EIGRP neighbors from your router shows the following information. Multiple copies of this command show that the neighbors never have an uptime of greater than 1 minute. What can you gather from this display?

```
Router# show appletalk eigrp neighbors
AT/EIGRP Neighbors for process 1, router id 83
Address                 Interface    Holdtime  Uptime    Q       Seq   SRTT  RTO
                                     (secs)    (h:m:s)   Count   Num   (ms)  (ms)
2345.27                 Ethernet0    49        0:00:47   0       277   4     20
2348.128                Ethernet1    43        0:00:22   0       233   4     20
```

A. EIGRP is fully operational and there are no problems, since EIGRP sends updates every few seconds anyway.

B. EIGRP needs to be configured on more than two interfaces to be operational.

C. Since the neighbors continually have a low uptime, there are quite possibly Physical Layer or serious congestion problems in this network.

D. EIGRP does not work for AppleTalk networks greater than 2000.

PING and TRACE

18. Which option of an AppleTalk PING allows you to change the number of echo packets that are sent from the source to the destination?

A. Repeat count

B. Datagram size

C. Timeout

D. Sweep range

19. By default, what is the maximum number of hops that an extended AppleTalk trace can survive?

A. 10

B. 20

C. 30

D. 40

AppleTalk Symptoms, Problems, and Action Plans

20. What is the best command to determine if a configuration error is the source of an AppleTalk connectivity problem?

A. SHOW APPLE ROUTE

B. SHOW APPLE INTERFACE

C. SHOW APPLE ZONE

D. SHOW APPLE NBP

21. What is the best command to determine if a ZIP storm is occurring in your network?

A. SHOW APPLE ROUTE

B. SHOW APPLE INTERFACE

C. SHOW APPLE ZONE

D. SHOW APPLE TRAFFIC

LAB QUESTION

Get two Cisco routers and connect them with a crossover cable via Ethernet ports. Enable AppleTalk routing on each router, and configure the Ethernet interfaces with the same cable range (1–10). Use the SHOW APPLE INTERFACE command to verify that the AppleTalk interfaces are not yet operational, due to the lack of one or more zones.

Configure the following zones on each AppleTalk interface: blue and red. Ensure that you use all lowercase letters. However, on one side, enter **blue** first, and on the other, enter **red** first. Is the interface operational?

SELF TEST ANSWERS

The Evolution of AppleTalk

1. ☑ **C. AARP.** AppleTalk uses the AppleTalk Address Resolution Protocol to dynamically select a unique Network Layer address.
   ☒ **A** is incorrect because NCP has nothing to do with AppleTalk. **B** is incorrect because ARP is an IP protocol, not an AppleTalk one. **D** is incorrect since AppleTalk does in fact dynamically acquire an address.

2. ☑ **B.** AppleTalk Phase I and Phase II can cause problems in the routers. AppleTalk Phase I and Phase II are sometimes incompatible in the routers.
   ☒ **A** is incorrect because the obsolescence of AppleTalk is truly subjective. Both **C** and **D** are incorrect because AppleTalk can easily coexist with other protocols.

3. ☑ **D.** LocalTalk is built into virtually every Apple device to allow for instant networking.
   ☒ **A** is incorrect because IP is a totally different Network Layer protocol. **B** is incorrect because Netopia is a company that enhanced the ease of use of LocalTalk. **C** is incorrect because EtherTalk refers to AppleTalk over Ethernet.

AppleTalk Connection Sequence

4. ☑ **B.** TVTalk does not exist.
   ☒ **A, C,** and **D** are actually proper AppleTalk media formats, but they are incorrect answers because the question asked which one was *not* a proper media format.

5. ☑ **A.** The user has not properly found the AppleTalk address, since 172.16.10.1 is the IP address. The address shown is an IP address, not an AppleTalk one, so it cannot be used to troubleshoot an AppleTalk network.
   ☒ **B** is incorrect because the AppleTalk operating system would never accidentally report an IP address. **C** is incorrect since the information shown is wrong, not incomplete. **D** is incorrect because AppleTalk does not use a subnet mask, the way IP does.

6. ☑ **D.** The AMT tracks each AppleTalk address and MAC address on a segment. The AMT tracks AppleTalk addresses and MAC addresses for each device.
   ☒ **A** is incorrect because there is no real correlation between IP addresses and AppleTalk addresses. **B** is incorrect because a routing table typically tracks destination interfaces. **C** is incorrect because normally network management stations track system uptime.

7. ☑ **B.** SHOW APPLE ARP.
   ☒ **A, C,** and **D** are incorrect because the commands SHOW APPLE AMT, SHOW APPLE AARP, and SHOW APPLE ARP-TABLE do not exist.

8. ☑ **A.** The network is configured with Phase I, which supports a total of only 254 users. Phase I supports a total of only 254 users, which is not appropriate for a 300-node LAN.
   ☒ **B** is incorrect because Phase II supports more than 254 users per cable range. **C** is incorrect because switch ports are not randomly bad. **D** is incorrect because the AMT table has nothing to do with user connectivity.

9. ☑ **D.** The cable range that has been blocked is used by AppleTalk clients to acquire an address. Cable range 65,280 through 65,534 is used by AppleTalk clients during the address discovery phase.
   ☒ **A** is quite possibly incorrect because a hacker would have problems destroying an entire network. **B** is incorrect because AppleTalk clients do not use this cable range for actual router-based network traffic. **C** is incorrect because this is a very serious network problem, not a user thing.

10. ☑ **D.** When there is no router present on the segment An AppleTalk client keeps its address in the 65,280 through 65,534 range if there is no router present to report the actual cable range of the segment.
    ☒ **A** is incorrect because there is obviously a time when this is true. **B** is incorrect in any AppleTalk router-based network. **C** is incorrect because this is an inappropriate cable range to apply to a router interface.

11. ☑ **B.** The two zones do not match (Engineering vs. engineering). The two zones configured are actually different because AppleTalk zones are case-sensitive.
    ☒ **A** is incorrect because at this point, there is no indication that there are bad ports on the routers. **C** is incorrect because a cable range mismatch would cause sporadic problems, not constant ones. **D** is incorrect because there is ample information to resolve the issue at this time.

12. ☑ **B.** Creating new names. NBP does not create the name structure in AppleTalk.
    ☒ **A, C,** and **D** show the actual functions of NBP, which is why they are incorrect for this question.

Cisco IOS Software Tools and Commands

13. ☑ **C.** More than 10 seconds have elapsed since an update was received about this network. AppleTalk networks become S (for *suspect*) when more than 10 seconds have elapsed between RTMP updates.

    ☒ **A** is incorrect because a routing update would not be suspect based on an incorrect zone assignment. **B** is incorrect because the route is obviously reachable (it is in the routing table). **D** is incorrect because RTMP can work up to 15 hops away, and this route is only 1 hop.

14. ☑ **D.** There is no cable range associated with the zone. Each AppleTalk zone must have at least one cable range associated with it. In this case, Boston is a ghost zone.

    ☒ **A** is incorrect because, from this display, there are no overlapping cable ranges reported (and this would not cause a zone problem anyway). **B** is incorrect because there is no way to verify if Boston is misspelled without some documentation. **C** is incorrect since a Cisco router can maintain many more than three zones.

15. ☑ **A.** The Boston zone is not permitted. Since the list is defined to deny any zones except those explicitly permitted, Boston is not permitted.

    ☒ **B** is incorrect because there is no way to verify from this screen how this access list is applied. **C** is incorrect since Boston is not even present in this display. **D** is incorrect since there is no way to verify the cable ranges in the Boston zone.

16. ☑ **B.** There is no problem here, since these represent the router interfaces. The " _ " time in the AARP table in the router shows directly connected interfaces, so this table does not report any particular problem.

    ☒ **A, C,** and **D** are all incorrect because this table does not indicate any particular AppleTalk problem.

17. ☑ **C.** Since the neighbors continually have a low uptime, there are quite possibly Physical Layer or serious congestion problems in this network. Because the neighbor uptime is continually low, there is either a Physical Layer problem or congestion on the wire.

    ☒ **A** is incorrect since it was mentioned that many successive SHOW screens had low uptime values, so everything is not OK. **B** and **D** are incorrect because they are simply not true.

PING and TRACE

18. ☑ **A.** The repeat count is used to configure the number of echo packets that are sent during a PING.

    ☒ **B, C,** and **D** are incorrect because, although they are configurable options in an extended PING, they do not control the number of echo packets.

19. ☑ C. The maximum number of hops for a trace is 30.
    ☒ A, B, and D are incorrect because they are not the default value.

AppleTalk Symptoms, Problems, and Action Plans

20. ☑ B. The best command to see if there are AppleTalk configuration errors is SHOW APPLE INTERFACE because most AppleTalk configuration are performed on the interface.
    ☒ A, SHOW APPLE ROUTE, shows the results of proper routing protocol configuration, which is enabled by default. C, SHOW APPLE ZONE, displays the list of all known AppleTalk zones learned by ZIP, which is also enabled by default. D, SHOW APPLE NBP, displays the dynamic naming convention used by AppleTalk.

21. ☑ D. The best command to see if there is a ZIP storm occurring is SHOW APPLE TRAFFIC, executed a few times in succession to see if the number of ZIP requests has gone up considerably.
    ☒ A, SHOW APPLE ROUTE, shows the AppleTalk routing table, which is not really affected by a ZIP storm. B, SHOW APPLE INTERFACE, shows the interface operation, which is operational with or without a ZIP storm. C, SHOW APPLE ZONE, displays the AppleTalk zones, not whether a zone storm is occurring.

LAB ANSWER

Again, AppleTalk is very picky about configuration parameters. The zones must be spelled identically on each end and configured in the same sequence on each end. The first router on the wire sets the necessary parameters for all other routers.

10

Diagnosing and Correcting Catalyst Problems

CERTIFICATION OBJECTIVES

N etworks have evolved from small proprietary LANs to encompass large enterprise-spanning configurations that are mission critical to the function and profitability of today's businesses. Originally, a shared-media LAN composed of hubs and a few servers was sufficient for most needs, but today's high performance environment is expected to deliver a variety of services efficiently, reliably, and effectively. To address these growing needs, techniques such as bridging, subnetting, and, more recently, virtual LANs (VLANs), trunking (both 802.1Q and Inter-Switch Link [ISL]), and multicasting were developed. Applications such as video to the desktop, voice over IP (VoIP), and interactive videoconferencing continue to place greater demands on the networks of today and tomorrow. LAN switching is the preferred method of network infrastructure to accommodate the growing bandwidth and quality of service (QoS) requirements of modern businesses.

Cisco's line of LAN switching products, known as the Catalyst family, includes a broad range of models, from the fixed configuration 1900, 2800, 2900, and 3500 series to the modular 4000 (the 4900 series is a special Layer 3 fixed configuration switch), 5000, 6000, and 8500 series. This chapter focuses on the Catalyst 5000 (Cat5K) and the Catalyst 6000 (Cat6K) series. However, most of the features and procedures discussed are applicable to other models in the Catalyst line.

The standard operating system (OS) on the Catalyst family of switches is known as the Catalyst OS (CatOS), on Revision 6.0 as of this writing. However, with the release of the Cat6K and the 8500 series, Cisco integrated switching services within the Cisco Internetwork Operating System (IOS) software. IOS, originally Cisco's OS for its router platform, is now being deployed across Cisco's entire hardware platform to simplify installation and management. With the advent of Layer 3 switching, a greater amount of switching functionality is being integrated into the base IOS platform. Commencing with release 12.0, such switching services and configurations can be performed using either CatOS or IOS on the Cat5K and the Cat6K, depending on the hardware platform and functionality desired. Today the Catalyst 3500 and 4000 series switches primarily run the CatOS. The Catalyst 8500 series runs IOS exclusively.

This chapter examines both OS releases and presents equivalent commands where applicable.

Be careful of the OS command you use to answer questions on the Cat5K or Cat6K. Both can run either the CatOS or IOS, depending on configuration and use. If either switch were in an access function (such as the closet), the best answer would be the CatOS command. If either one is in a distribution or core role (such as a network center or server farm use), the command should be the IOS version. Remember, Cisco wants you to choose the best answer, even if there is more than one correct answer.

CERTIFICATION OBJECTIVE 10.01

Catalyst Light-Emitting Diodes

One of the most important (and probably least glamorous) status indicator and troubleshooting tools you have is the Catalyst light-emitting diode (LED) displays. Depending on the module, you can get information on everything from link status, speed, collision rate, and duplex of the connection to mode the Supervisor module is operating in or if it had a boot failure.

The Cat5K is known for the vast number of available modules that can be inserted into its chassis; over 53 different modules are currently available. The Cat6K has more than 15 modules available, with more scheduled for release. This chapter focuses on the main Ethernet and Supervisor modules in the latest release that you are likely to encounter in new deployments. For the Cat5K, this is the Supervisor Engine III and the 24 port 10/100 Ethernet switching module. For the Cat6K, this chapter focuses on the Supervisor Engine 1-A, the 48 port 10/100 Enhanced QoS Ethernet module, and the 8 port Gig-Ethernet module. Details on all the modules can be obtained by searching Cisco's Web site at *www.cisco.com*.

The Catalyst 5000 Series

The Catalyst 5000 series has been the core of Cisco's networking infrastructure. The availability of networking modules spans a broad range of networking requirements, from Ethernet to Token Ring and FDDI modules. In this section, we focus on the Supervisor III and Ethernet modules and how to physically diagnose issues with these modules from the visible LEDs.

The Supervisor Module

The Cat5K can operate with one or two (for redundancy in the 5500 series) Supervisor modules. The Supervisor is required for the Cat5K to function; it controls all switching functions and backplane access. This module must go in slot #1 of the chassis, with the redundant Supervisor in slot #2. Figure 10-1 shows the base Supervisor III module with no uplinks installed.

A simple glance at the LED displays on the Supervisor module provides a wealth of information about the system status; these indicators are summarized in Table 10-1.

The Cat5K has a 3.6Gbps backplane that is composed of three separate 1.2Gbps backplanes in a cross-bar configuration. With Gigabit Ethernet interfaces, it is possible to saturate this backplane, with resultant packet loss. It is imperative that the switch-load LED stays below 90 percent; otherwise, network problems will occur. If you see high loading, you either have a spanning tree issue (discussed later in this chapter) or you have exceeded the capacity of the switch and should consider an upgrade.

Ethernet Modules

The main Ethernet modules that are currently deployed on the Cat5K are the 12- and 24-port 10/100 autosensing module for host access and the 9-port Gigabit EtherChannel switching module for backbones. However, a vast number of modules are available that support everything from CDDI to ATM to a 48-port RJ11 telco connector module. Figure 10-2 shows the 12-port 10/100 Ethernet card.

Most of the information that is needed to ascertain the link status is readily available by simply looking at the indicator LEDs on the card. These LED meanings are constant for all Ethernet/Fast Ethernet cards available for the Cat5K. Table 10-2 summarizes the meaning of the available LEDs.

FIGURE 10-1   The Catalyst 5500 Supervisor III module

TABLE 10-1	The Cat5K Supervisor III LED Indicators	

LED	State	Meaning
STATUS	–	Indicates the results of self and diagnostic tests
	Green	All tests pass
	Red	Failure (any test)
	Red	System boot process under way
	Orange	Redundant power supply is installed but not turned on
	Orange	Fan module failure
FAN	–	Indicates fan operation
	Green	All fans are functional
	Red	One or more fans are not functional
PS1	–	Indicates function of left-bay power supply
	Green	Operational
	Red	Not operational
	Off	Power supply is off or not installed
PS2	–	Indicates function of right-bay power supply
	Green	Operational
	Red	Not operational
	Off	Power supply is off or not installed
SWITCH LOAD	1% to 100%	Indicates the backplane traffic as a percentage
LINK 1 and LINK 2	–	Indicates status of PCMCIA Flash devices on the Supervisor III
ACTIVE	–	Indicates operational status of the Supervisor III
	Green	Supervisor III is up and operational
	Orange	Supervisor III is in standby mode

FIGURE 10-2	The 12-port 10/100 Ethernet card for the Cat5K

TABLE 10-2 The Cat5k Ethernet Module LED Indicators

LED	State	Meaning
MODULE STATUS	—	Results of self- and diagnostic tests
	Green	All tests pass
	Red	A test other than an individual port failed
	Orange	Module disabled, booting, or diagnostics running
LINKS	—	Individual port status
	Green	Port is up and operational
	Orange	Link disabled by software
	Flashing orange	Hardware failure
	Off	No signal detected
100Mbps	—	Display port speed
	Green	100Mbps
	Off	10Mbps

The Catalyst 6000 Series

The Cat6K is the first true Layer 3 switch that Cisco produced. With the advent of IOS version 12.0 switching services, when combined with hardware application-specific integrated circuits (ASICs), this switch provides the first true hardware wire-speed Layer 3 switching available from Cisco. The Netflow switching with a route switch module (RSM) or a route switch feature card (RSFC) that is available on the Cat5K is not true Layer 3 switching functionality; some people refer to it as a "router on a stick."

The Supervisor Module

The standard Cat6K Supervisor Engine 1 is currently available only with the CatOS. However, the current marketing trend is to deploy the Cat6K as a core/distribution-level switch and fully utilize its advanced Layer 3 wire-speed switching capabilities, combined with advanced QoS features. To meet this functionality, the Cat6K uses the Supervisor Engine 1-A-MSFC (multilayer switch function card) with IOS software (currently Version 12.1) as the preferred configuration. As with the Cat5K, the Cat6K Supervisor modules must be inserted into slots 1 and 2 (if redundancy is desired) in the chassis, and a Supervisor module is required for the Cat6K to function. Figure 10-3 shows a Cat6K Supervisor 1 module.

The LED indicators on the Supervisor 1 module provide an even greater depth of information than is available on the Cat5K Supervisor module. Table 10-3 lists the available information that can be readily scanned from the module LEDs.

The Catalyst 6500 series has what is called a *nonblocking architecture,* with a maximum backplane capacity of 256Gbps. That means that the backplane capacity is greater than the sum of all the module port capacities. Therefore, you should never see the switch load LED climb to maximum. If the LED does climb to maximum, you could have a cross-bar failure within the switch. This forces the Cat6K to revert to using the 32Gbps classic bus. This is a serious hardware failure and should be attended to immediately.

The Catalyst 6000 Ethernet Modules

The Cat6K can be outfitted with a number of modules. The primary modules are the 48-port 10/100 Ethernet switching modules and the Gigabit Ethernet modules. Newly released 48-port modules are even capable of supplying a 48-volt ring voltage to directly power IP telephones. As with all modules, a wealth of information is available at a glance, simply by looking at the status LEDs (shown in Table 10-4). For diagnostic troubleshooting, the LED meanings are constant across the entire Cat6K Ethernet module line. Regardless of whether you have the 10/100 card (shown in Figure 10-4), the Gigabit Interface Converter (GBIC) based Gigabit card (shown in Figure 10-5), or the Mechanical Transfer Registered Jack (MTRJ) connector-based modules, the LEDs remain the same.

FIGURE 10-3 The Catalyst 6000 Series Supervisor 1 module

TABLE 10-3	The Catalyst 6000 Supervisor LED Indicators	

LED	State	Meaning
STATUS	—	Supervisor engine status
	Green	All diagnostics pass, module is up and operational
	Orange	Module is booting or running diagnostics
	Orange	High-temperature warning, minor threshold
	Red	Diagnostic test fails, module is down
	Red	High-temperature warning, major threshold
SYSTEM	—	Shows chassis environmental status
	Green	All okay
	Orange	Power supply failure
	Orange	Power supply fan failure
	Orange	Redundant clock failure
	Orange	One VTT module fails
	Orange	VTT module overtemperature, minor threshold
	Red	Two VTT modules fail
	Red	VTT module overtemperature, major threshold
	Red	Supervisor module overtemperature, major threshold
ACTIVE	—	Supervisor module status
	Green	Supervisor module is active
	Orange	Supervisor module is in standby mode
PWR MGMT	—	Chassis power
	Green	Sufficient power for all modules
	Orange	Insufficient power
SWITCH LOAD	—	Indicates backplane load as a percentage
PCMCIA	Green	Lit when no card is present
LINK	—	Uplink port status
	Green	Port is operational
	Orange	Port has been disabled by software
	Flashing orange	Hardware failure
	Off	No signal detected

TABLE 10-4 The Catalyst 6000 Ethernet Module LED Indicators

LED	State	Meaning
STATUS	—	Module status
	Green	All diagnostics pass, module is up and operational
	Orange	Module is disabled from CLI
	Orange	High-temperature warning, minor threshold
	Red	Failed to download code or configuration; diagnostic error detected, module is down
	Red	Module is resetting
	Red	High-temperature warning, major threshold
LINK	—	Shows port and link status
	Green	Active and operational
	Orange	Port disabled from CLI
	Orange	Port initializing
	Flashing orange	Port is faulty and is disabled
	Off	Port not active or not connected

FIGURE 10-4 The Catalyst 6000 WS-6348-RJ-45 48 Port 10/100 Ethernet module

FIGURE 10-5 The Catalyst 6000 WS-6408-A-GBIC Gigabit Ethernet module with GBICs

LED Conclusion

The Catalyst series of switches provides a comprehensive level of visual information that is an invaluable aid to troubleshooting. Remember that it is best to start troubleshooting at the Physical Layer and work your way up. The visual LED displays provide a quick overview to the physical health of the connection as well as the entire Catalyst switch itself. If you know the LED meanings inside and out, you can save yourself significant time in troubleshooting a problem. If the STATUS LED is red or orange, you have a problem with your hardware; swap the module to see if that alleviates the problem. If the port LED is off, you probably have a cable issue. Orange indicates a software configuration, and green tells you to start working your way up the OSI layers.

exam
ⓦatch
Be careful interpreting the LEDs. They can and do have multiple meanings, depending on how a question is worded. Pay special attention to orange LEDs. They have the widest range of possible interpretations.

EXERCISSE 10-1

Matching LED Color with the Correct Meaning

To test your knowledge of the Catalyst LEDs, match the correct meaning with the LED color in Table 10-5. *Note:* All meanings must be in their correct answer areas; there should be no "spares."

Solution: 1:E, 2:A, 3:G, 4:B, 5:F, 6:C, 7:D.

TABLE 10-5 Match the LED Color with the Correct Meaning

LED	Color	Answer	Meaning
1. Cat5K Supervisor III STATUS	Red		A: Standby
2. Cat5K Supervisor III ACTIVE	Orange		B: Module is booting
3. Cat5K Ethernet Module STATE	Orange		C: Module is up
4. Cat6K Supervisor 1A STATUS	Orange		D: Faulty, disabled port
5. Cat6K Supervisor 1A SYSTEM	Red		E: Failure, any test
6. Cat6K Gigabit Ethernet module STATUS	Green		F: Overtemperature, major
7. Cat6K Gigabit Ethernet module LINK	Flashing orange		G: Link is software disabled

CiscoWorks 2000

You might be familiar with the previous-generation product known as CiscoWorks for Switched Internetworks (CWSI). This product has been replaced by the modular CiscoWorks 2000 package. CiscoWorks provides a comprehensive package of modules that allow you to fully monitor, troubleshoot, and configure a switched LAN. There are separate WAN and WAN switching versions. This chapter does not go into a detailed exploration of the workings of the CiscoWorks 2000 suite, since that topic could easily fill an entire book by itself. Rather, you should be familiar with what the individual modules do.

The CiscoWorks LAN management solution is composed of the following units:

- **Content Flow Monitor** Provides server information.

- **CiscoView** Provides detailed front and back views and configuration of all Cisco devices in the LAN. All LEDs and status information are displayed in CiscoView, as though you were at the corresponding device. For troubleshooting and status monitoring of the Physical Layer and hardware, this will be your primary tool.

- **Cisco Campus Manager** Provides detailed information and configuration of your logical and physical networks. If your Physical Layer shows no faults, this is where you would check for spanning tree issues, VLANs, and other Layer 2 issues. This is not merely a troubleshooting and status tool; it allows you to fully configure all Layer 2 services on your switches, just as though you were at the box using the command-line interface (CLI).

- **Cisco Traffic Director** With Traffic Director, you can pull detailed network statistics from your embedded remote monitoring (RMON) and switch probes. Remember, good network maintenance is proactive, not reactive, and with Traffic Director, you can keep track of and head off most network utilization issues before they become issues to your users.

CERTIFICATION OBJECTIVE 10.02

Cable and Media Distance Limitations

Cabling is one of the least considered but most troublesome aspects of networking. Cables are made, broken, rolled and tied into knots and balls, bent around corners, and generally abused without a second thought. However, more often than not, a network issue has been traced back to a faulty or marginal cable. The number-one rule regarding cabling is to certify or test all of your cabling with a cable tester. Unless your cabling is brand new, you never know if it has been excessively kinked, is susceptible to crosstalk, or its fiber been damaged. Many times, a customer reports intermittent network issues, and by testing the cable with a simple tester it was shown that the impedance was off or the cable was marginal. A quick cable change and the network is fully operational. Remember, you always start at the Physical Layer for connectivity.

Copper Cabling

Copper cabling comes in two basic types: shield twisted pair (STP) and unshielded twisted pair (UTP). In Europe, the predominant type of cabling is STP due to building requirements. In North America, due to lower costs and differing standards, UTP is the predominant cabling type. The physical networking characteristics of each type are the same; the only difference relates to the shielding on the STP that renders it relatively immune to electromagnetic (EM) radiation.

Category 3 Cabling

You should not install any Category 3 (Cat 3) cabling for new physical cabling plants. Cat 3 is an older standard based on telephone cable that was superseded by Category 5 (Cat 5) a number of years ago. You might find it in older implementations, but be warned: although it might run the old office shared LAN at 10Mbps half-duplex; it does not support any higher speeds. The best thing to do if you come across Cat 3 cable is to rip it out and replace it with Cat 5. Definitely suspect a cable issue if you have to troubleshoot a network and discover that it is composed of Cat 3 cable. If you do a lot of Token Ring work, you might come across Category 4 (Cat 4) cable. Cat 4 is an enhanced Cat 3 that supports data transition rates of up to 16MB. If you find Cat 4 cable in your network, it is probably best to get rid of it. As a trivia note, you could run into a 100BaseT implementation that runs over Cat 3 cable using a 4T+ signaling. This cable uses all four pairs in the cable for signaling. This type of cable is extremely rare and ranks with 100VG-ANYLAN in frequency. With Cat 3 cabling, you are limited to a maximum cable length of 100 meters between devices and a minimum cable length of 1 meter.

Category 5 Cabling

Cat 5 cable is the predominant cabling in use at this time. There is a trend toward the use of Cat 5 enhanced (Cat 5e) cabling to better prepare for gigabit copper installations, but normal Cat 5 is still predominant. With Cat 5 cabling, only two of the four pairs are used for signaling in the 100BaseTX standard. Cat 5 can handle speeds up to Gigabit Ethernet with the soon-to-be-released 802.3ab interface standard modules (shown in Table 10-6). With Cat 5 cable, you are still limited to the same 100-meter maximum distance as you are with Cat 3 cable.

Optical Networking

Copper cabling, although inexpensive, has issues with electrical interference and limited length. The 100-meter maximum length for copper is inadequate in many structures or campus environments. To overcome the distance and interference limitations of copper cable, optical cabling was developed. Optical cabling can be divided into two basic types: single mode and multimode fiber.

Single-Mode Fiber

Single-mode fiber optical cabling is composed of a fiber core with a nominal diameter of 8.7 microns (normally stated as 9 microns). Single-mode fiber is optimized for long distance transition using long-wavelength lasers. There are no

TABLE 10-6		10BaseT	100BaseTX	1000BaseCX
Segment Lengths Based on Copper Cable Type and Ethernet Base Type	Category 3	100m	NA (100m for 100BaseT4)	NA
	Category 5	100m	100m	25m/100m for AB

short-wavelength lasers for single-mode fiber cabling, due to the costs associated with this cable. It is possible to use single-mode fiber lasers in network lengths for Ethernet well in excess of 10,000 meters. Current long-haul (1000BaseZX) interfaces are pushing Ethernet out to distances of over 70 kilometers. For even higher speeds of 10GB, Ethernet can be pushed out to distances of over 50 kilometers.

Multimode Fiber

Multimode fiber optical cabling is the most commonly found cabling system in campus long-run networks. Multimode fiber is available in two standard types: 50 micron or 62.5 micron core diameters. Due to its lower cost, the majority of cable is the 62.5 micron variety. Multimode fiber, although able to utilize laser emitters, is normally used with LEDs due to the increased efficiencies of cost. However, it must be noted that although LEDs are common for 100BaseFX signaling, 1000BaseSX (short wavelength) and 1000BaseLX (long wavelength) use lasers exclusively.

Multimode fiber can be utilized in both half- and full-duplex modes of transmission, but it is utilized primarily for full-duplex transition. Half-duplex operations in 100BaseFX plants are limited to the standard Ethernet distance of 100 meters (shown in Table 10-7). Full-duplex 100BaseFX or 1000BaseSX have runs in excess of 400 meters, dependent on cabling diameter. You should be aware of the older 10BaseFL (FOIRL) standard that allows data communications up to 2000 meters per segment on multimode fiber. However, this type of connection is being phased out due to the superior bandwidth and longer range of 1000BaseLX connectivity and the advent of wireless LAN bridges that can offer 25Mbps over a line of site at distances up to 10 kilometers. (A discussion of wireless is beyond the scope of this book or the CIT exam.)

TABLE 10-7 Segment Length Based on Fiber Cable and Ethernet Base Types

	100BaseFX	1000BaseSX	1000BaseLX	1000BaseZX
Single mode	NA	NA	3000 meters	Over 70 Km
Multimode 62.5	100 meters half duplex; 400 meters full duplex	250 meters	550 meters	NA
Multimode 50	NA	550 meters	550 meters	NA

SCENARIO & SOLUTION

You are asked to design a campus network that will be composed of buildings that are spaced about 300 meters apart. Which cabling method will you use?	The 300 meters is the key in this case. Multimode fiber running at either gigabit or 100Base full duplex is the correct answer in this situation.
You have been asked to troubleshoot intermittent network problems in an electrical manufacturing facility. The network seems to be running okay generally, but during parts of the day, there are periods of network problems. The network wiring is new Category 5 UTP cabling. What could be the cause and recommended solution for this problem?	Because this is an electrical manufacturing facility, a large amount of EM radiation is probably being generated. Category 5 UTP is very susceptible to EM interference. The solution could involve replacing the Cat 5 UTP cabling with either Cat 5 STP or fiber cabling.

EXERCISE 10-2

Cable Media Types and Segment Distances

To test your knowledge of proper maximum cabling lengths, complete Table 10-8 by filling in the missing information, indicated by the capital letters A, B, C, and so on.

TABLE 10-8   Cable Media Types and Segment Distances

	A	100BaseTX	B	1000BaseLX
Cat 5 UTP	100 meters	C:	NA	NA
Single-mode fiber	NA	D:	NA	3000 meters
Multimode 62.5 fiber	NA	NA	400 meters full duplex	E:
Multimode 50 fiber	NA	NA	NA	F:

Solution: A: 10BaseT, B: 100BaseFX, C: 100 meters, D: NA, E: 550 meters, F: 550 meters.

CERTIFICATION OBJECTIVE 10.03

Catalyst Power-On Self Test

The power-on self test (POST) is the first line of troubleshooting and operation verification on the Catalyst series of switches. During the POST procedure, the system verifies the operational integrity of the entire chassis, power supply, and line modules present. Any failures of the POST process are indicated by the status LEDs on either the Supervisor or line card modules. For the Cat5K and Cat6K, the boot LED process is as follows:

1. The PS1 and PS2 LEDs on the Supervisor should become green.

2. The systems fans operate, and the fan LED on the Supervisor turns green.

3. The remaining LEDs on the Supervisor and line cards remain orange until the system is fully operational.

The detailed meanings of the LEDs have already been reviewed in the individual module section. Remember that all troubleshooting should follow a methodical stepwise process. If there is a problem at the physical level, attempting to track it down by examining the spanning tree parameters is of no use. Always eliminate physical problems before proceeding up the OSI layered model. The POST process shows you any problems that are occurring with the physical hardware of the Catalyst switch on a fairly general level. Any module that fails a POST should be replaced immediately. However, the visual POST LED reference is only the start of the tools that are available to troubleshoot and identify Physical Layer issues that can occur.

System Tests

This chapter has focused on the physical attributers of the Catalyst series. Now we'll commence an in-depth study of the various commands used to diagnose Physical Layer issues of the Catalyst switch. The basic methodology is the same for CatOS- and IOS-based switches. If a command equivalent exists in IOS, it is illustrated. However, be warned that the IOS is not as feature rich as the CatOS in terms of switching functions.

The SHOW BOOT Command

The SHOW BOOT command gives you information on the boot image used and stored in the Supervisor module. It gives you the OS version number and configuration boot register settings. This information is required if you need to place a call to TAC or to obtain the OS version number to check for available features. The syntax of the command is as follows:

```
CatOS: show boot
IOS: show bootflash
```

Here is an example of the SHOW BOOT command:

```
Console> show boot
BOOT variable = bootflash:cat5000-sup3.5-1-0-59.bin
CONFIG_FILE variable = slot0:cfgfile1
Configuration register is 0x10f
ignore-config: disabled
auto-config: recurring
console baud: 9600
```

The important information in this command is seen in the boot variable line. The image file is version 5-1-0-59. If you are checking for bugs or features available in a software release, this is where you obtain that information.

The SHOW MODULE Command

The SHOW MODULE command is one of the most basic troubleshooting commands available on the CatOS. It shows the status and type of modules installed in the Catalyst switch:

```
CatOS: show module [mod_num]
```

Here [mod_num] is the specific module in question. If you do not specify a module, all modules are listed. The status of each module, serial number, and module type is listed.

```
IOS: show module [mod_num | all]
```

If all is selected, the information on all modules is presented.

```
Console> show module
Mod Slot Ports Module-Type                  Model               Sub Status
--- ---- ----- ---------------------------- ------------------- --- --------
1   1    0     Supervisor III               WS-X5530            yes ok
3   3    9     Gigabit Ethernet             WS-X5410            no  ok

Mod Module-Name            Serial-Num
--- ------------------     ---------------
1                          000068394568
3                          00010395681

Mod MAC-Address(es)                        Hw     Fw      Sw
--- ------------------------------------- ------ ------- ---------------
1   00-e0-14-10-96-24 to 00-e0-14-10-9b-a3 1.3   3.1.2   6.2(0.48-Eng)ORL
3   00-10-7b-d6-05-98 to 00-10-7b-d6-05-a3 1.0   4.2(100) 5.2(1)

Mod Sub-Type Sub-Model Sub-Serial Sub-Hw
--- -------- --------- ---------- ------
1   EARL 1+  WS-F5520  0005755438 0.306
Console>
```

For troubleshooting purposes, four fields are important: the Status, Hw, Fw, and Sw fields. The Status field provides module operating status information. Valid results in this field are OK, disable, faulty, other, standby, or error. Any result other than OK or standby is indicative of either a hardware failure or a module being administratively disabled, which should be investigated. The Hw, Fw, and Sw fields provide the revision numbers of the hardware, firmware, and software, respectively. These are used to check for bugs or features that might be present or to file a report with TAC for further troubleshooting.

The SHOW PORT Command

The SHOW PORT command shows detailed information on a specific port. If a port is not specified, information for all ports is listed. Be careful of using this command without specifying a port or module. A fully loaded Cat5K or Cat6K could have in excess of 300 ports, so the resulting output can be very large and difficult to read through. This command not only verifies a module or port's POST status; it is also the most useful command for diagnosing cabling errors and a large variety of issues. Get to know this command very well:

```
CatOS: show port [mod_num[/port_num]]
```

The following is the output from this command for a single port, with a detailed analysis of the field meanings in Table 10-9:

```
Console> (enable) show port 4/1
Port  Name              Status     Vlan       Level  Duplex Speed Type
----- ----------------- ---------- ---------- ------ ------ ----- ------------
 4/1                    connected  1          normal   full   100 10/100BaseTX

Port  Security Secure-Src-Addr   Last-Src-Addr     Shutdown Trap     IfIndex
----- -------- ----------------- ----------------- -------- -------- -------
 4/1  disabled                                     No       disabled 58

Port     Broadcast-Limit Broadcast-Drop
-------- --------------- --------------
 4/1                   -              0

Port  Status     Channel    Channel    Neighbor                  Neighbor
                 mode       status     device                    port
----- ---------- ---------- ---------- ------------------------- ----------
 4/1  connected  off        not channel

Port  Align-Err  FCS-Err    Xmit-Err   Rcv-Err    UnderSize
----- ---------- ---------- ---------- ---------- ---------
 4/1       3384         16          0          0          0

Port  Single-Col Multi-Coll Late-Coll  Excess-Col Carri-Sen Runts     Giants
----- ---------- ---------- ---------- ---------- --------- --------- ---------
 4/1           0          0          0          0         0       521         0

Last-Time-Cleared
-------------------------
Thur Aug 17 2000, 12:11:52
Console>
```

TABLE 10-9   The SHOW PORT Field Meanings

Field	Meaning
Port	Module and port number. In this case, it is port 1 on Module 4.
Name	Name of the port (nothing configured).
Status	Status of the port. It could read return, not connected, connecting, standby, faulty, inactive, shutdown, disabled, or monitor. In this case, we are connected and live.

| TABLE 10-9 | The SHOW PORT Field Meanings (continued) |

Field	Meaning
Vlan	VLANs to which the port belongs. In this port, it is VLAN 1.
Duplex	Duplex setting for the port: auto, full, or half. In this case, duplex is full.
Speed	Speed setting for the port: auto, 10, or 100. In this case, speed is 100Mbps.
Type	Port type, which can be 100BaseFX MM, 100BaseFX SM, 10/100BaseTX, or RSM. In this case, the port is 10/100BaseTX.
Security	Status of whether port security is enabled or disabled. In this case, port security is disabled.
Secure-Src-Addr	Secure MAC address for the security-enabled port. There is none in this case.
Last-Src-Addr	Source MAC address of the last packet received by the port. None has been received by this port.
Shutdown	Status of whether the port was shut down because of security. This port was not.
Trap	Status of whether the port trap is enabled or disabled.. The port trap is disabled.
IfIndex	Number of the ifIndex. The ifIndex is 58.
Broadcast-Limit	Broadcast threshold configured for the port. None has been configured.
Broadcast-Drop	Number of broadcast/multicast packets dropped because the broadcast limit for the port was exceeded. A large reading here is indicative of a broadcast storm on your network. This could be due to a loop (an STP failure) or a bad NIC. In this case, this value shows 0.
Send admin	Flow-control administration. Possible settings: On indicates the local port sends flow control to the far end; Off indicates the local port does not send flow control to the far end; Desired indicates the local end sends flow control to the far end if the far end supports it.
FlowControl oper	Flow-control operation. Possible setting: Disagree indicates the two ports could not agree on a link protocol.
Receive admin	Flow-control administration. Possible settings: On indicates the local port requires the far end to send flow control; Off indicates the local port does not allow the far end to send flow control; Desired indicates the local end allows the far end to send flow control.
FlowControl oper	Flow-control operation. Possible setting: Disagree indicates the two ports could not agree on a link protocol.
RxPause	Number of pause frames received.
TxPause	Number of pause frames transmitted.
Unsupported Opcodes	Number of unsupported operating codes.

TABLE 10-9   The SHOW PORT Field Meanings *(continued)*

Field	Meaning
Align-Err	Number of frames with alignment errors. Errors here are normally indicative of a bad upstream network interface or bad cable.
FCS-Err	The number of valid size frames with FCS errors but no framing errors. Errors here would be due to a bad upstream port or NIC.
Xmit-Err	Number of transmit errors that occurred on the port (indicating that the internal transmit buffer is full). Errors here are normally a sign of congestion on the upstream link.
Rcv-Err	Number of receive errors that occurred on the port (indicating that the internal receive buffer is full). Errors here indicate that your backplane capacity has been exceeded.
UnderSize	Number of received frames less than 64 octets long (but that are otherwise well formed).
Single-Coll	Number of times one collision occurred before the port transmitted a frame to the media successfully.
Multi-Coll	Number of times multiple collisions occurred before the port transmitted a frame to the media successfully. On a full-duplex switched connection, there will be no collisions. However, on a half-duplex connection, collisions could be a sign of excessive network load.
Late-Coll	Number of late collisions (collisions outside the collision domain). This would normally indicate that the cable length has been exceeded.
Excess-Col	Number of excessive collisions that occurred on the port (indicating that a frame encountered 16 collisions and was discarded).
Carri-Sen	Number of times the port sensed a carrier (to determine whether the cable is currently connected and live).
Runts	Number of received runt frames (frames that are smaller than the minimum IEEE 802.3 frame size) on the port. This is normally caused by a bad NIC or upstream port.
Giants	Number of received giant frames (frames that exceed the maximum IEEE 802.3 frame size) on the port. Again, this is normally caused by a bad upstream port or NIC.
Last-Time-Cleared	Last time the port counters were cleared.
Data-rate mismatch	The number of valid size frames that experienced overrun or underrun.

TABLE 10-9   The SHOW PORT Field Meanings *(continued)*

Field	Meaning
Src-addr change	The number of times the last source address changed.
Good-bytes	The total number of octets in frames with no error.
Short-event	The number of times activity with a duration less than the ShortEventMax Time (74–82 bit times) is detected.

```
IOS: show interface
```

You can also use one of these special commands for further detailed information. This displays the administrative status of any nonrouting modules in the Cat6K:

```
show interfaces switchport [module module-number]
```

This displays the state or error disabled state of all interfaces in the chassis:

```
show interfaces status
```

This displays line errors that are seen by the specific module:

```
show interfaces counters errors [module mod_num]
```

The SHOW SYSTEM Command

The SHOW SYSTEM command shows basic system diagnostic information such as temperature alarms, bus utilization, and uptime:

```
CatOS: show system
```

On the IOS, no one comprehensive command gives you the same information. Rather, you must use two commands. The first shows the uptime, bus load, and MAC address on the Cat6K:

```
show catalyst6000 all
```

The second displays the environmental threshold settings:

```
show environment alarm
```

The SHOW TEST Command

The SHOW TEST command is one of the most powerful diagnostic commands to determine physical problems with Catalyst line modules. One of the problems with the commonly used SHOW MODULE command is that it does not tell why a module has failed. To view the results of a POST operation, you must physically view the console during the boot process. In contrast, the SHOW TEST command shows you the full POST results for each line module when the switch boots or the module is reset. This is a pure CatOS command. There is no equivalent in the IOS. The format of the command is:

```
show test [mod_num] where mod_num refers to the chassis slot
number
```

Summary

So far, this chapter has covered troubleshooting the Catalyst environment and the physical device. With the use of the diagnostic and status LEDs, combined with a series of diagnostic SHOW commands, you can troubleshoot and document any physical issue that occurs on the Catalyst box. Troubleshooting is methodical, as we stated before. Always eliminate the physical issues first. You can save yourself many hours of tracking down an issue that could be related to a component that failed a POST test or a box that sends out environmental alarms due to being located in an improperly ventilated wiring closet. The other aspect is for you to be proactive, not reactive. Use the SHOW commands on a regular basis to set a baseline for your equipment. That way, you can detect a trend and avert an issue before it happens.

EXERCISE 10-3

Command-Line Physical Diagnostic Commands

The visual information one can obtain from glancing at the LEDs on a Catalyst switch can provide some information, but frequently, more detailed information on the physical status of the port is required. Choose the proper command from the following list to complete the following statements:

1. To show the line errors seen by a particular line module in a Cat6K running IOS, you would issue the _____ command.

2. To obtain the CatOS version number on a Cat5K, use the
   _____ command.

3. To get port statistics from port 1 in module 3 on a Cat5K, use the
   _____ command.

4. To determine the status of a particular module in a Cat6K, use the
   _____ command.

5. To determine the results of POST tests, use the _____
   command.

Solution: 1: SHOW INTERFACES COUNTERS ERRORS, 2: SHOW BOOT,
3: SHOW PORT 3/1, 4: SHOW MODULE, 5: SHOW TEST.

Level 2 Troubleshooting

You know your hardware is working properly. You have verified all POST factors,
all the SHOW commands prove that your interfaces are up and functional, the
LEDs on all your modules are green, and your cables are fine. Everything should be
working. But your users are still complaining of problems. This is where Level 2
troubleshooting comes in. Why is this type of troubleshooting called Level 2?
Because switches and switch functionality operate at the second layer of the OSI
model. This chapter does not deal with troubleshooting Layer 3 issues (such as Layer
3 interVLAN routing or Layer 3 switching, which is really wire-speed routing in
hardware). Rather, the chapter focuses on troubleshooting the primary Data-Link
Layer functions, spanning tree, VLANs, and trunks in detail.

CERTIFICATION OBJECTIVE 10.04

Spanning Tree

Spanning tree is a special link-maintenance protocol that was developed to assure a
loop-free topology in a network. One of the easiest ways to bring a network to its
knees is to have loops within the network structure. Loops allow data packets to

have multiple paths to a destination and, in a worst-case scenario, be propagated in a perpetual loop that very quickly saturates the network, preventing all traffic from flowing. However, redundant network paths are desirable for fault tolerance. The spanning tree protocol was designed to provide for redundant network architecture while avoiding network loops.

Loop Avoidance

How is a loop avoided? The spanning tree protocol uses bridge port data units (BPDUs) to determine a single path to the root bridge. The BPDUs are used to calculate the lowest-weighted path to the root bridge. Any ports that represent an alternate but higher-weighted path to the root bridge are put in a blocking state. Switches continue to send BPDUs on their respective ports, and a port remains in a blocking state as long as it receives superior BPDUs from its neighbor. The important components of the protocol and BPDU packet are:

- **Bridge identifier**   This is a combination of the switch's MAC address and its priority.

- **Path cost**   Each port has a path cost that is inversely related to the port bandwidth.

- **Port priority**   The lower the priority of a port, the more it is a preferred path to the root.

Election of the Root Bridge

The first task of spanning tree is to elect a root bridge. The *root bridge* is the location that is used to determine the single nonlooping path structure. Although spanning-tree parameters should normally not be changed, the root bridge selection is one instance in which you should define the root bridge and not let the protocol determine it for you. If you let spanning tree select the root bridge and all switches are left with default priority of 32768, the switch with the lowest MAC address becomes the root bridge. This can be a serious problem if your network core is a pair of meshed redundant Cat5Ks but the spanning-tree algorithm has chosen a lowly Cat 1900 out in a closet as the root.

To counter this issue, use the SET SPANTREE ROOT CatOS command. This command lowers the priority of the switch to 8192 or one less than the value of the existing root switch (if the current root has a priority lower than 8192 and this switch has a lower MAC address):

```
console> (enable) set spantree root 1-100
VLANs 1-100 bridge priority set to 8192
VLANs 1-100 bridge max aging time set to 14 seconds.
VLANs 1-100 bridge hello time set to 2 seconds.
VLANs 1-100 bridge forward delay set to 9 seconds.
Switch is now the root switch for active VLANs 1-6.
Console> (enable)
```

Root Ports and Designated Ports

Root ports are the ports that the spanning-tree calculation has determined to have the lowest value to reach the root bridge. This can be thought of as the port with the most direct or best route to the root bridge. *Designated ports* are determined after the root ports are determined. The designated ports are ports that represent the lowest-cost path for each LAN segment to reach the root bridge. The easiest way to think of this is that the designated port is on the LAN segment side of the switch and the root port is the port from which the data from the segment will go out to reach the root bridge.

Port States

The chapter has discussed blocking and forwarding. However, every time the status of your bridged network changes, a spanning-tree recalculation takes place (and hopefully succeeds). Each port can work through four states (not including shutdown). In a spanning-tree state, the port is initially in a blocking state. In this state, it listens for and attends to BPDUs from other bridges, but it passes no data frames.

After blocking, a port transitions to a listening state. In this state, the port listens to data frames other than BPDUs but does not attend to them or store the MAC addresses.

After listening. a port moves to a learning state, in which a port learns the source MAC addresses and stores them in the CAM table. The switch does not forward packets at this time.

After the port learns associated MAC addresses, it enters the forwarding state and begins to pass packets normally. Forwarding on a port occurs if it receives inferior BPDUs indicating an indirect link. Failure to receive an inferior BPDU or a receipt of a superior BPDU prevents the port from transmitting packets.

This process (also called "walking the tree" by a number of network technicians) can take upward of 45 seconds or more for a simple port initialization to several minutes if a large network convergence is required.

The PORTFAST, UPLINKFAST, and BACKBONEFAST Commands

Picture this scenario: a user comes into her office in the morning and turns her computer on to log in to a Microsoft- or NetWare-based network. Everything seems fine, but the user cannot log in and gets a "Network not available" message. Your phone rings off the hook every morning with calls from users experiencing similar frustrations. The solution to this network scenario is to implement PORTFAST on the user switch ports.

Now consider this scenario: you have designed a redundant network topology with redundant links between your access, distribution, and core switches. With STP running, you think everything should be okay. A core or access connection is severed, and the network reconverges. Immediately, users call and complain, stating that their network connectivity has been terminated. You check, and your connectivity is fine; everything seems to be up and running. The solution to this problem is to implement either UPLINKFAST or BACKBONEFAST on the switches, depending on their particular purpose and connectivity.

Figure 10-6 provides a graphical representation of the parts of a network in which the various spanning-tree tuning parameters PORTFAST, UPLINKFAST, and BACKBONEFAST should be implemented.

The issues in the previously cited cases are due to the extended period of time it takes a port to go through all its states and the spanning tree to converge. The more complex the network, the longer this process can take. A simple user port might take over 45 seconds to go through the four states. During this time, the user's computer is unable to connect to the network (since the switch port is not forwarding) and fails to connect. If redundant ports do not initialize within 30 to 40 seconds, a user's TCP sessions are terminated.

At the user port level, use the PORTFAST command. This command bypasses the listening and learning states, forcing a port into a forwarding state immediately. If there is looping traffic, the port could be disabled about 45 seconds after detection of the loop; however, do not count on that occurring. Frequently, the 45-second interval for the spanning-tree port calculation to occur results in such a severe network traffic flood that BPDUs do not reach the open port and the loop is not

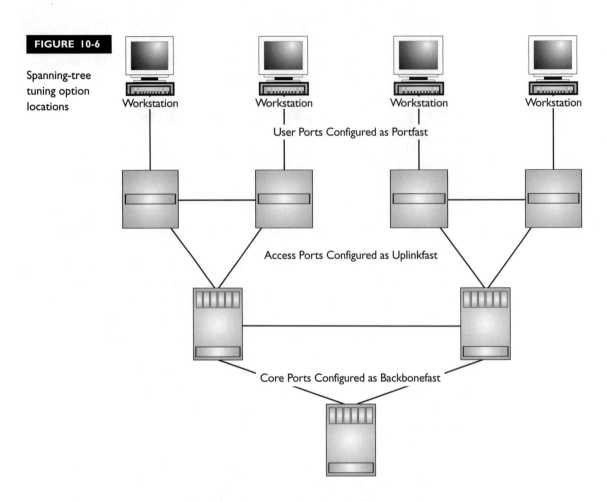

FIGURE 10-6

Spanning-tree tuning option locations

severed. Be careful that you use this command only on end-station ports (users or servers)! If you use it on trunk ports, you will immediately create the possibility for a loop that cannot be controlled by the spanning-tree protocol. There are many examples of networks brought to their knees by the use of this command on an improper port.

```
CatOS: Console> (enable) set spantree portfast mod_num/port_num
{enable | disable}
IOS: (config-if)#spanning-port portfast
```

For CatOS, the following is an example of how to enable PORTFAST on Port 4 of Module 2 on a Cat5K. The IOS version is given from the interface configuration prompt:

```
Console> (enable) set spantree portfast 2/4 enable
Warning: Spantree port fast start should only be enabled on
ports connected to a single host. Connecting hubs,
concentrators, switches, bridges, etc. to a fast start port can
cause temporary spanning tree loops. Use with caution.
Spantree port 2/4 fast start enabled.
Console> (enable)
```

UPLINKFAST is used only on Access Layer switches to ensure a fast and efficient failover if a trunk fails. Its purpose is to ensure that users experience no network issues if a trunk line connecting the closet switch to the distribution layer is downed. UPLINKFAST ensures a fast switchover to an alternate port if a root port or connection should fail. UPLINKFAST is a global configuration command. It changes the bridge priority to 49152 and increases the value of all spanning-tree interfaces by 3000. This makes it very unlikely that the switch would become a root bridge. Furthermore, when a root port failure is detected, UPLINKFAST automatically brings up the alternate root interface in forwarding mode without going through the previous states.

```
CatOS: set spantree uplinkfast enable
IOS: spanning-tree uplinkfast
```

BACKBONEFAST is a similar process to UPLINKFAST but is to be used only in meshed core networks that have redundant connections between devices. A key difference is that BACKBONEFAST detects indirect link failures in a meshed network instead of working with direct link failures. The command to enable backbone fast is:

```
CatOS: set spantree backbonefast enable
IOS: spanning-tree backbonefast
```

exam
ⓦatch

Spanning-tree optimization is one of the primary functions found in Catalyst switches. Know how to configure UPLINKFAST, BACKBONEFAST, and PORTFAST and where each would be used in a network for both CatOS and IOS.

SCENARIO & SOLUTION	
You have configured PORTFAST on all but the uplink ports of your Access Layer switches. In an attempt to provide for Network Layer redundancy, you cross-connect two of the switches together to provide an alternate path to the core, should one of the switches trunks fail. You enable UPLINKFAST on the switches. However, when you connect the switches, your network immediately crashes. What happened?	You were well meaning enough. but the problem was the PORTFAST configuration. It immediately forces a port into a forwarding mode. This immediately set up a loop in your network that caused it to go down. The expectation was that UPLINKFAST would have prevented that; however, because you did not disable PORTFAST on the cross-connected ports, UPLINKFAST had no effect. Remember, never use PORTFAST on uplink or redundant network ports.
You have a number of critical, time-sensitive applications running on your core servers. To ensure a robust fault-tolerant network, what can you implement on your core network switches to ensure a rapid recovery in case of a link failure?	For core switches, use BACKBONEFAST. BACKBONEFAST provides rapid failover in case of an indirect link failure in a core network. In a core network, make sure that you use *only* BACKBONEFAST, not PORTFAST or UPLINKFAST.

One STP Per VLAN

Cisco's enhancements to STP allow for one tree per VLAN, even over trunk ports. However, you have to be careful when you mix non-Cisco equipment with Cisco switches using trunk ports. Non-Cisco equipment that is 802.1q compliant passes only one instance of STP *per port*. This can pose a serious problem for STP convergence along that port path. However, if the initial and ending points are Cisco devices, the Cisco switches pass their STP information through the "cloud" of non-Cisco devices.

Load Sharing

A form of load balancing or sharing can be implemented using a meshed core with VLANs and STP port priorities. In this case, each core device is made a root bridge for a group of VLANs and a secondary root bridge for the other set. Port priorities are enabled so that each VLAN has a preferred path to its root bridge, with a secondary path to the other root bridge. This allows for a form of load balancing in which each VLAN is serviced by its primary root bridge but has a fallback capacity if one root should fail. This feature is currently not used that often due to the use of

EtherChannel trunks combined with server load balancers or load balancing-enabled IOS, as is found on the Cat6K.

Troubleshooting Spanning-Tree Issues

Spanning tree is one of those things that is taken for granted until something goes wrong in the network. Troubleshooting spanning-tree issues is more a case of avoidance than reaction. The basics of spanning-tree troubleshooting are:

- **Know your network**   This might seem like an obvious piece of advice, but many network administrators do not have an up-to-date network map listing network connectivity, redundancy, and other key network aspects. Such a map is absolutely essential.

- **Know the location of the root of each spanning tree**   The root should be in your core, but odds are, when you start investigating you might find that it is probably located elsewhere.

- **Know the location of all the blocked ports**   Do not enable PORTFAST on those ports, and keep the number of blocked ports to a minimum!

- **Know the location of redundancy**   This relates to the first point in the list.

If you experience a spanning-tree issue, you can get a segment of users who are suddenly "dead in the water" and unable to communicate with the network. The priority in this case is to get the users back online and deal with what caused the issue later. A key giveaway of a spanning-tree loop is the use of the SHOW SYSTEM command. It shows an extremely high backplane or CPU utilization. But what are some of the common causes of this situation?

on the
job

Spanning-tree issues are a fairly common occurrence. Very few network administrators are aware of what their root bridge is or, much less, where it is located. In troubleshooting network response issues, it is not uncommon to find that the root bridge is a lowly Catalyst 1900 or something equivalent sitting out in a closet somewhere instead of one of the main core switches. When checking out network responsiveness, always identify the root bridge. If it is not one of the core switches, use the SET SPANTREE ROOT command to set it to be the root bridge for its VLANs. You might find that many of your issues go away with this one simple modification.

Duplex Mismatch   If one side of a link is hardcoded to be full-duplex and the other side is left to autonegotiate, there is a potential duplex mismatch. The full-duplex side does not do a carrier sense but immediately starts sending frames. This causes a collision to occur with the receiving bridge side that defaults to a half-duplex setting. If the collision rate is high enough, the full-duplex bridge never receives a BPDU and assumes a failure condition. It then opens its blocked ports, creating a loop. This situation is extremely common in Access Layer switches that have utilized the UPLINKFAST spanning-tree command.

Unidirectional Link   A unidirectional link is another common error found in fiber optic cable installations. Fiber events could occur but go undetected and result in data being transmitted in only one direction. In this case, one switch assumes the link is down while the other assumes that everything is fine. This situation can cause an immediate network spanning-tree meltdown. To prevent this occurrence, high-end Cisco switches have a feature called Uni-Directional Link Detection (UDLD). Always enable this feature if your switch supports it. To enable UDLD globally, give the following command in privileged mode:

```
Console> (enable) set udld enable
```

If you suspect a spanning-tree issue, use the SHOW SYSTEM command to check for high backplane utilization, check your port status with the SHOW INTERFACE or SHOW PORT commands, and use the DEBUG SPANNING TREE command to check for BPDUs. The solution normally involves taking down the offending redundant links immediately so that network connectivity can be restored, then planning your network structure so that it does not occur again. For spanning-tree issues, the best solution is to be proactive, not reactive.

EXERCISE 10-4

Spanning-Tree Diagnosis

Troubleshooting a spanning-tree issue is normally a highly critical maneuver. Your network or a segment of it is down and you have to get it up right away. The key is to determine what has occurred and where so that you can remedy the situation as fast as possible. To diagnose a spanning-tree issue, follow these steps:

1. Check backplane utilization with the SHOW SYSTEM command. A high backplane utilization is a good indicator of a loop.

2. If there is only one segment down, use the SHOW PORT or SHOW INTERFACE command to check the status of all ports. See which ones are blocking and which ones are forwarding.

3. Use the SHOW CDP NEIGHBOR DETAILS command (discussed later in this chapter) to check for duplex mismatches.

4. If network convergence or startup time is an issue, use PORTFAST on end-user ports, UPLINKFAST on access-level ports, and BACKBONEFAST on core ports.

5. Down redundant links until your network stabilizes.

6. *Always know where your root bridge is. If necessary, set it to be one of your core switches.*

CERTIFICATION OBJECTIVE 10.05

Inter-Switch Link and Frame Tagging

Inter-Switch Link (ISL) is Cisco's version of the 802.1Q trunking protocol. It allows multiple VLANs to be passed down a single trunk while maintaining a separate instance of STP for each VLAN. Using a frame-tagging process that carries the VLAN information, the original datagram is encapsulated within the ISL frame without being modified.

ISL allows up to 1024 VLANs per trunking port. The VLAN identifier is a 15-bit value, but Cisco uses only 10 bits of this frame, resulting in the value of 1024.

All trunks, regardless of whether they are ISL or 802.1Q, are defined as point-to-point connections between devices. ISL trunks are primarily intended to connect switches to switches or routers to switches with multiple VLANs over a single physical port. This significantly reduces overhead infrastructure costs, since per-port costs can range into the thousands of dollars.

ISL encapsulates the original datagram within an ISL capsule. This process adds 30 octets to the length of the original frame and can result in an Ethernet frame of 1548 octets in length. Non-Cisco equipment sees such a frame as a giant and discards it. For that reason, use ISL on Cisco-to-Cisco equipment only. There are ISL network cards from various vendors for server connectivity. Thus, multiple VLANs can be sent down a single interface to a server.

ISL is the default encapsulation method on all Cisco ports configured as trunks. With the release of the Dynamic Trunking Protocol (DTP) in CatOS 4.1, configuration of ISL trunks has become almost automatic. All that needs to be done is for one of the ports to be set to desirable for trunking. This allows the automatic formation of an ISL trunk. Trunking must be manually configured in Cisco switches. ISL is recommended for all trunk links of 100Mbps full or higher. It is possible to configure ISL for trunks that are only 10Mbit in speed, as of CatOs 5.0 and IOS 12.0, but the associated overhead of ISL is an impractical use of the bandwidth. (Even though it can be done, it is not recommended to connect your 2500 series router via its 10Base-T port to your Cat switch using an ISL trunk.)

Internal Frame Tag and ISL

One of the big differences between 802.1Q and ISL is the position of the frame tags. In 802.1Q, only four octets are added to the original frame size. The VLAN identifier information is not added externally to the packet; rather, it is added inside the original frame, after the destination and source MAC addresses. ISL adds the VLAN information as an external 15-bit value (of which only 10 bits are used).

ISL Frame Format

The ISL frame format appends 30 octets onto the original datagram, which includes a second packet CRC with the original datagram CRC contained within the ISL packet. The ISDL frame consists of three primary parts: the ISL header, the original packet, and the FCS or CRC.

The ISDL header is composed of the following:

- **Destination address**   This is an ISL multicast address occupying the first 40 bits, currently set to 0x01_00_0C_00_00.

- **Type-frame type**   Currently used to indicate the frame type being encapsulated.

- **User-defined bits**   Currently used to define the priority of the packet.
- **Source address**   The MAC address of the sending trunk port.
- **Length**   An 18-bit field used to indicate the full length of the packet minus the above stated four fields.
- **The SNAP LLC field binary expression**
- **Organizational identifier of the source address**   The same as the first three octets of the MAC address.
- **VLAN ID**   A 15-bit value, of which Cisco uses 10 bits, to identify and support up to 1024 VLANs.
- **Index**   Contains the source port value of the frame.
- **Reserved**   Used only when FDDI or Token Ring packets are encapsulated within the ISL frame.
- **Original frame**   The original datagram with its own CRC value intact.
- **ISL CRC**   A new 32-bit CRC that is calculated for the entire frame.

exam
ⓦatch

ISL is Cisco's main trunking protocol. You need to know the ISL frame format very well.

Troubleshooting ISL Trunks

In ISL trunks, there are really only two problem scenarios: Either the trunk does not form or you have what is called a broken trunk.

Trunk Doesn't Form

If the trunk fails to come up automatically when the ports are connected (allowing that there are no Physical Layer issues), the issue is almost always a case of the ports being configured to differing trunking modes. The five trunking modes are:

- **Off**   The port never becomes a trunk and always sends normal Ethernet frames.
- **Auto**   The link becomes a trunk only if the other side requests it. This is the default for Cisco ISL-capable switch ports.
- **Desirable**   The trunk negotiates with the other side. The trunk becomes operational if the other side is Auto or On.

- **On**   The link trunks (sends only ISL frames) and responds to DTP. If the other side is Off, there are framing problems.

- **Nonegotiate**   The link does trunk but does not use DTP. This mode is used primarily to connect devices that do not understand DTP (such as server ISL NICs).

Know trunking modes and the differences between 802.1Q and ISL trunks with regard to spanning-tree parameters.

The recommended settings are Desirable in the network core connected to Auto at the network edge switch. Use one to one only if the link must always be a trunk.

Broken Trunk   A broken trunk is seen frequently in 802.1Q trunks. The native VLAN for Catalyst switches is VLAN 1, but 802.1Q does not tag frames in the native VLAN. Therefore, if the trunk port on each side of the trunk is set to a differing native VLAN, no communication is possible across the trunk.

Another form of broken trunk is seen when stations on the same VLAN but on different switches can no longer communicate and the trunks appear to be up. In this case, the VLANs were probably manually pruned on the switches during the trunk configuration process and no longer correspond on the trunk ports.

Troubleshooting a trunk port is a fairly simple task. There is one SHOW command in both the CatOS and IOS that gives you all the information needed to verify proper trunk configuration. Make sure that VLANs and trunk types are matched on both sides of the trunks, especially with respect to the native VLAN:

```
CatOS: show trunk detail (detail is optional)
IOS: show interfaces trunk
```

In a perfect world, we would all build our networks with Cisco Catalyst switches with ISL trunks. However, this is often not the case. Frequently, we have to mix hardware from differing manufacturers. If you do have a mixed environment, remember that you must use 802.1Q for your trunks. This is not the default on a Cisco switch and must be hard set. Remember, too, that 802.1Q trunks can pass only a single instance of a spanning tree for the trunking port. This can cause issues if you have designed your network to react with multiple instances of spanning tree (one for each VLAN on the trunk). You might need to redesign your network to prevent multiple instances of spanning tree from being conglomerated on the 802.1Q trunks.

VLAN Trunking Protocol and Propagation

VLAN Trunking Protocol (VTP) is a Layer 2 messaging protocol that acts to maintain VLAN information in a consistent basis across all Catalyst switches that are part of a common VTP domain. The default mode on a Cat5K and Cat6K is a VTP server with no domain name. Each switch can be configured to be part of only one VTP domain. With VTP, you only need to configure VLAN information on a single VTP server. The VLAN information is propagated out all trunk links to every switch in the VTP domain.

VTP is currently supported in two modes: VTP 1 and VTP 2. The default setting for Catalyst switches is Version 1; however, if you require support for Token Ring or FDDI, you must implement Version 2 on all switches within the VTP domain.

VTP Propagates the VLAN Table

VTP propagates the entire VLAN information table to all switches within the VTP domain. All VTP information is propagated on VLAN 1.

The VTP broadcasts include:

- VLAN IDs for both ISL and 802.1Q
- Emulated LAN names (if running LANE)
- 802.10 SAID values (for FDDI)
- VTP domain name
- VTP revision number
- VLAN configuration including maximum MTU size
- Frame format

A switch defines its group membership by the VTP domain name. Each switch can have only one VTP domain name and must be adjacent to switches within its domain area. (VTP conduits do not work.) A consistent VTP domain name must be employed on all switches within a VTP area.

VTP is by definition a trunking information protocol. It works only on links that are defined as ISL or 802.1Q trunks. If you are troubleshooting a VTP issue, make sure that you have working trunks between all your devices. VTP broadcasts are also confined to VLAN 1 only. This is the native VLAN for ISL trunks, but it might not be the native VLAN for 802.1Q trunks. Make sure that all 802.1Q trunks are set to use VLAN 1 as the native VLAN; otherwise, VTP information will not be propagated.

VTP is used to propagate VLAN information. VLANs are a Layer 2 construct; as such, VTP is a Layer 2 functional process. Because routers operate at Layer 3 of the OSI model, they are unable to propagate VTP information. Therefore, VTP functionality is limited to Catalyst switches only.

Three Modes of VTP

The following are the three modes of VTP:

- **Server** Server is the default mode for Catalyst series switches. In this mode, the switch can create, modify, and delete VLANs and specify configuration parameters for the entire VTP domain. By default, Catalyst switches are configured as a server with no domain.

- **Client** The VLAN information on a client switch cannot be directly modified. Instead, the switch listens for and modifies its VLAN information based on information supplied by the VTP server or propagated via other VTP clients.

- **Transparent** Transparent switches do not participate in VTP. They do not update nor listen to VTP broadcasts, but they do propagate VTP broadcasts out their trunk ports to other members of the VTP domain, assuming they are configured to be members of the same domain. Transparent switches are allowed to create, delete, and modify their own individual VLAN tables.

When to Use Each Mode

The root switch of your VTP domain should be configured as your VTP server. Each VTP domain should have only one VTP server. If you have a large number of switches in your internetwork or have a complex VLAN structure, the use of a VTP domain is recommended. Client mode should be configured on the remainder of the switches within a VTP domain. If you have a version of CWSI older than the current version (CWSI 2000), you must have your switches configured as either server or client. Earlier versions of CWSI do not recognize the transparent function. Transparent mode is not recommended as a long-term solution.

VTP Pruning

VTP pruning is extremely beneficial in environments that have multicast, broadcast, or unknown unicasts. This can include any environment that uses streaming multimedia applications, collaborative messaging, whiteboard, or ticker-tape applications. VTP pruning limits traffic on trunks to only those VLANs that are needed to access the resources across that trunk. VTP pruning is disabled by default. To enable VTP pruning, use the SET VTP PRUNING ENABLE command on any switch in the VTP domain. You can specify the VLAN range that is included in the VLAN pruning. VLAN 1 cannot be made prune eligible:

```
CatOS: set vtp pruneeligible vlans
IOS: Router(vlan)# vtp pruning
```

Troubleshooting VTP

VTP troubleshooting revolves around the effects of introducing a new switch to the network. Essentially, the domain is working fine, but the addition of new switch to the domain triggers a VTP meltdown. What this means is that all of a sudden, VLAN information disappears from your switches and the network stops working. Everything appears to be normal, but your VLAN database has now vanished from your server switch and all client switches.

This is a common occurrence if a switch that is added to a VTP domain has a higher revision number. A newly added Catalyst switch can be configured as either a client or a server, since both send VTP updates. The highest VTP revision in the domain is considered the valid one. Hence the newly added switch that has a high revision number (due to tests and sample configurations before it was attached to the network) overwrites the VLAN configuration on the Catalyst switches in the VTP domain. If this situation occurs, the only solution is to quickly reconfigure the VLANs on one of your VTP servers. You should also check revision numbers on any new switch before you introduce it to your network, or remember to configure VTP on a switch only *after* it is connected to your network. (Again, remember: proactive prevention is better than reaction in all cases!)

The easiest way to prevent this VTP meltdown is to reset the version number of the new switch. There is no command to simply reset the revision number to zero.

The way to accomplish this task is to rename the VTP domain to a bogus value and then restore it to the current one.

Use the SET VTP DOMAIN command to change the VTP domain to a bogus setting and then back again. To view the current VTP information, use the SHOW VTP DOMAIN command.

The equivalent IOS commands are SHOW VTP to view VTP information and VTP DOMAIN (*DOMAIN NAME*) to change the VTP domain name.

FROM THE CLASSROOM

Resetting the VTP Revision Number

Frequently, you configure a switch offline to test a configuration and then introduce the switch into the existing network. This can cause a problem with what is known as *VTP meltdown*. The preferred solution is to configure your switch for VTP when it is online. However, you should follow the procedure for resetting a switch's revision number if you have configured it as a VTP client offline and want to introduce it into the network. In this case, you are dealing with a Cat5K configured as a high-density closet switch named closet1. The switch was configured to support two VLANs, and the VTP domain name is set to Accounting. A SHOW VTP DOMAIN command displays the following output:

```
closet1 (enable) show vtp domain

Domain Name                          Domain Index VTP Version Local Mode  Password
------------------------------------ ------------ ----------- ----------- ----------
Accounting                           1            2           server      -

Vlan-count Max-vlan-storage Config Revision Notifications
@PD () = Box END


---------- ---------------- ---------------- --------------
7          1023             2                disabled

Last Updater    V2 Mode  Pruning  PruneEligible on Vlans
--------------- -------- -------- -------------------------
0.0.0.0         disabled disabled 2-1000
closet1 (enable)
```

The key field is the config revision value of 2. If this value is higher than the VTP revision number in the network, this switch wipes out the existing VLAN information as soon as the switch is introduced into the network. You have to reset the value of this register back to 0. To do this, reset the name to a bogus value and then back to the correct value by entering the following commands:

```
closet1 (enable) set vtp domain bogus
VTP domain bogus modified
```

Now reset the VTP domain name back to Accounting:

```
closet1 (enable) set vtp domain Accounting
VTP domain Accounting modified
```

A new SHOW VTP DOMAIN command verifies that the config register has been reset to 0 and the switch is safe to connect to the network:

```
closet1 (enable) show vtp domain
Domain Name                      Domain Index VTP Version Local Mode  Password
-------------------------------- ------------ ----------- ----------- ----------
Accounting                       1            2           server      -

Vlan-count Max-vlan-storage Config Revision Notifications
---------- ---------------- --------------- -------------
7          1023             0               disabled

Last Updater    V2 Mode  Pruning  PruneEligible on Vlans
--------------- -------- -------- ------------------------
0.0.0.0         disabled disabled 2-1000
closet1 (enable)
```

—*James Placer, CCDP, CCNP Voice, NNCSS, NNCDS, MCSE*

Another issue with VTP is that VTP information is not propagated to a switch via normal Ethernet ports. VTP can be propagated only along a trunk link. Use the SHOW TRUNK command to confirm that your switch is configured with a trunk port and that the proper encapsulation type is set (ISL or 802.1Q).

Don't Configure VTP Servers Offline

The point must be restated: if you configure VLANs into a VTP server offline, there is a chance that the configuration revision number will be greater than the one in the operational network. When the new switch joins the network, the bogus VLAN information wipes out the entire network. Always bring the new, empty switch up on the network and then configure the VTP information. That way, the revision number is always less than the existing revision number on the network, and you cannot override the existing VLAN information.

CERTIFICATION OBJECTIVE 10.07

Cisco Discovery Protocol

Cisco Discovery Protocol (CDP) is a Layer 2 Cisco-specific protocol that runs on all Cisco products. CDP is a media- and protocol-independent protocol that allows any Cisco device or network manager to learn the detailed device types and capabilities of directly connected Cisco devices. Each device sends out a CDP packet (which is a proprietary multicast frame of 0100.0ccc.cccc) that travels to adjacent devices. CDP packets are never forwarded past the adjacent Cisco device. However, other network devices flood the unknown multicast. CDP is one of the key troubleshooting tools for diagnosing network issues, because it is independent of media or higher-layer configurations. CDP uses a Cisco proprietary SNAP encapsulation and runs only at the Data-Link Layer. For that reason, CDP can be used over any media that supports Data-Link LayerSNAP encapsulation (FDDI, Ethernet, Token Ring, ATM, or Frame Relay).

CDP is a Data-Link Layer protocol only. It runs regardless of any VLAN or higher Network Layer configurations. CDP also runs on STP ports in a blocking state. If you have a valid physical connection between your LAN devices, CDP runs. CDP even functions over mismatched trunks, such as an ISL port trying to connect to an 802.1Q port.

Since CDP is a Data Link Layer protocol, all it needs to function is an appropriate and functional Physical Layer connection. CDP is a great way to determine if you have a Physical Layer issue. If you suspect that a box has a Physical Layer connection problem, use the SHOW CDP NEIGHBOR command and compare the device information returned with what is expected from your network diagram and cabling plant. If all devices are displayed, you have immediately eliminated a Physical Layer issue. This assumes that all the directly connected devices are Cisco products; remember that CDP is a Cisco proprietary protocol.

CDP Advertises Network Layer Information

One of the important aspects of CDP is that the CDP packets carry a detailed description of the physical capabilities of adjacent devices and full Network Layer information from those devices. This feature is extremely useful if you have physical connectivity but cannot obtain a network connection (as with Telnet) to a device. The command SHOW CDP NEIGHBORS DETAIL provides detailed information about neighboring devices, and it shows if duplex or native VLAN mismatches are present. Remember that a duplex mismatch is one of the key reasons for an STP failure causing a network loop, and native VLAN mismatches are one of the key issues in trunking failures. CDP provides an immediate diagnosis of either of those two error states.

The following are SHOW CDP commands:

```
Console> show cdp neighbors
* - indicates vlan mismatch.
# - indicates duplex mismatch.

Port      Device-ID                         Port-ID                    Platform
--------  --------------------------------  -------------------------  ------------
3/7       002267619                         3/5 *                      WS-C5000
3/6       002267619                         3/5                        WS-C5000
4/4       002267619                         4/5 #                      WS-C5000

Console> show cdp vlan
* - indicates vlan mismatch.
# - indicates duplex mismatch.

Port      Device-ID                         Port-ID                    NativeVLAN
--------  --------------------------------  -------------------------  ----------
3/7       002267619                         3/5 *                      1
3/6       002267619                         3/5                        1
4/4       002267619                         4/5 #                      1

Console> show cdp neighbors duplex
* - indicates vlan mismatch.
# - indicates duplex mismatch.
```

Port	Device-ID	Port-ID	Duplex
3/7	002267619	3/5 *	half
3/6	002267619	3/5	half
4/4	002267619	4/5 #	full

Remember that CDP is a Data-Link Layer protocol only. It verifies network availability at the physical and Data-Link Layer only. Many network configuration errors occur at the LLC or higher layers. CDP is only a start in your troubleshooting process and guides you to other issues that could be preventing network reachability. CDP might work, but you still cannot PING a device, for example. Use CDP as one of your first-line diagnostic tools in troubleshooting a network issue.

exam
ⓦatch

CDP is one of the most useful commands available. Make sure you are familiar with the various forms of the command and the information it provides.

CERTIFICATION OBJECTIVE 10.08

Diagnostic Commands

The Catalyst OS and IOS are rich in diagnostic and troubleshooting tools. This chapter has touched on a number of the more common ones, but be aware that there is a whole list of tools that can be used to diagnose a problem or verify the existing health of the internetwork. It is recommended that you become familiar with all of the following commands and use them on a regular basis to establish a baseline of your network activity. In-depth knowledge of how your network acts on a daily basis is invaluable if you have to troubleshoot a network issue. We can't overstate it: it is far better to be proactive than reactive if you are administering or troubleshooting a network.

This section does not cover the full depth of the available troubleshooting commands, but it is a summary of the most common ones that you should be using on a regular basis to monitor your network health.

The **SHOW SYSTEM** Command

Shows basic system uptime, utilization, and environmental counters:

```
CatOS: Console> show system
```

There is no direct IOS equivalent. Use the following commands to obtain the same information:

```
Router> show catalyst6000 all
Router> show environment status
```

The **SHOW INTERFACE** Command

Shows information on all interfaces, IP address, and up/down state. This is a command common to both CatOS and IOS:

```
Console> show interface
```

The **SHOW LOG** Command

The SHOW LOG command shows significant events that have occurred in the past with a relative time stamp. It is very useful to determine an event such as a switch reset and when it occurred:

```
CatOS: Console> show log
IOS: Router> show logging
```

The **SHOW CAM DYNAMIC** Command

This shows the dynamic CAM entries (MAC addresses) for all VLANs:

```
CatOS: Console> show cam dynamic
IOS: Router# show mac-address-table vlan
```

The **SHOW MAC** Command

This displays the MAC counter details:

```
CatOS: show mac
IOS: Router# show mac-address-table detail
```

The **SHOW MODULE** Command

This command shows all module details and is especially useful in troubleshooting the POST status of the module and microcode revisions. The command is the same in IOS and CatOS.

```
CatOS: Console> show module
```

The **SHOW PORT** Command

The SHOW PORT command shows detailed information about each port, the duplex and type, frames received, and error states. This is always a good troubleshooting place to check:

```
CatOS: Console> (enable) show port 3/1 (shows module 3 port 1)
IOS: Router# show interfaces type Ethernet (or trbf for token
ring)
```

The **SHOW CONFIG** Command

This command shows all nondefault running configuration parameters on the switch. Depending on the switch configuration, this can be a lengthy output but can provide detailed troubleshooting configuration information. Add the ALL option at the end to show nondefault and default configuration information:

```
CatOS: Console>(enable) show config {all}
IOS: Router>show running-config
```

The **SHOW SPAN** Command

If you have enabled port spanning (mirroring) to monitor network traffic on a port, this command shows the current SPAN settings. To show spanned port information on an IOS-based switch, you must use the SHOW RUNNING-CONFIG command:

```
CatOS: Console> (enable) show span
```

The **SHOW SPANTREE** Command

The SHOW SPANTREE command shows the spanning-tree information for a specific VLAN or module port. If you do not specify a VLAN, diagnostic information for VLAN 1 is displayed:

```
CatOS: Console> show spantree {vlan}
IOS: Router# show spanning-tree {active} {VLAN}
```

The SHOW TRUNK Command

This command shows details about all trunks configured on a switch. This is essential if you are hunting down ISL/802.1Q mismatches:

```
CatOS: Console> (enable) show trunk
IOS: Router# show interfaces switchport
```

The SHOW VLAN Command

This command shows all VLAN information and port assignments. If you suspect a VTP meltdown, use this command to check for VLANs. If they have all disappeared, you have a VTP issue:

```
CatOS:  Console> show vlan
IOS: Router# show spanning-tree vlan
```

The SHOW FLASH Command

This lists information on all files in Flash, including code revisions, filenames, and build dates:

```
CatOS: Console> show flash
IOS: Router> show bootflash:
```

The SHOW VTP DOMAIN Command

Every switch can belong to one and only VTP domain. This command allows you to check the current configured VTP domain. Remember that you could contribute to a VTP meltdown if you add a switch to a VTP domain. This command also shows VTP version and the device state (server, client, or transparent) and whether or not VTP pruning is enabled:

```
CatOS: Console> show vtp domain
IOS: Router# show vtp status
```

The SHOW CDP NEIGHBOR Command

This is one of the prime troubleshooting commands and an excellent way to validate connectivity between devices at the Physical Layer. CDP is on by default on all Cisco devices. The command is constant on Cisco operating systems:

```
OS: Console> show cdp neighbor {details}
```

exam
ⓦatch

For troubleshooting, the SHOW commands are your basic bread and butter. Know these commands and when to use them before you attempt to take the exam.

The following exercise allows you to diagnose and correct an issue with trunking ports that fail to propagate VTP information between two Cat5K switches.

EXERCISE 10-5

Diagnosing Trunking Issues

You have configured a trunk port between two Catalyst 5500 switches for 802.1Q trunking. Now the port is not passing VTP information (or so it would appear). How would you diagnose this problem?

The first step is to issue the SHOW CDP NEIGHBORS command on one of the Catalyst switches:

```
Console> show cdp neighbors
* - indicates vlan mismatch.
# - indicates duplex mismatch.

Port      Device-ID                          Port-ID                     Platform
--------  -------------------------------    -------------------------   ------------
4/6       002267619                          3/6 *                       WS-C5000
```

The Port-ID field indicates that there is a VLAN mismatch. Remember that if you have an 802.1Q trunk, the native VLAN must be set to VLAN 1. Checking the VLAN membership on the trunk on the other Catalyst shows Console> (enable) SHOW TRUNK:

```
* - indicates vtp domain mismatch
Port       Mode         Encapsulation  Status        Native vlan
--------   -----------  -------------  ------------  -----------
 3/6       nonegotiate  dot1q          trunking      2
```

The native VLAN has been set for 2 on this end. Resetting the native VLAN to 1 for this trunk port will fix the problem.

CERTIFICATION OBJECTIVE 10.09

The Switched Port Analyzer

In the days of a shared hub-based network, troubleshooting was much simpler. A packet sniffer was simply plugged into any port on a hub. Since the LAN was shared media, every packet that traversed the network was easily seen.

With the advent of switching, this is no longer the case. Switching allows each port to become its own collision domain. The only packets that are sent across the entire switch are broadcasts and multicasts. Often, broadcasts and multicasts do not help much in troubleshooting an individual issue.

To correct this potential problem, the switched port analyzer (SPAN) was created. SPAN allows you to mirror all traffic on a particular port or VLAN to a monitoring port. These packets are then sent out one particular port to a network sniffer or a dedicated RMON probe such as a Catalyst network with a monitor attached. Packet analysis is an excellent way to track down a problem related to a malfunctioning NIC or other hardware. If you see a large number of runts or giant frames on your network and can track the problem down to a particular segment, capturing those packets with a network analyzer gives you the MAC or network address of the offending hardware.

Configuration

Configuration of SPAN is very simple in either the CatOS- or IOS-based devices. On a Catalyst switch, you can SPAN only ports that are on the same module. If you are SPANning an entire VLAN to a port, only those ports that are on the same module and belong to the VLAN are mirrored.

To monitor a port, the command is:

```
CatOS: set span {src_mod/src_ports | src_vlan}
{dest_mod/dest_port}
```

To enable the SPAN on an IOS-based switch, you must be in interface configuration mode on the monitoring port. Then issue the following command:

```
(Conf-if)> port monitor (interface)
```

These commands immediately begin to forward packets to the monitoring port, so make sure that you do not have an active network or trunk connection on the port, since it is a very good way to saturate that link. You should always install your monitoring devices first, then enable port SPANning.

Catalyst Problem Isolation

The key to remember when a situation occurs on your network is to approach it in a methodical and level-headed manner. Work through the layers of diagnostics to locate the OSI layer at which the problem is occurring. Isolate the segment or segments the problem is on. You should have a detailed network diagram and baseline metrics collected well in advance of any issues. Remember, it is far more efficient (not to mention less stressful) to be proactive rather than reactive.

LEDs

The Catalyst LEDs are the first and greatest source of information. You can immediately get a visual indication of a physical problem exists with a chassis component or line card. All Catalyst cards can be hot swapped, so if you do have a marginal light, immediately change the affected component.

Status Light Color

Check the Supervisor module for status lights. Are they all green? If they are, your chassis is operating properly. If some are red or orange, you have a chassis hardware issue and normally require an immediate replacement of the affected part.

Port Light Color

Check your line module port status lights. Are they all green? If they are not, you have either a faulty cable or a bad port/line module. You might have something as simple as a cable pulled loose from a port. This happens much more frequently than you even dare have nightmares over. On the other hand, a port could be bad on the module. Change the cable to another port and see what happens.

Switch Configuration

If all of your LEDs are green, is your switch configured properly? Are all the ports enabled, or have some been administratively downed? Are VLANs or VTP settings correct? Start going up the list of issues, one at a time.

Physical Connections

It cannot be stressed enough to verify physical connectivity issues. Is a fiber cable damaged and transmitting in only one direction? Exposed cabling plants are very susceptible to damage, especially if you have an extensive fiber plant that is not in a conduit or a proper channel.

CDP Verifications

CDP is your number-one tool to verify that Physical Layer connections between adjacent switches are up and operational. Compare the results of CDP with your network diagram. If they do not match, you have a physical issue somewhere.

Layer 2 Path Between Switches

Switches are Layer 2 devices; make sure that Layer 2 configurations are correct. Check for things such as duplex mismatches, native VLAN mismatches on trunks, and improper trunk encapsulations. Remember that if your physical plant is okay, all you have to do is connect the Catalyst switches together and turn them on, and they will pass data. Misconfiguration on one or both ends of a link are common if people try to configure trunk or tune spanning-tree parameters. Be wary of PORTFAST; use it where you need it, but be sure you know on what ports it is enabled. Make sure you know the supposed location and actual location of the spanning-tree root bridge; where it should be and where it ends up are frequently two different locations.

CDP

CDP is again our main friend. CDP shows duplex and VLAN mismatches on trunks and ports. Remember that duplex mismatches are a very good way to precipitate a STP meltdown, whereas native VLAN mismatches and encapsulation mismatches prevent a trunk from forming or passing data. CDP shows all these issues quickly and effectively.

Trunking

All trunks must be of the same encapsulation. If you try to connect a Cisco switch to a non-Cisco switch, you must use 802.1Q trunking. Cisco devices use ISL as the default. Verify the trunk configuration and encapsulation, and make sure that the native VLAN is the same on both sides of a trunk.

VLAN Configuration

VTP might be of assistance in managing a large network, but remember that if you configure a VTP client or server offline and then connect it into a network, you could very easily have a VTP meltdown and have all your carefully configured VLAN information disappear. Be cognizant of any and all hardware and configuration changes on your network.

CERTIFICATION OBJECTIVE 10.11

Catalyst Symptoms, Problems, and Action Plans

The time has come to go through some common issues and common solutions to specific problems. The exact solution varies depending on the network condition and configuration, as shown in this section.

Switch Cannot Communicate with Local Devices

Local devices are defined as chassis components and modules and directly attached devices. You might not get statistics for a particular line module, power supply, or adjacent switch. You cannot Telnet into the switch from adjacent devices.

Power Supply

We never give the power supply much thought until it fails us. Most larger Catalyst switches have redundant power supplies and are capable of running with one if one goes bad. However, it is possible to have too great a drain on the power supply and therefore prevent modules from powering up. The Catalyst powers up modules in sequence, beginning with the Supervisor, until power supply limits are reached. Normally this is not an issue, but the Cat6K now has been issued with 48-port power modules that supply a 48-volt DC ring voltage to power IP phones. If you are using these modules, you can very easily exceed the power capacity of the Cat6K and have modules intermittently dropping out. Always verify power demands.

on the
() o b

Power loading will become a significantly greater concern in this coming year and the next. The growing trend is to converge your network and have your data network carry your voice and video traffic as well. On a current VOIP project, for example, we implemented the Catalyst 6509 switch configured with power line cards to enable IP phones. Unfortunately, as we started plugging phones into the modules, we ran out of power and ended up with a chassis that could run with only two-thirds of its card capacity. This was not an issue until we started using the powered IP phones. The solution was to increase the power supplies on the 6509s to handle the increased current load. Be aware of things such as power loading, which could have significant effects on functionality down the road.

Hardware

Are your modules running and are all ports enabled? Use the SHOW SYSTEM, SHOW CATALYST6000, SHOW INTERFACES, and SHOW RUNNING-CONFIG commands to verify that all ports are up and functional. Verify that all LEDs are green. If an LED is not green, it could indicate that you need to change the module or hardware device.

Cabling

Cabling is the number-one reason for LAN problems. Are all your segments within Ethernet guidelines? Are you using the correct cabling type? Switch-to-switch connections should be made using a cross-over cable. Host-to-switch connections are made using a straight-through cable. If using fiber, make sure the TX and RX connections are in the correct port. Verify Physical Layer connectivity with the SHOW CDP NEIGHBOR command.

Terminal Cannot Communicate with Switch

The primary means of communication with a switch is through the CLI. The terminal connection is established by a serial connection from a computer running a terminal program to the console port on the switch. Because the console port on the switch is configured in a fixed manner, failure to communicate with the console is normally due to external factors.

Misconfigured Console Port

By default, your terminal program must be configured for the proper serial port and set to 9600 baud, 8 bits, no parity, and 1 stop bit. Note that if the supervisor is from a Cat6K, you must use 2 stop bits, and terminal emulation should be set to VT100. If any of these parameters are incorrect, you either fail to connect or have gibberish on your screen.

Improper Cable

You must use the proper Cisco rolled cable to make the console connection. Even though it could have RJ45 connectors, that Cat 5 patch cord that was lying beside the switch does not have the proper pin-out. Keep the proper rolled cable handy at all times, or leave one attached to the switch; that way, it is there when you need it. The exception to this rule is the Supervisor III module on the Catalyst 5500, which allows you to select a DCE or DTE via a button. This allows the use of a straight-through cable if a rolled one is not available.

Server Cannot Communicate with Remote Devices on Another LAN

If a workstation or server cannot communicate across your LAN and you have verified that the Physical Layer functionality is intact, you have a number of Layer 2 and 3 issues that might need to be addressed. Because this is a switching troubleshooting session, it is assumed that all the devices are on the same VLAN or subnet. If they are not, Layer 3 troubleshooting needs to be performed, but that is another subject entirely.

IP Address Misconfiguration

A common problem is IP address misconfiguration. Can devices on the LAN reach each other? If they can, you probably have an incorrect IP setting on the machine. Check the assigned IP address, subnet mask, and default gateway on the device in question.

VLAN Mismatch

A VLAN mismatch can occur quite frequently if you are using 802.1Q trunks. If you are, make sure all trunking ports are configured for the same native VLAN. If you are using ISL trunks, make sure the same VLANs are configured on each trunk port. Use the SHOW VLAN and SHOW INTERFACE commands to verify these settings.

Port Timeout

Make sure that PORTFAST is enabled on the host port. Otherwise, a network timeout can occur. Use the SHOW CAM DYNAMIC command to make sure the switch is learning the MAC address of the host.

ISL/Trunking Problems

Make sure that all your trunk ports are the same encapsulation and are set for the same native VLAN. Use the SHOW TRUNK command or SHOW CDP NEIGHBOR to check for trunk and VLAN mismatches. Make sure that one end of your trunk is set to On or Desirable and the other is not set to Off.

Autonegotiation Problems

Most NICs should autonegotiate with Catalyst switch ports. However, autonegotiation does not always function properly. If you suspect an autonegotiation problem, check to make sure that the drivers for your NICs are current. If they are, set the Catalyst port and NIC to a similar speed and duplex.

VTP Isn't Propagating VLAN Information

VTP should send out full VLAN information to all your switches in the same VTP domain.

- **Trunk ports** VTP runs only over trunk ports. Use the SHOW TRUNK command to make sure all interswitch connections are via trunks.

- **VTP domain** Use the SHOW VTP DOMAIN command to make sure all switches are part of the same VTP domain. If you set a VTP password, that password must be constant on all switches in the VTP domain. Clear the VTP password using the SET VTP PASSWORD 0 command.

- **VTP meltdown** To avoid a VTP meltdown, never configure a switch offline. Always configure it online or reset the revision number by changing the VTP domain to a bogus name and back again. If you do have a VTP meltdown, recreate all your VLAN information on any VTP server and remember to not make the same mistake again.

CERTIFICATION SUMMARY

Troubleshooting a switched network is a methodical process that should be attacked in an organized and regimented manner. This chapter has addressed switching, both in a general manner and in conjunction with specialized CatOS and IOS tools.

Switching is a Layer 2 process. All troubleshooting must include both Layer 1 and Layer 2 functionality. At its core, switching is concerned with three processes: trunking, VLANs, and spanning tree. For trunking, beware of and know the differences between ISL and 802.1Q.

Spanning tree is one of the prime factors in a switched network. You need to be aware of Cisco's spanning-tree optimizations: PORTFAST, UPLINKFAST, and BACKBONEFAST, in both IOS and CatOS versions.

Be aware of CDP parameters and the meanings of the LEDs on the respective Supervisor modules.

The essentials of troubleshooting are the SHOW commands. They provide you with information on the status of your network and devices within the network. At this point, you should be able to recite the major SHOW commands. If you cannot, review the ones that you are unsure of.

Finally, when you are taking the test, remember that the key point is to fully read and comprehend the questions and ascertain the best answer. There could be more than one right answer, but you need to choose the best and most efficient answer. This choice applies to the fact that you have more than one OS for switching services. If you have a Cat5K question, the correct answer is the CatOS version of the command. If you have a Cat6K question, the correct answer is the IOS version of the command.

TWO-MINUTE DRILL

Here are some of the key points from each certification objective in Chapter 10.

Catalyst Light-Emitting Diodes

❑ Orange on a Supervisor means a hardware device has failed.

❑ Red means a diagnostic test has failed.

❑ Green means fully operational.

Cable and Media Distance Limitations

❑ Segment length is 100 meters for all Ethernet copper segments.

❑ Multimode fiber can extend to 400 meters for 100BaseFX and 550 meters for 1000BaseSX.

Catalyst Power-On Self Test

❑ During the POST process, the catalyst first verifies the functionality of the Supervisor module and all chassis components.

❑ The POST then verifies the functionality of all line modules. The LEDs show green during this phase.

❑ The POST process can be monitored from the CLI.

❑ Use the SHOW TEST command to give a detailed result of the POST tests.

Spanning Tree

❑ UPLINKFAST is used for access layer switches only.

❑ BACKBONEFAST is used on core switches only.

❑ PORTFAST is used for end-user host ports only.

❑ Know the configuration commands for CatOS and IOS very well!

Inter-Switch Link and Frame Tagging

❑ ISL encapsulates the original packet within a new header and uses a unique CRC.

❏ ISL maintains a separate instance of spanning tree for each VLAN carried on the trunk.

❏ ISL is unique to Cisco and is not compatible with 802.1Q trunking.

VLAN Trunking Protocol and Propagation

❏ All switches must be members of the same VTP domain.

❏ Switches can be servers, clients, or transparent.

❏ VTP uses a revision number to keep track of the most current level of VTP information.

❏ Introducing an offline configured switch into a VTP domain can trigger a VTP meltdown.

Cisco Discovery Protocol

❏ CDP is a Cisco proprietary Data-Link Layer protocol.

❏ CDP verifies network connection and is used to obtain adjacent device information.

❏ CDP runs by default on all Cisco devices.

❏ CDP provides information on duplex, VLAN, and trunking mismatches.

Diagnostic Commands

❏ The SHOW commands are the primary source of diagnostic information.

❏ SHOW INTERFACES (CatOS) and SHOW RUNNING-CONFIG (IOS) provide detailed interface information.

❏ SHOW TRUNK shows detailed trunking information.

The Switched Port Analyzer

❏ The SPAN is also known as port mirroring or the switch port analyzer.

❏ The SPAN directs all traffic from one switched port or VLAN to a specific port for monitoring with a network analyzer or RMON probe.

Catalyst Problem Isolation

❑ Always start with the Physical Layer and work up.

❑ Use CDP to verify Physical Layer connectivity and base network settings.

Catalyst Symptoms, Problems, and Action Plans

❑ Check terminal program settings if you cannot connect to the console port: 8 none and 1 for the Cat5K and 8 none and 2 for the Cat6K.

❑ Use proper cabling for switch-to-switch and switch-to-host connections.

❑ For trunking issues, use the SHOW TRUNK command to verify settings.

❑ Before beginning network troubleshooting, verify IP settings if workstations cannot communicate.

SELF TEST

The following questions will help you measure your understanding of the material presented in this chapter. Read all the choices carefully because there might be more than one correct answer. Choose all correct answers for each question.

Catalyst Light-Emitting Diodes

1. During the POST process, the status LED on a line module is orange. This means:
   A. A port on the module failed POST.
   B. POST is in process; please wait.
   C. A module ASIC failed.

2. On a Cat6K, if there is insufficient power for all the modules, the POWERMGMT LED is:
   A. Red
   B. Orange
   C. Green

Cable and Media Distance Limitations

3. The maximum distance for a Cat 5 100BaseTX Ethernet segment is:
   A. 25 meters
   B. 100 meters
   C. 400 meters
   D. 200 meters

4. You have a campus that needs to be connected back to your network operations center. The distance is 10 km. Which of the following types of cabling will you choose?
   A. Multimode fiber
   B. Multimode fiber with repeaters
   C. Single-mode fiber
   D. This is too long for a cable run. It is considered a WAN length, so you would use a router and some form of WAN technology.

Catalyst Power-On Self Test

5. To view the results of the POST tests from the CLI, you would use which command?

A. SHOW TEST

B. SHOW SYSTEM

C. SHOW INTERFACES SWITCHPORT

D. SHOW BOOT

6. The first visible LED during POST is which of the following?

A. PS1 and PS2 LEDs become green.

B. Fan LED turns green.

C. LEDs on the line cards turn orange.

Spanning Tree

7. To transition a port immediately to a forwarding state without going through the prior states, which of the following IOS commands would you use on a Cat6K?

A. CONSOLE> (ENABLE) SPANNING-PORT PORTFAST

B. CONSOLE> (ENABLE) SET SPANNINGTREE PORTFAST MOD NUMBER/PORT NUMBER

C. (CONFIG-IF)# SPANNING-PORT PORTFAST

D. (CONFIG-IF)# SET SPANNING TREE PORTFAST MOD NUMBER/PORT NUMBER

8. You want to have a rapid failover on your Access Layer Cat5K switches that are redundantly connected to your core. To ensure rapid failover in the event of a link failure, which of the following commands would you use?

A. CONSOLE>(ENABLE) SET SPANTREE UPLINKFAST ENABLE

B. CISCO# SET SPANTREE UPLINKFAST

C. CISCO# SPANNING-TREE UPLINKFAST

D. CONSOLE>(ENABLE) SET SPANNTREE BACKBONEFAST

Inter-Switch Link and Frame Tagging

9. ISL encapsulation adds how many octets to the length of the original frame?

  A. Four

  B. Eight

  C. Thirty

  D. Fifteen

10. The IOS command to show trunk information is which of the following?

  A. SHOW TRUNK DETAIL

  B. SHOW INTERFACES TRUNK

  C. SHOW TRUNK PORTS

  D. SHOW SWITCHPORT MODE TRUNK

VLAN Trunking Protocol and Propagation

11. To enable VTP pruning on a Cat5K, which of the following commands would you use?

  A. SET VTP PRUNEELIGIBLE {VLANS}

  B. VTP PRUNING

  C. VTP PRUNE VLAN1

  D. VTP PRUNING ENABLE

12. What problems, if any, are there with configuring VTP servers or clients offline?

  A. None; this is the correct procedure.

  B. You risk the chance of a VTP meltdown if the revision number is higher.

  C. It depends on whether the device is a VTP server or client.

Cisco Discovery Protocol

13. CDP operates at what level of the OSI model?

  A. Physical

  B. Network

  C. Data Link

  D. Transport

14. The command to get detailed information on adjacent Cisco devices using CDP is which of the following?

A. SHOW CDP NEIGHBORS

B. SHOW CDP NEIGHBORS DETAIL

C. SHOW CDP VLAN

D. SHOW CDP TRUNKS

Diagnostic Commands

15. If you needed to find out the last time a Cat5K was rebooted, which command would you use?

A. SHOW LOG

B. SHOW EVENTS

C. SHOW EVENTS RESTART

D. SHOW RUNNING-CONFIG

16. You need to determine the current operating configuration on a Cat6K switch. Which command would you use?

A. SHOW CONFIG

B. SHOW INTERFACE

C. SHOW RUNNING-CONFIG

D. SHOW CATALYST6000

The Switched Port Analyzer

17. You can SPAN which of the following to a monitoring port? Choose all that apply.

A. Any port on a switch

B. Any VLAN on a switch

C. Any port on the same module as the monitoring port

D. Any VLAN that belongs to a port on the same module as the monitoring port

18. To enable SPAN on a Cat5K switch, you would use which command?

A. SET SPAN 1/2 1/3

B. (CONF-IF)> PORT MONITOR 1/2

    C. SET MONITOR 1/3

    D. SET PORT SPAN 1/2 1/3

Catalyst Problem Isolation

19. Which of the following is the first step in isolating a problem?

    A. Look at the configurations of all of the switches to see if there is an issue.

    B. Check for trunking or VLAN changes.

    C. Eliminate Physical Layer problems.

20. The number-one tool for eliminating Physical Layer, trunking, and duplex mismatches is which of the following?

    A. A protocol analyzer

    B. RMON probes

    C. CDP

    D. LEDs

Catalyst Symptoms, Problems, and Action Plans

21. Your switch suddenly shows a very high bus and CPU utilization. What network event could have caused this situation? Choose all that apply.

    A. A bad NIC is flooding the network.

    B. STP convergence failed, resulting in a loop.

    C. There is a trunking mismatch.

22. You are trying to make a console connection to a Cat6K switch, but it keeps failing. The most common reason for this failure is which of the following?

    A. You have the wrong bit size.

    B. Your baud rate is incorrect.

    C. You have the wrong number of stop bits.

LAB QUESTION

You are asked to diagnose an interesting problem for a customer with a large, meshed switched LAN infrastructure. The core is composed of numerous meshed Catalyst 6509s that are connected to Catalyst 5500s in the closets. For the most part, the network runs just fine. However, at certain times and on certain days (with no apparent pattern), the network goes down for about a minute, and when connectivity is restored, some of the core trunks are in a blocking mode. This situation seems to last for only a short period of time (an hour or two) and then reverses itself. Along with the core computer room, a test lab, used for development work, is composed of meshed Catalyst 5000s connected to the core 6500s. Network load measurements are very low, never reaching over 15 percent. CPU and bus capacities are at correspondingly low levels. The local IT staff is getting frustrated at attempting to diagnose this issue and have called you in. What will you do troubleshoot this scenario, and what is causing the issue?

SELF TEST ANSWERS

Catalyst Light-Emitting Diodes

1. ☑ **B.** POST is in process; please wait. The status LED on a line module is orange while the POST process is occurring.
   ☒ **A** is incorrect because a failed port would be flashing orange. **C** is incorrect because it would cause the LED to be red.

2. ☑ **B.** Orange. POWERMGMT is orange if there is insufficient power.
   ☒ **A** is incorrect because there is no red state for the POWERMGMT LED on a Cat6K. **C** is incorrect because green indicates that there is sufficient power.

Cable and Media Distance Limitations

3. ☑ **B.** 100 meters. For all copper-based Ethernet segments, the maximum segment length is 100 meters, with the exception of 1000BaseTX, which is limited to 25 meters.
   ☒ **A, C,** and **D** are all incorrect distances.

4. ☑ **C.** Single-mode fiber. Current single-mode technology can extend the LAN to distances of 50 km and beyond.
   ☒ **A** is incorrect because it is limited to a length of 550 meters for 1000Base, 550 meters for 100Base, and 2000 meters for 10Base. **B** is incorrect because only two repeaters are allowed with multimode fiber. Hence the distance requirement cannot be met. **D** is incorrect because you can use single-mode fiber to run that length and extend your LAN.

Catalyst Power-On Self Test

5. ☑ **A.** The SHOW TEST command shows the POST results for all modules on a Cat5K.
   ☒ **B** is incorrect because the SHOW SYSTEM command shows general system states and variables. **C** is incorrect because the SHOW INTERFACES switch port shows the status of all nonrouting interfaces on a Cat6K. **D** is incorrect because the SHOW BOOT command shows the boot environment variables, including filename and version type.

6. ☑ **A.** During POST, the PS1 and PS2 LEDs first become green.
   ☒ **B** is incorrect because the fan LEDs become green during the second phase. **C** is incorrect because the line card LEDs become orange during the third phase, until the POST process is complete and the switch has booted.

Spanning Tree

7. ☑ **C.** (CONFIG-IF)# SPANNING-PORT PORTFAST. The question asked for a Cat6K. The preferred answer is an IOS-based command. In IOS, the SPANNING-PORT PORTFAST command is used from the configure interface prompt.
☒ **B** is incorrect for a Cat6K but is correct for a Cat5K running CatOS. **A** and **D** are incorrect because, although the commands are correct, they are used in the wrong OS.

8. ☑ **A.** CONSOLE>(ENABLE) SET SPANTREE UPLINKFAST ENABLE. The question stated a Cat5K, so we need the global CatOS version of the command.
☒ **B** is incorrect because this is the wrong way to do the IOS version of the command. **C** is incorrect because it is the IOS version of the command. **D** is incorrect because this command is used on core backbone switches only, not Access Layer switches.

Inter-Switch Link and Frame Tagging

9. ☑ **C.** ISL encapsulation adds 30 octets to the original frame.
☒ **A** is incorrect because 802.1Q encapsulation adds four octets. **B** and **D** are incorrect values.

10. ☑ **B.** SHOW INTERFACES TRUNK is the correct command to show trunk details in an IOS-based switch.
☒ **A** is the incorrect command to show trunk information but is correct for a CatOS-based switch. **C** and **D** are incorrect because they are not valid commands.

VLAN Trunking Protocol and Propagation

11. ☑ **A.** SET VTP PRUNEELIGIBLE {VLANS}. This is the global configuration command for the CatOS.
☒ **B** is the incorrect command to enable VTP pruning on a Cat5K but would be correct if given from the VLAN configuration mode on an IOS-based switch. **C** is incorrect because VLAN1 is never prunable. **D** is incorrect because there is no ENABLE modifier to the VTP PRUNING command.

12. ☑ **B.** You risk the chance of a VTP meltdown if the revision number is higher. If the revision number is higher, the switch overwrites all existing VLAN information in the VTP domain. This is known as a VTP meltdown.
☒ **A** is incorrect because the proper procedure is to configure VTP servers or clients online. **C** is incorrect because if both VTP servers and clients are updaters, this can cause a problem in either mode.

Cisco Discovery Protocol

13. ☑ **C.** Data Link. CDP, or Cisco Discovery Protocol, is a media-independent protocol that uses a SNAP frame format and operates at the Data-Link Layer. It can be used to verify Physical Layer functionality and it carries Network Layer information.
☒ **A** is incorrect because the Physical Layer is concerned only with the transmission of raw data. **B** is incorrect because CDP is not a routable protocol and operates at Layer 2 only. **D** is incorrect because there is no Transport Layer functionality in CDP.

14. ☑ **B.** The SHOW CDP NEIGHBORS DETAIL command gives detailed information about adjacent devices and their capabilities.
☒ **A** and **C** are valid CDP commands, but they are incorrect because the question asked for the detailed information. **D** is an incorrect format of the command.

Diagnostic Commands

15. ☑ **A.** The SHOW LOG command is used in CatOS-based switches to show the last time major events occurred.
☒ **B, C,** and **D** are incorrect because they are invalid commands in this case.

16. ☑ **C.** SHOW RUNNING-CONFIG displays the current running configuration of an IOS-based switch.
☒ **A,** SHOW CONFIG, works, but SHOW RUNNING-CONFIG is the preferred form of the command. **B,** SHOW INTERFACE, provides detailed information on the interfaces only, not the entire configuration of the switch. **D,** SHOW CATALYST6000, is used to display environmental and chassis parameters on a Cat6K.

The Switched Port Analyzer

17. ☑ **C** and **D.** You can SPAN any port or VLAN or range of ports or VLANs to a monitoring port, but they must be on the same module as the monitoring port. You cannot monitor ports or VLANs on differing modules.
☒ **A** is incorrect because the ports must be on the same module; you cannot SPAN across modules. **B** is incorrect for the same reason. The VLANs must reside on the same module on the switch.

18. ☑ **A.** The correct format of the SPAN command on a CatOS-based switch is SET SPAN *(SOURCE MODULE /PORT OR VLAN) DESTINATION MODULE/PORT.*
☒ **B** is incorrect because this is the IOS-based version of the command. It would be correct if you wanted to enable SPANning on an IOS-based switch. **C** is incorrect because there is no SET MONITOR command. **D** is incorrect because there is no SET PORT SPAN command.

Catalyst Problem Isolation

19. ☑ **C.** Eliminate Physical Layer problems. When you are troubleshooting, always work at the Physical Layer and proceed upward. This is by far the quickest and most efficient troubleshooting methodology. After you have eliminated physical issues, proceed to Layer 2 troubleshooting.

    ☒ **A** is incorrect because the configurations for each switch can be extremely large. First reduce the problem, then start looking at configurations. **B** is incorrect because you always eliminate Physical Layer problems first, then start looking at Layer 2 issues.

20. ☑ **C.** CDP is your number-one tool for troubleshooting a network. It works regardless of media or protocols and reports duplex and trunk mismatches. It verifies Physical Layer connectivity in the switch's adjacent topology.

    ☒ **A** and **B** are incorrect because protocol analyzers and RMON probes are useful in tracking down specific devices or events n a network, but they are not as useful for general, initial troubleshooting and diagnosis. **D** is incorrect because the LEDs will not provide information on trunking or duplex mismatches.

Catalyst Symptoms, Problems, and Action Plans

21. ☑ **A and B.** A high bus and CPU utilization is the trademark of either a malfunctioning NIC that is sending out a broadcast storm or STP convergence failing, and you now have a loop in your network.

    ☒ **C** is incorrect because a trunk mismatch results in *no traffic*, not too much traffic. In this case, a packet sniffer tells you immediately what the situation is. If all the packets are originating from one address, you have a bad NIC. Shut down the machine and replace the NIC. If STP failed, you have a high rate of collisions on the ports. In this case, immediately determine the blocking and nonblocking ports and stabilize your network by downing redundant links until the loop is removed. Afterward, you can troubleshoot what caused the loop, but your priority is to get the network up and running.

22. ☑ **C.** You have the wrong number of stop bits. In this case, any of the answers could be correct, but the question asked for the most common reason. The standard console setting for most Cisco equipment is 8 bits none parity and 1 stop bit. However, the question did specify the Cat6K. The Cat6K Supervisor is unique in the Cisco line in that is uses 2 stop bits for its console connection.

    ☒ **A** and **B** are incorrect because the question asks for the most common reason; 8 data bits and 9600 baud are the standard settings for *all* Cisco products. Only the Cat6K uses 2 stop bits, so standard settings of 8 none and 1 must be changed to 8 none and 2.

LAB ANSWER

As unusual as this scenario might seem, it is actually fairly common in most networks, especially legacy networks that have grown with no plan or organization and are connected together with no defined plan. A key to this scenario is that the situation is not constant and occurs only periodically. The other key is that the network disruption lasts for about a minute or more and, after network functionality is restored, some ports in the core are placed in a blocking state. These clues should be a dead giveaway as to the cause of the problem. The issue is the election of a new spanning-tree root bridge and a reconfiguration of network paths to the root bridge. In this case, the root of the tree is located in the Catalyst 6500s in the core. However, no spanning tree optimization was performed, and no spanning-tree planning was performed as the network was allowed to grow.

The culprit in this case is the meshed Catalyst 5000s in the R and D room. Because all spanning-tree parameters are set to default, these switches have the low MAC address and become the spanning-tree root when they are powered on. This forces a recalculation of the spanning tree (hence the one-minute network interruption) and then places some of the Catalyst 6500 ports in a blocking state to avoid loops. When the switches are powered off after the R and D staff leave, the tree returns to its normal operation. Determining what the root bridge was after a network interruption identified the cause of this problem. The solution was simply to set the Catalyst 6500s as root bridges for their respective VLAN using the SET ROOT command.

As this lab illustrates, learn the patterns and symptoms and the key causes appear for even some of the most vexing problems.

11

Troubleshooting VLANs on Routers and Switches

C hapter 10 discussed configuring and diagnosing Catalyst switches. This chapter studies, in detail, the virtual local area networks (VLANs) that Catalyst switches provide. Though a fairly new technology, VLANs have caught on like wildfire due to their flexibility and efficiency. These days, most enterprise networks have Catalyst switches in their backbones; in addition, Cisco provides inexpensive workgroup Catalyst switches that can provide switching and VLAN capability to the desktop. VLANs have become a standard part of network infrastructures.

Segmenting traffic into VLANs does provide some challenges, though. Routing between VLANs has been the most significant of these; routing has traditionally been a comparatively slow process. Fortunately, some of the high-speed routing technologies Cisco has developed have mitigated this concern a great deal. Chapter 5 detailed some of these technologies.

This chapter discusses troubleshooting VLAN-related problems, with a particular focus on communication between the VLANs (inter-VLAN routing). This chapter also examines more spanning-tree-related issues; segmenting broadcast domains on a Layer 2 device (such as a switch) can lead to some interesting scenarios. Finally, this chapter covers the most common "real-world" problems that arise when implementing a VLAN-based environment.

CERTIFICATION OBJECTIVE 11.01

Inter-VLAN Routing

Years ago, rising LAN traffic led to the need to segment broadcast domains. Routers were traditionally used to perform this segmentation. Figure 11-1 presents a classical LAN architecture.

Local traffic was confined to the LAN, and the router handled any inter-LAN communication. Servers and other workgroup resources were placed on the same LAN as its users, leading to the 80/20 rule, which states: 80 percent of traffic is confined to the local segment, and 20 percent is destined for a remote segment. For many years, network architects have been designing networks and placing resources based on this 80/20 algorithm.

The rise of switches, such as Cisco's Catalyst 1900 or 2900, led to a model similar to that shown in Figure 11-2.

A traditional
routed
environment

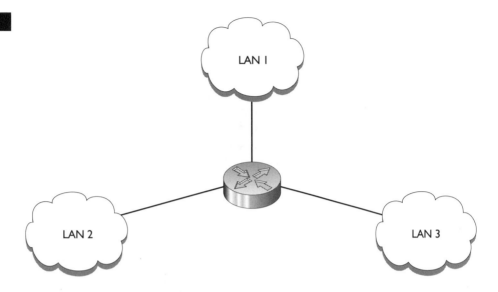

A traditional
routed and
switched
environment

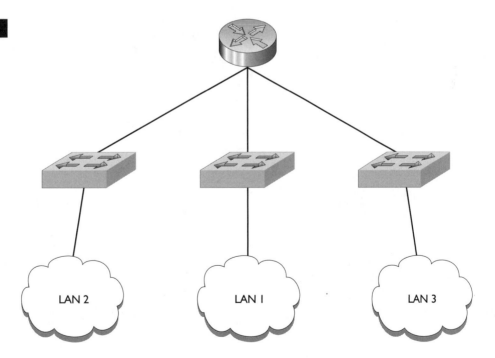

The switches segmented collision domains to servers and workstations. The router, in turn, directed traffic between the LANs. Resources were still placed close to the user, and the 80/20 rule still applied. However, the high-speed capability of switches greatly expanded the bandwidth available to the network—and applications began to quickly take advantage of this expansion.

The development of VLANs, as discussed in Chapter 10, led to the flexibility of segmenting broadcast domains wherever needed. Cisco Catalyst switches allowed network managers to group users based on function instead of location. Figure 11-3 demonstrates this model.

FIGURE 11-3 Segmenting a LAN using VLANs

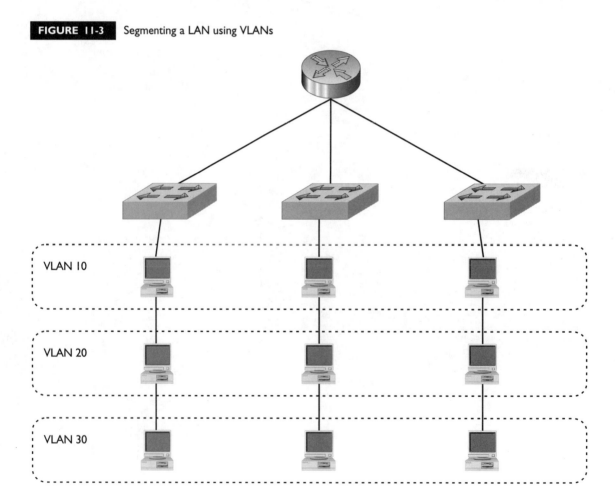

The Catalyst switches allow different ports to be placed into different broadcast domains, or VLANs. Furthermore, technologies such as VTP and trunking allow VLANs to distribute throughout an internetwork. This ability led to the creation of departmentalized subnets. Despite all their advantages, though, Catalyst switches cannot perform one vital function: they cannot switch or route packets between VLANs. This process, called *inter-VLAN routing,* must still be done on a router.

About the same time VLANs became widespread, the two other trends took shape. First, the Internet became a major resource; second, servers began to be migrated away from departments and consolidated into high-speed backbone networks. These types of environments have made the 80/20 rule obsolete, because most traffic has become destined for the remote resources. This is where networks stand today. Not only do they require high-speed workgroup and core switches, but they need high-speed routers to route between LANs and VLANs.

EXERCISE 11-1

Modern Network Design

Examine the network topology diagram in Figure 11-4. What is wrong with the design?

FIGURE 11-4   LAN design

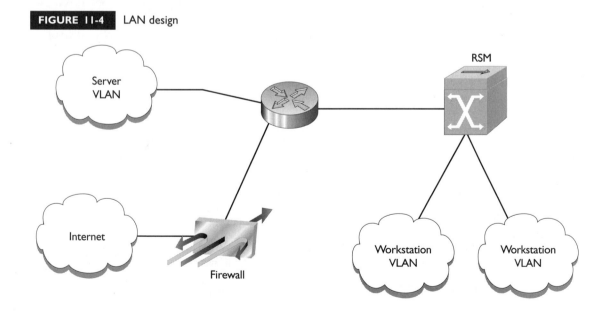

Solution: The server VLAN is located two hops away from the workstations. This design is probably the result of upgrading the central switch from an old Layer 2 switch (or hub) to a new Catalyst with an RSM. With the new design, the old router has become somewhat obsolete. The server VLAN can be directly connected to the switch to improve workstation performance. In theory, the firewall could also be connected to the switch, although security considerations might preclude you from doing so.

CERTIFICATION OBJECTIVE 11.02

Router and Switch Configuration

Traditionally, a router required one interface per subnet (or LAN) to which it was connected. If a router were to route between four LANs, it would require four interfaces. This topology can be applied to VLANs, too—you can place one interface into each VLAN to perform inter-VLAN routing, as shown in Figure 11-5.

Unfortunately, this approach does not scale very well. A large number of VLANs can require a burdensome (and expensive) number of interfaces. Fortunately, Cisco has provided two solutions to this problem: subinterfaces and route switch modules (RSMs).

FIGURE 11-5

One interface per VLAN routing

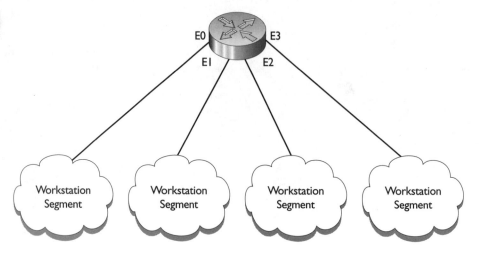

The "Router on a Stick" Configuration with Subinterfaces

The first approach to efficient inter-VLAN routing uses a VLAN trunk to deliver traffic from a switch to an external router. Recall from Chapter 10 that a trunk carries traffic from multiple VLANs throughout a switched fabric. Many Cisco routers support this type of trunking and can extend its routing functionality to the VLANs. This configuration, referred to as "router on a stick," is displayed in Figure 11-6.

Traffic within any VLAN is switched as it normally is, and traffic between VLANs is trunked to the router to be inter-VLAN routed. Performance can be very good if the router is equipped with one of the modern high-speed switching technologies, such as NetFlow switching. Both Cisco Inter-Switch Link (ISL) and IEEE 802.1Q trunking are supported.

A router on a stick is accomplished by defining logical subinterfaces on the trunk interface of the router. Each subinterface corresponds to a VLAN. Follow these three steps to configure subinterfaces:

1. Define the subinterface using this code:

```
(config)# interface fastethernet0/1.1
```

FIGURE 11-6 The "router on a stick" topology

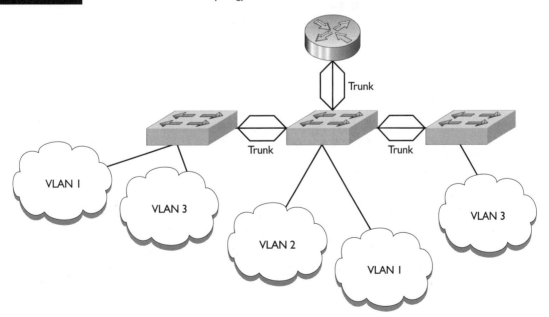

2. Define the encapsulation and VLAN number:

```
(config-subif)# encapsulation isl 20
```

This code defines the subinterface to use ISL encapsulation and carry traffic for VLAN 20. Possible encapsulation types are ISL and DOT1Q (802.1Q).

3. Assign an IP address to the subinterface:

```
(config-subif)# ip address 10.1.1.1 255.255.255.0
```

This is the router (or default gateway) address for end stations on the VLAN.

exam
ⓦatch

*Do not **assign an IP address to the main interface (interface FastEthernet0/1 in the preceding example). Assign IP addresses only to the subinterfaces.***

Switch Configuration in "Talking" to a Router

The switch port connected to the router must also be configured as a trunk port (as was described in Chapter 10). For example, enter privileged mode on the switch and use the following command:

```
Cat5000>(enable) set trunk 4/8 on 1-1000
```

- **4/8**   Sets the port you are configuring.
- **on**   Sets the trunking state.
- **1-1000**   Sets the VLANs for which the trunk will carry traffic.

RSM Configuration

Catalyst 5000 and 6000 series switches have the option of installing a router directly inside the switch. Originally devised as RSMs, they can be installed in almost any slot to connect the router directly to the switch backplane. (The speed of this connection depends on the specific hardware; it can vary from 400MB/s to many GB/s. The RSM provides Layer 3 routing services to the switch and, through trunks between the switches, can extend inter-VLAN routing services to the entire switching fabric. This topology is shown in Figure 11-7.

Configuration of an RSM differs slightly from configuring an external router. The direct connection means trunking and subinterfaces are not needed. Instead,

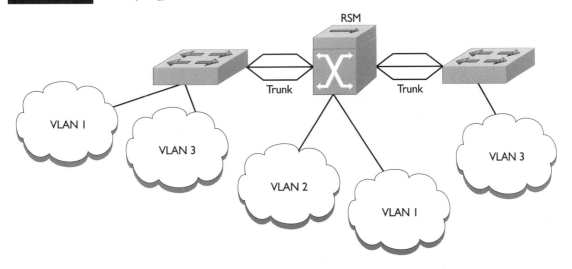

FIGURE 11-7 RSM topology

logical VLAN interfaces are defined on the RSM; these communicate directly with the VLANs in the switch fabric. RSM configuration consists of the following steps:

1. Define a VLAN interface:

```
(config)# interface vlan 20
```

This code defines the VLAN for which you are routing. It is functionally similar to the encapsulation ISL 20 command used in the router-on-a-stick configuration.

2. Assign an IP address to the VLAN interface:

```
(config-if)# ip address 10.2.2.2 255.255.255.0
```

This is the router (or default gateway) address for end stations on the VLAN.

Note: This text uses the term *RSM* to describe any one of a family of Cisco route modules for Catalyst 5000 and 6000 series switches. The following RSMs are offered:

■ **Route switch module (the original RSM)**   A full-size module that can be installed in a Catalyst 5000 series switch.

- **Route switch feature card (RSFC)**   This card, which replaced the RSM, is a daughtercard that can be installed on a Catalyst 5000 series Supervisor II G or Supervisor III G module.
- **Multilayer switch module (MSM)**   Similar to the RSM, the MSM is a full-size router module designed for the Catalyst 6000 series switches.
- **Multilayer switch feature card (MSFC)**   Similar to the RSFC, the MSFC is a daughtercard that comes installed on a Catalyst 6000 Supervisor IA or Supervisor II.

Configuring Bridging Between VLANs

Both an external router and an RSM can be configured to bridge between VLANs. The configuration is similar to standard IOS transparent bridging; you define a bridge group and add interfaces to this group. Bridging between VLANs can be used in the following scenarios:

- Nonroutable traffic such as local area transport (LAT) can be passed between VLANs.
- If the router receives a packet with a VLAN ID it does not understand, it transparently bridges that packet, if bridging is defined.
- With integrated routing and bridging (IRB) or concurrent routing and bridging (CRB), you can selectively route some protocols and bridge others. For example, you could choose to route IP but bridge IPX. See your Cisco documentation to learn more about configuring IRB or CRB.

Follow these steps to enable bridging between VLANs:

1. Define a bridge group and spanning-tree protocol.

   ```
   (config)# bridge 1 protocol ieee
   ```

   This code defines bridge group 1 to use the IEEE spanning-tree protocol.

2. Add interfaces to bridge group:

   ```
   (config)# interface fastethernet0/1.1
   ```

   This code adds interface FastEthernet0/1.1.

   ```
   (config-subif)# bridge-group 1
   ```

This code adds FastEthernet0/1.2 to the bridge group.

```
(config-subif)# interface fastethernet0/1.2
(config-subif)# bridge-group 1
```

EXERCISE 11-2

Inter-VLAN Routing Configuration

You have a new Catalyst 5000 series switch with an RSM. The switch has three VLANs defined: VLAN 100, 200, and 300. Configure the RSM to route between the VLANs. The default gateways for each VLAN are as follows:

```
VLAN 100 = 10.1.1.1 /24
VLAN 200 = 10.1.2.1 /24
VLAN 300 = 10.1.3.1 /24
```

Enter the RSM configuration commands here:

```
(config)#_____
(config-if)#_____
(config-if)#_____
(config-if)#_____
(config-if)#_____
(config-if)#_____
(config-if)#_____
(config-if)#_____
(config-if)#_____
```

Solution:

```
(config)# interface vlan 100
(config-if)# ip address 10.1.1.1 255.255.255.0
(config-if)# no shutdown
(config-if)# interface vlan 200
(config-if)# ip address 10.1.2.1 255.255.255.0
(config-if)# no shutdown
(config-if)# interface vlan 300
(config-if)# ip address 10.1.3.1 255.255.255.0
(config-if)# no shutdown
```

VLAN Design Issues

VLAN design issues, from a troubleshooting perspective, often center on the spanning-tree protocol (STP). A stable spanning tree is necessary for a healthy network; instability can bring a network to its knees in seconds. Review the following summary of the spanning-tree protocol:

- STP is designed to keep redundant links in a bridged network from forming loops. Cisco routers support two versions of STP: IEEE and DEC. They are incompatible; if both are used in the same LAN (or VLAN), loops can occur. (Note that Catalyst switches support only IEEE STP).

- STP bridges (switches and routers) elect a root bridge on every broadcast domain. Every other device must have only one path to this root bridge. If two or more paths exist, the port with the shortest path is used and the other port(s) are placed into *blocking* mode.

- STP topology is maintained with the use of bridge protocol data units (BPDUs). Every bridging (or switching) device on the network constantly sends out BPDUs to confirm connectivity to the root. A network change causes special topology change BPDUs to be immediately sent back to the root, informing it of the change.

- If a switch receives BPDUs on more that one port, it knows that it has more than one path to the root. The port with the shortest path moves to the forwarding mode; the others move to blocking.

STP Timers

Three STP timers impact your network design decisions:

- **Hello time** How often the switch sends out BPDUs; the default equals 2 seconds.

- **Forward delay** How long the switch stays in listening and learning states; the default equals 15 seconds.

- **Maximum age** How long the switch stores spanning-tree topology information; the default equals 20 seconds. If no BPDUs have been received for the maximum age time, the spanning-tree cycle starts over.

The root switch assigns all these timers, and their values are distributed in the BPDUs. Manually changing these values on the root switch distributes them to the rest of the local network.

Changing these timers on switches that are not the root has no effect once communication with the root is established; the root's settings override local settings.

Network Diameter

Network diameter can be defined as the maximum number of Layer 2 hops from one edge of a network to another—that is, the maximum number of switches one frame would have to pass to get from one end of the network to another. Your network diameter can directly affect some of your spanning-tree decisions (and vice versa).

Cisco recommends that a network diameter should never exceed seven hops; anything larger and spanning-tree convergence becomes an issue. Convergence is defined as the length of time it takes for a topology change to be detected and propagated throughout the network. During this convergence time, the MAC address table becomes obsolete because some of the entries might now be unreachable. For that reason, most of the MAC address table is quickly aged out.

Convergence time is a major issue in LAN stability. Unfortunately, many modern applications are sensitive to time delays and do not react well to network disconnects. If a network cannot respond quickly to changes, end stations (including servers) can quickly become disconnected and data can be lost. The larger a network gets, the longer convergence time becomes (because it takes time for the BPDUs to make it around the network). Cisco's seven-hop limit is a good compromise.

The default duration aging interval of a MAC address entry in most Cisco Catalyst switches is 5 minutes. That means that an entry will disappear if its station is not heard from in 5 minutes. As described, this can be much too long in periods of topology changes. Therefore, when a change is detected, the 5-minute interval is changed to the forward delay time (15 seconds by default). This delay time quickly ages out entries while giving high-traffic servers a chance to keep their entries.

The STP timers are closely tied to the seven-hop network diameter rule. For example, since the BPDU hello time is 2 seconds, the forward delay was calculated to be 15 seconds. If a BPDU is sent every 2 seconds and you can be, at most, seven hops away from the root switch, the longest it could ever take you to hear about it would be 2 x 7, or 14, seconds. Thus, if a switch has not heard anything for 15 seconds, it is allowed to move toward the forwarding state.

If your network diameter is greater than seven, you should change your forward delay and maximum age timers. You must make them long enough so that all switches get root switch advertisements and do not accidentally move into forwarding mode, causing a loop. Conversely, if your network diameter is smaller, you can adjust the timers accordingly. However, Cisco recommends against doing this. STP is not at all resource intensive, and problems with it can be disastrous, so Cisco recommends changing default settings only if you must.

on the
job

Instead of manually changing each of the STP timers on a Catalyst switch, Cisco provides the DIAMETER option of the SET SPANTREE ROOT command. When you define the diameter, the switch automatically adjusts the fwd-delay and max-age timers to their optimal values. For example:

```
Cat1>(enable) set spantree root 1-1000 diameter 4
```

This configures the network to have a diameter of 4; the STP timers are automatically adjusted as follows:
Forward delay – 9 seconds
Maximum aging – 14 seconds

STP in Routed VLANs

There are two ways of dealing with STP on VLAN-capable switches and routers: one spanning tree per VLAN or one large spanning tree. Per-VLAN Spanning Tree (PVST) is a proprietary Cisco mechanism that runs an instance of STP in each VLAN defined in a network. PVST has the following characteristics:

- It typically runs in ISL environments that use an RSM or external router to perform inter-VLAN routing.

- Trunk ports run an instance of STP for each VLAN on which they carry traffic.

- It requires more traffic and processing overhead than Common Spanning Tree (detailed in the following paragraphs) because the BPDU hello and change mechanisms are used on each VLAN.

■ Location of the root bridge can be optimized on a per-VLAN basis.

You can also run one large instance of SPT that covers all VLANs. This approach, part of the 802.1Q standard, is called Common Spanning Tree (CST):

■ CST is common in environments that bridge between VLANs; in fact, bridging between VLANs *requires* you to use one spanning tree.

■ By default, STP runs on VLAN1. This keeps BPDU traffic off the other VLANs.

■ Since there is only one root bridge, its placement cannot be optimized on a per-VLAN basis.

exam
ⓦatch
*Per-VLAN Spanning Tree and Common Spanning Tree are routed **VLAN** implementations. In bridged **VLAN** environments, the spanning trees of each **VLAN** are combined into one large spanning tree. However, this is not the same as CST. In bridged environments, BPDUs are transmitted to all **VLANs.** So, remember that if a **VLAN** environment uses bridging (including CRB and IRB), one large spanning tree is created.*

Default VLANs

Several VLANs are provided by default on Catalyst switches, as outlined in Table 11-1.
Cisco recommends that VLAN1 not be used for production data traffic. Instead, it should be set aside for network management functions. Regular data VLANs should be created as needed.

TABLE 11-1   Default VLANs on Catalyst Switches

VLAN	Type	VLAN ID	802.10 SAID
default	Ethernet	1	100001
fddi-default	FDDI	1002	101002
token-ring-default	Token Ring	1003	101003
fddinet-default	FDDI-net	1004	101004
trnet-default	tr-net	1005	101005

SCENARIO & SOLUTION

What are the three main STP timers, and what are their default values?	Hello time = 2 seconds Forward delay = 15 seconds Max aging = 20 seconds
What is the maximum network diameter recommended by Cisco?	Seven hops.
What are the two spanning-tree protocols supported by Cisco routers?	IEEE and DEC.

EXERCISE 11-3

Placement of the Root Bridge

Examine the network diagram in Figure 11-8.

FIGURE 11-8

Network diagram
for Exercise 11-3

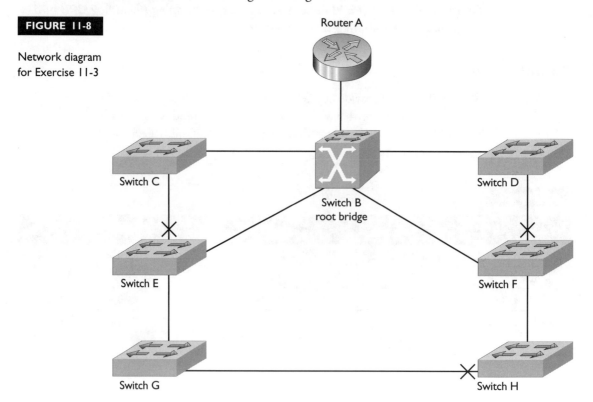

The switches have been booted up with their default configurations. Switch B has been elected root bridge, and three ports have been blocked. Is this the optimal configuration? If not, how could it be improved?

Solution: Yes, Switch B is the optimal choice. It is central to the network. Spanning-tree convergence will be fastest to this device. Also note that the blocked ports are furthest from the root bridge and thus furthest from the center of the network. Therefore, they are well placed.

CERTIFICATION OBJECTIVE 11.04

VLAN Troubleshooting

Troubleshooting begins long before problems occur. Being prepared is the first step of solid troubleshooting skills. Documentation of VLAN and STP information is vital when things start going down, but sometimes that information is hard to come by during outages. Be sure to have on hand the following information about your network:

- Network diagrams:
  - Layer 2 topology map
  - Layer 3 topology map
  - Application flow diagrams

- VLAN information:
  - Port maps of all VLANs
  - VTP information
  - Inter-VLAN routing configuration

- STP information:
  - Location of root bridge
  - Location of redundant links and blocked ports

Troubleshooting Strategies

■ **Bridging between router ISL subinterfaces**   Remember that if you bridge between subinterfaces of an external router, you create one large spanning tree for all your VLANs. This can impact your network diameter. It can also make the router the best choice for the root bridge.

■ **Placement of the root bridge**   It is almost always right to manually set the root bridge (using the bridge priority parameters). The root bridge should be placed centrally in the network; this minimizes spanning-tree convergence time. In multi-VLAN environments (with STP topologies in each VLAN), the root bridge should be placed in the center of each VLAN.

■ **STP timers**   Remember that all bridges (switches) inherit their STP timer values from the root bridge. Changing timers on any other bridges is ineffective; make all changes on the root.

■ **STP consistency**   Make sure that all bridges use the same STP, either IEEE or DEC. Differing protocols in the same tree can cause loops. Remember that Catalyst switches only support IEEE.

■ **VTP and external routers**   Remember that inter-VLAN routers do not support VTP. Your VLANs are not automatically extended to them as they are to your VTP client switches. You must manually create VLAN interfaces and subinterfaces on any router.

on the
job

Misconfiguring the router is a common mistake in configuring inter-VLAN routing. Make sure your VLAN encapsulation and VLAN identifiers are identical on the router and VTP server switch.

■ **Maximize timers during periods of instability**   When the network is having problems and you suspect spanning-tree problems (such as redundant links), try increasing the spanning-tree timers to their maximum values: 30 seconds for forward delay and 40 seconds for maximum age. This prevents STP from making the problems worse. Be aware, though, that these increases delay convergence time when the network becomes stable again.

EXERCISE 11-4

Troubleshooting VLANs

A client has the network layout shown in Figure 11-9.

All devices are connected by ISL trunks, and VTP and VTP pruning are both used. The router performs inter-VLAN routing for all VLANs. Each VLAN runs its own instance of STP.

The client calls with difficulties on VLAN 2. Network response is extremely slow; CPU utilization on Switch E is close to 100 percent. The rest of the VLANs do not seem to be badly affected. Which of the following could be the problem?

A. Switch E has lost VTP communications with the rest of the network.

B. The blocked port on Switch E has begun forwarding, creating a loop.

FIGURE 11-9   Troubleshooting VLANs

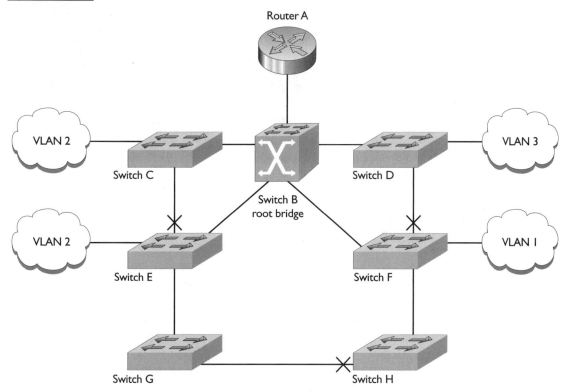

C. A workstation on VLAN 2 has a faulty NIC.

D. A workstation on VLAN 3 has a faulty NIC.

Solution: B. The blocked port on Switch E has begun forwarding, creating a loop. Spanning-tree loops can cause links to become flooded with frames. Those frames should not be forwarded to other VLANs, however. Also, a faulty NIC can rarely bring an entire VLAN to a halt.

Router VLAN Diagnostic Tools

Chapter 10 detailed tools you could use in troubleshooting VLAN operation on Catalyst switches. This chapter looks at similar tools that can be used to troubleshoot external and internal routers that perform the inter-VLAN routing function.

As discussed earlier, many Cisco routers support VLAN trunks to Catalyst switches. In addition, RSMs and RSFCs are routers placed directly in the switch chassis. These routers can then be used to route (or even bridge) between VLANs. Remember, though, that by default each VLAN on a trunk runs a separate instance of the spanning-tree protocol (under PVST).

Troubleshooting in these areas uses a subset of IOS commands that are similar to their Catalyst counterparts but have output with the look and feel of the IOS.

The SHOW VLANS Command

Use the SHOW VLANS command to display information about the VLANs configured on an external router as well as their corresponding router interfaces (subinterfaces). Compare this output with that from your Catalyst switch to make sure your VLAN IDs and encapsulations are consistent. The following is output from a model 7500 router with a VLAN trunk connected to interface FastEthernet1/0:

```
R7500# show vlans
Virtual LAN ID:  20 (Inter Switch Link Encapsulation)
    VLAN Trunk Interface:    FastEthernet1/0.1
    Protocols Configured:    Address:    Received:        Transmitted:
            IP              10.20.0.1    1244                1245
Virtual LAN ID:  30 (Inter Switch Link Encapsulation)
    VLAN Trunk Interface:    FastEthernet1/0.2
    Protocols Configured:    Address:    Received:        Transmitted:
            IP              10.30.0.1    4538                74458
Virtual LAN ID:  40 (Inter Switch Link Encapsulation)
    VLAN Trunk Interface:    FastEthernet1/0.3
    Protocols Configured:    Address:    Received:        Transmitted:
            IP              10.40.0.1    45758               4532
```

- **Virtual LAN ID**   The VLAN number you are receiving and routing packets for. The VLAN encapsulation protocol is also shown.

- **VLAN Trunk Interface**   The logical subinterface that is receiving traffic for the VLAN.

- **Protocols configured**   The protocols with network addressing defined on the subinterface.

- **Address**   The Network Layer address assigned to the subinterface. For IP networks, this should be the default gateway for end stations on the VLAN.

The **SHOW SPAN** Command

SHOW SPAN displays the current spanning-tree configuration of an IOS device; STP timers, path costs, and root information are all shown. In addition, complete port information is given—each port, its state, and its addressing. Observe the following output of a Catalyst 6000 series RSM that is bridging between VLANs (meaning one large spanning tree):

```
RSM6000> sh span
 Bridge group 1 is executing the ieee compatible Spanning Tree protocol
  Bridge Identifier has priority 32768, address 00d0.d335.86a0
  Configured hello time 2, max age 20, forward delay 15
  Current root has priority 10, address 00b0.8e02.7000
  Root port is 4 (Vlan1), cost of root path is 4
  Topology change flag not set, detected flag not set
  Number of topology changes 4672 last change occurred 00:26:28 ago
        from Vlan40
```

```
 Times:  hold 1, topology change 35, notification 2
         hello 2, max age 20, forward delay 15
 Timers: hello 0, topology change 0, notification 0, aging 300
Port 4 (Vlan1) of Bridge group 1 is forwarding
   Port path cost 4, Port priority 128, Port Identifier 128.4.
   Designated root has priority 10, address 00b0.8e02.7000
   Designated bridge has priority 10, address 00b0.8e02.7000
   Designated port id is 131.129, designated path cost 0
   Timers: message age 2, forward delay 0, hold 0
   Number of transitions to forwarding state: 1
   BPDU: sent 4673, received 2635018
. . . . . . . . . . . . . . . .
Port 10 (Vlan150) of Bridge group 1 is forwarding
   Port path cost 4, Port priority 128, Port Identifier 128.10.
   Designated root has priority 10, address 00b0.8e02.7000
   Designated bridge has priority 32768, address 00d0.d335.86a0
   Designated port id is 128.10, designated path cost 4
   Timers: message age 0, forward delay 0, hold 0
   Number of transitions to forwarding state: 1
   BPDU: sent 2635023, received 1643
```

This command also includes some useful troubleshooting counters:

- **Configured hello time 2, max age 20, forward delay 15**   These timers are set to defaults.

- **BPDU sent and received**   You can use this command multiple times to see if BPDUs are being sent or received for any given port.

- **Number of topology changes and time change occurred**   Counters to get current topology change information.

- **Timers: message age 0, forward delay 0, hold 0**   Current values for the individual interfaces are shown. The message age is the time since the last BPDU was received. Since these interfaces are all forwarding, the forward delay and hold are all zero; these timers are not active.

The SHOW BRIDGE Command

If a Catalyst switch bridges between VLANs, SHOW BRIDGE on the RSM can be used to display the current bridging table. MAC addresses and their corresponding VLANs are displayed. Observe the following from the RSM of a Catalyst 5000 switch:

```
RSM5000> sh bridge
Total of 300 station blocks, 275 free
Codes: P - permanent, S - self
Bridge Group 1:
   Address         Action     Interface     Age    RX count    TX count
0200.0000.0201    forward     Vlan20         0          38           0
00d0.796e.dad9    forward     Vlan152        0      869237           0
0050.dac1.fff8    forward     Vlan20         0      569451      426278
0600.0104.0900    forward     Vlan30         0      167412      157772
. . . . . . . . . . . . . . .
00c0.852c.16ce    forward     Vlan40         0          40           0
4200.0102.c32d    forward     Vlan30         0        1189        1185
```

Use this command to determine if an end station is communicating successfully with the bridging mechanism of the RSM.

The **SHOW INTERFACE** Command

SHOW INTERFACE on a VLAN interface of an RSM shows the packets that have been received and routed (or bridged) by the virtual interface. This command is similar to other SHOW INTERFACE commands; see the following example output from a Catalyst 6000 series RSM:

```
RSM6000> sh int vlan 20
Vlan20 is up, line protocol is up
  Hardware is Cat6k RP Virtual Ethernet, address is 00d0.d335.86a0 (bia
00d0.d335.86a0)
  Internet address is 10.0.22.4/24
  MTU 1500 bytes, BW 1000000 Kbit, DLY 10 usec,
     reliability 255/255, txload 1/255, rxload 1/255
  Encapsulation ARPA, loopback not set
  ARP type: ARPA, ARP Timeout 04:00:00
  Last input 00:00:00, output never, output hang never
  Last clearing of "show interface" counters never
  Queueing strategy: fifo
  Output queue 0/40, 0 drops; input queue 0/75, 20499 drops
  5 minute input rate 10000 bits/sec, 8 packets/sec
  5 minute output rate 5000 bits/sec, 6 packets/sec
     122524352 packets input, 7766146 bytes, 1 no buffer
     Received 57309986 broadcasts, 0 runts, 0 giants, 0 throttles
     0 input errors, 0 CRC, 0 frame, 0 overrun, 0 ignored
     90423880 packets output, 3540415222 bytes, 0 underruns
```

```
0 output errors, 1 interface resets
0 output buffer failures, 0 output buffers swapped out
```

Some of the more important fields in troubleshooting VLANs include:

- **Hardware**   The RP hardware.

- **Internet address**   IP address information for the router interface. This is the default gateway for end stations on the VLAN.

- **5 minute input/output rates**   Use these counters to determined if the router is being overburdened (or used at all).

- **Input errors/output errors**   Data link frame error conditions are reported, similar to a standard Ethernet interface.

See Chapter 3 for a more detailed description of the output of this command.

The SHOW ARP Command

SHOW ARP displays the ARP table of an RSM or external router:

```
RSM6000> sh arp
Protocol   Address          Age (min)   Hardware Addr    Type    Interface
Internet   10.0.12.9                1   0800.3e00.5890   ARPA    Vlan20
Internet   10.0.16.13              10   0010.8355.2034   ARPA    Vlan60
Internet   10.0.14.15             140   0004.00b0.565d   ARPA    Vlan40
Internet   10.0.12.8                0   0030.9440.5850   ARPA    Vlan20
. . . . . . . . . . . . . .
Internet   10.0.19.6                1   0004.accb.5d3f   ARPA    Vlan70
Internet   10.0.16.9               75   0004.0008.9f0e   ARPA    Vlan60
Internet   10.0.19.11             121   0004.0088.9a3d   ARPA    Vlan70
```

Use SHOW ARP to track down IP/MAC address mappings. Often this is the easiest way to determine the MAC address of a remote device.

The SHOW IP CACHE Command

SHOW IP CACHE displays the contents of a router's fast cache in memory. Recall from Chapter 5 that routers configured for fast caching cache next-hop and MAC header information of recently routed packets. When a packet comes destined for an address contained in the cache, the router uses the cached next-hop and MAC header to expedite processing. Observe the following output from a Catalyst 5000 series RSM:

```
RSM5000# sh ip cache
IP routing cache 525 entries, 112800 bytes
   1156690 adds, 1156165 invalidates, 0 refcounts
Minimum invalidation interval 2 seconds, maximum interval 5 seconds,
   quiet interval 3 seconds, threshold 0 requests
Invalidation rate 0 in last second, 0 in last 3 seconds
Prefix/Length           Age         Interface       Next Hop
1.0.0.0/8               8w0d        Vlan200           10.0.120.5
4.0.0.0/8               00:05:47    Vlan200           10.0.120.5
10.0.12.0/24            00:40:25    Vlan20            10.0.12.2
. . . . . . . . . . . . . . . .
10.1.12.250/32          00:10:03    Vlan20            10.0.12.250
10.1.13.12/32           00:09:40    Vlan30            10.0.13.12
```

Use this command to troubleshoot inter-VLAN routing difficulties. Note that on some routers, MAC header information is displayed, and on others (such as the above), it is not.

The DEBUG VLAN PACKET Command

Use DEBUG VLAN PACKET to determine if packets that are being received by a router are being forwarded correctly. If a packet comes into a router destined for a VLAN not defined on the router, it is reported. Observe the following output from a model 7500 series router:

```
R7500# debug vlan packet
Virtual LAN packet information debugging is on
VLAN: Received ISL encapsulated UNKNOWN packet bearing colour ID 16
      on interface FastEthernet0/1.1 which is not configured to
      route or bridge this packet type.
VLAN: Received ISL encapsulated UNKNOWN packet bearing colour ID 16
      on interface FastEthernet0/1.1 which is not configured to
      route or bridge this packet type.
VLAN: Received ISL encapsulated UNKNOWN packet bearing colour ID 16
      on interface FastEthernet0/1.1 which is not configured to
      route or bridge this packet type.
```

Packets are being received on trunk port FastEthernet0/1.1, destined for VLAN 16. However, the router does not have VLAN 16 defined, so the packets are dropped.

on the
ⓘob

*Unlike most other debug commands, **DEBUG VLAN PACKET** does not report normal activity—only errors, such as the ones shown in the example. If you run this command on a router and see no output, do not be concerned; most likely, inter-VLAN routing is working correctly.*

SCENARIO & SOLUTION

What command shows the VLANs that are configured on an external IOS router?	SHOW VLANS
What command displays the current bridging table on an IOS device?	SHOW BRIDGE
What command shows MAC addresses mapped to their IP addresses?	SHOW ARP
What command could you use to determine the MAC address of the root bridge?	SHOW SPAN

EXERCISE 11-5

Using Troubleshooting Tools

Observe the network diagram shown in Figure 11-10.
You execute a SHOW VLANS on RouterA:

```
RouterA# show vlans
Virtual LAN ID:  1 (Inter Switch Link Encapsulation)
    VLAN Trunk Interface:    FastEthernet1/0.1
    Protocols Configured:    Address:      Received:        Transmitted:
        IP               10.1.1.1      2233             3435
Virtual LAN ID:  2 (Inter Switch Link Encapsulation)
    VLAN Trunk Interface:    FastEthernet1/0.2
    Protocols Configured:    Address:      Received:        Transmitted:
        IP               10.1.2.1      234              2345
Virtual LAN ID:  3 (Inter Switch Link Encapsulation)
    VLAN Trunk Interface:    FastEthernet1/0.3
    Protocols Configured:    Address:      Received:        Transmitted:
        IP               10.1.3.1      4548             5634
```

FIGURE 11-10 Using troubleshooting tools diagram for Exercise 11-5

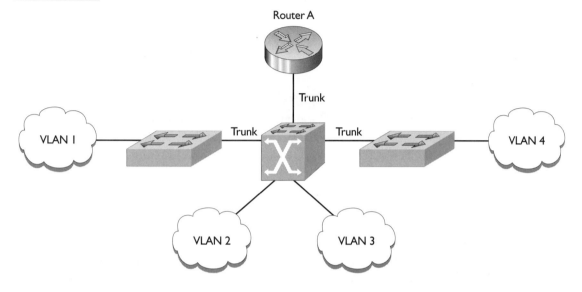

Then you run a DEBUG VLAN PACKET on RouterA and see the following output:

```
RouterA# debug vlan packet
Virtual LAN packet information debugging is on
VLAN: Received ISL encapsulated UNKNOWN packet bearing colour ID 4
      on interface FastEthernet1/0.1 which is not configured to
      route or bridge this packet type.
VLAN: Received ISL encapsulated UNKNOWN packet bearing colour ID 4
      on interface FastEthernet1/0.1 which is not configured to
      route or bridge this packet type.
```

What is happening here?

Solution: A station on VLAN1 is trying to communicate with a station on VLAN4. However, VLAN4 has not been defined on RouterA; therefore, it does not know what to do with these packets.

CERTIFICATION OBJECTIVE 11.06

Router and Switch Problem Isolation

The process of troubleshooting VLAN environments follows the general troubleshooting model studied so far: start at the bottom of the OSI model and work your way up. If you can quickly determine at which layer the problem originated, troubleshooting becomes much easier; there are fewer possible culprits. When you first encounter a VLAN problem, try to isolate it to one of three possible areas: the Physical Layer, a switch, or the router. This chapter discusses all three of these areas.

Physical Layer

As always, troubleshooting starts at the Physical Layer (some networking texts state that 90 percent of network failures are due to cabling problems). Things to check or verify at the physical level are:

- **Physical interface status**   Check the interface's LED. Use SHOW INTERFACE (IOS) or SHOW PORT (CatOS) to determine if it is physically up or down.

- **Duplex configuration**   Both ends of a network connection must be configured at the same duplex level (full or half); SHOW INTERFACE (IOS) or SHOW PORT (CatOS) shows what it is set to. Duplex problems are covered in more detail later in the chapter.

- **Data link connectivity**   Use SHOW CDP NEIGHBOR to determine if a device is successfully communicating with its neighbors. CDP was covered in Chapter 10.

Switch Configurations

If physical communications are up, VLAN and switching problems can be caused by incorrect VLAN, VTP, or STP configurations. Check or verify the following areas:

- **VLAN configuration** Make sure ports are in the correct VLAN; use SHOW VLAN on the switch to determine VLAN membership. Also remember that SPAN ports do not communicate normally to the network (see Chapter 10). Use SHOW SPAN to determine if any ports are in SPAN mode.

- **VTP parameters** Make sure VTP is configured properly on all switches. Usually a network has one or more VTP servers and the rest VTP clients. Also check VTP version and security parameters (see Chapter 10 for more details). Improperly configured VTP prevents VLAN information from being distributed throughout the network.

- **STP configurations** Make sure all switches run the same STP protocol and the root bridge is set in the center of the network. Check network diagrams for ports that should be blocking and verify that they have not started forwarding. Also ensure that the STP timers are sufficient for your network diameter. SHOW SPAN (IOS) or SHOW SPANTREE (CatOS) displays all this information. STP problems can create bridging loops that can grind a network to a halt.

Router Configuration

If communications within a VLAN are up but inter-VLAN communication is not, the router is usually the suspect. Since routers do not communicate using VTP, they must be manually configured separately from the switch. Check the following areas:

- **External router configuration** Make sure all VLANs you are routing for are defined on the router. You must be using the same trunking protocol as on the switch. SHOW VLAN displays the trunking configuration. Compare the VLANs on the router with those defined on the switch.

- **RSM configuration** Make sure each VLAN is defined as an interface. Use the NO SHUTDOWN command to enable a VLAN (they are shut down by default). SHOW INTERFACE displays all configured VLAN interfaces on a router.

- **Routing protocols** Inter-VLAN routing is done through the use of routing tables (like any other routing). Check the table with SHOW IP ROUTE, and check the routing protocol status with SHOW IP PROTOCOL.

SCENARIO & SOLUTION

What protocol distributes VLAN information to switches in a switch fabric?	Virtual Trunking Protocol (VTP).
What Cisco proprietary protocol can be used to confirm data link connectivity between two Cisco devices?	Cisco Discovery Protocol (CDP).

EXERCISE 11-6

Troubleshooting an RSM

Examine the network diagram shown in Figure 11-11.

A station on VLAN4 is having trouble communicating with a station of VLAN1. You suspect a routing issue, so you run SHOW IP ROUTE on the RSM and receive this output:

```
RSM1> sh ip route
     10.0.0.0/8 is variably subnetted, 3 subnets
C       10.1.2.0/24 is directly connected, Vlan2
C       10.1.3.0/24 is directly connected, Vlan3
C       10.1.4.0/24 is directly connected, Vlan4
```

FIGURE 11-11   Troubleshooting an RSM network diagram

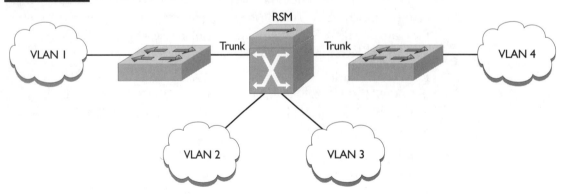

What might be the problem? Choose all that apply.

   A. VTP is not configured properly to communicate with the RSM.

   B. Interface VLAN1 is not defined on the RSM.

   C. Interface VLAN4 is not defined on the RSM.

   D. Interface VLAN1 is administratively shut down.

   E. Interface VLAN4 is administratively shut down.

Solution: B and **D.** Since VLAN1 does not appear in the routing table, it is probably either shut down or not defined. The same cannot be true of VLAN4, since it appears in the table. In addition, VTP does not communicate with RSMs.

CERTIFICATION OBJECTIVE 11.07

Router VLAN Symptoms, Problems, and Action Plans

Some problems appear over and over again—in all kinds of environments. Being prepared for these common problems can save you time and energy in critical situations. (It can also make you look smart.) This chapter discusses some of the most common VLAN problems you might encounter, how to diagnose them, and how to fix them.

Slow or Unreliable Performance Within a VLAN

Slow or intermittent performance problems can be some of the most difficult to pin down (down links are much easier to figure out). The following are some of the most common causes:

■ **Bad adapter** A bad network adapter (either on an end station or a bad port on a switch) can cause a multitude of problems. Sometimes bad adapters corrupt packets or send fragments. Another symptom is jabbering—when a bad adapter floods the network with runt packets. Use SHOW INTEFACES to check the error counters on an interface. If the counters are rapidly increasing, something on that segment is likely malfunctioning. Replacing the adapter should fix this problem.

e x a m
ⓦ a t c h

You can reset the error counters to zero; that makes it easier to see the rate at which they are increasing. Use the CLEAR COUNTERS [INTERFACE] command.

■ **Full-duplex vs. half-duplex mismatch** If one side of a connection is configured half-duplex and the other full-duplex, the symptom is intermittent problems, not a fully down state. You see excessive fragments accumulating on the interface (again, use SHOW INTERFACES to see this). Often, a device does not correctly autonegotiate duplex settings with another device. The easiest solution is to manually configure all network devices to the proper duplex setting.

on the
ⓘ o b

Duplex mismatches can happen between two Cisco devices as well. Manually set duplex settings do not always negotiate, so if two interfaces have negotiated half-duplex, and you then manually set one to full-duplex, the other side might not auto-adjust itself.

■ **Cabling issue** Bad network cables can cause intermittent problems, as can EMI. Like most other connectivity problems, try swapping with a known good cable.

Flooded Network: Spanning-Tree Loop

A loop in the spanning tree can quickly cause the network to become completely saturated. If you suspect a loop has occurred, use one of the following commands to determine if a device is being overloaded:

■ **(IOS) SHOW INTERFACE** *INTERFACE* Look at the load statistic and the input and output queues to see if the device has more packets than it can handle. In addition, look for excessive collisions, fragments, and the like.

■ **(IOS) SHOW PROCESSES CPU** Look at CPU utilization; if it is unusually high, you could have a overload problem.

■ **(CatOS) SHOW PORT** *SLOT/PORT* Look for collisions, alignment errors, and FCS errors. These statistics are similar to the IOS SHOW INTERFACES counters.

FROM THE CLASSROOM

Duplex Mismatches Explained

How can a duplex mismatch cause intermittent problems instead of a complete loss of connectivity? Observe Figure 11-12.

1. Since neither side is aware of a duplex mismatch, they both send data as normal. Recall, though, that to achieve full-duplex, that device must disable CSMA/CD.

2. Both devices send data at the same time, and a collision occurs. Switch A, which is still using CSMA/CD, learns of the collision and waits its time to resend the frame. Workstation B,

however, does not know about the collision and keeps sending data.

3. The result is a loss of synchronization between the two devices and data lost in packets that were not resent.

Collisions caused by duplex mismatches are often *late collisions*, or collisions that occur late during the transmission of the packet. (Normally Ethernet collisions occur early in the packet transmission.) SHOW INTERFACE ETHERNET displays a *late collisions* counter. Remember, though, they will be detected only on the switch running CSMA/CD (half-duplex).

—Don Dettmore, CCNP, MCSE, CNE

■ **(CatOS) SHOW SYSTEM**   This shows CPU utilization on a Catalyst.

To determine if a loop exists, use your network documentation to check all the ports that should be in blocking state. Make sure none of them have started forwarding. You can use SHOW SPAN (IOS) or SHOW SPANTREE (CatOS) to quickly see the spanning-tree status of all ports.

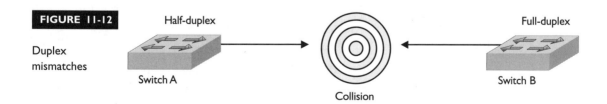

FIGURE 11-12

Duplex mismatches

Half-duplex

Switch A

Collision

Full-duplex

Switch B

If a loop does exist, disable (or unplug) the offending port. When the network is stable again, examine your spanning tree structure (network diameter, STP timers, etc.) to determine what may have caused the loop.

Loops can also easily occur in FastEtherchannel environments. Recall that Fast Etherchannel is a method of bonding multiple physical Fast Ethernet links into one logical link. Under normal (non-Etherchannel) conditions, multiple paths to the same destination would be considered an STP loop, and all ports but one would be blocked. Using FastEtherchannel allows the multiple links to be combined into one large pipe without having STP disable any of the ports. Unfortunately, if any of the FastEtherchannel ports are misconfigured, a loop could occur.

on the *Job* *Try to configure your FastEtherchannel almost simultaneously on the two switches. If one switch is configured for FastEtherchannel and the other not configured immediately afterward, the initial switch detects a loop and blocks redundant ports. Subsequent configuration of FastEtherchannel will not automatically reenable the port.*

Local Devices Cannot Communicate to Devices Beyond the Router

If devices with a VLAN are communicating with each other but not with devices on other VLANs, the problem is either a VLAN setting or a network protocol (IP) setting. These are some of the most common problems:

- **IP misconfiguration**   Make sure the end station has its IP address, subnet mask, and default gateway set correctly. (The default gateway is usually the culprit.) In addition, check the IP address on the router.

- **VLAN inconstency**   Ensure that the end station's switchport is assigned to the correct VLAN (or to a VLAN at all). Use SHOW VLAN to see the VLAN status of each port.

- **ISL/trunking problem**   Check the VTP status of your switches; use SHOW VLAN on each switch to see if the VLANs are being distributed throughout the network. Check VTP pruning to make sure you have not accidentally pruned some VLANs off necessary trunks.

- **Router misconfiguration**   Verify that all VLANs are properly created and configured on the router (or RSM). Make sure that the VLAN IDs match and that the IP address of the VLAN matches the end station's default gateway. Use SHOW IP ROUTE to verify that the end station's destination has an entry in the routing table.

EXERCISE 11-7

Examining a Catalyst 6000 Series Switch

Examine the following output from a Catalyst 6000 switch port:

```
CAT6000# sh port 3/5
Port  Name               Status      Vlan       Duplex Speed Type
----- ------------------ ----------  ---------- ------ ----- ------------
3/5                      connected   50            full  1000 1000BaseSX
Port  Security Violation Shutdown-Time Age-Time Max-Addr Trap     IfIndex
----- -------- --------- ------------- -------- -------- -------- -------
3/5   disabled shutdown            0        0        1 enabled       18
Port      Broadcast-Limit Broadcast-Drop
--------  --------------- --------------------
3/5                    -                    0
Port    Send FlowControl   Receive FlowControl   RxPause TxPause Unsupported
        admin    oper      admin    oper                         opcodes
-----   -------- --------   -------- --------    ------- ------- -----------
3/5     desired  on        off      off         0       0       0
Port  Status      Channel                Admin Ch
                  Mode                   Group Id
----- ----------  -------------------- ----- -----
3/5   connected   auto silent             67    0
Port  Align-Err FCS-Err    Xmit-Err   Rcv-Err    UnderSize
----- --------- ---------- ---------- ---------- ---------
3/5        1454       1334          0       2165       2443
Port  Single-Col Multi-Coll Late-Coll  Excess-Col Carri-Sen Runts     Giants
----- ---------- ---------- ---------- ---------- --------- --------- ------
3/5            0          0          0          0         0      1665      0
Last-Time-Cleared
-------------------------
Sun Jul 2 2000, 09:18:59
```

What can you likely conclude from this? Choose all that apply.

A. This is a trunk port.

B. There could be a duplex mismatch.

    C. The port is detecting a high number of collisions.

    D. The port is detecting a high number of faulty frames.

Solution: B and **D.** The error, alignment, and FCS counters have significant numbers; this is frequently a sign of a duplex mismatch. The port is not running CSMA/CD (full duplex), so collisions are not being detected. This is not a trunk port; it is assigned to VLAN50.

CERTIFICATION SUMMARY

This chapter has shown most aspects of VLAN operation—and what can go wrong. First, inter-VLAN routing—how it is set up and configured—was covered. Both internal and external routers were examined. Next, VLAN design and troubleshooting issues were discussed; most of this discussion involved VLAN configuration and the spanning-tree protocol. Next, we looked at the various Cisco commands used to diagnose VLAN problems. Note how similar they are to the troubleshooting tools discussed in the previous chapters. Finally, the chapter covered problem isolation, common symptoms, and solutions. What was learned in designing the topology could be directly applied to troubleshooting as well.

Most VLAN problems are fairly straightforward and not too difficult to diagnose and solve. (The exception is spanning tree; it can sometimes be tricky to figure out). Most important, though, this chapter emphasized the need for up-to-date documentation and diagrams. These usually make the difference between quick solutions and extended outages. To put it bluntly, a successful network engineer is almost always a well-prepared one.

✓ TWO-MINUTE DRILL

Here are some of the key points from each certification objective in Chapter 11.

Inter-VLAN Routing

❑ High-end switches and routers have begun to obsolete the 80/20 rule. With virtual LANs (VLANs), workgroups are logically assigned and servers are consolidated to high-speed backbones.

❑ Inter-VLAN routing is the process of routing packets between VLANs. This task cannot be performed by a switch; it must be performed by a router or a route switch module (RSM).

Router and Switch Configuration

❑ To configure a trunk form an external router to a Catalyst switch, define a subinterface for each VLAN you intend to route.

❑ To configure an RSM to route between VLANs, define a logical VLAN interface for each VLAN on the switch.

VLAN Design Issues

❑ Many VLAN design issues revolve around the spanning-tree protocol. Optimizing STP parameters can have an important effect on how your network deals with instability.

❑ In routed VLAN environments, you can choose between one STP instance per VLAN or one for the entire switched fabric. In bridged VLAN environments, you must have one STP instance for the switched fabric.

VLAN Troubleshooting

❑ Be prepared for network problems. Have your network properly documented. Sometimes important information will not be available during outages.

❑ Avoid having spanning tree exacerbate network problems by maximizing the STP timers during periods of instability.

Router VLAN Diagnostic Tools

❏ Use SHOW VLANS to see the different VLANs and trunks configured on your external router.

❏ Use SHOW BRIDGE and SHOW SPAN to look at the Layer 2 characteristics of your router or RSM.

❏ Use DEBUG VLAN PACKET to diagnose inter-VLAN routing problems on your router or RSM. Remember that this command reports only error conditions.

Router and Switch Problem Isolation

❏ Always start troubleshooting with the Physical Layer. Problems here include faulty hardware and cables and incorrect duplex settings.

❏ Work your way up the OSI model when troubleshooting. After the Physical Layer, examine Layer 2 devices (switches), then Layer 3 devices (routers/RSMs).

Router VLAN Symptoms, Problems, and Action Plans

❏ Poor network performance can be caused by a variety or problems—from physical problems such as faulty hardware to Layer 2 problems such as spanning-tree loops.

❏ Inter-VLAN problems usually involve configuration errors on the workstation (IP addressing errors) or on the router (routing protocol misconfigurations).

SELF TEST

The following questions will help you measure your understanding of the material presented in this chapter. Read all the choices carefully because there might be more than one correct answer. Choose all correct answers for each question.

Inter-VLAN Routing

1. A router is used to segment which of the following?

   A.   Broadcast domains

   B.   Collision domains

   C.   VTP Domains

   D.   NT Domains

2. A customer has bought a new Catalyst switch and defined two VLANs: VLAN 30 and VLAN 40. Unfortunately, stations on VLAN 30 cannot communicate with stations on VLAN 40 (and vice versa). What must he do?

   A.   Use the SET IP ROUTE CatOS command to configure routes between the VLANs.

   B.   Use a router (or RSM) to route between the VLANs.

   C.   Make sure the VLANs are not using different versions of the spanning-tree protocol.

   D.   Configure a VTP domain on the switch.

3. A client wants to use RSMs to perform interVLAN routing in his Catalyst-based LAN. What is the minimum number of RSMs he must purchase?

   A.   One

   B.   One per catalyst

   C.   One per VLAN

   D.   One per routing protocol

Router and Switch Configuration

4. Configuring an external router to route between VLANs involves which of the following? Choose all that apply.

   A.   Defining a subinterface for each VLAN you are routing for

    B. Choosing a trunking protocol

    C. Defining the VTP domain on the router

    D. Creating a trunk between the router and switch

5. You are creating a trunk on a model 7500 series router. Subinterface FastEthernet0/2.2 will carry traffic for VLAN50. The trunking protocol being used is InterSwitch Link. Choose the correct command from the following.

    A. (CONFIG-SUBIF)# TRUNK 50 ISL

    B. (CONFIG-SUBIF)# TRUNK ISL 50

    C. (CONFIG-SUBIF)# ENCAPSULATION 50 ISL

    D. (CONFIG-SUBIF)# ENCAPSULATION ISL 50

VLAN Design Issues

6. How does spanning tree work in bridged VLAN environments?

    A. One spanning tree per VLAN

    B. One spanning tree per broadcast domain

    C. One spanning tree per collision domain

    D. One spanning tree for the entire network

7. Cisco recommends that VLAN1 be used for:

    A. All network traffic

    B. Network management

    C. Spanning-tree protocol

    D. VTP traffic

8. Would you recommend IEEE and DEC spanning-tree protocols coexisting on the same LAN?

    A. Yes

    B. No

9. Observe the LAN diagram shown in Figure 11-13. Does this met Cisco's network diameter recommendation?

    A. Yes

    B. No

FIGURE 11-13 Network diameter

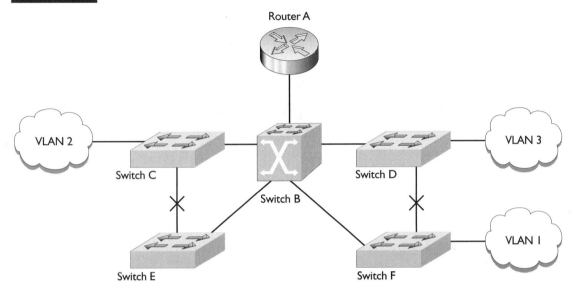

VLAN Troubleshooting

10. A Catalyst switch receives BPDUs on two of its ports (both are in the same VLAN). What will the switch most likely do?

    A. Place both ports in blocking mode.

    B. Place one port in forwarding mode and the other in blocking mode.

    C. Place both ports in forwarding mode.

    D. Place one port in forwarding mode and the other in learning mode.

Router VLAN Diagnostic Tools

11. A client calls with a spanning-tree question. He would like to know if his model 7500 series router is the root bridge. What command on the router displays the MAC address of the root bridge?

    A. SHOW BRIDGE

    B. SHOW ROOT-BRIDGE

    C. SHOW SPAN

    D. SHOW SPANTREE

12. Which command on a 7500 series router displays trunking information?

    A. SHOW VLAN

    B. SHOW TRUNK

    C. SHOW VLAN TRUNK

    D. SHOW VTP

13. A device on your network is malfunctioning. Your router logs indicate its MAC address but not its IP address. Which IOS command most likely helps you find its IP address?

    A. SHOW BRIDGE

    B. SHOW VLAN

    C. SHOW ARP

    D. DEBUG BRIDGE

14. Which of the following are recommended ways of checking an interface's physical and data link connectivity status? Choose all that apply.

    A. Check the interface's LED

    B. SHOW INTERFACE

    C. SHOW CDP NEIGHBOR

    D. SHOW IP EIGRP NEIGHBOR

Router and Switch Problem Isolation

15. A client is experiencing network instability, so you direct him to increase his spanning-tree timers to their maximum to minimize the effect of STP on the network problems. What values should he increase? Choose all that apply.

    A. Maximum age

    B. Minimum age

    C. Forward delay

    D. BPDU priority

16. Observe the network diagram shown in Figure 11-14. You want to change the STP forward delay time. On which machine(s) should you make this change?

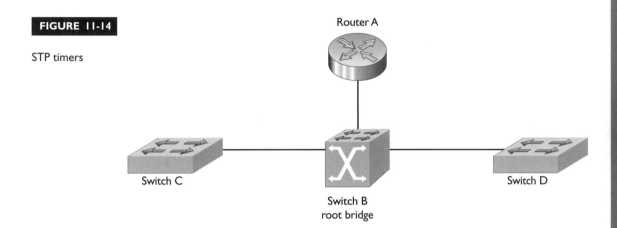

FIGURE 11-14

STP timers

Router A

Switch C

Switch B
root bridge

Switch D

A. Router A

B. Switch B

C. Router A and Switch B

D. Switches B, C, and D

Router VLAN Symptoms, Problems, and Action Plans

17. A PC is connected directly to a Catalyst 5000 series switch. The PC NIC is set to half-duplex, but the switch is set to full-duplex. What will most likely be the result? Choose all that apply.

A. A complete loss of connectivity between the PC and switch

B. Collisions will occur, but the PC will not be aware of them

C. Collisions will occur, but the switch will not be aware of them

D. Frames will be lost

18. You have a model 7500 series router that trunks to your Catalyst switch and routes between VLANs. You enter DEBUG VLAN PACKET on the router, but for 5 minutes you see no output. What is the most likely explanation?

A. The router has stopped routing packets between VLANs.

B. Your routing protocol has stopped receiving updates.

C. You have not configured any VLANs on the router.

D. Your router is functioning properly.

19. A workstation that is directly connected to a Catalyst switch is experiencing slow network performance. Which of the following could be a cause? Choose all that apply.

    A. Duplex mismatch between the workstation and switch

    B. A bridging loop in the network

    C. EMI

    D. VTP is misconfigured on the switch

20. A workstation cannot communicate with workstations on a different VLAN. It communicates fine with stations on its own VLAN. Which of the following could be the cause? Choose all that apply.

    A. The workstation has an incorrect default gateway configured.

    B. The workstation has an incorrect subnet mask configured.

    C. The workstation NIC has an incorrect duplex setting configured.

    D. The workstation has an incorrect VLAN configured.

LAB EXERCISE

Examine the network diagram shown in Figure 11-15. You must set up a trunk between interface FastEthernet2/1 on the router and port 1/1 on the switch according to the following guidelines:

FIGURE 11-15   Chapter 11 lab diagram

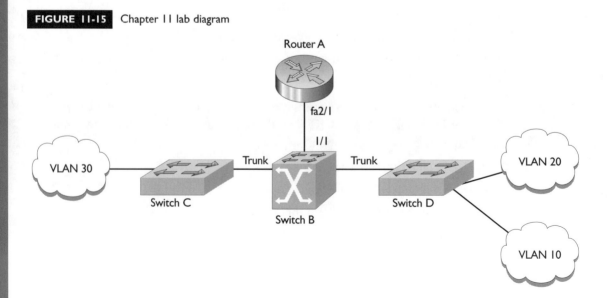

■ The router will route between VLANs 10, 20, and 30.

■ The default gateways for the VLANs are as follows:

```
VLAN 10 = 10.1.10.1 /24
VLAN 20 = 10.1.20.1 /24
VLAN 30 = 10.1.30.1 /24
```

■ ISL is the trunking protocol.

■ The trunk will carry traffic for all VLANs (including future VLANs).

Enter the configuration commands for the router below:

```
(config)#_____
(config-subif)#_____
(config-subif)#_____
(config-subif)#_____
(config-subif)#_____
(config-subif)#_____
(config-subif)#_____
(config-subif)#_____
(config-subif)#_____
```

Enter the configuration command for the switch below:

```
CAT5000(enable) _____
```

SELF TEST ANSWERS

Inter-VLAN Routing

1. ☑ **A.** Broadcast domains. A router segments broadcast domains.
   ☒ **B, C,** and **D** are incorrect because a switch segments collision domains, and VTP domains are logical domains defined on a switching fabric. NT domains are irrelevant to the question.

2. ☑ **B.** Use a router (or RSM) to route between the VLANs. A switch cannot route between VLANs by itself; it needs a router to do this.
   ☒ **A** is incorrect because SET IP ROUTE is used only for direct switch communications. **C** and **D** are incorrect because neither STP nor VTP are involved in inter-VLAN routing.

3. ☑ **A.** One RSM can route for an entire LAN as long as trunks are configured between the switches.
   ☒ **B, C,** and **D** are incorrect because they would exceed minimum requirements.

Router and Switch Configuration

4. ☑ **A, B,** and **D.** You must define subinterfaces that correspond with VLANs. Choose a trunking protocol (ISL or 802.1Q) and create the trunk link.
   ☒ **C** is incorrect because VTP is not supported on most external routers.

5. ☑ **D.** (CONFIG-SUBIF)# ENCAPSULATION ISL 50 is the correct syntax.
   ☒ **A, B,** and **C** are incorrect because their syntax is incorrect.

VLAN Design Issues

6. ☑ **D.** One spanning tree for the entire network. When bridging between VLANs is configured, there is one spanning tree for the entire network.
   ☒ **A** and **B** are incorrect because in routed VLAN environments, there is one spanning tree per VLAN or broadcast domain. **C** is incorrect because there is never one spanning tree per collision domain.

7. ☑ **B.** Network management. Cisco recommends that VLAN1 be used for management, not normal network usage.
   ☒ **A** is incorrect because traffic will typically be divided among the VLANs. **C** is incorrect because Cisco recommends the VLAN spanning tree. **D** is incorrect because VTP traffic is not confined to a specific VLAN; it is a trunking protocol.

8. ☑ **B.** No. IEEE and DEC should not coexist in the same LAN because that could cause loops.
☒ **A,** yes, is incorrect because IEEE and DEC should not coexist in the same LAN.

9. ☑ **A.** Yes. Cisco recommends a network diameter of 7 or less.
☒ **B,** no, is incorrect because the diagram does met Cisco's network diameter recommendation.

VLAN Troubleshooting

10. ☑ **B.** Place one port in forwarding mode and the other in blocking mode. If a switch detects BPDUs on two ports, the spanning-tree protocol places one of the ports in blocking mode to prevent loops. The other port moves to forwarding mode.
☒ **A, C,** and **D** are incorrect because all would be incorrect spanning-tree responses.

Router VLAN Diagnostic Tools

11. ☑ **C.** SHOW SPAN. This command shows detailed spanning-tree information of a router.
☒ **A, B,** and **D** are incorrect because SHOW BRIDGE shows the bridge table, not spanning-tree information; SHOW ROOT-BRIDGE is not a real command, and SHOW SPANTREE is the CatOS command.

12. ☑ **A.** SHOW VLAN displays VLAN and trunk information for configured trunk ports.
☒ **B, C,** and **D** are incorrect because they are not valid commands on an IOS router.

13. ☑ **C.** SHOW ARP shows MAC-to-IP address mappings.
☒ **A** is incorrect because SHOW BRIDGE shows MAC addresses, but only their associated port. **B** and **D** are incorrect because they would not show useful IP address information.

14. ☑ **A, B,** and **C.** Checking the interface's LED shows an interface's physical status. SHOW INTERFACE can show its physical and data link status. SHOW CDP NEIGHBOR shows data link connectivity to neighbors.
☒ **D** is incorrect because SHOW IP EIGRP NEIGHBOR shows no output. You do not necessarily have a physical or data link problem.

Router and Switch Problem Isolation

15. ☑ **A** and **C.** Maximum age and forward delay are the spanning-tree timers that determine how often topology change BPDUs are sent.
☒ **B** and **D** are incorrect because they are not spanning-tree timers.

16. ☑ **B.** Switch B. You must change STP timers only on the root bridge.

☒ **A, C,** and **D** are incorrect because all other bridges learn their timer values from the root.

Router VLAN Symptoms, Problems, and Action Plans

17. ☑ **C** and **D.** Collisions will occur, but the switch will not be aware of them, and frames will be lost. The full-duplex side has CSMA/CD disabled, so it is not aware of collisions and does not resend data (resulting in lost frames).

☒ **A** is incorrect because some successful data transfer still occurs. **B** is incorrect because the half-duplex side runs CSMA/CD, so it is aware of collisions.

18. ☑ **D.** DEBUG VLAN PACKET produces output only when it receives packets for VLANs it does not know. If you see no output, your router is most likely routing packets normally.

☒ **A, B,** and **C** are the least likely explanations of why you would see no output.

19. ☑ **A, B,** and **C.** All cause slow and unreliable network performance.

☒ **D** is incorrect because although it can cause some VLANs to be inaccessible, it does not cause slow performance.

20. ☑ **A** and **B.** The workstation has an incorrect default gateway configured, and the workstation has an incorrect subnet mask configured. Both are necessary to properly communicate outside your own subnet.

☒ **C** is incorrect because it would cause disruption in all communications. **D** is incorrect because you do not configure VLANs on workstations.

LAB ANSWER

<u>Router:</u>

```
(config)# interface fastethernet2/1.1
(config-subif)# encapsulation isl 10
(config-subif)# ip address 10.1.10.1 255.255.255.0
(config-subif)# interface fastethernet2/1.2
(config-subif)# encapsulation isl 20
(config-subif)# ip address 10.1.20.1 255.255.255.0
(config-subif)# interface fastethernet2/1.3
(config-subif)# encapsulation isl 30
(config-subif)# ip address 10.1.30.1 255.255.255.0
```

<u>Switch:</u>

```
CAT5000(enable) set trunk 1/1 on
```

12

Diagnosing and Correcting Frame Relay Problems

F rame Relay is appreciated as an extremely reliable yet affordable means of switching packets around. The necessary switching infrastructure can be provided by public entities, usually telcos, or private concerns. Frame Relay allows multiple logical, software-defined connections, or *permanent virtual circuits (PVCs),* to use a single link in a manner that makes efficient use of available bandwidth. Similar to other connection-oriented protocols such as the older X.25 in structure, Frame Relay takes advantage of advances in modern, faster wide area networks (WANs) by essentially throwing caution to the wind and dispensing with many of the error-correction mechanisms present in X.25.

The purpose of this chapter is to explore the tools available within the Cisco Internetwork Operating System (IOS) and to address techniques that can be used to troubleshoot problems on Frame Relay networks.

CERTIFICATION OBJECTIVE 12.01

Frame Relay Diagnostic Tools

Troubleshooting any WAN, such as the Frame Relay network in Figure 12-1, should follow a layered approach. In Figure 12-1, the display consists of basic components needed for a connection to a Frame Relay network. For the sake of consistency, this chapter follows the first three layers of the Open Systems Interconnection (OSI) model. Frame Relay is a Layer 2 protocol, but at the Data Link layer, you should approach initial troubleshooting at the Physical Layer. Ask

FIGURE 12-1   Basic Frame Relay Network

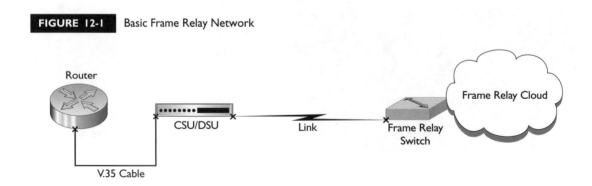

TABLE 12-1   A Frame Relay Frame

Flag	Frame Relay Header	Data	FCS	Flag
1 byte	2 bytes	Variable	2 bytes	1 byte

yourself these questions: is the CSU/DSU configured correctly? Is the V.35 cabling that connects your serial interface to the CSU/DSU connected? Are all the various light-emitting diodes (LEDs) on the router and CSU/DSU indicating connectivity?

The Frame Relay frame in Table 12-1 is bracketed by 1-byte flags at the beginning and end of each frame, has a data field of variable size, and has a Frame Check Sequence (FCS) field, usually used for cyclic redundancy check (CRC). The field that distinguishes Frame Relay is the 2-byte address field. This field contains the actual circuit identification, or *Data Link Connection Identifier (DLCI)*.

The DLCI part of the Frame Relay address field consists of a total of 10 bits over the 2 bytes of the address field, as illustrated in Table 12-2. The DLCI section is where the logical connection that is multiplexed into the physical channel is defined. The DLCI has local significance, so you can have different DLCIs that refer to the same circuit on distinct ends of a connection.

The kernel of the Frame Relay header is the DLCI field. Other fields in the Frame Relay header are briefly described in Table 12-3. The Forward Explicit Congestion Notification (FECN) and Backward Explicit Notification (BECN) fields are utilized within the Frame Relay network to communicate congestion information. The Discard Eligible (DE) field helps the switches "decide" which frames to drop in the event of congestion.

exam
ⓦatch

If you want to pass your exam, be sure that you have an in-depth understanding of the material presented in this chapter. If you then see a choice in a test that looks unfamiliar, you will know it is incorrect.

TABLE 12-2   Breakdown of the Frame Relay Header

Byte 1				Byte 2				
DLCI	C/R	EA		DLCI	FECN	BECN	DE	EA
Bits 3–8	Bit 2	Bit 1		Bits 5–8	Bit 4	Bit 3	Bit 2	Bit 1

TABLE 12-3	Description of Fields Within Frame Relay Header
Field	**Description**
DLCI	Data Link Connection Identifier: Local significance, reflects logical connection within multiplexed physical channel
C/R	Command/response field: currently unused
EA	Extended address bit: currently unused
FECN	Forward Explicit Congestion Notification: bit set in frame, informs the data terminating equipment (DTE) of congestion encountered en route
BECN	Backward Explicit Congestion Notification: bit set in frame, informs DTE of congestion on reverse path
DE	Discard Eligible: bit set in frame to let network switches know to drop low-priority frames if there is congestion

The SHOW CONTROLLERS SERIAL Command

To verify that you have connectivity at Layer 1, the following Cisco SHOW commands' output shed light. Line 3 of the SHOW CONTROLLERS SERIAL command in Figure 12-2 shows that Serial 0 is using a V.35 DCE cable and provides clocking of 125,000 bits per second. The output of this command would detect a DCE (Data Communications Equipment)or Data Terminal Equipment (DTE) cable, regardless of clock rate settings.

Figure 12-3 shows similar output; however, here a V.35 DTE cable is being used and the router is not providing a clock rate. As a DTE, the interface receives its

FIGURE 12-2 Output of the SHOW CONTROLLERS SERIAL command for DCE (some output omitted)

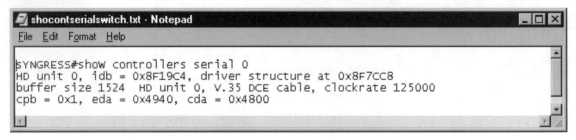

```
shocontserialswitch.txt - Notepad
File  Edit  Format  Help

SYNGRESS#show controllers serial 0
HD unit 0, idb = 0x8F19C4, driver structure at 0x8F7CC8
buffer size 1524  HD unit 0, V.35 DCE cable, clockrate 125000
cpb = 0x1, eda = 0x4940, cda = 0x4800
```

FIGURE 12-3 Output of the SHOW CONTROLLERS SERIAL command for DTE (output omitted)

```
shocontserial.txt - Notepad                                                    _ □ ×
File  Edit  Format  Help
Syngress#show controllers serial 0
HD unit 0, NIM slot 0, NIM type code 12, NIM version 5
idb = 0x609B6C68, driver structure at 0x609BC170, regaddr = 0x3C000000
buffer size 1524  Universal Serial: DTE V.35 cable
cpb = 0x0, eda = 0x71CC, cda = 0x71E0
RX ring with 32 entries at 0x40007000
00 bd_ptr=0x7000 pak=0x609BCFEC ds=0x4000A60C status=80 pak_size=251
01 bd_ptr=0x7014 pak=0x609C4874 ds=0x40022CA4 status=80 pak_size=81
cpb = 0x0, eda = 0x7800, cda = 0x7800
```

clocking from the CSU/DSU (and ultimately the service provider). If no cable is attached to this interface or if the cable is attached upside down, the output indicates "no cable" where Figure 12-3 indicates "DTE V.35 cable."

The SHOW INTERFACES SERIAL Command

In order to further check the Layer 1 issues, the SHOW INTERFACES SERIAL command is useful. The first line in Figure 12-4 shows us that serial interface is up. This indicates a good physical link from end to end. The third line from the bottom in Figure 12-4 shows 0 interface resets. A large number could indicate hardware failure at the CSU/DSU or switch. The last line in Figure 12-4 shows 0 carrier transitions; a large number here, particularly in conjunction with interface resets, could also indicate physical link problems. We look at this screen in more depth later in the chapter.

Given that all is well at Layer 1, let's look at Layer 2. Most of the Cisco IOS commands outlined in this chapter work at this layer. The Local Management Interface, which is the process Frame Relay uses to manage PVCs, needs to have a consistent configuration between the router and the Frame Relay switch it is using at each end. Each router could have a different Local Management Interface (LMI) type as long as its LMI type matched the adjacent Frame Relay switch. The Frame Relay provider defines the DLCI, which is used locally. The DLCI is mapped to a Layer 3 address, and defines the logical "channel" that shares the physical bandwidth. The DLCI field is part of the Frame Relay header, which in turn is part of the frame. Misconfigured DLCI values, improper mapping, and LMI type mismatches are common problems at Layer 2.

FIGURE 12-4 The SHOW INTERFACES SERIAL command to examine Layer 1 problems

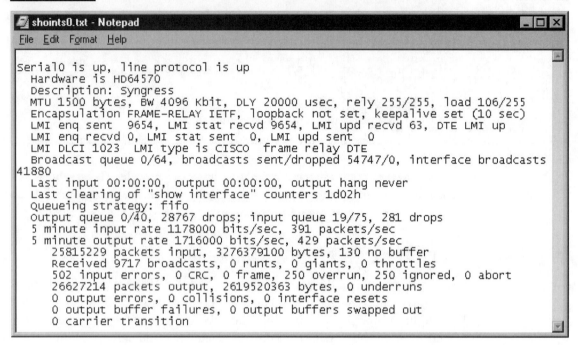

```
shoints0.txt - Notepad                                        _ □ X
File  Edit  Format  Help

Serial0 is up, line protocol is up
  Hardware is HD64570
  Description: Syngress
  MTU 1500 bytes, BW 4096 Kbit, DLY 20000 usec, rely 255/255, load 106/255
  Encapsulation FRAME-RELAY IETF, loopback not set, keepalive set (10 sec)
  LMI enq sent  9654, LMI stat recvd 9654, LMI upd recvd 63, DTE LMI up
  LMI enq recvd 0, LMI stat sent  0, LMI upd sent  0
  LMI DLCI 1023  LMI type is CISCO  frame relay DTE
  Broadcast queue 0/64, broadcasts sent/dropped 54747/0, interface broadcasts
41880
  Last input 00:00:00, output 00:00:00, output hang never
  Last clearing of "show interface" counters 1d02h
  Queueing strategy: fifo
  Output queue 0/40, 28767 drops; input queue 19/75, 281 drops
  5 minute input rate 1178000 bits/sec, 391 packets/sec
  5 minute output rate 1716000 bits/sec, 429 packets/sec
     25815229 packets input, 3276379100 bytes, 130 no buffer
     Received 9717 broadcasts, 0 runts, 0 giants, 0 throttles
     502 input errors, 0 CRC, 0 frame, 250 overrun, 250 ignored, 0 abort
     26627214 packets output, 2619520363 bytes, 0 underruns
     0 output errors, 0 collisions, 0 interface resets
     0 output buffer failures, 0 output buffers swapped out
     0 carrier transition
```

At Layer 3, the issues one is likely to encounter are generally associated with IP address errors, such as improperly configured access lists and mistakes made with associating DLCIs to subinterfaces.

Often it is useful to work at the political level, sometimes referred to as Layer 9, if you are dealing with a public carrier as part of the network troubleshooting process. In any event, your ability to provide guidance to your carrier to assist its piece of the troubleshooting process will be facilitated by a clear understanding of the issues affecting your side of the network.

exam
ⓦatch
Although it is possible to abbreviate router commands, it makes good sense to know what you are abbreviating. For example **SH INT S 0** *will work as well as the full text command of* **SHOW INTERFACES SERIAL 0** *but is not the complete and accurate command.*

The **CLEAR COUNTERS SERIAL** Command

The counters reported by the output of the SHOW INTERFACES SERIAL command and other interface-specific commands indicate statistics accrued since the last time the router booted or since the last time the counters were cleared, whichever is more recent. Thus to get a good sense of what is happening on the interface, it makes sense to clear the counters to develop a baseline of events.

EXERCISE 12-1

Clear Counters

In this exercise, you will log on to your router, clear the counters, observe the results, and then repeat to view to accrual of counters.

Telnet to the router and access privileged mode:

1. Type **clear counters serial** *n* (*n* = interface number of the interface you want to view).

2. Type **show interface serial** *n*.

3. Wait 1 minute.

4. If there is traffic on the link, you will observe that the counters will increment.

This exercise reflects a very important part of the repertoire necessary for successful troubleshooting. With judicious use of the CLEAR COUNTERS command, you can take "snapshots" of the way an interface is behaving. Having an accurate sense of exactly how rapidly an interface is accruing errors is critical if you are going to make informed choices on what intervention to make.

In Figure 12-5, the SHOW INTERFACES SERIAL 0 command has been issued. Note that the interface has accrued four interface resets since the last clearing of counters.

FIGURE 12-5 Output of SHOW INTERFACES SERIAL before clearing counters

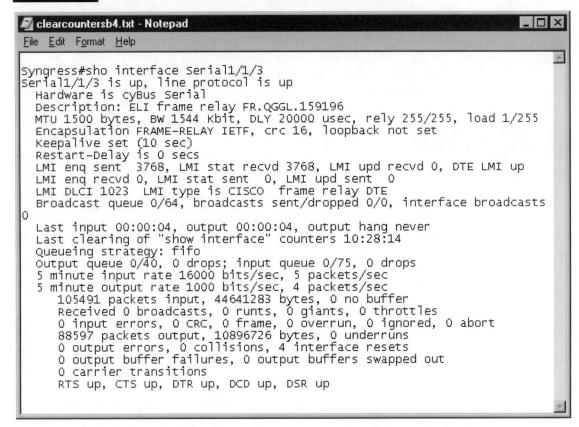

In Figure 12-6, the counters are cleared and the SHOW INTERFACES SERIAL command is issued again. The counters are reset. All the statistics start over. Note that the interface reset counter returns to zero.

The SHOW INTERFACES SERIAL Command

The SHOW INTERFACES SERIAL command provides a wealth of information about the status of your Frame Relay connection. From the output displayed after

FIGURE 12-6   SHOW INTERFACES SERIAL after clearing counters

```
clearcountersafter.txt - Notepad                                      _ □ ×
File  Edit  Format  Help
Syngress#clear counters Serial1/1/3
Clear "show interface" counters on this interface [confirm]y
Syngress#
Syngress#show interfaces Serial1/1/3
Serial1/1/3 is up, line protocol is up
  Hardware is cyBus Serial
  Description: ELI frame relay FR.QGGL.159196
  MTU 1500 bytes, BW 1544 Kbit, DLY 20000 usec, rely 255/255, load
1/255
  Encapsulation FRAME-RELAY IETF, crc 16, loopback not set
  Keepalive set (10 sec)
  Restart-Delay is 0 secs
  LMI enq sent  2, LMI stat recvd 2, LMI upd recvd 0, DTE LMI up
  LMI enq recvd 0, LMI stat sent  0, LMI upd sent  0
  LMI DLCI 1023  LMI type is CISCO  frame relay DTE
  Broadcast queue 0/64, broadcasts sent/dropped 0/0, interface
broadcasts 0
  Last input 00:00:01, output 00:00:06, output hang never
  Last clearing of "show interface" counters 00:00:25
  Queueing strategy: fifo
  Output queue 0/40, 0 drops; input queue 0/75, 0 drops
  5 minute input rate 20000 bits/sec, 4 packets/sec
  5 minute output rate 1000 bits/sec, 4 packets/sec
     120 packets input, 54872 bytes, 0 no buffer
     Received 0 broadcasts, 0 runts, 0 giants, 0 throttles
     0 input errors, 0 CRC, 0 frame, 0 overrun, 0 ignored, 0 abort
     113 packets output, 5563 bytes, 0 underruns
     0 output errors, 0 collisions, 0 interface resets
     0 output buffer failures, 0 output buffers swapped out
     0 carrier transitions
```

you enter this command, you can gather statistics regarding the status of the connection (see Figure 12-7).

The information in Figure 12-7 indicates that Serial0 is up and that the line protocol is also up. Five other states could be reflected in such output:

- **Serial0 is down, line protocol down**   Indicates that the router is not able to get carrier detect (CD), caused by bad cables, hardware, router, or CSU/DSU.

- **Serial0 is up, line protocol is down**   Could be a problem with configuration on the local or remote router or a malfunctioning or misconfigured CSU/DSU or router.

FIGURE 12-7 Output of SHOW INTERFACES SERIAL command

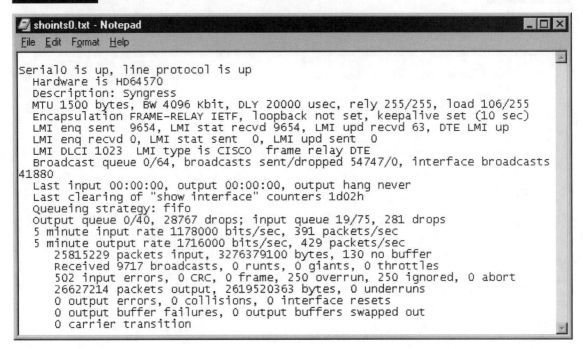

- **Serial0 is up, line protocol is up (looped)** Somewhere in the circuit there is a loop and the circuit doubles back toward you. A loop could be a result of a CSU/DSU or router interface being inadvertently or intentionally looped, or it could be a physical loop somewhere in the circuit. Looping is intentionally used to troubleshoot circuits.

TABLE 12-4 SHOW INTERFACES SERIAL Command

Line from Figure 12-7	Description
Serial0 is up, line protocol is up	Indicates that the line protocol is up. If line protocol were down and the serial interface showed as down, it would indicate problems with the CSU/DSU, router hardware, malfunctioning switches on the telco side, or misconfiguration of the interface. If the serial interface is up and the line protocol is down, you need to look at Layer 2 issues such as encapsulation, configuration, or LMI mismatches.

TABLE 12-5 Frame Relay Encapsulation

Line from Figure 12-7	Description
Encapsulation FRAME-RELAY IETF, loopback not set, keepalive set (10 sec)	Displays the encapsulation type. In the example, it is set to FRAME-RELAY IETF. (*IETF* stands for Internet Engineering Task Force.) Encapsulation must be set to the same setting on both sides of the link. It can be Frame Relay or IETF. If the keepalive is not manually Set, it will default to 10 seconds. If the keepalive is not set, inverse Address Resolution Protocol (ARP) does not work and all FR maps must be manually set.

- **Serial0 is up, line protocol is down (disabled)**   Most likely caused by a faulty CSU/DSU or router hardware; could also be caused by many errors received from your provider (see Table 12-4).

- **Serial0 is administratively down, line protocol is down**   Means that the SHUTDOWN command has been issued on the interface.

The line displayed in Table 12-5 addresses encapsulation. This is also where you can look to see whether or not the interface has been configured in loopback mode. You can also observe that the keepalives will be sent at the default 10-second interval. If you want change the default keepalive interval, you can do so with the KEEPALIVE command.

on the
Ů o b   *If you are not sure that the equipment on the other end of the link is a Cisco router, use the IETF encapsulation. The default encapsulation is Frame-Relay.*

In Table 12-6, you can see that the Cisco LMI type uses DLCI 1023. American National Standards Institute (ANSI) and q933a use DLCI 0. Frame Relay DTE indicates that the interface is functioning as a DTE device. This means that the interface is functioning as a source or recipient of Frame Relay frames. If the output were Frame Relay DCE, it would indicate that the interface was a DCE and is acting as a Frame Relay switch.

TABLE 12-6 LMI DLCI and Type

Line from Figure 12-7	Description
LMI DLCI 1023 LMI type is CISCO Frame Relay DTE	Indicates that the example is using the Cisco LMI, which uses DLCI 1023. The three LMI types you could see are Cisco, ANSI, and Q.933a.

TABLE 12-7	LMI Information

Line from Figure 12-7	Description
LMI enq sent 9654, LMI stat recvd 9654, LMI upd recvd 63, DTE LMI up LMI enq recvd 0, LMI stat sent 0, LMI upd sent 0	This line represents an overview of the LMI traffic over the interface.

The output outlined in Table 12-7 represents an overview of the LMI traffic traversing the interface. The following list defines the fields. Later in the chapter we look at LMI traffic in more depth:

- **LMI enq sent**   LMI inquiries sent out of the interface.
- **LMI stat recvd**   LMI status packets received.
- **LMI upd recvd**   LMI updates received.
- **DTE LMI up**   Status of LMI interface.
- **LMI enq recvd**   Number of LMI inquiries received on the interface.
- **LMI stat sent**   Number of LMI status packets sent.
- **LMI upd sent**   Number of LMI update packets sent.

Carrier transitions are an interruption in the carrier signal; they can be caused by line drops, interface resets, or CSU/DSU faults and are registered by the counter referenced in Table 12-8. If a remote CSU/DSU drops and then comes back up, you should see two carrier transitions.

The input errors, outlined in Table 12-9, should be viewed from the perspective of the relative number of errors you are getting to the amount of time it has been since your counters have been cleared. One percent of your total traffic could generate a large number of errors, particularly if you have not cleared counters for a while.

TABLE 12-8	Carrier Transitions

Line from Figure 12-7	Description
0 carrier transitions	This is a particularly useful statistic if you suspect that you are having multiple carrier transitions, which is a likely indicator that your line is unstable and possibly having intermittent connectivity or "flaps."

TABLE 12-9	CRC Errors

Line from Figure 12-7	Description
17282 input errors, 0 CRC, 0 frame, 8636 overrun, 8636 ignored, 0 abort	If the input errors exceed 1 percent of your total traffic or you are seeing an excessive number of CRC errors, it is likely that you have a noisy serial line, your cables are too long, or your network is connected to faulty telco equipment.

The SHOW FRAME-RELAY LMI Command

The SHOW FRAME-RELAY LMI command shows information related to the LMI. This command can give valuable insight into the status of the Frame Relay network. Using this command, you can determine LMI types, DTE or DTE configuration, and numerous statistics related to LMI messages received. The information displayed in Figure 12-5 indicates that interface serial 0 is configured for Frame Relay and is a DTE. Serial 0 is using the Cisco LMI type, and the interface has not accumulated any invalid LMI messages since the counters were last cleared. Serial 0 has received a message back for every one of the 9826 LMI status messages sent; it has received 63 inquiries and has had three timeouts. It is important to interpret the data in conjunction with knowledge of how long it has been since the counters were last cleared.

SCENARIO & SOLUTION

Why are there different LMI types?	The original standard, LMI, was further developed and augmented by the subsequent ANSI and q933a.
What is the most widely supported type?	The original standard, LMI (Cisco to a Cisco router), followed by ANSI and q933a or International Telecommunications Union (ITU).
Does the LMI type need to be the same on both sides of the link?	No. The LMI type needs to be the same between the router and the Frame Relay switch. Thus two routers could use different LMI types if their respective switches are different.

Verify LMI Type by Interface

If you want to view interface-specific LMI information, simply add the interface name to your SHOW FRAME-RELAY LMI command (for example, SHOW FRAME-RELAY LMI SERIAL *n*, where *n* = interface number.

Verify LMI Packets Flowing In and Out

If you cannot see the LMI exchange as evidenced by the status messages sent and received, the descriptions in Figure 12-8 indicate potential problems that can occur with the LMI messages as they traverse the interface.

The various LMI fields that you will see referenced in the SHOW FRAME-RELAY LMI output are outlined in Table 12-10. The fields that are most useful for troubleshooting purposes are the first field and the fields Status Enq. Sent and Status msgs Rcvd, one up from the bottom of the screen. The first field gives basic information regarding interface number, type, and LMI flavor in use. The two fields at the bottom help you see whether or not the status messages are being exchanged. We examine LMI exchanges in more detail later in the chapter when we look at the DEBUG SERIAL INTERFACE command.

Autosense vs. Static Configuration

Cisco routers with IOS 11.2 or later can *autosense* the LMI type. If the router is not explicitly configured for a specific LMI type, it autosenses. To autosense, the router sends out a status request to the switch in each of the three LMI types: ANSI, q933a,

---

FIGURE 12-8   Output of the SHOW FRAME-RELAY LMI command

```
LMI Statistics for interface Serial0 (Frame Relay DTE) LMI TYPE = CISCO
  Invalid Unnumbered info 0        Invalid Prot Disc 0
  Invalid dummy Call Ref 0         Invalid Msg Type 0
  Invalid Status Message 0         Invalid Lock Shift 0
  Invalid Information ID 0         Invalid Report IE Len 0
  Invalid Report Request 0         Invalid Keep IE Len 0
  Num Status Enq. Sent 9826        Num Status msgs Rcvd 9826
  Num Update Status Rcvd 63        Num Status Timeouts 3
```

TABLE 12-10 SHOW FRAME-RELAY LMI Fields

Line from Figure 12-8	Description
LMI Statistics	Signaling or LMI specification: CISCO, ANSI, or ITU-T.
Invalid Unnumbered Info	Number of received LMI messages with an invalid unnumbered information field.
Invalid Prot Disc	Number of received LMI messages with an invalid protocol discriminator.
Invalid dummy Call Ref	Number of received LMI messages with invalid dummy call references.
Invalid Msg Type	Number of received LMI messages with an invalid message type.
Invalid Status Message	Number of received LMI messages with an with an invalid status message.
Invalid Lock Shift	Number of received LMI messages with an invalid lock shift type.
Invalid Information ID	Number of received LMI messages with an invalid information identifier.
Invalid Report IE Len	Number of received LMI messages with an invalid report IE length.
Invalid Report Request	Number of received LMI messages with an in valid report request.
Invalid Keep IE Len	Number of received LMI messages with an invalid keep IE length.
Num Status Enq. Sent	Number of LMI status inquiry messages sent.
Num Status Msgs Rcvd	Number of LMI status messages received.
Num Update Status Rcvd	Number of LMI asynchronous update status messages received.
Num Status Timeouts	Number of times the status message was not received within the keepalive time value.
Num Status Enq. Rcvd	Number of LMI status inquiry messages received.
Num Status Msgs Sent	Number of LMI status messages sent.
Num Status Enq. Timeouts	Number of times the status inquiry message was not received within the T392 DCE timer value.
Num Update Status Sent	Number of LMI asynchronous update status messages sent.

and Cisco, respectively. The switch should respond to one of the requests, and the router in turn configures itself to suit the appropriate LMI type. In certain situations, such as when the router's adjacent switch is set to autosense, you need to manually set the LMI type. The command to achieve this task in interface configuration mode is FRAME-RELAY LMI-TYPE {ANSI | CISCO | Q933A}. If LMI is disabled, autosense does not work, and if keepalive is disabled, LMI does not work.

EXERCISE 12-2

Manually Set LMI Type

As mentioned earlier, there are times when you must manually configure the LMI type in your router. Of the three LMI types, the original LMI type, CISCO, allowed for only unidirectional requests and responses between router and the adjacent Frame Relay switch. The ANSI and q933a types augmented the original specification slightly to allow for the bidirectional communication allowed in some switches. If you are working with a public network, you must use the type of LMI that the connected switch is using. If you are building a private network, you need to determine which of the standards best suits your needs:

1. Telnet to your router and get into configuration mode.

2. Enter interface configuration mode by typing **interface serial** *n* (*n* = interface number).

3. For CISCO LMI, type **frame-relay lmi-type cisco**.

4. For ANSI LMI, type **frame-relay lmi-type ansi**.

5. For Q933A LMI, type **frame-relay lmi-type q933a**.

6. Press Ctrl-Z to exit configuration mode.

7. Type **copy running-config startup-config** to save.

Setting the LMI in this fashion is very useful if the equipment to which you are connecting is a different type than the equipment you are using locally.

exam
Ⓦatch

Cisco routers autosense the LMI type providing that you are using IOS 11.2 or later. In CISCO IOS 11.1 and earlier, the default LMI type is CISCO.

The SHOW FRAME-RELAY MAP Command

The SHOW FRAME-RELAY MAP command, as shown in Figure 12-9, reveals mapping between networks layer protocols and DLCIs. The output also indicates the status and encapsulation of all the Frame Relay interfaces. In this example,

FIGURE 12-9 Output from SHOW FRAME-RELAY MAP

```
showframemap.txt - Notepad                                              _ □ ×
File  Edit  Format  Help

Syngress#show frame-relay map
Serial0.71 (up): point-to-point dlci, dlci 71(0x47,0x1070), broadcast, IETF, BW = 128000
         status defined, active
Serial0.75 (up): point-to-point dlci, dlci 75(0x4B,0x10B0), broadcast, IETF, BW = 128000
         status defined, active
Serial0.51 (up): point-to-point dlci, dlci 51(0x33,0xC30), broadcast, BW = 56000
         status defined, active
Serial0.48 (up): point-to-point dlci, dlci 48(0x30,0xC00), broadcast, BW = 128000
         status defined, active
Serial0.17 (up): point-to-point dlci, dlci 17(0x11,0x410), broadcast, BW = 56000
         status defined, active
Serial0.62 (up): point-to-point dlci, dlci 62(0x3E,0xCE0), broadcast, IETF, BW = 512000
         status defined, active
Serial0.56 (up): point-to-point dlci, dlci 56(0x38,0xC80), broadcast, BW = 128000
         status defined, active
Serial0.74 (up): point-to-point dlci, dlci 74(0x4A,0x10A0), broadcast, IETF, BW = 1534000
         status defined, active
Serial1 (up): ip 203.201.2.3 dlci, dlci 75(0x4B,0x10B0), broadcast, IETF, BW = 1534000
status defined, active
```

Serial 1 is configured as a point-to-multipoint interface and the subinterfaces are configured as point to point.

The output described in Table 12-11 illustrates how a functional subinterface, configured with the FRAME-RELAY INTERFACE-DLCI subinterface configuration, looks to the SHOW FRAME-RELAY MAP command.

The line from Figure 12-9 referenced in Table 12-12 indicates a major interface, Serial1, with a IP address mapped to it. Given that multiple logical circuits are generally associated with a Frame Relay major interface, any Layer 3 address information needs to be associated with, or mapped to, a circuit's DLCI; otherwise, the interface will not know where to send traffic. If a major interface, or

TABLE 12-11 The FRAME-RELAY INTERFACE-DLCI Command on Subinterfaces

Line from Figure 12-9	Description
Serial0.51 (up): point-to-point dlci, dlci 51(0x33,0xC30), broadcast, BW = 56000 status defined, active	Figure 12-9 indicates a subinterface configured with the FRAME-RELAY INTERFACE-DLCI command. The output also shows the DLCI number and displays the bandwidth set by the router administrator.

TABLE 12-12	Distant Layer 3 Addresses Are Shown on Major Interfaces, Not Subinterfaces

Line from Figure 12-9	Description
Serial1 (up): ip 203.201.2.3 dlci, dlci 75(0x4B,0x10B0), broadcast, IETF, BW = 1534000 status defined, active	Figure 12-9 shows a major interface with a Layer 3 address mapped to it. Although Layer 3 addresses can be mapped to a remote subinterface, the distant Layer 3 address will be displayed only if mapped to a major interface. To associate a Layer 3 address with a subinterface, simply assign an IP address to the interface.

subinterface, is not explicitly mapped to an IP address, it will attempt to use a process called *Frame Relay inverse ARP* to discover the remote IP address.

The SHOW FRAME-RELAY PVC Command

The SHOW FRAME-RELAY PVC command displays the status of every PVC but also can be used to examine a specific PVC. The output also indicates DTE or DCE, dependent on whether the router is functioning as a switch. This command is invaluable for assessing problems associated with specific logical channels. The out put of the SHOW FRAME-RELAY PVC command, as shown in Figure 12-10, allows you to look at the DLCI of specific PVCs, input and output byte counts, packets dropped, FECN and BECN information, DE statistics, and the creation and last modified times for the PVC. Table 12-13 (page 744) indicates active versus inactive status of output shown in Figure 12-10.

In this chapter, you have seen a lot of acronyms. This might be a good time to review a few of them.

SCENARIO & SOLUTION

Acronym	Definition
What do the letters DLCI stand for?	Data Link Connection Identifier
What do the letters PVC stand for?	Permanent Virtual Circuit
What do the letters CSU/DSU stand for?	Channel Service Unit /Data Service Unit
What do the letters LMI stand for?	Local Management Interface

FIGURE 12-10 Output from SHOW FRAME-RELAY PVC

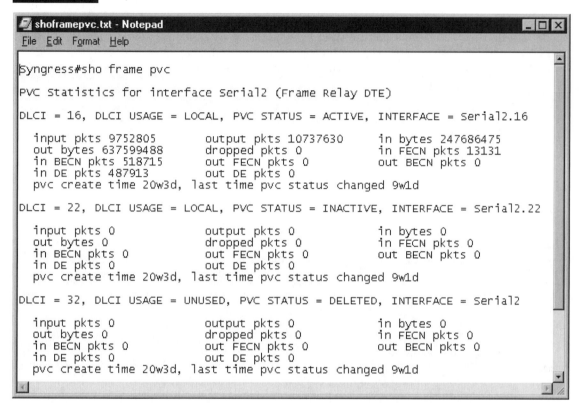

```
shoframepvc.txt - Notepad

File   Edit  Format  Help

Syngress#sho frame pvc

PVC Statistics for interface Serial2 (Frame Relay DTE)

DLCI = 16, DLCI USAGE = LOCAL, PVC STATUS = ACTIVE, INTERFACE = Serial2.16

   input pkts 9752805        output pkts 10737630      in bytes 247686475
   out bytes 637599488       dropped pkts 0            in FECN pkts 13131
   in BECN pkts 518715       out FECN pkts 0           out BECN pkts 0
   in DE pkts 487913         out DE pkts 0
   pvc create time 20w3d, last time pvc status changed 9w1d

DLCI = 22, DLCI USAGE = LOCAL, PVC STATUS = INACTIVE, INTERFACE = Serial2.22

   input pkts 0              output pkts 0             in bytes 0
   out bytes 0               dropped pkts 0            in FECN pkts 0
   in BECN pkts 0            out FECN pkts 0           out BECN pkts 0
   in DE pkts 0              out DE pkts 0
   pvc create time 20w3d, last time pvc status changed 9w1d

DLCI = 32, DLCI USAGE = UNUSED, PVC STATUS = DELETED, INTERFACE = Serial2

   input pkts 0              output pkts 0             in bytes 0
   out bytes 0               dropped pkts 0            in FECN pkts 0
   in BECN pkts 0            out FECN pkts 0           out BECN pkts 0
   in DE pkts 0              out DE pkts 0
   pvc create time 20w3d, last time pvc status changed 9w1d
```

exam
🐦 **a t c h**   *It is a good idea to acquaint yourself with what the various acronyms that you encounter actually stand for. Not only will you impress your friends, but sometimes the lengthy version is actually descriptive and helpful in understanding concepts.*

Loopback Tests

Loopback testing is a critical part of the Frame Relay troubleshooting process. Most problems that you are likely to encounter can be isolated using a thorough series of

TABLE 12-13 Active vs. Inactive Status

Line from Figure 12-10	Description
DLCI = 16, DLCI USAGE = LOCAL, PVC STATUS = ACTIVE, INTERFACE = Serial2.16	Indicates that DLCI 16 has an active status and is associated with subinterface Serial2.16.
DLCI = 22, DLCI USAGE = LOCAL, PVC STATUS = INACTIVE, INTERFACE = Serial2.22	Shows that DLCI 22 is inactive. This could indicate that the router at the other end of the connection is not configured properly or is not up.
DLCI = 32, DLCI USAGE = UNUSED, PVC STATUS = DELETED, INTERFACE = Serial2	Reports that DLCI 32 has been deleted. Indicates that the DLCI association has been changed by your provider.
BECN packets in and out	Number of BECN packets traversing the logical circuit with the bit set on.
FECN packets in and out	Number of FECN packets traversing the logical circuit with the bit set on.
pvc create time 20w3d, last time pvc status changed 9w1d	Indicates the create timer of the PVC and the last time the status was changed.

loopback tests. A very useful tool for loopback testing is a *loopback plug* or *receptacle,* essentially a way of looping the physical wires to achieve a "hard loop." Most CSU/DSUs also allow a looped configuration. Telco engineers often have the capability to loop your CSU/DSU and their equipment remotely. Loopback testing is something of a blunt instrument; you can use it only on major interfaces.

EXERCISE 12-3

Loopback Testing

This exercise outlines the steps you would take to do full loopback testing on a typical Frame Relay network, as illustrated in Figure 12-11. If you do not have access to a network that has all the components listed in Figure 12-11, you could simulate most of the elements with which you would typically deal using a router connected to a CSU/DSU:

1. Log on to Router 1 and enter enable mode.

2. From interface configuration, enter the LOOPBACK command, followed by Ctrl-Z. If your router is functioning properly, you should see that the line is up and looped when you perform a SHOW INTERFACES SERIAL command. You should also be able to see that LMI traffic counters are incrementing.

3. Use the extended PING command to ping the Layer 3 address of the interface. This action can be compared with pinging the 127.0.0.1 address on a local host: it will not tell you much, but it comes in handy if you have a bad serial card.

4. If all is well, remove the LOOPBACK command from the interface config.

5. Next, move to the local CSU/DSU and place it in local loop mode. (You can also use a loopback plug at this stage.)

6. Perform Steps 3–7 again. This process will test the connection between router and CSU/DSU.

7. If all is well here, you need to make a choice as to how soon to bring your provider into the troubleshooting process. This choice also depends somewhat on whether you have access to the remote end of the connection. Try to check both ends before calling the telco.

FIGURE 12-11 Loopback testing

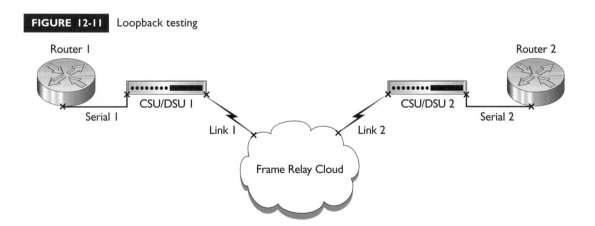

8. If you decide and are able to check the other end of the link, have an assistant either hard-loop the CSU/DSU or set it in remote loop mode. If you are then able to ping your LOCAL interface's Layer 3 address, you are probably looking at a problem with the remote network. Simply repeat Steps 1–7 to isolate the problem.

9. At this stage, you might want to reboot the CSU/DSUs because, when you call the telco representatives, he or she is sure to ask whether you've done so.

10. Call your provider or telco representative and let him or her know that the provider/telco has a problem on its network and needs to fix it. Invite the telco to loop to your CSU/DSU in order to test. If you have done your end of the testing well, it will make working with the provider much more smooth.

on the **job**

Debug commands are critical tools if you are going to get more than a superficial perspective of potential problems with your Frame Relay network. Judicious use of the array of debug commands available for troubleshooting can pinpoint the exact source of a problem. Efficient use of these commands can improve your job security, too. On production networks, it is important to carefully apply some of the more processor-intensive debug commands, particularly if you are already dealing with an overworked router.

The DEBUG SERIAL INTERFACE Command

The DEBUG SERIAL INTERFACE command is useful in determining whether or not you are having any problems with timing across the serial link. One drawback with using this information with a Frame Relay connection is that you will not see output if LMI is down. Some texts recommend enabling HDLC encapsulation on the interface to troubleshoot. The problem with this approach is that you have to be able to control both ends of the physical link, which is not usually possible when working with public network providers. You could enable High Level Data Link

FIGURE 12-12   Output from the DEBUG SERIAL INTERFACE command

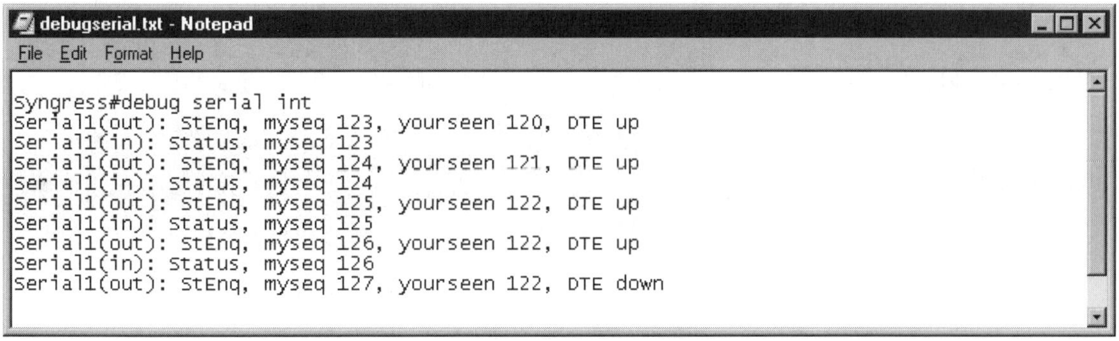

```
debugserial.txt - Notepad                                          _ □ ×
File  Edit  Format  Help
Syngress#debug serial int
Serial1(out): StEnq, myseq 123, yourseen 120, DTE up
Serial1(in): Status, myseq 123
Serial1(out): StEnq, myseq 124, yourseen 121, DTE up
Serial1(in): Status, myseq 124
Serial1(out): StEnq, myseq 125, yourseen 122, DTE up
Serial1(in): Status, myseq 125
Serial1(out): StEnq, myseq 126, yourseen 122, DTE up
Serial1(in): Status, myseq 126
Serial1(out): StEnq, myseq 127, yourseen 122, DTE down
```

control (HDLC) over the link in a private or lab setting where you have routers on both sides of a physical link.

Figure 12-12 looks at a production Frame Relay interface that is connected to a physically broken link. In this situation, when the LMI does not see an incremented response from the switch for three out of six consecutive keepalive events, you will see the DTE go down. In Figure 12-12, you can see that for the first three lines, the myseq, mineseen, and yourseen messages each increment by 1. In the next four lines of Figure 12-12, the seen packets stop incrementing. This essentially means that communications have been lost with the router at the other end of the connection. Note that the LMI continues to attempt to establish a keepalive dialog, and when it sees three consecutive keepalives, it brings the DTE back up.

The output displays keepalives traversing the link. Table 12-14 explains the keepalive types that you will see referenced after you issue the DEBUG SERIAL INTERFACE command.

TABLE 12-14

Keepalive Types

Type	Description
Myseq	Keepalives sent from your side of the link.
Yourseen	Keepalives sent from the other side of the link.

TABLE 12-15   Description of DEBUG SERIAL INTERFACE Output Before Failure

Lines from Figure 12-12	Description
Serial1(out): StEnq, myseq 123, yourseen 120, DTE up Serial1(in): Status, myseq 123 Serial1(out): StEnq, myseq 124, yourseen 121, DTE up Serial1(in): Status, myseq 124 Serial1(out): StEnq, myseq 125, yourseen 122, DTE up Serial1(in): Status, myseq 125	Output indicates that Serial1 is functional. Note that keepalives are incrementing and that you can track the passage of packets in and out of the interface.

In Table 12-15, the keepalives are incrementing, indicating that the routers on both sides of the link are communicating.

But now we see the backhoe-induced fiber failure (BIFF), the severing of a physical link within the network connecting the two machines at both sides of the link. This cessation of traffic is indicated in Table 12-16.

The DEBUG FRAME-RELAY LMI Command

This command, as illustrated in Figure 12-13, allows you to see whether or not LMI is being exchanged between your router and its adjacent switch in the Frame Relay

TABLE 12-16   Description of DEBUG SERIAL INTERFACE Output After Failure

Line from Figure 12-12	Description
Serial1(out): StEnq, myseq 126, yourseen 122, DTE up Serial1(in): Status, myseq 126 Serial1(out): StEnq, myseq 127, yourseen 122, DTE down	When the physical link is broken, the LMI brings the DTE down. This process is initiated when the yourseen packets cease to increment for three out of six consecutive keepalive events. Yourseen and mineseen not incrementing is bad news. The fact that the mineseen and yourseen keepalives are not incrementing reflects the loss of connectivity. The myseq keepalives continue to increment. When the difference between the myseq and mineseen exceeds two out of six consecutive packets, the line protocol drops.

FIGURE 12-13 Output of the DEBUG FRAME-RELAY LMI command

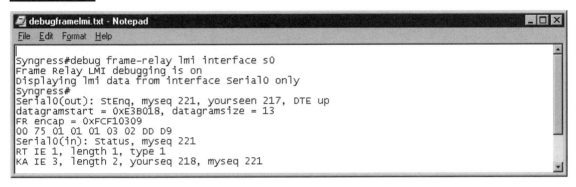

```
debugframelmi.txt - Notepad
File  Edit  Format  Help

Syngress#debug frame-relay lmi interface s0
Frame Relay LMI debugging is on
Displaying lmi data from interface Serial0 only
Syngress#
Serial0(out): StEnq, myseq 221, yourseen 217, DTE up
datagramstart = 0xE3B018, datagramsize = 13
FR encap = 0xFCF10309
00 75 01 01 01 03 02 DD D9
Serial0(in): Status, myseq 221
RT IE 1, length 1, type 1
KA IE 3, length 2, yourseq 218, myseq 221
```

network. DEBUG FRAME-RELAY LMI is fairly useful because you can issue the command without fear of overwhelming the router with a great deal of output. This command can be issued in a major interface-specific manner.

Table 12-17 breaks down and explains the elements in the output of the DEBUG FRAME-RELAY LMI command. The line outlined in Table 12-18 allows you to see more information about the elements of the PVC and display DLCI status.

The DEBUG FRAME-RELAY EVENTS Command

The DEBUG FRAME-RELAY EVENTS command displayed in Figure 12-14 and Table 12-19 allows analysis of packets coming into the network. The output of this command also displays Frame Relay ARP replies and requests. Contrary to popular

TABLE 12-17 DEBUG FRAME-RELAY LMI Exchange Elements

Lines from Figure 12-13	Description
Serial0(out): StEnq, myseq 221, yourseen 217, DTE up	This is a query sent out by the router to the switch; it also tells us that DTE is up.
Serial0(in): Status, myseq 221	This is the switch responding to the router.
RT IE 1, length 1, type 1	Report Type Information Element (RTIE) indicates the length, in bytes, and the type.
KA IE 3, length 2, yourseq 218, myseq 221	KeepAlive Information Element (KAIE) indicates length and counts keepalive packets traversing the logical circuit.

TABLE 12-18 Full LMI Status

Line from Figure 12-13	Description
PVC IE 0x7, length 0x6, dlci 17, status 0x2, bw 56000	This line displays information regarding the PVC elements and DLCI. Note that you can also observe the bandwidth configured on the interface.

FIGURE 12-14 Output of the DEBUG FRAME-RELAY EVENTS command

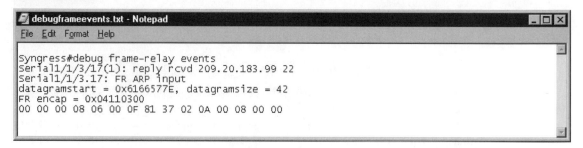

```
debugframeevents.txt - Notepad
File  Edit  Format  Help

Syngress#debug frame-relay events
Serial1/1/3/17(1): reply rcvd 209.20.183.99 22
Serial1/1/3.17: FR ARP input
datagramstart = 0x6166577E, datagramsize = 42
FR encap = 0x04110300
00 00 00 08 06 00 0F 81 37 02 0A 00 08 00 00
```

opinion (and some textbooks), this command does not generally create a lot of output. Frame Relay's use of ARP has similarities to the IP implementation but uses the DLCI rather than the MAC address to discover protocol information from remotely linked devices.

exam
ⓦatch
It will serve you well to have a clear idea of what each debug screen actually does so that you can utilize them in appropriate circumstances. Understanding the debug functions will minimize the possibility of misapplication. An exception due to the limited output that it generates is DEBUG FRAME-RELAY LMI.

TABLE 12-19 DEBUG FRAME-RELAY EVENTS Command Output

Line from Figure 12-14	Description
Serial1/1/3/17(1): reply rcvd 209.20.183.99 22	Frame Relay ARP reply received from host 209.20.183.99 on DLCI 22.
Serial1/1/3.17: FR ARP input	Frame Relay ARP packet received.
00 00 00 08 06 00 0F 81 37 02 0A 00 08 00 00	Ethernet type code 0x0806 or ARP.

FIGURE 12-15   Output of the DEBUG FRAME-RELAY PACKET command

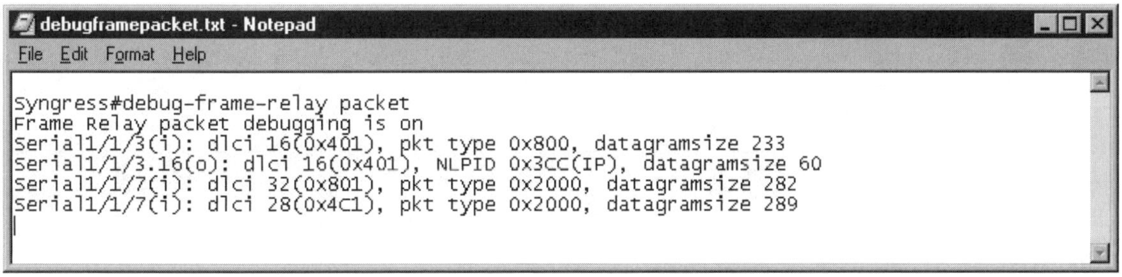

```
debugframepacket.txt - Notepad                                    _ □ ×
File  Edit  Format  Help

Syngress#debug-frame-relay packet
Frame Relay packet debugging is on
Serial1/1/3(i): dlci 16(0x401), pkt type 0x800, datagramsize 233
Serial1/1/3.16(o): dlci 16(0x401), NLPID 0x3CC(IP), datagramsize 60
Serial1/1/7(i): dlci 32(0x801), pkt type 0x2000, datagramsize 282
Serial1/1/7(i): dlci 28(0x4C1), pkt type 0x2000, datagramsize 289
```

The DEBUG FRAME-RELAY PACKET Command

The DEBUG FRAME-RELAY PACKET command, shown in Figure 12-15, allows you to analyze packets traversing each Frame Relay interface. This command allows you to view information about each packet. Figure 12-15 details include the major interface, subinterface, DLCI involved, packet types, whether the packet is coming in or leaving the interface, protocol ID information, ARP requests, and datagram size. Cisco recommends using this command on interfaces with fewer than 25 packets per second of traffic.

The breakdown of the DEBUG FRAME-RELAY PACKET command displayed in Table 12-20 shows how the output provides information related to specific interfaces and PVCs. You can track a particular protocol to a specific interface and develop conclusions based on the absence of certain protocol information for a specific interface. Table 12-20 shows some debug output of a router with two major Frame Relay interfaces.

TABLE 12-20   DEBUG FRAME-RELAY PACKET Command Output

Line from Figure 12-15	Description
Serial1/1/3(i): dlci 16(0x401), pkt type 0x800, datagramsize 233 Serial1/1/3.16(o): dlci 16(0x401), NLPID 0x3CC(IP), datagramsize 60	These two lines show that an IP packet came in on Serial1/1/3 DLCI 16 and that a packet was sent out from DLCI 16 on subinterface Serial1/1/3.16.
Serial1/1/7(i): dlci 32(0x801), pkt type 0x2000, datagramsize 282 Serial1/1/7(i): dlci 28(0x4C1), pkt type 0x2000, datagramsize 289	These two lines indicate Cisco Discovery Protocol (CDP) packets destined for the PVCs associated with DLCIs 28 and 32.

TABLE 12-21 A Sampling of Packet Codes

Packet Type?	Code	Packet Type?	Code
RFC 1294 (only for IP)	0xCC	IP on 3MB net	0x0201
XNS	0x0600	IP on a 10MB Network	0x0800
IP ARP	0x0806	Frame Relay ARP	0x0808
DEC MOP booting protocol	0x6001	DEC MOP console protocol	0x6002
DEC LAT on Ethernet	0x6004gg	RARP	0x8035
Apple EtherTalk	0x809b	AppleTalk ARP	0x80f3

For readers interested in more depth on this topic, more packet type codes are included in Table 12-21. The table presents a sampling of some of the packet codes that you could encounter in the output of Cisco debug commands. Knowing these codes is not necessary to pass the test.

CERTIFICATION OBJECTIVE 12.02

Problem Isolation in Frame Relay WANs

Narrowing the location of a problem is the key to troubleshooting. Bear in mind that Frame Relay is a rather magnificent amalgam of diverse media and technologies. Therefore, it can break down. Knowing where it is broken, at what layer and physical location, could transform your worst nightmare into job security. For this reason, take a methodical, layered approach to your troubleshooting efforts.

In Figure 12-16, a typical Frame Relay network is displayed. Router 1 connects via a CSU/DSU and a physical link to the Frame Relay cloud. The switches in the cloud continue the circuit to another physical link, CSU/DSU, and finally Router 2. Each physical link can carry multiple PVCs. It might be helpful to keep the whole picture in mind when troubleshooting the component parts. Use the following list as a guide:

1. **Physical link** Check your cables. You can use the SHOW INTERFACES SERIAL command to see whether or not input errors are accruing. You can also check by replacing the cable with a known good cable and by using various cable testers.

2. **PVC configuration** Check to see that the encapsulation, LMI type, assignments, and so on are correct.

3. **Layer 2 to 3 mapping** Check to ensure that the network is configured properly at the IP level.

4. **Remote side** Check that all is well at the remote side of the network. Use the same sequence as indicated in Steps 1–3.

FIGURE 12-16 Typical Frame Relay network

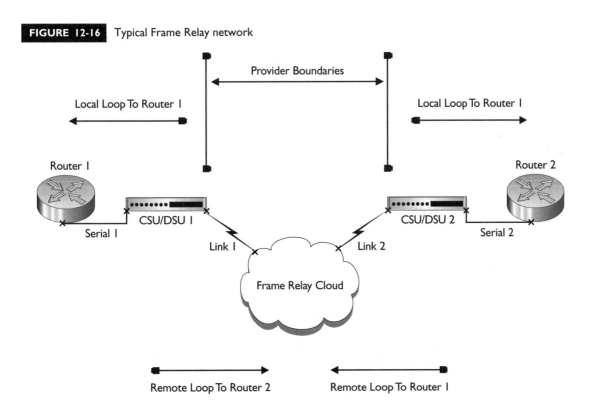

TABLE 12-22 Frame Relay Network Issues and Problems

Issue	Potential Problem
New installation does not work	Circuit is not ordered or provisioned correctly
Failure after successful operation	Router, cable failure, IP error, software problem
Failure at certain times	Congestion
Intermittent problems	Bad serial cable, congestion, CSU/DSU problems

Table 12-22 outlines some issues that might arise with your Frame Relay network and some possible problems that cause or contribute to the issue. Table 12-23 lists methods for gathering more information about the location of potential problems.

on the
Job *It pays to keep a record of your circuit identification numbers. Being able to provide your telco correct circuit information in the "heat of the moment," when a circuit is down and the pressure is on, is as important as all the other parts of the troubleshooting puzzle.*

TABLE 12-23 Information About Potential Frame Relay Network Problems

Potential Problem	For Further Information
Bad hardware or cables	Use the SHOW RUNNING CONFIGURATION or SHOW INTERFACES SERIAL command or cable testers.
CSU/DSU problems	Use the SHOW INTERFACES SERIAL command and check for input errors.
Congestion	Use the SHOW BUFFERS command to determine possible drops. Use the SHOW INTERFACES SERIAL command to evaluate traffic load on the major interface; are resets increasing? Use a protocol analyzer to assess the amount of broadcast traffic.
IP problems	Use the SHOW IP ROUTE command to evaluate routing tables.
Provisioning problems	Work with the provider to ensure that everyone has the same provisioning information.

SCENARIO & SOLUTION

How do I display keepalive messages?	Use the DEBUG SERIAL INTERFACE command.
How do I determine what LMI messages the switch and router are exchanging?	Use the DEBUG FRAME-RELAY LMI command.
How do I display debug information about packets coming in to the interface and determine which application is using a given DLCI?	Use the DEBUG FRAME-RELAY EVENTS command.
How do I display debug information about packets traversing the interface?	Use the DEBUG FRAME-RELAY PACKET command.

It can get a little confusing to keep track of the array of debug commands. The previous is a consolidation of the more useful commands.

EXERCISE: 12-4

Checking That the Correct DLCI Is Assigned

You are troubleshooting a new Frame Relay installation and cannot achieve connectivity. You have ruled out cabling issues and suspect that you might have configured the subinterface with inaccurate DLCI information. Perform the following exercise to check that the DLCI assigned is the one you think it is:

1. Log on to you router. (You do not need to be in enable mode.)

2. Type **show frame-relay pvc interface serial** n x (n = interface number, x = DLCI you *think* should be there).

3. If you see output, it should indicate statistics on the DLCI and PVC.

4. If you do not see output, perform a **show frame-relay pvc interface serial** n (n = interface number) by itself.

5. You will either see nothing or a different DLCI than you expected.

CERTIFICATION OBJECTIVE 12.03

Frame Relay Symptoms, Problems, and Action Plans

Once you have isolated a problem, it is important to develop a plan of action. As with all troubleshooting, it is a good idea to take a methodical approach—take one step at a time so that you do not compound your problem by introducing errors.

Various intermittent problems and means to respond to them are outlined in Table 12-24. Problems that are occasional are often the most difficult to resolve. It is a good idea to take a step-by-step approach, documenting changes that you make and noting times and conditions when you see the problem occur.

When you see problems occurring as the load increases, as outlined in Table 12-25, it is important to rule out hardware issues before you suspect that congestion could be the problem. You can do this by taking a look at the actual byte count coming over a major interface or by looking at the load on a subinterface using the

TABLE 12-24   Action Plans for Addressing Intermittent Connectivity

Issue	Action Plan
Bad V35 cable	Check cabling by issuing a SHOW INTERFACES SERIAL command; replace if needed.
Bad CSU/DSU	Check for errors with the SHOW INTERFACES SERIAL command; swap out unit and test.
Congestion	Reduce broadcast traffic, implement queuing, increase bandwidth, improve efficiency of bandwidth usage.

TABLE 12-25	Action Plans for Addressing Connection Failures as Load Increases

Issue	Action Plan
Dirty serial line	Use the SHOW SERIAL INTERFACES command to ascertain errors; check cables and hardware.
Congestion	Analyze traffic patterns, implement priority queuing. Ultimately, the bandwidth for the PVC may need to be increased.

SHOW INTERFACES SERIAL command. In addition, if you are seeing a high number of interface resets or broadcasts, you could lean toward congestion as an issue. Table 12-26 lists the actions you could take to address congestion.

The issues outlined in Table 12-27 address some of the problems that are likely to occur and some actions that can be taken when a functioning Frame Relay network fails. Although the pressure is much greater to achieve a resolution quickly when the network is not functioning at all, it is perhaps even more important to proceed methodically.

Table 12-28 addresses a network that has never worked. Of course, any of the other problems outlined in this section of the chapter could come into play with a

TABLE 12-26	Action Plans for Addressing Connection Failures at Particular Time of Day

Issue	Action Plan
Congestion	Schedule large file transfers at low-usage times; increase bandwidth, queuing.

TABLE 12-27   Action Plans for Addressing Connection Failures After Some Period of Time

Issue	Action Plan
Unshielded cables too close to EMI source	Reroute cables.
Hardware failure	Confirm problem with loopback tests and the SHOW INTERFACES SERIAL command.
Routing convergence	Make sure routing is correct by using the SHOW IP ROUTE and SHOW IP PROTOCOL commands.
Buffer problems	Check buffer status with the SHOW BUFFERS command.
Clocking problem	Check settings of CSU/DSU and correct; check cable length. You can also set the encapsulation to HDLC to test whether or not you are running a private Frame Relay network over a point-to-point circuit.

new installation. Table 12-28 mentions the CLEAR FRAME-RELAY-INARP command. Frame Relay inverse ARP is a process that is used to discover the remote protocol address on a link. If you make changes to the subinterface configuration, you need to issue the command to change the information about the remote link that the router possesses. If you simply delete the subinterface, you need to reboot the router to completely remove the configuration.

TABLE 12-28   Action Plans for Addressing a Connection That Never Worked

Issue	Action Plan
Circuit not provisioned	Work with provider to get the circuit installed and functional.
Configuration	Review all aspects of configuration using the OSI layers as a guide.
Subinterface misconfigured	Remove the subinterface and reconfigure or issue a CLEAR FRAME-RELAY-INARP command.

SCENARIO & SOLUTION

I configured a subinterface with the wrong DLCI. How do I fix this?	Simply reconfigure the subinterface with the correct DLCI, then issue a CLEAR FRAME-RELAY INARP command
What does *inarp* mean?	It stands for *inverse ARP*. It enables Frame Relay to discover remote Layer 3 address information; it depends on the Frame Relay header to exchange protocol information.
Does inarp need to be configured?	Inverse ARP works when no specific mapping has been configured.

EXERCISE 12-5

Checking the Serial Interface for Input Errors

Because you are not seeing an inordinate amount of traffic, you have come to suspect that the "congestion" reported on your network is a hardware problem. You now want to begin the process of looking more closely at your network. The following exercise takes you through the steps of performing a SHOW INTERFACES SERIAL command.

1. Log on to your router.

2. Type **show interfaces serial***n* (*n* = number of the interface). Your screen should look something like the one shown in Figure 12-17.

3. Look at the highlighted line in Figure 12-17 and notice that there is a high number of input errors.

4. Repeat the command.

5. See if the errors are continuing to accrue. Clear counters if it makes the output easier to discern.

Using this output this way is useful in that you can get a real-time picture of what is happening on the machine. In this case, it is plain to see that there are many input errors, possibly indicating a bad serial connection.

FIGURE 12-17   Output of the SHOW SERIAL INTERFACES command

```
shoints0input errors.txt - Notepad                                    _ □ ×
File  Edit  Format  Help
Serial0 is up, line protocol is up
  Hardware is HD64570
  Description: Syngress
  MTU 1500 bytes, BW 4096 Kbit, DLY 20000 usec, rely 255/255, load 106/255
  Encapsulation FRAME-RELAY IETF, loopback not set, keepalive set (10 sec)
  LMI enq sent   9654, LMI stat recvd 9654, LMI upd recvd 63, DTE LMI up
  LMI enq recvd 0, LMI stat sent   0, LMI upd sent   0
  LMI DLCI 1023  LMI type is CISCO  frame relay DTE
  Broadcast queue 0/64, broadcasts sent/dropped 54747/0, interface broadcasts
  Last input 00:00:00, output 00:00:00, output hang never
  Last clearing of "show interface" counters 1d02h
  Queueing strategy: fifo
  Output queue 0/40, 28767 drops; input queue 19/75, 281 drops
  5 minute input rate 1178000 bits/sec, 391 packets/sec
  5 minute output rate 1716000 bits/sec, 429 packets/sec
     25815229 packets input, 3276379100 bytes, 130 no buffer
     Received 9717 broadcasts, 0 runts, 0 giants, 0 throttles
     50289879 input errors, 0 CRC, 0 frame, 250 overrun, 250 ignored, 0 abort
     26627214 packets output, 2619520363 bytes, 0 underruns
     0 output errors, 0 collisions, 0 interface resets
     0 output buffer failures, 0 output buffers swapped out
     0 carrier transitions
     DCD=up  DSR=up  DTR=up  RTS=up  CTS=upw
```

FROM THE CLASSROOM

To Subinterface or Not To Subinterface

In a discussion I had with another manager of network operations recently, he pointed out that he viewed the question of whether or not to use subinterfaces in Frame Relay networks as a "religious matter"—that the balance was about level on the question. This is simply not the case, for several reasons. When you configure a major interface with static maps—for example, interface serial0, you get the following output:

```
ip address 207.202.234.2 255.255.255.0
frame-relay-map ip 207.202.234.3 16
frame-relay-map ip 207.202.234.4 17
frame-relay-map ip 207.202.234.5 18
```

FROM THE CLASSROOM

Figure 12-18 represents how a network configuration appears when configured using the preceding configuration. The dark lines indicate PVC paths through the network. In this configuration, all PVC paths are configured on a single major interface.

There is a possibility that, depending on the protocols used, routing difficulties could arise due to split horizon. Split horizon precludes backup paths if a PVC goes away. In addition, when the Frame Relay network becomes larger, this type of configuration can become difficult to scale and manage. On the other hand, when we configure subinterfaces like this:

```
interface serial0
no ip address
encapsulation frame-relay

interface s0.16 point to point
ip address 207.202.234.1 255.255.255.252
frame-relay interface-dlci 16

interface s0.17 point to point
ip address 207.202.234.4 255.255.255.252
frame-relay interface-dlci 17

interface s0.18 point to point
ip address 207.202.234.9 255.255.255.252
frame-relay interface-dlci 18
```

Figure 12-19 displays a network that is using subinterfaces. Now, even though the major interface is still in use, it is separated into subinterfaces. These are seen by routing protocols as distinct interfaces. You now have separate point-to-point networks connecting the routers. Again, Figure 12-19 represents the PVC paths only.

This configuration allows for configuration of multiple point-to-point networks on the same physical channel. It is routable, scalable, friendly to routing protocols, and arguably easier to troubleshoot. If you are concerned about IP address usage, you can set up unnumbered interfaces to conserve address space. Finally, subinterfaces allow greater freedom in Frame Relay network design because each PVC can have more distinct qualities.

—Nick Guy, CCNP, MCSE

FIGURE 12-18

A Frame Relay
network using
single interface

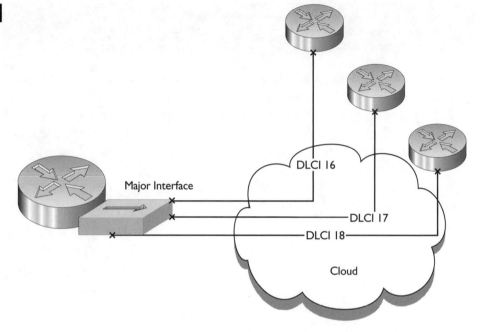

FIGURE 12-19

A Frame Relay
network using
subinterfaces

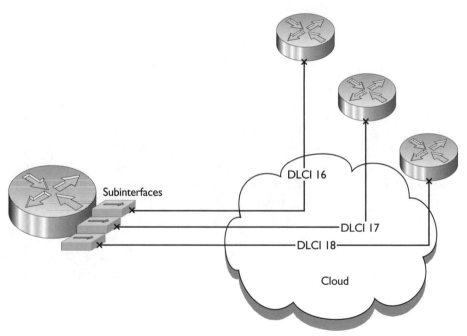

CERTIFICATION SUMMARY

This chapter addressed many aspects of what can go wrong with an installation of Frame Relay. The chapter also addressed some strategies and described tools that can be used to address and troubleshoot problems when they occur.

The importance of being able to clearly diagnose Frame Relay problems cannot be overemphasized. If you are successful and accurate when it comes to troubleshooting problems within your network, your ability to resolve problems in your partnership with your provider will increase and your customers will experience less downtime.

TWO-MINUTE DRILL

Here are some of the key points from each certification objective in Chapter 12.

Frame Relay Diagnostic Tools

❑ The SHOW INTERFACES SERIAL command can be used to troubleshoot Layer 1 and Layer 2 problems.

❑ The SHOW FRAME-RELAY LMI command lets you view LMI statistics. Is your router talking to the switch?

❑ The SHOW FRAME-RELAY PVC command lets you look at LMI information for individual PVCs.

❑ The SHOW FRAME-RELAY MAP command lets you observe Layer 2 to Layer 3 mapping.

❑ The SHOW CONTROLLERS SERIAL command displays information about cables attached to the interface.

Problem Isolation in Frame Relay WANs

❑ Make sure that your cables are good.

❑ Use the SHOW INTERFACES SERIAL command to check your hardware.

❑ Use the SHOW FRAME-RELAY LMI command to confirm that the DLCIs match PVC output.

❑ Use the SHOW FRAME-RELAY MAP command to check Layer 2 to Layer 3 mapping.

❑ Use the PING command to check router-to-router Layer 3 connectivity.

Frame Relay Symptoms, Problems, and Action Plans

❑ If your lines are congested, you need to manage traffic and priority queues or find a way to increase bandwidth.

❑ If the connection has never worked, you quite likely need to get in touch with your provider.

❑ If you suspect a timing problem, check your CSU/DSU.

❑ Use the SHOW INTERFACES SERIAL command to check for possible hardware problems.

❑ If routing is broken, use a combination of PING and loopback tests.

SELF TEST

The following questions will help you measure your understanding of the material presented in this chapter. Read all of the choices carefully because there might be more than one correct answer. Choose all correct answers for each question.

Frame Relay Diagnostic Tools

1. Which of the following identifiers is used to distinguish software-defined logical connections that are established permanently?

   A. PVC

   B. DLCI

   C. LMI

   D. IETF

2. You are setting up a new Frame Relay network and have determined that the router at the other side of the link is configured with the default Cisco Frame Relay encapsulation. You issue the SHOW INTERFACES SERIAL command and receive the output shown in Figure 12-20.

FIGURE 12-20   Output of SHOW INTERFACES SERIAL command

```
shoints0question2.txt - Notepad
File  Edit  Format  Help

Serial0 is up, line protocol is down
  Hardware is HD64570
  Description: Syngress
  MTU 1500 bytes, BW 4096 Kbit, DLY 20000 usec, rely 255/255, load 1/255
  Encapsulation FRAME-RELAY IETF, loopback not set, keepalive set (10 sec)
  LMI enq sent  9654, LMI stat recvd 9654, LMI upd recvd 63, DTE LMI up
  LMI enq recvd 0, LMI stat sent  0, LMI upd sent  0
  LMI DLCI 1023  LMI type is CISCO  frame relay DTE
  Broadcast queue 0/64, broadcasts sent/dropped 54747/0, interface broadcasts 41880
  Last input 00:00:00, output 00:00:00, output hang never
  Last clearing of "show interface" counters 1d02h
  Queueing strategy: fifo
  Output queue 0/40, 0 drops; input queue 19/75, 0 drops
  5 minute input rate 0 bits/sec, 0 packets/sec
  5 minute output rate 0 bits/sec, 0 packets/sec
     0 packets input, 0 bytes, 0 no buffer
     Received 0 broadcasts, 0 runts, 0 giants, 0 throttles
     0 input errors, 0 CRC, 0 frame, 0 overrun, 0 ignored, 0 abort
     0 packets output, 0 bytes, 0 underruns
     0 output errors, 0 collisions, 0 interface resets
     0 output buffer failures, 0 output buffers swapped out
```

What is the best action to take to resolve the problem?

A. Log on to the router and clear the counters in order to see how traffic is incrementing.

B. Log on to the router and run a FRAME-RELAY LMI-TYPE command to resolve the problem.

C. Log on to the router, get into enable mode, interface config depending on mapping preferences, and change the encapsulation.

D. Call the Frame Relay provider and inform it that its line is down and that it needs to fix the line before you can continue.

3. What are valid LMI types? Choose all that apply.

A. Adtran

B. Cisco

C. q931

D. VTY100

E. ANSI

F. q933a

4. What DLCI does the Cisco LMI type use?

A. 0

B. 1023

C. 900

D. 999

5. Your team is troubleshooting a Frame Relay installation, and you see no active DLCIs when you issue a SHOW FRAME-RELAY PVC command. After looping your CSU/DSU locally, you start to see DLCI information. Which of the following actions should you take next?

A. Check your V.35 cable for problems

B. Check for router interface/hardware problems

C. Call your provider

D. Check your CSU/DSU

6. What version of the Cisco IOS will autosense LMI? Choose all that apply.

A. 11.2

B. 12.0

C. 10.2

D. 11.1

7. You are trying to establish why your network is getting intermittent connectivity at 8:00 a.m., just at the time when people are coming in to work. You suspect that problem is that everyone coming in to the office is checking their e-mail and temporarily oversubscribing the serial line. What are some steps you could take to improve the situation? Choose all that apply.

A. Set up priority queuing on the router.

B. Schedule file transfers and other network traffic at times when the network is a little less busy.

C. Increase the bandwidth that your Frame Relay network is using.

D. Schedule e-mail-related activity for later in the day.

8. You are looking at the output of the SHOW FRAME-RELAY PVC command when you notice that you are getting rather a lot of packets with the FECN bit set. What does this mean?

A. There is congestion in the direction in which traffic is heading.

B. There is congestion in the direction in which traffic is not heading.

C. You need more bandwidth.

D. You need to institute priority queuing.

Problem Isolation in Frame Relay WANs

9. You suspect that the reason your installation of a Frame Relay circuit is not going well is due to an inaccurate DLCI assigned to the PVC with which you are working. What are some steps that you could take to take care of the problem? Choose all that apply.

A. Log on to your router and issue a SHOW FRAME-RELAY PVC command to see whether or not the correct DLCI is indeed associated with the circuit.

B. Log on to your router and issue a DEBUG FRAME-RELAY LMI command to get DLCI information.

C. Log on to you router and issue a SHOW INTERFACES SERIAL command.

D. Log on to you router and issue a SHOW FRAME-RELAY INTERFACE-DLCI MISMATCH command.

10. You want to determine whether or not you have a noisy or otherwise intermittently faulty serial line connection. You want to get more information about the situation. Which of the following is the most useful first step to take?

    A. Replace the suspect cable with another one and see if the problem goes away.

    B. Examine the configuration of all the other equipment on the line—CSU/DSUs, routers, switches—in a methodical manner.

    C. Log on to you router and issue a SHOW INTERFACES SERIAL command and examine the input errors.

    D. Disconnect the cable and test it with a breakout box.

11. Which of the following could cause a problem with Layer 3 traffic?

    A. Bad timing on the circuit

    B. Misconfigured access list

    C. Noisy serial cable

    D. Faulty CSU/DSU

12. You have finished your configuration of your Frame Relay WAN installation and would like to see if the remote side of the cloud is able to communicate with the equipment on the local side. You have already established that both sides have "serial up" and "line protocol up." What is the next step?

    A. Issue the DEBUG FRAME-RELAY PACKET command on the router to determine if you are getting traffic.

    B. Issue a DEBUG FRAME-RELAY LMI command to see if you are getting LMI from the router on the other side of the link.

    C. Ping the interface on the other side.

    D. Issue a SHOW FRAME-RELAY REMOTE command.

13. You are getting intermittent connectivity. Which of the following could cause the problem? Choose all that apply.

    A. Congested/overutilized serial line

    B. Faulty router hardware

    C. Timing problems

    D. Noise from equipment or other lines

14. Your Frame Relay network has been working without fail and suddenly ceases to function. It has fallen to you to troubleshoot the connection. Assuming that you have already established that you cannot ping across the WAN connection, what would you do next? 1: Check that the physical link is OK. 2: Check that the remote side of the connection is OK. 3: Check that your Layer 2 to Layer 3 mapping is OK. 4: Check PVC configuration. Select the sequence of steps that would most effectively address the problem.

    A. 1, 2, 3, 4

    B. 3, 1, 4, 2

    C. 4, 1, 3, 2

    D. 1, 2, 4, 3

Frame Relay Symptoms, Problems, and Action Plans

15. You have problems with your connections failing over the Frame Relay interface when the load increases. What could you do when the problem is occurring to help diagnose the cause of the failure?

    A. Issue a DEBUG FRAME-RELAY EVENTS command to ascertain whether or not you are getting consistent traffic over the connection.

    B. Issue a SHOW *PROTOCOL* ROUTE command to see whether or not you are getting congestion-oriented routing failure.

    C. Issue a SHOW SERIAL INTERFACES command and watch for input errors.

    D. Issue a SHOW CONTROLLERS V.35 command to see whether or not there are cable errors.

16. What is an appropriate command to use to investigate possible routing abnormalities on your Frame Relay network? Choose all that apply.

    A. SHOW IP ROUTE

    B. SHOW INTERFACE STATUS

    C. SHOW IP INTERFACES BRIEF

    D. SHOW IP PROTOCOL

    E. SHOW IP ACCESS-LIST

17. You need to troubleshoot a connection that appears to be a problem with the Frame Relay portion of the link. You want to observe data regarding the yourseen element. What do you do next to continue the troubleshooting process?

    A. Issue a DEBUG FRAME-RELAY LMI command to observe keepalive information.

    B. Issue a DEBUG FRAME-RELAY EVENTS to measure LMI traffic.

    C. Issue a DEBUG FRAME-RELAY PACKET to measure packet loss.

    D. Issue a DEBUG SERIAL INTERFACE to see if keepalives increment.

18. You have been troubleshooting your Frame Relay network and have determined that there is a configuration problem on the local router. That configuration problem is that the relevant subinterface has been misconfigured and refers to the wrong DLCI. In order to fix the problem, what must you do? Choose all that apply.

    A. Simply change the DLCI reference to reflect the correct DLCI.

    B. Remove the subinterface and add it back in with the correct information.

    C. Issue a CLEAR IP command.

    D. Replace the DLCI on the subinterface and issue a CLEAR FRAME-RELAY-INARP command.

19. As part of your plan to respond to a congested network, you want to see whether or not LMI exchanges are being adversely affected. What is the best debug command to use?

    A. DEBUG FRAME-RELAY EVENTS

    B. DEBUG FRAME-RELAY LMI

    C. DEBUG FRAME-RELAY PACKET

    D. DEBUG INTERFACE SERIAL

20. What is a DTE?

    A. A CSU/DSU

    B. A V.35 cable

    C. A router interface

    D. An NIU

FIGURE 12-21 Lab setup

Serial Interface   Serial Interface

Router 1   ×————————— V.35 DCE/DTE Cable —————————×   Router 2

LAB QUESTION

It is rather difficult to simulate problems with a production Frame Relay network without affecting your customers or workers adversely. It is a good thing to be able to look at various problems in a lab setting so that when you encounter various problems on a production network, you will have some familiarity with how particular problems presents themselves. This exercise simulates a private Frame Relay network using two Cisco routers. Please refer to Figure 12-21 for the setup of this lab.

1. Obtain two Cisco routers and a DTE/DCE cable. (This type of cable is available from any outlet that sells Cisco cables.)

2. Connect the routers; plug the DTE end into one Serial 0 interface and the DCE end into the Serial 0 interface of the other router.

3. Using a Cisco management cable or Ethernet connection, configure each router to the specifications in Table 12-29.

4. At this point, you should be able to bring up each subinterface, serial0.1, on both routers.

TABLE 12-29   Lab Router Configuration

Router 1 (DTE cable) Frame-Relay switching interface Serial0 no ip address encapsulation Frame-Relay Frame-Relay intf-type dce Frame-Relay lmi-type cisco interface Serial0.1 point-to-point ip address 192.168.1.1 255.255.255.252 Frame-Relay interface-dlci 16	Router 2 (DCE cable) interface Serial0 no ip address encapsulation Frame-Relay clockrate 64000 interface Serial0.1 point-to-point ip address 192.168.1.2 255.255.255.252 Frame-Relay interface-dlci 16

5. Issue a SHOW INTERFACES SERIAL 0 on either router and note the output.

6. Issue a SHUTDOWN command on the router opposite from the one on which you issued a SHOW SERIAL INTERFACES SERIAL 0 command.

7. Reissue the SHOW INTERFACES SERIAL 0 command on the original router and note the output.

   What, if anything, has changed about the output, and why?

SELF TEST ANSWERS

Frame Relay Diagnostic Tools

1. ☑ **B.** DLCI, which stands for Data Link Connection Identifier, is used to identify the individual logical connections or PVCs and SVCs within a Frame Relay network.
    ☒ **A** is incorrect because PVC refers to the actual virtual circuit, not its identifier. **C** is incorrect because LMI refers to the Local Management Interface. **D** is incorrect because IETF stands for the Internet Engineering Task Force, which sets various Internet-related standards.

2. ☑ **C.** Log on to the router, get into enable mode, interface config depending on mapping preferences, and change the encapsulation. The output shows that the Frame Relay encapsulation type is IETF. If the other side of the connection were not specifically configured as IETF, chances are you will not have a useful connection.
    ☒ **A** is incorrect because the counters have yet to increment anything, which tells you something but not enough to warrant issuing the command. **B** is incorrect because you won't get any LMI when line protocol is down. **D** is incorrect because you will not win many friends at your provider if you take this action.

3. ☑ **B, E,** and **F.** Cisco, ANSI, and q933aare the three LMI types that are in use. The most common is Cisco, followed by ANSI and q933a, to a lesser degree.
    ☒ **A** is incorrect because Adtran manufactures CSU/DSUs. **C** is incorrect because q931 is used to look at B-channel information on Integrated Services Digital Network (ISDN) connections. **D** is incorrect because VTY100 is a type of screen emulation.

4. ☑ **B.** The 1023 DLCI is used by the Cisco application of LMI.
    ☒ **A** is incorrect because DLCI 0 is used by ANSI and q933a. **C** and **D** are incorrect because DLCI 900 and 999 are not reserved DLCIs for any LMI type.

5. ☑ **C.** Call your provider.
    ☒ **A, B,** and **D** are essentially ruled out if you can see DLCI information after you put the CSU/DSU into a loop. This is so because you have established that there is a reasonable chance that the cables are good and that the other hardware is in good shape, since you have been able to "bounce" traffic off the local side of the CSU/DSU.

6. ☑ **A** and **B.** 11.2 and 12.0. Cisco routers running an IOS of 11.2 or later will autosense LMI.
    ☒ **C** and **D** are incorrect because 10.2 and 11.1 are earlier versions than 11.2.

7. ☑ **A.** Set up priority queuing on the router. This answer is correct and is designed for burst situations.

☒ **B** is incorrect because it would be difficult to implement without negatively affecting the people on the LAN. **C** is not a good solution because the congestion is only at one part of the day and could be addressed with queuing. **D** is incorrect because scheduling e-mail activity is not realistically workable.

8. ☑ **A.** There is congestion in the direction in which traffic is heading. Forward Explicit Congestion Notification (FECN) is a notification that informs the DTE device that congestion was encountered en route in the same direction as the frame was traveling.

☒ **B** is incorrect because if the Backward Explicit Congestion Notification (BECN) bit was set it would indicate that there was congestion in the direction opposite to the path of the frame. **C** and **D** are incorrect because you do not need more bandwidth or queuing because these notifications are from the Frame Relay network itself to assist upper layer protocols with flow control.

Problem Isolation in Frame Relay WANs

9. ☑ **A and B.** Log on to your router and issue a SHOW FRAME-RELAY PVC command to see whether or not the correct DLCI is indeed associated with the circuit, and log on to your router and issue a DEBUG FRAME-RELAY LMI command to get DLCI information. You should be able to see whether or not the suspect DLCI is indeed associated with the circuit, and you should see information about the pertinent DLCI in the output.

☒ **C** is incorrect because SHOW INTERFACE SERIAL will not give you information about DLCIs on the interface except those associated with various LMI types. **D** is incorrect because SHOW FRAME-RELAY INTERFACE-DLCI MISMATCH is a made-up command.

10. ☑ **C.** Log on to you router and issue a SHOW INTERFACES SERIAL command and examine the input errors. This is the least invasive first step, and the input errors will indicate whether or not you are having any problems with the line.

☒ **A** might work but would not rule out interference from nearby equipment and will bring the line down. **B** and **D** are also things that you could do, but they would not be the *first* thing you would do.

11. ☑ **B.** An access list error could easily cause the router to drop packets. This is easily mistaken for other problems.

☒ **A** is incorrect because bad timing would cause global connection problems. **C** and **D** are also incorrect because they are likely to be Layer 1 or 2 problems, not Layer 3.

12. ☑ **C.** Ping the interface on the other side. This question is a little bit tricky but, given that the line and serial are up, why not simply ping and be done with it?

☒ **A** is incorrect because it is overkill to try this command before a ping. **B** is incorrect because LMI does not come from the router on the other side of the link; it originates locally. **D** is incorrect because it is an invalid command.

13. ☑ **A, B, C,** and **D.** All these could cause problems that could be sporadic.

☒ There are no incorrect choices.

14. ☑ **D.** 1, 2, 4, 3. It makes sense to first check the physical connection, then to do the same on the other side of the link.

☒ **A** is incorrect because you would check the layer information, the PVC, before looking at the Layer 3 information. **B** is incorrect because you could not check Layer 2 or 3 before checking the remote side. **C** is incorrect because you would not check the PVC configuration before checking the cable.

Frame Relay Symptoms, Problems, and Action Plans

15. ☑ **C.** Issue a SHOW SERIAL INTERFACES command and watch for input errors. You can see input errors accumulating if you have a dirty serial line, and you will likely see other errors such as CRC errors.

☒ **A** is incorrect because there is no real correlation between Frame Relay events and load-induced failure; it just tells you packets are coming in. **B** is incorrect because this is not a routing issue. **D** is total fantasy, although it would be nice.

16. ☑ **A, C, D,** and **E.**

☒ **B** is incorrect because SHOW INTERFACE STATUS only gives up/down and caching information.

17. ☑ **D.** Issue a DEBUG SERIAL INTERFACE to see if keepalives increment. This command enables you to see the yourseen keepalive sequences over the interface.

☒ **A, B,** and **C** are incorrect because they do not display the keepalive data.

18. ☑ **D.** Replace the DLCI on the subinterface and issue a CLEAR FRAME-RELAY-INARP command. This action will clear the entries in the router's inverse ARP table and cause the router to remap its DLCI to interface mappings.

☒ **A** is incorrect because you run the risk of not actually changing the mapping. **B** is incorrect because you need to reboot the router to completely remove the subinterface information. **C** is incorrect because there is no such command as CLEAR IP.

19. ☑ **B.** DEBUG FRAME-RELAY LMI will show you LMI information and whether keepalives are incrementing.

 ☒ **A** is incorrect because DEBUG FRAME-RELAY EVENTS looks at all packets received and is not specifically focused on LMI. **C** and **D** are incorrect for similar reasons—DEBUG FRAME-RELAY PACKET and DEBUG INTERFACE SERIAL look at all packets traversing the Frame Relay interface.

20. ☑ **C.** A router interface. In a standard Frame Relay implementation, the router interface plays the role of the data terminating equipment (DTE).

 ☒ **A** is incorrect because a CSU/DSU does not terminate data; it is more like a modem. **B** is incorrect because, although a V.35 can affect the interface, the DTE is still the interface. **D** is incorrect because an NIU is your connection to the provider network.

LAB ANSWER

Figure 12-22 shows the output before the opposite interface is put into shutdown or administrative mode. Both the serial and line protocol are up.

FIGURE 12-22 Output before shutdown

```
noshut.txt - Notepad                                                    _ □ ×
File  Edit  Format  Help
Serial0 is up, line protocol is up
  Hardware is HD64570
  MTU 1500 bytes, BW 1544 Kbit, DLY 20000 usec,
      reliability 254/255, txload 1/255, rxload 1/255
  Encapsulation FRAME-RELAY, loopback not set
  Keepalive not set
  Restart-Delay is 0 secs
  Broadcast queue 0/64, broadcasts sent/dropped 439/139, interface broadcasts 14
  Last input 02:07:16, output 00:00:21, output hang never
  Last clearing of "show interface" counters 1d02h
  Queueing strategy: fifo
  Output queue 0/40, 0 drops; input queue 0/75, 0 drops
  5 minute input rate 0 bits/sec, 0 packets/sec
  5 minute output rate 0 bits/sec, 0 packets/sec
     444 packets input, 83250 bytes, 0 no buffer
     Received 0 broadcasts, 0 runts, 0 giants, 0 throttles
     1 input errors, 1 CRC, 0 frame, 0 overrun, 0 ignored, 1 abort
     1210 packets output, 148401 bytes, 0 underruns
     0 output errors, 0 collisions, 2620 interface resets
     0 output buffer failures, 0 output buffers swapped out
     416 carrier transitions
     DCD=up  DSR=up  DTR=up  RTS=up  CTS=up
```

Note that, now that the remote interface has been shut down, the local interface also drops. The serial interface drops because the remote interface is shut down and not available. The line protocol also drops because the remote serial interface is unavailable.

This exercise is intended to give you a sense of the testing scenarios you can simulate with a lab setup like the one displayed in Figure 12-23. Most of the situations covered in this chapter can be emulated.

FIGURE 12-23   Output after shutdown

```
Serial0 is down, line protocol is down
  Hardware is HD64570
  MTU 1500 bytes, BW 1544 Kbit, DLY 20000 usec,
     reliability 255/255, txload 1/255, rxload 1/255
  Encapsulation FRAME-RELAY, loopback not set
  Keepalive not set
  Restart-Delay is 0 secs
  Broadcast queue 0/64, broadcasts sent/dropped 436/137, interface broadcasts 14
  Last input 02:04:45, output 00:08:54, output hang never
  Last clearing of "show interface" counters 1d02h
  Queueing strategy: fifo
  Output queue 0/40, 0 drops; input queue 0/75, 0 drops
  5 minute input rate 0 bits/sec, 0 packets/sec
  5 minute output rate 0 bits/sec, 0 packets/sec
     442 packets input, 82694 bytes, 0 no buffer
     Received 0 broadcasts, 0 runts, 0 giants, 0 throttles
     0 input errors, 0 CRC, 0 frame, 0 overrun, 0 ignored, 0 abort
     1207 packets output, 147540 bytes, 0 underruns
     0 output errors, 0 collisions, 2620 interface resets
     0 output buffer failures, 0 output buffers swapped out
     415 carrier transitions
     DCD=down  DSR=down  DTR=up  RTS=up  CTS=down
```

13

Diagnosing and Correcting ISDN Problems

CERTIFICATION OBJECTIVES

I ntegrated Services Digital Network (ISDN) has become one of the more popular WAN technologies since its rise in the early 1990s. Both large corporations and small offices/home offices (SOHOs) alike take advantage of ISDN's flexibility to fulfill a variety of WAN needs. Three markets in particular fuel the demand for ISDN services. First, ISDN is an excellent backup technology for primary WAN links such as Frame Relay; it can be used on demand in case of failure or overload. Second, ISDN offers a good price-to-performance ratio to the small business market, for intermittent connectivity to headquarters locations as well as the Internet. Finally, ISDN has been the method of choice for telecommuters whose bandwidth requirements often exceed the capabilities of the analog modem for dial-up access to corporate networks. Even though ISDN now faces fierce competition from new technologies such as xDSL and cable modems, its flexibility and its large installed base ensure a place for ISDN in the network infrastructure of the future.

CERTIFICATION OBJECTIVE 13.01

BRI Overview

ISDN provides high-speed data, voice, and video communication over conventional plain old telephone service (POTS) phone lines. It does so on a "per call" basis, just as a standard phone does. You can place a data "call" to your office and disconnect when you are finished. Typically, you are charged only for the time the line is in use, making ISDN very cost effective. And unlike most other WAN technologies, ISDN devices can call different locations from the same line. For example, after calling the office, you can disconnect and place a new call to the Internet. This combination of features makes ISDN the most flexible WAN technology available.

If ISDN and analog modems both use POTS, what makes ISDN so much faster than analog? The answer is simple: ISDN communications are completely digital, from end to end. Standard modem signals are analog to the telephone company central office (CO), where they are converted to digital. These analog signals use pulse-code modulation (PCM), just as regular phone conversations do, and significant overhead is involved in converting PCM to digital signaling—hence the slower speeds. ISDN's pure digital signaling allows it to attain speeds more than twice those of conventional dialup modems. Figure 13-1 illustrates the difference between the two technologies.

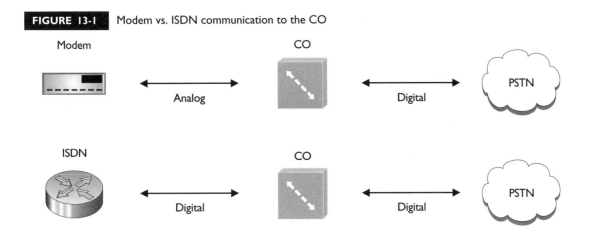

FIGURE 13-1 Modem vs. ISDN communication to the CO

Once ISDN traffic arrives at the CO, it moves onto the public switched telephone network (PSTN), where it is delivered to its destination using the Signaling System 7 (SS7) signaling protocols, just like any other phone conversation. The ISDN interface to the CO is called basic rate interface, or BRI.

2B+D = 3 DS0s

The ISDN BRI standard, originally devised by the International Telecommunications Union-Telecommunications (ITU-T) specification in 1968, uses time division multiplexing (TDM) to define three distinct channels: two Bearer (B) channels and one D channel. The B channels operate at 64KB/s each; the D channel operates at 16KB/s. In addition, 48KB/s are used for Physical Layer maintenance (bit synchronization and the like), bringing the total to 192KB/s—or three DS0s (DS0 stands for *digital signal zero*). These channels are commonly referred to as *2B+D*.

ISDN also defines another standard: primary rate interface (PRI). PRI operates over T1 circuits (DS1), which include (in North America) 24 channels: 23 64KB/s B channels and 1 64KB/s D channel. In Europe, PRI includes 30 64KB/s B channels and 1 64KB/s D channel. This chapter, however, focuses on troubleshooting ISDN BRI only.

Differences Between B Channels and the D Channel

The BRI B channels carry user traffic—data, voice, and/or video—and can reach speeds of up to 128KB/s. Usually, the B channels are encapsulated using Point-to-Point Protocol (PPP), although the Cisco proprietary High-Level Data Link Control (HDLC) is also sometimes used. Communication over the B channels does not begin until a call is established via the D channel.

The D channel carries link establishment, call setup, call maintenance, and call teardown traffic utilizing the Q.921 and Q.931 protocols. When an ISDN device is plugged in, it establishes communication with the CO via a D channel. Later, when a call is placed, call setup is established over the D channel. The D channel is relatively quiet during a call, but it comes alive again when a call is ended, negotiating the call teardown phase.

The differences between the B and D channels are summarized in Table 13-1.

ISDN and the OSI Model

The ISDN D channel maps to the first three layers of the OSI model, as shown in Figure 13-2 and described in the following list:

- ISDN Layer 1 is similar to the OSI Physical Layer; it describes the line coding and framing of ISDN data at the physical (electrical) level. It is described by ITU recommendation I.430 and covers communication between the S/T interface and the NT1.

- ISDN Layer 2 correlates roughly with the OSI Data Link layer; it utilizes the Link Access Procedure D-Channel (LAPD) protocol, described by ITU recommendation Q.921. LAPD is derived from HDLC, another WAN data

TABLE 13-1   Differences Between B and D Channels

Channel	Bandwidth (KB/s)	Protocols	Function
B	64	PPP, HDLC	Voice, video, data
D	16	Q.921, Q.931	Call maintenance, data link setup

FIGURE 13-2   ISDN layers mapped to the OSI model

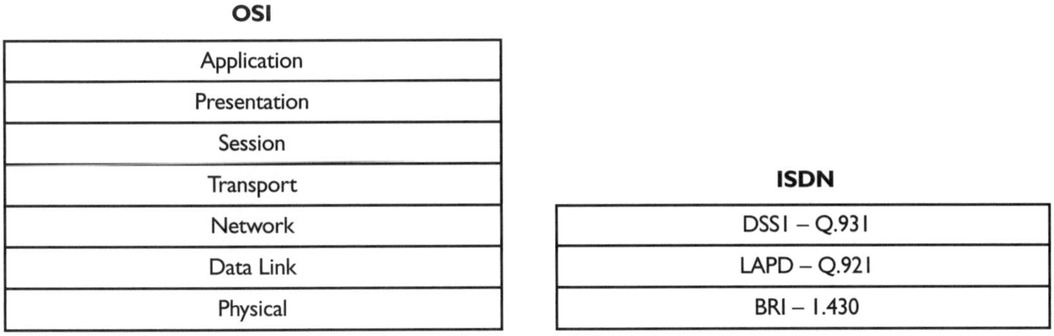

OSI

Application
Presentation
Session
Transport
Network
Data Link
Physical

ISDN

DSS1 – Q.931
LAPD – Q.921
BRI – I.430

link protocol, and is closely related to Link Access Procedure Balanced, or LAPB (used in X.25), and Link Access Procedures to Frame, or LAPF (used in Frame Relay).

■ ISDN Layer 3 maps to the OSI Network Layer and uses the Digital Subscriber Signaling System 1 (DSS1) protocol (or a portion thereof) and is described by ITU recommendation Q.931.

It is important to remember that the ISDN Layer 2 and 3 protocols (Q.921 and Q.931) operate only on the D channel. The B channels use standard WAN protocols (such as PPP). *Note:* Q.921 and Q.931 are the ITU specifications on the use of LAPD and DSS1 protocols, respectively. Most technical texts, however, refer to Q.921 and Q.931 as the protocols themselves. For the sake of clarity and consistency, this text follows the latter course.

EXERCISE 13-1

Troubleshooting Basic ISDN Connectivity

A client contacts you with an ISDN problem. The client is installing a new ISDN connection to back up a T1, and she cannot get the router to initiate a call. At your instruction, the client types **show isdn status** and reports the following output:

```
Router#sh isdn st
Global ISDN Switchtype = basic-dms100
ISDN BRI1/0 interface
        dsl 8, interface ISDN Switchtype = basic-dms100
```

```
Layer 1 Status:
    DEACTIVATED
Layer 2 Status:
    Layer 2 NOT Activated
Spid Status:
    TEI Not Assigned, ces = 1, state = 1(terminal down)
        spid1 configured, no LDN, spid1 NOT sent, spid1 NOT valid
Layer 3 Status:
    0 Active Layer 3 Call(s)
```

Which of the following could be the problem?

1. Configuration of service profile identifiers (SPIDs)

2. Configuration of PPP authentication

3. Configuration of routing protocols

4. The ISDN cable

Solution: The correct answer is 4: the ISDN cable is bad. Note in the output that LAYER 1 STATUS = DEACTIVATED; therefore, the problem is at Layer 1. Only Answer 4 could cause Layer 1 to go down. Answers 1 and 2, configuration of SPIDs and PPP uthentication, are required for Layer 2 and 3 call activation, and Answer 3, configuration of routing protocols, is required to initiate a call.

CERTIFICATION OBJECTIVE 13.02

ISDN Reference Points

ITU-T standards define specific device types in an ISDN network as well as the communication links—called *reference points*—that connect these devices. The following devices are defined:

- **Terminal endpoint 1 (TE1)**   An ISDN-aware device that communicates using ISDN protocols. A Cisco router with a BRI interface is a TE1.

- **Terminal endpoint 2 (TE2)**   A non-ISDN aware device such as a PC.
- **Terminal adapter (TA)**   A device that connects a TE2 to an ISDN network.
- **Network termination unit 2 (NT2)**   A customer premises ISDN switch, an NT2 can connect multiple TEs to a single ISDN link. A PBX commonly functions as an NT2.
- **Network termination unit 1 (NT1)**   An ISDN-specific device that converts the four-wire cable used by the customer to the two-wire facility used by the telephone company local loop. In North America, the NT1 is the demarc point; in Europe, it usually resides at the CO.
- **Line termination (LT)**   A CO device that functions similarly to the NT1.
- **Exchange termination (ET)**   The ISDN switch at the phone company.

Figure 13-3 illustrates the classical ISDN configuration. Figures 13-4 and 13-5 show common configurations you are most likely to see in the field. These figures also include the reference points, which are discussed in the next section.

FIGURE 13-3   A classical ISDN configuration

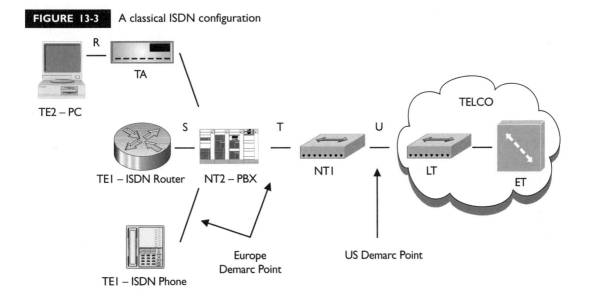

FIGURE 13-4 A small office ISDN configuration

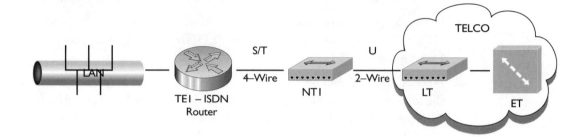

The reference points are the interfaces between the various device types and are specifically defined by the ITU-T standard as follows:

- **U** The U (User) reference point covers communication between the NT1 and the LT over existing phone company two-wire cabling. The ITU has not defined a standard for the U interface; in North America, it is defined by the American National Standards Institute (ANSI) and uses 2B1Q line coding. Europe's standard is similar but uses 4B3T line coding.

- **S/T** The ITU defines the S (System) reference point as the interface between a TE1 (or TA) and the NT2, where the T (Terminal) reference point connects the NT1 and NT2. However, the two points use the same signaling and are frequently combined into one device (an S/T interface). An example of such a device was shown in Figure 13-4.

FIGURE 13-5 A residential ISDN connection to the Internet

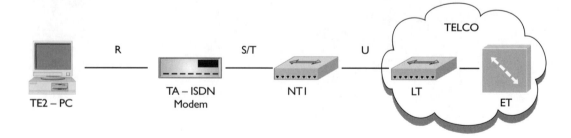

■ **R** The R (Reference) point is the interface between a TE2 and a TA. It can use a variety of standard physical-layer communication protocols, such as V.35, V.24, and EIA/TIA-232-C.

EXERCISE 13-2

ISDN Reference Points

A client in Atlanta calls you with a question about an ISDN router he just received. His office in London, where the router was previously in use, sent it to his office. It has an S/T interface and a U interface, but the engineer is not sure which one to plug into their NT1—or if either one will work at all. What do you think?

Solution: Use the S/T interface and it should work fine. Remember the following two points about North American and European ISDN:

■ In North America, the NT1 is on-site and provides an S/T interface to the customer's router. In Europe, there is no NT1 at the customer site; the S/T interface is provided directly to the customer.

■ The S/T interface is an accepted standard throughout the world. However, the U interface has no accepted standard; different versions are in use in Europe and North America.

CERTIFICATION OBJECTIVE 13.03

The ISDN S/T Interface

As previously stated, the S/T interface is a four-wire connection from the customer ISDN device(s) to the NT1. Defined by the ISO8877 standard, the S/T interface is similar to a standard twisted-pair LAN cable with an RJ-45 connector. The two pairs of wires are twisted together to minimize crosstalk.

FROM THE CLASSROOM

The CO ISDN Switch

The CO switch runs special software that allows it to act as an ISDN BRI switch. Unfortunately, the various ISDN switch vendors chose to implement the ISDN standard in various ways. The result is differing and incompatible communication methods. As a result, you must configure the switch type in the Cisco router.

The IOS configuration commands to configure your switch type are as follows:

```
router4#config term
router4#(config) isdn switch-type your-switch-type
```

Your ISDN service provider must supply the SWITCH-TYPE parameter. If it is necessary to change your switch type after the initial configuration, be aware that a reload of the router is also necessary. In addition, keep in mind that the Cisco IOS can support multiple ISDN switch types on the same router if you are running IOS 11.3T or higher code. In this case, enter an ISDN SWITCH-TYPE command in global configuration mode (as just shown), and configure different switch types on a per-interface basis.

Be aware that the SWITCH-TYPE entered in this command is a software setting and is not necessarily the same as the hardware or vendor of the actual switch. In North America, the most common BRI switch types are the basic-5ess, the basic-dms100, and the basic-ni1. In Europe, the most common BRI switch type is the basic-net3.

There are a few major differences, and many minor ones, among the various vendors' ISDN switch implementations. The most noticeable is the requirement (or lack thereof) of SPIDs to be configured on your end. The basic-ni1 and basic-dms100 switches generally require them, whereas the basic-5ess varies. In Europe, the basic-net3 almost never requires SPIDs. Other differences include the use of endpoint identifiers (by basic-ni1 and basic-5ess) and the different methods of handling orphan terminal endpoint identifiers (TEIs) after a link goes down.

—Don Dettmore, CCNP, MCSE, CNE

The pin-outs, as well as their usage, are depicted in Figure 13-6. The primary pins used are 3–6, which alternate positive and negative charges. As current flows into the positive line, it flows out of the negative, maintaining no net charge.

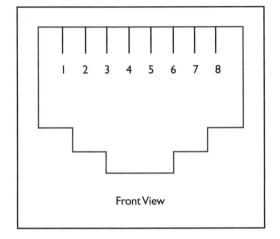

FIGURE 13-6   ISDN RJ-45 connector and pin-outs

Front View

Pin	Function
1	Power +
2	Power –
3	TE –> NT +
4	NT –> TE +
5	NT –> TE –
6	TE –> NT –
7	Power –
8	Power +

EXERCISE 13-3

ISDN Cabling

Scenario: A client calls you with an ISDN cabling emergency. A worker accidentally cut the cable that connects the ISDN router and the NT1. It is a high-priority line, and they would like you on site immediately to make a new cable. What do you tell them?

Solution: Tell them to relax. A standard straight-through LAN cable (RJ45 twisted pair) works just fine.

CERTIFICATION OBJECTIVE 13.04

ISDN S/T Line Framing

At the physical level, an ISDN S/T interface frame is 48 bits long and is transmitted 4000 times per second, for a total bandwidth of 192KB/s (48 bits/frame * 4000 frames/sec = 192KB/sec). The breakdown of a frame is shown in Table 13-2.

TABLE 13-2	Data	Bits/Frame	Total Bandwidth (in KB/s)
Frame Breakdown	B channel 1	16	64
	B channel 2	16	64
	D channel	4	16
	Physical Layer maintenance	12	48

ISDN uses alternate mark inversion (AMI) signaling, meaning that a 1 is transmitted by a lack of a charge and a 0 is transmitted by alternating positive and negative charges. The frame differs slightly in format, depending on which way it is traveling. For example, NT-to-TE frames are 2 bits offset from TE-to-NT frames. In addition, TE-to-NT frames lack activation (A) its and collision avoidance (E, S, M) bits. The actual ISDN frame format can be seen in Figure 13-7 and is described in the following list:

■ **Synchronization bits**   F, FA, and N bits are used to create AMI line-code violations, which provide framing and synchronization.

■ **Bearer channels**   These are the B channels. Note that only 32 out the 48 bits of each frame actually contain user data.

FIGURE 13-7   S/T interface frame format

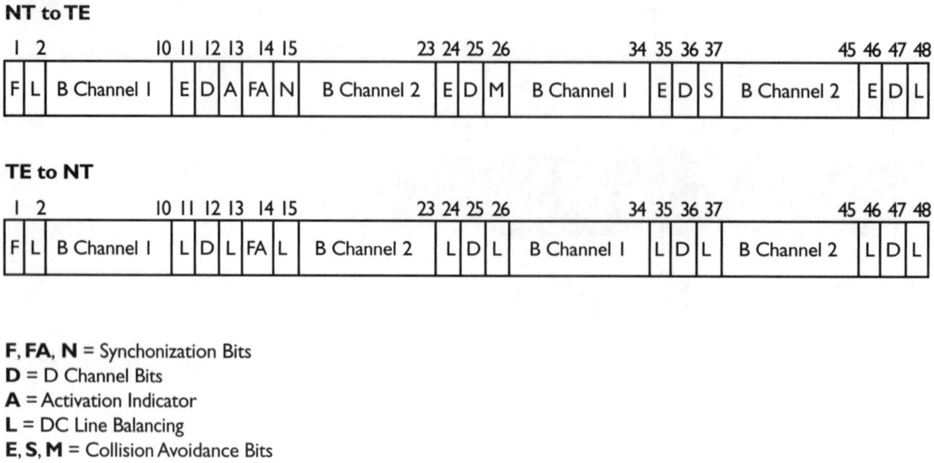

NT to TE

| 1 2 | | 10 11 12 13 14 15 | | | | | | 23 24 25 26 | | | | 34 35 36 37 | | | | 45 46 47 48 |
| F | L | B Channel 1 | E | D | A | FA | N | B Channel 2 | E | D | M | B Channel 1 | E | D | S | B Channel 2 | E | D | L |

TE to NT

| 1 2 | | 10 11 12 13 14 15 | | | | | | 23 24 25 26 | | | | 34 35 36 37 | | | | 45 46 47 48 |
| F | L | B Channel 1 | L | D | L | FA | L | B Channel 2 | L | D | L | B Channel 1 | L | D | L | B Channel 2 | L | D | L |

F, FA, N = Synchonization Bits
D = D Channel Bits
A = Activation Indicator
L = DC Line Balancing
E, S, M = Collision Avoidance Bits

- **Data channel** The four D bits are the D channel data.

- **Activation indicator** This bit (aptly named) indicates whether the line is active or not.

- **DC line balancing** Using AMI, there must be no net DC signal. L bits are used to balance the DC voltage.

- **Collision avoidance** Up to 8 TEs can share one BRI link; the E, S, and M bits are used to avoid contention for the D channel. The E (Echo) bits are actually the D bit data from the previously received frame.

S/T Layer 1 Activation

The physical activation process uses the activation indicator bit. It normally starts when the TE is plugged into an active line and consists of the following four steps:

1. The TE initiates activation of the S/T interface by sending the 01111110 (7E in hex) to the NT. This combination is known as the *flag*; it comes from the HDLC protocol.

2. The NT responds by sending frames with the A bit set to 0. (Note that the B, D, and E bits are also set to 0.)

3. The TE synchronizes with these frames and responds; however, the A bit is still set to 0.

   The NT synchronizes with the TE's frames, and begins sending frames with the A bit set to 1. The S/T interface is now considered active.

EXERCISE 13-4

Troubleshooting Layer 1 Problems

Scenario: One of your clients has an ISDN BRI for WAN backup to their remote offices. A remote office has reported that it can dial in on B channel 1 when the BRI is unoccupied, but it is unable to dial in on the second B channel when the first is occupied. They suspect a problem with timing and bit synchronization. Could this be the problem?

Solution: No, this is obviously not a Layer 1 problem. Since calls to the first B channel are successful, ISDN Layer 1 must be functioning properly. Remember that every ISDN frame contains data from both B channels and the D channel. Therefore, if Layer 1 has a problem, all channels have a problem.

Since only one channel is affected, the problem is most likely a configuration error on that specific channel. Use SHOW ISDN STATUS to check you SPIDs and local directory numbers (LDNs). (We cover this topic in more detail later.)

ISDN Q.931 Call Setup

When the time comes to actually place a call to a remote location, the Q.931 protocol handles call SETUP messages, which are then sent over to the D channel and encapsulated in the Q.921 frames. Call setup is generally a four-step process, although many variations exist (based on the CO ISDN switch). The four message types generally used are *SETUP, CALL PROCEEDING, ALERTING,* and *CONNECT:*

- **SETUP** When the TE initiates an ISDN call, it sends a SETUP message to the CO switch. Based on the information in the SETUP message, the CO switch will route the call to its destination over the PSTN.

- **CALL PROCEEDING** Although the CO switch is connecting to the remote destination, it will send a CALL PROCEEDING message back to the originating router to let it know all is going well.

- **ALERTING** Next, the remote ISDN switch can (but is not required to) send an ALERTING message back to the originating TE. This message simply means that the phone is ringing at the remote end. You will not see this message frequently when placing data calls.

- **CONNECT** If the call is successful and a connection is made, the remote TE will send a CONNECT message back to the originating TE.

Q.931 Message Format

Examining the contents of a Q.931 message can be very useful when troubleshooting call setup problems. The Q.931 message format is shown in Figure 13-8 and summarized as follows:

- **Protocol discriminator**   Set to 8 for Q.931.

- **Length of call reference**   Tells the length of the following Call Reference field.

- **Call reference**   Used to distinguish between calls being made over the same D channel. It also contains a flag that indicates whether or not the message was sent from the call originator or call receiver:

  1. Flag = 0: From call originator

  2. Flag = 1: From call receiver

- **Message type**   Indicates the type of Q.931 message. Some message types include:

  1. SETUP: 0x05

  2. ALERTING: 0x01

  3. CALL PROCEEDING: 0x02

  4. DISCONNECT: 0x45

- **Information elements (IEs)**   Transmit information about call setup and maintenance. The IEs contained in a message depend on the message type. Some of the more notable IEs are as follows:

  1. **Bearer capability**   Specifies connection parameters, such as connection mode (packet or circuit) and data transfer rate (56KB/s or 64KB/s).

  2. **Channel identification**   Identifies which B channel the call is on.

FIGURE 13-8

S/T interface
frame format

8   1
Protocol Discriminator (1 byte)
Length of Call Reference (1 byte)
Call Reference (1–2 bytes)
Message Type (1 byte)
Information Elements (1–n bytes)

3. **Calling party number**   The call originator's number.

4. **SPID**   Service profile identifier of the calling side.

Troubleshooting ISDN Calls

A client calls you with an ISDN problem. He is installing a new ISDN line, and he cannot ping the remote side. At your instruction, he types **show isdn status** and reports the following output:

```
Router4#sh isdn st
Global ISDN Switchtype = basic-5ess
ISDN BRI1/0 interface
        dsl 8, interface ISDN Switchtype = basic-5ess
    Layer 1 Status:
        ACTIVE
    Layer 2 Status:
        TEI = 64, Ces = 1, SAPI = 0, State =
MULTIPLE_FRAME_ESTABLISHED
        TEI = 73, Ces = 2, SAPI = 0, State =
MULTIPLE_FRAME_ESTABLISHED
    Spid Status:
        TEI 64, ces = 1, state = 5(init)
            spid1 configured, spid1 sent, spid1 valid
            Endpoint ID Info: epsf = 0, usid = 1, tid = 0
        TEI 73, ces = 2, state = 5(init)
            spid2 configured, spid2 sent, spid2 valid
            Endpoint ID Info: epsf = 0, usid = 0, tid = 0
    Layer 3 Status:
        0 Active Layer 3 Call(s)
```

What is the next step?

Solution: The next step depends on whether or not the router is actually dialing and getting disconnected or if it is not dialing at all. If it is dialing and disconnecting, you might try DEBUG ISDN Q931 or DEBUG PPP NEGOTIATION events to gain insight into what is happening during the call establishment process. If the router does not dial at all, try using DEBUG DIALER and check your DDR statements. We discuss this topic in more detail later.

PPP and Multilink PPP

Now that we've covered the D channel, it is time to examine the B channels. HDLC is the Cisco default Layer 2 encapsulation for the data-carrying B channels. Frame Relay can also be supported. However, PPP offers several qualities the others do not, making it far and away the protocol of choice.

Although it is based on HDLC (like so many data link protocols), PPP is an open protocol. One vendor's PPP should interoperate with any other vendor's PPP, as long as both comply with the PPP standards. This is a refreshing change from HDLC, which is vendor specific. A router running Cisco HDLC can communicate only with other Cisco HDLC devices.

PPP also adds numerous capabilities that other data link protocols do not offer. Authentication is provided using Password Authentication Protocol (PAP) and Challenge Handshake Authentication Protocol (CHAP). IP address assignment is supported by the Internet Protocol Control Protocol (IPCP). Compression, and bundling of channels (multilink) are some of the other options. This flexibility and these features are achieved through PPP's Link Control Protocol (LCP) and Network Control Protocol (NCP) layers. LCP carries the link establishment and maintenance datagrams (remember, this is B channel only), and the NCPs carry the Layer 3 (IP or IPX) traffic.

PPP Multilink

Used in conjunction with ISDN, Multilink PPP (MPP) is a particularly attractive offering. With MPP, both B channels can be combined into one logical pipe for data transfer, allowing the two 64KB/s channels to approach 128KB/s of bandwidth. To do this, PPP segments data packets and gives them sequence numbers. It then sends them across both B channels, alternating from one to another (a process known as *inverse multiplexing*) and reassembling them at the destination.

In addition, MPP is not limited to a single BRI interface or only two channels. It can be spread across multiple channels and interfaces to provide very large pipes for efficient data transfer.

Multilink Multichassis PPP (MMP) extends the capabilities of MPP by allowing channels coming into *different* routers be combined into one multilink bundle. For example, your company can accommodate a large number of remote users by having multiple PRIs come into multiple access servers that all share a single dial-in number. If the access servers are all members of a *stack group*, calls coming into separate access servers can still be bundled into one multilink pipe.

EXERCISE 13-6

Identifying PPP Protocols

Scenario: Dynamic Host Configuration Protocol (DHCP) is an open standard protocol used to dynamically assign IP addresses to clients. DHCP is most similar to which of the following PPP protocols?

A. MPP

B. IPCP

C. LCP

D. NCP

Solution: B: IPCP. Like DHCP, IPCP assigns an IP address to a client during the LCP negotiation phase of PPP startup.

CERTIFICATION OBJECTIVE 13.07

ISDN BRI Diagnostic Tools

The Cisco IOS provides a wide variety of SHOW and DEBUG commands to use in diagnosing and troubleshooting ISDN. SHOW commands in particular can be used to view just about everything you would want to know about the current status and configuration of a router. Use SHOW CONTROLLERS to see detailed information on the physical interfaces. SHOW INTERFACES typically shows more Layer 2-based information as well as useful traffic and error counters. Several SHOW ISDN commands are provided to give status and history information about ISDN interfaces and calls. Other commands, such as SHOW DIALER and SHOW PPP MULTILINK, give very specific ISDN information

Use the DEBUG commands for troubleshooting purposes only. They can provide valuable low-level details of exactly what is passing through the router, but they are very resource intensive. Be very careful when using DEBUG commands in production environments, because improperly used, they can quickly consume all system resources and crash a router. Cisco recommends using access lists with DEBUG to view only the traffic you are trying to see.

The SHOW INTERFACES BRI 0 Command

To find general Layer 2 information and D channel statistics, use the SHOW INTERFACE BRI *BRI#* command, where *BRI#* is the interface you want to see:

```
Router4>sh int bri 0
BRI0 is up, line protocol is up (spoofing)
  Hardware is BRI with integrated NT1
  Internet address is 10.1.101.200/32
  MTU 1500 bytes, BW 64 Kbit, DLY 20000 usec, rely 255/255, load 1/255
  Encapsulation PPP, loopback not set
  Last input 00:00:00, output 00:00:00, output hang never
  Last clearing of "show interface" counters never
  Input queue: 0/75/49 (size/max/drops); Total output drops: 0
  Queueing strategy: weighted fair
  Output queue: 0/1000/64/0 (size/max total/threshold/drops)
    Conversations  0/1/256 (active/max active/max total)
    Reserved Conversations 0/0 (allocated/max allocated)
  5 minute input rate 0 bits/sec, 0 packets/sec
  5 minute output rate 0 bits/sec, 0 packets/sec
    118073 packets input, 496372 bytes, 0 no buffer
    Received 0 broadcasts, 11 runts, 0 giants, 0 throttles
    49 input errors, 6 CRC, 43 frame, 0 overrun, 0 ignored, 26 abort
    118083 packets output, 472668 bytes, 0 underruns
    0 output errors, 0 collisions, 4 interface resets
    0 output buffer failures, 0 output buffers swapped out
    5 carrier transitions
```

■ **Spoofing**   If the D channel is up, the interface indicates LINE PROTOCOL IS UP (SPOOFING), whether a call is active or not. Spoofing is the router's way of pretending that the interface is up/up, even when no B channels are connected. This is done to keep the interface's IP subnet in the routing table. Remember that packets will not be routed to a down interface.

- **Protocols shown here** This command also gives brief information about the Layer 2 protocol assigned to the interface (PPP, in this case) as well as its IP address (if assigned).

exam
ⓦatch

Be sure to remember that LINE PROTOCOL IS UP does not mean that either B channel is up. To find out if B channels are up, use the SHOW INTERFACE BRI # 1 2 command.

The **SHOW INTERFACES BRI 0 1** Command

The SHOW INTERFACE BRI # 1 command shows detailed Layer 2 information about B channel 1. Use this command when you want to see B channel status, statistics, and errors:

```
Router4>sh int bri 0 1
BRI0:1 is up, line protocol is up
  Hardware is BRI with integrated NT1
  MTU 1500 bytes, BW 64 Kbit, DLY 20000 usec, rely 255/255, load 1/255
  Encapsulation PPP, loopback not set, keepalive set (10 sec)
  LCP Open, multilink Open
  Last input 00:00:04, output 00:00:04, output hang never
  Last clearing of "show interface" counters never
  Queueing strategy: fifo
  Output queue 0/40, 0 drops; input queue 0/75, 0 drops
  5 minute input rate 0 bits/sec, 0 packets/sec
  5 minute output rate 0 bits/sec, 0 packets/sec
     153 packets input, 4847 bytes, 0 no buffer
     Received 0 broadcasts, 0 runts, 0 giants, 0 throttles
     0 input errors, 0 CRC, 0 frame, 0 overrun, 0 ignored, 0 abort
     153 packets output, 4474 bytes, 0 underruns
     0 output errors, 0 collisions, 0 interface resets
     0 output buffer failures, 0 output buffers swapped out
     11 carrier transitions
```

- **Bearer channel 1** All the information from this output is specific to B channel 1. Encapsulation, LCP status, and multilink status are all listed, as are input/output and error counters.

- **Up/down states** Unlike the SHOW INTERFACE BRI # command, which *always* reports LINE PROTOCOL IS UP (SPOOFING), SHOW

INTERFACE BRI # 1 gives you the actual up/down status of B channel 1. If a call is active on B Channel 1, the line protocol is up; otherwise, it is down.

exam
Ⓦatch

The statistics (packets input and so forth) shown using the SHOW INTERFACE BRI INT# command are for the D channel. To see similar statistics for the B channels, use the SHOW INTERFACE BRI# 1 2 command.

The **SHOW INTERFACES BRI 0 2** Command

```
Router4>sh int bri 0 2
BRI0:2 is down, line protocol is down
  Hardware is BRI with integrated NT1
  MTU 1500 bytes, BW 64 Kbit, DLY 20000 usec, rely 255/255, load 1/255
  Encapsulation PPP, loopback not set, keepalive set (10 sec)
  LCP Closed, multilink Closed
  Closed: IPCP, CDPCP
  Last input never, output never, output hang never
  Last clearing of "show interface" counters never
  Queueing strategy: fifo
  Output queue 0/40, 0 drops; input queue 0/75, 0 drops
  5 minute input rate 0 bits/sec, 0 packets/sec
  5 minute output rate 0 bits/sec, 0 packets/sec
     0 packets input, 0 bytes, 0 no buffer
     Received 0 broadcasts, 0 runts, 0 giants, 0 throttles
     0 input errors, 0 CRC, 0 frame, 0 overrun, 0 ignored, 0 abort
     3 packets output, 312 bytes, 0 underruns
     0 output errors, 0 collisions, 0 interface resets
     0 output buffer failures, 0 output buffers swapped out
     1 carrier transitions
```

- **Bearer channel 2**   Similar to the previous command, SHOW INTERFACE BRI # 2 gives detailed Layer 2 information for B channel 2.

- **Up/down states**   Shows the up/down status of B channel 2.

exam
Ⓦatch

To reset SHOW INTERFACE BRI # counters to zero, use the CLEAR COUNTERS BRI # command. However, to reset the SHOW INTERFACE BRI # 1 2 counters, you must reboot the router. Resetting the counters can be very useful when troubleshooting; it is often important to see whether or not error counters are incrementing.

The SHOW CONTROLLER BRI 0 Command

Use the SHOW CONTROLLER BRI # command to see detailed information about the ISDN Physical Layer:

```
Router4#sh contr bri 0
BRI interface 0 with integrated NT1
Layer 1 is ACTIVATED. (ISDN L1 State F7)
Master clock for slot 1 is bri interface 0.
Total chip configuration successes: 235, failures: 0, timeouts: 0
D Channel Information:
  Interrupt Queue Element(index=1747): interrupt is enabled
  RX ring entries: 5, buffer size 1548
...  ...  ...  ...  ...
  Channel state: UP  Channel IDB: 80960148
...  ...  ...  ...  ...
B1 Channel Information:
...  ...  ...  ...  ...
  Channel state: UP  Channel IDB: 80965DB4
...  ...  ...  ...  ...
  Bandwidth: 64, idle channel: Unassigned, idle ts bitfield: 0x0
  0 missed datagrams, 0 overruns
  0 bad datagram encapsulations, 0 memory errors
  0 transmitter underruns, 0 throttles, 0 enables, 0 bad interrupt elements
B2 Channel Information:
...  ...  ...  ...  ...
Channel state: UP  Channel IDB: 8096BA20
...  ...  ...  ...  ...
  Bandwidth: 64, idle channel: Unassigned, idle ts bitfield: 0x0
  0 missed datagrams, 0 overruns
  0 bad datagram encapsulations, 0 memory errors
  0 transmitter underruns, 0 throttles, 0 enables, 0 bad interrupt elements
```

The listing has been abbreviated; this command produces a ton of output! Although most of it is useful only for Cisco engineers, several handy pieces of information can be gleaned:

- Layer 1 status, including both B channels, is shown.

- Physical layer buffers and bandwidth are listed.

- Several Layer 1 statistics and error counters are presented to aid in troubleshooting.

The **SHOW ISDN STATUS** Command

The most frequently used command when troubleshooting IDSN is SHOW ISDN STATUS. This command shows a quick summary of the current status of all three ISDN layers. Examine the following output from a Cisco 2601 router:

```
Router4>show isdn status bri 1/0
Global ISDN Switchtype = basic-dms100
ISDN BRI1/0 interface
        dsl 8, interface ISDN Switchtype = basic-dms100
    Layer 1 Status:
        ACTIVE
    Layer 2 Status:
        TEI = 80, Ces = 1, SAPI = 0, State =
MULTIPLE_FRAME_ESTABLISHED
        TEI = 89, Ces = 2, SAPI = 0, State =
MULTIPLE_FRAME_ESTABLISHED
    Spid Status:
        TEI 80, ces = 1, state = 5(init)
            spid1 configured, spid1 sent, spid1 valid
            Endpoint ID Info: epsf = 0, usid = 1, tid = 0
        TEI 89, ces = 2, state = 5(init)
            spid2 configured, spid2 sent, spid2 valid
            Endpoint ID Info: epsf = 0, usid = 0, tid = 0
    Layer 3 Status:
        0 Active Layer 3 Call(s)
    Activated dsl 8 CCBs = 0
    The Free Channel Mask:  0x80000003
    Total Allocated ISDN CCBs = 0
```

- **ISDN layer 1—physical connection**   Layer 1 status is ACTIVE; physical connectivity to the basic-dms100 switch has been established.

- **ISDN Layer 2**   Successful Layer 2 establishment is indicated by STATE = MULTIPLE_FRAME_ESTABLISHED. This means that the TE can send more than one frame before receiving an acknowledgment—a requirement for ISDN.

- **ISDN SPID Status**   Both SPIDs have been sent to the basic-dms100 switch and have been validated. Also note that the assigned TEIs are shown with their states. The most common TEI states are as follows:

1: Terminal down
3: Await establishment
5: Initialized
8: Established

However, not all ISDN switches report state 8 (established); some report 5 when successfully established. TEIs are covered in more detail later in the chapter.

■ **ISDN Layer 3 Call Status**   Layer 3 has 0 active calls; neither B channel is sending data at the moment. Note that although both B channels are down and no user data is being sent, the D channel is up and actively communicating with the basic-dms100 switch.

The SHOW DIALER Command

Use the SHOW DIALER command to find the dialer's current activity as well as a brief history of call usage and the reason a call was initiated:

```
Router4#sh dialer
BRI0 - dialer type = ISDN

Dial String      Successes   Failures    Last called   Last status
8005551212              16          0     00:01:21       successful   Default
0 incoming call(s) have been screened
0 incoming call(s) rejected for callback

BRI0:1 - dialer type = ISDN
Idle timer (600 secs), Fast idle timer (20 secs)
Wait for carrier (30 secs), Re-enable (15 secs)
Dialer state is multilink member
Dial reason: ip (s=10.1.247.1, d=10.1.1.1)
Current call connected 00:01:21
Connected to 8005551212 (0dc0.0424.4a5d)

BRI0:2 - dialer type = ISDN
Idle timer (600 secs), Fast idle timer (20 secs)
Wait for carrier (30 secs), Re-enable (15 secs)
Dialer state is idle
```

■ **Dial strings**   The numbers that have been dialed, the current call status, and the time of the last call are all reported.

■ **B channels in use**   Both B channels are shown, including their current status and timers.

The SHOW PPP MULTILINK Command

To see the status of channels using the PPP Multilink option, use SHOW PPP MULTILINK:

```
Router4#sh ppp mult
Bundle 00c0.0504.4a2d, 2 members, Master link is Virtual-Access1
Dialer Interface is BRI0
  0 lost fragments, 0 reordered, 0 unassigned, sequence 0x0/0x558 rcvd/sent
  0 discarded, 0 lost received, 83/255 load
Member Links: 2 (max not set, min not set)
BRI0:1
BRI0:2
```

■ **MPP**   BRI0:1 (BRI0 channel 1) and BRI0:2 (BRI0 channel 2) are bound together to form one multilink bundle. The load is reported as 83/255; this must be greater than the DIALER LOAD-THRESHOLD to have triggered the second call. *Note:* SHOW PPP MULTILINK also shows the status of MMP if it is configured.

The DEBUG ISDN Q921 Command

Q.921 on the D channel encapsulates Layer 3 information to reliably transport call setup and teardown messages to and from the CO ISDN switch. The Q.921 frame format is shown in Figure 13-9.

■ **Flag**   Marks the beginning and end of each frame. It is the same as the HDLC flag, 01111110 (7E in hex).

■ **Address**   Used for Layer 2 identification; contains several components.

■ **Service access point identifier (SAPI)**   Identifies the type of Layer 3 information contained in the frame. It is similar to other Layer 2 protocol mechanisms, such as Ethernet's Type field.

■ **Command/response (C/R)**   The frame is either a command or a response.

■ **Address extension bits (EA0, EA1)**   If set, indicate the end of the Address field.

■ **Terminal endpoint identifier (TEI)**   Uniquely identifies each TE. Since multiple devices (TEs) can share a single ISDN link, the CO switch must distinguish between them by assigning each a TEI.

FIGURE 13-9 The Q.921 frame format

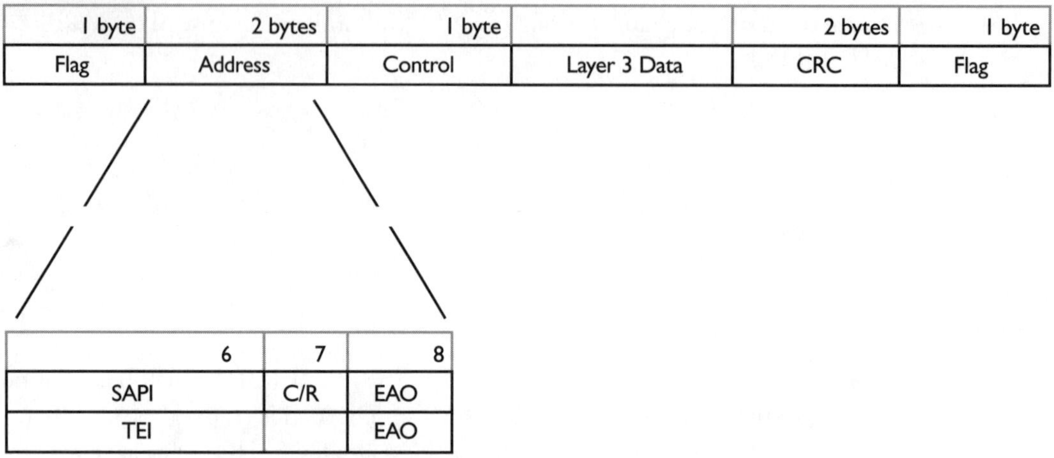

1 byte	2 bytes	1 byte		2 bytes	1 byte
Flag	Address	Control	Layer 3 Data	CRC	Flag

	6	7	8
SAPI		C/R	EAO
TEI			EAO

DEBUG ISDN Q921 is a useful command for troubleshooting Layer 2 connectivity problems; it shows the Layer 2 activity between the TE and the CO switch. The following samples show different stages of ISDN Layer 2 communications:

```
00:04:00: ISDN BR1/0: TX ->  IDREQ  ri = 86  ai = 127
00:04:02: ISDN BR1/0: TX ->  IDREQ  ri = 1463  ai = 127
00:04:04: ISDN BR1/0: TX ->  IDREQ  ri = 24872  ai = 127
00:04:06: ISDN BR1/0: TX ->  IDREQ  ri = 29609  ai = 127
00:04:30064771071: ISDN BR1/0: RX <-  IDASSN  ri = 29609  ai = 104
00:04:06: %ISDN-6-LAYER2UP: Layer 2 for Interface BR0, TEI 104 changed to up
```

- **IDREQ and IDASSN** When a TE comes online, it transmits an IDREQ to the CO switch to ask for a TEI. In the DEBUG output above, the TE keeps sending IDREQs (each with a different reference indicator: ri) until it hears a response. Note that in the IDREQ, ai = 127 (all ones) and requests any TEI.

The CO switch answers IDREQs with an IDASSN. In this case, ASSN ID (ai) = 104, meaning that the TE has been assigned TEI = 104.

```
01:05:37: ISDN BR1/0: TX ->  SABMEp sapi = 0  tei = 80
01:05:37: ISDN BR1/0: RX <-  UAf sapi = 0  tei = 80
01:05:37: %ISDN-6-LAYER2UP: Layer 2 for Interface BRI0, TEI 80 changed to up
```

■ **SABME and UA**   Once an identity has been established and a TEI assigned, the TE attempts to establish multiple-frame communication with the ISDN switch. This simply means that the TE is able to send multiple frames before receiving an acknowledgment from the ISDN switch. The TE sends a Set Asynchronous Balanced Mode Extended (SABME) message in order move to the MULTIPLE FRAME ESTABLISHED state. The ISDN switch should respond with an unnumbered acknowledgment (UA). If the SABME and UA exchange succeeds, ISDN can move to the information transfer phase. At this point, Layer 2 is UP.

```
01:05:38: ISDN BR1/0: RX <-  IDCKRQ  ri = 0  ai = 80
01:05:38: ISDN BR1/0: TX ->  IDCKRP  ri = 16568  ai = 80
```

■ **IDCKRQ and IDCKRP**   Once Q.921 communications have been established, the CO switch will periodically send an ID Check Request (IDCKRQ) to verify that the TEIs are still in use. Active TEIs respond to the IDCKRQ with an ID Check Response (IDCKRQ).

■ **IDREM**   If a station does not respond to IDCKRQs, the CO switch removes its TEI from use by issuing an ID Remove (IDREM).

```
01:05:37: ISDN BR0: RX <- INFOc sapi = 0  tei = 80  ns = 0  nr = 0  i =
0x08018575
01:05:37: ISDN BR1/0: TX -> RRr sapi = 0  tei = 80  nr = 1
```

■ **INFO and RR**   Information frames are sent once Q.921 has been established and data transfer has begun. The receiver can respond with Receiver Ready (RR) if it is ready for more data or Receiver Not Ready (RNR) if it is busy.

■ **DISC**   A disconnect (DISC) frame ends multiple-frame communication and brings Layer 2 down. Like the SAMBE, it is acknowledged with a UA.

The DEBUG DIALER Command

Once Q.921 has been established, the router is ready to place a call. If problems arise in this area (calling the wrong number, never placing a call, etc.), use the DEBUG DIALER command to monitor the dialer's activity (or lack thereof):

```
00:02:13: BRI0 DDR: Dialing cause ip (s=10.1.247.1, d=10.1.1.1)
00:02:13: BRI0 DDR: Attempting to dial 8005551212
```

```
00:02:14: %LINK-3-UPDOWN: Interface BRI0:1, changed state to up.
00:02:14: %ISDN-6-CONNECT: Interface BRI0:1 is now connected to 8005551212
00:02:15: %LINK-3-UPDOWN: Interface Virtual-Access1, changed state to up
00:02:15: Virtual-Access1 DDR: dialer protocol up
```

DEBUG DIALER reports the dialer's state: if it is calling, whom it is calling, and why it is calling. In the output, an attempted IP connection from 10.1.247.1 to 10.1.1.1 has caused the router to place a call to 8005551212.

Problems with the dialer usually result from incorrect DIALER LIST or DIALER MAP statements. DIALER LIST controls what traffic is permitted to initiate an ISDN call; DIALER MAP controls what numbers are called and the parameters associated with calls. These are the first places to check if the router is not dialing when you think it should be.

The DEBUG ISDN Q931 Command

Once Layer 2 has been successfully established, calls can be initiated and received. You can monitor the call setup and call teardown process by examining the contents of incoming and outgoing Q.931 messages using the DEBUG ISDN Q931 command.

The following DEBUG ISDN Q931 output illustrates the call establishment process:

```
00:09:20: ISDN BR1/0: TX ->  SETUP pd = 8  callref = 0x01
00:09:20:          Bearer Capability i = 0x8890
00:09:20:          Channel ID i = 0x83
00:09:20:          Called Party Number i = 0x80, '8005551212'
00:09:90194313899: ISDN BR1/0: RX <-  CALL_PROC pd = 8  callref = 0x81
00:09:90194313216:          Channel ID i = 0x89
00:09:90194354176: ISDN BR1/0: RX <-  CONNECT pd = 8  callref = 0x81
00:09:21: %LINK-3-UPDOWN: Interface BRI1/0:1, changed state to up
00:09:21: %ISDN-6-CONNECT: Interface BRI1/0:1 is now connected to 8005551212
00:09:21: ISDN BR1/0: TX ->  CONNECT_ACK pd = 8  callref = 0x01
00:09:22: %LINK-3-UPDOWN: Interface Virtual-Access1, changed state to up
00:09:23: %LINEPROTO-5-UPDOWN: Line protocol on Interface BRI1/0:1, changed
state to up
```

■ **SETUP** The TE initiates a call by transmitting a SETUP message to the CO switch. It includes several IEs such as bearer capability (0x8890 = 64MB/s), channel ID (B Channel 1), and called party number.

exam
ⓦatch

The bearer capability reports the ISDN data transfer rate for a B channel call. Bearer capability mismatches are a common cause of ISDN problems and can be easily seen with DEBUG ISDN Q931. The default data transfer rate on a B channel is 64KB/s. However, under some circumstances (particularly long distance calls), the maximum supported speed on your ISDN link will be 56KB/s. If your interface is configured incorrectly, the call will drop. You can manually set the data transfer rate of a call with the DIALER MAP command.

■ **CALL PROCEEDING**   While the CO switch is routing the call over the PSTN to its final destination, it sends a CALL_PROC (call proceeding) message back to the TE.

Note that in our example, the TE uses the value 0x83 for the channel ID, whereas the CO switch uses the value 0x89 to refer to the same channel. This is normal and does not apply only to Channel ID. Each side can use its own identifiers for different IEs, so long as they are unique to that device. For example, the TE uses 0x01 for this call's call reference value, whereas the CO switch uses 0x81.

■ **CONNECT**   The remote ISDN TE responds with a CONNECT message, indicating it has successfully received the call and made a connection.

■ **CALLED and CALLING NUMBER verification**   The initial SETUP message *can* contain CALLED NUMBER and CALLING NUMBER IEs. These can be used for call screening purposes: to accept calls only from numbers that are approved. The ISDN ANSWER1, ISDN ANSWER2 and ISDN CALLER interface configuration commands are used for this purpose.

When an ISDN call ends, for whatever reason, the terminating side sends a DISCONNECT message. The opposite side responds with a RELEASE message, which is followed by a RELEASE_COMP message. The following DEBUG ISDN Q931 output illustrates a DISCONNECT caused by the idle timer expiring:

```
00:59:50: %ISDN-6-DISCONNECT: Interface BRI1/0:1  disconnected from
 8005551212 00c0.0504.4a2d, call lasted 602 seconds
00:59:50: ISDN BR1/0: TX -> DISCONNECT pd = 8  callref = 0x04
00:59:50: Cause i = 0x8090 - Normal call clearing
00:59:51: ISDN BR1/0: RX <- RELEASE pd = 8  callref = 0x84
00:59:51: %LINK-3-UPDOWN: Interface BRI1/0:1, changed state to down
00:59:51: ISDN BR1/0: TX -> RELEASE_COMP pd = 8  callref = 0x04
00:59:51: %LINEPROTO-5-UPDOWN: Line protocol on Interface BRI1/0:1,
 changed state to down
```

```
00:59:51: %LINEPROTO-5-UPDOWN: Line protocol on Interface Virtual-Access1,
changed state to down
```

The DISCONNECT message includes the CAUSE IE, which can be a very useful troubleshooting tool. The most common cause code is *normal call clearing* (0x8090), which is fairly generic; it can mean anything from idle-timer expiration to dropped physical connections. However, some other CAUSE codes can be very insightful and can include the following:

- Channel unacceptable
- Number changed
- Destination out of order
- Invalid number format
- No route to destination

This information is most useful when ISDN calls do not make it through the initial call-establishment process.

on the **Job**

You can manually end an ISDN call with the CLEAR INTERFACE BRI # command.

After Q.921 comes up (see DEBUG ISDN Q921 earlier in this section), the SPIDs are sent to the CO switch and validated. This must happen before Q.931 call setup takes place. SPID verification is a relatively simple exchange: the TE transmits an INFORMATION frame containing the SPID, and the CO switch acknowledges with an endpoint ID (EID). The following DEBUG ISDN Q931 output illustrates this process:

```
00:07:48: ISDN BR0: TX ->  INFORMATION pd = 8  callref = (null)
      SPID Information i = '80055512120101'
00:07:49: ISDN BR0: RX <-  INFORMATION pd = 8  callref = (null)
      ENDPOINT IDent i = 0x8180
00:07:49: ISDN BR0: Received EndPoint ID
00:07:49: ISDN BR0: RX <-  INFORMATION pd = 8  callref = (null)
      Locking Shift to Codeset 5
00:07:49:          Codeset 5 IE 0x2A  i = 0x808001, 'P'
00:07:49: ISDN BR0: TX ->  INFORMATION pd = 8  callref = (null)
      SPID Information i = '80055512120101'
00:07:49: ISDN BR0: RX <-  INFORMATION pd = 8  callref = (null)
      ENDPOINT IDent i = 0x8080
```

```
00:07:49: ISDN BR0: Received EndPoint ID
00:07:49: ISDN BR0: RX <-  INFORMATION pd = 8  callref = (null)
        Feature Indicate i = 0xB900
```

The **DEBUG BRI** Command

DEBUG BRI tracks all activity on a BRI interface; it generates a great deal of output and can be somewhat difficult to sift through. However, it can be helpful for troubleshooting interfaces that unexpectedly go down or up. Observe the following output of a B channel coming up:

```
03:05:34: BRI0:1: Enabled channel B1
03:05:34: BRI0: Wrote command 0x14 to SID
03:05:34: %LINK-3-UPDOWN: Interface BRI0:1, changed state to up
03:05:34: %ISDN-6-CONNECT: Interface BRI0:1 is now connected to 8005551212
```

Notice that all the activity of the BRI interface is shown—including its interaction with different parts of the internal system. This includes activation of B channels.

The **DEBUG PPP NEGOTIATION** Command

When the ISDN Q.931 CONNECT message has been sent, PPP can begin passing data over the B channel. The first step of this operation is to agree with the remote side on the PPP options that will be used. PPP's LCP performs this negotiation, which can be seen with the DEBUG PPP NEGOTIATION command:

```
03:07:19: %ISDN-6-CONNECT: Interface BRI1/0:1 is now connected to 8005551212
03:07:19: BR1/0:1 PPP: Treating connection as a callout
03:07:19: BR1/0:1 PPP: Phase is ESTABLISHING, Active Open
03:07:19: BR1/0:1 LCP: I CONFREQ [REQsent] id 23 len 29
03:07:19: BR1/0:1 LCP:    MagicNumber 0xDB7FAE1B (0x0506DB7FAE1B)
03:07:19: BR1/0:1 LCP:    AuthProto PAP (0x0304C023)
03:07:19: BR1/0:1 LCP:    MRU 1564 (0x1104061C)
03:07:19: BR1/0:1 LCP: O CONFREJ [REQsent] id 23 len 6
03:07:19: BR1/0:1 LCP:    MRU 1564 (0x110405F4)
03:07:19: BR1/0:1 LCP: I CONFACK [REQsent] id 13 len 24
03:07:19: BR1/0:1 LCP:    MagicNumber 0x312C0A3D (0x0506312C0A3D)
03:07:19: Vi1 IPCP: O CONFREQ [REQsent] id 2 len 10
03:07:19: Vi1 IPCP:    Address 10.1.101.200 (0x03060A0165C8)
03:07:19: Vi1 IPCP: I CONFNAK [REQsent] id 1 len 10
03:07:19: Vi1 IPCP:    Address 10.1.101.200 (0x03060A0165C8)cal
```

- **LCP**   A few common PPP options that Cisco routers negotiate are AuthType, MRU, ACompression, PCompression, MagicNumber, and AsyncMap. Of these options, AuthType *must* be agreed on or the connection will drop. What is so special about the AuthType option? It defines which authentication protocol (if any) will be used to initiate this connection. The two authentication methods available on the Cisco router are PAP and CHAP.

- **CONFREQ**   The initiating TE sends a Configuration Request (CONFREQ) asking for the options that it would like. In the output, you can see that the TE has asked for a Magic Number (which is a PPP mechanism), an Authentication Protocol (PAP), and a Maximum Receive Unit (1564 bytes).

- **CONFACK**   The remote TE agrees to a parameter by sending a Configuration Acknowledgment (CONFACK). In our output, it has agreed the requested Magic Number.

- **CONFNAK**   The remote TE can also reject a CONFREQ by sending a Configuration Negative Acknowledgment (CONFNAK). You can see that at the end of the conversation, the IPCP asked for an IP address, and the TE denied it.

- **CONFREJ**   If the remote TE receives a CONFREQ for a parameter it doesn't recognize, it sends a Configuration Rejection (CONFREJ). Cisco does not use the MRU parameter, so you may frequently see a CONFREJ for that.

The DEBUG PPP AUTHENTICATION Command

Authentication problems end a B channel call before it has begun—in the LCP negotiation phase. If your calls are quickly becoming disconnected and you suspect PPP authentication failures, use DEBUG PPP AUTHENTICATION to view the process. If you understand the PPP authentication, the debug output is very easy to understand and troubleshoot.

The two PPP authentication protocols are PAP and CHAP; here we look at CHAP.

exam
ⓦatch

CHAP, the recommended authentication protocol, is the successor to PAP. CHAP is preferred because it encrypts the password before sending it over the wire. PAP sends its password in clear text, making it vulnerable to hackers. Also note that if a Cisco router calls another Cisco router, this CHAP process occurs in both directions. However, if a PC PPP client (such as Windows Dial-Up Networking) dials into the router, only the PC is challenged.

```
00:35:28: %ISDN-6-CONNECT: Interface BRI1/0:1 is now connected to 8005551212
00:35:28: BR1/0:1 PPP: Treating connection as a callout
00:35:29: BR1/0:1 PPP: Phase is AUTHENTICATING, by the peer
00:35:29: BR1/0:1 AUTH: Started process 0 pid 31
00:35:29: BR1/0:1 CHAP: O CHALLENGE id 1 len 28 from "Router1"
00:35:29: BR1/0:1 CHAP: I RESPONSE id 1 len 28 from "Router2"
00:35:29: BR1/0:1 CHAP: O SUCCESS id 1 len 4
00:35:29: %LINK-3-UPDOWN: Interface Virtual-Access1, changed state to up.
```

- **Challenge**   CHAP uses a three-way handshake authentication process. The first step is the challenge, or Code 1, where the local TE sends a challenge to the remote TE. This challenge includes the TE's authentication name (often the hostname), an ID value, and a random number. In the output, only HOSTNAME (Router1) is listed in the outgoing (O) challenge.

- **Response**   The remote TE receives the challenge and extracts the host name, ID, and random number. If the hostname matches a value in the authentication database, it feeds the hostname's password along with the ID and random number into an encryption algorithm (a process known as *hashing*). The resulting encrypted (hashed) value, the ID, and the remote TE's authentication name (the hostname) are all sent back to the local TE as a response, or Code 2.

- **Success**   When the original TE receives the response, it looks up the remote TE's hostname in its own authentication database and retrieves the password. It then feeds this password, the ID, and the original random number into its own hashing mechanism. If the resultant value is equal to the hashed value it just received in the response, authentication is successful and a CHAP success packet is sent to the remote TE. This success packet is known as a Code 3.

- **Failure**   If the compared values do not match, authentication is unsuccessful and a failure (Code 4) packet is sent back to the remote TE. The connection now drops.

Password misconfiguration is the most common mistake made when configuring CHAP. For CHAP to be successful, the passwords for remote routers must be identical on each router. For example, if Router1 is configured with USERNAME ROUTER2 PASSWORD AQUAMAN, Router2 must be configured with USERNAME ROUTER1 PASSWORD AQUAMAN. Also, the correct hostname must be sent in the PPP message (usually configured with the DIALER MAP command).

The **DEBUG IP PACKET** Command

DEBUG IP PACKET is useful for diagnosing a variety of IP problems. It reports all IP packets passing through the router, including their source, destination, and next-hop addresses. It can give a great deal of insight into the routing process on the router. However, it can also overload the router. As with all DEBUG commands, you should use it with great care. (Using an access list is a great idea with this command.)

The following DEBUG IP PACKET TRACE shows a normal packet traveling through a Cisco router. Note that both the source and destination addresses are displayed:

```
20:26:21: IP: s=10.1.101.200 (local), d=10.1.1.1 (BRI1/0), len 44, sending
20:26:21: IP: s=10.1.2.2 (BRI1/0), d=10.1.101.200 (BRI1/0), len 56, rcvd
```

DEBUG IP PACKET also reports encapsulation errors when it sees them. With ISDN, this is usually symptomatic of a PPP negotiation failure. Try using DEBUG PPP NEGOTIATION to further troubleshoot this problem.

Now that you have a better idea of SHOW and DEBUG commands, please refer to the following Scenario & Solution.

SCENARIO & SOLUTION

What SHOW commands tell you if the D channel is up on interface BRI0?	SHOW INTERFACE BRI 0 SHOW ISDN STATUS
Which SHOW commands tell you the current status of B channel 1 on interface BRI0?	SHOW INTERFACE BRI 0 1 SHOW DIALER
What DEBUG command would you use if you suspected Layer 1 problems?	DEBUG BRI
What DEBUG commands would you use if your router dials and then quickly disconnects?	DEBUG ISDN Q931 DEBUG DIALER DEBUG PPP NEGOTIATION DEBUG PPP AUTHENTICATION

EXERCISE 13-7

Troubleshooting ISDN Activation

Examine the following DEBUG BRI output. What went wrong?

```
00:01:41: ISDN BR1/0: TX ->  IDREQ  ri = 86  ai = 127
00:01:43: ISDN BR1/0: TX ->  IDREQ  ri = 1463  ai = 127
00:01:45: ISDN BR1/0: TX ->  IDREQ  ri = 24872  ai = 127
00:01:47: BRI1/0: Wrote command 0x15 to SID
00:01:47: ISDN BR1/0: TX ->  IDREQ  ri = 29609  ai = 127
00:01:47: ISDN BR1/0: RX <-  IDASSN  ri = 29609  ai = 64
00:01:47: ISDN BR1/0: TX ->  SABMEp sapi = 0  tei = 64
00:01:47: ISDN BR1/0: RX <-  UAf sapi = 0  tei = 64
00:01:47: %ISDN-6-LAYER2UP: Layer 2 for Interface BR1/0, TEI 64 changed to
up
00:01:47: ISDN BR1/0: TX ->  INFOc sapi = 0  tei = 64  ns = 0  nr = 0  i =
0x08007B3A0E3430373239343235363530313030
00:01:47:     INFORMATION pd = 8  callref = (null)
       SPID Information i = '80055512120100'
00:01:48:     INFORMATION pd = 8  callref = (null)
       ENDPOINT IDent i = 0x8180
00:01:48: ISDN BR1/0: Received EndPoint ID
00:01:48: ISDN BR1/0: TX ->  IDREQ  ri = 44602  ai = 127
00:01:48:   INFORMATION pd = 8  callref = (null) Locking Shift to Codeset 5
00:01:48:          Codeset 5 IE 0x2A  i = 0x808001, 'P'
00:01:48: %ISDN-6-LAYER2UP: Layer 2 for Interface BR1/0, TEI 73 changed to
up
00:01:48: ISDN BR1/0: TX ->  INFOc sapi = 0  tei = 73  ns = 0  nr = 0  i =
0x08007B3A0E343037323933323737313330313030
00:01:48:     INFORMATION pd = 8  callref = (null)
       SPID Information i = '81055512130100'
00:01:48: ISDN BR1/0: RX <-  RRr sapi = 0  tei = 73  nr = 1
00:01:48:     INFORMATION pd = 8  callref = (null)
       Cause i = 0x82E43A - Invalid IE contents
00:01:48: ISDN BR1/0: TX ->  RRr sapi = 0  tei = 73  nr = 1
00:01:48: %ISDN-4-INVALID_SPID: Interface BR1/0, Spid2 was rejected
00:01:58: ISDN BR1/0: TX ->  RRp sapi = 0  tei = 64 nr = 2
```

Solution: Layer 2 activation went fine until line 27, when the second SPID was sent. Lines 30 and 32 indicate that SPID2 was invalid (probably due to a typo).

CERTIFICATION OBJECTIVE 13.08

Problem Isolation in ISDN BRI WANs

Problem isolation in ISDN BRI environments conforms to the standard problem-solving procedure: start from the bottom and work your way up. Without any other guidance, you should troubleshoot a problem in the following order:

1. Verify the Physical Layer.
2. Verify ISDN Layer 2.
3. Verify ISDN Layer 3.
4. Verify Dial-on-Demand Routing (DDR) configurations.
5. Verify PPP and authentication.

Physical Layer

The Physical Layer covers communication between the router (BRI S/T interface) and the NT1. Without the Physical Layer, none of the other layers could begin functioning, so your troubleshooting should always start there. Remember that you can check Physical Layer status with SHOW ISDN STATUS and SHOW CONTROLLER BRI 0. Typical problems with the Physical Layer include the following:

- **Cabling problems**   Cabling and cable connectors fail frequently; inspecting and swapping cables should be the first thing you try when troubleshooting the Physical Layer.

- **Electromagnetic interference (EMI)**   As with most electrical cabling, EMI is always a concern.

- **Faulty TE of NT1**   Examine CPU utilization, buffer statistics, input/output errors, and the like. If possible, try to swap equipment.

ISDN Layer 2

ISDN Layer 2 involves communication between the TE and the CO ISDN switch. Problems usually involve misconfiguration of one of these devices. Typical Layer 2 problems include the following:

- **ISDN switch type**   Configuring the wrong ISDN switch type prevents Layer 2 from coming up. Remember that there are many differences between switch types, so successful Q.921 negotiation cannot occur unless this parameter is correct.

- **TEI Negotiation**   The TEI value ranges between 0 and 127. The CO switch usually dynamically assigns it. Dynamic values range from 64 to 126 (64 and 65 are typically used). If directed, you can manually assign a TEI value (between 0 and 63) with the ISDN STATIC-TEI interface configuration command.

- **Telco problems**   Believe it or not, sometimes the phone company makes a mistake. Once you have verified that your configuration is correct, call the Telco and have them verify theirs.

ISDN Layer 3

ISDN Layer 3 covers end-to-end communications between the two TE devices. Problems with call setup and teardown are covered in ISDN Layer 3. Some common problems include the following:

- **Wrong SPIDs**   Layer 2 will come up, even with misconfigured SPIDs. In fact, some CO switches do not even verify the SPIDs until a call is placed. Use SHOW ISDN STATUS to verify that your SPIDs have been corrected.

- **Bearer capability**   Remember that many exchanges will not support 64KB/s end to end. Use the DIALER MAP statement to set the proper speed.

- **Telco problems**   Again, errors by the telephone company can cause problems in this area.

DDR Configurations

DDR configuration issues include the following:

- **Defining interesting traffic** Check your DIALER LIST and DIALER-GROUP commands.

- **Routing issues** Make sure your routing protocols know how to get to the next hop.

- **Dialing issues** Check your DIALER MAP (or DIALER STRING) statements to make sure you are dialing the correct number for the appropriate next hop.

on the job

Forgetting the DIALER LIST command is a very common mistake. Even if you want any traffic to trigger an ISDN call, you still must configure a DIALER LIST and apply it with DIALER-GROUP.

PPP and Authentication

Once a call has been initiated and answered, PPP options are usually the cause of problems. Authentication misconfigurations probably account for 95 percent of these problems. Check your USERNAME/PASSWORD statements, and make sure you are using the correct authentication type. Remember that the username sent with the CHAP request is configured with the DIALER MAP statement. With PAP, you can also use the PPP PAP SENT-USERNAME command. In addition, don't forget the ENCAPSULATION PPP statement!

Now that you have a better grasp of problem isolation, please refer to the following Scenario & Solution.

SCENARIO & SOLUTION

What is the first thing to check when you're having ISDN problems?	The Physical Layer—cabling.
What is the most common cause of Layer 2 problems?	The wrong ISDN switch-type is configured.
What is the most common PPP problem?	Misconfigured authentication.

Troubleshooting with DEBUG BRI

Look at the following output from DEBUG BRI. At which layer do you think the problem is occurring?

```
00:02:30: BRI1/0: Wrote command 0xFF to SID
00:02:30: BRI1/0: state F2, IS F1, event LSD
00:02:30: BRI1/0: Wrote command 0x1B to SID
00:02:30: BRI1/0: Line signal detected, changing state F2 to F3
00:02:30: BRI1/0: Wrote command 0xFF to SID
00:02:30: BRI1/0: state F3, IS F3, event AP
00:02:30: BRI1/0: Wrote command 0x92 to SID
00:02:30: BRI1/0: Activation Pending, changing state F3 to F6
00:02:33: BRI1/0: Wrote command 0xFF to SID
00:02:33: BRI1/0: state F6, IS F7, event AI
00:02:33: BRI1/0: Port activated, changing state F6 to F7
00:02:33: Drop all frames if there is any
00:02:33: ISDN BR1/0: TX ->  IDREQ  ri = 86  ai = 127
00:02:35: ISDN BR1/0: TX ->  IDREQ  ri = 1463  ai = 127
00:02:37: ISDN BR1/0: TX ->  IDREQ  ri = 24872  ai = 127
00:02:39: %ISDN-6-LAYER2DOWN: Layer 2 for Interface BR1/0, TEI 255
changed to down
```

Solution: Lines 10 and 11 indicate that the activation indicator has been received, so Layer 1 is up. The IDREQ is the first step of Layer 2 activation, and it fails. Therefore, there is a Layer 2 problem.

CERTIFICATION OBJECTIVE 13.09

ISDN Symptoms, Problems, and Action Plans

Now that we have established a troubleshooting process, we examine some of the more common problems you will face in ISDN environments.

ISDN Router Does Not Dial

Nothing is more frustrating than configuring an ISDN router and watching it just sit there, refusing to initiate a call. Obviously, a multitude of problems could cause this situation to occur. This section covers the most common scenarios, which include the following:

- **Bad SPID, LDN, called number**   Mistyped SPIDs and LDNs (when required) prevent a router from ever placing a call. Fortunately, this problem is easy to diagnose: use SHOW ISDN STATUS to see if the CO switch has accepted them. If you are dialing the wrong number, the call will obviously fail. Use DEBUG DIALER or DEBUG ISDN Q931 and verify that your called number is correct.

on the
Job

SPIDs and LDNs can cause much confusion. Your provider assigns you SPIDs, which are tied to the line provided to you. They work only on that line. Most providers create the SPIDs by adding two to four other digits to the 10-digit telephone number assigned to that line; these digits usually designate the services you are paying for.

The LDNs are the local phone numbers on which your TE may receive ISDN calls, so they are usually similar to the SPIDs (with only seven of the digits, of course). Some providers insist that you configure LDNs. LDNs may also be used in hunt-group or rollover configurations, in which the second B channel answers the same phone number as the first B channel when the first is busy.

- **Incorrect DDR—dialer-list, dialer-group, dialer map, dialer string**   If ISDN Layers 1–3 have been verified and the router still does not dial, DDR is likely the culprit. DDR defines the trigger for a call as well as the destination of the call.

You must define what "interesting" traffic can trigger a call. Use the DIALER-LIST global configuration command to do this. You can define interesting traffic by protocol or tie it to an access list. The DIALER-GROUP interface configuration command ties an interface (or dialer) to a dialer list.

The DIALER MAP and DIALER STRING interface configuration commands define the number the router dials to place a call. Use the DIALER STRING command if an interface dials only one number. DIALER MAP should be used if different numbers are called based on the destination of the "interesting" packets.

DIALER MAP also allows different options such as connection speed and hostname for authentication.

Problems can arise if an interesting packet triggers a call but there is no next hop in the routing table or the next hop is not tied to a destination ISDN number. In troubleshooting, make sure that your routing tables contain information about destination addresses and your DIALER MAPs know how to reach these destinations.

 on the job

Be very careful about configuring routing protocols over ISDN interfaces. Companies have been known to install an ISDN line for intermittent usage and forget this step, only to get their first month's bill and see that the routing protocol activated the link every 30 seconds for the entire month. Explain that one to your boss!

■ **No ISDN switch defined**   If no ISDN switch type is defined, neither Layer 2 nor Layer 3 comes up, precluding a call from being placed. The switch type can be configured in global configuration mode or interface configuration mode (for the specified interface).

Users Cannot Connect

Sometimes you find that users cannot dial into your router. This situation can arise from a variety of problems. Assuming that Layers 1 and 2 are up, use DEBUG ISDN Q931 to determine whether or not you are receiving Q.931 messages:

■ **Bad hardware**   A faulty NT1 or BRI interface (on the router) can keep calls from being accepted. Needless to say, so can faulty cabling. Use SHOW CONTROLLERS BRI and SHOW INTERFACES BRI to look for input/output errors, encapsulation errors, and other Physical Layer problems.

■ **Misconfigured router**   The routing protocols must be configured to recognize the remote node from which users are calling. Unless there is a next hop back to the user, no traffic will ever be returned. Check your static route statements, dialer maps (which define the next hops), and routing protocols to troubleshoot this problem.

ISDN Call from Router Does Not Go Through

Sometimes there is no answer to a known good destination. It could appear that the call is never placed, but it is possible that Q.931 was never established. Use DEBUG ISDN Q931 to determine if the call is being placed and, if so, the reason it is being disconnected. The Cause field of the DISCONNECT message is the first place to start looking:

- **Bad hardware**   A faulty NT1 or BRI interface (on the router) can cause calls to be dropped or never accepted. However, this situation usually cannot be discernible from the DISCONNECT message. Use SHOW CONTROLLERS BRI and SHOW INTERFACES BRI to check for errors. Often, you have to swap hardware or have the Telco look at your equipment.

- **Misconfigured Telco**   As stated earlier, misconfigurations at the Telco can cause all sorts of calling problems.

ISDN Router Cannot Ping the Remote Side

When you are unable to ping the remote side, usually one of two things has happened: either the call was never placed or the call was made and then dropped before the B channels came up.

Problems with CHAP authentication, such as misconfigured passwords or wrong authentication types, cause a router to quickly drop the call. The call connects but drops 2 to 3 seconds later, after LCP negotiation. Use DEBUG PPP AUTHENTICATION to find where in the process the problem is occurring, and check your USERNAME/PASSWORD statements.

On the other hand, a misconfigured router could prevent a call from ever being placed. A routing table entry for the next-hop destination is required to initiate the dialer. If no entry exists, the dialer will not place a call. Check your routing table with SHOW IP ROUTE, and use DEBUG IP PACKET to discover whether or not IP packets are making it out and back in.

Second ISDN B Channel Does Not Come Up

If a call on B channel 1 successfully comes up, the ISDN Layers 1, 2, and 3 are all operational. If B channel 2 does not come up, either your DIALER LOAD

THRESHOLD or your DIALER MAPS are misconfigured. Use SHOW INTERFACE BRI 0 1 2 and SHOW DIALER to verify the states of each B channel:

■ **Load threshold misconfiguration**   If you are using PPP Multilink, the DIALER LOAD THRESHOLD interface configuration command determines the amount of traffic that will trigger a call on the second channel. Remember that the DIALER LOAD THRESHOLD range is from 1 to 255, where 1 is a 0 percent load and 255 is 100 percent (so 128 would be 50 percent). Furthermore, remember to use the INBOUND, OUTBOUND, or EITHER keyword to identify which direction of traffic flow should trigger the call.

■ **Misconfigured router**   If your second B channel should be calling a different destination from the first, routing is most likely the issue. Check the routing table to make sure the destination networks have listed next hops, and make sure your DIALER MAP statements accurately map those next hops to destination numbers. Use SHOW DIALER MAPS to view the configured dialer maps.

Now that you have a better grasp of common problems, please refer to the following Scenario & Solution.

SCENARIO & SOLUTION

Why won't the router dial?	Check the DDR statements. Monitor with DEBUG DIALER.
What if I ping and get no response?	Check the dialing process with DEBUG DIALER. Verify PPP authentication and negotiation with DEBUG PPP NEGOTIATION and DEBUG PPP AUTHENTICATION.
What if I ping and get "Destination host unreachable" or "Destination network unreachable" messages?	Check the routing tables for valid next-hop addresses for the desired network.

EXERCISE 13-9

Troubleshooting Disconnects

Scenario: Your client has an ISDN router that connects to a satellite office. During the course of troubleshooting, you capture the following DEBUG ISDN Q931 output:

```
00:59:50: %LINK-3-UPDOWN: Interface Virtual-Access1, changed state to down
00:59:50: %ISDN-6-DISCONNECT: Interface BRI1/0:1  disconnected from 8005551212
00c0.0504.4a2d, call lasted 602 seconds
00:59:50: ISDN BR1/0: TX ->  DISCONNECT pd = 8  callref = 0x04
00:59:50: Cause i = 0x8090 - Normal call clearing
00:59:51: ISDN BR1/0: RX <-  RELEASE pd = 8  callref = 0x84
00:59:51: %LINK-3-UPDOWN: Interface BRI1/0:1, changed state to down
00:59:51: ISDN BR1/0: TX ->  RELEASE_COMP pd = 8  callref = 0x04
00:59:51: %LINEPROTO-5-UPDOWN: Line protocol on Interface BRI1/0:1, changed state
to down
00:59:51: %LINEPROTO-5-UPDOWN: Line protocol on Interface Virtual-Access1, changed
state to down
```

Which side (yours or the remote site) most likely initiated the disconnect? How can you tell?

Solution: Your side most likely initiated the disconnect. Observe in Line 4 that your router transmitted the DISCONNECT message. The remote side responded (with the RELEASE message) and you followed with a RELEASE_COMP.

CERTIFICATION SUMMARY

ISDN installation and configuration are not exactly the most intuitive processes in the world. This chapter's goal was to provide you with a solid understanding of the underlying technology, provide the tools for proper troubleshooting, and examine the most common errors made in the field. We saw that the Cisco IOS provides a wealth of information through its SHOW and DEBUG commands. You should be able to use these commands to track down virtually any ISDN problem you encounter.

The architects of ISDN intended to create an open architecture. Evidence of their success can be seen in ISDN's widespread use and adoption in other related industries. Now that you know and understand how ISDN operates in Cisco data networks, you will find it easy to apply this knowledge to other ISDN-related technologies. In addition, new technologies—technologies that will bring the Internet to the masses and provide a completely networked world in the future—will ride on top of the foundation ISDN has provided.

TWO-MINUTE DRILL

Here are some of the key points from each certification objective in Chapter 13.

BRI Overview

❑ ISDN basic rate interface (BRI) is a "last-mile" technology that allows digital connections over the same copper wires that deliver analog plain old telephone service (POTS).

❑ The ISDN BRI connection consists of three time division multiplexed (TDM) channels: two 64KB/s B channels and one 16KB/s D channel. These channels are commonly referred to as *2B+D*.

ISDN Reference Points

❑ The NT1 converts the four-wire signals from the terminal endpoint (TE) to the two-wire signaling on the telephone company's network.

❑ In North America, the most common BRI switch types are the basic-ni1 (National ISDN 1), the basic-dms100 (Northern DMS-100), and the basic-5ess (AT&T 5ESS). SPIDs are normally required for the basic-ni1 and the basic-dms100; they are optional on the basic-5ess. In Europe, the basic-net3 (NET3 switch) switch type is used; SPIDs are generally not used in Europe.

ISDN S/T Interface

❑ The S/T interface uses a straight-through cable similar to a standard LAN patch cable. Pins 3–6 are used to transfer bits.

ISDN S/T Line Framing

❑ The ISDN physical frame is 48 bits long; its format differs depending on the direction in which it is traveling.

❑ Layer 1 activation requires the following events: The TE begins the process by signaling 01111110 until the NT1 returns at least three 48-bit frames with the A (Active) bit set to 0. An active Layer 1 connection is indicated when the NT1 starts sending frames with the A bit set to 1.

ISDN Q.931 Call Setup

❑ ISDN calls progress through a series of Q.931 events from call establishment to call teardown. Each Q.931 event is given a name, called the *message type.*

❑ By far the most informative of the Q.931 messages, the SETUP message is the first place to look once you've verified the Physical Layer, the Data Link layer (Q.921), and DDR. All the Q.931 message-type packets contain fields called *information elements (IEs).* In the SETUP message, these IEs contain information vital to the call establishment procedure. The most important IEs in the SETUP packet are the bearer capability, called party number, calling party number, and the call reference value.

PPP and Multilink PPP

❑ PPP adds to HDLC capabilities for authentication, compression, IP address assignment, and bundling of multiple B channels, in addition to many other standardized and proprietary features.

❑ Multilink PPP uses inverse multiplexing to combine two or more B channels into one *logical pipe* for increased bandwidth.

ISDN BRI Diagnostic Tools

❑ The Cisco IOS offers numerous SHOW commands that display current information about ISDN. SHOW ISDN STATUS shows a quick snapshot of all three ISDN layers; SHOW INTERFACES BRI shows useful information about both B and D channels.

❑ DEBUG commands can be used to track down problems and see every ISDN event that occurs. DEBUG ISDN Q921 and DEBUG ISDN Q931 show these protocols in action. DEBUG DIALER and DEBUG PPP NEGOTIATION offer insight into Layer 3 problems.

Problem Isolation in ISDN BRI WANs

❑ Problem isolation in ISDN BRI WANs follows the same troubleshooting procedure as any other area: start from the bottom of the OSI model and work your way up.

❑ The five areas to check when troubleshooting are the ISDN Physical Layer, ISDN Layer 2, ISDN Layer 3, DDR configuration, and PPP options.

ISDN BRI Symptoms, Problems, and Action Plans

❑ Faulty hardware can cause a multitude of hard-to-track-down problems. Use SHOW INTERFACES BRI to look at the counters for hardware errors.

❑ Incorrect routing and dialing configurations can cause many connection issues. Know how to use DIALER MAP, DIALER STRING, DIALER-LIST, DIALER-GROUP, and DIALER LOAD-THRESHOLD commands.

SELF TEST

The following questions will help you measure your understanding of the material presented in this chapter. Read all the choices carefully because there might be more than one correct answer. Choose all correct answers for each question.

BRI Overview

1. A client wants to buy a videoconferencing package. The packages available require varying amounts of dedicated bandwidth. Which of the following packages will a single ISDN BRI support? Choose all that apply.

   A. 56KB/s

   B. 64KB/s

   C. 144KB/s

   D. 192KB/s

2. Which of the following OSI model layers has a corresponding ISDN layer?

   A. Session

   B. Presentation

   C. Data Link

   D. Application

ISDN Reference Points

3. Which of the following statements are true about the ISDN U interface? Choose all that apply.

   A. It can use a standard serial (RS-232) interface.

   B. It uses the existing two-wire Telco infrastructure.

   C. It connects an NT1 to the phone company.

   D. It connects a TA to an NT.

4. A client is not sure whether his switch type requires SPIDs. Which of the following *almost never* requires SPIDs?

   A. Basic-ni1

   B. Basic-5ess

   C. Basic-net3

   D. Basic-dms100

ISDN S/T Interface

5. Which two of the following cable types could be used to connect an ISDN router (S/T interface) to an NT1? Choose all that apply.

   A. Straight-through ISDN cable

   B. Crossover ISDN cable

   C. Straight-through LAN (RJ45) cable

   D. Crossover LAN (RJ45) cable

   E. Straight-through telephone (RJ11) cable

   F. Crossover telephone (RJ11) cable

6. What pins carry the bits on a four-wire S/T interface cable?

   A. 1, 2, 7, and 8

   B. 1–4

   C. 3–6

   D. 5–8

ISDN S/T Line Framing

7. ISDN framing and synchronization bits use what mechanism?

   A. Collision avoidance

   B. AMI line-code violations

   C. Activation indicator

   D. D channel balancing

8. A customer calls with a question about his ISDN connection to the Internet. He has read that ISDN BRI provides three DS0s and wonders why he does not get 192KB/s of bandwidth. What do you tell him?

   A. He *does* get 192KB/s.

   B. North American facilities can handle only 128KB/s.

C. The other 64KB/s is dedicated to the D channel.

D. The other 64KB/s is dedicated to the D channel and the Physical Layer.

ISDN Q.931 Call Setup

9. Which is *never* a part of the Q.931 SETUP message?

   A. Bearer capability

   B. Called party number

   C. Calling party number

   D. Cause code

10. A client from Georgia calls with an ISDN issue. She has a remote user in Maine dialing in via ISDN. She can see the call being placed, but it is quickly dropped every time. Which of the following could be the problem? Choose all that apply.

    A. Bearer capability mismatch

    B. Invalid SPID

    C. Wrong PPP authentication type

    D. Misconfigured DIALER-LIST

PPP and Multilink PPP

11. A client asks why PPP is preferred over HDLC in ISDN environments. Which of the following advantages would you tell him about? Choose all that apply.

    A. PPP has authentication.

    B. PPP supports compression.

    C. PPP Multilink is a benefit.

    D. PPP can carry IP traffic.

12. Look at the following debug output:

```
02:45:13: %ISDN-6-CONNECT: Interface BRI1/0:1 is now connected to
8005551212 00c0.0504.4a2d
02:45:14: BR1/0:2 MLP: Multilink up event pending
02:45:14: BR1/0:2 MLP: 00c0.0504.4a2d, multilink up
02:45:15: %LINEPROTO-5-UPDOWN: Line protocol on Interface BRI1/0:2,
changed state to up
```

```
02:45:19: %ISDN-6-CONNECT: Interface BRI1/0:2 is now connected to
8005551212 00c0.0504.4a2d
```

This exchange shows which of the following?

A. PPP authentication

B. Q.921 activation

C. PPP Magic Number negotiation

D. PPP Multilink activation

ISDN BRI Diagnostic Tools

13. Layer 2 status from the SHOW ISDN STATUS command should report which of the following?

A. MULTIPLE FRAME ESTABLISHED

B. TEI ASSIGNED

C. SAMBE

D. UA

14. Which tool would you use to discover the cause of an ISDN DISCONNECT message?

A. DEBUG ISDN Q931

B. DEBUG BRI

C. DEBUG PPP DIALER

D. DEBUG PPP MULTILINK

15. Examine the following output:

```
03:07:19: Vi1 IPCP: I CONFREQ [REQsent] id 2 len 14
03:07:19: Vi1 IPCP:    CompressType 0x002D (0x0204002D)
03:07:19: Vi1 IPCP:    Address 10.0.0.21 (0x03060A010313)
03:07:19: Vi1 IPCP: O CONFNAK [REQsent] id 2 len 8
03:07:19: Vi1 IPCP:    CompressType 0x002D (0x0204002D)
```

Which of the following statements is true about the exchange?

A. The router requested an IP address and was accepted.

B. The router requested an IP address and was turned down.

C. The router requested a compression type and was accepted.

D. The router requested a compression type and was turned down.

Problem Isolation in ISDN BRI WANs

16. Where should you generally start your ISDN troubleshooting efforts?

A. ISDN Physical Layer

B. ISDN Layer 2

C. ISDN Layer 3

D. PPP authentication

17. What command associates a next hop with an ISDN number to be dialed?

A. DIALER-LIST

B. DIALER MAP

C. DIALER LOAD-THRESHOLD

D. DIALER STRING

ISDN BRI Symptoms, Problems, and Action Plans

18. Your company cannot get its new ISDN line to come up. The phone company comes out to check the U interface with an oscilloscope. What layer are they troubleshooting?

A. Physical

B. Data Link

C. Network

D. Q.931

19. Examine the following output from SHOW INTERFACE BRI 1/0:

```
Router4>sh int bri 1/0
BRI1/0 is up, line protocol is up (spoofing)
Hardware is BRI with integrated NT1
Internet address is 10.1.101.200/32
MTU 1500 bytes, BW 64 Kbit, DLY 20000 usec, rely 255/255, load 1/255
Encapsulation PPP, loopback not set
Last input 00:00:00, output 00:00:00, output hang never
Last clearing of "show interface" counters never
Input queue: 0/75/49 (size/max/drops); Total output drops: 0
Queueing strategy: weighted fair
Output queue: 0/1000/64/0 (size/max total/threshold/drops)
Conversations  0/1/256 (active/max active/max total)
Reserved Conversations 0/0 (allocated/max allocated)
```

```
5 minute input rate 0 bits/sec, 0 packets/sec
5 minute output rate 0 bits/sec, 0 packets/sec
118073 packets input, 496372 bytes, 0 no buffer
Received 0 broadcasts, 8322 runts, 0 giants, 0 throttles
10654 input errors, 432 CRC, 665 frame, 0 overrun, 0 ignored 776 abort
118083 packets output, 472668 bytes, 0 underruns
0 output errors, 0 collisions, 4 interface resets
0 output buffer failures, 0 output buffers swapped out
5 carrier transitions
```

If this interface were having problems placing and dropping calls, what would you suspect?

A. ISDN Physical Layer

B. ISDN Layer 2

C. ISDN Layer 3

D. PPP authentication

20. An ISDN router places a call, connects, and then drops after 3 seconds. Which of the following could be the problem?

A. Incorrect DIALER LOAD-THRESHOLD

B. Incorrect DIALER MAP

C. Incorrect PPP authentication

D. Incorrect DIALER-LIST

LAB QUESTION

You are to set up an ISDN BRI router to connect with a remote router across town. The router's hostname is Router5, and it will use the BRI0 interface. Use the following specifications to fill in the router configuration worksheet located in Table 13-3.

■ ISDN switch type = National ISDN 1.

■ SPID 1 = 999555121201010, SPID = 99955512130101.

■ The BRI interface IP address is 10.1.1.1 (class C). The remote address is 10.1.1.2.

■ Use a static route to send all local traffic across the link.

■ Activate the link for all IP traffic.

■ The remote dial number is 5557777.

■ Use PPP encapsulation, PPP Multilink, and CHAP authentication.

■ The remote router's name is router4 and its CHAP password is *boxter*.

■ Have the second channel come up if the first is 50 percent or greater capacity in either direction.

TABLE 13-3	(config)	Hostname Router5
	(config)	_____
Router	(config)	_____
Configuration for	(config)	_____
Lab Question	(config)	_____
	(config-if)	_____
	(config-if)	_____
	(config-if)	_____
	(config-if)	_____
	(config-if)	_____
	(config-if)	_____
	(config-if)	_____

SELF TEST ANSWERS

1. ☑ **A and B.** 56KB/s and 64KB/s. ISDN supports a maximum of 128KB/s of data transfer.
   ☒ **C and D** are incorrect because only 128KB/s are available to the B channels. Even though ISDN is three DS0s (192KB/s), the other 64KB/s are used for the D channel and Physical Layer signaling.

2. ☑ **C.** The OSI Data Link Layer corresponds to ISDN Layer 2.
   ☒ **A, B,** and **D** are incorrect because none of these OSI layers has a corresponding ISDN Layer.

ISDN Reference Points

3. ☑ **B and D.** It uses the existing two-wire Telco infrastructure, and it connects a TA to an NT. The U reference point connects the NT1 to the LT (at the CO) over the phone company's existing two-wire infrastructure.
   ☒ **A and C** are incorrect because they describe the R reference point.

4. ☑ **C.** Basic-net3. SPIDs are almost never used in Europe, where the basic-net3 switch is used.
   ☒ **A and D,** basic-ni1 and basic-dms100, almost always require SPIDs. **B,** basic-5ess, usually depends on your provider.

ISDN S/T Interface

5. ☑ **A and C.** Standard straight-through cables are correct for the S/T interface.
   ☒ **B and D** are incorrect because crossover cables will not work with ISDN. **E and F** are incorrect because the S/T interface is four-wire, not two-wire, like the standard RJ11 telephone interface.

6. ☑ **C.** Pins 3–6 carry the positive and negative signals that are the bits.
   ☒ **A, B,** and **D** are all incorrect; pins 1, 2, 7, and 8 sometimes carry power and are sometimes not used at all.

ISDN S/T Line Framing

7. ☑ **B.** The F bits use bipolar line-code violations to clearly demarcate frames.
   ☒ **A and C** are Physical Layer mechanisms but do not provide framing and synchronization. **D,** channel balancing, does not mean anything.

8. ☑ **D.** The other 64KB/s is divided between the D channel (16KB/s) and Physical Layer maintenance (48KB/s).

   ☒ **A, B,** and **C** are incorrect because they are all untrue.

ISDN Q.931 Call Setup

9. ☑ **D.** Cause code is part of the DISCONNECT message, not the SETUP message.

   ☒ **A, B,** and **C** are all incorrect because they are usually IEs in the SETUP message.

10. ☑ **A and C.** Both bearer capability mismatches and wrong PPP authentication types cause quick drops. Note that with a bearer capability mismatch, the call never actually connects. With wrong PPP authentication type, the call connects for about two seconds, then disconnects.

    ☒ **B and D** are both incorrect; if either condition exists, a call is never placed.

PPP and Multilink PPP

11. ☑ **A, B,** and **C.** PPP has authentication, PPP supports compression, and PPP Multilink are all options PPP offers that HDLC does not.

    ☒ **D** is incorrect because PPP and HDLC can both carry IP.

12. ☑ **D.** The output shows that both B channels are connected and Multilink is bonding the channels.

    ☒ **A, B,** and **C** are incorrect because none deals with the connection of multiple B channels.

ISDN BRI Diagnostic Tools

13. ☑ **A and B.** If Layer 2 is operational, SHOW ISDN STATUS should report both MULTIPLE FRAME ESTABLISHED and which TEI is assigned.

    ☒ **C and D** are both Layer 2 mechanisms, but neither is reported in SHOW ISDN STATUS.

14. ☑ **A.** DEBUG ISDN Q931 shows the DISCONNECT message, which includes the CAUSE IE.

    ☒ **B, C,** and **D** are incorrect because none contains information about the CAUSE IE.

15. ☑ **D.** The router first sends a CONFREQ requesting both a compression type and an IP address. The CONFNAK, in response, rejects the compression type.

    ☒ **A and B** are both incorrect because no answer was given to the IP address request. **C** is incorrect because the compression type received a CONFNAK.

Problem Isolation in ISDN BRI WANs

16. ☑ **A.** ISDN Physical Layer. ISDN troubleshooting is similar to most networking troubleshooting methodologies: verify the bottom layers first and work your way up. The Physical Layer is the lowest level at which to start.

    ☒ **B, C,** and **D** are all incorrect because starting from a middle layer leads to nebulous troubleshooting results. For example, if ISDN Layer 2 is not functioning, you do not know for sure if Layer 2 is truly the problem until you verify Layer 1. Therefore, always start from the bottom layer.

17. ☑ **B.** DIALER MAP is used to associate a next hop with an ISDN number.

    ☒ **A,** DIALER-LIST, is incorrect because it is used to define interesting traffic. **C,** DIALER LOAD THRESHOLD, is incorrect because it defines the traffic load required to bring up a second channel. **D,** DIALER STRING, is incorrect because it defines a certain interface to dial a specific ISDN number.

ISDN BRI Symptoms, Problems, and Action Plans

18. ☑ **A.** Physical. The U interface is the two-wire phone company cable.

    ☒ **B, C,** and **D** are incorrect because an oscilloscope could be used only to check cabling.

19. ☑ **A.** ISDN Physical Layer. The huge number of input errors means either cable problems or a faulty device.

    ☒ **B, C,** and **D** are incorrect. No ISDN Layer 2 problems are indicated. This output gives no information about ISDN Layer 3 or PPP authentication.

20. ☑ **C.** PPP authentication problems would cause a call to connect and then immediately drop.

    ☒ **A, B,** and **D** are incorrect. A call would never be placed if DIALER MAP and DIALER-LIST were misconfigured. If DIALER LOAD-THRESHOLD were wrong, one call would be placed and a second would never come up.

LAB ANSWER

The configuration should read as follows:

```
(config)Hostname Router5
(config)isdn switch-type basic-ni
(config)dialer-list 1 protocol ip permit
(config)ip route 0.0.0.0 0.0.0.0 10.1.1.2
(config)username router4 password boxter
```

```
(config-if)ip address 10.1.1.1 255.255.255.0
(config-if)encapsulation ppp
(config-if)ppp authentication chap
(config-if)ppp multilink
(config-if)dialer load-threshold 128
(config-if)dialer-group 1
(config-if)dialer map ip 10.1.1.2 name router5 5557777
```

A

About the CD

T his CD-ROM contains the CertTrainer software. CertTrainer comes complete with ExamSim, Skill Assessment tests, the e-book (electronic version of the book), and DriveTime. CertTrainer is easy to install on any Windows 98/NT/2000 computer and must be installed to access these features. You may, however, browse the e-book directly from the CD without installation.

Installing CertTrainer

If your computer CD-ROM drive is configured to autorun, the CD-ROM will automatically start up upon inserting the disk. From the opening screen you may either browse the e-book or install CertTrainer by pressing the *Install Now* button. This will begin the installation process and create a program group named "CertTrainer." To run CertTrainer use START | PROGRAMS | CERTTRAINER.

System Requirements

CertTrainer requires Windows 98 or higher and Internet Explorer 4.0 or above and 600 MB of hard disk space for full installation.

CertTrainer

CertTrainer provides a complete review of each exam objective, organized by chapter. You should read each objective summary and make certain that you understand it before proceeding to the SkillAssessor. If you still need more practice on the concepts of any objective, use the "In Depth" button to link to the corresponding section from the Study Guide.

Once you have completed the review(s) and feel comfortable with the material, launch the SkillAssessor quiz to test your grasp of each objective. Once you complete the quiz, you will be presented with your score for that chapter.

ExamSim

As its name implies, ExamSim provides you with a simulation of the actual exam. The number of questions, the type of questions, and the time allowed are intended to be an accurate representation of the exam environment. You will see the following screen when you are ready to begin ExamSim:

When you launch ExamSim, a digital clock display will appear in the upper left-hand corner of your screen. The clock will continue to count down to zero unless you choose to end the exam before the time expires.

There are three types of questions on the exam:

- **Multiple Choice**   These questions have a single correct answer that you indicate by selecting the appropriate check box.

- **Multiple-Multiple Choice**   These questions require more than one correct answer. Indicate each correct answer by selecting the appropriate check boxes.

- **Simulations**   These questions simulate actual Windows 2000 menus and dialog boxes. After reading the question, you are required to select the appropriate settings to most accurately meet the objectives for that question.

Saving Scores as Cookies

Your ExamSim score is stored as a browser cookie. If you've configured your browser to accept cookies, your score will be stored in a file named *History*. If your browser is not configured to accept cookies, you cannot permanently save your scores. If you delete this History cookie, the scores will be deleted permanently.

E-Book

The entire contents of the Study Guide are provided in HTML form, as shown in the following screen. Although the files are optimized for Internet Explorer, they can also be viewed with other browsers including Netscape.

Help

A help file is provided through a help button on the main ExamSim Gold screen in the lower right-hand corner.

Upgrading

A button is provided on the main ExamSim screen for upgrades. This button will take you to www.syngress.com where you can download any available upgrades.

Glossary

10Base2   Ethernet specification using 50-ohm thin coaxial cable and a signaling rate of 10-Mbps baseband.

10Base5   Ethernet specification using standard (thick) 50-ohm baseband coaxial cable and a signaling rate of 10-Mbps baseband.

10BaseFL   Ethernet specification using fiber-optic cabling and a signaling rate of 10-Mbps baseband, and FOIRL.

10BaseT   Ethernet specification using two pairs of twisted-pair cabling (Category 3, 4, or 5): one pair for transmitting data and the other for receiving data, and a signaling rate of 10-Mbps baseband.

10Broad36   Ethernet specification using broadband coaxial cable and a signaling rate of 10-Mbps.

100BaseFX   Fast Ethernet specification using two strands of multimode fiber-optic cable per link and a signaling rate of 100-Mbps baseband. A 100BaseFX link cannot exceed 400 meters in length.

100BaseT   Fast Ethernet specification using UTP wiring and a signaling rate of 100-Mbps baseband. 100BaseT sends link pulses out on the wire when there is no data traffic present.

100BaseT4   Fast Ethernet specification using four pairs of Category 3, 4, or 5 UTP wiring and a signaling rate of 100-Mbps baseband. The maximum length of a 100BaseT4 segment is 100 meters.

100BaseTX   Fast Ethernet specification using two pairs of UTP or STP wiring and 100-Mbps baseband signaling. One pair of wires is used to receive data; the other is used to transmit. A 100BaseTX segment cannot exceed 100 meters in length.

100BaseX   100-Mbps baseband Fast Ethernet specification based on the IEEE 802.3 standard. 100BaseX refers to the whole 100Base family of standards for Fast Ethernet.

80/20 rule   General network standard that 80 percent of traffic on a given network is local (destined for targets in the same workgroup); and not more than 20 percent of traffic requires internetworking.

AAL (ATM adaptation layer)   Service-dependent sublayer of the Data-Link Layer. The function of the AAL is to accept data from different applications and present it to the ATM layer in 48-byte ATM segments.

AARP (AppleTalk Address Resolution Protocol)   The protocol that maps a data-link address to an AppleTalk network address.

ABR (area border router)   Router located on the border of an OSPF area, which connects that area to the backbone network. An ABR would be a member of both the OSPF backbone and the attached area. It maintains routing tables describing both the backbone topology and the topology of the other area.

access list   A sequential list of statements in a router configuration that identify network traffic for various purposes, including traffic and route filtering.

accounting   Cisco command option that, when applied to an interface, makes the router keep track of the number of bytes and packets sent between each pair of network addresses.

acknowledgment   Notification sent from one network device to another to acknowledge that a message or group of messages has been received. Sometimes abbreviated ACK. Opposite of **NAK**.

active hub   A multiport device that repeats and amplifies LAN signals at the Physical Layer.

active monitor   A network device on a Token Ring that is responsible for managing ring operations. The active monitor ensures that tokens are not lost, or that frames do not circulate indefinitely on the ring.

address   A numbering convention used to identify a unique entity or location on a network.

address mapping   Technique that allows different protocols to operate together by associating addresses from one format with those of another.

address mask   A string of bits, which, when combined with an address, describes which portion of an address refers to the network or subnet and which part refers to the host. *See also* **subnet mask.**

address resolution   A technique for resolving differences between computer addressing schemes. Address resolution most often specifies a method for mapping Network Layer addresses to Data-Link Layer addresses. *See also* **address mapping.**

Address Resolution Protocol   *See* ARP.

administrative distance   A rating of the preferability of a routing information source. Administrative distance is expressed as a value between 0 and 255. The higher the value, the lower the preference.

advertising   A process in which a router sends routing or service updates at frequent intervals so that other routers on the network can maintain lists of usable routes or services.

algorithm   A specific process for arriving at a solution to a problem.

AMI (alternate mark inversion)   The line-code type that is used on T1 and E1 circuits. In this code, zeros are represented by 01 during each bit cell, and ones are represented by 11 or 00, alternately, during each bit cell.

ANSI (American National Standards Institute)   An organization of representatives of corporate, government, and other entities that coordinates standards-related activities, approves U.S. national standards, and develops positions for the United States in international standards organizations.

AppleTalk A suite of communications protocols developed by Apple Computer for allowing communication among their devices over a network.

application layer Layer 7 of the OSI reference model. This layer provides services to end-user application processes such as electronic mail, file transfer, and terminal emulation.

ARP (Address Resolution Protocol) Internet protocol used to map an IP address to a MAC address.

ASBR (autonomous system boundary router) An ASBR is an ABR connecting an OSPF autonomous system to a non-OSPF network. ASBRs run two protocols: OSPF and another routing protocol. ASBRs must be located in a nonstub OSPF area.

asynchronous transmission Describes digital signals that are transmitted without precise clocking or synchronization.

ATM (Asynchronous Transfer Mode) An international standard for cell relay suitable for carrying multiple service types (such as voice, video, or data) in fixed-length (53-byte) cells. Fixed-length cells allow cell processing to occur in hardware, thereby reducing latency.

ATM adaptation layer *See* AAL.

ATM Forum International organization founded in 1991 by Cisco Systems, NET/ADAPTIVE, Northern Telecom, and Sprint to develop and promote standards-based implementation agreements for ATM technology.

AUI (attachment unit interface) An interface between an MAU and a NIC (network interface card) described in the IEEE 802.3 specification. AUI often refers to the physical port to which an AUI cable attaches.

auto-discovery A mechanism used by many network management products, including CiscoWorks, to build a map of a network.

autonomous system   A group of networks under a common administration that share in a common routing strategy. Sometimes abbreviated AS.

B8ZS (binary 8-zero substitution)   The line-code type that used on T1 and E1 circuits. With B8ZS, a special code is substituted whenever eight consecutive zeros are sent over the link. This code is then interpreted at the remote end of the connection.

backoff   The retransmission delay used by contention-based MAC protocols such as Ethernet, after a network node determines that the physical medium is already in use.

bandwidth   The difference between the highest and lowest frequencies available for network signals. The term may also describe the throughput capacity of a network link or segment.

baseband   A network technology in which a single carrier frequency is used. Ethernet is a common example of a baseband network technology.

baud   Unit of signaling speed equal to the number of separate signal elements transmitted in one second. Baud is synonymous with bits per second (bps), as long as each signal element represents exactly one bit.

B channel (bearer channel)   An ISDN term meaning a full-duplex, 64-kbps channel used to send user data.

bearer channel   *See* B channel.

BECN   Backward explicit congestion notification. A Frame Relay network facility that allows switches in the network to advise DTE devices of congestion. The BECN bit is set in frames traveling in the opposite direction of frames encountering a congested path.

best-effort delivery   Describes a network system that does not use a system of acknowledgment to guarantee reliable delivery of information.

BGP (Border Gateway Protocol)   An interdomain path-vector routing protocol. BGP exchanges reachability information with other BGP systems. It is defined by RFC 1163.

binary   A numbering system in which there are only two digits, ones and zeros.

bit stuffing   A 0 insertion and deletion process defined by HDLC. This technique ensures that actual data never appears as flag characters.

BNC connector   Standard connector used to connect coaxial cable to an MAU or line card.

BOOTP (Bootstrap Protocol)   Part of the TCP/IP suite of protocols, used by a network node to determine the IP address of its network interfaces, in order to boot from a network server.

BPDU   Bridge Protocol Data Unit. A Layer 2 protocol used for communication among bridges.

bps   Bits per second.

BRI (Basic Rate Interface)   ISDN interface consisting of two B channels and one D channel for circuit-switched communication. ISDN BRI can carry voice, video, and data.

bridge   Device that connects and forwards packets between two network segments that use the same data-link communications protocol. Bridges operate at the Data-Link Layer of the OSI reference model. A bridge will filter, forward, or flood an incoming frame based on the MAC address of the frame.

broadband   A data transmission system that multiplexes multiple independent signals onto one cable. Also, in telecommunications, any channel with a bandwidth greater than 4 KHz. In LAN terminology, a coaxial cable using analog signaling.

broadcast   Data packet addressed to all nodes on a network. Broadcasts are identified by a broadcast address that matches all addresses on the network.

broadcast address   Special address reserved for sending a message to all stations. At the Data-Link Layer, a broadcast address is a MAC destination address of all 1s.

broadcast domain   The group of all devices that will receive the same broadcast frame originating from any device within the group. Because routers do not forward broadcast frames, broadcast domains are typically bounded by routers.

buffer   A memory storage area used for handling data in transit. Buffers are used in internetworking to compensate for differences in processing speed between network devices or signaling rates of segments. Bursts of packets can be stored in buffers until they can be handled by slower devices.

bus   Common physical path composed of wires or other media, across which signals are sent from one part of a computer to another.

bus topology   A topology used in LANs. Transmissions from network stations propagate the length of the medium and are then received by all other stations.

byte   A series of consecutive binary digits that are operated upon as a unit, usually eight bits.

cable   Transmission medium of copper wire or optical fiber wrapped in a protective cover.

cable range   A range of network numbers on an extended AppleTalk network. The cable range value can be a single network number or a contiguous sequence of several network numbers. Nodes assign addresses within the cable range values provided.

CAM   Content-addressable memory.

carrier   Electromagnetic wave or alternating current of a single frequency, suitable for modulation by another, data-bearing signal.

Carrier Detect   *See* CD.

Carrier Sense Multiple Access With Collision Detection   *See* CSMA/CD.

Category 5 cabling   One of five grades of UTP cabling described in the EIA/TIA-586 standard. Category 5 cabling can transmit data at speeds up to 100 Mbps.

CCITT (Consultative Committee for International Telegraphy and Telephony)   International organization responsible for the development of communications standards. Now called the ITU-T. *See* ITU-T.

CCO   Cisco Connection Online. Self-help resource for Cisco customers. Available 24 hours a day, seven days a week at http://www.cisco.com. The CCO family includes CCO Documentation, CCO Open Forum, CCO CD-ROM, and the TAC (Technical Assistance Center).

CD (Carrier Detect)   Signal that indicates whether an interface is active.

CDDI (Copper Distributed Data Interface)   The implementation of FDDI protocols over STP and UTP cabling. CDDI transmits over distances of approximately 100 meters, providing data rates of 100 Mbps. CDDI uses a dual-ring architecture to provide redundancy.

CDP   Cisco Discovery Protocol, used to discover neighboring Cisco devices, and used by network management software. The CiscoWorks network management software takes advantage of CDP.

cell   The basic data unit for ATM switching and multiplexing. A cell consists of a five-byte header and 48 bytes of payload. Cells contain fields in their headers that identify the data stream to which they belong.

CHAP (Challenge Handshake Authentication Protocol)   Security feature used with PPP encapsulation, which prevents unauthorized access by identifying the remote end. The router or access server determines whether that user is allowed access.

checksum   Method for checking the integrity of transmitted data. A checksum is an integer value computed from a sequence of octets taken through a series of arithmetic operations. The value is recomputed at the receiving end and compared for verification.

CiscoWorks   Network management package that provides a graphical view of a network, collects statistical information about a network, and offers various network management components.

CIDR (classless interdomain routing)   Technique supported by BGP4 and based on route aggregation. CIDR allows routers to group routes together in order to cut down on the quantity of routing information carried by the core routers. With CIDR, several IP networks appear to networks outside the group as a single, larger entity. With CIDR, IP addresses and their subnet masks are written as four octets, separated by periods, followed by a forward slash and a two-digit number that represents the subnet mask.

CIR (committed information rate)   The rate at which a Frame Relay network agrees to transfer information under normal conditions, averaged over a minimum increment of time. CIR, measured in bits per second, is one of the key negotiated tariff metrics.

circuit switching   A system in which a dedicated physical path must exist between sender and receiver for the entire duration of a call. Used heavily in telephone networks.

client   Node or software program, or front-end device, that requests services from a server.

CLNS (Connectionless Network Service)   An OSI Network Layer service, for which no circuit need be established before data can be transmitted. Routing of messages to their destinations is independent of other messages.

CMU SNMP   A free command-line SNMP management package that comes in source code form. Originally developed at the Carnegie Mellon University, and available at http://www.net.cmu.edu/projects/snmp/.

collision   In Ethernet, the result of two nodes transmitting simultaneously. The frames from each device cause an increase in voltage when they meet on the physical media, and are damaged.

collision domain   A group of nodes such that any two or more of the nodes transmitting simultaneously will result in a collision.

congestion   Traffic in excess of network capacity.

connectionless   Term used to describe data transfer without the prior existence of a circuit.

console   A DTE device, usually consisting of a keyboard and display unit, through which users interact with a host.

contention   Access method in which network devices compete for permission to access the physical medium. Compare with **circuit switching** and **token passing**.

cost   A value, typically based on media bandwidth or other measures, that is assigned by a network administrator and used by routing protocols to compare various paths through an internetwork environment. Cost values are used to determine the most favorable path to a particular destination—the lower the cost, the better the path.

count to infinity   A condition in which routers continuously increment the hop count to particular networks. Often occurs in routing algorithms that are slow to converge. Usually, some arbitrary hop count ceiling is imposed to limit the extent of this problem.

CPE (customer premises equipment)   Terminating equipment, such as terminals, telephones, and modems, installed at customer sites and connected to the telephone company network.

CRC (cyclic redundancy check)   An error-checking technique in which the receiving device performs a calculation on the frame contents and compares the calculated number to a value stored in the frame by the sending node.

CSMA/CD (carrier sense multiple access collision detect)
Media-access mechanism used by Ethernet and IEEE 802.3. Devices use CSMA/CD to check the channel for a carrier before transmitting data. If no carrier is sensed, the device transmits. If two devices transmit at the same time, the collision is detected by all colliding devices. Collisions delay retransmissions from those devices for a randomly chosen length of time.

CSU (channel service unit)   Digital interface device that connects end-user equipment to the local digital telephone loop. Often referred to together with DSU, as CSU/DSU.

datagram   Logical unit of information sent as a Network Layer unit over a transmission medium without prior establishment of a circuit.

data-link layer   Layer 2 of the OSI reference model. This layer provides reliable transit of data across a physical link. The Data-Link Layer is concerned with physical addressing, network topology, access to the network medium, error detection, sequential delivery of frames, and flow control. The Data-Link Layer is divided into two sublayers: the MAC sublayer and the LLC sublayer.

DCE (data circuit-terminating equipment)   The devices and connections of a communications network that represent the network end of the user-to-network interface. The DCE provides a physical connection to the network and provides a clocking signal used to synchronize transmission between DCE and DTE devices. Modems and interface cards are examples of DCE devices.

D channel   Data channel. Full-duplex, 16-kbps (BRI) or 64-kbps (PRI) ISDN channel.

DDR (dial-on-demand routing)   Technique whereby a router can automatically initiate and close a circuit-switched session as transmitting stations demand. The router spoofs keepalives so that endstations treat the session as active. DDR permits routing over ISDN or telephone lines using an external ISDN terminal adapter or modem.

DECnet   Group of communications products (including a protocol suite) developed and supported by Digital Equipment Corporation. DECnet/OSI (also called DECnet Phase V) is the most recent iteration and supports both OSI protocols and proprietary digital protocols. Phase IV Prime supports inherent MAC addresses that allow DECnet nodes to coexist with systems running other protocols that have MAC address restrictions. *See also* **DNA**.

dedicated line   Communications line that is indefinitely reserved for transmissions, rather than switched as transmission is required. *See also* **leased line**.

de facto standard   A standard that exists because of its widespread use.

default gateway   Another term for default router. The router that a host will use to reach another network when it has no specific information about how to reach that network.

default route   A routing table entry that is used to direct packets when there is no explicit route present in the routing table.

de jure standard   Standard that exists because of its development or approval by an official standards body.

delay   The time between the initiation of a transaction by a sender and the first response received by the sender. Also, the time required to move a packet from source to destination over a network path.

demarc   The demarcation point between telephone carrier equipment and CPE.

demultiplexing   The separating of multiple streams of data that have been multiplexed into a common physical signal for transmission, back into multiple output streams. Opposite of multiplexing.

destination address   Address of a network device to receive data.

DHCP (Dynamic Host Configuration Protocol)   Provides a mechanism for allocating IP addresses dynamically so that addresses can be reassigned instead of belonging to only one host.

discovery mode   Method by which an AppleTalk router acquires information about an attached network from an operational router and then uses this information to configure its own addressing information.

distance vector routing algorithm   Class of routing algorithms that use the number of hops in a route to find a shortest path to a destination network. Distance vector routing algorithms call for each router to send its entire routing table in each update to each of its neighbors. Also called Bellman-Ford routing algorithm.

DLCI (data-link connection identifier)   A value that specifies a virtual circuit in a Frame Relay network.

DNA (Digital Network Architecture)   Network architecture that was developed by Digital Equipment Corporation. DECnet is the collective term for the products that comprise DNA (including communications protocols).

DNIC (Data Network Identification Code)   Part of an X.121 address. DNICs are divided into two parts: the first specifying the country in which the addressed PSN is located and the second specifying the PSN itself. *See also* **X.121**.

DNS (Domain Name System)   System used in the Internet for translating names of network nodes into addresses.

DSP (domain specific part)   Part of an ATM address. A DSP is comprised of an area identifier, a station identifier, and a selector byte.

DTE (data terminal equipment)   Device at the user end of a user-network interface that serves as a data source, destination, or both. DTE connects to a data network through a DCE device (for example, a modem) and typically uses clocking signals generated by the DCE. DTE includes such devices as computers, routers and multiplexers.

DUAL (Diffusing Update Algorithm)   Convergence algorithm used in EIGRP. DUAL provides constant loop-free operation throughout a route computation by allowing routers involved in a topology change to synchronize at the same time, without involving routers that are unaffected by the change.

DVMRP (Distance Vector Multicast Routing Protocol)   DVMRP is an internetwork gateway protocol that implements a typical dense mode IP multicast scheme. Using IGMP, DVMRP exchanges routing datagrams with its neighbors.

Dijkstra algorithm   Dijkstra's algorithm is a graph algorithm use to find the shortest path from one node on a graph to all others. Used in networking to determine the shortest path between routers.

dynamic routing   Routing that adjusts automatically to changes in network topology or traffic patterns.

E1   Wide-area digital transmission scheme used in Europe that carries data at a rate of 2.048 Mbps.

EIA/TIA-232   Common Physical Layer interface standard, developed by EIA and TIA, that supports unbalanced circuits at signal speeds of up to 64 kbps. Formerly known as RS-232.

EIGRP Enhanced IGRP. A multiservice routing protocol supporting IPX, AppleTalk, and IP. BGP is used for interconnecting networks and defining strict routing policies.

encapsulation The process of attaching a particular protocol header to a unit of data prior to transmission on the network. For example, a frame of Ethernet data is given a specific Ethernet header before network transit.

endpoint Device at which a virtual circuit or virtual path begins or ends.

enterprise network A privately maintained network connecting most major points in a company or other organization. Usually spans a large geographic area and supports multiple protocols and services.

entity Generally, an individual, manageable network device. Sometimes called an alias.

error control Technique for detecting and correcting errors in data transmissions.

Ethernet Baseband LAN specification invented by Xerox Corporation and developed jointly by Xerox, Intel, and Digital Equipment Corporation. Ethernet networks use the CSMA/CD method of media access control and run over a variety of cable types at 10 Mbps. Ethernet is similar to the IEEE 802.3 series of standards.

EtherTalk Apple Computer's data-link product that allows an AppleTalk network to be connected by Ethernet cable.

EtherWave A product from Netopia (formerly Farallon) used to connect AppleTalk devices with LocalTalk connectors to Ethernet networks. They are an alternative to LocalTalk-to-EtherTalk routers.

explorer packet Generated by an endstation trying to find its way through a SRB network. Gathers a hop-by-hop description of a path through the network by being marked (updated) by each bridge that it traverses, thereby creating a complete topological map.

Fast Ethernet   Any of a number of 100-Mbps Ethernet specifications. Fast Ethernet offers a speed increase ten times that of the 10BaseT Ethernet specification, while preserving such qualities as frame format, MAC mechanisms, and MTU. Such similarities allow the use of existing 10BaseT applications and network management tools on Fast Ethernet networks. Based on an extension to the IEEE 802.3 specification. Compare with **Ethernet**. *See also* **100BaseFX**; **100BaseT**; **100BaseT4**; **100BaseTX**; **100BaseX**; **IEEE 802.3**.

FDDI (Fiber Distributed Data Interface)   LAN standard, defined by ANSI X3T9.5, specifying a 100-Mbps token-passing network using fiber-optic cable, with transmission distances of up to 2 km. FDDI uses a dual-ring architecture to provide redundancy. Compare with **CDDI**.

FECN (forward explicit congestion notification)   A facility in a Frame Relay network to inform DTE receiving the frame that congestion was experienced in the path from source to destination. DTE receiving frames with the FECN bit set can request that higher-level protocols take flow-control action as appropriate.

file transfer   Category of popular network applications that features movement of files from one network device to another.

filter   Generally, a process or device that screens network traffic for certain characteristics, such as source address, destination address, or protocol, and determines whether to forward or discard that traffic or routes based on the established criteria.

firewall   Router or other computer designated as a buffer between public networks and a private network. A firewall router uses access lists and other methods to ensure the security of the private network.

Flash memory   Nonvolatile storage that can be electrically erased and reprogrammed as necessary.

flash update Routing update sent asynchronously when a change in the network topology occurs.

flat addressing A system of addressing that does not incorporate a hierarchy to determine location.

flooding Traffic-passing technique used by switches and bridges in which traffic received on an interface is sent out all of the interfaces of that device except the interface on which the information was originally received.

flow control Technique for ensuring that a transmitting device, such as a modem, does not overwhelm a receiving device with data. When the buffers on the receiving device are full, a message is sent to the sending device to suspend transmission until it has processed the data in the buffers.

forwarding The process of sending a frame or packet toward its destination.

fragment Piece of a larger packet that has been broken down to smaller units.

fragmentation Process of breaking a packet into smaller units when transmitting over a network medium that is unable to support a transmission unit the original size of the packet.

frame Logical grouping of information sent as a Data-Link Layer unit over a transmission medium. Sometimes refers to the header and trailer, used for synchronization and error control, which surround the user data contained in the unit. The terms cell, datagram, message, packet, and segment are also used to describe logical information groupings at various layers of the OSI reference model and in various technology circles.

Frame Relay Industry-standard, switched Data-Link Layer protocol that handles multiple virtual circuits over a single physical interface. Frame Relay is more efficient than X.25, for which it is generally considered a replacement.

frame relay cloud   A generic term used to refer to a collective frame relay network. For frame relay carrier customers, it generally refers to the carrier's entire frame relay network. It's referred to as a "cloud" because the network layout is not visible to the customer.

frequency   Number of cycles, measured in hertz, of an alternating current signal per unit of time.

FTP (File Transfer Protocol)   An application protocol, part of the TCP/IP protocol stack, used for transferring files between hosts on a network.

full duplex   Capability for simultaneous data transmission and receipt of data between two devices.

full mesh   A network topology in which each network node has either a physical circuit or a virtual circuit connecting it to every other network node.

gateway   In the IP community, an older term referring to a routing device. Today, the term router is used to describe devices that perform this function, and gateway refers to a special-purpose device that performs an application layer conversion of information from one protocol stack to another.

GB   Gigabyte. Approximately 1,000,000,000 bytes.

GBps   Gigabytes per second.

Gb   Gigabit. Approximately 1,000,000,000 bits.

Gbps   Gigabits per second.

giants   Ethernet frames over the maximum frame size.

GNS (Get Nearest Server)   Request packet sent by a client on an IPX network to locate the nearest active server of a particular type. An IPX network client issues a GNS request to solicit either a direct response from a connected server or a response from a router that tells it where on the internetwork the service can be located. GNS is part of the IPX SAP.

half duplex   Capability for data transmission in only one direction at a time between a sending station and a receiving station.

handshake   Sequence of messages exchanged between two or more network devices to ensure transmission synchronization.

hardware address   *See* MAC address.

HDLC (High-Level Data Link Control)   Bit-oriented synchronous Data-Link Layer protocol developed by ISO and derived from SDLC. HDLC specifies a data encapsulation method for synchronous serial links and includes frame characters and checksums in its headers.

header   Control information placed before data when encapsulating that data for network transmission.

hello packet   Multicast packet that is used by routers for neighbor discovery and recovery. Hello packets also indicate that a client is still operating on the network.

Hello protocol   Protocol used by OSPF and other routing protocols for establishing and maintaining neighbor relationships.

hierarchical addressing   A scheme of addressing that uses a logical hierarchy to determine location. For example, IP addresses consist of network numbers, subnet numbers, and host numbers, which IP routing algorithms use to route the packet to the appropriate location.

holddown   State of a routing table entry in which routers will neither advertise the route nor accept advertisements about the route for a specific length of time (known as the holddown period).

hop   Term describing the passage of a data packet between two network nodes (for example, between two routers). *See also* **hop count**.

hop count   Routing metric used to measure the distance between a source and a destination. RIP uses hop count as its metric.

host   A computer system on a network. Similar to the term node except that host usually implies a computer system, whereas node can refer to any networked system, including routers.

host number   Part of an IP address that designates which node is being addressed. Also called a host address.

hub   A term used to describe a device that serves as the center of a star topology network; or, an Ethernet multiport repeater, sometimes referred to as a concentrator.

ICMP (Internet Control Message Protocol)   A Network Layer Internet protocol that provides reports of errors and other information about IP packet processing. ICMP is documented in RFC 792.

IEEE (Institute of Electrical and Electronics Engineers)   A professional organization among whose activities are the development of communications and networking standards. IEEE LAN standards are the most common LAN standards today.

IEEE 802.3   IEEE LAN protocol for the implementation of the Physical Layer and the MAC sublayer of the Data-Link Layer. IEEE 802.3 uses CSMA/CD access at various speeds over various physical media.

IEEE 802.5   IEEE LAN protocol for the implementation of the Physical Layer and MAC sublayer of the Data-Link Layer. Similar to Token Ring, IEEE 802.5 uses token passing access over STP cabling.

IGP (Interior Gateway Protocol)   A generic term for an Internet routing protocol used to exchange routing information within an autonomous system. Examples of common Internet IGPs include IGRP, OSPF, and RIP.

InARP   Inverse Address Resolution Protocol, a basic Frame Relay protocol that allows routers on the frame network to learn the protocol addresses of other routers.

interface   A connection between two systems or devices; or in routing terminology, a network connection.

Internet   Term used to refer to the global internetwork that evolved from the ARPANET, that now connects tens of thousands of networks worldwide.

Internet protocol   Any protocol that is part of the TCP/IP protocol stack. *See* TCP/IP.

internetwork   Collection of networks interconnected by routers and other devices that functions (generally) as a single network.

internetworking   General term used to refer to the industry that has arisen around the problem of connecting networks together. The term may be used to refer to products, procedures, and technologies.

Inverse ARP (Inverse Address Resolution Protocol)   Method of building dynamic address mappings in a Frame Relay network. Allows a device to discover the network address of a device associated with a virtual circuit.

IP (Internet Protocol)   Network Layer protocol in the TCP/IP stack offering a connectionless datagram service. IP provides features for addressing, type-of-service specification, fragmentation and reassembly, and security. Documented in RFC 791.

IP address   A 32-bit address assigned to hosts using the TCP/IP suite of protocols. An IP address is written as four octets separated by dots (dotted decimal format). Each address consists of a network number, an optional subnetwork number, and a host number. The network and subnetwork numbers together are used for routing, while the host number is used to address an individual host within the network or subnetwork. A subnet mask is often used with the address to extract network and subnetwork information from the IP address.

IPX (Internetwork Packet Exchange)   NetWare Network Layer (Layer 3) protocol used for transferring data from servers to workstations. IPX is similar to IP in that it is a connectionless datagram service.

IPXCP (IPX Control Protocol)   The protocol that establishes and configures IPX over PPP.

IPXWAN   A protocol that negotiates end-to-end options for new links on startup. When a link comes up, the first IPX packets sent across are IPXWAN packets negotiating the options for the link. When the IPXWAN options have been successfully determined, normal IPX transmission begins, and no more IPXWAN packets are sent. Defined by RFC 1362.

ISDN (Integrated Services Digital Network)   Communication protocol, offered by telephone companies, that permits telephone networks to carry data, voice, and other source traffic.

ISL (Inter-switch Link)   Cisco's protocol for trunking VLANs over Fast Ethernet.

ITU-T (International Telecommunication Union Telecommunication Standardization Sector)   International body dedicated to the development of worldwide standards for telecommunications technologies. ITU-T is the successor to CCITT.

jabbers   Long, continuous frames exceeding 1518 bytes that prevent all stations on the Ethernet network from transmitting data. Jabbering violates CSMA/CD implementation by prohibiting stations from transmitting data.

jam pattern   Initiated by Ethernet transmitting station when a collision is detected during transmission.

KB Kilobyte. Approximately 1,000 bytes.

Kb Kilobit. Approximately 1,000 bits.

KBps Kilobytes per second.

Kbps Kilobits per second.

keepalive interval Period of time between keepalive messages sent by a network device.

keepalive message Message sent by one network device to inform another network device that it is still active.

LAN (local-area network) High-speed, low-error data network covering a relatively small geographic area. LANs connect workstations, peripherals, terminals, and other devices in a single building or other geographically limited area. LAN standards specify cabling and signaling at the physical and Data-Link Layers of the OSI model. Ethernet, FDDI, and Token Ring are the most widely used LAN technologies.

LANE (LAN emulation) Technology that allows an ATM network to function as a LAN backbone. In this situation LANE provides multicast and broadcast support, address mapping (MAC-to-ATM), and virtual circuit management.

LAPB (Link Access Procedure, Balanced) The Data-Link Layer protocol in the X.25 protocol stack. LAPB is a bit-oriented protocol derived from HDLC.

LAPD (Link Access Procedure on the D channel) ISDN data link layer protocol for the D channel. LAPD was derived from the LAPB protocol and is designed to satisfy the signaling requirements of ISDN basic access. Defined by ITU-T Recommendations Q.920 and Q.921.

LAPF Data link standard for Frame Relay.

late collision   Collision that is detected only after a station places a complete frame of the network.

latency   The amount of time elapsed between the time a device requests access to a network and the time it is allowed to transmit; or, amount of time between the point at which a device receives a frame and the time that frame is forwarded out the destination port.

LCP (Link Control Protocol)   A protocol used with PPP, which establishes, configures, and tests data-link connections.

leased line   Transmission line reserved by a communications carrier for the private use of a customer. A leased line is a type of dedicated line.

link   Network communications channel consisting of a circuit or transmission path and all related equipment between a sender and a receiver. Most often used to refer to a WAN connection. Sometimes called a line or a transmission link.

link-state routing algorithm   Routing algorithm in which each router broadcasts or multicasts information regarding the cost of reaching each of its neighbors to all nodes in the internetwork. Link state algorithms require that routers maintain a consistent view of the network and are therefore not prone to routing loops.

LLC (Logical Link Control)   Higher of two Data-Link Layer sublayers defined by the IEEE. The LLC sublayer handles error control, flow control, framing, and MAC-sublayer addressing. The most common LLC protocol is IEEE 802.2, which includes both connectionless and connection-oriented types.

LMI (Local Management Interface)   A set of enhancements to the basic Frame Relay specification. LMI includes support for keepalives, a multicast mechanism; global addressing, and a status mechanism.

load balancing   In routing, the ability of a router to distribute traffic over all its network ports that are the same distance from the destination address. Load balancing increases the utilization of network segments, thus increasing total effective network bandwidth.

local loop A line from the premises of a telephone subscriber to the telephone company central office.

LocalTalk Apple Computer's proprietary baseband protocol that operates at the data-link and Physical Layers of the OSI reference model. LocalTalk uses CSMA/CA and supports transmissions at speeds of 230.4 Kbps.

loop A situation in which packets never reach their destination, but are forwarded in a cycle repeatedly through a group of network nodes.

MAC (Media Access Control) Lower of the two sublayers of the Data-Link Layer defined by the IEEE. The MAC sublayer handles access to shared media.

MAC address Standardized Data-Link Layer address that is required for every port or device that connects to a LAN. Other devices in the network use these addresses to locate specific ports in the network and to create and update routing tables and data structures. MAC addresses are 48 bits long and are controlled by the IEEE. Also known as a hardware address, a MAC-layer address, or a physical address.

MAN (metropolitan-area network) A network that spans a metropolitan area. Generally, a MAN spans a larger geographic area than a LAN, but a smaller geographic area than a WAN.

Mb Megabit. Approximately 1,000,000 bits.

Mbps Megabits per second.

media The various physical environments through which transmission signals pass. Common network media include cable (twisted-pair, coaxial, and fiber optic) and the atmosphere (through which microwave, laser, and infrared transmission occurs). Sometimes referred to as physical media.

Media Access Control   *See* MAC.

mesh   Network topology in which devices are organized in a segmented manner with redundant interconnections strategically placed between network nodes.

message   Application layer logical grouping of information, often composed of a number of lower-layer logical groupings such as packets.

MSAU (multistation access unit)   A wiring concentrator to which all endstations in a Token Ring network connect. Sometimes abbreviated MAU.

multiaccess network   A network that allows multiple devices to connect and communicate by sharing the same medium, such as a LAN.

multicast   A single packet copied by the network and sent to a specific subset of network addresses. These addresses are specified in the Destination Address field.

multicast address   A single address that refers to multiple network devices. Sometimes called a group address.

multiplexing   A technique that allows multiple logical signals to be transmitted simultaneously across a single physical channel.

mux   A multiplexing device. A mux combines multiple input signals for transmission over a single line. The signals are demultiplexed, or separated, before they are used at the receiving end.

NAK (Negative acknowledgment)   A response sent from a receiving device to a sending device indicating that the information received contained errors.

name resolution   The process of associating a symbolic name with a network location or address.

NAT (Network Address Translation)   A technique for reducing the need for globally unique IP addresses. NAT allows an organization with addresses may conflict with others in the IP address space, to connect to the Internet by translating those addresses into unique ones within the globally routable address space.

NBMA (nonbroadcast multiaccess) Term describing a multiaccess network that either does not support broadcasting (such as X.25) or in which broadcasting is not feasible.

NBP (Name Binding Protocol) AppleTalk transport level protocol that translates a character string name into the DDP address of the corresponding socket client.

NCP (Network Control Protocol) Protocols that establish and configure various Network Layer protocols. Used for AppleTalk over PPP.

NDS (NetWare Directory Services) A feature added in NetWare 4.0 as a replacement for individual binaries. NDS allows NetWare and related resources to be grouped in a tree hierarchy to better provide central administration.

NetBIOS (Network Basic Input/Output System) An application programming interface used by applications on an IBM LAN to request services from lower-level network processes such as session establishment and termination, and information transfer.

netmask A number, usually used as a bit-mask, to separate an address into its network portion and host portion.

NetWare A network operating system developed by Novell, Inc. Provides remote file access, print services, and numerous other distributed network services.

network Collection of computers, printers, routers, switches, and other devices that are able to communicate with each other over some transmission medium.

network interface Border between a carrier network and a privately owned installation.

network layer   Layer 3 of the OSI reference model. This layer provides connectivity and path selection between two end systems. The Network Layer is the layer at which routing takes place.

NLSP (NetWare Link Services Protocol)   Link-state routing protocol for IPX based on IS-IS.

node   Endpoint of a network connection or a junction common to two or more lines in a network. Nodes can be processors, controllers, or workstations. Nodes, which vary in their functional capabilities, can be interconnected by links, and serve as control points in the network.

NVRAM (nonvolatile RAM)   RAM that retains its contents when a device is powered off.

ODI   Novell's Open Data-Link Interface.

OSI reference model (Open System Interconnection reference model)   A network architectural framework developed by ISO and ITU-T. The model describes seven layers, each of which specifies a particular network. The lowest layer, called the Physical Layer, is closest to the media technology. The highest layer, the application layer, is closest to the user. The OSI reference model is widely used as a way of understanding network functionality.

OSPF (Open Shortest Path First)   A link-state, hierarchical IGP routing algorithm, which includes features such as least-cost routing, multipath routing, and load balancing. OSPF was based on an early version of the IS-IS protocol.

out-of-band signaling   Transmission using frequencies or channels outside the frequencies or channels used for transfer of normal data. Out-of-band signaling is often used for error reporting when normal channels are unusable for communicating with network devices.

packet   Logical grouping of information that includes a header containing control information and (usually) user data. Packets are most often used to refer to

Network Layer units of data. The terms datagram, frame, message, and segment are also used to describe logical information groupings at various layers of the OSI reference model, and in various technology circles. *See also* **PDU.**

packet analyzer   A software package (also sometimes including specialized hardware) used to monitor network traffic. Most packet analyzer packages will also do packet decoding, making the packets easier for humans to read.

packet burst   Allows multiple packets to be transmitted between Novell clients and servers in response to a single read or write request. It also allows file transfer to greatly improve throughput by reducing the number of acknowledgments.

packet starvation effect   On Ethernet, when packets experience latencies up to 100 times the average, or completely starve out due to 16 collisions. Occurs as a result of the CSMA/CD implementation.

PAP   Password Authentication Protocol. Authentication protocol that allows PPP peers to authenticate one another. The remote router attempting to connect to the local router is required to send an authentication request. Unlike CHAP, PAP passes the password and host name or username in the clear (unencrypted). PAP does not itself prevent unauthorized access, but merely identifies the remote end. The router or access server then determines if that user is allowed access. PAP is supported only on PPP lines.

partial mesh   Term describing a network in which devices are organized in a mesh topology, with some network nodes organized in a full mesh, but with others that are only connected to one or two other nodes in the network. A partial mesh does not provide the level of redundancy of a full mesh topology, but is less expensive to implement. Partial mesh topologies are generally used in the peripheral networks that connect to a fully meshed backbone. *See also* **full mesh; mesh.**

PDU (protocol data unit)   The OSI term for a packet.

physical layer   Layer 1 of the OSI reference model; it corresponds with the physical control layer in the SNA model. The Physical Layer defines the specifications for activating, maintaining, and deactivating the physical link between end systems.

Ping (packet internet groper)   ICMP echo message and its reply. Often used in IP networks to test the reachability of a network device.

poison reverse updates   Routing updates that explicitly indicate that a network or subnet is unreachable, rather than implying that a network is unreachable by not including it in updates. Poison reverse updates are sent to defeat large routing loops.

port   1. Interface on an internetworking device (such as a router). 2. In IP terminology, an upper-layer process that receives information from lower layers. Ports are numbered, and each numbered port is associated with a specific process. For example, SMTP is associated with port 25. A port number is also known as a well-known address. 3. To rewrite software or microcode so that it will run on a different hardware platform or in a different software environment than that for which it was originally designed.

PPP (Point-to-Point Protocol)   A successor to SLIP that provides router-to-router and host-to-network connections over synchronous and asynchronous circuits. Whereas SLIP was designed to work with IP, PPP was designed to work with several Network Layer protocols, such as IP, IPX, and ARA. PPP also has built-in security mechanisms, such as CHAP and PAP. PPP relies on two protocols: LCP and NCP. *See also* **CHAP; LCP; NCP; PAP; SLIP.**

presentation layer   Layer 6 of the OSI reference model. This layer ensures that information sent by the application layer of one system will be readable by the application layer of another. The presentation layer is also concerned with the data structures used by programs and therefore negotiates data transfer syntax for the application layer.

PRI (Primary Rate Interface)   ISDN interface to primary rate access. Primary rate access consists of a single 64-kbps D channel plus 23 (T1) or 30 (E1) B channels for voice or data. Compare to **BRI.**

protocol   Formal description of a set of rules and conventions that govern how devices on a network exchange information.

protocol stack   Set of related communications protocols that operate together and, as a group, address communication at some or all of the seven layers of the OSI reference model. Not every protocol stack covers each layer of the model, and often a single protocol in the stack will address a number of layers at once. TCP/IP is a typical protocol stack.

proxy ARP (proxy Address Resolution Protocol)   Variation of the ARP protocol in which an intermediate device (for example, a router) sends an ARP response on behalf of an end node to the requesting host. Proxy ARP can lessen bandwidth use on slow-speed WAN links. *See also* **ARP**.

PVC (permanent virtual circuit)   Permanently established virtual circuits save bandwidth in situations where certain virtual circuits must exist all the time, such as during circuit establishment and tear down.

Q.921   ITU (International Telecommunication Union) standard document for ISDN Layer 2 (Data Link layer).

Q.931   ITU (International Telecommunication Union) standard document for ISDN Layer 3.

query   Message used to inquire about the value of some variable or set of variables.

queue   A backlog of packets stored in buffers and waiting to be forwarded over a router interface.

RAM   Random-access memory. Volatile memory that can be read and written by a computer.

reassembly   The putting back together of an IP datagram at the destination after it has been fragmented either at the source or at an intermediate node. *See also* **fragmentation**.

reload   The event of a Cisco router rebooting, or the command that causes the router to reboot.

reverse path forwarding   If a packet server receives a packet through different interfaces from the same source, the server drops all packets after the first.

reverse Telnet   Using a router to connect to a serial device, frequently a modem, in order to connect out. For example, telnetting to a special port on an access router in order to access a modem to dial out. Called "reverse" because it's the opposite of the router's usual function, to accept calls into the modem.

RFC (Request For Comments)   Document series used as the primary means for communicating information about the Internet. Some RFCs are designated by the IAB as Internet standards.

ring   Connection of two or more stations in a logically circular topology. Information is passed sequentially between active stations. Token Ring, FDDI, and CDDI are based on this topology.

ring topology   Network topology that consists of a series of repeaters connected to one another by unidirectional transmission links to form a single closed loop. Each station on the network connects to the network at a repeater.

RIP (Routing Information Protocol)   A routing protocol for TCP/IP networks. The most common routing protocol in the Internet. RIP uses hop count as a routing metric.

RMON (Remote monitor)   A set of SNMP standards used to collect statistical network information. RMON is divided into groups, with each additional group providing more statistical information.

ROM (read-only memory)   Nonvolatile memory that can be read, but not written, by the computer.

routed protocol   Protocol that carries user data so it can be routed by a router. A router must be able to interpret the logical internetwork as specified by that routed protocol. Examples of routed protocols include AppleTalk, DECnet, and IP.

router   Network Layer device that uses one or more metrics to determine the optimal path along which network traffic should be forwarded. Routers forward packets from one network to another based on Network Layer information.

routing   Process of finding a path to a destination host.

routing metric   Method by which a routing algorithm determines preferability of one route over another. This information is stored in routing tables. Metrics include bandwidth, communication cost, delay, hop count, load, MTU, path cost, and reliability. Sometimes referred to simply as a metric.

routing protocol   Protocol that accomplishes routing through the implementation of a specific routing algorithm. Examples of routing protocols include IGRP, OSPF, and RIP.

routing table   Table stored in a router or some other internetworking device that keeps track of routes to particular network destinations and, in some cases, metrics associated with those routes.

routing update   Message sent from a router to indicate network reachability and associated cost information. Routing updates are typically sent at regular intervals and after a change in network topology. Compare with **flash update**.

RSRB (remote source-route bridging)   Equivalent to an SRB over WAN links.

RTMP (Routing Table Maintenance Protocol)   The protocol used by AppleTalk devices to communicate routing information. Structurally similar to RIP.

runts   Ethernet frames that are smaller than 64 bytes.

SAP (service access point)   1. Field defined by the IEEE 802.2 specification that is part of an address specification. Thus, the destination plus the DSAP define the recipient of a packet. The same applies to the SSAP. 2. Service Advertising Protocol. IPX protocol that provides a means of informing network routers and servers of the location of available network resources and services.

segment   1. Section of a network that is bounded by bridges, routers, or switches. 2. In a LAN using a bus topology, a segment is a continuous electrical circuit that is often connected to other such segments with repeaters. 3. Term used in the TCP specification to describe a single Transport Layer unit of information.

serial transmission   Method of data transmission in which the bits of a data character are transmitted sequentially over a single channel.

session   1. Related set of communications transactions between two or more network devices. 2. In SNA, a logical connection that enables two NAUs to communicate.

session layer   Layer 5 of the OSI reference model. This layer establishes, manages, and terminates sessions between applications and manages data exchange between presentation layer entities. Corresponds to the data flow control layer of the SNA model. *See also* **application layer; Data-Link Layer; Network Layer; Physical Layer; presentation layer; Transport Layer.**

sliding window flow control   Method of flow control in which a receiver gives a transmitter permission to transmit data until a window is full. When the window is full, the transmitter must stop transmitting until the receiver acknowledges some of the data, or advertises a larger window. TCP, other transport protocols, and several Data-Link Layer protocols use this method of flow control.

SLIP (Serial Line Internet Protocol)   Uses a variation of TCP/IP to make point-to-point serial connections. Succeeded by PPP.

SNAP (Subnetwork Access Protocol)   Internet protocol that operates between a network entity in the subnetwork and a network entity in the end system.

SNAP specifies a standard method of encapsulating IP datagrams and ARP messages on IEEE networks.

SNMP (Simple Network Management Protocol)   Network management protocol used almost exclusively in TCP/IP networks. SNMP provides a means to monitor and control network devices, and to manage configurations, statistics collection, performance, and security.

SNMP Manager   Software used to manage network devices via SNMP. Often includes graphical representation of the network and individual devices, and the ability to set and respond to SNMP traps.

SNMP Trap   A threshold of some sort which, when reached, causes the SNMP managed device to notify the SNMP manager. This allows for immediate notification, instead of having to wait for the SNMP manager to poll again.

socket   Software structure operating as a communications endpoint within a network device.

SONET (Synchronous Optical Network)   High-speed synchronous network specification developed by Bellcore and designed to run on optical fiber.

source address   Address of a network device that is sending data.

spanning tree   Loop-free subset of a network topology. *See also* **Spanning-Tree Protocol**.

Spanning-Tree Protocol   Developed to eliminate loops in the network. The Spanning-Tree Protocol ensures a loop-free path by placing one of the bridge ports in "blocking mode," preventing the forwarding of packets.

SPF (shortest path first algorithm)   Routing algorithm that sorts routes by length of path to determine a shortest-path spanning tree. Commonly used in link-state routing algorithms. Sometimes called Dijkstra's algorithm.

SPIDs (Service Profile Identifers)   These function as addresses for B channels on ISDN BRI circuits. When call information is passed over the D channel, the SPIDs are used to identify which channel is being referred to. SPIDs are usually some variant of the phone number for the channel.

split-horizon updates   Routing technique in which information about routes is prevented from being advertised out the router interface through which that information was received. Split-horizon updates are used to prevent routing loops.

SPX (Sequenced Packet Exchange)   Reliable, connection-oriented protocol at the Transport Layer that supplements the datagram service provided by IPX.

SRB (source-route bridging)   Method of bridging in Token Ring networks. In an SRB network, before data is sent to a destination, the entire route to that destination is predetermined in real time.

SRT (source-route transparent bridging)   IBM's merging of SRB and transparent bridging into one bridging scheme, which requires no translation between bridging protocols.

SR/TLB (source-route translational bridging)   Method of bridging that allows source-route stations to communicate with transparent bridge stations, using an intermediate bridge that translates between the two bridge protocols.

standard   Set of rules or procedures that are either widely used or officially specified.

star topology   LAN topology in which endpoints on a network are connected to a common central switch by point-to-point links. A ring topology that is organized as a star implements a unidirectional closed-loop star, instead of point-to-point links. Compare with **bus topology**, **ring topology**, and **tree topology**.

static route   Route that is explicitly configured and entered into the routing table. Static routes take precedence over routes chosen by dynamic routing protocols.

subinterface   A virtual interface defined as a logical subdivision of a physical interface.

subnet address   Portion of an IP address that is specified as the subnetwork by the subnet mask. *See also* **IP address; subnet mask; subnetwork.**

subnet mask   32-bit address mask used in IP to indicate the bits of an IP address that are being used for the subnet address. Sometimes referred to simply as mask. *See also* **address mask; IP address.**

subnetwork   1. In IP networks, a network sharing a particular subnet address. 2. Subnetworks are networks arbitrarily segmented by a network administrator in order to provide a multilevel, hierarchical routing structure while shielding the subnetwork from the addressing complexity of attached networks. Sometimes called a subnet.

SVC (switched virtual circuit)   Virtual circuit that can be established dynamically on demand, and which is torn down after a transmission is complete. SVCs are used when data transmission is sporadic.

switch   1. Network device that filters, forwards, and floods frames based on the destination address of each frame. The switch operates at the Data-Link Layer of the OSI model. 2. General term applied to an electronic or mechanical device that allows a connection to be established as necessary and terminated when there is no longer a session to support.

T1   Digital WAN carrier facility. T1 transmits DS-1-formatted data at 1.544 Mbps through the telephone-switching network, using AMI or B8ZS coding. Compare with **E1**. *See also* **AMI; B8ZS.**

TCP (Transmission Control Protocol)   Connection-oriented Transport Layer protocol that provides reliable full-duplex data transmission. TCP is part of the TCP/IP protocol stack.

TCP/IP (Transmission Control Protocol/Internet Protocol) Common name for the suite of protocols developed by the U.S. DoD in the 1970s to support the construction of worldwide internetworks. TCP and IP are the two best-known protocols in the suite.

TDR Time-domain reflectometer. A TDR test is used to measure the length of a cable, or the distance to a break. This is accomplished by sending a signal down a wire, and measuring how long it takes for an echo of the signal to bounce back.

TEI Terminal endpoint identifier. Field in the LAPD address that identifies a device on an ISDN interface.

TFTP Trivial File Transfer Protocol. Simplified version of FTP that allows files to be transferred from one computer to another over a network.

three-way handshake The three required packets to set up a TCP connection. It consists of a SYN packet, acknowledged by a SYN+ACK packet, which is finally acknowledged by an ACK packet. During this handshake, sequence numbers are exchanged.

throughput Rate of information arriving at, and possibly passing through, a particular point in a network system.

timeout Event that occurs when one network device expects to hear from another network device within a specified period of time, but does not. A timeout usually results in a retransmission of information or the termination of the session between the two devices.

token Frame that contains only control information. Possession of the token allows a network device to transmit data onto the network. *See also* **token passing**.

token passing Method by which network devices' access the physical medium is based on possession of a small frame called a token. Compare this method to circuit switching and contention.

Token Ring   Token-passing LAN developed and supported by IBM. Token Ring runs at 4 or 16 Mbps over a ring topology. Similar to IEEE 802.5. *See also* **IEEE 802.5; ring topology; token passing.**

TokenTalk   Apple Computer's data-link product that allows an AppleTalk network to be connected by Token Ring cables.

transparent bridging   Bridging scheme used in Ethernet and IEEE 802.3 networks. Allows bridges to pass frames along one hop at a time, based on tables that associate end nodes with bridge ports. Bridges are transparent to network end nodes.

transport layer   Layer 4 of the OSI reference model. This layer is responsible for reliable network communication between end nodes. The Transport Layer provides mechanisms for the establishment, maintenance, and termination of virtual circuits, transport fault detection and recovery, and information flow control.

tree topology   A LAN topology that resembles a bus topology. Tree networks can contain branches with multiple nodes. In a tree topology, transmissions from a station propagate the length of the physical medium, and are received by all other stations.

twisted-pair   Relatively low-speed transmission medium consisting of two insulated wires arranged in a regular spiral pattern. The wires can be shielded or unshielded. Twisted-pair is common in telephony applications and is increasingly common in data networks.

UDP (User Datagram Protocol)   Connectionless Transport Layer protocol in the TCP/IP protocol stack. UDP is a simple protocol that exchanges datagrams without acknowledgments or guaranteed delivery, requiring that error processing and retransmission be handled by other protocols. UDP is defined in RFC 768.

unicast   Regular IP packet sent from a single host to a single host.

UTP (unshielded twisted-pair)   Four-pair wire medium used in a variety of networks. UTP does not require the fixed spacing between connections that is necessary with coaxial-type connections.

virtual circuit   Logical circuit created to ensure reliable communication between two network devices. A virtual circuit is defined by a VPI/VCI pair, and can be either permanent or switched. Virtual circuits are used in Frame Relay and X.25. In ATM, a virtual circuit is called a virtual channel. Sometimes abbreviated VC.

VLAN (virtual LAN)   Group of devices on one or more LANs that are configured (using management software) so that they can communicate as if they were attached to the same wire, when in fact they are located on a number of different LAN segments. Because VLANs are based on logical instead of physical connections, they are extremely flexible.

VLSM (variable-length subnet masking)   Ability to specify a different length subnet mask for the same network number at different locations in the network. VLSM can help optimize available address space.

VTY   Virtual Terminal. VTYs work like physical terminal ports on routers so they can be managed across a network, usually via Telnet.

WAN (wide-area network)   Data communications network that serves users across a broad geographic area and often uses transmission devices provided by common carriers. Frame Relay, SMDS, and X.25 are examples of WANs. Compare with **LAN** and **MAN**.

wildcard mask   32-bit quantity used in conjunction with an IP address to determine which bits in an IP address should be matched and ignored when comparing that address with another IP address. A wildcard mask is specified when defining access list statements.

X.121   ITU-T standard describing an addressing scheme used in X.25 networks. X.121 addresses are sometimes called IDNs (International Data Numbers).

X.21   ITU-T standard for serial communications over synchronous digital lines. The X.21 protocol is used primarily in Europe and Japan.

X.25   ITU-T standard that defines how connections between DTE and DCE are maintained for remote terminal access and computer communications in public data networks. X.25 specifies LAPB, a Data-Link Layer protocol, and PLP, a Network Layer protocol. Frame Relay has to some degree superseded X.25.

ZIP broadcast storm   Occurs when a route advertisement without a corresponding zone triggers the network with a flood of Zone Information Protocol requests.

Zone Information Protocol (ZIP)   A protocol used in AppleTalk to communicate information about AppleTalk zone names and cable ranges.

Zone Information Table (ZIT)   A table of zone name to cable range mappings in AppleTalk. These tables are maintained in each AppleTalk router.

zone   In AppleTalk, a logical group of network devices.

INDEX

10BaseT cabling, 152
10-Mbps hubs(Ten), 131
100BaseT cabling, 152, 507, 617
100BaseTX
   signaling in, 617
100-Mbps hubs or switches, 153, 166

A

ABRs (area border routers), 315, 319,
  322, 379
Access control lists (ACL), 445
Access layer, 633, 636, 662, 666, 672

Access lists, 44, 250, 405, 460,
  468-469, 496, 500-501, 509, 519,
  526, 540, 573, 583, 586, 730, 797
ACK (acknowledge) packets, 358, 362,
  433-434
Active monitor, 143, 145-146
Address space, 291, 369, 761
Addressing stations, 123
adjacencies, 379, 381, 392
Adjacency database (OSPF), 243
Administrative distance, 294, 343,
  370, 372, 430
   redistribution and, 459

C

P

S

T

Z